Women's Realities, Women's Choices

HUNTER COLLEGE WOMEN'S STUDIES COLLECTIVE

Ülkü Bates • Florence Denmark • Virginia Held • Dorothy O. Helly • Shirley Hune • Susan Lees • Sarah B. Pomeroy • Carolyn Somerville • Sue Rosenberg Zalk *second edition*

Women's Realities, Women's Choices

AN INTRODUCTION TO WOMEN'S STUDIES

**Hunter College
Women's Studies
Collective**

New York   Oxford
OXFORD UNIVERSITY PRESS
1995

Oxford University Press

Oxford   New York   Toronto
Delhi   Bombay   Calcutta   Madras   Karachi
Kuala Lumpur   Singapore   Hong Kong   Tokyo
Nairobi   Dar es Salaam   Cape Town
Melbourne   Auckland   Madrid

and associated companies in
Berlin   Ibadan

Library of Congress Cataloging-in-Publication Data
Women's realities, women's choices : an introduction to women's
studies / Hunter College Women's Studies Collective. — 2nd ed.
p. cm.   Includes bibliographical references and index.
ISBN 0-19-505883-6
1. Women's studies—United States.   I. Hunter College.
Women's Studies Collective.
HQ1181.U5W653   1995   305.4'0973—dc20   94-13648

9 8 7 6 5 4 3 2 1
Printed in the United States of America
on acid-free paper

THE AUTHORS

Ülkü Ü. Bates was born in Romania and grew up in Turkey. She studied at the Universities of Istanbul, Turkey, and Freiburg, Germany, and received her Ph.D. in the History of Islamic Art from the University of Michigan. She has traveled widely and has done research on Islamic archaeology and architecture in the Middle East. She has written on the art and architecture of Anatolia (Turkey), Ottoman Cairo, and Istanbul. She is a professor of art history and has one son.

Florence L. Denmark received her Ph.D. in Social Psychology from the University of Pennsylvania. She has been the Thomas Hunter Professor of Psychology at Hunter College of the City University of New York, and at present is the Robert Scott Pace Distinguished Professor of Psychology at Pace University, where she is Chair of the Department of Psychology. A past president of the American Psychological Association and the International Council of Psychologists, she has edited and authored numerous books and articles on the psychology of women and has been the recipient of many professional awards and honors. She is the mother of three children, the stepmother of three others, and has two grandchildren.

Virginia Held is a professor of Philosophy and a professor of Women's Studies at Hunter College and the Graduate School of the City University of New York. Among her books are *Feminist Morality: Transforming Culture, Society and Politics* (1993), *Rights and Goods: Justifying Social Action* (1984), and *The Public Interest and Individual Interests* (1970). She has been a Fellow at the Center for Advanced Studies in the Behavioral Sciences and has had

Fulbright and Rockefeller fellowships. She is on the editorial board of five journals in the areas of philosophy and political theory. She has also taught at Yale, Dartmouth, UCLA, and Hamilton. She has two children and three grandchildren.

Dorothy O. Helly is Professor of History and Women's Studies at Hunter College and the Graduate School of the City University of New York, where she also teaches in the Women's Studies Certificate Program. Educated at Smith College and Harvard University, her scholarly fields are Victorian England, British Colonialism, and Women's History. At Hunter College she has been a dean (1977–83) and coordinator of Women's Studies (1984–87); since 1987 she has co-facilitated a university faculty development seminar on balancing the curriculum for gender, race, ethnicity, and class. She is on the editorial boards of *The Journal of Women's History* and the *Women's Studies Quarterly;* she co-chaired the Program Committee for the Seventh Berkshire Conference on the History of Women (1987) and the Fourth International Interdisciplinary Congress on Women (1990). She is co-editor of *Gendered Domains: Rethinking the Public and the Private in Women's History* (1992). She has a daughter.

Shirley Hune was born in Toronto, Canada, a third-generation Chinese Canadian, and received her Ph.D. from the George Washington University in American Civilization. She has published in the areas of U.S. immigration policy, third world politics, human rights and migrant workers, and Asian American studies. She is a past president of the Association for Asian American Studies and is actively involved in curriculum transformation. At Hunter College she was professor of Educational Foundations and Associate Provost. She joined the University of California, Los Angeles, in 1992 and is Associate Dean for Graduate Programs in the Graduate Division and Professor of Urban Planning in the School for Public Policy and Social Research. She has two adult stepchildren and four grandchildren.

Susan H. Lees is Professor of Anthropology and Acting Dean of the Division of Social Sciences at Hunter College and a member of the Ph.D. Program in Anthropology and the Women's Studies Certificate Program at the Graduate Center of the City University of New York. She received her undergraduate education in anthropology at the University of Michigan. She has carried out fieldwork in Latin America and in Israel, primarily in rural communities, and has published extensively about human ecology and rural development. She has co-edited the interdisciplinary journal *Human Ecology* since 1977. She has two sons and a stepdaughter.

Sarah B. Pomeroy is the author of *Goddesses, Whores, Wives, and Slaves: Women in Classical Antiquity* (1975; 1994), *Women in Hellenistic Egypt from Alexander to Cleopatra* (1984; 1989), and *Xenophon's Oeconomicus: A Social and Historical Commentary* (1994). She is a coauthor of *Women in the Classical World: Image and Text* (1993) and editor of *Women's History and Ancient History* (1991). She is now writing *The Family in Classical and Hellenistic Greece*. She was the first director of the women's studies programs at Hunter College and the Graduate School of the City University of New York, and the first Chair of the Women's Classical Caucus. She teaches Classics, History, and Women's Studies at Hunter College and the Graduate School for the City University of New York. She has two daughters, one son, one son-in-law, one grandson, and one granddaughter.

Carolyn M. Somerville received her Ph.D. in Political Science from the University of Michigan. She teaches comparative and international politics in the Department of Political Science and the Women's Studies Program at Hunter College of the City University of New York. In 1992–93 she was acting director of the Women's Studies Program. She is on the graduate faculty at the City University of New York. Her published works include *Drought and Aid in the Sahel: A Decade of Development Cooperation*, as well as articles on the debt crisis and democracy in Senegal. Her current research explores the impact of the domestic transition on women in Mozambique. She is the mother of a four-year-old.

Sue Rosenberg Zalk studied at New York University and received her Ph.D in psychology from Yeshiva University. She is a professor in the Department of Education Foundations at Hunter College and is on the faculty of the Ph.D. Programs in Social-Personality Psychology and Educational Psychology at the Graduate School and University Center of the City University of New York, where she also serves as Ombuds Officer. She is the former director of the Center for the Study of Women and Society at the Graduate School of the City University of New York and past president of the Division of Women's Issues of the New York State Psychological Association. She is editor of *Sex Roles: A Journal of Research* and on the Board of Directors of The Feminist Press. She has done research and published in the fields of racial attitudes, psychology of women, gender role development, and multicultural curriculum. She is coauthor of *Expectant Fathers* (1978) and co-editor of *Revolutions in Knowledge: Feminism in the Social Sciences* (1992).

The authors dedicate the second edition of this book to all those who have brought joy to our lives, to the Hunter College Women's Studies Community which has sustained us, to the many friends and colleagues who have made our work a pleasure, and not least to all the feminists and activists everywhere whose work we celebrate in these pages.

FOREWORD TO THE FIRST EDITION

The publication of any book is reason enough for a celebration. This particular volume deserves fireworks. It symbolizes the coming of age of the women's studies movement. Indeed, the substance of this book represents years of struggle by courageous scholar-teachers, to be taken seriously by their more traditional colleagues.

That a women's studies program has produced a textbook is also a tribute to progressive elements in higher education in the United States. Women's studies programs and courses, more specifically scholarship on women, are now so widely accepted that there is scarcely a college or university without some offerings.

Hunter College's long commitment to the education of women makes it a particularly fitting place for launching this text. No institution has sent more women on for doctoral studies. Our graduates include a Nobel Prize winner, and leaders in education, the arts, and business.

This effort by a collective of our most distinguished faculty fills us with pride. It also allows us to recommit ourselves to the elimination of sexism in higher education

April 1983   DONNA E. SHALALA, PH.D.
President, Hunter College
of the City University
of New York

FOREWORD TO THE SECOND EDITION

Women's studies has come of age, and the progress of the last dozen years can now be measured by the changes presented in this volume.

The sophistication of women's studies is evident on these pages from the greater representation of women of color and sexual diversity to the inclusion of women globally, historically, and in the present. New feminist thinking deals with the relationship between the state and its citizens, the nature of the gendered division of labor, and the complexities of caring, women's health, reproductive issues, and the problems of aging.

No one claims there are any easy answers to the problems identified here, but what needs to be done has been spelled out clearly. Everywhere women face the need to shape the policies that will transform domestic worlds, places of employment, educational institutions, and health and welfare systems.

The authors of this book have succeeded in bringing the developments of the last dozen years front and center. The changes appear in every chapter, and in a new chapter on Gender and Race. It was my pleasure to be the president of Hunter College when the first edition of this important work was published, and I appreciate the opportunity on the occasion of the second edition to salute the achievement of its authors once again. I join with them in the belief that words matter.

September 1994   DONNA E. SHALALA, PH.D.

PREFACE

The first edition of this book was the first textbook written for introductory women's studies courses. Unlike other comprehensive women's studies textbooks that were described as multidisciplinary but were actually either collections of individual chapters, each written from the perspective of a single discipline, or collections of readings with an editor's prefatory remarks, this book was interdisciplinary throughout, with authors from different disciplines writing and rewriting each chapter. We hoped that its use would encourage and regularize the teaching of women's studies introductory courses.

By now an enormous amount of work has been done in the area of women's studies, much of it interdisciplinary. This edition of our textbook updates the first, trying to incorporate within it the greatly strengthened and enlarged insights of feminist theory and practice, the painstaking research on women, and the exciting rethinking that has been developing in nearly all areas of inquiry in the past decade.

Our book can be visualized as organized in a series of concentric rings. In Part I, "Defining Women," we start with the innermost ring, the woman as person. We ask: What are the cultural "givens" that seemed to define women in the past, and how do women, looking out from the center, see ourselves, our own body images, our minds, our social place? How do our racial, ethnic, and class identities, as we see them, affect our own experiences and outlooks?

Then, in Part II, "The Family Circle," we look at women in terms of our closest human relationships. How have these relationships (woman as daughter, sister, wife, and mother) been defined and imposed on us? How do women see them, and how might we reshape these relationships to take account of our own choices? How have women shaped our own place in lesbian households and in nonkinship structures (e.g., communal groups and religious communities)? In Part III, "Women in Society," we look at the widest sphere of human interactions, the society at large. Here we look at the place of women in social institutions related to religion, health, education, work, and political power, and at how women's roles have changed and are changing through time. In addition to a final chapter entitled "Changing the Present: A Look to the Future," questions and suggestions within each chapter also point the way toward social change.

We recognize that to place the person or self in the center of the circle is to focus on the individual—on personal growth, awareness, action—in contrast to stressing the collective movement, shared goals, and broader social change that greatly affect individuals. We are aware that many feminists believe that there can be no real personal liberation without radical social change and that the appropriate emphasis must be on collective efforts to bring about that change. The authors of this book differ on the degree to which we adhere to one or the other position, but we agree that they are closely interconnected. In many places in this book the self is stressed, but awareness of the need for basic social change through collective effort is also always present.

It should be pointed out that this book itself

was a collective effort. We did not merely divide the chapters among the authors; instead, each of us has contributed to each chapter. No aspect of women's lives is isolated from any other, whether it be personal, familial, or societal. Divisions are arbitrary, and the chapter titles and book organization are designed to provide a possible conceptual framework. We believe that the concept of concentric circles presents a visual image that meshes with the experiences and perspectives of most readers.

Thus, our book attempts to go from the center, the self, outward, to examine the implications of the ways women have existed and how we may wish to reshape our own existence in society. At each level we observe the contradiction between the social or cultural "givens" that generally have been structured by men in their own interests and what we perceive to be women's own realities. We consider what women's realities are, and how we can change our current realities to reflect better women's possible choices. The title we have selected, and retained, acknowledges the gap between women's realities and women's choices. Our book is an effort to help bridge that gap.

We expect courses in women's studies using this textbook to be cooperative ventures between teachers and students, for we are all breaking new ground. We gain from each other's insights and disparate experiences as we share our progress. The writing of this textbook gained from such sharing.

The original edition of this textbook had a gestation period of over four years. In 1978–1979 the authors participated in an interdisciplinary seminar directed toward designing a curriculum for an "Introduction to Women's Studies" and training faculty in interdisciplinary perspectives. Meetings open to interested members of the Hunter College community were held weekly as the core group proceeded in a year-long discussion. The seminar meetings were recorded on tape and transcribed. In addition, minutes were taken. For each topic, participants offered remarks from the perspective of our disciplines; one or two presented extended comments; and all contributed bibliographical sources from our own fields. The outline of this textbook is based on the material developed for that course. By now, thousands of copies of this book have been used in classrooms throughout the world, and have been read by large numbers of interested readers outside of classrooms.

Oxford University Press asked us to prepare a second edition, and after debating the merits of doing so, we decided to proceed. One of the original authors, under the pressure of other responsibilities, had to withdraw. Two scholars able to strengthen the book's inclusion of racial and cultural diversity were added to the group of authors. Again, each chapter was revised, as it had been written, by authors from various disciplines and discussed by the whole group.

Throughout this book, we its authors use the pronoun *we* to refer to women everywhere, in any period of history. The choice requires an explanation and some personal history.

We the authors originally decided to try to take the point of view of women, to speak for women as subjects (we) rather than as objects (them), to speak, that is, for all of "us." The device of the pronoun, using "women . . . we" rather than "women . . . they" appealed to us, so we tried using it.

We immediately ran into difficulties. The device struck some readers as awkward and artificial: "We the authors" did not take part in the French Revolution nor did we personally suffer the outrage of slavery; how could we presume to speak for all women? Was it not either disrespectful or just silly to pretend to do so?

We decided that the manuscript should be rewritten, using *they* to refer to women collectively and in the contexts we were describing, and *we* to refer only to us the authors.

It was at this stage when the chapters were initially put together that many of us authors saw the book as a whole for the first time. As we read it over, we realized what had been lost in relegating women, again, to the voiceless "they," the "other," where patriarchy has always worked to put all of us.

After much rethinking and lengthy discussion of fresh criticism and reactions from new readers, we the authors revised the perspective of the book yet again, again trying to speak, however haltingly, for all women. We the authors do not presume for a minute to be able to do so. We are only a small number of women with restricted backgrounds and limited experiences. We are of course not pretending to be able to give adequate voice to the experiences of all women. But the authors of this book together with all those who read it and teach with it may together be quite a large number of women with quite varied backgrounds. We use the device of speaking of "us women" in the hope that those who read this book, men as well as women, can be encouraged to see the world from the point of view of *women*, from the points of view of all of *us*, from *our* diverse perspectives. We hope the device of identifying with whatever women are being discussed in this book will help the reader make this shift of perspective. It can also be effective in making us think about subject perspective when we discuss relationships between women, as between sisters or mothers and daughters.

History, literature, philosophy, the arts, and the sciences have until very recently been made largely by men from the point of view of men. Men have seen themselves as the subjects, the "we" of mankind even though, in general, only a small number of privileged men have taken part in this process. We the authors of this book want to make clear that all women are the "we" of womankind, and must be part of the "we" of humankind. We the authors of this book on women want to try to open the eyes of readers to the extent to which it feels new and different to begin to see human experience from *our* points of view, the points of view of *women*. As women, we hope that all women can come to experience the world through women's eyes, to understand what this shift in perspective means, and to work toward using this new lens to bring all that has been left out back into focus.

In revising the book we again considered the difficulties in using *we* for women distant in cultural context, ways of life, and global location from us the authors. But, again, we the authors decided to keep the perspective of women, of the *we* who are all, in our often unnoticed ways, transforming the world.

The National Endowment for the Humanities awarded us a grant to write the first edition of this textbook for the basic course in women's studies, and we are grateful for that support. This grant permitted us free time in which to write and discuss our work and enabled us to carry out extensive evaluations of drafts of various chapters that were used experimentally in classrooms. The manuscript of the first edition was read by three outside evaluators, Nancy Hartsock, Joyce Ladner, and Catharine Stimpson, and we are grateful for their comments as well as for those of several other specialists who evaluated individual chapters. Innumerable others who have read and used the book have given us the benefit of their comments and suggestions, and we thank them.

We are grateful to Spencer Carr who originally offered us a contract with Oxford University Press for this book and to the editors there, including Valerie Aubrey and, more recently, David Roll, Gioia Stevens, and Susan Hannan, for editorial support during the lengthy process of its revision.

The book has been written and revised collectively, not only by the authors whose names appear on the title pages of the two editions, but by the many others who have participated in the processes of writing, evaluating, and reworking this text. The authors themselves have been drawn from many different disciplines at Hunter College. Hunter College was the first free municipal college for women and has maintained its tradition of providing education of the highest quality for an increasingly diverse student body. We are pleased to express our appreciation for the support we have received from the Hunter College administration for the original project and for this second edition.

New York
September 1994

CONTENTS

Boxes

Women's Realities, Women's Choices

Introduction to Women's Studies

Women's Studies and Feminism

History of Women's Studies

How Does Women's Studies Study Women?

The Need for Women's Studies

Missing Information about Humans

Misconceptions about Humans

Old and New Processes of Inquiry

Knowledge of Men

Women's Studies: Issues and Goals

Race, Social Class, and Other Group Identities

Women's Studies as an Academic Discipline

Women's Studies and Gender Studies

Women's Studies as a Source of Strength

How This Book Presents Women's Studies

Women's studies is not simply the study of women. It is the study of women that places women's own experiences in the center of the process. It examines the world and the human beings who inhabit it with questions, analyses, and theories built directly on women's experiences.

In the past, both women and men studied women from the perspective of men only. All theories about human beings, our nature and our behavior, have been "man" made. Knowledge about ourselves and our world has usually been divided—for the purpose of study—into distinct "fields" or "disciplines." Such fields have a long past, as in the case of history or philosophy. Other fields or disciplines such as sociology, economics, or psychology have developed as distinct approaches to knowledge only in the past century or two. Still other ways of studying the world or parts of the world, such as communications, computer sciences, or African American studies, have even more recent origins.

However long these areas of study have been in existence, each involves a relatively distinctive approach to knowledge. Each also involves an explicit set of observations of what is perceived to be true and rests on an implicit set of assumptions and ethical views. These observations and assumptions provide us with guidelines for human action. Yet, if these observations and assumptions reflect a predominantly masculine perspective on reality, the interpretations they give rise to may not be as true for women as for men. They often do not reflect women's experiences of reality, and they are often poor guides for women. They represent, in fact, men's studies without awareness of their limitations, in contrast with the new field of men's studies now developing which calls attention to issues of gender and questions traditional assumptions about men and men's roles. Women's studies focuses on women's experiences and points of view. It seeks to provide observations and to develop assumptions that can help us understand women's realities. And it seeks to provide the kind of information that can enable women to choose more knowledgeably how they wish to act in and to shape the world.

Women's studies is both a complement and correction to established disciplines and a new academic discipline of its own. In both respects, it requires other fields to reexamine and revise the basic assumptions and theories on which they rest. As a new discipline, women's studies not only challenges basic methods and presuppositions in established disciplines but also crosses the boundaries between them, giving fresh views of their subject matter and creating a coherent new way of seeing the world.

Women's studies contributes to change of

a fundamental kind as a result of its search for knowledge. Its role in the academic community and in the feminist movement is still under discussion. Its distinct perspectives, issues, and goals are continually being formulated, debated, revised, and reformulated. This is an exhilarating process and a challenging one, both intellectually and politically, for all of us in women's studies.

Women's Studies and Feminism

Feminism has been defined in various ways, but it is widely agreed that it is committed to overcoming the devaluation of women. Feminism insists that women be valued for the attributes we ourselves choose to value, not for those imposed on us valued by others for their purposes. Feminism rejects cultural images that denigrate women, social structures that treat women as subordinate, and behavior that fails to accord women equality. When we support feminism, we strive to contribute to the cooperative efforts of women to shape our own destinies.

Aligning with feminism means rejecting the assignment of social roles with their corresponding norms according to whether a person is female or male. As feminists we reject evaluations that esteem presumably "masculine" qualities such as being aggressive and autonomous when found in men, while deploring these qualities in women. And we affirm the moral importance, for men as well as women, of various presumably "feminine" qualities such as being caring and compassionate. Any quality may appear in any human being and should be evaluated on its own merits, not in terms of the gender of the person in whom it appears. Understanding that cultural attitudes and beliefs about women have often been based on false premises and faulty observations, feminists are working to replace ignorance and fantasy with views that have greater validity. Realizing that discriminatory laws and customs have oppressed women, that this oppression is disgraceful and harmful to all human beings, and that we can through our persistent and collective efforts bring about change for the better, feminists seek such change.

We may differ in our immediate goals and the directions in which we choose to focus our energies. For some, the focus of feminism is on personal change; for others, the core of feminism lies in collective efforts and shared goals. Feminists also differ on whether equality and freedom for women can occur in society as it is currently structured or whether a radical transformation of the social structure is required. Whichever positions we take, we gain strength through mutual support.

Feminists recognize that it is not only women who have been oppressed. Much recent work among feminists has been devoted to better understanding the oppression of racism, class position, and discrimination on grounds of sexual orientation or ethnic identity. These affect women differently; for all women to be liberated, concerted efforts are needed to overcome many different kinds of oppression.

Feminism reflects intellectual, ethical, and political positions that can be espoused by women or men. Women's studies, which can be studied by women and men, is the outgrowth of a realization that much more needs to be known about women, and much more needs to be thought about from the points of view of women. As a scholarly discipline, importantly motivated by feminist concerns, women's studies receives support from feminist commitment outside the academic community and provides understanding and activities that can help women's efforts both inside and outside the academy.

History of Women's Studies

The development of an academic manifestation of feminism has been a relatively recent addition to the history of feminism. Although there were scattered courses in areas such as women's history or women in literature, women's studies was not taught under that name on American college campuses until 1970. In the late 1960s, however, concurrent with the civil rights, students' rights, and antiwar movements and the creation of black studies, courses sprang up across the country exploring the status of women, discrimination experienced in public roles and private lives, and gender bias in general in society, literature, and learning. Dozens of courses, some official, some unofficial, were launched in a variety of contexts by instructors with many different academic backgrounds but most often in the liberal arts: the humanities, sociology, psychology, and history. During the next six years, such courses proliferated on American campuses. Instructors in high schools as well as in colleges exchanged syllabi and ideas about how to teach in the feminist mode. While many of the courses were incorporated into the curriculum of existing disciplines such as psychology or history, special programs for a concentration—a minor or a major—in women's studies were also developed at several colleges and universities.

From 1970 to 1976, women's studies began to be articulated as a distinctive, increasingly integrated field. Journals in women's studies were established, including, in the United States alone, *Feminist Studies, Women's Studies, Signs, Quest, Sex Roles,* and the *Women's Studies Quarterly.* Anthologies of writing and full-length books in women's studies were published. These began to establish the field as a discipline. The National Women's Studies Association was founded in 1977 to facilitate the sharing of information among individuals involved in women's studies and other feminist pursuits. By the early 1990s, some form of women's studies curriculum was offered at over 2,000 of more than 3,000 accredited colleges and universities in the United States, and women's studies were growing throughout the world (Chamberlain and Bernstein, 1992).

The roots of the discipline are in feminist critiques of existing scholarship and higher education, for academic fields had virtually overlooked women's experiences and points of view, the contributions of women scholars and writers had gone unrecognized, and women were grossly underrepresented among academics (Chamberlain, 1988). By now there has been a virtual explosion of scholarly books and articles on women, and feminist perspectives are transforming much of the work in specific fields as varied as literature and poetry, health and medicine, history, psychology, philosophy, law, political science, economic development, communications, and management. Profound questions are being raised about many of the assumptions on which such academic disciplines rest, and about the ways human beings have organized and should organize the societies in which women and men live.

How Does Women's Studies Study Women?

Every discipline uses concepts and theories about how our universe functions and uses specific methods devised to pursue inquiry. Women's studies incorporates concepts and methods other disciplines have developed to the extent that they are gender-neutral, that is, so long as they do not make assumptions that reflect a primary focus on men's realities. It marshals the new scholarship on women, whatever the source, and builds on it to understand women's experiences in the past and present, to analyze women's situations, and to clarify the courses of action women can choose.

For example, to understand changes in childrearing practices in a particular situation, we may wish to draw from the field of biology to understand how lactation works, from economics to examine the conditions under which women make decisions about how to rear infants, from psychology to consider why women perceive conditions as we do, from anthropology to appreciate the cultural contexts of child-rearing practices, from nutrition to weigh the effects of different practices on mothers and children, from politics and law to discern the formal support systems, or lack of them, for particular decisions, and so forth. The questions asked may be different from those usually asked in established disciplines, but the means by which they are answered may rely heavily on developed fields of knowledge.

Many questions raised in women's studies call for findings and theorizing that other disciplines have not produced or even considered. These questions may involve other groups of people who have traditionally been neglected by the established disciplines. We know little directly about women in antiquity, and even less about slave women, because we rely on documentary material written by men about men's experiences, largely those of privileged men. How can we find out more about women in these periods? Feminist historians have been developing alternative methods and in focusing on the history of women have reconceptualized whole periods of history (for example: Pomeroy, 1975; White, 1985; Anderson and Zinsser, 1988).

Again, we have learned that various psychological tests, such as personality or I.Q. tests, have been gender biased and culturally biased and may not tell us about the emotional makeup or reasoning abilities of the members of groups not part of the dominant class. How can we devise tests that are bias-free and that tell us what we want to know? Women's studies is beginning to identify its own needs for special methods and to diverge, where appropriate, from traditional approaches.

A distinctive characteristic of women's studies, inherited from its earliest days during the 1960s, has been the development of collective modes of production. Although women who are scholars, professionals, artists, and the like often work alone, we also often pool our resources (knowledge, skills, energy) for collective work that does not emphasize individual achievement but rather the shared product made possible only by cooperative group effort.

The strengths gained from this kind of action are twofold. First, collective action provides mutual support in a difficult endeavor. Establishing a new discipline, like breaking into a field from which one has been excluded, is hard work and can be psychologically alienating; the collective mode helps individuals by reconfirming values in the context of a group. Second, many problems require the insights of more than one individual. Women's studies develops as a new discipline by drawing from various fields of knowledge both to challenge established ideas and to work out new ones. Women need one another's perspectives to figure out how to fit the pieces together. The excitement already generated by this process has been enormous. It has spurred new collaborative modes of study and work to bring together all that we know to define and redefine the study of women—and to reassess what we know about men and society as well.

The Need for Women's Studies

Some academicians argue that the other established disciplines study women as well as men. When we look more closely, however, we see how unsatisfactory most established disciplines are in the way they represent women and women's points of view. We uncover many gaps in our knowledge of women and misconceptions about women and we question whether established approaches to inquiry can correct them. Even today, as more information about women has become available within traditional disciplines, we find that the scholars responsible for such break-throughs have read "women's studies" scholarship to develop the women-focused questions they have applied to their own fields. And women's studies as a discipline becomes all the richer for the interchange of information.

Missing Information about Humans

For many years archaeologists of prehistory refined theories about human origins based on increasing knowledge about tools and behavior associated with what is generally a man's activity: hunting. But when feminist anthropologist Sally Slocum (1975) asked what *women* were doing, it was realized that little or nothing was known of women's activities in preagricultural communities. Historians may have imagined that they knew a great deal about the Renaissance until feminist historian Joan Kelly (1987) asked: Did *women* have a Renaissance? What were women doing during that period in Europe? One focus of problems in women's studies is the search for "missing information" about women: as providers of food, as writers, thinkers, and artists, as traders and producers of crafts, in the past and at present.

One reason women have been "invisible" has to do with the way our "silence" about ourselves has been sustained. Women have generally tended to be excluded from recorded public discourse and confined to the "domestic sphere" of home and family and to less valued "woman's work." Because women were only rarely taught to write, there is relatively little direct documentary material about most of our foremothers' lives. Compared to the numbers of male artists, few women were engaged in creating the painting, sculpture, and architecture that historians traditionally study, and work of lasting value done by women was often forgotten through neglect. Many creative women tended to use

such forms as music, dance, weaving, tapestry making, quilting—forms that are fragile, ephemeral, and anonymous. Women still are poorly represented in the world of the arts establishment, among those who decide which paintings will be hung in museums and which books published. There have been few women participants in the scholarly world in the past, and even today women are few in number in many academic disciplines.

Not only have women had fewer opportunities to express ourselves to others, but scholars and critics in the past did not select as interesting the things that women recorded or did. Why should this be so? One obvious answer is that these scholars and critics (generally men) felt that the restricted set of activities open to women was simply not very important: what was important was what men did—governing, fighting, producing "great" works of art. While it is true that the course of social events has largely been directed by men's activities, it is also true that much of what men have done has been directed toward *controlling* what women do, or are thought to do.

The lack of interest in women can also be traced to a more general devaluation of women. Our work has often been ignored because it was done by women. That is why some women in the past chose to write under male pen names, such as George Eliot (Marian Evans) and George Sand (Amandine-Aurore-Lucile Dudevant).

It is also a distortion of history, however, to think that the course of social events has been directed by men's activities alone. Men's wars could not have been fought and male-controlled industrialization could not have taken place without the integral support of women's work and activities. Women maintained the army supply lines of early modern Europe and entered the civilian and military labor force in twentieth-century warfare (Hacker, 1981). Economic and social changes in men's lives could not have taken place in the same way without concurrent—if different—changes in women's lives, but these have been largely overlooked.

Today economic planners are beginning to ask what the impact of technological development is on women around the world. Educators are looking at the effects of particular pedagogical methods on girls' learning of mathematical concepts. In this way we are beginning to get a new view of phenomena we once thought we understood, from the explanation of the origins of culture, to the events of a historical period, to the processes of economic development, to the impact of primary school teaching, to the development and use of ideologies like that of public and private spheres (Helly and Reverby, 1992). The raising of our consciousness is opening our eyes to the realities that have shaped the lives of women/men, and have constrained their interactions in society in general.

Women are becoming more visible. Our collective efforts to participate in the determination of our lives—for instance, by demanding the rights to vote and hold office, to control our own reproduction, to perform almost every kind of work, or to control our own property—have raised basic questions about what women are, what we do, how we feel, and what we value for ourselves and for society. These questions have affected scholarship and the arts as well as the social and legal world. To the extent that such questions help us to become aware of our own potential, they encourage our more active participation in these areas. These questions make it more difficult for women and men to ignore women. They force a rethinking of deeply held assumptions. They counteract the general devaluation of women as human beings and increase the chances for women to make choices that will shape the world that shapes our lives.

Misconceptions about Humans

The discovery that a great deal of information is missing about humans has contributed to a second discovery: Some very serious misconceptions about humans, particularly about women, are widely believed. In some cases, these misconceptions are the result of too narrow a focus of study. When historians assumed that the Renaissance meant the same things in the lives of women and of men, they failed to ask the questions that would prove otherwise (Ferguson et al., 1986). Although they noted that upper-class men became more dependent politically on their princes, they failed to see how upper-class women lost not only the possibility for political power but also the power to achieve sexual or any other kind of independence from their domestic roles. Anthropologists, writing about "Man the hunter" in the Paleolithic period, concluded that hunted animals provided the entire food supply for these ancient populations. Questions about what preagricultural women were doing led to the discovery that among some contemporary "hunting" societies, up to 80 percent of the diet consisted of vegetable foods gathered by women (Tanner, 1981; Haraway, 1989).

Feminist research has uncovered a large number of misconceptions about women's bodies, mental capacities, activities, and achievements. This book addresses many of these misconceptions and their implications for a better and broader understanding of human nature and society.

Old and New Processes of Inquiry

The discipline of women's studies searches to understand how these misconceptions in other disciplines came about, how they affect these disciplines today, and how we might improve processes of inquiry to develop better knowledge. The historian who wishes to understand why we know so little about women's activities during a particular period might observe that only a limited set of written documents was used to study that time and place, primarily those relating to "public" events or leaders. This historian might then look for other kinds of sources—such as those dealing with local and family records. These records add new kinds of information and also yield new insights into the previously used materials. The economist who asks how women contributed to development in post-colonial African nations might observe that calculations of the Gross National Product were based on men's wage labor and ignored unpaid agricultural production largely done by women. To find out what that production was, the economist might have to develop new means of collecting data and new types of analysis. She or he might decide that it is necessary to re-examine certain basic concepts such as "work" (should it be defined in terms of wages?) and "production" (should it be defined in terms of markets?), as well as to examine the whole notion of how an economy functions, thus challenging established assumptions.

Women's studies may begin with questions about women, but it leads to many other questions about men and societies and about the methods we use to find out about them. In some cases, it is discovered that old research tools can serve new purposes; in other cases, it is found that new methods may be required. When questions such as these are pursued, they can radically alter the way whole areas of knowledge can be conceptualized (Zalk and Gordon-Kelter, 1992). For instance, most of moral theory can be seen to be gender-biased; it has given priority to the norms of "public" life where men have predominated and has discounted as of little moral significance the "personal" interactions largely conducted by women; it has given priority to the rules and rationality traditionally associated with men over the sensitivity and caring traditionally as-

sociated with women (Held, 1993). Again, the field of modern economics, built as it is on assumptions about "economic man"—as basically self-interested and motivated above all to achieve an ever-increasing satisfaction of his desires as efficiently as possible—can be seen to require rethinking from the point of view of, for instance, mothers more concerned with the well-being of our children and of our relations with them than with the rational satisfaction of our own self-interest in isolation. Economics has been among the established fields slowest to reflect that basic change required by feminist critiques, but by 1993, the rethinking was well underway (Couglin, 1993).

Knowledge of Men

Women's studies raises questions about all that we have been taught and all that we have learned. It has become increasingly clear that if women are not well understood, neither are men. Because female and male roles are intricately interwoven, a distorted perspective of one sex must of necessity involve a misunderstanding of the other. Just as social systems based on beliefs about "natural" gender roles perpetuate stereotyped female roles, so do they perpetuate stereotypic male roles. Just as these systems pressure women to conform to their notions of a "feminine" ideal, so do they pressure men to conform to a "masculine" ideal. This pressure is not only detrimental to women but is a handicap to men. Women's studies will inevitably contribute to our knowledge about men. Women's liberation will, we believe, also stimulate the liberation of men.

Women's Studies: Issues and Goals

Like any academic discipline, women's studies has multiple goals and confronts many issues, although it may be more explicit than most disciplines about what it hopes to accomplish.

Race, Social Class, and Other Group Identities

Individual persons come to women's studies and feminism from a variety of cultural and social backgrounds. As members of different races, economic classes, ethnic and religious groups, age groups, and with different sexual orientations, we bring with us different interests and concerns that sometimes make it difficult to arrive at a consensus.

Those of us who were brought up as or find ourselves members of oppressed groups may find it particularly difficult to see what we have in common with those whom we have learned to classify as members of privileged, dominant groups. Women and men alike may be viewed as undifferentiated "enemies," to be feared, hated, and resisted. To attain some measure of self-esteem, we have learned to emphasize and positively express our differences and to value features that distinguish us as a group. We do not want to be "assimilated" according to the values of others but insist on being accepted on our own terms.

Our identity as a member of a less privileged group depends on our consciousness of the history of our oppression by others. Freedom from racial, class, ethnic, or homophobic oppression may rank highest among our priorities, and to focus attention on a division *within* our groups, between women and men, may seem to us a betrayal of our common cause. How can we concern ourselves with the problems of the women among our oppressors, or even with our own experiences of sexism in our particular group, when the men in our group daily suffer oppression from more privileged groups and classes? We may feel that our very survival depends on unity within our group and that our men cannot be blamed for conditions not of their own making. Perhaps when *these* conditions change, we argue,

we can worry about the relations between the sexes. Right now, the quality of those relations is determined by the social position of our group as a whole.

Thus, African American women may rightfully argue that relations with African American men are shaped by racist discrimination that denies African American men equal opportunities. What can these relations have in common with relations between white women and men? While Native American women may have suffered oppression by a sexist society, sexism itself seems a much lesser evil than genocide. Jewish women in Israel or Palestinian women in the West Bank, and those who identified with them, may have felt that given an ever-present threat of violence, concern about women's equality must be deferred. The oppression of an entire economic class by those born into a privileged class may seem to some to be a greater injustice than sexism. Women who are lesbians may feel closer to gay men who can understand the exclusion lesbians experience than to straight women who do not.

Those of us, then, who deal with day-to-day problems of enormous dimensions arising from racial, class, ethnic, and other oppression may find it hard to focus on a form of oppression shared by others who do not suffer directly from these same problems. Still, the various kinds of discrimination we experience in whatever group we belong to arise from some similar sources. Racism, sexism, class oppression, and homophobia all assign people roles based on stereotypes, on supposed attributes used to provide rationalization for exploitation or disdain. To fight against one kind of discrimination is to aid the fight against other kinds. Just as feminism in the nineteenth century arose along with the struggle against slavery and with an awareness of other exploited groups in society, so the twentieth-century women's movement began in part in connection with the civil rights movement and is increasingly allied with many other movements for social justice. And women who fight against any form of oppression do well to join in the fight against sexism as well.

As those of us from relatively more silenced groups increasingly gain a hearing for the expression of our concerns, experiences, and points of view (Anzaldúa, 1990; Collins, 1990; hooks, 1989, 1990; Ling, 1991; Williams, 1991), women who lack adequate awareness of these experiences can learn from them and can incorporate these different points of view into our own thinking. Women who have been relatively privileged may need to work hard to become conscious of the double and triple burdens of those of our gender who have suffered other types of oppression. And those of us who have been part of groups oppressed for reasons other than gender may have to face the fact that sexism exists in our own group. Fighting discrimination against women in general—in the job market, in gaining education, in becoming trained professionals, and in leading dignified personal lives free of domestic violence and with a heightened self-esteem—cannot but help every woman, regardless of group or class affiliation. The more we identify the barriers women face, the clearer our different perspectives will become, and the more the diversity of perspectives can contribute to better formulating of feminist goals, understanding how to reach them, and addressing the concerns of all women everywhere (Albrecht and Brewer, 1990).

Like members of any other oppressed group taking a first step toward change, women begin by recognizing the characteristics that distinguish us as a group, in the view of outsiders and in our own view. We emphasize those distinctive characteristics of our group that we value and that we believe ought to be a source of pride. This emphasis on group distinctiveness and unity gives us the political and psychological strength we need

to demand the right to be accepted on our own terms. While as women we may welcome the help of men who recognize the oppression we have suffered, we do not wish to depend on it or to compromise our own views to obtain it. In a context of practical politics, compromise may be appropriate. In a context of women's studies, it is not.

Women's Studies as an Academic Discipline

People in women's studies differ as to whether the new scholarship about women should be developed as a separate academic discipline or whether it should be integrated entirely within the established academic disciplines. The study of women as a specific focus emerged within the established academic disciplines. Individuals who received our training in a particular field such as literature, history, psychology, or philosophy became discontented with existing knowledge, perspectives, and research methodologies regarding women and began to pursue the study of women within our own disciplines. In this way, specialties such as the psychology of women, women's history, and women's literature emerged. All this new scholarship provided a powerful impetus to create new theories and concepts from a nonsexist perspective. Focusing on women from a particular disciplinary perspective is not the same as drawing from many disciplines to answer questions that focus on women. Different disciplines ask different kinds of questions and often use discipline-based methods to find the answers. For this reason, many people now believe that the field of women's studies should be its own discipline, and not simply a focus on women integrated into the already existing fields. By 1987 there were some 500 programs in women's studies in the United States, and 49 percent of all colleges and universities offered concentrations in the field (Zinsser, 1993).

As women's studies grows as a discipline,

with a special focus on the study of women, universities have begun to offer advanced work in women's studies. Master's level and even doctoral programs exist, although they are a slowly growing phenomenon. As in other disciplines, individuals in women's studies are also very likely to specialize in some particular area of the study of women, as the field is too broad for anyone to be an "expert" in all its aspects.

Women's studies allows scholars to draw information about women from all the other academic disciplines and to select from that scholarship whatever perspectives, information, and approaches are most useful to a particular question. Doing so has allowed women's studies scholars to develop their own conceptual frameworks and to build new theories from them while engaging in research projects that will test, revise, and expand these theories. In practice, the study of women need not be confined to one approach. It can be part of established disciplines as well as a discipline on its own.

The study of women provides a basis for critical examination both of existing disciplines and of the social practices they study. Women's studies sharpens our awareness of the connections between ideas and behavior. The importance to women's studies of the connected perspectives of race, ethnicity, class, age, sexual orientation, religion, and physical abilities has placed women's studies scholars in the forefront of efforts to transform knowledge and the curriculum that flows from it. These efforts since the late 1970s have done much to challenge what is taught and how it is taught (Andersen and Collins, 1992; Culley and Portuges, 1985; Fiol-Matta and Chamberlain, 1994; Luke and Gore, 1992; Minnich, 1990; Rothenberg, 1992; Zalk and Gordon-Kelter, 1992). Knowing the effects of ideas, institutions, and patterns of behavior on the place of diverse women in society provides us with a basis for criticism in both moral and practical terms. It helps us understand our complex past and plan our future.

Women's Studies and Gender Studies

Part of the rethinking about women and society that took place in the earliest years of the modern women's movement was the introduction of the concept of "gender." *Gender* was proposed as a word that would distinguish between an individual's biological sex and the characteristics, roles, and sense of self that were formed by social expectations after birth. The use of the word *gender* instead of *sex* when referring to an individual's "femaleness" or "maleness" was intended to imply this social construction of realities and its effect on an individual's choices. The usage allowed scholars to pursue in a careful, analytical manner the effects of particular contexts on those realities and choices and social interaction in general.

We therefore interpret the choice of *gender* rather than *women* in describing a program of studies, as in *gender studies*, deliberately to signify that the focus of the scholarship lies in the interaction of the sexes and not a focus on studying issues specifically from women's perspectives. For this reason, the authors of this book continue to use *women* and *women's studies* as the central organizing principle of our text to reaffirm our original commitment to placing women in the center of our study. We use *gender* to acknowledge our awareness of the social construction of "femininity" and "masculinity" in different cultural contexts. We believe, however, that there must be a core study of women's experiences, focusing directly on women's lives and what they have created, in order to balance the omissions of knowledge that are centuries old and hamper us still in some of the formative concepts of other disciplines (Zalk and Gordon-Kelter, 1992). Such a focus continues to be required to supply us with the critical knowledge we need to reassess what we think we know about women, to bring that new information to the study of gender relations between the sexes, andthereby to add to the sum of human knowledge.

Women's Studies as a Source of Strength

One of the most important achievements of women's studies as an academic discipline has been to recover the successes of women in the past and to sustain the work women are now doing. Many isolated women in the past accomplished extraordinary things that have been buried through lack of interest by those controlling cultural life. Previous feminist ferment produced significant social change and outstanding academic and intellectual efforts that were then submerged by waves of reaction. Examples of losses that have been recovered are Christine de Pizan's *Book of the City of Ladies* (1405, 1982) and Elizabeth Cady Stanton's *The Woman's Bible* (1895–1898, 1972). Similarly, today's exchanges of books between the United States, Europe, Asia, and Africa—works of imagination and scholarship—create a new global women's community that looks for knowledge and information, theory and literature, from multiple sources reflecting many differing realities. Women need to ensure that today's women's movement remains strong and is not submerged again; the history of feminist gains followed by grievous losses should serve as a warning of what can happen and make clear the importance of keeping knowledge about women alive and growing.

An institutional base for women's studies at as many universities and colleges as possible will help to make visible the work women have done and are now doing, even when such work is unwelcome in the wider society. Independent centers for research on women, community-based women's organizations, lobbying in government circles, and organizing for

political and cultural influence can all gain from women's studies. And women's studies can in turn gain knowledge from what is found in women's practical endeavors and experiences—especially from women's work for women, such as battered women's shelters, rape crisis centers, and the work to keep abortion clinics safe and available to all women.

Women's studies also provides a basis for action in specific and practical ways for the individual, both as a student and in later life. While we are in college, women's studies courses expand our perspectives on what we are taught in other courses, providing us with a basis for evaluating what we are taught and for relating such knowledge in a meaningful way to our lives.

Whatever our major fields of interest in school most of us will use our education in the nonacademic world. What we learn from women's studies may help us to make better decisions about how to live and work and vote, how to express ourselves, and how to fight for our ideals. Women's studies gives us an increased awareness of ourselves (women and men), which may help us to understand our personal pasts and futures. These personal issues—such as choosing a career, making decisions about human relationships, and planning our futures—touch us all in one way or another. Women's studies is not a "how-to" course, but it does bring the issues and implications of our personal decision making into sharper focus.

How This Book Presents Women's Studies

The field of women's studies is still so new it has no traditional subgrouping, no standard way of presenting materials, not even a general agreement about its definition. In this book, we have tried to present the discipline as we see it, in the continuing process of defining itself. As far as possible, we have avoided disciplinary boundaries in order to focus on our subject, women, as human beings.

We begin with a focus on women as individual persons; we then move to women in the family, and, lastly, to women in society. The order could readily be reversed; indeed, many may prefer to view things that way. We have visualized the subject matter as three concentric circles. Moving from the self outward, we have sought to suggest that what occurs in each circle has profound reverberations through the others.

Women are not one group of people with common backgrounds, experiences, and perspectives. When we wrote the first edition of this book, a dozen years ago, there was much more information on white, middle-class women and on women in the majority classes of more industrialized countries than on the rest of us, including women from industrially developing nations. As women's studies has grown and as more women with diverse backgrounds are reflecting on our experiences, literature by and about the latter women has developed, and this edition of our book incorporates the rich insights, new information, and wider data such material provides.

We have grappled with the issue of language in several ways. To begin with, we are very conscious of the changes that occur in self-identity and self-presentation as they translate into language usages. We have moved from the first edition's blanket term *black* to designate only African Americans to that explicit terminology; we are aware of the multiplicity of ethnicities involved in the U. S. census heading "Hispanic," and have substituted the term *Latinos/Latinas* where appropriate and more specific ethnic designations where more appropriate. We have continued to use the term *Native American*, although at times we also write *Native American Indian*, because we learn that there is a shift going on in the usage of that terminology. Even more difficult phraseology that gets repeated as

shorthand language causes us problems. For example, *developing nations* and *developed countries* seem to us to refer clearly to issues involving the economy and efforts to change the bases for economies, but there is somehow a hint of noneconomically related "development" implying hierarchical scales of value that we wish to dismiss from our usage. We have therefore chosen to use terms like *economically developing nations* and *industrially developed countries* to make our understanding of that issue evident. The term *Third World* has its roots in Cold War terminology, and we use it only when it seems to be claimed by women in areas so designated. A particularly troublesome term because of its prevalence in social science literature is *minorities*. Here we understand the term to refer strictly to groups whose numerical presence within a larger group brings with it lack of power and privilege claimed by the dominant group. Within the United States "minority" groups may in fact be part of global majority populations for whom the political realities of citizenship include acting strategically from the vantage point of less privileged positions. On the whole we try to avoid the term, substituting what we believe is more pertinent to any context, reference to the issues of poverty and racial and ethnic minority status that frame people's lives. On occasion we have even used with some reluctance the contrasting terms *white* and *nonwhite* as a shorthand to designate some kinds of dominant and nondominant positions vis-à-vis power and privilege. We know we have not "solved" these linguistic issues to our own satisfaction, but we think it important that the readers of this textbook be conscious of our choices and the need to understand that contexts require choices of language all the time.

One last word about the approach of this book. It must be apparent by now that when we authors write about women, we use the pronouns *we* and *our*. We have discussed this decision in detail in the preface and refer the reader to it, but some attention to this technique seems appropriate here. In using *we* when referring to women, we the authors do not intend to imply that we speak for all women; indeed, we are very much aware of the diversity among women. We know that we may be accused of a cultural ego-/ethnocentricity, just as we have accused men who, using generic *he*, claim to speak for women as well as men. There is a considered point of view behind our use of *we*, and our commitment to that point of view has made us willing to take the risks inherent in employing this technique.

First, our use of *we* is an attempt to make a statement about previous writing about women. Historically, women have been written *about*; they have been presented as passive objects in all forms of communication. The use of *we* and *our* is an attempt to place women before the reader as the subjects, the actors. Our second goal is to try, through this technique, to instill in the reader a sense of participation with all women in the shared aspects of our histories, and identification with women's realities and women's choices in every setting and every age. Such identification, across our differences—real as they are—is the meaning to us of sisterhood, and we still believe in sisterhood, not as an essentialism that denies differences but as a practical political stance upon which we can found coalitions of interests toward shared goals.

As we have noted in our preface, we the authors are aware that the reader may find this usage jarring at first. We hope that the reader's response will provoke thought about this matter. There is a danger that many readers may feel excluded when first reading *we* in reference to groups of women—older women, women of the past, women of another culture—with whom these readers do not identify. We suggest that readers think about the factors that account for such differences of subjectivities, and consider what—beyond these differences—women may still have in common. Clearly, understanding women and women's experiences historically, across classes, cultures, generations, and sexual orientations, indeed across all the barriers that potentially divide us, requires a heightened awareness of both our differences and our similarities. We need to understand the consequences of being assigned membership in a human group socially labeled "women."

Summary

Women's studies examines the world and those who inhabit it in the light of women's own experiences of that world. It complements and corrects established disciplines as well as constituting a discipline of its own.

Feminism is based on the high evaluation of women as human beings and rejects the assignment of roles based on gender. Women's studies receives support from feminists in and out of academic life and arms us with knowledge. Women's studies has grown on American college campuses since the late 1960s. It marshals new feminist scholarship from various disciplines and builds on it to create new concepts and theories. Much of this work is done as a collective effort.

Women's studies programs are necessary because they fill in missing information about women in history and correct misconceptions about women's bodies, mental capacities, activities, and achievements. In the process of doing so, women's studies is developing new lines of inquiry that focus on women and our views. Women's studies is also adding to our knowledge of men.

Women's studies serves as an academic discipline that can develop and keep alive knowledge of the past and present work of women. It is a source of strength for the women's movement and a basis for action to bring about greater social justice and personal development for women of all groups.

Increasingly, women's studies takes account of and reflects the experiences and insights of women bearing the burdens of racial, class, ethnic, and other subordinations along with the burden of gender subordination. The women's movement is concerned with oppression from all sources. To understand and work for the liberation of women contributes to the fight against all oppression.

References

Albrecht, Lisa, and Brewer, Rose M., editors. *Bridges of Power: Women's Multicultural Alliances*. Philadelphia: New Society Publishers, 1990.

Andersen, Margaret L., and Collins, Patricia Hill, editors. *Race, Class, and Gender: An Anthology*. Belmont, Calif.: Wadsworth Publishing Company, 1992.

Anderson, Bonnie S., and Zinsser, Judith P. *A History of Their Own: Women in Europe from Prehistory to the Present*. 2 vols. New York: Harper & Row, 1988.

Anzaldúa, Gloria, editor. *Making Face, Making Soul. Haciendo Caras: Creative and Critical Perspectives by Feminists of Color*. San Francisco: Aunt Lute Books, 1990.

Chamberlain, Mariam K., editor. *Women in Academe: Progress and Prospects*. New York: Russell Sage, 1988.

Chamberlain, Mariam K., and Bernstein, Alison. "Philanthropy and the Emergence of Women's Studies." *Teachers College Record* 93:3 (Spring 1992):556–68.

Collins, Patricia Hill. *Black Feminist Thought: Knowledge, Consciousness, and the Politics of Empowerment*. New York and London: Routledge, 1990.

Coughlin, Ellen K. "Feminist Economist vs. 'Economic Man': Questioning a Field's Bedrock Concepts." *Chronicle of Higher Education* (June 30, 1993):8–9.

Culley, Margo, and Portuges, Catherine, editors. *Gendered Subjects: The Dynamics of Feminist Teaching*. Boston: Routledge and Kegan Paul, 1985.

Ferguson, Margaret W., Quilligan, Maureen, and Vickers, Nancy J., editors. *Rewriting the Renaissance: The Discourse of Sexual Difference in Early Modern Europe*. Chicago and London: The University of Chicago Press, 1986.

Fiol-Matta, Liza, and Chamberlain, Mariam, editors. *Women of Color and the Multicultural Curriculum: Transforming the College Classroom*. New York: The Feminist Press of the City University of New York, 1994.

Hacker, Barton C. "Women and Military Institutions in Early Modern Europe: A Reconnaisance." *Signs* 6 (1981):643–71.

Haraway, Donna. *Primate Visions: Gender, Race, and Nature in the World of Modern Science*. New York and London: Routledge, 1989.

Held, Virginia. *Feminist Morality: Transforming Culture, Society, and Politics*. Chicago: University of Chicago Press, 1993.

Helly, Dorothy O., and Reverby, Susan M., editors. *Gendered Domains: Rethinking Public and Private in Women's History* (Essays from the Seventh Berkshire Conference in the History of Women). Ithaca and London: Cornell University Press, 1992.

hooks, bell. *Talking Back: Thinking Feminist, Thinking Black*. Boston: South End Press, 1989.

———. *Yearning: Race, Gender, and Cultural Politics*. Boston: South End Press, 1990.

Kelly (Kelly-Gadol), Joan. "Did Women Have a Renaissance?" In *Becoming Visible: Women in European History*, edited by Renate Bridenthal, Claudia Koonz, and Susan Stuard. 2nd ed. Boston: Houghton Mifflin, 1987.

Ling, Amy. "I'm Here: An Asian American Woman's Response." In *Feminisms: An Anthology of Literary Theory and Criticism*, edited by Robyn R. Warhol and Diane Price Herndl. New Brunswick, N.J.: Rutgers University Press, 1991.

Luke, Carmen, and Gore, Jennifer, editors. *Feminisms and Critical Pedagogy*. New York and London: Routledge, 1992.

Minnich, Elizabeth Kamarck. *Transforming Knowledge*. Philadelphia: Temple University Press, 1990.

Pizan, Christine de. *The Book of the City of Ladies.* 1405. Translated by Earl Jeffrey Richards. New York: Persea, 1982.

Pomeroy, Sarah B. *Goddesses, Whores, Wives, and Slaves: Women in Classical Antiquity.* New York: Schocken Books, 1975.

Rothenberg, Paula S., editor. *Race, Class, & Gender in the United States: An Integrated Study*, 2nd ed. New York: St. Martin's Press, 1992.

Slocum, Sally. "Woman the Gatherer: Male Bias in Anthropology." In *Toward an Anthropology of Women*, edited by Rayna R. Reiter. New York: Monthly Review Press, 1975.

Stanton, Elizabeth Cady. *The Woman's Bible.* 1895–1898. Reprint. New York: Arno Press, 1972.

Tanner, Nancy M. *On Becoming Human.* New York: Cambridge University Press, 1981.

White, Deborah Gray. *Ar'n't I a Woman? Female Slaves in the Plantation South.* New York and London: Norton, 1985.

Williams, Patricia J. *The Alchemy of Race and Rights.* Cambridge Mass.: Harvard University Press, 1991.

Zalk, Sue Rosenberg, and Gordon-Kelter, Janice, editors. *Revolutions in Knowledge: Feminism in the Social Sciences.* Boulder, Co.: Westview, 1992.

Zinsser, Judith P. *History and Feminism: A Glass Half Full.* New York: Twayne Publishers, 1993.

Part *I*

Defining Women

Introduction

What is a "woman"? What is it that allows us to say of someone that she is a woman? When we think about these questions we realize that they are not simple. One response might be: "Which woman?" We are different. We belong to different racial, ethnic, cultural, and national groups, we live different lives in different classes and times, some of us are mothers and some are not, some are lesbians, some are not. Yet we understand that to study women in all our complexity we need a conception of the people we are studying. What is it about women that leads us to group ourselves together and to refer to women's studies as a discipline?

One common definition of "woman" that is generally taken as incontestable comes from the biological sciences: women are that group of the human species whose typical members are able to conceive, carry a fetus, give birth, and lactate. Is that an acceptable definition of woman? Certainly women are much more than this. We are whole and active persons, not merely "walking wombs."

Recorded history reveals a range of images of women and of views on how to define women. These images and views have represented how men saw, imagined, and thought about women, not how women saw, imagined,

and thought about ourselves directly, though the dominant images and ideas of a culture shape how all the people in it see themselves and others. More recently, people trained in various areas of knowledge have suggested conceptions of women that focus on the biology or psychology or social roles of women; various disciplines have tried to capture women in the discipline's own particular picture of women's bodies, emotions, or behavior. This has left us without a sense of woman as a subject of experience, as the embodiment of an "I," rather than as an object of others' views or of scientific study. We have lacked a sense of woman as a whole person.

Many of the different disciplines have basic similarities. Researchers often study the effects of biology on behavior and emotions as well as the way psychological processes act on the body. Psychology has roots in philosophy as well as physiology. Anthropologists frequently employ economic or psychological theories to explain their findings. The symbols and images that appear in literature and the arts reappear in diverse fields. And conclusions from one discipline affect the thinking and approaches to the study of another. Thus we see many overlapping premises and perspectives. The problem with this is that much information is gathered and many theories are built on common misconceptions and biases. This is especially true in the case of women.

Where do these underlying assumptions come from? They come from the beliefs, teachings, and experiences of the people who contribute to the disciplines. These individuals generally come from similar educational backgrounds infused with a history of attitudes and beliefs about women. Their conclusions are frequently generalized to women who have never actually been studied, and especially not studied from women's points of view. All these disciplines have been dominated by men. In all cultures men's experiences differ from women's, yet it is nearly always men who define women. As a result, women learn to see ourselves through men's definitions, and must struggle to unlearn this way of seeing.

The definition of women as "baby makers" is almost universal. That women have the babies is hardly debatable. What are questionable are the conclusions drawn from this biological fact, such as that what women are and do must be determined by our reproductive capacities. Women give birth and lactate; therefore, it has been thought, it is natural for us to be the caretakers, and for our entire lives to be shaped by this. Gender roles, the roles which society prescribes for women and men, are based on such definitions. Questionable

conceptions of women and men are often put forward as explanations, and a cycle of faulty reasoning evolves.

Women need not read the professional literature to know how we have been seen and thought about. Definitions are communicated in direct as well as subtle ways in all cultures. They are communicated in social roles; in myths, rituals, folklore, and now media images; in the symbols and values of a culture; and in the language used to express ideas. Inevitably, the persons described are pressured to fit the symbols and definitions used to describe them, thereby lending what is seen as support for the original, biased definition.

The attitude, however subtle, that permeates definitions of women is the view of women as "the other." Thus, women have been thought of primarily as those who are "not men." Women have been seen as those who are "other than" what has been thought to be the foremost example of human: man. There has been an emphasis in much thinking and research on the differences between women and men. Women have been defined by comparison: *less* rational, *more* frivolous, *closer to* nature, *more* nurturing, *less* aggressive, for example. Women have been conceptualized in terms of our endocrine and reproductive systems—that which makes us *different* from men. Men have been viewed as the norm, and women as a deviation from that norm. What is identified as "male" has been viewed as "ideal," and thus "male" characteristics have been highly valued. By comparison, women's characteristics have been devalued because we have been viewed as defective or incomplete males, inherently less than "ideal," and even less than human.

The implications and consequences of such definitions of women affect our daily lives. They mold our sense of self from childhood to old age. They affect how we are brought up and evaluated. They undergird the legal system we live in and the public policy that affects our control over our bodies in matters of contraception, abortion, and sexual coercion. They shape our society's approaches to women's educational and occupational opportunities, and to women's physical and mental health. Most important, the process of defining what a women is also tells women what society thinks they *should* be. In the course of socialization and education, and in recent years of media indoctrination, these definitions of women communicate to us what we should aspire to. They impose on women the expectations of society, and provide a framework within which to censor women who do not, or will not, conform to those expectations.

What have clearly been missing are women's self-definitions. As feminists increasingly move into the various disciplines of academic study, we are questioning underlying assumptions and definitions in our histories, our cultures, and our specialized fields. We are proposing new questions to be asked and new methods of inquiry, and we are offering alternative interpretations of findings. We are revealing the faulty premises and biased reasoning of previous thought. Women's studies as a discipline is not constrained by the narrower focus of other fields. It can study women as whole people. Using the new insights of feminists in domains other than the academic and in various disciplines, women's studies provides an integrated understanding of the lives and experiences of a wide range of different women.

The chapters in Part I look at the ways in which the question "What is a 'woman'?" has been answered. They take a critical look at the images and conceptions, the assumptions and research, that have been used in answering the question, and they analyze how these affect women and men. The chapters also address the ways in which women have defined ourselves over the years and in different cultures and circumstances. They consider the changes that are occurring, the rebellious voices that are being raised, and the new directions that are being pursued.

One might ask whether it is helpful to rehearse past definitions of women. It is our be-lief that the traditional perspectives on women are very much a part of our heritage and are inseparable from the lives women have led. An understanding of what has existed can help women clarify where we want to go as we in-creasingly develop our own views of who and what we are.

chapter **1**

Imagery and Symbolism in the Definition of Women

No man would consent to be a woman, but every man wants women to exist. "Thank God for having created woman." "Nature is good since she has given women to men."

SIMONE DE BEAUVOIR

The Meaning of Imagery and Symbolism

Experience, Perception, and the Symbolic Construction of Reality

Classification and Perception. If we were suddenly transported to another world, where none of the objects, smells, sounds, colors, or other sensations were anything like what they are on earth, we would feel greatly confused. Our senses might be open to everything, but we would have difficulty knowing what we were experiencing. Until we learned to classify what we sensed, we would have no clear perception of this strange world. What we perceive is dependent on the way we order our experience. We select certain characteristics and say that they typify an object; other characteristics are dismissed as unimportant and are erased from our consciousness. The ordering that we do in our minds structures our experience for us and renders it intelligible. Without some order, there is no meaning.

The capacity to organize our perceptions is innate, but we must learn the categories we will use to classify them. In our first years of life, we learn from people around us distinctions that have meaning within our own cultural settings. We learn to distinguish colors such as green from yellow, objects that are food from those that are "not to eat," and things that are for girls from things that are for boys. Soon we take the meanings of our classificatory system so much for granted that we cease to question. We believe that we are perceiving "reality" even though, to a large extent, we are seeing only our culture's interpretation of it.

When we need to teach a child or a stranger the distinctions meaningful to us, we see how arbitrary they are. A little boy needs to be taught that he cannot wear silk panties or ruffled dresses. These are arbitrarily classified as "feminine," although there is nothing intrinsically feminine about fine material or personal adornment. Through distinctions such as these, children quickly learn to identify gender by clothing. A modern American child might easily be confused by the dress of a Scottish bagpiper or a traditional Arab chieftain.

In organizing our experience, we make use of *symbols* to give meaning to our perceptions. A symbol, such as a word, a color, or an object, is used arbitrarily to represent something else. Paper money is a cultural or public symbol, a representation widely understood and agreed upon by members of our society. There can be private symbols as well, representations that individuals make to themselves in their own dreams and fantasies.

Our perceptions of women and men are shaped by our symbolic constructs of "femininity" and "masculinity." We select very particular features of personality and physical shape to focus on and to emphasize while we ignore others. We reinterpret what we see according to these preconceptions about what is important. The symbols we allow to represent "feminine" and "masculine" are often arbitrary. For example, we may designate round hips as a feminine characteristic, but both sexes can (and do) have round hips. In any culture, the social construct of "femininity," dependent as it is on symbols, is artificial.

An *image* is an idea or picture formed in the mind. It may be composed of symbols, or it may serve as a symbol itself. The Statue of Liberty is an image formed out of symbols representing womanhood, light, and strength; as a symbol itself it represents liberty, welcome, security—and also the United States, particularly New York City. Imagery is a medium of expression that depends on the symbolic association of the perceiver.

The Shaping of Reality. Not only do we interpret and construct the reality of the external world through the application of names and symbols, but the same names and symbols gradually construct us. Consider our appearance. In places where most people have an image of women as persons who wear makeup, jewelry, and skirts, women who are eager to be perceived as "feminine" do indeed wear makeup, jewelry, and skirts. Social constructs also influence more profound matters of conduct, personality, and intellect. To conform to a cultural representation of femininity, we may think of ourselves as being—and act as though we were—physically weak, incapable of understanding mathematics, and preoccupied with getting married and having babies. Furthermore, such constructs govern the behavior of others toward the individual in such a way as to reinforce the actuality of the image. If women are assumed to be incapable of

learning mathematics, we will not be taught mathematics.

As children, we learn to view ourselves and to behave according to others' perceptions and expectations of us. Cultures vary widely in their attribution of characteristics to femininity and masculinity. In some cultures, women are thought to be naturally strong and hardy, while in others we are thought to be delicate and needing to remain indoors and be protected. A pale skin is therefore associated with femininity, and a darker skin with robustness and masculinity. African American women have experienced the politics of skin color and hair that do not replicate the dominant image of feminine beauty (Okazawa-Rey et al., 1986).

Imagery and Symbolism in the Definition of Women

We live in a world doubly shaped by mental constructions. We perceive "reality" in terms of the categories we have learned, and we shape ourselves and others to conform to the images we have created. We learn to classify objects and to combine symbols into imagery in subtle, inexplicit ways, so that we are not even aware of how we learned what we have learned. Understandings about the meanings of symbols are conveyed through language, through art and literature, through popular media and folklore. This chapter is about these symbolic media, the images they convey about women, and the significance of their representations for women's behavior and ideas about ourselves.

It is important to remember that to the extent that symbolic expression, through whatever medium, is dominated by one segment of society, the imagery conveyed is that group's imagery. If men, not women, are the artists, then the image of women depicted in painting and sculpture will be men's images; women's images of ourselves will not be conveyed either to men or to ourselves. If women have access to the products of this creativity as "consumers"—if, for example, we read but do not speak or write—then the perceptions of women who listen and read will be shaped by a one-sided view of reality. In the history of the world's best-documented civilizations, men have indeed predominated as the creators of symbolic expressions. This results in an imbalance, a lack of reciprocity: Men have been the providers of images and women and men have been the recipients.

The Function of Images and Symbols

The images built out of our symbol-controlled perceptions are usually grouped into categories and classified in different ways depending on our immediate purposes. Different sorts of purposes will result in classification of the same objects in different ways. We may have three articles of clothing: a pink sweater with a ruffle, a bikini, and swimming trunks. We may classify the two bathing suits together if we are interested in function, but we may classify the sweater and the bikini together if we are interested in the gender of the wearer.

How does this apply to classification of people? For some purposes, Aristotle (384–322 B.C.E.) classified women and children together. Since he believed that neither had fully developed rationality, he concluded that the male should rule both females and children and be responsible for them. This attitude, pervasive in Aristotle's time and culture, was reflected in a social system wherein women and children were excluded from public life. In modern America we often find similar attitudes.

How is this type of classification represented symbolically? A "feminine" woman may affect childish mannerisms such as baby talk. Womanhood may be idealized as essentially childlike and associated with innocence, unworldliness, and vulnerability; the "ideal"

woman portrayed in a novel or play may be vested with these characteristics. Thus, the cultural classification of women and children together, in opposition to men, is represented in a variety of symbolic images, some contributed by men, but some contributed by women as we create ourselves to fit the classificatory system that exists. It is obvious that in a classificatory system that views women as the polar opposites of men, but erotically connected only with men, lesbians will have no natural place.

Heterosexism involves the negative representation of gays and lesbians. In Texas, four people were murdered during one year because of their sexual orientations. Advocates of gay and lesbian rights claim that such incidents are related to the proliferation of anti-gay images and messages in the media (*New York Times*, August 30, 1994).

Realistic images of lesbians and gays have been rare in literature and art. Faderman points out that before the lesbian-feminist movement of the 1970s, lesbian writers were compelled to create male characters for their own voices (Cruikshank, 1982). The secrecy that has shrouded homosexuality has contributed to the negation of artistic and intellectual achievements by lesbians and gay men (Duberman et al., 1989). The past decade has witnessed an increase in scholarship that aims to reclaim gay and lesbian history (Lilly, 1990).

Negative images have only recently been challenged in the fictional and nonfictional works of gay and lesbian writers of color. *The Gilda Stories* (Gomez, 1991), *Between the Lines: an Anthology by Pacific/Asian Lesbians* (Chung and Lemeshewsky, 1987), *Compañeras: Latina Lesbians* (Ramos, 1987) are all recent works that fill this void (de Lauretis, 1991).

The Use of Symbols and Their Influence

A woman does not need to be told explicitly that women are separate from and considered unequal to men. We learn this in many dif-

Women, Writing, & Language

I shall speak about women's writing: about *what it will do*. Woman must write her self: must write about women and bring women to writing, from which they have been driven away as violently as from their bodies—for the same reasons, by the same law, with the same fatal goal. Woman must put herself into the text—as into the world and into history—by her own movement.

* * *

Every woman has known the torment of getting up to speak. Her heart racing, at times entirely lost for words, ground and language slipping away—that's how daring a feat, how great a transgression it is for a woman to speak—even just open her mouth—in public. A double distress, for even if she transgresses, her words fall almost always upon the deaf male ear, which hears in language only that which speaks in the masculine.

It is by writing, from and toward women, and by taking up the challenge of speech which has been governed by the phallus, that women will confirm women in a place other than that which is reserved in and by the symbolic, that is, in a place other than silence. Women should break out of the snare of silence. They shouldn't be conned into accepting a domain which is the margin or the harem.

(Cixous, 1981:245; 251)

ferent ways, through various symbolic media, including language, myths, fantasies, and artifice.

Language. The language that women use for thought and speech contains the message of inequality in many forms. We learn that *man* means people and that *he* is the standard singular pronoun. One "masters" material; one does not "mistress" it. "Patrons" support the arts; "matrons" serve as custodians in prisons. *Patronage* describes the condescending help the wealthy or important person offers the poor or less influential one. *Matronage* has not been a word at all until recently, when some feminists have begun to use it in support of women's causes.

These verbal matters are not frivolous and insignificant. Such use of language teaches the young girl that men are the doers and that women are valued mainly for our looks and our amenability. When there are only postmen and firemen and spokesmen, the young girl may assume that only men "man" these posts. (In the new language that feminists are

forming, the word *staff* will serve for *man* in this context.) *Effeminate* is always a "bad" word meaning weak, flaccid, irresolute. *Feminine* is a "nice" word as applied to women, but applied to anything else it is likely to be uncomplimentary. Language has always expressed a people's cultural biases, whatever they are; sexism is only one of them. In other ways, for example, our language is phallocentric. Consider how metaphors reflect a male-centered view of the world in the way that they reflect the close linkage implied between the male sex and machines. Wanting to provide "input," a male "plugs into" a conversation to get its "thrust" and "penetrate" the problem. Or consider how ideas are referred to as "seminal," not "germinal."

Myths, Fantasies, and Artifice. More insidious perhaps than the spoken word, because their messages are subliminal, are myths and fantasies. The story of Adam and Eve, an origin myth for Jews, Christians, and Muslims, begins with the creation of man by God "in his own image." Here we learn that man came first and

---

Women in Nature and Society

. . . for a woman, wanting to become a man proves that she escapes her initial programming. But even if she would like to, with all her strength, she cannot become a man. For becoming a man would demand from a woman not only the external appearance of a man but his consciousness as well, that is, the consciousness of one who disposes by right of at least two "natural" slaves during his life span. This is impossible and one feature of lesbian oppression consists precisely of making women out of reach for us, since women belong to men. Thus a lesbian *has to* be something else, a not-woman, a not-man, a product of society, not a product of nature, for there is no nature in society.

(Wittig, 1981:49)

---

that God is like man (because man is like God). Eve was made as a companion to Adam and constructed from his rib. This tells us that women are subordinate to men in that we are made from them (but not the reverse), and that we exist to serve men's needs. The next event in the creation myth is that Eve, succumbing to temptation, leads Adam into sin. From this we learn that women are morally weak and that our weakness leads men into trouble. In this case, the trouble is great; Adam and Eve are expelled from paradise and are cursed. The curse itself is interesting: Adam's curse is that he shall have to work for a living, and Eve's is that she shall bear children in pain. This suggests that it is men, not women, who engage in productive labor, and furthermore that it is right and proper that childbirth be painful (see Chapter 10).

Cultural imagery, largely originating in men's minds, expresses ideas about women and our roles. The messages conveyed are complex; there may be contradictions and multiple aspects and many levels of communication. The symbolic devices themselves constitute the creative content of culture: literature (spoken and written), sculpture and painting, ritual, dance, drama, clothing, and other ways that humans use their imaginations to express their ideas.

Some Predominant Imagery

Various art forms in different cultures and different historical periods have expressed certain basic ideas of women in similar ways. We will now take a look at some of the ways that women have been represented through symbolic constructs by examining five themes that commonly appear in many cultures around the world—frightening females, venerated madonnas, sex objects, earth mothers, and "misbegotten men." These themes may not be universal, but they are also not confined to any type of culture or geographical region. And although the messages conveyed are not necessarily consistent, contradiction itself makes a statement, as we shall see later in this chapter.

Frightening Females

Men's fear of women is expressed in a vast number of different symbolic modes. Rituals and beliefs suggesting that women's anatomical parts or physiological processes are polluting have been found to be extremely widespread. Women in many cultures are secluded during and after childbirth and during menstruation, after which we must undergo a purification ritual lest we contaminate men. In

The Hindu Goddess Kali portrays woman as monster. This goddess is assigned the attributes of death and destruction, and is usually depicted wih four arms, red palms and eyes, and bloodstained tongue, face, and breasts; her hair is matted with blood, her eyes are crossed, and she has fang teeth. She sometimes wears strings of skulls around her neck, while her earrings resemble corpses. Sometimes her waist is depicted as girdled by snakes. (Nelson Gallery—Atkins Museum, Kansas City, Missouri [Nelson Fund])

some cultures, men are prohibited from sexual intercourse with women prior to engaging in religious rituals or warfare. Many religions prohibit the participation of women in the most sacred ceremonies and even forbid our witnessing these rituals; we are not to touch or see the most sacred ritual objects, or we will pollute them. Such practices may all be interpreted as expressing fear of women.

Folk tales present a more direct image of women as fearsome objects. Witches, sorcerers, and other semisupernatural figures able to transform men by spells are frequently females. Sometimes these threatening figures are deceptively beautiful, but often they are old and ugly. In the Western heritage of fairy tales, the wicked stepmother has no male counterpart; she is the embodiment of evil—selfish, powerful, and dangerous to men and children alike.

Female deities and mythical women are also often portrayed as evil, dangerous, and powerful. In Greek mythology, numerous female monsters threaten men: Scylla squeezes men's bones together and eats them, while Charybdis, the whirlpool, draws men into her watery depths (see Chapter 10).

These cultural expressions of men's fear of women have inspired numerous explanatory treatises. Psychohistorical arguments rest on Freudian analysis, which begins with early-childhood conflicts that become projected in fantasies. Sociologist Philip Slater (1968) argues that the close, stifling relationship of mothers and sons in ancient Greece accounts for the terrifying females of Greek mythology. He claims that mothers, confined to the women's quarters, vented their baffled energies on their small and defenseless sons, whose understandable fears were the basis for the bloodthirsty female figures of myth they grew up to write about.

Some nineteenth-century social thinkers, such as Johann Jacob Bachofen, author of *Mother Right* (1861), as well as a few contemporary feminists, have argued that myths representing female figures as powerful and dominant over men have a historical explanation. They believe that at an earlier stage of human history, women ruled. This form of social organization, called *matriarchy*, was later overthrown by men. Awesome, uncivilized female figures are interpreted, in this argument, as representative of a more ancient order, a mirror image of and threatening to patriarchy, the more recent rule of men.

A number of anthropologists have sought the explanation for men's fear of women in social conditions (Ember, 1978). Some conclude that fear of women is greatest where women are most oppressed. Expressed fear of women may or may not be universal; it is certainly variable in its manifestation.

Venerated Madonnas

While women are perhaps most widely portrayed as objects of fear, we are also idealized as objects of love and veneration. The wicked witch has a counterpart in the fairy godmother; the destructive goddess has a counterpart in the heavenly madonna. Woman in this guise is self-sacrificing, pure, and content. Her job is to make men (and children) feel happy and successful. This message is conveyed in sex manuals and child-rearing manuals alike. The madonna construct is fascinatingly unbiological; she has no blemishes and no body functions. One imagines that she does not menstruate, urinate, defecate, or even perspire.

Incorporated in the image of the Virgin Mary, the madonna has existed in Western culture for centuries: She is the young, beautiful, and pure woman who is at once mother and virgin, source of comfort and support, fulfilled in giving, submerged in the male figures who make use of her (God and Jesus). She is symbolically represented as the new Eve, whose obedience and humility redeemed

Benazir Bhutto (born 1953), elected prime minister of Pakistan in 1993, a predominantly Muslim country. A glamorous woman, born to a wealthy and political family, Bhutto was educated in the West. Her father, also a prime minister in Pakistan, was executed in a political upheaval and members of his family were exiled abroad. About 1980, Benazir Bhutto returned to Pakistan to rise in the political arena against many odds, including the opposition of her mother, who supported her son against her daughter Benazir. In September 1994, Bhutto led her country's delegates to the United Nations Conference on Population and Development in Cairo and made a bold speech defending the rights of women. Two other women prime ministers of Muslim countries, Turkey and Bangladesh, stayed away from the conference, pressured by conservative groups. The imagery and symbolism of a woman, even of a prime minister, is defined by the society in which she lives. It is a courageous defiance on the part of Benazir Bhutto to break through these constructed images. (Reuters/Bettmann Newsphotos)

"mankind" from the curse the first Eve brought upon "him." Through her perpetual virginity, she serves as a symbol of the "good" woman. Through her maternal nature, she nourishes and comforts her offspring in this vale of tears.

How do we account for this image, the converse of the frightening witch? The warm and nurturing relationships small children can enjoy with their mothers may provide the basis for the mythical madonna figures. But madonnalike images do not predominate where women are more equal to men; rather, they sometimes seem to accompany the fearsome images as foil or counterpart in situations of inequality (Cornelison, 1976; Wolf, 1969). They may be understood not only as idealizations but also as wish fulfillments: women deranged and declawed; women now sanctified for our compliance with men's wishes. The "good" woman, stripped of her dangerous elements, desires nothing, demands nothing, and receives worship, not equality.

Sex Objects

Images of women as witches or madonnas leave out an inescapable fact. The first image suggests that sexual relations with women are dangerous to men; the second suggests that sexual relations are unnecessary. But sexual relations with women obviously occur, and without them men cannot have children. The idea of woman as sex object focuses on male sexual gratification. Images of women as sex objects are affected, however, by other notions about women. If we are perceived as dangerous, then before we can be sexually attractive, our dangers must be overcome. If "good" women are pure and asexual, then the objects of sexual desire and release must be invented as "bad," impure.

Pornography, which attempts to reduce human beings to sexual objects, manipulates images of women to appeal to male fantasies.

While the nonerotic witch-woman may consume men (the vagina is sometimes imagined to have teeth), the erotic sex object offers herself to be "eaten." She is displayed as merchandise and popularly called "sugar," "honey," "peach." She may be reduced to a bodily part and called "cunt" or "pussy." If her bodily parts are perceived as threatening, they may be rendered more harmless by being portrayed as childlike. If she is perceived as being too pure to be accessible, her breasts and buttocks may be exaggerated. The adult female may be depicted as bound and helpless, or she may be portrayed as the irresistible seductress. "Hard" pornography does not confine itself to binding women but displays scenes of mutilation; breasts are sliced off, throats bleed, and genitals are penetrated with broken glass. Vulnerable women, debased, in chains, and totally available to male penetration, constitute the fantasy of hard pornography.

Anti-pornography feminists speak out against pornography because it is degrading to women, promotes violence toward women, and perpetuates sexist images of women in general (Russell, 1993). However, feminist responses to the problem vary.

Some anti-pornography feminists (notably Catharine MacKinnon, 1993, and Andrea Dworkin, 1979) promote legislation against images deemed to be degrading to women. Others (Burstyn, 1985; Ellis et al., 1986; Vance, 1990) who fear that such legislation can lead to an erosion of crucial First Amendment rights, favor social policies that promote nonsexist education and the protection of women from sexual violence or its effects (by establishing rape crisis centers, battered women's shelters, and abortion services).

In addition, some feminist critics have pointed out that the pornography debate has been collapsed into a general censure of erotic female images. For example, Carol Vance (1984) points out that this focus may inadver-

---

The Masculine Mystique

Instead of yielding to the affective self, as implied by sensuality, the warrior hero must fight another battle, treating sex as war (between the sexes), making conquests, gaining victories. Even the contemporary vision of the sexual expert is more a matter of a "job-well-done" than shared delight.

... The official macho attitude requires that women, in their delicacy, dependence, timidity, gullibility, and softness, are to be used and enjoyed, like a peach plucked ripe from a tree and discarded just as easily. A young man told me that his father advised him to practice the four f's: "Find 'em, feel 'em, fuck 'em, and forget 'em." Contempt blossoms into hatred: women are stupid, dangerous, wheedling. The only exceptions are those who cannot be contemplated as sexual partners—mothers and sisters, for example, or nuns.

(Ruth, 1980:47, 49)

---

tently reinforce sexual shame and inhibition among women, or falsely suggest that women are not interested in erotic images (Lewallen, 1989). According to this view, it is not women's sexuality or nudity that is objectionable per se, but the way in which images of women are manufactured to reinforce in print the social, political, and economic subjugation of women to men in reality.

Earth Mothers

If the depiction of women as sex objects depends largely on cultural artifice, the counterpart, the earth mother, is seen as embodying what is "natural." Sherry Ortner (1974), an anthropologist, sees the universal devaluation of women as related directly to the symbolic association of women and "nature." Her argument runs as follows: Every culture controls and transforms nature by means of symbols and artifacts. "Culture" is equated with human consciousness and its products (thought and technology), which humans use to control "nature." Culture is superior to nature, for it can transform nature according to its needs or wishes. Women have been associated with

"nature" and men with "culture"; hence, women are seen as inferior to men, and able to be controlled by them.

Women are not identified solely with nature, but are held to be closer to it than men. There are three reasons for this position: (1) Because women also participate in culture, we are considered intermediate between culture and nature. However, what is distinctive about women's physiology is connected with our reproductive role, and our bodily involvement with reproduction is greater than men's. Thus, we are seen as more a part of nature than are men. (2) Because women nurture infants and children, we are associated with children, who have not yet acquired culture (and are therefore closer to nature). Again, however, women are intermediate between culture and nature because our role is to socialize children, that is, to transform "natural" humans into "cultural" ones. Women who care for children are kept closer to domestic cycles, hence to the "natural" family, than men, who circulate in the more artificial "cultural" settings of society beyond the family. (3) Woman's psyche is thought to be closer to nature. Women deal more with what is concrete,

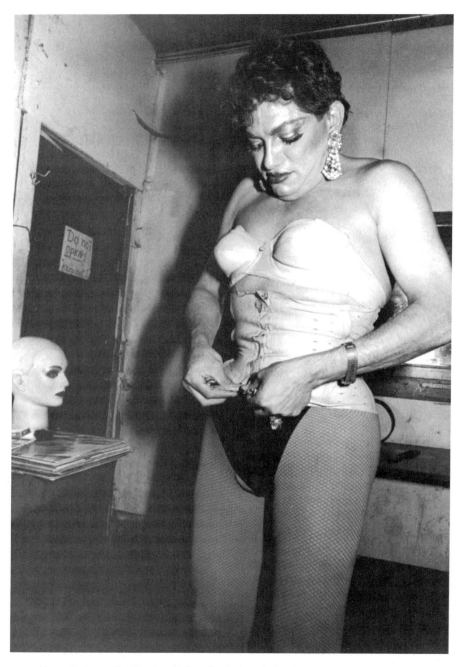

Escuelita An overstated image of a "woman" is reflected on this "queen" as he dresses in drag. The corset that pinches the waistline, the bikini underpants, the mesh stockings, the fake eyelashes, the chunky jewelry are all playful comments on the way a "woman" designs her exterior image. (Photograph by Hope Wurmfeld, 1988)

while men deal more with what is abstract. This results from the difference between the ways females and males are socialized by their mothers (Ortner, 1974).

Women, seen as being closer to nature than men, are accordingly consigned to lower status. Men have culturally manipulated their ideas about women to clarify their own position with regard to controlling nature. The representations of women in cultural imagery—mythology, art forms, ritual, and so forth—are affected by the relations between men, culture, and nature.

Woman as "Misbegotten Man"

In all the foregoing cultural constructs of femininity, women remain a distinctive and formidable presence, but woman as "misbegotten man" very nearly disappears. In the male-centered conceptual world, man is the toolmaker, the doer of deeds, the thinking being. Women who engage in these activities are "like men." Women of ambition who succeed in training our intellects, despite all the obstacles, are said to "think like men."

The subsuming of women under the category "man" that has taken place in the conceptions prevalent in much theorizing has led to the virtual disappearance of women from conscious thought. When Aristotle proclaimed man a "political" (i.e., civilized) animal, he certainly did not mean to include women. The "brotherhood of man" is not a sisterhood. When anthropologists refer to "man the hunter" or literary scholars refer to "man the hero," it is hard to believe they mean to include women. In many respects, this systematic exclusion of women expresses the image of woman as part of nature, and perhaps not fully human. This final image more emphatically denies women a place in culture, because we are neither threats, saints, sex objects, nor earth mothers; we simply are not there.

The Effect of the Images on Women

It would be a mistake to assume that any one image of the female is predominant in a society or at a particular time; in fact, the apparently contradictory images are different expressions of the same idea: woman as "other," the anomalous being who is both like and unlike man. As anthropologist Claude Levi-Strauss (1964) argues, a myth cannot be understood in isolation from the full repertoire of the mythology of a society.

The message that the imagery of women conveys lies not only in its content (woman is dangerous, woman is natural) but also in its form, the opposition of extreme elements: good *versus* evil, natural *versus* artificial. All these images serve to set us apart as "other," to make us more creatures of the imagination than real people. We are conceptualized only in our parts, not as whole human beings.

This kind of conceptualization, according to sociologist Nancy Chodorow (1978), reflects a male way of thinking, a tendency to deal with categories rather than people, which results from the socialization process applied to boys (see Chapter 4). That it predominates in a culture attests to male control over symbolic construction itself—over language, religion and ritual, literature, and the arts.

Although the imagery we have discussed may well originate in the male mind, women certainly subscribe to it and use it. We socialize our children to live in a male-dominated world. We teach our daughters to be feminine and our sons to be masculine (however those terms may be construed).

Do women conform to male images simply to survive, knowing that we must placate men? Do we adopt male fantasies because we have none of our own? No. It appears more likely that women's own imagery has been hidden as a result of male control of symbolic communication. Since women have for the most part been confined to the domestic world, our thoughts rarely emerge in public. Denied opportunities to speak or write or paint or engage in public ritual, we cannot communicate our imagery in any lasting way to one another or to men. Men may, in any case, ignore what women produce because they devalue it. If, in other cultures or other times, historians or anthropologists had the opportunity to observe women's imagery, they paid little or no attention to it. Most historians and anthropologists have been men, trained by men. They have been communicating with men about what interests men (Ardener, 1975).

It was suggested earlier that social imagery provides a rationalization for the real social order. The social distancing established by the notion of women as "other" provides an excuse for the actual devaluation of women, for the treatment of women as less than human, for exploitation and abuse, for the denial of our rights to self-determination. The same ideological devices are used against various ethnic groups and social classes exploited by the elite of a stratified and unequal social order. As a result, women in these communities face the consequences of a double burden of devaluation. This makes the challenge to change it formidable.

Changing Reality by Changing Images

If our sense of ourselves, and of the ways we feel and act, is shaped by predominant social images of gender, than presumably our perceptions, feelings, and behavior can be changed in part by a change in imagery.

It is often argued that "the production of meaning is inseparable from the production of power" (Chadwick, 1990). Feminists contest images perceived to represent women negatively, often by creating diverse alternatives in academia, art, and literature.

In the 1970s, scholarship on women set out to disprove that unequal status of women around the world is biologically determined (and therefore "natural"). This was seen by feminists as an essential first step in combatting images of women that suggested that women were inferior to men.

Women, Culture and Society (Rosaldo and Lamphere, 1974) locates women's subordination, which in this work is deemed to be universal, within a culturally prescribed role as mother and nurturer. Most notably, anthropologist Sherry Ortner and sociologist Nancy Chodorow provided theoretical frames within which to view women's universal subordination.

Sherry Ortner (1974) proposed a nature/culture dichotomy, by which women are universally associated with untamed nature. Mothering roles link women indelibly to biological processes, and private home sphere. Men, on the other hand, are depicted as having superseded and civilized their own "natures," and are associated with the superior public sphere of social life.

Nancy Chodorow (1978) argued that male and female roles were reinforced in children through different relationships between mother and sons or daughters.

Another anthology criticized, or took a different approach from, this early work. *Toward an Anthropology of Women* (Reiter, 1975) suggested that the nature/culture dichotomy and models of child socialization are most useful in describing Western, middle-class cultures, and cannot be used to generalize about women from non-Western cultures. Moreover, this volume questioned the universality of the nature/culture dichotomy on historical grounds. Reiter's volume thus shifted analytic focus from a search for universals to a deeper understanding of how the experiences of women around the world may differ (Morgan, 1989).

Recent works, such as *Gender and Kinship: Toward a Unified Analysis* (Collier and Yanagisako, 1987) and *Gender at the Crossroads of Knowledge: Feminist Anthropology in the Post-*

modern Era (di Leonardo, 1991), explore the perspectives of women of various ethnicities, nationalities, races, and classes to understand our experiences. In these volumes, neither the experience of being a woman nor the meaning of female gender itself is taken to be everywhere the same. Thus, there has been a move away from the search for universal symbols of women's experience to the recognition that diverse groups of women may interpret the same cultural images differently. Perhaps most important, it is also understood that women can and must produce our own symbols to represent our own experiences.

Perhaps the most important contributions to the understanding of the diversity of women's experience have come from women of color, such as Cherríe Moraga and Gloria Anzaldúa, bell hooks, Angela Davis, and Barbara Smith, among many others (Ginsburg and Tsing, 1990). Two of these important contributions are *This Bridge Called My Back* (Moraga and Anzaldúa, 1983), *Making Face, Making Soul—Haciendo Caras: Creative and Critical Perspectives by Feminists of Color* (Anzaldúa, 1990). They include statements of third world feminism, including the work of women of diverse national, ethnic, and racial backgrounds.

As Angela Davis (1989) points out, it is essential that mainstream feminism not overlook the experiences and contributions of women of color. Such an omission can never be benign, as Patricia Hill Collins notes, since

> suppressing the knowledge produced by any oppressed group makes it easier for dominant groups to rule because the seeming absence of an independent consciousness in the oppressed can be taken to mean that subordinate groups willingly collaborate in their own victimization. Maintaining the invisibility of black women and our ideas is critical in structuring patterned relations of race, gender and class inequality that pervade the entire social structure (Collins, 1990:5).

Women's oppression is three-tiered: economic, political, and ideological. The last, the subject of this chapter, is represented by "controlling images" of women (Collins, 1990). According to bell hooks, African Americans have made the least progress in the realm of representation. Whereas improvements have been made in education and employment, images of African Americans in the media are often stereotypical and negative. Whites may see African Americans through the lens of such negative images, and African Americans may see themselves the same way (hooks, 1992). Negative stereotypes are so dominant that they can affect women's esteem for one another. For example, hooks points out that African-American feminists and other feminists of color must be careful not to dissociate themselves from one another while competing for places within the white feminist hierarchy (hooks, 1990).

Changes in Appearance and Conduct

Two recent works, *The Beauty Myth* (Wolf, 1991) and *Backlash* (Faludi, 1991), view the glamorous female image promoted by the commercial fashion industry as dangerous to women. Many women undergo time-consuming and/or dangerous cosmetic procedures in order to allay self-esteem problems aggravated by the proliferation of images of female "perfection."

An alternative perspective is offered by Camille Paglia (1992), who assails feminists for what she regards as dull rhetoric. Beauty, to Paglia, is not a male demand to which women subordinate their energies, but rather an elemental part of female nature, whose sensuality can overwhelm and conquer men. While these two positions are clearly irreconcilable, real women living in a post-modern age may have trouble neatly staking out their own positions on these issues.

Madonna is the cultural icon who best represents this tension. A "perfect blonde," she is at once a consumer and a promoter of the "beauty myth," and she is also a strong, ambitious, successful, talented modern woman (Schwichtenberg, 1993). Ginsburg and Tsing point out that contemporary society offers many ways of being a woman. The question is whether "diversity and change disguise the stable contours of oppression . . . or . . . reveal the shapes of creative resistance and empowerment" (1990:1).

Participating in Imagery Construction: An Example

An important function of the expression arts—literature, drama, poetry, painting and sculpture, and music—is the creation of imagery with which we can see, express, and order the world. Women artists have a very significant role to play in orienting women to our own female identities, as we will see later in this chapter. Here we will look at an effort to change popular imagery which illustrates the challenges and possible achievements of altering consciousness-changing language.

It is no longer news that much of our daily language, spoken and written, is sexist. Such use of language tends to reinforce sexist behavior and organization in our society, to promote stereotyping by gender, and to perpetuate inequality. Feminists have urged those involved in the public media to change their use of language and other imagery in favor of nonsexist usage.

An entirely new language is not necessary to present equal treatment of the sexes. Very conservative change, using common, traditional language, but with balance, can be effective (Miller and Swift, 1980). Many book publishers now have explicit editorial policies about nonsexist usage. One publisher has issued guidelines to eliminate sexist assumptions from all its publications to encourage "a greater freedom for all individuals to pursue

their interests and realize their potentials" (Guidelines . . . McGraw-Hill, n.d.:3).

Guidelines concerning language usage suggest that the terms *man* and *mankind*, when used to denote humanity at large, should be replaced by *human being, person, humanity,* or *people.* The term *man-made* can be replaced by *artificial, synthetic, constructed,* and so forth. Occupations can be denoted by nonsexist terms, as Table 1.1 shows.

To avoid repetition of the pronouns *she, he, her,* and *his,* authors can use plurals terms or words like *personal* and *individual.* Instead of: "The student can buy his or her books at the campus bookstore," we can write, "Students can buy their books . . ." or "The student can buy books for personal use at the campus bookstore." When a single student is being discussed, the gender of the pronoun can be alternated in different cases: "She may graduate with honors if . . ." or "He must fulfill the following requirements . . ." The inclusion of the phrase *and women* in "men and women" can signal an author's sensitivity to the issue of sexism in language.

There is nothing difficult or jarring about these changes for either the writer or the reader. They are minor, easily achievable reforms of language usage. Some writers have attempted more radical changes, but the extent to which they can affect usage is not yet clear.

Table 1.1 Nonsexist Occupational Terms

Congressman	Representative
Fireman	Firefighter
Mailman	Mail carrier
Salesman	Salesclerk, sales representative, salesperson
Insurance man	Insurance agent
Chairman	Chairperson, chair, presiding person
Cameraman	Camera operator
Policeman	Police officer
Spokesman	Spokesperson

Source: Adapted from *Guidelines* . . . McGraw-Hill, n.d.:13.

Women Define Ourselves

The courageous motto written by the nine-teenth-century mathematician Sonya Koval-evsky on a prize-winning essay was "Say what you know, do what you must, come what may" (Osen, 1974). This is splendid advice for those who know that they do know something and have a strong sense of what they must do. But self-definition is problematical for many women. We have not been taught to use our critical faculties, and we have little self-esteem and few ways to develop it apart from society's narrowly approved means. The deepest prob-lems may revolve around our internalization of society's views, our lack of realization that we have a "self" to fulfill, or even that we have any wishes beyond those of pleasing our fam-ilies or others around us. In what follows, we will look at ways in which women have searched for self through art and literature.

Women's Search for Self through Art

Historical Perspective. A few examples from the his-tory of women as painters illustrate the prob-lem of gaining self-definition. As Ann Suth-erland Harris says, "Most women artists before the nineteenth century were the daughters of artists. Those who married often married artists as well. Most women artists be-fore 1800 were trained by their fathers, or by their husbands or some other male relative" (Harris and Nochlin, 1977:41).

Men were more or less free to choose such a field of endeavor, but women could not think of taking up painting without the ap-proval, chaperonage, support, and teaching of a male relative. As a result, we painted as we were taught to paint. Marietta Robusti (1550–1590), daughter of the great Tintoretto, learned to paint with her brothers in her fath-er's studio and learned, as they all did, to paint in their father's manner. Her paintings of her father's friends for the silversmith's guild may

never be identified, lost as they are among Tintoretto's works (Greer, 1979).

To be taught to write or to paint by imitat-ing a style is not unusual; but to be an accom-plished artist, one must learn independence of mind and judgment, qualities not stressed in the training of women. Writing of another era, Linda Nochlin acknowledges the high price women paid:

> The result of ... discriminatory attitudes—whether veiled or overt—was often achieve-ment at a level of competent mediocrity by those women artists tenacious enough to pur-sue professional careers.... Simply being persistent enough to devote a lifetime of effort to being a serious artist was a considerable ac-complishment for a nineteenth-century woman, when marriage and its concomitant domestic duties so often meant the end of even the most promising careers. (Harris and Nochlin, 1977:57)

But there were women artists who did fol-low a personal vision. Their works are often mistaken for the work of a male artist of the same school because they are so fine and so representative of the work of the mentor. The painting of the Dutch artist Judith Leyster (1609–1660), for example, was drawn into the more famous works of Frans Hals, even though their stylistic differences are obvious.

Leyster, born about thirty years after Hals, was respected in her own time. She was men-tioned in Ampzing's description of Haarlem in 1628 and listed as a member of the Haarlem Guild in 1633 (Harris and Nochlin, 1977). Yet some of her works were identified as the works of other artists, men like Hals and her hus-band, Jan Molenaer. It is possible to recognize her paintings by her signature, a monogram JL attached to a star (from her father's brew-ery, the Leyster or Lodestar). One of her works was found to bear her monogram crudely altered to an interlocking "FH"—ap-parently to suggest identification with Frans

Hals (Greer, 1979). In her paintings Leyster shows "mothers combing their children's hair and women sewing by the fireside while their children play beside them.... That Leyster was the first to paint such themes cannot be proved but she conveys greater sympathy for the daily lives of women and their social situations than do the men in her circle who on occasion turned to similar subjects" (Harris and Nochlin, 1977:138). It was only later, when Nicolaes Maes, a follower of Rembrandt, and Pieter de Hooch, a Delft artist, began to portray household scenes in the 1650s that such themes became widely popular in Holland.

The point is clear: How can women's accomplishments be known if our works do not remain attached to our names or if they are dismissed because done by a woman? How can subsequent generations of women avoid being discouraged by the assumption that there have been no important women artists? We should not, then, permit the question "Why were there no great women artists?" since we dispute what it presumes. Notice the careful phrasing of the questions put by Harris and Nochlin in their important book and catalog for the exhibition of *Women Artists: 1550–1950.*

> Why was the Renaissance almost over before any woman artists achieved enough fame for their works to be treasured and thus preserved and for their accomplishments to be noted by contemporary biographers? Why did women artists not reach the historical status of Giotto, so to speak, until almost two hundred fifty years after he had become prominent? What made it possible for a small but growing number of women to have successful careers as painters after 1550 but prevented them from having any significant impact before that date? (Harris and Nochlin, 1977:13).

For us to know of women artists, their potential had to have been valued enough in their own time so they could be taught the craft and left free to pursue it; and then their work had to be valued enough to be kept under their own names so biographers could learn of it and preserve these names for us.

Wendy Slatkin (1993) points out that the perception that women do not create art has to do with the systematic exclusion of women artists from textbooks. In New York a group of women artists calling themselves the Guerrilla Girls have protested the exclusion of women artists from galleries and museums (Chadwick, 1990).

In the past, the designation of much of women's work as mere "craft" rather than "high art" has caused our creations to be devalued. Some contemporary women are reviving such skills as weaving and quilting and are finding a special pleasure in the collaborative nature of much of their creative work. The weaving, pottery, and clothing created by anonymous women inspired feminist artists such as Joyce Kozloff (b. 1942) to redefine the limits of their art (Field and Fine, 1987).

Contemporary Feminist Imagery. Feminism has created a new context within which women artists may work, with feminist critics commenting on our work. Feminist artists are beginning to flourish. The multiplicity of our work demonstrates that there is no single form of expression that must be labeled "feminist."

Some contemporary feminists, like women artists of the past, record and interpret women's lives and fantasies about such experiences as birth, motherhood, food preparation, and being in the presence of other women. In 1971 Judy Chicago and Miriam Shapiro, two feminist artists, along with their students, created a "Womanhouse." This environment "included a dollhouse room, a menstruation bathroom, a nude womannequin emerging from a (linen) closet, a bridal staircase, a pink kitchen with fried egg-breast decor, and an elaborate bedroom in which a seated woman perpetually made herself up and brushed her hair" (Lippard, 1976). Like other feminist artists, Judy Chicago availed herself of the freedom of the twentieth century to express herself through explicitly female sexual imagery.

Working for six years with hundreds of other women and a few men, Chicago created "The Dinner Party," a work that celebrates women's heritage and employs arts traditionally cultivated by women, including needlework, lacemaking, and china painting. On an equilateral triangular table that measures forty-eight feet on each side, thirty-nine places are set for goddesses and women, from prehistoric earth goddesses to the contemporary American artist Georgia O'Keeffe (1887–1986). The table rests on a floor of triangular tiles on which the names of 999 women are written. The triangular shape is based on the configuration of women's pubic mound. For the plates, Chicago adapted the imagery of flowers and butterflies to represent the female genitalia. This imagery derives from the work of O'Keeffe, who developed the painting of flowers into a serious subject but who herself denied that being a woman influenced her painting. "The Dinner Party" is controversial even among feminists. Some question its artistic merit; others express concern that the one plate of an African American—Sojourner Truth—does not use the imagery of all the others (Pois, 1979, 1981; Kuby, 1981).

Feminist artists are also critical of the Art establishment. Artists such as Karen Finley protest the commodification of art by creating public art and performance art, which cannot be stored in a gallery to acquire value through time. Others, such as Jenny Holzer, Barbara Kruger, Silvia Kolbowski, Marie Yates, and Mary Kelly, have critiqued dominant media constructions of women through their own art (Chadwick, 1990).

The work of other feminist artists does not explicitly express a feminist identity. Louise Nevelson (1899–1987), one of the most successful artists of the twentieth century, was best known for her assemblages of machinery, building materials, and welded metal. Nevertheless, Nevelson attributed the special genius of her creativity to being a woman.

Women's Search for Self through Literature

The earliest woman writer in Western literature whose works are extant is Sappho, who lived on the Greek island of Lesbos in the sixth century B.C.E. She wrote poetry for and about a group of younger women who spent time with her before they departed for marriage. The emotions expressed by Sappho run the gamut from love to jealousy to hate, and they were all inspired by women. Although she lived in a male-dominated culture, Sappho asserts women's values. She would not trade her daughter for limitless treasure; she appreciates the beauty of other women; and she prefers love to war. Despite her preoccupation with women's culture, Sappho was admitted into the mainstream of classical literature because of her technical versatility. Male poets could adopt her erotic imagery for homosexual or heterosexual purposes.

Sappho's poetry is an artistic rearrangement and interpretation of reality, though it appears to be frank and personal. In fact, most women's literature is personal to such a degree that the confessional style of writing has been labeled "feminine" even when men employ it (Kazin, 1979). Owing to the circumstances of our lives, women writers have often turned inward to explore the private sphere.

Discovering Models in Women's Culture. Virginia Woolf once said, "Anonymous was a woman." In the past, it was often difficult for women to maintain respectability if we made our writing public (Bernikow, 1974). As in the case of paintings, many works of literature whose creators are now unknown may have been produced by women. According to historian S. D. Goitein

"The Dinner Party" by Judy Chicago celebrates women of myth and history. A central motif for the decoration of the plates is the vaginal shape, which traditionally has signified women's hidden sex identity, with implications of shame, weakness, and inferiority. The transformation of such an image into a celebration of women's greatness and achievements represents the work of feminist artists bent on self-definition. (© Judy Chicago, 1979. Photo by Michael Alexander)

(1978), the poet who composed the Song of Songs (also known as the Song of Solomon) was female. Her dream of bringing her beloved into her mother's house was unlikely to be realized in the society of the Old Testament patriarchs, in which brides moved to their husband's place of residence (see Chapter 7). Her description of herself is a model for women who feel ambiguity or self-hatred about our appearance: The poem may demonstrate the positive effect of romantic love on a woman's self-esteem.

Instead of working anonymously, or as an amateur, Aphra Behn (1640–1689) became the first woman author in England actually to support herself through writing. Restoration

"Moon Garden Wall II." Louise Nevelson (1908–1986) combined everyday objects and discarded scraps of metal to achieve this original, vibrant, and intriguing sculptured panel. She created an extraordinary environment, never seen in such a composition before. One of the foremost artists of the twentieth century, Nevelson considered her art feminine because of its emphasis on creating a new life out of ordinary matter. (1961–75, wood painted black, 96 × 72 × 24 inches. The Pace Gallery. Photo by Al Mozell)

Louise Nevelson: "My Whole Life Is Feminine"

I feel that my works are definitely feminine. . . . There is something about the feminine mentality that can rise to heaven. The feminine mind is positive and not the same as a man's. I think there is something feminine about the way I work. . . . The creative concept has no sex or is perhaps feminine in nature. The means one uses to convey these conceptions reveal oneself. A man simply couldn't use the means of say, finger-work to produce my small pieces. They are like needlework.

I have always felt feminine . . . very feminine. . . . Men don't work this way; they become affixed, too involved with the craft or technique. They wouldn't putter, so to speak, as I do with these things. The dips and cracks and detail fascinate me. My work is delicate; it may look strong, but it is delicate. True strength is delicate. My whole life is in it, and my whole life is feminine, and I work from an entirely different point of view. My work is the creation of a feminine mind—there is no doubt. What I wear every day and how I comb my hair all has something to do with it. The way you live a life. And in my particular case, there was never a time that I ever wanted to be anything else. I was interested in being myself. And that is feminine. I am not very modest, I always say I built an empire.

(Glimcher, 1976:23–24)

literature is tolerant of talk of sex, but Aphra Behn showed courage and originality in speaking of the game of love from a woman's viewpoint. "The Disappointment" is about premature ejaculation. In "A Thousand Martyrs I Have Made," she writes about sexual pleasures. But in another poem, "To Alexis in Answer to His Poem Against Fruition," she recounts a common experience that women faced after satisfying a lover's pleas. Aphra Behn was labeled a prostitute for her outspokenness (Bernikow, 1974).

The Heroine. The word *heroine* is ambiguous. It has been applied to both the female protagonists in a literary work and to females whose actions are admirable. By what criteria are we to judge those heroines of Greek tragedy who, motivated by personal concerns, threatened the masculine fabric of the state? Queen Clytemnestra slew her husband, Agamemnon, upon his triumphant return from Troy in order to avenge his sacrifice of their daughter Iphigenia. Antigone dared to disobey the edict of the king, Creon, by giving her brother, a traitor, a proper burial. Clytemnestra was murdered by her son, and Antigone, condemned to death, committed suicide. Are these women heroines or villains? Our answer clearly depends on who we are and the period of history in which we live. Doubtless some members of the Athenian audience in the fifth century B.C.E. sympathized with Clytemnestra and Antigone for the wrongs they suffered but condemned their actions. Women's experimental theater groups nowadays reenact the old myths so as to leave no doubt that, in our assertion of female values, Clytemnestra and Antigone are heroines in every sense of the word.

In *The Woman Warrior* (1976), Maxine Hong Kingston conjures up a myth derived from stories told by women in her family. A Chinese American girl living a humdrum life in San Francisco envisions herself as a warrior woman in China fighting barbarians, bandits, and even the emperor. She takes vengeance on

---

Song of Solomon

I am black, but comely, O ye daughters of Jerusalem, as the tents of Kedare, as the curtains of Solomon. . . .

I am the rose of Sharon, and the lily of the valleys. . . .

I found him whom my soul loveth: I held him, and would not let him go, until I had brought him into my mother's house, and into the chamber of her that conceived me. . . .

How beautiful are thy feet with shoes, O prince's daughter! The joints of thy thighs are like jewels, the work of the hands of a cunning workman.

Thy navel is like a round goblet, which wanteth not liquor: thy belly is like a heap of wheat set about with lilies.

Thy two breasts are like two young roses that are twins.

Thy neck is as a tower of ivory; thine eyes like the fishpools in Heshbon, by the gate of Bathrabbim: thy nose is as the tower of Lebanon which looketh toward Damascus.

Thine head upon thee is like Carmel, and the hair of thine head like purple. . . .

How fair and how pleasant art thou, O love, for delights!

This thy stature is like a palm tree, and thy breasts to clusters of grapes. . . .

I would lead thee, and bring thee into my mother's house. . . .

(Song of Solomon, 1:5, 2:1, 3:4, 7:1–7, 8:2)

Hebrew Scriptures, Authorized (King James) Version

---

behalf of the people of her village whose grievances were inscribed on her back with knives. Heroines are women who do not accept their fate passively. They think, choose, and act.

The search for self—even for the duration of a summer—is a luxury that has been enjoyed by few of the world's women (Trilling, 1978), but that does not mean the theme should be rejected as unimportant (Jelinek, 1980). The written text need not reveal—directly or distortedly—the experience of the majority. We are looking forward to a world where more options will be available to greater numbers of women. Literature serves as a testing ground for new models.

The paucity of books relating to the experiences of women of color, which critique negative stereotypes of women of color as well as provide alternative images, has been partially rectified in the 1980s and 1990s. Novels such as *The Color Purple* (Walker, 1982) and *Beloved* (Morrison, 1987) have been widely read and acclaimed. Toni Morrison was awarded the Nobel Prize for literature in 1993. Important nonfiction works by women of color include *Home Girls: A Black Feminist Anthology* (Smith, 1983), *Borderlands/La Frontera* (Anzaldúa, 1987), *Women of Color in U.S. Society* (Baca Zinn and Dill, 1994), and *Black Popular Culture* (Wallace, 1992).

Women's Words. Language itself shapes social realities, for words are our primary system of communication. Some people claim that changes in language are an important step in developing awareness of reality and that such changes are essential for reforming society. But language is controlled by those in power and enables them to structure women's individual and collective unconscious. If men have labeled, named, and catalogued everything and have thus forged our system of thought, then women must think and write in a dialect

Aphra Behn: To Alexis in Answer to His Poem Against Fruition

Man! our great business and our aim,
For whom we spread our fruitless snares,
No sooner kindles the designing flame,
But to the next bright object bears
The Trophies of his conquest and our shame:
Inconstancy's the good supreme
The rest is airy Notion, empty dream!

Then, heedless Nymph, be rul'd by me
If e're your Swain the bliss desire;
Think like Alexis he may be
Whose wisht Possession damps his fire;
The roving youth in every shade
Has left some sighing and abandon'd Maid,
For tis a fatal lesson he has learn'd,
After fruition ne'er to be concern'd.

(Bernikow, 1974:71–72)

and mode that is foreign to us (Spender, 1980). Feminist scholars are now attempting to determine whether there is a distinct language, a distinct quality of the imagination, and a separate literary style that are natural to women (Todd, 1980; Cixous, 1981; Tannen, 1990).

According to Robin Lakoff's analysis (1975), women's language has been shaped by socialization. Our vocabulary is expected to be ladylike, and our phraseology and intonation are shaped by our role as language teachers to young children.

> WOMEN'S LANGUAGE: Oh dear, you've put the peanut butter in the refrigerator again, haven't you?
> MEN'S LANGUAGE: Shit, you've put the damn peanut butter in the refrigerator again.

Such differences are being dispelled as women enter the workforce and the locker room, and as men take on a larger share in childrearing.

On the one hand, some women argue that the goal of women authors should be to employ the standard language and to write of common human experience, rather than to examine the truths particular to female life. According to Helen Vendler, "Our young women poets, however loyal their interest in the work of their female predecessors and contemporaries, are still finding the best poetry available to them in the pages of Shakespeare, Milton, Keats, and Wordsworth" (Vendler, 1981:33). She is not convinced that this array of male predecessors must be inhibiting, though she admits that "no woman can fail to hope for the appearance of a woman poet of Shakespearean or Keatsian power" (ibid.).

On the other hand, it is possible to argue that powerful female poets already exist in the Western tradition, though they may not be appreciated by students whose teachers are prejudiced by sexist values. Sappho, for example, may be viewed as at least as admirable a poet as, say, Keats.

Women's Identity in Utopia. Science fiction is a kind of laboratory for testing suppositions and presenting new paradigms. Women's utopian science fiction attempts to create better worlds for everyone but pays particular attention to what is beneficial for women. Feminist writers disagree about whether to emphasize the differences between the sexes in such a world and to honor women's distinctive characteristics, especially the ability to bear children. Should the goal, instead, be *androgyny* (blending of female and male), with the separate identities of the sexes reduced to a minimum? Some feminists prefer a separate women's culture, and others prefer freedom from gender (Ketchum, 1980).

In a complicated work called *The Female Man*, Joanna Russ (1975) tells the stories of Jeanine, Janet, Joanna, and I, who turn out to be all aspects of Woman—women of the past, present, and future, all conflicting, and all carried within each woman, shaped as she is by her temporal, cultural, and personal environment. Russ uses science fiction to explore women's multifaceted nature, freed of the restrictions of society. Ursula Le Guin's *The Left Hand of Darkness* (1976) considers a world in which people are androgynous and anyone may go into "Kemmer," the sexual cycle, and give birth. Critics have objected that her central character is still male, referred to by the male pronoun throughout, so that the old error of men being the norm and women the deviates—the other—is perpetuated even in this inventive book.

Marge Piercy's *Woman on the Edge of Time* (1976) also uses the science fiction genre to suggest two opposing possible futures. To include all women, Piercy takes pains to make her work multiethnic and multiracial. Her visions of two different possible futures, one sexist and one nonsexist, are conveyed in part

through terms that underscore social inequality and equality. In the nightmarish sexist future, women are designated *fems*. If we are not "richies" (members of the upper class), we try to survive as "contracties" (women who arrange to get a contract for sexual service to men). The contracts range for periods of a night or a month to several years; only a "bulgie" (a shapely woman) can get a long-term contract. Reproduction is limited mainly to women who are professional babymakers, "moms." Women are generally considered useful only for sexual entertainment. If we fail to get a "prospect" (client), we might end up in a "knock-shop" (house of prostitution); by forty, we are useless, hence likely to be "ashed" (cremated). If we misbehave, we might be sent to an "organbank" so our organs can be used for someone else.

The nonsexist utopian future has sex and sexuality, but not gender. The pronouns *him* and *her* are replaced by *per*, for "person." People select their own names at adolescence. These names have no particular gender reference but reflect the personalities and preferences of their owners: Luciente, Jack-rabbit, Bee, Red Star. Distinctions are not made by sex in coupling; there are "handfriends" and "pillowfriends" among women and men and between them. The term *mother* applies to all parents, regardless of sex; there are no fathers. All babies are created in laboratories (breeders), not born from women; and through hormonal control, both females and males can (and do) breast-feed. The people who are closest friends form a "core," but there are no marriages or nuclear families. Each child has three "co-mothers" who are usually not lovers ("sweet friends"). Although every person might have various kinds of friends, including lovers, co-mothers, and handfriends, everyone has a room of "per" own, a private living space within the community. Only babies live together.

By her use of *per* and *co-mother* and *core* and

a variety of other terms, Piercy challenges us to see the sexism implicit in the institutional arrangements that standard terms for social relationships represent. She suggests that in a society not governed by sexual stereotyping, a whole new set of concepts, and therefore new language, would be necessary.

The Propagation of Feminist Imagery

Is there a female aesthetic? If so, what are the artistic principles by which we may evaluate works created by women about women's experience for a female audience?

The problem of self-definition through art extends to criticisms of women's work by a cultural establishment dominated by men. Consider needlepoint, quilt making, and painting on porcelain. These are termed *crafts* or *arts*, as in "arts and crafts"—not art. Such terms demonstrate that political power defines reality. The one who classifies grants needlepoint the status of craft and painting the status of art. The bases of the categorizer, whether male, white, wealthy, industrial or ethnic, poor, or agrarian will help determine whether the world so classified will be lauded or criticized.

Contemporary strategies are developing to aid women's self-definition. One strategy has long been known to women in small communities—that of using the support of other women. Just as the larger society has found that people sharing a common concern gain strength from meeting together, so women have learned to use our common experiences to illuminate and support ourselves, to show that we are not alone in our experience as women.

Networking is another variation of this strategy. Having observed the way "old boys' networks" operate, women are trying to develop our own networks. This is the importance of the increasing numbers of women's regional, national, and even international con-ferences. Women are learning that in helping each other we constitute a force of considerable magnitude in the world.

Groups have formed in which women band together to gain and sustain employment and to enjoy and participate in women's culture. Collectives have formed in this country and elsewhere to display media other than the written word. Music groups are flourishing, as are graphics collectives and galleries to exhibit women's work. The National Museum of Women in the Arts in Washington, D.C., has assembled a collection of art created by women in many media, including sculpture, painting, ceramic, and metalwork.

Conclusions: Being Whole

The efforts of many feminists in a wide variety of professions—including writing, law, health, and art—have been directed toward establishing an idea of woman as a whole human being. Women should not be reduced to the subordinate member of a relationship (wife of x, mother of y, secretary of z) or a body part (breasts, uterus, legs). This complex process implies, to many, a radical rethinking of what human beings are and what our society has made of us.

Most feminists today reject self-definitions that deny any one of our parts as much as we reject a self-definition in terms of one or more of these characteristics. We do not, that is, deny the fact that we have families, children, lovers, friends, or dependents: Our obligations to and pleasures with others are emphatically a part of our lives. We seek to incorporate these parts into our perceptions, into our work, and into our activities. This may mean working for certain practical changes, such as accommodations for children in the workplace or in other public places (movie theaters, restaurants, and so forth) so we can take our children with us when we want to.

Maya Lin (b. 1959). Women have been image makers; one of the most frequently visited and celebrated national images is the *Vietnam Memorial* in Washington, D.C., on the Mall. In its understated and pure form, the memorial represents abstract concepts of remembrance, sadness, loss, and love among other feelings that we link with the war in Vietnam. The visual impact of this image of the Vietnam war is stunning and serene. Maya Lin was in her early twenties and a student in the school of architecture at Princeton University when she won the design competition for the Vietnam Memorial in 1981. The "image" of the Vietnam memories is a gift to the nation from the creative mind of this woman. In 1986 another of Maya Lin's creations, *The Civil Rights Memorial*, was placed in Montgomery, Alabama. (AP/World Wide Photos)

Being whole also means accepting and taking pride in one's physical self, not feeling ashamed or awkward or limited because of bodily parts and processes or sexual preferences. This acceptance entails adopting different attitudes toward menstruation, childbirth, menopause, and sexuality, as well as toward breasts and vaginas and legs. Women see these things in terms of what they mean for us, not simply in terms of what they may mean for others. From this perspective, older images of women (witch, polluter, saint, savior) make no sense whatsoever.

Should our new view of ourselves actually become established, through art and literature, medicine and law, many women and men would be obliged to reexamine self-identities and self-definitions. Men, in particular, would have to seek new self-images. If men have defined themselves as "not-woman," characterizing manliness in terms of male superiority toward, conquest of, or disdain for women, the concept of manhood, too, would have to be rethought. Once "woman" along with "man" means "human," we can begin reconceptualizing everything in which difference and contrast has been an organizing principle.

Nor are there secrets, mysteries, or privileges of sex. Women would give this up in exchange for the ability to express ourselves. Menstruation and menopause are neither dirty secrets nor sacred mysteries. No longer hidden and no longer threatening, they cannot be used to manipulate others. Having insisted that we are not *simply* nurturers, consolers, and sources of pleasure for men and for children, women must admit to our human shortcomings and admit the competence of others, including men, to be nurturers, consolers, and sources of pleasure.

It should not be surprising that the effort to create an image of oneself, true to one's own experience and knowledge, is difficult. Any difficult endeavor depends considerably on the extent of cooperation and support people receive from one another. Women who have sought to change our self-images have depended mainly on other women. The literature of feminism is filled with references to support groups and networks of women who share ideas and motivations and time and effort. In this, women have cooperated as they have in the past, whether to bring about change or just to survive in the face of pressure, work, and resistance.

Summary

The ideas that women and men have had about who we are, how we relate to one another, and what our potential is are the products of our cultures. An important part of any culture is its system of symbolic representations of reality—the attribution of *meaning* to perception. We (or our cultures) shape our perception of what is "out there" on the basis of the ways we have learned to *interpret* reality. These perceptions, or "images," are social creations whose shape and origin need to be explained rather than accepted at face value.

Notions of what women are have been shaped by social imagery. Society conveys imagery through ordinary language, social behavior, and creative works. The images themselves have served to set women aside from humanity by reducing us to one or a few aspects of our personalities, physiologies, or behavior. Thus, the image of women as either witch, madonna, sex object, earth mother, or misbegotten man reduces us to something less than whole human beings. This symbolic reduction of women then becomes a rationale for unequal treatment of women and for our own self-devaluation. Women often shape ourselves according to this demeaning imagery simply to survive in a world dominated by men. This imagery is damaging. Why is it so widespread and how can we change it? One important factor in explaining the biased imagery is the predominance of *men* in producing and disseminating it: Men have dominated the fields of public discourse and professional activity in the past. Few women have had the opportunity to present our views of ourselves, although feminist scholars are now discovering many self-defining women whom men's history has hidden. Now, many more women are self-consciously producing images of women, drawing from our own life experiences and perceptions and guided by a feminist appreciation for women's worth. We have examined some of the past obstacles and current strategies that enhance this development.

Imagery and symbolism are of great importance in shaping not only works of art but all perceptions of reality, including those to be discussed in the next chapters. The ways that scientists and scholars have perceived women have been no less influenced by the subtle constructions of culture than have the perceptions of artists, writers, and poets.

Discussion Questions

1. Describe a woman and a man whom you know. (You may use yourself as one of the characters.) Note the difference in language you have used to describe each.
2. Tell a fairy tale or folk tale or the words of a song that a woman told you when you were young. Which of the stereotypes that we have discussed in this chapter appear in

this tale? What message is being conveyed to the listener?

3. Examine a woman's fashion magazine. Discuss the images that fashion imposes upon women. What "feminine" qualities are emphasized? What qualities are ignored? What sorts of women are not shown in the photos? If you were designing clothing, what would you create?

4. Does the curtailment of pornography infringe on freedom of expression?

Recommended Readings

De Lauretis, Teresa. *Alice Doesn't: Feminism, Semiotics, Cinema.* Bloomington: Indiana University Press, 1984. With a title from the Looking-Glass world of Lewis Carroll's Alice, de Lauretis suggests feminism must explore the "labyrinth of language" that often means more than one wants it to mean. She uses film criticism to examine "the representation of woman as spectacle—body to be looked at, place of sexuality, and object of desire—so pervasive in our culture" (4). She asks, "How do we envision women as subjects in a culture that objectifies, imprisons and excludes, woman?" (10)

Kaplan, E. Ann. *Women & Film: Both Sides of the Camera.* New York and London: Methuen, 1983. The development of feminist film criticism beginning in the early 1970s focused in particular on the question of the male gaze, seen as having a "controlling power over female discourse and female desire" (2). Kaplan explores this concept of image-making through a number of specific films. She includes in her introduction a useful glossary to the language of feminist film criticism.

Modeleski, Tania. *Loving with a Vengeance: Mass-produced fantasies for women,* orig. pub. 1982. New York and London: Routledge, 1988. A study of three forms of popular culture designed for a female audience, Harle-

quin romances, Gothic novels, and television soap operas. Modeleski examines the way each type of narrative contains elements of resistance to the subservient role women are expected to play, yet show women ultimately endorsing the patriarchal myths and institutions which subordinate them.

Mulvey, Laura. *Visual and Other Pleasures.* Bloomington and Indianapolis: Indiana University Press, 1989. Essays reflecting the positions the author has explored over time to take on the political issues of culture as they unfolded in the women's movement and the art world from 1971. She pursues the issues of cinematic pleasure and voyeurism and the gradual development of theoretical tools to examine the image of woman as a signifier of sexuality, bringing new questions about image and representation.

Ringer, R. Jeffrey, editor. *Queer Words, Queer Images: Communication and the Construction of Homosexuality.* New York and London: New York University Press, 1994. Among the proliferation of books on Lesbian Theory and Queer Theory, this volume has a section on the portrayals of lesbians and gay men in the media. Issues include the way television portrays homosexuality and AIDS, heterosexism, and lesbian and gay characters.

References

Ardener, Edwin. "Belief and the Problem of Women." In *Perceiving Women,* edited by Shirley Ardener. London: Dent, 1975.

Anzaldúa, Gloria. *Borderlands/La Frontera: The New Mestiza:* San Francisco: Aunt Lute Books, 1987.

Anzaldúa, Gloria, editor. *Making Face, Making Soul—Haciendo Caras: Creative and Critical Perspectives by Feminists of Color.* San Francisco: Aunt Lute Books, 1990.

Baca Zinn, Maxine, and Dill, Bonnie Thornton, editors. *Women of Color in U.S. Society.* Philadelphia: Temple University Press, 1994.

Bachofen, Johann Jakob. *Myth, Religion and Mother Right*. Selected Writings of J. J. Bachofen. 1861. Reprint. Translated by Ralph Manheim. Princeton: Princeton University Press, 1967.

Beauvoir, Simone de. *The Second Sex*. 1949. Translated by H. M. Parshley. New York: Knopf, 1953.

Bernikow, Louise. *The World Split Open: Four Centuries of Women Poets in England and America, 1552–1950*. New York: Vintage, 1974.

Burstyn, Varda, editor. *Women Against Censorship*. Vancouver, B.C.: Douglas and McIntyre, 1985.

Chadwick, Whitney. *Women, Art, and Society*. London: Thames and Hudson, 1990.

Chodorow, Nancy. *The Reproduction of Mothering: Psychoanalysis and the Sociology of Gender*. Berkeley: University of California Press, 1978.

Chung, C. A., and Lemeshewsky, A. K., editors. *Between the Lines: An Anthology by Pacific/Asian Lesbians*. Santa Cruz, Calif.: Dancing Bird Press, 1987.

Cixous, Hélène. "The Laugh of the Medusa." In *New French Feminisms*, edited by Elaine Marks and Isabelle de Courtivron. New York: Schocken, 1981. Originally published as "Le rire de la meduse," 1975.

Collier, Jane, and Yanagisako, Sylvia. *Gender and Kinship: Essays toward a Unified Analysis*. Stanford: Stanford University Press, 1987.

Collins, Patricia Hill. *Black Feminist Thought: Knowledge, Consciousness, and the Politics of Empowerment*. New York: Routledge, 1991.

Cornelisen, Ann. *Women of the Shadows: The Wives and Mothers of Southern Italy*. Boston: Little, Brown, 1976.

Cruikshank, Margaret. *Lesbian Studies: Present and Future*. New York: The Feminist Press, 1982.

Davis, Angela. *Women, Culture, Politics*. New York: Random House, 1989.

de Lauretis, Teresa. "Queer Theory: Lesbian and Gay Sexualities, An Introduction." *differences: A Journal of Feminist Cultural Studies* 3, 2 (1991): iii–xviii.

di Leonardo, Micaela. *Gender at the Crossroads of Knowledge: Feminist Anthropology in the Postmodern Era*. Berkeley: University of California Press, 1991.

Duberman, Martin B., Vicinus, Martha, and Chauncey, George. *Hidden From History: Reclaiming the Gay and Lesbian Past*. New York: New American Library, 1989.

Dworkin, Andrea. *Pornography: Men Possessing Women*. New York: G.P. Putnam, 1979.

Ellis, Kate, et al., editors. *Caught Looking: Feminism, Pornography and Censorship*. New York: Caught Looking, Inc., 1986.

Ember, Carol. "Men's Fear of Sex with Women: A Cross-Cultural Study." *Sex Roles* 4 (1978): 657–78.

Faludi, Susan. *Backlash: The Undeclared War Against American Women*. New York: Crown Publishers, 1991.

Field, Richard S., and Fine, Ruth E. *A Graphic Muse: Prints by Contemporary American Women*. New York: Hudson Hills Press, 1987.

Gamman, Lorraine, and Marshment, Margaret, editors. *The Female Gaze: Women as Viewers of Popular Culture*. Seattle: The Real Comet Press, 1989.

Ginsburg, Faye, and Tsing, Anna Lowenhaupt, editors. *Uncertain Terms: Negotiating Gender in American Culture*. Boston: Beacon Press, 1990.

Glimcher, Arnold B. *Louise Nevelson*. New York: Dutton, 1976.

Goitein, Solomon D. *A Mediterranean Society. The Jewish Communities of the Arab World as Portrayed in the Documents of the Cairo Geniza*. vol. 3. *The Family*. Berkeley: University of California Press, 1978.

Gomez, Jewelle. *The Gilda Stories*. Ithaca, N.Y.: Firebrand Books, 1991.

Greer, Germaine. *The Obstacle Race*. New York: Farrar, Straus, & Giroux, 1979.

Guidelines for Equal Treatment of the Sexes in McGraw-Hill Book Company Publications. New York: McGraw-Hill, n.d.

Harris, Ann Sutherland, and Nochlin, Linda. *Women Artists: 1550–1950*. New York: Knopf, 1977.

hooks, bell. *Black Looks: Race and Representation*. Boston: South End Press, 1992.

hooks, bell. *Yearning: Race, Gender and Cultural Politics.* Boston: South End Press, 1990.

Jelinek, Estelle C., editor. *Women's Autobiography: Essays in Criticism.* Bloomington: Indiana University Press, 1980.

Kazin, Alfred. "The Self as History: Reflections on Autobiography." In *Telling Lives, The Biographer's Art,* edited by Mark Pachter. Washington, D. C.: New Republic Books, 1979.

Ketchum, Sara Ann. "Female Culture, Womanculture and Conceptual Change: Toward a Philosophy of Women's Studies." *Social Theory and Practice* 6 (1980):151–62.

Kingston, Maxine Hong. *The Woman Warrior.* New York: Knopf, 1976.

Kuby, Lolette. "The Hoodwinking of the Women's Movement." *Frontiers* 6 (1981):127–29.

Lakoff, Robin. *Language and Woman's Place.* New York: Harper & Row, 1975.

Le Guin, Ursula. *The Left Hand of Darkness.* New York: Harper & Row, 1976.

Levi-Strauss, Claude. *The Raw and the Cooked.* 1964. Translated by John and Doreen Weightman. New York: Harper & Row, 1969.

Lewallen, Alice. "Lace: Pornography for Women?" In *The Female Gaze: Women as Viewers of Popular Culture,* edited by Lorraine Gamman and Margaret Marshment. Seattle: The Real Comet Press, 1989.

Lilly, Mark, editor. *Lesbian and Gay Writing: An Anthology of Critical Essays.* Philadelphia: Temple University Press, 1990.

Lippard, Lucy R. *From the Center: Feminist Essays on Women's Art.* New York: Dutton, 1976.

MacKinnon, Catharine A. *Only Words.* Cambridge: Harvard University Press, 1993.

Miller, Casey, and Swift, Kate. *The Handbook of Nonsexist Writing.* New York: Lippincott and Crowell, 1980.

Moraga, Cherríe, and Anzaldúa, Gloria, editors. *This Bridge Called My Back: Writings by Radical Women of Color.* Latham, N.Y.: Kitchen Table/Women of Color Press, 1983.

Morgen, Sandra, editor. *Gender and Anthropology: Critical Reviews for Research and Teaching.* Washington, D.C.: American Anthropological Association, 1989.

Morrison, Toni. *Beloved.* New York: Knopf, 1987.

Okazawa-Rey, Margo, Robinson, Tracy, and Ward, Janie Victoria. "Black Women and the Politics of Skin Color and Hair." *Women's Studies Quarterly* 14 (1986):13–14.

Ortner, Sherry. "Is Female to Male as Nature Is to Culture?" In *Woman, Culture and Society,* edited by Michelle Z. Rosaldo and Louise Lamphere. Stanford: Stanford University Press, 1974.

Osen, Lynn M. *Women in Mathematics.* Cambridge, Mass.: MIT Press, 1974.

Paglia, Camille. *Sex, Art, and American Culture.* New York: Vintage Books, 1992.

Piercy, Marge. *Woman on the Edge of Time.* New York: Knopf, 1976.

Pois, Anne Marie. "The Dinner Party." *Frontiers* 4 (1979):72–74.

———. "A Reply to Kuby's Review." *Frontiers* 6 (1981):129–30.

Ramos, Juanita. *Compañeras: Latina Lesbians.* New York: Latina Lesbians History Project, 1987.

Reiter, Rayna Rapp. *Toward an Anthropology of Women.* New York: Monthly Review Press, 1975.

Rosaldo, Michelle Zimbalist, and Lamphere, Louise, editors. *Woman, Culture and Society.* Stanford: Stanford University Press, 1974.

Russ, Joanna. *The Female Man.* New York: Bantam, 1975.

Russell, Diana E. H., editor. *Making Violence Sexy: Feminist Views on Pornography.* New York: Teachers College Press, 1993.

Ruth, Sheila. *Issues in Feminism: A First Course in Women's Studies.* Boston: Houghton Mifflin, 1980.

Schwichtenberg, Cathy, editor. *The Madonna Connection: Representational Politics, Subcultural Identities, and Cultural Theory.* Boulder, Co.: Westview Press, 1993.

Slater, Philip. *The Glory of Hera.* Boston: Beacon, 1968.

Slatkin, Wendy. *The Voices of Women Artists.* Englewood Cliffs, NJ: Prentice-Hall, 1993.

Smith, Barbara, editor. *Homegirls: A Black Feminist Anthology.* Latham, New York: Kitchen Table/Women of Color Press, 1983.

Spender, Dale. *Man Made Language.* Boston: Routledge & Kegan Paul, 1980.

Tannen, Deborah. *You Just Don't Understand: Women and Men in Conversation.* New York: Morrow, 1990.

Todd, Janet, editor. *Gender and Literary Voice.* New York: Holmes & Meier, 1980.

Trilling, Diana. "The Liberated Heroine." *Times Literary Supplement.* October 13, 1978:1163–67.

Vance, Carol, editor. *Pleasure and Danger: Exploring Female Sexuality.* Boston: Routledge and Kegan Paul, 1984.

Vance, Carol S. "Negotiating Sex and Gender in the Attorney General's Commission on Pornography." In *Uncertain Terms: Negotiating Gender in American Culture,* edited by Faye Ginsburg and Anna Lowenhaupt Tsing. Boston: Beacon Press, 1990.

Vendler, Helen. Review of Margaret Homan's "Women Writers and Pietic Identity." *New York Review of Books.* February 19, 1981:33.

Walker, Alice. *The Color Purple.* New York: Washington Square Press, 1982.

Wallace, Michelle. *Black Popular Culture.* Seattle: Bay Press, 1992.

Wittig, Monique. "One Is Not Born a Woman." *Feminist Issues* 1 (1981):47–54.

Wittig, Monique. *The Straight Mind and Other Essays.* Boston: Beacon Press, 1992.

Wolf, Eric R. "Society and Symbols in Latin Europe and in the Islamic Near East: Some Comparisons." *Anthropological Quarterly* 42 (1969):287–301.

Wolf, Naomi. *The Beauty Myth: How Images of Beauty Are Used Against Women.* New York: William Morrow and Company, 1991.

Ideas about Women's "Nature"

Is there a women's nature? What should the words *women* and *nature* be taken to mean? Can women choose what to be? What are equality and freedom? Philosophers have traditionally dealt with such fundamental questions as these. Yet philosophers in the past have dealt only very inadequately with fundamental questions concerning women.

In this chapter, we look at various philosophical definitions of women and at the concepts of equality and freedom. We will examine feminist viewpoints on these issues and see how feminist philosophers are changing ideas about women, and about women's "nature," and are exploring women's experiences and points of view.

Definitions and Theories

When people want to know the meaning of a word, they look in a dictionary. But dictionaries are written by people (usually male) and can be rewritten. For the most part, they merely record usage at a given time; usage can change, and the ideas that people have can cause usage to change. Ideas change for many reasons, but it is philosophers (also usually male) who suggest what our ideas about fundamental matters *ought* to be.

Definitions are starting points or building blocks. They give us the terms with which we can make assertions about what is in fact the case, or about what is normatively valid. We can consider whether these assertions are true or false, depending on the evidence and arguments. For instance, once we have defined *swan* without requiring whiteness to be part of the definition, we can look for empirical evidence of whether or not there are black swans (there are).

We also need definitions to construct theories, both theories about what is and theories about what ought to be. Human beings need theories to deal with life and experience—to understand the world and to act in it. For instance, it is a theory about what it is to be a "person" that allows us to think we are the same persons as when we were children. It is a theory that lets us expect that the sun will rise tomorrow because it has risen every previous day. (Of course, we now have a *different* theory to explain this than people had before Copernicus showed that the earth revolves around the sun.)

A definition may reflect an assumed theory. For instance, we are assuming one theory if we define *earth* as "center of the universe" and another if we define *earth* as "planet in the solar system." Definitions of *woman* have often reflected faulty theories that men had about the "nature" of women. This is partly because men's ideas and writings on the subject of women have been irrational, erroneous, and unclear. And the very language in which women have been considered and talked about has contained hidden, implicit sexism (Vetterling-Braggin, 1981). Definitions of women have usually been the result of fear or ignorance and have almost always been affected by the distorted perspective of one part of humanity seeing another part as "other" than itself, and drawing unjustified inferences from this partial perspective.

Woman as "Other"

The philosopher Simone de Beauvoir's extraordinarily rich and perceptive book *The Second Sex* first appeared in 1949, at a time when there was no women's liberation *movement* to sustain the sorts of views she presented. Better than anyone, she explored the implications of defining women as "other." The dominant view, she writes, is that it is men who are agents in the world: They act, they make history, they are conscious, they think and work and rule. She shows that whenever the concepts of the "self," or of the self as "agent," had been developed, they had *male* exemplars. From the perspective of the male agent, women are "other," "different." Men look upon women as other than themselves. Man, the agent, acts. Woman, the "other," exists.

Man is active; woman is passive. According to this view, woman is a part of nature or of the external world on which and with which man, who is human and conscious, acts. Yet she is sufficiently conscious to be able to recognize man's humanity and achievement. By being a conscious "other," woman is able to affirm him in his manhood in a way in which inert matter (or nature) cannot. In possessing this passive yet conscious "other," man both asserts himself and reassures himself about his selfhood and his humanity.

To understand *himself* as a human being,

man, the subject, needs other human beings rather than merely nature. Other *men* do not serve this purpose, however. They only present him with an interminable conflict. Each man, de Beauvoir writes, "aspires to set himself up alone as sovereign subject. Each tries to fulfill himself by reducing the other to slavery." Since all men are trying to triumph over all other men, conflict is constant.

Woman presents man with neither "the hostile silence of nature" nor the opposing will that leads other men to strive to be master: "woman is defined exclusively in her relation to man." Such definitions, de Beauvoir continues, are truly *man*-made. "Representation of the world, like the world itself, [is] the work of men; they describe it from their own point of view, which they confuse with absolute truth" (1953:143).

It is possible to question de Beauvoir's assumption that the archetype of the "free agent" is the ideal of human life, but as an existentialist, she saw that ideal as what all human beings should consciously become.

Since men have held the positions of power and privilege that have enabled them to label and to define from their own perspective, it is not surprising that their view of women as "other" has led to many unjustifiable theories and false assertions. Secure in their own experience of the world, they have felt little need to question their views (Hartsock, 1983). The more we as women understand ourselves and interpret our experience in our own terms, the less likely we are to accept the misconceptions that have prevailed throughout history as valid ideas about "woman" and women's "nature." We will recognize these views as claims, usually false, about what women are like, and recommendations, usually invalid, about how women should behave.

Women can begin with ostensive definitions, definitions which *point* to the entities designated. In this case, the entities are real. *They are us.* We are women. Any definition of

Simone de Beauvoir (1908–1986), photographed here in 1964, fifteen years after the publication of *The Second Sex*, had been all her life an activist in political causes and a member of French intellectual circles. Her essential contribution to modern feminism was to point out that most of what had ever been written and considered important had been written by men, and in consequence women were always portrayed as acted upon, the eternal "other," in relation to the male agent. (Wide World Photos)

De Beauvoir Looks Back

This book was first conceived . . . almost by chance. Wanting to talk about myself, I became aware that to do so I should first have to describe the condition of woman in general; first I considered the myths that men have forged about her. . . . in every case, man put himself forward as the Subject and considered the woman as an object, as the Other . . .

. . . I began to look at women with new eyes and found surprise after surprise lying in wait for me. It is both strange and stimulating to discover suddenly, after forty, an aspect of the world that has been staring you in the face all the time which somehow you have never noticed. One of the misunderstandings created by my book is that people thought I was denying there was any difference between men and women. On the contrary, writing this book made me even more aware of those things that separate them; what I contended was that these dissimilarities are of a cultural and not of a natural order.

(Beauvoir, 1964: 185–87)

women that does not refer to women as we know ourselves to be is faulty. Of course, there is a catch in "and know ourselves to be," because in the past we have too often only known ourselves through the eyes and languages and theories of men. We have lacked the confidence to know ourselves directly. But as we increasingly see for ourselves our own reality and express it in our own words and ways, we can reject the definitions of women that belie that reality. Let us now look at some of the distorted philosophical definitions that have prevailed in the past.

Philosophical Definitions of Women

In writing about women, male philosophers have by and large shared in the distorted views characteristic of their times and places, however original or antitraditional their views may have been on other issues (Mahowald, 1978). There have been a few notable exceptions, such as Plato (c. 427–347 B.C.E.), Condorcet (1743–1794), and John Stuart Mill (1806–1873), but the list is distressingly short. The implication is not that the philosophical mode of inquiry is suspect, but that feminist philos-

ophers must make sure philosophy is enriched by women's views and women's realities. Contemporary feminist philosophers are striving to do this (Harding and Hintikka, 1983; *Hypatia*; Jaggar, 1983; Ruddick, 1989).

A so-called definition of *woman* which has had an enormous and pervasive influence on vast segments of human thought, however ludicrous we can recognize it to be, is that which holds that "a woman is a defective man." This view was suggested by Aristotle in the fourth century B.C.E. Aristotle was one of the most influential philosophers of ancient Greece. His work was rediscovered by Christian theologians in medieval Europe; they referred to him as "the" philosopher and adapted many of his views.

Aristotle's view of women was based partly on a theory that among animal species, females have less vital heat than males. He reasoned that woman, lacking this heat, was unable to impart shape to what flowed away as menstrual blood. Woman's part in conception was merely to supply the container, the "flower pot," one might say, in which the distinctive seed, implanted by a man, grows (Whitbeck, 1976). "We should look on the

---

Contemporary Efforts to Define "Woman"

In the case of most classical theories, claims about women's nature were explicit, although definitely not accorded a central place in the total system. In contemporary times, systematic political philosophers . . . have rarely discussed women directly. Nevertheless, the very silence of contemporary philosophers on this topic is significant. Either it suggests that standard moral or political theories, such as natural rights theory, utilitarianism or even the theory of alienation, apply without modification to women, or it suggests that they do not apply to women at all. In other words, from contemporary philosophers' silence about women one might infer either that there are no differences between women and men that are relevant to political philosophy or that women are not part of the subject matter of political philosophy at all.

Feminists break this silence. Their critique of women's position in contemporary society demonstrates that every aspect of social life is governed by gender. In other words, it reminds us that all of social life is structured by rules that establish different types of behavior as appropriate to women and men. Feminists subject these rules to critical scrutiny, arguing that, in many cases if not all, they are oppressive to women.

(Jaggar, 1983:21)

---

female," Aristotle said, "as being as it were a deformity, though one which occurs in the ordinary course of nature" (Aristotle, 1943).

Aristotle therefore thought of woman as both a "monstrosity" and "an accidental necessity of *the species*, the norm of which species is obviously male" (Lange, 1983:12). It followed that women were lesser, "defective" men or inferior to men, and this theory of sex difference was "interwoven in a consistent manner into the fabric of his philosophy" (ibid.:2).

Although we can now dismiss Aristotle's "biological theory" of woman's nature as mistaken, we have to appreciate its long-lasting significance. We need only look to modern theories of women as "defective men," such as the influential views of Sigmund Freud (1856–1939), to understand the point. Freud's conception of females as psychologically defective because, lacking penises, he thought they are anatomically defective, will be discussed in Chapter 4.

The view of women as "defective men" was thought to be confirmed by the attributes assigned to being "feminine" in the Western tradition. The concept of "feminine" was always shaped by the concept of what constituted "masculinity." The belief that "reason" characterized "masculinity" was pervasive. If "male" meant being rational, "female" meant being irrational, emotional, and intuitive. The task of rationality was to dominate over the inferior parts of the soul, over Nature, over the emotions, and over the body, each of which came thus to be identified with the "feminine," or with "woman's nature" (Lloyd, 1984). Western philosophers since Aristotle have assigned women subordinate roles in the work of creating knowledge, that is, in the life of the mind and the use of "reason." We shall investigate these ideas again in many other contexts (see, for example, Chapters 4, 10, and 11).

In terms of biology, of course, the "facts" imagined by Aristotle and others are false. We

> **The "Maleness" of Reason and Woman's "Nature"**
>
> What exactly does the "maleness" of Reason amount to? . . . Our ideas and ideals of maleness and femaleness have been formed within structures of dominance—of superiority and inferiority, "norms" and "difference," "positive" and "negative," the "essential" and the "complementary." . . . And the male-female distinction itself has operated not as a straightforwardly descriptive principle of classification, but as an expression of values. . . . What is valued—whether it be odd as against even numbers, "aggressive" as against "nurturing" skills and capacities, or Reason as against emotion—has been readily identified with maleness. Within the context of this association of preferred traits, it is not just incidental to the feminine that female traits have been construed as inferior—or, more subtly, as "complementary"—to male norms of human excellence. Rationality has been conceived as transcendence of the feminine; and the "feminine" itself has been partly constituted by its occurrence within this structure.
>
> (Lloyd, 1984:103–4)

now understand that both the woman's ovum and the male's sperm contain essential chromosomes to create the genes that form the embryo. A discussion of facts, however, is not the end of the matter. The more significant question is why anyone would suppose that from any such "facts" about such a biological process or reality, conclusions of an evaluative kind could be drawn. To suppose that a woman is a *defective* man or less *important* as a human being or of lesser worth or that she *ought* to be ruled by men or ought to be passive, does not follow from *any* facts of biology or psychology.

The contemporary version of such arguments is that women have some biologically based trait, such as being less aggressive, which is properly reflected in society, as in having men dominate women in all major activities. But no such conclusion can follow from any statement of biological fact. Even if it were true that men are innately more aggressive, society might be organized so as to restrain far more than it now does, or even punish, the aggressiveness of men, rather than to reinforce and reward it.

Because women give birth to babies, it has often been supposed that this is our primary function, and that it is somehow fitting that we be confined to the role of mother, nurturer, or homemaker. Again, no such conclusion follows from the biological facts, but innumerable thinkers, from ancient times to the present, have made such gross mistakes of reasoning when the subject was women.

Aristotle, again, gives us a good example. He assumed that we could understand what a thing *is* by understanding what it does, as when we see that a knife is a thing whose function is to cut. The function of woman, he thought, is to bear children, whereas the function of man is rational activity. He did not argue that the function of man was to beget children. He also argued that since the function of woman is not the same as the function of man, virtue for women is different from virtue for men. A woman's virtue could only be found in serving men. A "good woman" is one who produces children and confines herself to this function.

Aristotle had a hierarchical view of human society. He thought it right and proper for free, adult males to rule over women, children, and slaves, for he believed that only some adult males are capable of being fully rational. Aristotle held that slaves, both female and male, lack the ability to deliberate, that children have this ability only in an underdeveloped form, and that in all women the ability is only partial or defective. We now recognize such theories of intelligence, or reasoning ability, to be false. But again, *even if there were* a difference of intelligence, this would not entitle us to conclude that those with greater intelligence *ought* to be in a privileged position in society. Society can be based on equal rights even if persons are "naturally" different in intelligence, strength, or psychological tendencies. (See discussion in Chapter 14.)

Arguments drawn from biology or psychology to justify social advantages claimed have taken many forms. We need to be on guard against the many current misuses of such arguments about women.

Contemporary Feminist Views

Feminist Morality. Contemporary feminists have begun to consider the implications of understanding the traditional ideals of rationality and objectivity as "male" rather than as universal (Lloyd, 1984). Interest in the issue was intensified by the studies of moral development made by Carol Gilligan and others (Gilligan, 1982; Lyons, 1983). Gilligan has shown that the most widely accepted theory of moral development, that of Lawrence Kohlberg, is, like Freud's theories, male-biased. Proposed as a universal theory, but based on an interpretation of the cognitive development of eighty-four boys, Kohlberg's scale of moral development was constructed to represent progress in moral reasoning. On Kohlberg's scale, the highest level of achievement is seen as the internalization of formal, abstract principles or rules of justice. Gilligan set out to study women to determine why they seemed to become stalled at the middle stage of Kohlberg's scale, a situation that implied that we are deficient in the development of moral judgment.

Gilligan found that, in general, "men and women follow different paths to moral development," and that there exists a morally "different voice" from the one that Kohlberg identified as "definitive of mature moral judgment" (Tronto, 1987:647). Studying a group of women making real-life decisions regarding abortions, Gilligan discovered that instead of applying abstract rules of justice, her subjects were concerned with preserving actual human relationships and expressing care for those for whom they felt responsible. This "ethic of care" was a different way of interpreting moral problems from that enunciated by the "ethic of justice" of Kohlberg's scale. As Gilligan put it:

> This conception of morality as concerned with the activity of care centers moral development around the understanding of responsibility and relationships, just as the conception of morality as fairness ties moral development to the understanding of rights and rules (1982:19).

Although Gilligan's analysis suggests *how* women and men act and think about themselves, it does not explain *why* they develop differently, or whether an "ethic of care" is inferior or superior to an "ethic of justice." One danger, according to some of Gilligan's critics, is that the idea of a morally "different voice" lends itself to biological typecasting such as has been used through the centuries to keep us in our "place," confine us to a "separate sphere," and assign us the world's dirty work by praising our capacities for selfless devotion to others. Some feminists suggest that women's different moral expression may result from our historically subordinate social position (Nicolson, 1983; Tronto, 1987;

What Is "Natural" for Women?

What does it mean . . . to say that nature intends for us to do certain things? We know what it means to say that "I intend to pack my suitcase," but what sense can it make to say that nature intends for us to do one thing rather than another? (One) use of "natural" reduces to saying "this is what most animals do." To the extent that this is the meaning of the term, it will be hard to get a notion of value out of it. The fact that something happens a lot does not argue for or against it. . . .

Teleological uses of "natural" automatically set up an evaluative context; knowing the function of "X" makes it possible for us to evaluate "X" on grounds of functioning well. But . . . teleological uses have to be morally evaluated: a good bomb is one that destroys, but is a good bomb morally good?

(Pierce, 1971: 162, 171) By permission of
Basic Books, Inc., Publishers, New York.

1993). Political scientist Joan Tronto draws upon a study of moral development among white, black, and Chicano children, which found that white children scored higher than the other two groups on Kohlberg's scale; she asks whether a study of these other groups would "indicate that, as Gilligan found to be true for women, their moral views were not underdeveloped but simply not captured by the categories used by the scale" (Tronto, 1987:650). Tronto and others see a lack of caretaking experiences by privileged males leaving them morally deprived, misleading them into thinking that moral beliefs can be expressed in abstract, universalistic terms "as if they were purely cognitive questions, like mathematical formulae" (ibid.:652; Chodorow, 1978).

Feminist philosophers have been exploring the kinds of morality that might adequately reflect the experience of women (Baier, 1985; Card, 1991; Held, 1993; Tong, 1993). Perhaps an "ethic of care" should be combined with an "ethic of justice," or perhaps the context of caring relationships between actual persons and of concern for the next generation should be the primary context for the development of moral thinking (Noddings, 1984; Kittay and Meyers, 1987; Jaggar, 1989; Ruddick, 1989).

Rethinking "Knowledge." Feminist theorists have explored questions of whether there are distinct approaches to knowledge characteristic of women's experience. Many theorists suggest that even the physical sciences and certainly the social sciences will have to be understood very differently if they are to reflect the points of view of women as fully as they reflect those of men (Harding and Hintikka, 1983; Lloyd, 1984; Harding, 1987; Zalk and Gordon-Kelter, 1990).

In one field after another, radical reconceptualizations are seen to be required to overcome the bias that has been built into what has been taken to be "knowledge." Not only have topics of interest to women, but of less interest to men, such as rape, the sexual abuse of children, employment patterns among women, or the histories of women's lives, been simply left out of traditional disciplines, but the very concepts and assumptions with which inquiry has proceeded have reflected a male rather than a universal point of view.

> **"Women's Nature": To Be Caretakers**
>
> [W]omen not only define themselves in a context of human relationship but also judge themselves in terms of their ability to care. Women's place in man's life cycle has been that of nurturer, caretaker, and helpmate, the weaver of those networks of relationships on which she in turn relies. But while women have thus taken care of men, men have, in their theories of psychological development, as in their economic arrangements, tended to assume or devalue that care. When the focus on individuation and individual achievement extends into adulthood and maturity is equated with personal autonomy, concern with relationships appears as a weakness of women rather than as a human strength.
>
> (Gilligan, 1982:17)

And feminists of color have shown how the perspectives of race and gender overlap and interact, requiring radical rethinking of what has been thought of as impartial and objective knowledge (Collins, 1991; Williams, 1991).

For example, to suppose that the objects of study in psychology are individuals and their states (as when an individual is in a state of fear, or an individual is in a state of sexual arousal) rather than relationships between individuals, may reflect a masculine "way of seeing" (Harding and Hintikka, 1983). Or to conceptualize social and political and economic life as characterized by contracts between rationally self-interested "men" may again be the result of male bias rather than the reflection of a gender-neutral view (DiStefano, 1983; Held, 1993). Or to categorize all persons as "male" or "female" may ignore how identities formed by being black or Latina or lesbian may sometimes be even more fundamental (Spelman, 1988; Anzaldúa, 1990).

Examining such issues as these makes clear that "knowledge" is seldom the impartial, objective, unbiased enterprise it has often been claimed to be. To a significant degree, it rests on ideological assumptions, and among the most pervasive of such assumptions is that the point of view of relatively privileged white, Western men is the appropriate one from which to construct and to understand "human civilization" and "scientific truth."

Feminists are increasingly concerned with the ways knowledge ought to contribute to human liberation, rather than, as much of it has, to human oppression. And we are asking how to proceed, in constructing theory, in ways that will listen to those excluded from dominant discourses, not only by gender but also by race and class and sexual orientation (Collins, 1991; Lugones and Spelman, 1983; Williams, 1991).

Language and Continental Feminism. Contemporary feminists have considered the issues of defining gender and understanding the meaning of gender differences from a number of perspectives. Some of these call into question in especially fundamental ways the language we use to understand ourselves, gender, and difference. Among theorists who call themselves poststructuralists, usually working in a Continental rather than Anglo-American philosophical tradition, language is seen as reflective of struggles for power.

In the past, as we have seen, ideas about "woman's nature" have sought confirmation by reference to nature and science; ideas about women as "defective men" have flourished in

> ### "Women's Nature": Learning Silence
>
> Anecdotal reports as well as research on sex differences indicate that girls and women have more difficulty than boys and men in asserting their authority or considering themselves as authorities . . . ; in expressing themselves in public so that others will listen . . . , in gaining [the] respect of others for their minds and their ideas . . . ; and in fully utilizing their capabilities and training in the world of work. . . . In everyday and professional life, as well as in the classroom, women often feel unheard even when they believe they have something important to say. Most women can recall incidents in which either they or female friends were discouraged from pursuing some line of intellectual work on the grounds that it was "unfeminine" or incompatible with female capabilities. Many female students and working women are painfully aware that men succeed better than they in getting and holding the attention of others for their ideas and opinions. All women grow up to deal with historically and culturally engrained definitions of femininity and womanhood—one common theme being that women, like children, should be seen and not heard.
>
> (Belenky et al., 1986:4–5)

psychoanalytic and moral development theories; there have been specific social and historical accounts of the meaning of "woman's nature." The conviction that differences between women and men are ultimately biological have been used as a major ideological support of structures of male dominance, including a gender division of labor that devalues work done by women because it is done by women (see Chapter 13).

We have also begun to discover that the meanings attached to "women's nature" or biological difference have changed over time, reshaped with the emergence of the medical profession in the nineteenth century, for example, or the rise of psychiatry in the twentieth (Foucault, 1978; 1986). In poststructuralist terms, the different processes by which meanings are shaped are called "discourses." Poststructuralist feminists speak of language as the site of battles within a discourse over meanings. For example, assumptions, as in the "discourse" called *sociobiology*, that motherhood and childrearing are "natural" for women, carry many political, social, and economic messages with regard to women who do not choose to become mothers as well as those who do. As one observer notes, "Where women seek to challenge the assertion which biological theories make about their nature, they are told that they are going against nature itself" (Weedon, 1987:130). "Natural femininity and masculinity," as depicted in much sociobiological discourse, "necessarily fit women and men for different types of jobs and social and familial tasks" (ibid.). Differences between "woman's nature" and "man's nature" are presented as fixed and, by virtue of the tasks assigned, hierarchical, and men have the greater access to the power that determines the nature of society.

Yet sociobiologists characteristically assume that as scientists they are independent of particular social and moral values and interests, and that the language they use is merely a tool for expressing facts, rather than the material out of which conflicting versions of the facts are constructed. If, however, meanings are contested and our very subjectivity constantly being constructed in the context of the battle going on over those meanings, how can we understand gender differences?

Some feminists worry that contemporary Continental efforts to undermine previous, biased claims to "truth" and "objectivity" are now being used, in turn, to undermine the insights of feminists. If all discourses and theories are relative and without foundation, feminist criticisms and reconstructions of them are as dismissible as those they replace (Hartsock, 1989–90; Smyth, 1992).

We look next at the concepts of "equality" and "liberty" and the structures of thought in which they have been embedded. We will consider what *women* may choose to mean by such terms, and what we may decide about "women's nature."

Ideas of Equality

The first major repudiation of the hierarchical traditions that characterized much of Western thought from the time of Aristotle occurred in the seventeenth and eighteenth centuries. Enlightenment philosophers deliberately rejected notions of original sin and of the innate inferiority of some men compared with others. They emphasized instead the essential equality of men and the importance of liberty. This liberating movement formed the background of the new American nation in the late eighteenth century and its ideas have helped to shape the society of the United States to a significant extent ever since. The familiar words of the American Declaration of Independence express the dominant ideas of the liberal tradition: "We hold these truths to be self-evident, that all men are created equal; that they are endowed by their Creator with certain inalienable rights; that among these, are life, liberty, and the pursuit of happiness. That, to secure these rights, governments are instituted among men, deriving their just powers from the consent of the governed."

The ideas of the Enlightenment that inspired the Declaration of Independence formed a liberal tradition that encouraged the further development of political democracy. As it has been developed in the West, political liberalism requires such aspects of political democracy as periodic free elections, an independent judiciary, laws that respect the rights of citizens to be treated fairly, and a government that is responsive to the will of its citizens as expressed through the political process.

In the expansive economic developments of the nineteenth century, traditional liberalism fostered the acceptance of "laissez-faire," the view that government should not interfere with the economic activity of its citizens. This political policy allowed the relatively unrestrained growth of capitalist forms of economic production and corporate ownership. Liberalism did not require economic institutions to be democratic, for that would be interfering with the free exercise of what were thought to be rights to private property. Though government may, and later did, enact laws that businesses must obey, the liberal view regards economic activity as part of the "private sphere." The term *private enterprise* specifically indicates that economic activity is considered appropriately *outside* the sphere of democratic political control and decision, that it is to be free to develop (its critics would say free to exploit) without governmental interference. Criticism of exploitative capitalism also developed in the nineteenth century, and there were calls for political restraints on "free enterprise" along with more radical demands for the overthrow of capitalism. Many contemporary social critics point out that the modern corporation is an extraordinarily undemocratic institution and that the vast disparities of wealth and income and inherited position between rich and poor in an economic system such as that of the United States are incompatible with the spirit and principles of democracy.

In the tradition of political liberalism, democracy applies to the political sphere of activity, not to the economic. This view of democracy continues to dominate opinion in the United States and to a lesser extent in Western Europe. Many socialists also advocate democracy. But democratic socialism argues that economic activity ought to be organized to serve the needs of the whole society rather than allowing individuals to own the means of production and to profit from this private ownership. The liberal tradition and the alternative democratic socialist tradition differ in their views of the sort of economic system we ought to have, but both claim to be democratic.

The liberal tradition has made the concepts of freedom and equality central to our ways of thinking. Most of us characteristically begin our discussions of what society ought to be like with commitments to democracy, to freedom, to equality, and to the rights of individuals. But liberalism has not applied these principles in a satisfactory way to women.

Liberalism and Feminism

Feminists often take for granted the principles that liberalism first espoused, such as that people have rights to be free and to be treated as equals, and that social arrangements ought to be based on consent and not simply imposed by the strong on the weak. These ideas were developed in Europe and America in the seventeenth and eighteenth centuries but, until very recently, had not been applied to women as well as to men, even in the political domain. Women were only given the vote, an absolute minimum of political equality, in England in 1918 and 1928, in the United States in 1920,

in France in 1945, and in Switzerland in 1971. But liberal ideas are the foundations on which feminists have often built, and many continue to do so. They offer us conceptions of freedom and equality and suggest principles to which we should commit ourselves.

In the early seventeenth century in England, the dominant view was that represented by Robert Filmer (c. 1588–1653), who held that political authority should be based on inherited title, with the rulers of nations standing toward their subjects as a father toward his wife and children. Filmer advocated benevolent patriarchy throughout society. With the rise of democratic liberalism, this view of government was replaced. Thomas Hobbes (1588–1679) and John Locke (1632–1704) saw government as based on a hypothetical contract between free and equal individuals. The purpose of government was to protect the rights of individual citizens and to serve the interests of those who contracted to establish and maintain government. The great documents of political freedom and equality such as the Declaration of Independence and the French Declaration of the Rights of Man reflect these views. Society was to be based on principles of equality and freedom.

The citizens for whom liberal government was thought legitimate, however, turned out to be male heads of households. The interests of women were thought to be covered by taking account of the interests of these men. As James Mill (1773–1836) expressed it as late as 1820 with respect to who should be permitted to vote:

> One thing is pretty clear, that all those individuals whose interests are indisputably included in those of other individuals, may be struck off without inconvenience. In this light may be viewed all children up to a certain age, whose interests are involved in those of their parents. In this light also, women may be re-

garded, the interest of almost all of whom is involved either in that of their fathers or in that of their husbands. (James Mill, 1821:21)

Most liberal thinkers were not explicit on the subject of women. They took the family as given, and they saw women as confined to the family. They neither included women in the political realm as free and equal citizens nor considered the possibility of relations *within* the family becoming egalitarian and consensual. As Susan Okin writes in her important study *Women in Western Political Thought,* "Whereas the liberal tradition appears to be talking about individuals, as components of political systems, it is in fact talking about male-headed families. . . . Women disappear from the subject of politics" (Okin, 1979:202).

Not all of the fathers of democracy and liberalism were so reticent. Jean-Jacques Rousseau (1712–1778), one of the most important figures of the Enlightenment on the European continent, argued that liberal principles could not and must not be applied to women, or government would be impossible. He exemplified the contradiction between an egalitarian view of men in society and an inegalitarian view of women in relation to men. In his book *Émile* (1762), he maintained that women must learn to submit to man's will and to find happiness in doing so. It was according to nature, Rousseau argued, for the woman to obey the man.

Since the essence of being human, for Rousseau, is freedom, women in his conception are less than fully human. Rousseau argued that within the family, there must be a dominant authority (which must be the father); without the rule of the man within the family, society would fall apart.

Rousseau was unwilling either to apply the principles of freedom and equality to relations between women and men in the family *or* to apply to the wider society his conception of the necessity for clear lines of authority in the family. If Rousseau was right that not even two persons with ties of affection and common concerns can reach decisions on the basis of mutuality rather than domination and submission, it would suggest that there is little hope for the democratic, consensual organization of any larger society that he so passionately advocated. On the other hand, if the liberal and democratic view of government is correct—that is, if government should be based not on tradition or force but on consent between free and equal individuals—it is remarkable that its adherents have been so unwilling to extend such ideas to that bastion of tradition and coercion, the family (Kofman, 1988; Okin, 1989).

Along with many others, Rousseau invoked nature to keep women from sharing in the principles of the Enlightenment. The so-called philosopher of freedom declared that:

> Nature herself has decreed that woman, both for herself and her children, should be at the mercy of man's judgment. . . . When the Greek women married, they disappeared from public life; within the four walls of their home they devoted themselves to the care of their household and family. This is the mode of life prescribed for women alike by nature and reason. (1966: 328–30)

Wollstonecraft

Mary Wollstonecraft (1759–1797) is perhaps the first woman philosopher to make a place for herself in history, although few histories of philosophy mention her. Writing in England in the late eighteenth century, she shared fully in the Enlightenment's rejection of all authority based on arbitrary power and its reliance on human reason alone to assure endless human progress. She was a journalist and author, struggling to live on her own earnings and concerned that other middle-class women were unable to find ways of sus-

Mary Wollstonecraft, a courageous opponent of Rousseau's view that women should be subordinate to men, argued in her book *A Vindication of the Rights of Woman* (1792) that the principles of freedom and equality are as valid for women as for men. (Sophia Smith Collection [Women's History Archive], Smith College, Northampton, Mass. 01063)

taining economic independence. She was aware of the contradictions between society's maxims about "woman's nature," women's idleness and weakness, and the barriers society placed around women's ability to gain their economic livelihood (Eisenstein, 1981). She argued forcefully against Rousseau's view that women are inferior in reasoning and that virtue in a woman is thus different from virtue in a man. She wrote in 1792:

> Men, indeed, appear to me to act in a very unphilosophical manner when they try to secure the good conduct of women by attempting to keep them always in a state of childhood. . . . It is a farce to call any being virtuous whose virtues do not result from the exercise of its own reason. This was Rousseau's opinion respecting men: I extend it to women. (1967:50, 52)

Wollstonecraft said that women had been taught to be creatures of emotion rather than of reason. Instead, we should have educations comparable to those that enable at least those men not corrupted by too much wealth to become rational and responsible beings. She was not discouraged by the magnitude of the changes needed in human behavior; along with many other Enlightenment thinkers, she celebrated the distance already traveled by men.

To Wollstonecraft, the principles of the Enlightenment were correct principles that ought to apply fully to women as well as to men (see Chapter 11). Unfortunately, Rousseau's ideas rather than Mary Wollstonecraft's appealed to those who have made history and the history of ideas in their own image. What gains women made in the political turmoil of the eighteenth century were soon lost, even in theory (see Chapter 15).

Various rationalist philosophers on the European continent continued to maintain that women are defective in rationality, however

admirable in other respects, such as beauty or sensitivity. In Germany, the influential philosopher Immanuel Kant (1724–1804) developed a morality based on reason alone, seeing the fundamental principle of morality as required by rationality. Since women in his view are emotional rather than rational beings, we are not capable of fully moral action. Kant's identification of pure reason with traits defined as "masculine," fitting into the preceding views of male philosophers about "woman's nature," were powerful precursors of later psychological theories and theories of development, which also measured human nature in masculine terms. Kant's own vision of morality was deeply marked by his assumptions about sexual difference (Lloyd, 1984). Thus the great moral principles enunciated so forcefully by Kant, which added to the liberal tradition of respect for individual rights the concept of respect for persons *as* persons, were simply not applicable to women.

Mill and Taylor

Almost all the giants of the liberal tradition excluded women from the political world in one way or another, but there were a few exceptions. John Stuart Mill (1806–1873), the son of James Mill, argued for an end to the subjection of women (1869, 1970). Mill's life-long companion and eventual wife, Harriet Taylor (1807–1858), helped him develop his feminist positions. Mill argued that the liberal requirements of equal rights and equal opportunities should be extended to women and that women ought to be able to own property, to vote, to receive education, and to enter into any profession for which we were qualified. These views were the height of radicalism in mid-nineteenth-century England, but discussions of Mill through the 1960s usually failed to include his ideas on women among his important writings.

Mill's arguments ran counter to those of the

Harriet Taylor Mill left us only a small legacy of her writing, but her views about women and the issues of women's emancipation were essential to the analysis made of this subject by the nineteenth-century philosopher John Stuart Mill. (The London School of Economics, The British Library of Political and Economic Science)

French philosopher Auguste Comte (1798–1857), often considered the "father of sociology." Comte asserted that women are biologically inferior to men and will always be so. Biology, he claimed, was already "able to es-tablish the hierarchy of the sexes, by demonstrating both anatomically and physiologically that, in almost the entire animal kingdom, and especially in our species, the female sex is formed for a state of essential childhood"

(Okin, 1979:220). Mill rejected the view that observable deficiencies found among women are due to innate inferiority. He argued that since women have never been given a chance to gain the same education and intellectual development as men, we cannot know what our capacities are. It may well be, he thought, that the environment rather than any innate incapacity has caused women to achieve less than men so far.

Mill believed that society would benefit if women were given all the educational opportunities given men. But even he thought that although women should be free to choose a career, marriage itself was a career. Despite Harriet Taylor's objections, he continued to think that while men could have both parenthood and an occupation, women could have only one or the other.

Harriet Taylor's own writings on women were even more forceful than Mill's in demanding equality for women. She derided the faulty arguments through which men tried to support their refusal to accord women equality.

Apart from maxims of detail, which represent local and national rather than universal ideas: it is an acknowledged dictate of justice to make no degrading distinctions without necessity. . . . When that which is interdicted includes nearly everything which those to whom it is permitted most prize, and to be deprived of which they feel to be most insulting; when not only political liberty but personal freedom of action is the prerogative of a caste; when even in the exercise of industry almost all employments which task the higher faculties in an important field, which lead to distinction, riches, or even pecuniary independence, are fenced round as the exclusive domain of the predominant class . . . the miserable expediencies which are advanced as excuses for so grossly partial a dispensation, would not be sufficient, even if they were

real, to render it other than a flagrant injustice. . . .

The world were once persuaded that the supreme virtue of subjects was loyalty to kings, and are still persuaded that the paramount virtue of womanhood is loyalty to men. . . . Self-will and self-assertion form the type of what are designated as manly virtues, while abnegation of self, patience, resignation, and submission to power . . . have been stamped by general consent as preeminently the duties and graces required of women. The meaning being merely, that power makes itself the center of moral obligation, and that a man likes to have his own will, but does not like that his domestic companion should have a will different from his. (H. Taylor Mill, 1970:97)

Liberal Feminism

Contemporary liberal feminists, like liberal feminists of the past, view biological difference as irrelevant to the question of women's rights. This view that "woman's nature" is not significantly different from human nature leads to efforts to prove that women share most capacities with men; it emphasizes educational and occupational opportunities (Jaggar, 1983). "Liberal feminists believe that the treatment of women in contemporary society violates, in one way or another, all of liberalism's political values, the values of equality, liberty, and justice" (ibid.:175–76). Contemporary liberal feminists fight discrimination against women, particularly in areas such as education, employment, constitutional rights, and rights to reproductive freedom. It was the desire to end all sex-biased laws that led to the attempt to pass the Equal Rights Amendment in the 1970s (see Chapter 14). These efforts continue, as do efforts to assure the rights of lesbians, and as do battles against sexual double standards and against sexual harassment and rape.

Liberal feminists continue the task begun

by Wollstonecraft and the Mills: to extend liberal principles to women, not only when we enter the so-called public realm but also within the family. Equality, it is argued, can never be realized for most women if we are forced by social convention or law to choose between parenthood and a career while men can have both. The marriage contract can never be a free and voluntary agreement as long as women are forced by economic necessity to marry or stay married, and as long as the terms of the contract are so clearly unfair, within what used to be the standard marriage—the entire responsibility of child care and household tasks falling on the mother, and the opportunity for economic independence open only to the father (Okin, 1989). And since wives, and especially mothers, perform hard work in the home for very long hours, the economic value of this work should be recognized.

Some feminists favor wages for housework. But pay for housework (as distinct from support payments to provide for children) may do little to change the unjustifiable division of labor within the household that assigns tasks on the basis of gender. A more plausible liberal solution is the equal sharing of housework and child care and of the responsibility to support the family economically (Bem and Bem, 1993).

Liberal feminists also call for the equalization of women and men in the realms of political life and economic activity, where liberals have always professed commitment to equality of opportunity (though not to "economic democracy"). The liberal tradition should be seen to imply that women have an equal right to as much education as men, to develop an occupation that is as fulfilling, to hold public office, to choose to have or not have children, and to be a parent with some leisure for further self-development.

To make equality of opportunity a reality, special efforts of "affirmative action" to open up opportunities for qualified women in nontraditional employment, such as police and fire departments, have been tried. The rationale behind affirmative action is to give qualified women and the men of subordinated racial and ethnic groups, who have consistently experienced a pattern of discrimination in the past, a right to be considered, sometimes even ahead of similarly qualified white men, until discrimination is overcome. Providing women and subordinated men such openings has been resisted by those who were previously given preference for such positions in these occupations. Despite some advances made in opening up opportunities previously closed, much remains to be done. Other efforts, such as to achieve equal pay for work of "comparable worth" (see Chapter 13), also continue toward the goal of equality of opportunity.

The resistance of many men and of society to the changes that their own traditions indicate should be made tells us something about the extent to which self-interest rather than a commitment to principles of equality motivates the behavior of the fortunate (see Chapter 14). As Joan Kelly pointed out (1984), during many of the great periods of "progressive" change in history, such as classical Athenian civilization, the Renaissance, and the French Revolution, women not only failed to share in the progress, but actually suffered a "relative loss of status." But among the strongest arguments feminists can make is that the traditions of liberalism and democracy inherently require many of the changes we seek (Eisenstein, 1981).

The Concept of Freedom

In addition to concerning ourselves with equality, feminists need to develop principles of freedom for women. In doing so, we may recognize that freedom for women will have to be very different from the freedom advocated by the liberal tradition, which is essentially a freedom to be left alone without interference. This concept of freedom was developed by such theorists as Hobbes and Locke with the self-sufficient farmer or tradesman in mind. It was assumed that if such a "free man" had no property, he could always acquire some unoccupied territory belonging to no one—of which there was still at that time thought (however erroneously) to be a considerable amount. Left alone by those who might rob or kill him and by a government that ought, according to this view, do no more than protect his life and property from attack, he would be free.

This conception of freedom is sadly out of date for all those in contemporary industrial society who do not already own substantial amounts of property—whether land or capital or a satisfactory, safe income. It is particularly unsatisfactory for women. Poverty-stricken people who are taking care of small children, for example, need to have basic necessities provided, not just to be left alone. People need to have jobs made available if they cannot find employment. The traditional image of the strong individual, able to fend for himself and acquire what he needs through his labor with no help from society, is a romantic image that simply does not apply to today's society or to most women. There is no empty land there for the taking. A person may try to sell her or his labor but find no one to buy it. In contemporary society, people need to be enabled to be free, not just to be left alone to cope with their deprivations (Held, 1984).

The liberal tradition offers the basis on which our ideas of freedom and equality might be developed so women can enjoy the individual rights to which "all men" have long been thought to be entitled. In recent years, many feminists in this country have been working within this tradition and expanding on it. We argue for rights to basic necessities such as

food, shelter, and medical care, and for a woman's right to decide for herself whether to have a child or an abortion. We argue for rights to employment—that is, to actually *have* a job—as well as to be treated fairly in trying to get a job and in advancing within it. We argue for a meaningful kind of "equality before the law," plainly stated in the Constitution and then substantively interpreted. Women can never be liberated without a more satisfactory idea of what freedom is than the one so far recognized in the law of the United States.

Conservative Sentiments and Feminism

Conservatives have often claimed to be concerned about many aspects of life important to women and valued by us: the family, the voluntary association, the moral standards of society. Traditionally, conservatives have upheld ties of family and friendship against the more calculated and competitive relations advocated by traditional liberalism. The conservative tradition has understood the emotional value of ethnic traditions and the role of habits of discipline or responsibility. A liberal sometimes appears willing to decide everything in the marketplace; to a conservative, there are things that should not be bought and sold, such as a person's honor.

In some respects, the sentiments of feminists parallel those of conservatives. Feminists, too, understand the importance of family relations although we have different notions of what constitutes a family. We, too, resist the calculations of liberal self-interest and commercialism. But conservatives have so far shown no inclination to transform their views in a way that would be compatible with feminism. The traditional values conservatives try to uphold include that of the place of woman: in the home, as wife and mother, giving emotional support to a husband who supports her economically. And conservatives nearly always undermine their credibility by upholding economic as well as social privileges at odds with the moral principles they espouse.

Conservatives (even more so than traditional liberals) favor less governmental regulation of the activities of business corporations. Yet conservatives (unlike liberals) favor more governmental regulation of the sexual behavior of individuals. The idea that the activities of a large corporation, which affect the lives of millions, are "private" while what consenting adults do in bed is "not private" does not stand up well to critical reflection. Nor does the claim that conservatives respect women, if at the same time they expect women to "stay in their place."

Socialism and Feminism

Many feminists look to the socialist tradition as the most satisfactory source of ideas for a women's movement that will improve society (Jaggar, 1983). These feminists see conservatism as conserving a sexist status quo and fear that liberalism will merely promote an even more generalized pursuit of self-interest than already exists. Socialist feminists fear that too many of the few women in a liberal capitalist system who will taste success will learn to scramble for self-advancement in the corporate hierarchy, striving for profits regardless of the good of society, just as men do. And too many other women will simply be left out, especially poor women, Third World women, and women whose racial and ethnic heritages differ from those who have traditionally controlled society.

These feminists claim that liberalism has never paid enough attention to economic issues because of its concern with political issues and its tradition of laissez-faire. Women could gain all sorts of legal rights such as the right to vote, the right to equal admission to professional schools, the right to join certain clubs, and even the right to abortion, and still be left in a condition of economic dependency thoroughly damaging to our self-respect and our efforts to win liberation.

The unfortunate effect of the economic dependence of women was recognized by Karl Marx (1818–1883) and Friedrich Engels (1820–1895). In *The Origin of the Family, Private Property, and the State* (1884), Engels argued that the institutional and cultural manifestations of a given historical period, including the monogamous family, result from economic causes. At that stage of human development at which property began to be accumulated by men (though it is not clear, some feminists note [Flax, 1981], why it was *men* who did the accumulating), men became the first ruling class.

In the middle-class family of Western capitalism, as seen by Marx and Engels, the wife had sold herself sexually for economic support. In the eyes of many other writers as well, the wife and mother in the successful bourgeois family of Victorian times was "elevated" to a position of powerlessness: cared for by hired servants, flattered but sexually imprisoned, denied any chance for self-development or personal freedom.

Women of the lower classes, meanwhile, were economically exploited in factories and needle trades and as domestic servants even more brutally than were men. Economic and social "progress" by late in the century had moved many married women from the factory into the home. They aspired to the status and promised security of the middle-class wife, not realizing how few could achieve it or how unsatisfactory this goal could turn out to be. The point was well made by Charlotte Perkins Gilman (1860–1935), the author of *The Yellow Wall-Paper* (1899) and of *Women and Economics*, published in 1898:

When the woman, left alone with no man to "support" her, tries to meet her own economic necessities, the difficulties which confront her prove conclusively what the general economic status of women is. . . . We see the human mother worked far harder than a mare, laboring her life long in the service, not of her children only, but of men; husbands, brothers, fathers, whatever male relative she has. . . . The human female, the world over, works at extra-maternal duties for hours enough to provide her with an independent living, and then is denied independence on the ground that motherhood prevents her working! (Gilman, 1966:10, 19–20, 21)

The Marxist view held that the working class must gain control of the means of production and thus end the exploitation of workers by capitalists. In this view, if women enter the labor force in large numbers, our problems will be soluble along with the problems of the working class. Marxist feminists, however, recognize that this picture needs revision.

Democratic socialism in Western Europe and elsewhere has come closer to representing the ideals of Marxism than did the communism of the former Soviet Union and the Eastern European States. But it has not escaped the notice of feminists that social-democratic men, along with capitalist and communist men, have, at least until recently, still expected "their" women to do the dishes and to bring up the children. Social-democratic men have often had great difficulty taking women seriously and acknowledging us as intellectual equals (Sargent, 1981). They have argued that attention to the concerns of women should not be allowed to deflect attention from the "real" struggle: the struggle of the working class (Funk and Mueller, 1993; Posadskaya et al., 1994).

Socialist Feminism

The lack of awareness among traditional Marxists of the views and problems of women has resulted in the development of a socialist feminist position. This has been one of the leading positions among Western feminists concerned with the formulation and expression of feminist theory (Jaggar, 1983; Kelly, 1984).

Socialist feminists such as Sheila Rowbotham and Juliet Mitchell argue that many transformations of the economy called for by socialists are necessary before women—confined primarily to the lowest-paying and least secure jobs—can begin to gain real economic independence. Capitalism is responsible for at least a significant part of the oppression of women throughout the world. For society to begin to provide what women need rather than what is profitable for corporations, many specific demands made by socialists will have to be accepted. All feminists can enthusiastically join socialists in demanding publicly funded child care and medical care, decent housing for all, and nonexploitative jobs for all who can work. And we can join with socialists in working for the changes in corporate capitalism that will be necessary to make these possible.

But socialist feminists also recognize that traditional socialism has failed to understand the specific ways in which women are oppressed *as women* and not merely as workers (Gould, 1976; Sargent, 1981; Jaggar, 1983). Socialist feminists emphasize that the traditional gender division of labor *within* the family as well as outside it will have to disappear, that men will have to learn to have as much regard for women as they have for each other, and that feminist alternatives—such as women-centered communities and lesbian families—will have to be recognized as legitimate.

Socialist feminists have contributed to the analysis of women's oppression a version of the theory of alienation (Bartky, 1990). Some see women in contemporary society as "alien-

> ### Capitalist Oppression
>
> Oppression is not an abstract moral condition but a social and historical experience. Its forms and expression change as the mode of production and the relationships between men and women, men and men, women and women, change in society. Thus, while it is true that women were subordinated to men before capitalism and that this has affected the position of women in capitalist society, it is also true that the context of oppression we fight against now is specific to a society in which the capacity of human beings to create is appropriated by privately owned capital and in which the things produced are exchanged as commodities.
>
> (Rowbotham, 1973:xiii)

ated from all aspects of their own labor, from other women and from children." Since male-dominant culture defines masculinity and femininity as opposites—active/passive, intellectual/intuitive, inexpressive/emotional, strong/weak, dominant/submissive, to the extent women and men conform to these definitions, "they are bound to be alienated from each other, holding incompatible views of the world" (Jaggar, 1983:316). They will also have incompatible interests: "men in maintaining their dominance, women in resisting it. And to the extent that women and men conform to gendered definitions of humanity, they are bound to be alienated from themselves" (ibid.). The result is that women overdevelop their capacities for nurture and altruism and that men become excessively competitive. Both represent distortions of human possibilities.

Radical Feminism

Radical feminists often start thinking about women's oppression by looking at the way sexuality is socially constructed. In Catharine MacKinnon's view, men sexualize hierarchy; the male sexual role "centers on aggressive intrusion on those with less power. Such acts of dominance are experienced as sexually arousing, as sex itself" (MacKinnon, 1989; 316).

Radical feminism sees the basic hierarchy with regard to sexuality as extended by society to all aspects of social life. This creates two cultures: the visible world of male culture, which is divided into national boundaries, and the invisible world of women's culture, which exists universally "within every culture" (Jaggar, 1983:249). According to radical feminists, dominant male culture portrays a picture of social reality in which men are, and should be, positive, forceful, aggressive, dominant, objective, strong, and intellectual, while women are, and are in most cases even valued for being, passive, emotional, intuitive, mysterious, unresponsible, quarrelsome, childish, dependent, evil, and submissive. Liberal feminists and socialist feminists often seem to accept this picture as an accurate depiction of social reality, but see it as socially constructed. Liberal feminists believe women have as much potential for autonomy and rationality as men and socialist feminists see the contrast in terms of women's social oppression and alienation (Jaggar, 1983).

Radical feminists claim that the picture of reality presented by male culture conceals the destructive values that underlie this culture and "obscures the positive contributions of the female culture" (Jaggar, 1983:251). For instance, male culture seems to focus on death and on dying for gods or countries, while relegating human birth and childrearing to mere "natural" events (Hartsock, 1984; Held, 1993). Radical feminists think liberal and socialist feminists have internalized the values of male culture, and that their efforts for change are a striving to make women into men by men's standards. Radical feminists revalue the attributes assigned to women in men's culture and reclaim them with new meanings for "womanculture." It is to radical feminism that we owe the slogan "the personal is political" (Jaggar, 1983:255).

Radical feminists view patriarchy as a system of pervasive domination by males, most clearly expressed in efforts to control women's bodies. Hence, radical feminists view failures to provide adequate contraception and abortion as aspects of compulsory motherhood, and motherhood as it is institutionalized under patriarchy as one of the bases for women's oppression. Other aspects of women's sexual oppression under patriarchy include rape, prostitution, and pornography (MacKinnon, 1987). This focus on women's oppression in intimate relations is a contribution to feminist thought by radical feminists, just as liberal feminists contribute an analysis of barriers to equal job opportunities and socialist feminists an analysis of what women need for full participation in the public world.

It follows from the radical feminist view of women's oppression that heterosexual relationships are always in danger of being reduced to male control of female bodies, whether expressed in marriage, motherhood, prostitution, or intimate relations of shorter or longer duration. From that perspective, separatism may be an answer, and separatism may take the form of sexual celibacy or lesbianism, which may or may not take a sexual form. Charlotte Bunch, for example, writes:

> Being a Lesbian means ending identification with, allegiance to, dependence on, and support of heterosexuality. It means ending your personal stake in the male world so that you join women, individually and collectively, in the struggle to end your oppression. Lesbianism is the key to liberation and only women who cut their ties to male privilege can be trusted to remain serious in the struggle against male dominance (Bunch, 1975:36)

For some radical feminists, the very fact that lesbianism is sexual makes it political. As Adrienne Rich expresses it: "Lesbianism is a threat to the ideological, political, personal, and economic basis of male supremacy. The Lesbian threatens the ideology of male supremacy by destroying the lie about female inferiority, weakness, passivity, and by denying women's 'innate need for men'" (Rich, 1980:648).

If the goal of radical feminism, however, is women's control over our own bodies, it must embrace women's choices to mother as well as not to mother, even to embark on the hazardous venture of heterosexual relations. In addition, recognition must be given to the different experiences of race, ethnicity, and class among women. Some groups of women, African American women, Hispanic women of various cultures, working-class women, for example, all have some interests in common with the men of our groups because we have also been oppressed as a group.

Some feminists consider themselves radical because they see the overthrow of gender domination as the most fundamental and radical change possible in human history and society. Some think this change can occur within as well as by rejecting close relationships with men, and many believe that racial and class oppression are in important ways dependent on gender domination.

Where Do We Go from Here?

Why the Issue of "Women's Nature" Remains Important

Contemporary feminists are confronted with the problem of constructing appropriate conceptions of equality and difference. Women are different from men in some ways that should be recognized. On the other hand, women are entitled to equality. If equality of treatment does not mean sameness of treatment, how should it be understood?

Some difficulties in deciding were illustrated by the Equal Employment Opportunity Commission (EEOC) case against Sears, Roebuck, which was initiated in 1979 and decided in the courts in 1986.

During the trial, two historians, Rosalind Rosenberg and Alice Kessler-Harris, testified on opposite sides (Milkman, 1986; Rosenberg, 1986; Kessler-Harris, 1986; Scott, 1988). The arguments presented by the Sears lawyers and by Rosalind Rosenberg asserted that women as a group, however their behavior was determined, by culture or patterns of socialization, differed fundamentally from men and therefore did not want the commission sales jobs that men historically filled. Sears claimed, therefore, and used Rosenberg's testimony to bolster their claim, that "woman's nature," not employer discrimination, explained the Sears hiring patterns. EEOC, on its side, with Alice Kessler-Harris as its expert witness, argued that Sears's hiring practices constituted unequal treatment of women because they were based on and therefore maintained in practice the incorrect notion that there were fundamental differences between its women and men employees. The judge held for Sears on grounds that he was convinced on the evidence that the lack of women in sales commission jobs was the result of women's "nature," not Sears's discriminatory practices. Many feminists disa-

greed with that decision. In the words of historian Joan Scott:

> Equality-versus-difference was the intellectual trap within which historians argued. . . . Feminists cannot give up "difference"; it has been our most creative tool. We cannot give up equality, at least as long as we want to speak to the principles and values of our political system. . . . How then do we recognize and use notions of sexual difference and yet make arguments for equality? The only response is a double one: the unmasking of the power relationship constructed by posing equality as the antithesis of difference and the refusal of its consequent dichotomous construction of political choices. (Scott, 1988: 43–44)

The oppositional pairing of "equality-versus-difference" misrepresents the relationship of both terms; it certainly gets in the way of constructive feminist politics. As Scott puts it, the political notion of equality depends on an acknowledgment of the existence of difference. Demands for equality have rested on implicit and usually unrecognized arguments from difference; if individuals or groups were identical or the same there would be no need to ask for equality (Scott, 1988).

We must refuse to oppose equality to difference and insist continually on differences, as the condition of individual and collective identities and as that which should be respected equally in ways that will not disadvantage or devalue the different (Littleton, 1987; Young, 1986).

The concept of "women's nature" has proven difficult for contemporary feminism. After several early years of an ideal of "androgyny," which sought changes that would minimize differences between the sexes, feminists began to celebrate difference and to build theories recognizing women's unique experiences and contributions to culture. Some feminists are concerned that "woman"

> **On Equality**
>
> What the sameness standard fails to notice is that men's differences from women are equal to women's differences from men. There is an *equality* there. Yet the sexes are not socially equal. The difference approach misses the fact that hierarchy of power produces real as well as fantasied differences, differences that are also inequalities. What is missing in the difference approach is what Aristotle missed in his empiricist notion that equality means treating likes alike and unlikes unlike, and nobody has questioned it since. Why should you have to be the same as a man to get what a man gets simply because he is one? Why does maleness provide an original entitlement, not questioned on the basis of *its* gender, so that it is women—women who want to make a case of unequal treatment in a world men have made in their image (this is really the part Aristotle missed)—who have to show in effect that they are men in every relevant respect, unfortunately mistaken for women on the basis of an accident of birth?
>
> (MacKinnon, 1987:37)

at the core of such theories, in its emphasis on the uniqueness of women's experience, "maternal thinking," "voices," and "ways of knowing," is too close at heart to an *essentialist* view of "women's nature."

Essentialism is the view that there is an essential, innate, human nature based on biological realities. In the past, biological thinking about women has underpinned a doctrine of "separate spheres," tying women as a group to our "natural" domestic place, supposedly "for our own good." Essentialist thinking was often couched in universals, forcing all women into a single grouping because difference from "man" was seen as the paramount characteristic of "woman." Critics of essentialism have emphasized that "women's nature" has been socially and culturally constructed, and is subject to significant change over time and place. Increasingly there have been an exploration and a celebration of differences among women, an appreciation of the complexities of subjective identities. The question of "women's nature" must now be broached in terms of a multitude of racial, ethnic, religious, class, and sexual identities and histories. Still, with-

out falling into essentialism, women can affirm our distinct contributions. Feminist philosopher Linda Alcoff suggests we take a "positional perspective." She says:

> The concept of positionality allows for a determinate though fluid identity of woman . . . woman is a position from which a feminist politics can emerge rather than a set of attributes that are "objectively identifiable." Seen in this way, being a "woman" is to take up a position within a moving historical context. (Alcoff, 1988:435)

Principles in Action

What the goals of feminism should include is a subject of much discussion among feminists, and there are healthy debates among us. Feminists are engaged in much innovative thinking about the kind of world we should work for and about the actions that ought to be taken to advance our goals.

All feminists put great emphasis on freedom. The term *women's liberation* expresses this. Women universally have a great deal of

Identity as a Point of Departure

As the history of revolutionary movements in this century has shown, and as the most recent developments in feminist theory confirm beyond a doubt (developments that have been prompted by the writings of women of color, Jewish women, and lesbians, and that can be sustained only by a serious, critical, and self-critical attention to the issues they raise), consciousness is not the result but the term of a process. Consciousness of self, like class consciousness or race consciousness (e.g., my consciousness of being white), is a particular configuration of subjectivity, or subjective limits, produced at the intersection of meaning with experience. (I have never, before coming to this country, been conscious of being white; and the meaning, the sense of what it means to be white has changed for me greatly over the years.) In other words, these different forms of consciousness are grounded, to be sure, in one's personal history; but that history—one's identity—is interpreted or reconstructed by each of us within the horizon of meanings and knowledges available in the culture at given historical moments, a horizon that also includes modes of political commitment and struggle. . . .

In this perspective, the very notion of identity undergoes a shift: identity is not the goal but rather the point of departure of the process of self-consciousness, a process by which one begins to know that and how the personal is political, that and how the subject is specifically and materially en-gendered in its social conditions and possibilities of existence.

(de Lauretis, 1986:8–9)

experience with what it is like to *be dominated.* Feminists advocate societies that are *not* characterized by relations of domination and subordination. We are, in a sense, the true "democrats," advocating for people in every sphere of life a freedom and equality that will enable all to live with dignity and respect.

In regard to economic issues, feminists sometimes start with the workplace. We advocate units of economic activity in which a concern for the environment and for providing satisfying work is more important than either profits or high salaries. We seek work arrangements that will encourage cooperative and egalitarian rather than hierarchical and coercive interaction among members.

Just as in the household, the question must be asked outside the home: What work *needs to be done?* Obviously, much of the work that gets done in both business and bureaucratic societies does *not* need to be done: People are persuaded to buy things they do not need so that corporations can increase their sales and dividends. Officials try to multiply the occasions on which they can exercise their authority over citizens, regardless of whether this serves a useful purpose. On the other hand, important work often is not done: Children go uncared for and inexpensive housing goes unbuilt because those with the capital to invest do not believe there is adequate profit to be made in these areas.

Feminists deciding what work needs to get done begin with the meeting of real human needs. The next questions may concern how to divide the work so that each person does her or his fair share, and how to structure it so it is done cooperatively, with a minimum of hierarchy. Then attention may be turned to making work as joyful and creative an activity as possible.

A feminist business that produces a product

Gloria Steinem on Feminist Labels

In the label department . . . I would prefer to be called simply "a feminist." After all, the belief in the full humanity of women leads to the necessity of totally changing all male-supremacist structures, thus removing the model and continuing support for other systems of birth-determined privilege. That should be radical enough. However, because there are feminists who believe that women can integrate or imitate existing structures (or conversely; that class or race structures must be transformed *first*, as a precondition to eliminating sexual caste), I feel I should identify myself as a "radical feminist." "Radical" means "going to the root," and I think that sexism *is* the root, whether or not it developed as the chronologically first dominance model in prehistory. . . . the tolerance of a habit as pervasive as male-dominance not only creates an intimate model for oppression as "natural," but builds a callousness to other dominations—whether based on race, age, class, sexuality, or anything else.

(Steinem, 1978:92–93)

---

or performs a service genuinely useful to women, that uses its earnings to train other women and to help us increase our economic independence, will not be a "business" in the usual sense (Woodul, 1976). It may respond voluntarily to community or regional or even national planning. It should certainly take responsibility for maintaining the health of its workers or neighbors and preserving the environment of future children, and it may be expected to do so without government intervention. Though it may well seek to expand, its goal will not simply be to maximize profits and increase its control over others, but to perform useful work in ever more humanly satisfying ways.

How should the changes needed in society be brought about? Those with power in corporations, and those with power in bureaucracies, whatever the form of the economic system, are predominantly male. Women must usually work from the bottom up. We must organize, persuade, and build our strength gradually and steadily.

Feminists emphasize that women do not want to be liberated in order to be increasingly like men. A basic aspect of feminist thought

will continue to resist such absorption into male structures of domination and oppression. Feminists often start by attempting to make our immediate communities more humane and cooperative places to live and work. We may go on to develop ways of governing ever wider communities that will enhance rather than pollute and destroy our environments. We may change the culture from one that induces greed and egotism to one that fosters mutuality and respect, and in which disputes are settled without violence or war (Ruddick, 1989), or imperialistic ventures.

Women are finally choosing for ourselves the conceptions of women with which we wish to live.

Summary

Definitions of women have often reflected faulty theories that men have had about the "nature" of women. Distorted definitions result from men seeing women as something "other" than themselves and drawing unjustified inferences from this perspective. Men tend to view themselves as active subjects and women as passive objects.

Aristotle's early definition of woman as "defective man" has had enormous influence on human thought. Biological "facts" about women, regardless of their validity, should not be misused to draw evaluative conclusions about women's rights.

Contemporary feminists are exploring whether women may have a distinctive approach to moral problems, which traditional moral theories have omitted or undervalued.

We are also coming to see that what has been thought to be impartial and objective "knowledge" has often represented the point of view of men only. Changes will be needed in what we think of as knowledge, even in the sciences.

Some contemporary feminists emphasize the way language and our most basic concepts result from one group having imposed its conceptual schemes on others. We need to propose more adequate meanings of, for instance, "equality" and "freedom" than those of patriarchal culture.

Philosophers of the Enlightenment rejected hierarchical traditions of Western political thought—but not for women. The liberal principles of equality and freedom that helped to shape our nation applied to men and to male heads of households. Many liberal thinkers were silent on the subject of women. Jean-Jacques Rousseau, however, was outspoken in his opinion that the existence of society required woman's subordination to man. Many philosophers believed that women were deficient in rationality.

The Enlightenment philosopher Mary Wollstonecraft argued that women had not yet been taught to favor reason rather than emotion and that we should have an education comparable to men's. John Stuart Mill also believed women's capacities would increase with more education. His wife, Harriet Taylor, argued even more forcefully for women's equality.

Contemporary liberal feminists favor equality in the home as well as in the public realm, holding that wives and husbands should share equally in child care and household tasks. Affirmative action programs are needed to provide women with equal job opportunities.

Feminists today are concerned with freedom as well as with equality. But the liberal idea of freedom—freedom to be left alone—is clearly inadequate in contemporary industrial society. We must be able to meet our basic needs in order to be free. We need to have various economic and social rights recognized, such as the rights to adequate food and shelter, to pursue education whether or not we have the money, and to have a job made available to anyone who seeks work.

Some conservative views coincide with feminist concerns for the family and moral values. But conservatives oppose feminism on the place of women, maintaining that woman's place is only, or primarily, in the home.

Some feminists have been influenced by the socialist tradition. Since traditional Marxism did not understand many of the problems of women, socialist feminism has developed its own positions. It focuses on the oppression of women as women, not merely as workers.

Radical feminism moves beyond the ideas familiar in any existing social theories. It emphasizes aspects of sexuality and reproduction as the sources of women's oppression, and appreciates the values and strengths of women's culture.

Although feminists frequently disagree, we all share one goal: to overcome the oppression of women. We are interested in work that meets human needs, with the work fairly divided and cooperatively organized. We believe society should be governed with a minimum of domination and subordination.

Women no longer have to accept the conceptions that others have had about us and about society. We can choose for ourselves what ideas to accept, and what to work for.

Hillary Rodham Clinton (1947–) is a graduate of Wellesley College and Yale Law School. She worked as a staff attorney for the Children's Defense Fund, was a full-time partner in a law firm, chaired an education committee that set public school standards in Arkansas, and headed President Clinton's Task Force on National Health Care Reform. Since her husband entered politics in the early 1980s, she has become the target of controversial debate; her admirers and opponents disagree on her public image: whether she should fit in the standard role expected of the First Lady, remaining in the background as a silent supporter of her husband and working at noncontroversial tasks, or following the precedent of Eleanor Roosevelt, be herself an intelligent, ambitious, and professional woman committed to her ideals in working for the American people. At the heart of the controversy are the constructed issues of the "image" and the "nature" of womanhood, as they are represented in the person of the First Lady. (White House Press Office)

Discussion Questions

1. Do women have a "choice"? Discuss the ways in which women can or cannot choose to (a) "accept" subordinate roles, (b) believe in the "natural" inferiority of women, (c) act as free and responsible persons, and (d) do what we would rather do than what others would like us to do.
2. In what ways can you see a male rather than a universal point of view as predominant in (a) traditional moral theory, (b) a social science with which you are familiar?
3. What would be needed for women to have (a) legal equality, (b) equal opportunities, (c) equality within the family, and (d) full equality?
4. Why is freedom in the sense of freedom from governmental interference insufficient for the liberation of women?
5. Discuss the importance of feminist theory in your own experience. Has it helped you to understand, to choose, to act? If so, how? What are the major areas in which you think feminist theory needs to be improved?

Recommended Readings

Al-Hibri, Azizah Y., and Simons, Margaret A., editors. *Hypatia Reborn: Essays in Feminist Philosophy*. Bloomington and Indianapolis: Indiana University Press, 1990. Essays from the first three issues of *Hypatia*, 1983–85, focusing on many of the issues raised in this chapter, including a separate section on Beauvoir and feminist philosophy.

Beauvoir, Simone de. *The Second Sex*, 1949. Translated by H. M. Parshley. New York: Vintage, 1974. A classic book on how women have been thought about, and how we can begin to think for ourselves about ourselves.

Harding, Sandra, editor. *Feminism and Methodology—Social Science Issues*. Bloomington: Indiana University Press, 1987. A collection of essays showing how different "knowledge" looks, and will have to become, from a feminist perspective.

Jaggar, Alison M. *Feminist Politics and Human Nature*. Totowa, N.J.: Rowman & Allanheld, 1983. An important book for understanding the theories of liberal feminism, traditional Marxism, radical feminism, and socialist feminism. Jaggar gives the reader an excellent framework for reading further on her own.

Lloyd, Genevieve. *The Man of Reason: "Male" and "Female" in Western Philosophy*. Minneapolis: University of Minnesota Press, 1984. Lloyd demonstrates that Western philosophers have celebrated the ideal of "reason" in ways that, upon close investigation, required the rejection of whatever, at various stages of history, was associated with the female.

Phillips, Anne, editor. *Feminism and Equality*. New York. New York University Press, 1987. An examination of the implications of inequality, oppression, and subordination for women, this book explores the issues of equality (political, economic and social, sexual) and difference (sexual, class, racial).

References

Alcoff, Linda. "Cultural Feminism Versus Post Structuralism: The Identity Crisis in Feminist Theory." *Signs* 13:3 (Spring 1988):405–36.

Anzaldúa, Gloria, editor. *Making Face, Making Soul-Haciendo Caras: Creative and Critical Perspectives by Women of Color*. San Francisco: Aunt Lute Books, 1990.

Aristotle. *The Generation of Animals*. vols. 1 and 4. Translated by A. L. Peck. Cambridge, Mass.: Harvard University Press, 1943.

Baier, Annette. "What Do Women Want in a Moral Theory." *Nous* XIX:1 (March 1985):53–63.

Bartky, Sandra. *Femininity and Domination. Studies*

in the Phenomenology of Oppression. New York: Routledge, 1990.

Beauvoir, Simone de. *The Second Sex.* 1949. Translated by H. M. Parshley. New York: Knopf, 1953.

———. *Force of Circumstance.* Translated by Richard Howard. New York: Putnam, 1964.

Belenky, Mary Field, Clinchy, Blythe McVicker, Goldberger, Nancy Rule, and Tarule, Jill Mattuck. *Women's Ways of Knowing: The Development of Self, Voice, and Mind.* New York: Basic Books, 1986.

Bem, Sandra, and Bem, Daryl. "Homogenizing the American Woman." In *Feminist Frameworks*, edited by Alison M. Jaggar and Paula S. Rothenberg. New York: McGraw-Hill, 3rd ed, 1993.

Bunch, Charlotte. "Lesbians in Revolt." In *Lesbianism and the Women's Movement*, edited by Nancy Myron and Charlotte Bunch. Baltimore: Diana Press, 1975.

Card, Claudia, editor. *Feminist Ethics.* Lawrence: University Press of Kansas, 1991.

Chodorow, Nancy. *The Reproduction of Mothering: Psychoanalysis and the Sociology of Gender.* Berkeley: University of California Press, 1978.

Collins, Patricia Hill. *Black Feminist Thought: Knowledge, Consciousness, and the Politics of Empowerment.* New York and London: Routledge, 1991.

De Lauretis, Teresa. "Feminist Studies/Critical Studies: Issues, Terms, and Contexts." In *Feminist Studies/Critical Studies*, edited by Teresa de Lauretis. Bloomington: Indiana University Press, 1986.

DiStefano, Christine. "Masculinity as Ideology in Political Theory: Hobbesian Man Considered." *Hypatia:* A Special Issue of *Women's Studies International Forum* 6:6 (1983): 633–44.

Eisenstein, Zillah. *The Radical Future of Liberal Feminism.* New York: Longman, 1981.

Engels, Friedrich. *The Origin of the Family, Private Property, and the State.* 1884. Translated by Alec West. Edited by Eleanor Burke Leacock. New York: International Publishers, 1972.

Fauk, Nanette, and Mueller, Magda, editors. *Gender Politics and Post-Communism: Reflections from Eastern Europe and the Former Soviet Union.* New York and London: Routledge, 1993.

Flax, Jane. "Do Feminists Need Marxism?" In *Building Feminist Theory: Essays from Quest, a Feminist Quarterly.* New York: Longman, 1981.

Foucault, Michel. *The History of Sexuality.* Translated by Robert Hurley. New York: Pantheon, 1978, 1986. vol. 1: *An Introduction;* vol. 2: *The Use of Pleasure.*

Gilligan, Carol. *In a Different Voice. Psychological Theory and Women's Development.* Cambridge, Mass.: Harvard University Press, 1982.

Gilman, Charlotte Perkins. *Women and Economics.* 1898. Reprint, edited by Carl Degler. New York: Harper Torchbooks, 1966.

———. *The Yellow Wall-Paper.* 1899. Reprint. Afterword by Elaine R. Hedges. New York: Feminist Press, 1973.

Gould, Carol. "Philosophy of Liberation and the Liberation of Philosophy." In *Women and Philosophy*, edited by Carol Gould and Marx Wartofsky. New York: Putnam, 1976.

Harding, Sandra, editor. *Feminism and Methodology. Social Science Issues.* Bloomington: Indiana University Press, 1987.

Harding, Sandra, and Hintikka, Merrill B., editors. *Discovering Reality: Feminist Perspectives on Epistemology, Metaphysics, Methodology, and Philosophy of Science.* Dordrecht, Holland: D. Reidel, 1983.

Hartsock, Nancy C. M. "Postmodernism and Political Change: Issues for Feminist Theory." *Cultural Critique* 14 (Winter 1989–90):15–33.

———. "The Feminist Standpoint: Developing the Ground for a Specifically Historical Feminist Materialism." In *Discovering Reality*, edited by Sandra Harding and Merrill Hintikka. Dordrecht, Holland: D. Reidel, 1983.

———. "Prologue to a Feminist Critique of War and Politics." In *Women's Views of the Political World of Men*, edited by Judith H. Stiehm. Dobbs Ferry, N.Y.: Transnational Pub., 1984.

Held, Virginia. *Feminist Morality Transforming Culture, Society, Politics.* Chicago: University of Chicago Press, 1993.

———. *Rights and Goods. Justifying Social Action.* New York: Free Press/Macmillan, 1984.

Hypatia. A Journal of Feminist Philosophy. Bloomington: Indiana University Press, 1983–present.

Jaggar, Alison. "Feminist Ethics: Some Issues for the Nineties." *Journal of Social Philosophy* xx 1989:91–107.

———. *Feminist Politics and Human Nature.* Totowa, N.J.: Rowman and Allanheld, 1983.

Kelly, Joan. *Women, History, and Theory: The Essays of Joan Kelly.* Chicago: University of Chicago Press, 1984.

Kessler-Harris, Alice. "Written Testimony." In "Women's History Goes on Trial: *EEOC v. Sears, Roebuck and Company.*" *Signs* 11:4 (Summer 1986):767–79.

Kittay, Eva Feder, and Meyers, Diana T., editors. *Women and Moral Theory.* Totowa, N.J.: Rowman & Allanheld, 1987.

Kofman, Sarah. "Rousseau's Phallocratic Ends." *Hypatia* 3:3 (Fall 1988):123–36.

Lange, Lynda. "Woman Is Not a Rational Animal." In *Discovering Reality*, edited by Sandra Harding and Merrill Hintikka. Dordrecht, Holland: D. Reidel, 1983.

Littleton, Christine. "Reconstructing Sexual Equality." *California Law Review* 25 (1987):1279–1337.

Lloyd, Genevieve. *The Man of Reason: "Male" and "Female" in Western Philosophy.* Minneapolis: University of Minnesota Press, 1984.

Locke, John. *Two Treatises of Government.* 1690. Reprint. Edited by Peter Laslett. New York: Mentor, 1965.

Lugones, María, and Spelman, E. V. "Have We Got a Theory for You! Feminist Theory, Cultural Imperialism and the Demand for 'the Woman's Voice.' " *Women's Studies International Forum* 6:6 (1983):573–81.

Lyons, Nona. "Two Perspectives: On Self, Relationships, and Morality." *Harvard Educational Review* 53:2 (May 1983):125–45.

MacKinnon, Catharine. *Feminism Unmodified: Discourses on Life and Law.* Cambridge Mass.: Harvard University Press, 1987.

———. "Sexuality, Pornography, and Method: 'Pleasure under Patriarchy.' " *Ethics* 99:2 (January 1989):314–46.

Mahowald, Mary Briody, editor. *Philosophy of Woman, Classical to Current Concepts.* Indianapolis: Hackett, 1978.

Milkman, Ruth. "Women's History and the Sears Case." *Feminist Studies* 12:2 (Summer 1986):375–400.

Mill, Harriet Taylor. "The Enfranchisement of Women (1851)." In John Stuart Mill and Harriet Taylor Mill, *Essays on Sex Equality.* Edited by Alice S. Rossi. Chicago: University of Chicago Press, 1970.

Mill, James. "Government." Written for the 1820 supplement to the *Encyclopaedia Britannica.* Reprinted as a pamphlet. London, 1821.

Mill, John Stuart. "On the Subjection of Women (1869)." In Mill and Mill, *Essays on Sex Equality.* Edited by Alice S. Rossi, Chicago: University of Chicago Press, 1970.

Mitchell, Juliet. *Woman's Estate.* New York: Vintage, 1973.

Nicholson, Linda J. "Women, Morality, and History." *Social Research* 50:3 (Autumn 1983):514–36.

Noddings, Nel. *Caring: A Feminine Approach to Ethics and Moral Education.* Berkeley: University of California Press, 1984.

Okin, Susan Moller. *Women in Western Political Thought.* Princeton: Princeton University Press, 1979.

———. *Justice, Gender, and the Family.* New York: Basic Books, 1989.

Pierce, Christine. "Natural Law Language and Women." In *Woman in Sexist Society: Studies in Power and Powerlessness*, edited by Vivian Gornick and Barbara Moran. New York: Basic Books, 1971.

Plato. *The Republic.* Translated by H.D.P. Lee. Baltimore: Penguin, 1955.

Posadskaya, Aanastasia, et al., editors. *Women in Russia: A New Era in Russian Feminism.* Translated by Kate Clark. London and New York: Verso, 1994.

Rich, Adrienne. "Compulsory Heterosexuality and Lesbian Existence." *Signs* 5:4 (Summer 1980):631–60.

Rosenberg, Rosalind. "Offer of Proof." In "Women's History Goes on Trial: *EEOC v. Sears, Roebuck and Company.*" *Signs* 11:4 (Summer 1986):757–55.

Rousseau, Jean-Jacques. *Émile* (1762). Translated by Barbara Foxley. New York: Dutton, 1966.

Rowbotham, Sheila. *Woman's Consciousness, Man's World.* Baltimore: Pelican, 1973.

Ruddick, Sara. *Maternal Thinking.* Boston: Beacon Press, 1989.

Sargent, Lydia, editor. *Women and Revolution: A Discussion of the Unhappy Marriage of Marxism and Feminism.* Boston: South End Press, 1981.

Scott, Joan W. "Deconstructing Equality-Versus-Difference: Or, The Uses of Poststructuralist Theory for Feminism." *Feminist Studies* 14:1(Spring 1988):33–50.

Smyth, Ailbhe. "A (Political) Postcard From a Peripheral Pre-Postmodern State (of mind) or How Alliteration and Parentheses Can Knock You Down Dead in Women's Studies." *Women's Studies International Forum* 15 (May–June 1992):331–37.

Spelman, Elizabeth V. *Inessential Woman: Problems of Exclusion in Feminist Thought.* Boston: Beacon Press, 1988.

Steinem, Gloria. "From the Opposite Shore, or How to Survive Though a Feminist." *Ms* 7 (1978):65–67, 90–94, 105.

Tong, Rosemarie. *Feminine and Feminist Ethics.* Belmont, CA: Wadsworth, 1993.

Tronto, Joan C. "Beyond Gender Difference to a Theory of Care." *Signs* 12:4 (Summer 1987):644–63.

———. *Moral Boundaries: A Political Argument for an Ethics of Care.* New York and London: Routledge, 1993.

Vetterling-Braggin, Mary. *Sexist Language.* Totowa, N.J.: Littlefield, Adams, 1981.

Weedon, Chris. *Feminist Practice and Poststructuralist Theory.* Oxford: Blackwell, 1987.

Whitbeck, Caroline. "Theories of Sex Difference." In *Women and Philosophy*, edited by Carol C. Gould and Marx W. Wartofsky. New York: Putnam, 1976.

Williams, Patricia J. *The Alchemy of Race and Rights.* Cambridge, Mass.: Harvard University Press, 1991.

Wollstonecraft, Mary. *A Vindication of the Rights of Woman.* 1792. Reprint. New York: Norton, 1967.

Woodul, Jennifer. "What's This About Feminist Businesses?" *Off Our Backs* 6 (1976):24–26.

Young, Iris Marion. "The Ideal of Community and the Politics of Difference." *Social Theory and Practice* 12 (1986):1–26.

Zalk, Sue Rosenberg, and Gordon-Kelter, Janice, editors. *Revolutions in Knowledge: Feminism in the Social Sciences.* Boulder, Co.: Westview, 1990.

chapter 3

Women's Bodies

Biological Definitions of Women

Some Biological Dilemmas in Defining Women

How Is a Woman Defined Biologically?

The Female Reproductive System and the Life Cycle

Childhood

Adolescence: Puberty and Female Reproductive Maturity

Female Reproductive Cycle

Adulthood and Childbearing

Midlife and Our Later Years

Our Sexual Selves

Western Attitudes about Female Sexuality

The Scientific Study of Sexuality: Female Sexual Response

Sexuality Across the Life Span

Lesbian Sexuality

Older Women and Sexuality

Phallocentric and Heterosexual Bias in Research of Female Sexuality

Biological Definitions of Women

All societies categorize people as male or female. Presumably, this classification is based on a biological difference. In this chapter, we ask: Do physiological characteristics define "woman"?

Our understanding of the biological "facts," however, is shaped by the ideas of the people who formulate the questions and the language they use to express their observations. These people—scientists—are like all human beings, products of their culture, class, and gender experiences. Their investigations and conclusions about female and male characteristics necessarily reflect the perspectives and expectations of the dominant male culture (Haraway, 1989; Hubbard et al., 1982; Longino and Doell, 1987; Keller, 1985).

When biologists speak of the "male" hormone androgen as "masculinizing" fetal sex organs, they appear to be using simple, descriptive terms. In fact, they are bringing their observations within well-worn paths of human expectations and meaning that derive much from the specific culture, society, and identity of the person using the term. The language of sexual dualism carries with it far more than simple biology; when biologists use it to define what the sexes are, an extra, often hidden, explanation of social expectations is always present.

Some Biological Dilemmas in Defining Women

What physiological characteristics do we look for in distinguishing women from men? The most obvious are body shape and height. For example, men, on the average, are taller than women. But does that make a six-foot-tall woman, who is taller than most men, not a woman? An obvious physiological difference is seen in the genital organs. But what about people with genital "abnormalities"? Do we assign these people to yet another gender? Reproductive anatomy seems basic: Women have the machinery for gestation (pregnancy), and men do not. But what about the woman who cannot have children? Does that biological fact make her not a woman?

Hormonal differences between the two sexes are often suggested as explanations for differences in behavior as well as physiology. Women and men have some hormones in approximately equal amounts. There are, in addition, so-called female hormones and male hormones, but such references are misleading. All people have both "female" and "male" hormones in varying amounts, and even within one gender the variation in amount of

U.S.A.'s Florence Griffith-Joyner raises her arms in jubilation after winning the women's 100-meter dash at the 1988 Olympics in Seoul, Korea. A woman's body is capable of wondrous accomplishments.

each set of hormones is great. It also varies for any one person in moments of stress, on different days, and at different times of life.

Chromosomes are an obvious place to turn for a way to define a woman biologically. Most people have a genetic combination that results in the development of physical characteristics labeled "female" or "male." However, there are other genetic combinations that are neither simply "female" nor "male." There are people whose genetic makeup appears to be that of one sex but who are born with the genitals of the "other" sex. They are usually considered, by themselves and by others, and show the behavior expected of, the gender they are assigned, regardless of their chromosomal makeup.

The Problem with "Averages." Sexual dimorphism (difference in shape or form between the sexes) refers to a statistical average of the frequency or degree of specific differences. While this may be useful in describing large groups, it tells nothing about individuals. We may find that there is tremendous overlap between groups, and that the variations *within* any one group may be greater than the difference between the two groups. For example, in the 1979 New York City Marathon, the first woman to complete the race, Grete Waitz, ran faster than over 99 percent of the men who reached the finish line. There was roughly a sixteen-minute difference in running time between her and the first man to finish. There was over a five-hour difference in running time between the first man and the last man to finish.

Variations within a Sex and between the Sexes. Physical differences between females and males are sometimes emphasized, such as greater upper-body muscle mass in men. Two primary factors influence these differences—genetic traits and environment (e.g., nutrition, exercise). The African Watusi and Pygmies are known, re-

spectively, for their great and small heights. Women within these groups are usually smaller than the men, but the Watusi female is taller than the average non-Watusi male, and the average non-Pygmy female is taller than the Pygmy male. Similarly, women in any society whose activities require physical strength might be stronger and more muscular than men who do not engage in strenuous endeavors. Thus, to say *all* women are smaller or weaker than men is obviously misleading.

Discussions of secondary sex characteristics imply artificial polarities along dimensions of height, weight, musculature, body hair, breast size, and the pitch of the human voice. While the "average" woman differs from the "average" man on these dimensions, all of these characteristics fall on a continuum. Body shape and even height, for example, may be influenced to a great extent by nutrition and exercise.

Some scientists differentiate women and men on the basis of hormonal fluctuations in women. Some critics of women's participation in politics, for example, have argued that hormonal fluctuation might cause erratic behavior, which would preclude responsible decision making. But men, too, have hormonal variations and fluctuations (McFarlane et al., 1988). For example, the steroid hormones that are produced by the adrenal glands fluctuate on a twenty-four-hour (or circadian) cycle (Luce, 1970) and affect emotions.

How Is a Woman Defined Biologically?

A woman is a member of the species *Homo sapiens*, all of whom are mammals, and mammals are defined by the female function of nursing their young. When scientists talk about the biology of women, however, the two systems that mediate their perception are the endocrine and reproductive systems—in other words, the systems that make women "not male."

In contrast, the "biology of man" refers not only to the physiology of male reproduction and endocrinology, but to those biological systems common to both women and men. This narrow definition of the biology of women has resulted in the misapplication of medical knowledge about men to women and a dearth of research on women's health, which has had detrimental consequences for women's health. In this chapter, we concentrate on a discussion of the implications of the reproductive and endocrine systems, with the clear understanding that such a presentation is only a small part of the whole woman.

Chromosomes and Gender. Current scientific opinion holds that a person's sex is primarily determined by her or his chromosomal makeup. Most human beings have forty-six chromosomes, arranged in twenty-three pairs in each cell. Each chromosome has approximately twenty thousand genes in it. These genes contain what is called the genetic code, the program for the development of characteristics inherited from the parents. All cells in the body have these forty-six chromosomes with the exception of the sex cells, or gametes. The *gametes* are the *ova* (eggs) in the female and

the *sperm* in the male. Each of these cells has only twenty-three chromosomes—one chromosome from each of the 23 pairs.

At conception, twenty-three chromosomes from the ovum and twenty-three chromosomes from the sperm pair up. The fertilized egg, called a *zygote*, has forty-six chromosomes, or twenty-three pairs. One of these pairs will determine if the fetus is a genetic female or genetic male. In females this pair of chromosomes is made up of X chromosomes, making an XX pattern; in males the pattern is XY. All ova, then, having only one set of the twenty-three pairs, will always carry an X chromosome. Male sperm will carry either an X or a Y chromosome. Thus, if the ovum is fertilized by a sperm carrying an X chromosome, there will be an XX pattern and a genetic female. If the egg is fertilized by a sperm carrying a Y chromosome, there will be an XY pattern, and a genetic male. The accompanying illustration depicts this chromosomal determination of sex. As we will see below, it is the presence of the Y chromosome that initiates a sequence of events that results in the development of male reproductive organs.

What we currently know about the Y chro-

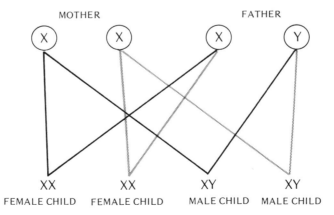

MOTHER   FATHER

X   X   X   Y

XX   XX   XY   XY
FEMALE CHILD   FEMALE CHILD   MALE CHILD   MALE CHILD

mosome is that it carries little other genetic information (except for the gene for hairy ears, which is why females do not inherit this trait). The X chromosome, in contrast, is rich with genetic information. This explains a number of things about sex-linked inherited characteristics and diseases. A number of characteristics (for example, balding in some men, or hemophilia, the "bleeding disease") are carried on the X chromosome. If a man gets an X chromosome with a disease-carrying trait (which can only come from his mother), he will have the disease or condition. The Y chromosome offers no resistance, no counteraction. Females, in contrast, are much less vulnerable to inherited diseases or traits because they have two X chromosomes. If a female receives one X chromosome that is carrying one of these traits, and one that is not, she will most likely not show the trait. She would have to get two X chromosomes carrying that characteristic, one from her mother and one from her father, a much less frequent occurrence.

This chromosomal division into female or male is not as simple as it appears, however. Occasionally, chromosomal anomalies occur at conception. For example, such chromosomal combinations as XO, XXY, XXX, or XYY have been found. Since a gene on the Y chromosome triggers the development of the male reproductive system, those genetic combinations with a Y chromosome (even XXY) will develop male genitals. Most people with these genetic variations have some physiological developmental problems and are sterile.

It is tempting to define females biologically as individuals who have two X chromosomes and no Y chromosome, and males as those who receive at least one Y chromosome. But a clearer understanding of the role of genes shows the inadequacy of such an approach.

A fertilized ovum multiplies again and again, and different parts of the mass of cells become different body systems and organs. Slowly it takes on the form of the human fetus.

The genetic code then communicates to the cells how to proceed with our development. But genes are not traits or organs in and of themselves. They are like a blueprint, indicating the direction something should take. Genes merely reflect the potential for development; any genetic program requires a particular environment in which to evolve. This is an important fact to remember whenever we think about the contributions of genes to any behavior or trait.

The nature of the genetic contributions will vary depending on the environment in which that trait develops. If females and males are not exposed to the same environment, we have no way of knowing whether their differences reflect genetic potentials. Even the development of genetically linked traits can be modified by environmental events.

This interaction between the genetic code and the environment also applies to the determination of the fetus's reproductive organs. The chromosomal blueprint merely starts this process. A range of things can modify or change it.

Intrauterine Events. Generally, for the first six weeks of gestation, both genetic females and genetic males have an identical, undifferentiated *gonad* (sex organ). If the *embryo*[1] has a Y chromosome, a gene on the chromosome will release a substance that will cause the inner layer of the gonad to develop into testicles. In the absence of this substance, the outer layer of this gonad will develop into an ovary.

Primitive genital duct structures for the female internal reproductive organs (the Mullerian duct) and for the male (the Wolffian duct) exist as two parallel systems in both XX and XY fetuses. The Mullerian duct system has the potential to develop into the uterus

---

[1]*Embryo* is the term for the growing fetus from the second week through the second month of pregnancy.

Adam-out-of-Eve

The primacy of the embryonic female morphology forces us to reverse long held concepts on the nature of sexual differentiation. Embryologically speaking, it is correct to say that the penis is an exaggerated clitoris, the scrotum is derived from the labia majora, and that the original libido is feminine, etc. The reverse is true only for the birds and reptiles. For all mammals, modern embryology calls for an Adam-out-of-Eve myth!

(Sherfey, 1972:46)

Copyright @1972 by Random House. Reprinted by permission.

and the fallopian tubes. The Wolffian system has the potential to develop into the male internal reproductive system. Which of these systems develops depends on the presence or absence of certain hormones. Newly formed testicles release hormones, one of which will suppress the development of the Mullerian duct system. The other hormone will stimulate the growth of the Wolffian system, causing the development of male internal organs. In the absence of these hormones, the Wolffian duct system will spontaneously degenerate and the Mullerian system will develop into the female internal reproductive organs—even in a genetic male. At present, scientists know of no special hormones needed for female internal reproductive organs to develop. It seems this will occur if the hormones released by the testicles fail to be introduced into the system. These hormones, then, are critical for the development of male internal reproductive structures. If there is any interference in the production of these hormones, a genetic male could develop some female internal organs.

A similar process occurs in the development of the external genitalia at the end of the third fetal month. Prior to that time, one undifferentiated structure exists in both genetic female and male fetuses. After the third month, the release of fetal hormones from the testicles will cause the system to differentiate into a penis. If the release of these hormones, called

androgens, does not occur, the structure will differentiate into a vagina and clitoris, even in a genetic male fetus. As one can see, many of the sexual organs in females and males have evolved out of the same embryonic tissues. We say they are homologous. They are also similar in function (analogous). Table 3.1

Table 3.1 Homologous and Analogous Sexual Organs

Female Ovaries	Male Testicles
Shaft of the clitoris (connects the head of the clitoris to the pubic bone)	Corpus cavernosum (cylindrical body inside the penis)
Glans of clitoris (head of the clitoris)	Glans of penis (head)
Labia majora (outer lips)	Scrotum (houses the testicles)
Labia minora (inner lips)	Bottom side of the penis
Bulb of the vestibule (sensitive tissues around the opening of the vagina)	Bulb of the penis (base of the penis and corpus spongiosum (cylindrical body in the penis)
Bartholin's glands (glands on each side of the vaginal opening)	Cowper's glands (glands inside the penis)

Source: Adapted from *The New Our Bodies, Ourselves* by the Boston Women's Health Book Collective, Inc. (New York: Simon & Schuster, 1976), rev. ed. 1992. Reprinted by permission of Simon & Schuster, a Division of Gulf and Western Corp.

shows examples of homologous and analogous sexual organs.

A genetic condition or an interference in the events dictated by the genetic blueprint may result in persons born with internal or external organs different from their chromosomal sex. Occasionally, fetal testicles do not produce sufficient androgens or the genetic male fetus is unable to use these hormones when they are produced (called *androgen insensitivity*). In these cases, a person will be born with the external genitals of a female. These individuals are labeled and raised as females; they identify themselves as women and they assume gender-appropriate roles (Money and Ehrhardt, 1972).

Similarly, androgens may be introduced into the system of a genetic female fetus. When born, such persons are referred to as *androgenized females.* Depending on the extent of the androgenizing influences, these genetic females may be born with female internal reproductive organs and an enlarged clitoris or with what appears to be a normal penis with an empty scrotum (Money and Ehrhardt, 1972). This condition may be the result of a hereditary disorder or an externally induced disorder. The latter occurred in the 1950s, for example, when some pregnant women were given progestin, a synthetic hormone, to prevent miscarriages.

Scientists have recently isolated a gene on the X chromosome that has doubled (duplicated itself) in some chromosomal males, apparently causing, to varying degrees, the prenatal development of female genitals and/or reproductive organs. This occurred even though these individuals produced the required hormones for the development of male organs. As a result, scientists are now speculating that there may be a gene that contributes to the prenatal development of female organs in girls, as well (Angier, 1994). Little is known about this possibility; however, this research highlights the complexity of the development and determination of biological sex and challenges the strongly held assumption that it is predetermined and binary (either female or male). The biological events that lead up to being labeled "female" or "male" at birth demonstrate that what appears on the surface to be the clearest biological definition of woman or man—that is, one's genetic and reproductive makeup—is far from being that simple or clear.

The Female Reproductive System and the Life Cycle

Generally, the prenatal period is unproblematic, and people are born with a genital reproductive structure readily assigned by society as either "female" or "male."

In contrast to our other biological systems, the reproductive system remains relatively inactive during the childhood years. Like the rest of the body, however, it too will develop, grow, mature, and age, setting the parameters of the so-called childbearing years. Societal attitudes about women's roles and cycles define the value attached to our reproductive stage and, often, how we are treated. The ability to conceive brings with it different meanings and consequences in various cultures and, inevitably, affects how we feel about ourselves at different life stages. Nonetheless, no society ignores that stage in our lives, and it is a concrete marker in our development. This section addresses the female reproductive system in developmental stages throughout the life span. For a summary and illustration of the genital and reproductive system of the mature female, see "Female Internal and External Genital Structure."

Childhood

Girls' skeletal and neurological systems tend to be more advanced at birth, and girls mature more rapidly than boys; otherwise, girls and boys are physiologically virtually the same. Their bodies are shaped similarly, size differences are negligible, and there is little difference in the level of sex hormones (estrogen and androgens) that flow through their systems. Males, however, are more vulnerable to physiological distress. Far from being the "stronger sex," male fetuses are more likely to suffer prenatal problems and to abort spontaneously. Male children are also more vulnerable to childhood diseases and developmental problems (Jacklin, 1989).

While stereotypes prevail about behavioral differences between girls and boys, research suggests remarkably few, and even these are not consistently or cross-culturally supported by solid evidence linking them to biological sex. However, the gender assignment made at birth is followed by a long socialization process by which children's behavior is encouraged to conform to a society's gender roles (see Chapter 5).

Adolescence: Puberty and Female Reproductive Maturity

Puberty marks the physiological transition from childhood to reproductive maturity. It is marked by menstruation in females and by the production of sperm in males. In cultures that define a block of years as a transitional stage between childhood and adulthood, the onset of puberty is frequently viewed as the beginning of adolescence. In cultures that do not define an adolescent developmental stage, puberty signals entrance into the adult world, and the young adult is expected to assume adult responsibilities and roles. Sometimes adolescents are initiated into adulthood with some formal ritual or celebration, called *rites of passage* or *puberty rites.*

In Western cultures, the median age of the onset of puberty in females is about twelve. On the average, females reach puberty two years earlier than males. Beginning with pu-

berty and continuing throughout the reproductive years, there are marked differences in the production of hormones that regulate the reproductive capacity of females and males.

Exactly what triggers the sequence of biological events that leads to the onset of puberty is not known. It is thought that at this point in development, the hypothalamus (a gland in the brain) signals other body organs to begin the production of sex hormones—estrogen and progesterone in the female. The girl's nipples and then breasts begin to develop, pubic hair appears, hair begins to grow in the armpits, and the sexual and reproductive organs grow larger. The girl's body begins to experience a spurt of growth and to assume the characteristics of an adult woman (e.g., hips widen). These developments continue throughout the teenage years, but about one to two years after their onset, menstruation begins, and the female reproductive cycle is set into motion.

Female Reproductive Cycle

Three main glands—the hypothalamus, the pituitary, and the ovaries—govern the reproductive cycle by secreting hormones into the blood. These hormones communicate regulatory messages between the glands. At the point where the body experiences low levels of the hormones estrogen and progesterone, the hypothalamus, which is sensitive to fluctuating levels of hormones, produces a hormone called follicle-stimulating-hormone-release factor (FSH-RF). This hormone stimulates the pituitary gland, which in turn produces another hormone called follicle-stimulating hormone (FSH). FSH does just what its name says: It stimulates the follicles in the ovaries to grow. The maturing follicle produces estrogen, which causes the endometrium, or uterine lining, to grow thick. When the follicle reaches maturity, it releases an ovum, which is expelled from the ovary.

Female Internal and External Genital Structure

Vulva—the external genital area (clitoris, outer lips, inner lips, and vaginal opening).

Mons—soft fatty tissue lying in front of the pubic bone. It is the area above where the crotch begins. It contains pubic hair.

Labia Majora ("outer lips")—hair-covered, soft, fatty area between the legs.

Labia Minora ("inner lips")—surrounded by the labia majora, hairless folds of skin which frame the vaginal opening. The labia minora meet toward the front of the woman to cover the *clitoris*. The covering is called the *hood*. The labia minora consists of erectile tissues. It is very sensitive and responds to sexual arousal by filling up with blood (vasocongestion).

Clitoris—highly sensitive piece of erectile tissue just covered by the labia minora where they meet in the front of the body (clitoral hood). The head or tip of the clitoris is called the *glans*. During sexual arousal, the clitoris fills with blood and swells, extending out from its hood. Prior to orgasm, it withdraws again. The clitoris is the most sensitive part of the female genital structure. Its sole purpose is to receive and send messages about sexual arousal. There was for some years a debate about whether the clitoris in the "mature" woman loses much of its importance and the vagina becomes the primary organ of sexual arousal. We believe now that this is not the case and that regardless of the source of sexual arousal, the clitoris plays a primary role, even if it is not stimulated directly.

Urinary Opening (urethral orifice)—small hole below the clitoris. This is the opening for the urethra, the small tube that leads to the bladder and from which urine is expelled.

Vaginal Opening—just below the urinary opening, this is a larger opening that leads to the vagina. It may be partially covered by a thin membrane, called the hymen. The hymen is generally stretched or ruptured by sexual or physical activity.

Bartholin's Glands—two glands on either side of the vaginal opening. They secrete a small amount of fluid.

Perineum—area between the labia minora and the *anus* (opening to the rectum).

Vagina—the canal which extends from the uterus to the outside of the body ("vaginal opening"). During sexual arousal, the vagina "sweats" or lubricates. This is caused by the increase in blood flow through the vaginal tissue.

Fornix—end of the vagina.

Cervix—base of the uterus.

Os—opening in the cervix leading to the inside of the uterus.

Uterus ("womb")—a pear-shaped, muscular organ located between the bladder and the rectum. The fetus develops in the uterus. The outer third of the lining (*endometrium*) of the uterus is shed during menstruation.

Fundus—the top of the uterus.

Fallopian tubes—two tubes extending outward from the top of the uterus. The outer ends of the fallopian tubes are funnel-shaped and fringed (*fimbria*). They wrap around the ovaries but do not actually touch them. When a woman ovulates, the ovum travels down the fallopian tube to the uterus.

Ovaries—two almond-shaped organs, each located on one side of, and slightly behind, the uterus. These glands produce the hormones (estrogen and progesterone) that are responsible for the development and release of the mature ova.

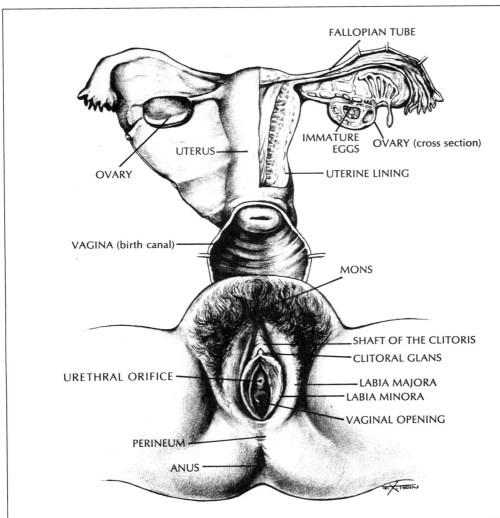

FALLOPIAN TUBE

IMMATURE EGGS

OVARY (cross section)

UTERUS

UTERINE LINING

OVARY

VAGINA (birth canal)

MONS

SHAFT OF THE CLITORIS

CLITORAL GLANS

URETHRAL ORIFICE

LABIA MAJORA

LABIA MINORA

VAGINAL OPENING

PERINEUM

ANUS

Illustration from: S. Bittman and S. R. Zalk, *Expectant Fathers*. New York: Hawthorne Books, 1978.
Artist: F.X. Tobin.

"The Abandoned Doll" by Suzanne Valadon (1867–1938) captures the moment at which the girl is changing into a young woman. The girl is examining herself in the mirror and looking at the changes; the older woman appears as a mother figure, explaining and supportive. The doll, the symbol of childhood, lies at their feet, no longer claiming the girl's attention but symbolic of a turning point in her life. (1921, Galerie Spiess, Paris)

This event is referred to as *ovulation* (see the illustration on page 102 showing phases of the menstrual cycle).

Just prior to ovulation, the mature follicle will also secrete progesterone. This hormone helps to create a nourishing and retentive environment for the fertilized ovum should conception occur. If the ovum is fertilized, the matured follicle, now called *corpus luteum*, will continue the secretion of progesterone and estrogen. When fertilization does not occur, the follicle will slowly disintegrate, decreasing the amount of these hormones. With this decrease of estrogen and progesterone, the uterus can no longer hold its lining. It sheds a portion of the endometrium, the process of *menstruation*. The remaining endometrium will form the new lining. Now the hypothalamus responds to the fact that there are low levels of estrogen and progesterone in the body and releases FSH-RF, beginning the cycle all over again.

Menstruation is simply one part of an integrated body cycle. Although ovulation and menstruation are tied together, it is possible to menstruate without ovulating and to ovulate without menstruating. Some women may fail to menstruate at all (amenorrhea) or do so irregularly (see Chapter 12). What is more, this genetically programmed biological sequence is reactive to environmental events, physical health, and emotional state. Age of *menarche* (first menstruation) as well as regularity of menstruation, for example, is affected by nutrition, weight, stress, and even light (or length of day). There is a relationship between total weight and the percentage of body fat and the menstrual cycle. Women whose weight or level of body fat drops below a critical level may stop menstruating altogether or do so irregularly. This is common among *anorexic*[2] females and often occurs with dancers

and athletes whose lean bodies have little fat and much muscle.

Attitudes about Menstruation. In some parts of the world, menarche is accompanied by initiation rituals. These events may celebrate the female's passage into womanhood, or conversely, they can be based on a negative, hostile, and fearful attitude toward menstruating and menstrual blood. Many societies treat the menstruating woman as unclean and in need of isolation, especially from men. This may oblige a woman to remain in a segregated hut during menstruation or to avoid touching a man, his food, or his weapon (sometimes we are even forbidden to make eye contact with men). In these cultures, menstrual blood is viewed as polluting or dangerous. Some of the customs also dictate that women purify ourselves at the end of the menstrual period in various ritualistic ways (Weideger, 1977).

A young woman's feelings and attitudes about menstruation can affect her self-esteem, family relationships, feelings of autonomy, and sexual behavior (Golub, 1983). Negative feelings are more likely to be associated with distressing reactions. Surveys of pre- and postmenarche Western women indicate that women are quite ambivalent about menstruation. Many women report experiencing both positive and negative feelings, such as excitement and pride along with fear and embarrassment. In Western societies women's reactions to menarche and menstruation vary tremendously. Societal attitudes communicated through language, media, and hygienic protocol shape attitudes and opinions.

Euphemisms for menstruation pervade our language. This effort to avoid public embarrassment suggests menstruation carries the taint of an unclean excretory function. Products related to menstrual hygiene are now advertised widely in magazines, newspapers, and television but rarely make direct references to menstruation. It is still common to hear the

---

[2]Anorexia is a condition in which an individual refuses or feels unable to eat.

1. DAY OF CYCLE

MP   OVULATION   MP

1 2 3 4 5 6 7 8 9 10 11 12 13 14 15 16 17 18 19 20 21 22 23 24 25 26 27 28 29 30 31

2. BASAL TEMPERATURE

3. OVARIAN CHANGES

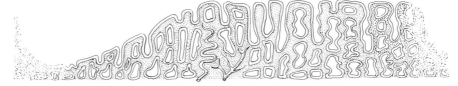

——————FOLLICULAR PHASE—————— ————LUTEAL PHASE————

4. ENDOMETRIAL CHANGES

5. OVARIAN HORMONE LEVELS

ESTROGENS

PROGESTERONE

Phases of the menstrual cycle:

1. Ovulation usually occurs midpoint between menstrual periods (MP).
2. At the time of ovulation, basal temperature (temperature upon waking in the morning) rises slightly.
3. These changes occur in the ovary prior to ovulation, at ovulation (day 14), and after ovulation if conception does not occur.
4. The lining (endometrium) of the uterus sheds during menstruation and then grows thick again.
5. Estrogen and progesterone levels are high around the time of ovulation and then gradually diminish; the diminished levels cause the endometrium lining to shed. (Adapted from D. Jensen, *The Principles of Physiology*, 2d ed. New York: Appleton, 1980.)

statements, "I have the curse," "My friend is visiting," or "It's that time of the month." The degree of preparedness for and accurate knowledge about menstruation is a powerful factor in how a woman reacts to menstruating. The more prepared and knowledgeable, the more positive the experience and related perceptions. According to one large survey, almost 40 percent of the women interviewed felt inadequately prepared and ignorant (Rierdan, 1983). Most females learn about menstruation from their mothers and turn to them for support. A mother's attitude toward menstruation shapes her daughter's reactions (see Golub, 1983, and Travis, 1988, for literature review).

Also associated with menstruation is the notion that it is an illness. During the Victorian era in England, male medical doctors urged women to act as invalids when they were menstruating, but autobiographical sources suggest that only a few did, and only upper-class women could afford to do so (Showalter and Showalter, 1972; Digby, 1989; Jalland, 1986). Most women do not have the resources to treat menstruation as a sickness, and most do not "feel sick." Nevertheless, this association between menstruation and infirmity is often met in the workplace where it has been used to discriminate against women. Menstrual cramps may occur, but in most cases this condition is not debilitating. As is the case with any bodily function, menstruation may cause discomfort to a disabling degree in some women. Exercise, biofeedback techniques, and medication can help alleviate discomfort.

However, menstruation is a natural bodily function. Women may engage in any activity while menstruating, including bathing, swimming, sexual intercourse, or exercise. Nonetheless, both society and professional literature have perpetuated myths about menstruation that have helped to keep women in subordinate roles (Parlee, 1974, 1978).

Since menstruation is an observable function, it has been easy to perpetuate such myths.

Menstruation and Moods. Menstruation has been used to make a charge of mental instability in women. Recent research has discovered that certain mood and emotional states may have a biochemical basis. These feelings may be brought about by the hormonal changes that occur during *many* cycles, not just the menstrual cycle. It must be kept in mind that other cycles and changes in other hormones, in both women and men, affect psychological responses (Luce, 1970). It is also worth noting that emotional distress can alter hormone levels (Sommer, 1978). In addition, environmental, emotional, and biological factors interact in complex ways, so no one factor can be singled out as the primary cause of hormonal fluctuations in women and men.

Some women experience what has been loosely termed a *premenstrual syndrome.* Typical symptoms include water retention, cramps, headaches, irritability, anxiety, and tension. Actually, a total of 150 symptoms have been cited at different times (Moos, 1969). It is difficult to come up with a definition that conforms to most women. There is little agreement as to how many women experience the syndrome. The proportion reported varies from 15 percent to 95 percent, depending on the definition of the term used and the researcher using it (Paige, 1973). It is important to note that these symptoms are reactions all people have at different times in their lives in response to stress, regardless of the phase of their hormonal cycle. Any stress experienced by women is frequently attributed to premenstrual (or menstrual, or postmenstrual) reactions. Women who have experienced such reactions have been called hysterical and hypochondriacs. We have been accused, among other things, of rejecting our femininity. Arguments such as these have been used as an excuse to keep women from positions of power and authority. Recent research comparing mood fluctuations of women and men over menstrual and other cycles, however, found no pattern specifically related to menstrual cycle or gender (McFarlane et al., 1988; McFarlane and Williams, 1994).

As we noted earlier, both women and men have hormonal cycles (Luce, 1970; Ramey, 1972; McFarlane et al., 1988). Men's cycles are more difficult to chart because of the absence of an observable event such as menstruation. When researchers have undertaken projects to determine cyclic functioning in males, they report an interaction between hormone fluctuations and mood and functioning. But little research attention has been given to these male cycles.

Nonetheless, women are inclined to label mood changes as related to their menstrual cycle. Studies suggest that as many as 50 percent of North American adult women report experiencing premenstrual syndrome. However, longitudinal studies of these women indicate that most experience similar emotional highs and lows at other times in their cycle and these do not differ from men's mood changes over a lunar month (McFarlane and Williams, 1994). The readiness to label women's, but not men's, emotional phases as biologically precipitated reflects the stereotype of women as emotionally unstable due to menstrual hormonal cycles and the equally unsupported stereotype of men's freedom from cyclical mood changes and, as a result, relative emotional stability. This research strongly calls into question the recent decision by the American Psychiatric Association to include premenstrual syndrome (called Premenstrual Phase Dysphoric Disorder) in the *Psychiatric Diagnostic and Statistical Manual*, the standard guidebook for psychiatric/psychological diagnoses. The research challenges the validity,

meaningfulness, and usefulness of this diagnosis. The implications for women are complex, and controversy over this issue is ongoing in the medical, psychiatric, and psychological community.

Adulthood and Childbearing

Many women are able to conceive for almost forty years, beginning shortly after menarche and ending with *menopause* (the cessation of ovulation), which usually occurs between the ages of forty-eight and fifty-two. The likelihood of conceiving steadily diminishes and the probability of miscarriage increases for women past the age of forty.

The Physiology of Pregnancy. The biology of pregnancy is obviously closely tied to the hormonal cycle governing ovulation and menstruation. Women are born with all of our ova, which are stored in the ovaries. At the time of ovulation, one ovum (sometimes more) matures. When the ovum leaves the ovary, it is swept into the funnel-like end of one fallopian tube. The ovum then makes the journey down the tube to the uterus, a trip that takes about six days. If the ovum is not fertilized, it either disintegrates or is sloughed off in vaginal secretions. If fertilization by a sperm does take place, this is called *conception*. Since the ovum is only viable for about twenty-four hours, fertilization must occur in the upper third of the fallopian tube. The sperm has to travel through the vagina, through the uterus, and into the fallopian tube. Sperm live longer than the ovum, so women can conceive if we have had intercourse shortly before we ovulate.

As the fertilized ovum (zygote) travels down the fallopian tube, the cell multiplies over and over again. When it reaches the uterus, it attaches to the uterine wall, and a *placenta* begins to develop. The placenta is a broad, flat organ that joins the woman by means of the umbilical cord to the fetus. The developing placenta secretes a hormone that signals the *corpus luteum* (the mature follicle after it has released the egg) to continue its production of hormones that will keep the uterine lining proliferated and secreting. Occasionally, the fertilized ovum implants in the fallopian tube. This is called a *tubal* or *ectopic* pregnancy. It is not a viable pregnancy and usually requires surgery.

Nutrients are carried by the woman's blood into the placenta and pass through a placental barrier to the fetus. Thus, the woman's diet and ingestion of chemicals and substances may affect the development of the fetus and the health of the child. The fetus and woman have separate circulatory systems, and there is no exchange of blood between them. The fetus continues to grow inside the uterus, and the different body parts will develop from the embryonic tissues according to a genetic code. This sequence of developments is dictated by the genetic code and is the same for all human fetuses.

The expanding uterus as the fetus grows is what gives women the "pregnant look." This expansion also causes an increased need to urinate (the uterus places pressure on the bladder) and shortness of breath later on in the pregnancy (the uterus takes up more space, decreasing the area in which the lungs can expand when the woman inhales).

In normal development, the fetus has all of its organs months before birth and only the respiratory system is not functioning. The infant begins breathing independently only after emerging from the mother. That is the significance of the baby's first cry at birth. It is this immature respiratory system that provides the greatest risk to a baby born prematurely.

The biology of pregnancy is just one aspect of this nine-month period. Attitudes and beliefs about pregnant women vary and can help us understand what pregnancy means, and how women react to this event in specific societies and situations (see Chapter 8).

The Biology of Birth. Most human pregnancies last nine months. The birth process is called *labor*. Exactly what triggers labor is not known. Late in the pregnancy, the woman may become aware of some "practice" contractions. These contractions serve to prepare the uterus for birth by beginning the effacement (thinning) and dilation (opening) of the cervix. There are several indications that labor will begin soon. Some women notice a mucus discharge streaked with blood. The membrane of the amniotic sac (which contains the fetus) may rupture and the amniotic fluid be expelled through the vagina. It may drip out and hardly be noticed, or it may come with a gush. The beginning of labor itself is signaled by a pattern of regular contractions. Health care professionals tend to divide labor into three stages. The first stage can take anywhere from two to twenty-four hours or more. As the labor progresses, the contractions are more frequent, last longer, and are stronger. These contractions cause the cervix to efface and dilate so that the fetus can pass out of the uterus and into the woman's vagina.

Most fetuses are head-down when labor begins. This position makes it easier for the fetus to fit through the woman's pelvis and is least likely to cause complications. Some fetuses do present themselves in other positions, the most common being the breech (buttocks-down) position.

The first stage of labor ends when the cervix is completely effaced and dilated. The second stage of labor is the fetus's movement through the birth canal (the vagina); it ends when the baby is born. This second stage usually lasts from one-half hour to two hours. We will be told to push or bear down, to help the process along (unless large amounts of anesthesia have been given).

The third stage of labor is the delivery of the placenta. This occurs within minutes or up to one-half hour after the birth. Certain hormones are produced that cause the uterus to contract and to expel the placenta. If the mother breast-feeds immediately after birth, the sucking newborn will stimulate the production of these hormones. Breast-feeding also speeds up the return of the uterus to its nonpregnant size.

Some of us are unable to have vaginal deliveries. This may occur, for example, if the pelvis is too small for the fetus to pass through, or if the cervix fails to efface and dilate sufficiently. Sometimes the fetus or the pregnant woman is in physical distress, necessitating a speedy delivery. When these events occur in our society, a cesarean procedure is performed. This involves surgical removal of the baby by cutting through the abdominal wall and into the uterus. The placenta is also removed in this way.

Cesarean procedures have spared many women and newborns birth-related health complications. Nonetheless, the frequency of cesarean procedures and the study of demographic patterns have led women's health care advocates to claim that a substantial number of cesareans are not medically indicated or motivated and that unnecessary procedures are performed at a higher rate on select groups of women. This is discussed in Chapter 12.

Postpartum or "Lying-in" Period. After childbirth, women's bodies readjust to the nonpregnant state. This occurs very rapidly compared to the slow and continuous adjustment of the body to the pregnant state over nine months. It takes about six weeks for the uterus to return to the nonpregnant state, but the changes in the circulatory system are rapid, occurring within the first twenty-four hours after the birth.

During the postpartum period, women experience uterine bleeding similar to the menstrual period, and lactation, the production of milk, begins. Often we feel fatigued because of the stress on our bodies and the limited sleep cycle permitted by a newborn infant. Traditions, circumstances, and personal preferences dictate the time a culture allots for a woman to readjust during this period.

Women experience a significant hormonal alteration after childbirth. This alteration, coupled with sleep deprivation and the need to adjust to a newborn, can affect our emotional response. Many women experience a let-down or transient period of depression. Our social support systems at this time are important. In many places in the world, this period is a time when women take care of other women. But in the United States, with its high degree of mobility and modern emphasis on technology, women may frequently be isolated from kin or even friends, a situation that may increase our stress. A small percentage of women experience a severe and chronic depression that persists for weeks or even longer, and requires professional help.

Breast-feeding. Women not only carry and give birth to babies but also we are born with the biological capacity to feed our young. During pregnancy, the placenta produces hormones that prepare the mammary glands in the breast for secreting milk. These hormones also inhibit the production of milk-forming chemicals until after the birth. The first few days after childbirth, a high-protein secretion called *colostrum* is produced. Two or three days after the birth, the mother starts to produce milk. *Lactation* refers to the production of milk after childbirth. Two hormones are involved—one for production and one for secretion. The sucking baby stimulates the production of these hormones; thus, the more women nurse, the more milk we produce. If we stop nursing, milk production will cease.

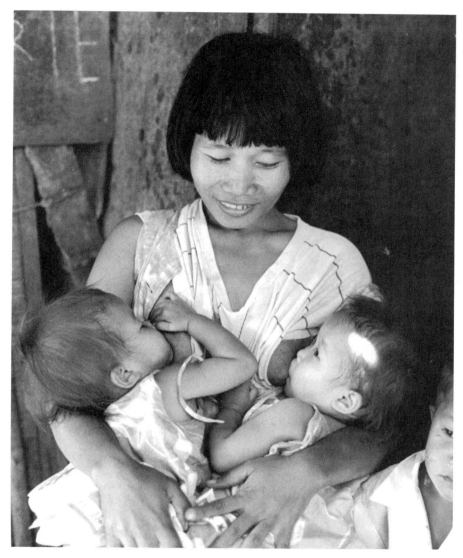

Woman nursing two babies in the Philippines. A biological "fact," that a woman is endowed with the capacity to feed the young, may be a great source of joy for the mother. Breast-feeding is considered a superior nutritional alternative to commercially produced formulas.

Lactation may inhibit ovulation, but this is not a reliable means for contraception. Women may begin ovulating again before the first menstrual flow, so we may not get an indication that we are once more fertile. However, many things can affect both the experience and physiology of lactation and breast-feeding and these will affect each other. Our health, our bodies (e.g., characteristics of our nipples), our feelings, cultural attitudes, responsiveness of the newborn, all interact with the biological process.

Reproductive Technology. Within the last decade, scientists have developed drugs and medical technologies to correct or "sidestep" many conditions that result in infertility. These have been called "reproductive technologies."

There are many factors that can cause infertility. For example, the sperm may be inadequate for fertilization; there may be problems with ovulation or the viability of the ova; the fallopian tubes may be blocked; or there may be an infection, a disease, or antibodies that interfere with conception. Often the reason is not known. Some women can conceive but are unable to carry the fertilized ovum to term.

Male fertility drugs are sometimes effective in increasing the viability of sperm, and some conditions that interfere with sperm production respond to surgery. Similarly, women may be placed on a drug regimen, for example, to stimulate ovulation or to make the uterus more receptive for pregnancy. Surgery may be performed to open blocked fallopian tubes.

One of the least invasive reproductive technology procedures involves the mechanical introduction of sperm into the vagina (*artificial insemination*). While this procedure increases the possibility of conception when the preferred donor has a low sperm count or sperm motility, couples may use artificial insemination with donor sperm when the male partner is infertile or when donor sperm decreases the

possibility of a genetic disease to the offspring. The child is genetically related to the woman and the woman is the birthing mother.

Increasingly, however, artificial insemination has become the method of choice for women who do not want to solicit the cooperation of a particular male, contend with paternal "rights," or have sexual intercourse with a man. Artificial insemination has assisted women without partners and lesbian couples in producing biological offspring.

The reproductive technology known as *in vitro fertilization* has several applications that are considerably more drastic and are the subject of controversy and debate. This reproductive technology involves removing ova from a woman's body and fertilizing them outside the body ("in vitro" means "in glass"). The fertilized ova are then placed into the woman's uterus or fallopian tube. A woman can also provide fertilized (in vitro) ova to another woman, sometimes called a "surrogate" mother or a woman engaged in "contract motherhood," who will gestate the embryo for the woman whose ovum initiated the child. Or a woman can receive the fertilized ova of another woman, carry a surviving embryo to term, and keep the child. Fertilized ova can be frozen and thawed and re-placed for up to five years, but the ratio of success is low. Placement of in vitro fertilized ova can also be painful and expensive. A woman who does not ovulate or whose ova are not viable, but who is capable of a full-term pregnancy, can carry another woman's child, or a woman who produces ova but cannot be pregnant or complete a pregnancy can have her fertilized ova implanted in another woman's body. The reality of the physiology of reproduction has been altered by medical intervention.

Biology, Technology, and Definitions of Women. Reproductive technologies are controversial and the center of considerable and heated debate. These are discussed further in the chapter on women and health (Chapter 12). What concerns us here is the implications they have for biological definitions of women. Biology has been considered the most agreed upon and uncontroversial criterion for defining women, but technological developments in biological processes are now rapidly rendering such definitions problematic. Reproductive technologies can drastically change women's relationships to childbearing. They challenge accepted definitions of motherhood and fatherhood and biological roles in procreation.

Midlife and Our Later Years

In the United States, life expectancy has increased tremendously during the twentieth century, and, as a result, our society has gradually revised its definition of "old age" and its views of adults whose age has passed half a century. Today, the average life expectancy of women in the United States is seventy-eight. Here, the average woman will live one-third of her life beyond her reproductive years.

If society defines women biologically, specifically in terms of our reproductive systems, then how does society define us when we are past our reproductive years? Both medical and lay people view a woman beyond childbearing years primarily in terms of her inability to bear children. Doing so, they unfortunately define a woman as a "baby maker" and ignore the rest of the woman—her body, her competencies, and her still-untapped potential.

Menopause. The physiological changes that signal the end of the reproductive stage are referred to as the *climacteric*. Colloquially, this transition is frequently termed *the change of life*. The cessation of menstruation, the most obvious change, is called *menopause*.

Most women go through menopause sometime between the ages of forty-five and fifty-five. Gradually menstrual bleeding will become less regular until cessation. Biologically,

our ovaries are no longer responding to the hormones from the pituitary gland. As a result, we no longer ovulate, and our ovaries stop producing estrogen and progesterone. By the time we have gone through menopause, our estrogen production will have decreased to one-sixth of what it was in our fertile years. The decrease of estrogen in our bodies causes a thinning of the vaginal walls, a decrease in vaginal lubrication, and a loss of muscle tone. Women may experience hot flashes, episodes of warmth and flushing accompanied by perspiration. We may experience other physical symptoms such as dizziness, headaches, and tingling sensations. These feelings can be explained by the decreased estrogen and resulting hormonal imbalance, as it takes the body some time to adjust to the changes.

"Going crazy" has been a stereotype associated with menopause in Western cultures and serves to label and degrade women and our menopausal experiences. Where menopause is viewed negatively, popular characterizations of menopausal women include rapid mood change, depression, and irrationality. These characterizations reflect and reinforce these cultures' higher valuation of young women and women's reproductive functions. The adverse effects of these stereotypes are not limited to older women. They are also harmful to younger women, who view menopause with dread. Young women's attitudes and fear about menopause are considerably more negative than those held by menopausal and postmenopausal women (Eisner and Kelly, 1980).

Hormonal shifts can affect emotional states and some women do experience a low period that has been termed *menopausal depression*. This usually passes. Nonetheless, a relationship between the biological events of menopause and mental health and physical health are questionable. There is some suggestion that menopausal women may be more vulnerable to life's stresses (e.g., death in the family, unemployment, marital conflict) than pre- and postmenopausal women, but even this is not evidence of a hormonal connection (Greene, 1990).

On the contrary, a relationship between estrogen levels and depression has not been found with women experiencing a natural menopause, and menopausal women do not report greater emotional distress or more psychologically related physical symptoms than premenopausal women. The best predictors of depression in menopausal women are life stresses and premenopausal health status (Ballinger et al., 1987; McKinlay et al., 1987; Leiblum and Swartzman, 1986; Greene 1990). Women who experience surgical menopause (removal of the ovaries prior to menopause) do have greater distress, owing to the rapid reduction in hormones. Research strongly suggests that attitudes and beliefs about menopause and its symbolic meaning are pivotal factors in a woman's reactions to menopause. While these vary among women within a specific culture, cross-cultural studies support the position that attitudes and beliefs about menopause are culturally defined. In societies that have little use or respect for women past childbearing years and in which, as a result, older women are treated poorly, menopause is likely to exacerbate emotional and physical symptoms. In contrast, in cultures where a multiplicity of roles are available, where women view menopause as freedom from menstruation and the risk of pregnancy, and an indication of increased social status, depression and nonspecific physical symptoms are less likely to ensue (Griffen, 1979; Bart, 1971; Datan, 1990; Flint, 1975).

Women's Prime of Life. The belief that the postmenopausal years are traumatic to women is merely a social stereotype. In reality, individual factors such as health, attitudes, and life circumstances, as well as cultural factors, determine the quality of our midlives.

Cross-cultural research indicates that for many women, the quality of life improves in their middle and postmenopausal years (Greer, 1992). In some societies, midlife women are accorded greater status, authority, and autonomy; in others, midlife is accompanied by a reduction in physical labor. The absence of children provides some women with the time, space, and energy to pursue new directions (Mitchell and Helson, 1990; Brown and Kerns, 1985; Todd et al., 1990). Many women experience what Margaret Mead termed "postmenopausal zest."

Our Older Bodies. Throughout the world, people are living longer, and a majority of the elderly are women. It is estimated that by the year 2010, about 14 percent of the population in the United States will be over the age of 65 and that forty years later, in 2050, this age group will constitute 25 percent of the population. Almost everywhere, women live longer than men. While life expectancy varies by class and ethnic group, the pattern is consistent. However, the difference in life expectancy between females and males, and the ratio of elderly females to males, is considerably smaller in industrially developing countries than in industrialized countries. The greater the cultural devaluation of women, the smaller the female-male life expectancy ratio. For example, it is estimated that Latin American women born in 1985–1990 will live five years longer than Latin American men, while in Africa, the difference will be three years. In Asia, as a whole, women are expected to live 1.7 years longer. However, life expectancy for women and men in India is about the same, and men are expected to live one year longer than women in Bangladesh (Heisel, 1989; Grau and Susser, 1989).

The greater the devaluation of females and

level of poverty, the fewer resources are invested in daughters as compared to sons (e.g., medical care, nutrition). As a result, females from poor countries are in poorer health than males while they also face a greater risk of health complications and death from childbirth than do women from wealthier countries. While the percentage of male deaths is greater than that for females at all ages in most countries, that difference diminishes as unequal treatment increases. The more similar the treatment of women and men, including their nutrition and health care, the longer women live as compared to men. The degree to which women and men are treated differently is not associated with *men's* life expectancy (Heisel, 1989). Nonetheless, women tend to live longer than men. Why? What are the implications of this trend to our lives in our later years?

Some researchers attribute the differences between women's and men's longevity to environmental influences, specifically gender differences in life-style, such as substance abuse, work-related stresses, cigarette smoking, and recklessness (see Rodin and Ickovics, 1990, for literature review). Two biological explanations have been proposed to account for gender differences in mortality. The first suggests that women have a genetic advantage; the second, a hormonal advantage. Investigators favoring the genetic explanation attribute the longer life expectancy of women to their extra X chromosome, which diminishes their risk of developing sex-linked diseases; some also speculate that the additional genetic material may provide protection from other physical disorders. Males, having only one X chromosome, lack this additional and redundant genetic information, and the Y chromosome carries little significant information other than that necessary for the development of the male reproductive system. Those who propose that women have a hor-

monal advantage cite the body of research that suggests that estrogen reduces the risk of heart disease, a major cause of death among adults and more frequent among men than women.

Although we live longer, we are not necessarily healthier. While women are biologically more predisposed to develop some conditions associated with aging than are men (e.g., loss of bone mass), many diseases are more common among older women than men, simply because women live longer.

Our Sexual Selves

What exactly is "sexuality"? Is it a psychological quality? A sequence of behaviors and physiological responses? A potential? Is there a universal definition rooted in the biology of *homo sapiens*? Sexual behavior is a complex interaction between physiological responses, cultural attitudes, and emotional states. It is shaped by prevailing social expectations and personal experiences.

Beliefs about sexuality and sexual behavior are woven into the fabric of all societies throughout recorded history. These beliefs were imposed by a small and select group of citizens (almost always men) whose position and status accorded them the authority. While these changed over time and varied across cultures, all of them assumed a universal "truth," claiming either a biological explanation or a spiritual/religious teaching. Sexual behaviors that did not conform were judged as evidence of abnormality or sin. Thus these beliefs were a way of controlling sexual behavior and served to maintain the cultural status quo.

Beliefs about female sexuality are not rooted in biology, as is evident from cultural variations. For example, two groups, the Trobriand Islander and the Kwoma and Mataco (Malinowski, 1932), believe women's sex drive is stronger than men's. The prevailing belief in Southwest Pacific societies is that there is no gender difference in sex drive (Marshall, 1971). Conversely, in many societies there is a belief that a man's sex drive is stronger than a woman's.

Western Attitudes about Female Sexuality

Female sexuality has been associated with reproduction; so assumptions and attitudes about our sexuality once more are interwoven into cultural views of women as procreators. The view of women as childbearers, on the one hand, and as objects of men's sexual desires, on the other, pervades social and scientific perspectives on female sexuality. Men, not women, have defined female sexuality.

Historically, philosophers, rulers, religious teachers, and more recently, medical professionals and even politicians have fostered the moral norms of the culture that dictate ideas about female and male sexuality. In the late Middle Ages, Western secular law considered nonprocreative sex a "crime against nature." The authoritative voice of the medical profession was increasingly applied to beliefs about human sexuality in the eighteenth and nineteenth centuries and "unnatural" (e.g., masturbation, oral-genital sex) or even "natural" sexual behavior in excess was believed to cause illnesses and disabilities.

The United States, along with many other countries, has "inherited" a legacy of Victorian attitudes about sexuality. These beliefs have tended to dichotomize women into the "good" woman (virginlike) and the "bad" (whorelike) one. The good woman had no sexual desire but complied to satisfy her husband's need and to have children. The sexual woman was viewed as sick and dangerous. The concept of sex as dirty and dangerous gradually changed over time to the belief that sex is good—but only for men. Although this stan-dard is changing to some extent, it has followed us into the 1990s.

It was during the sexually repressive Victorian era that Havelock Ellis and Sigmund Freud, among others, began to write about human sexuality and to legitimize it as a topic of study (Robinson, 1976). Freud, the founder of psychoanalysis, stated that women were indeed beings with sexual needs, and that the repression of sexual expression was a cause of neurosis in women. This was in contrast to prevailing attitudes of the time, which held that sexual expression was a cause of, and evidence of, neurosis. Freud based his ideas primarily on the recollections of women who consulted him for help. His theories evolved out of his interpretation of these women's underlying emotional dynamics and unconscious motives. While he believed women should express our sexuality, he also believed that our fulfillment could only come about in the form of vaginal orgasm (as distinct from clitoral orgasms, which Freud considered "masculine" and childish) and the subsequent bearing and nurturing of children. Although in many ways Freud began a liberation of female sexuality, his theories had components that passed on yet another set of masculine standards against which women were to judge ourselves (see Chapter 4).

Psychoanalytic theories dominated Western beliefs about sexuality for the following decades and represented a new set of assumptions about "normal" sexual behavior and roles for women. In the 1940s and 1950s, Alfred Kinsey (1953) conducted an extensive survey of the sexual behavior of women and men. His findings, based on interviews, astonished his contemporaries. He found many people engaging in a range of sexual behaviors considered to be atypical by standards of that time. Masturbation, homosexuality, and oral-genital sex were found to be practiced by a significant proportion of the population.

The Scientific Study of Sexuality: Female Sexual Response

Masters and Johnson (1966) studied human sexual responses in the laboratory. They divided the human response cycle into four phases. Masters and Johnson's findings for females are shown in Table 3.2.

Masters and Johnson note remarkable similarity in the sexual responses of females and males. However, males, unlike females, have a refractory period after orgasm in which they cannot get another erection regardless of the amount of stimulation. For young men, this may last but a few minutes; for older men it may last for hours. Women, in contrast, can move back and forth between the plateau and orgasmic phase without returning to the nonaroused state.

Masters and Johnson's "phases" are just one way of categorizing sexual responses; other researchers have outlined different divisions. Helen Singer Kaplan (1979), for example, outlines a three-phase model of human sexual response: the desire phase, the excitement phase, and the orgasmic phase.

Sexual excitement can be triggered by fantasy, visual images, odors, tactile sensations, and emotional responses. Regardless of the source of stimulation, the physical responses detected in the laboratory are the same. Masters and Johnson argue that all orgasms are physiologically the same, regardless of the source of stimulation—intercourse, manual or oral stimulation from one's partner, or masturbation—although the orgasms may differ in intensity or be subjectively experienced differently. Research on whether all orgasms are similar still continues, as does the debate on this matter.

Masters and Johnson's research was an influential corrective to long-held heterosexist and androcentric beliefs about female sexuality. For example, their finding that orgasms result from clitoral stimulation, and that the phases of female sexual response are the same regardless of the source of stimulation, rejects the notion that a woman's full sexual satisfaction *requires* sexual intercourse with a man. Their studies indicated that women generally reach orgasm more quickly and with greater intensity from manual stimulation of the clitoris, especially when we stimulate ourselves. This finding suggests that delays or failure to achieve orgasm during intercourse may be a result of techniques that are not compatible with our physiological responsiveness.

Table 3.2 Phases of the Female Sexual Response

Excitement
1. Vaginal lubrication.
2. Venous dilation of the external genitalia.
3. Clitoral engorgement (filling with blood) causing the clitoris to swell.
4. Vaginal expansion.
5. Erection of the nipples.

Plateau
1. Outer third of the vagina becomes engorged with blood, narrowing the passageway.
2. Inner two-thirds of vagina expands.
3. Uterus rises up.
4. Purple coloration of nipples and areola.
5. Clitoris retracts under its hood but remains extremely sensitive.

Orgasmic
1. Vasocongestion reaches a critical point and the muscles of the lower vagina and uterus contract (the orgasm), which expels the congestion.
2. There are approximately 8–15 contractions, of which the first 5–6 are most intense.

Resolution
1. Genitalia return to the nonaroused state.
2. Clitoris returns to its usual position and size.
3. Vagina returns to a relaxed state (10–15 minutes).
4. Coloration of nipples returns to prearoused state.
5. If the woman does not have an orgasm, the resolution phase takes longer, and she may feel discomfort in her genitals.

While laboratory studies of sexuality and physiological sexual responses have discredited many old assumptions and raised new possibilities, they are limited in addressing the varied and changing experience and meaning of sexuality to the individual. Tiefer (1987) argues that sex is a social construction. She questions the privileged position of biology in its study, stating that sex cannot be reduced to objective measures or divorced from its social and personal context.

Sexuality Across the Life Span

Humans are sexual beings throughout their lives, although sexual experience, expression, and meaning change at different life stages. Even children are sexual beings, but it is not the sexuality we generally attribute to adults. Sigmund Freud outlined distinct stages of sexual development. The child's sexuality is expressed in the need for and pleasure derived from tactile stimulation—being held, and stroked—and from gratification of bodily functions. And children, as they explore their bodies in the process of learning about themselves, find pleasure in contact with their genitals.

Most societies acknowledge puberty as the beginning of adult sexuality. In societies that are more permissive, it is a time of increased sexual interest, curiosity, and expression. Both hormonal and social factors account for sexual interest and behavior, although these factors are extremely complex and little understood.

It appears that androgens contribute to sexual desire in both female and male adolescents, although their influence on sexual behavior is unclear. There is considerable evidence that social and contextual factors are much more important determinants of adolescent sexual behavior. These include cultural and societal attitudes, peer and family influence, and individual dynamics (see Brooks-Gunn and Furstenberg, 1989, for an overview). There has been some suggestion that female sexual desire is affected by the menstrual cycle and that it peaks during ovulation, when estrogen levels are high. However, this is not true for all women, particularly those practicing the rhythm method of birth control, suggesting psychological factors as pivotal (Adams et al., 1978). Males also have hormonal cycles, and research suggests these may influence sexual desire. However, this has received little study. The attention to the relationship between fluctuations in sexuality and hormonal cycles in women, and not men, once more reflects societal attitudes that female sexuality is tied to procreation and that women, not men, are controlled by their hormones.

The common stereotype is that males have stronger sexual drives than females. There is, however, little evidence to support this. Males do tend to begin sexual intercourse earlier in life and to have more sexual experiences, but this gap is rapidly diminishing in Western countries (see Brooks-Gunn and Furstenberg, 1989, for review), and the numbers of women and men engaged in heterosexual relations are nearly equal.

Women are socialized for a particular kind of sexual behavior. In spite of the increasing liberalization of sexual attitudes, women in America are taught a male perspective on sexuality. At puberty, the social pressure on us to play the role of sex object increases. Attention is given to the way we look, and various parts of our bodies are decorated to accentuate the role. The sexual attention of males is treated as a mark of our worth.

The female is supposed to be passive, the male active. Sexual inexperience is more likely to be approved in the female than in the male, since the male is socialized to be the "teacher." Frequently, young men learn about sex from "locker-room" talk, pornography, and masturbation, hardly experiences that would inform them about female sexual pleasures. Under such dichotomized roles, it is difficult for women to teach men about our sexual needs.

Traditionally, investigations of sexuality emphasized satisfaction for men and procreation for women, although homosexuality among men was discussed. The fact that many women find sexual satisfaction in each other was given little attention. Today there is a significant increase in literature on this topic (see, for example, Faderman, 1981; Hite, 1976; Jay and Young, 1977; Sissley and Harris, 1977; Vida, 1978).

Popular writings have up to now depicted romantic sexual unions in which the innocent female virgin is initiated into sexual pleasure by the worldly, experienced man. The picture generally portrayed is "penis-in-vagina" sex, with orgasm depicted as automatic. Since society has conditioned women to acquiesce to men's preferences, it is only natural that men should project their sexual preferences onto women. One consequence of this has been noted by Laws and Schwartz (1977) in their discussion of sexual foreplay. The term *foreplay* generally refers to sexual contact that precedes intercourse (note the heterosexual focus of the term). Men generally view foreplay as something they have to do to make the woman more receptive, but of little intrinsic value. Yet, if we think for a moment about what foreplay involves, we discover that for women it is often the main event.

In reporting their own sexual experience, women say that they like the holding and hugging, physical closeness and murmuring, kissing, touching, and caressing. It is only from a male point of view that such contact is foreplay (Laws and Schwartz, 1977).

For women, sexuality seems to be more diverse, in contrast to the phallic-centered sexuality of men. Laws and Schwartz note how female sexuality may differ from that of men:

Rather than hurry-up, goal-oriented activity, with overtones of achievement anxiety, sexual encounter has a quality of flow, a continuous high, punctuated by incidents like orgasm. Women do not necessarily conceptualize a sexual episode as "before and after" orgasm. From the female point of view the term "foreplay" is a misnomer. Women like foreplay before, during, and after. As a social construction, foreplay clearly embodies male priorities and practices in the sexual encounter. (ibid:56)

Lesbian Sexuality

The exclusion of research on lesbian sexuality results in a misrepresentation of the sexuality of heterosexual women as well. For example, the sexuality of older lesbian couples is not as influenced by the cultural value placed on youth and attractiveness. We are not as sexually self-conscious about the process of aging. In addition, older lesbians do not have to deal with possible discomfort during intercourse due to changes in the vagina or with made penile erectile problems (Cole and Rothblum, 1990).

Lesbians, like heterosexual women, prefer romance, physical closeness, and intimacy—sex is less "goal-oriented." However, internalized homophobia may cause discomfort about sexual expressions, and negative experience with men may increase hesitancy. Lesbians have sex less often than heterosexuals and male homosexuals. Since lesbians are subject to social pressures, we lack norms for frequency (Clunis and Green, 1988). Lesbian couples report greater intimacy in sharing and fewer inhibitions due to gender role.

Homosexuality and heterosexuality are on a continuum. Many heterosexuals have had homosexual experiences, and many people who engage only in heterosexual sex have homosexual fantasies.

Older Women and Sexuality

The double standard toward aging is reflected in beliefs about sexuality, which, in turn, influence how we view ourselves. In societies that value maturity in men and youth and attractiveness in women, older women are considered less sexually desirable to men. They are also assumed to be "asexual," that is, relatively uninterested in sexual intimacies. No longer able to procreate and lacking the attributes culturally labeled "attractive," their sexuality is no longer acknowledged. In older women, diminished interest in sex is viewed as less problematic than in men.

Both women and men in their later years report a decline in sexual interest and frequency of sexual activities with age. Physiological changes, as a result of decreased estrogen, can have implications for sexual interest, response, and activities in postmenopausal woman. However, many women are unbothered by these bodily changes. Research on the relationship between levels of estrogen and sexuality is inconclusive.

However, as with adolescence, sexuality occurs and takes on meaning within a cultural context, and there is considerable evidence that psychological and social factors account for more of the variation in the effects of aging on postmenopausal women's sexuality than do hormonal changes. A most obvious influence is the fact that women live longer than men; so as we age there are increasingly fewer available male partners for heterosexual women. Societal definitions of "sexy" and attitudes toward older women, as well as gender role prescriptions, contribute to feelings of unattractiveness and discourage older women from initiating sexual intimacies or expressing sexual needs and preferences. Such attitudes are compounded when male partners adhere to these standards and reinforce them. Gender stereotypes, supported by the fact that meno-

pause is a concrete marker of both life stage and physiological transitions, have, once more, allowed research to focus on women's reproductive cycles and hormonal functioning and incorrectly to suggest that male sexuality is stable, while female sexuality is dominated by biological events. There has been little consideration of aging on male sexuality and how this may affect female sexual patterns. Nonetheless, research clearly indicates that this relationship cannot be ignored (see, for example, Formanek, 1990; Rice, 1989; Leiblum, 1990; Morokoff, 1988).

Sexual arousal and orgasm take more time as men age and diminishing erections are more common. While one might speculate that this should be compatible with aging patterns of female sexual response, it does not conform with cultural gender role expectations. Older men's slower sexual pace conflicts with the stereotype of "masculinity." When this challenge to his "manliness" is reinforced by a misunderstanding of the more gradual progression of sexual responsiveness in his female partner, sexual contact is likely to be avoided. Similarly, women may avoid sexual intimacies if they experience the slower sexual response of their male partners as evidence of their sexual undesirability, or as undermining their partners' sexual esteem. An ensuing cycle of sexual dissatisfaction and discouragement is probable.

Phallocentric and Heterosexual Bias in Research of Female Sexuality

Virtually all research on human sexuality across the life span rests on three assumptions that render findings suspect, in general, and strongly question the validity of "knowledge" about female sexuality, in particular. This is true for studies on adolescent patterns of sexual behavior, sexuality during the reproductive years, and sexual responses and aging.

These are (1) defining sexual relations as sexual intercourse; (2) defining sexual desires, responses, and activities as goal-directed activities leading toward orgasm; and (3) assuming that biological and social science research perspectives will reveal universal and objective "rules" of human sexual behavior. The first of these denies the reality of sexual relations between partners of the same sex as well as the significance and poignancy of sexual contacts that do not culminate in sexual intercourse. The second ignores the range of physical intimacies that individuals experience as sexual and gratifying that are neither directed toward nor result in orgasms. The third assumes that sexuality can be divorced from its social, cultural, and situational context (Tiefer, 1987).

Summary

Biologists have looked to genetic and hormonal factors to explain behavioral differences between women and men. But research lends little support to the view that these assumed differences even exist. Biological and physical attributes are frequently used in defining "woman." Scientists, who have traditionally been men, reflect the biases of the culture. These biases can be seen in language, research questions pursued, and in conclusions drawn. In the study of women, biologists generally focus on those aspects of women that distinguish us from men, such as secondary sex characteristics and reproductive anatomy. Average differences between males and females in physical and behavioral attributes, such as physical strength and height, are frequently cited. An average, however, is a statistical concept. The range of differences within any one sex is greater than the average difference between the sexes.

All people receive half of their genes from their mother and half from their father. Genetic females have an XX chromosomal pair and genetic males have an XY chromosomal pair. The sex genes received at conception, however, are only the beginning of a series of intrauterine events that determine the reproductive and genital structure of the fetus. As a result, events can occur, or fail to occur, that cause genital variations. The environment the fetus grows in is as important an element in the development of genitals and reproductive organs as is the genetic contribution.

Puberty for most women is signaled by the onset of menstruation. Throughout women's reproductive years, our bodies experience a cycle of hormonal events. Menopause marks the cessation of this reproductive cycle. Research suggests that hormonal shifts may affect women's moods, but it also indicates that men may be subject to emotional swings as a result of hormonal events. What are frequently ignored in the discussion of hormones and moods are cultural and social attitudes regarding the physical events that accompany these hormonal changes. Thus, most societies have attitudes and beliefs about menstruation that reflect negative attitudes toward women. Cultural beliefs have also affected societies' reactions to the physiological events of pregnancy, birth, the postpartum period, and breast-feeding.

New reproductive technologies have been developed to correct or "sidestep" many conditions causing infertility; these are often controversial. Such technologies challenge the traditional understandings of the reproductive roles of women and men that are the basis for the most widely accepted biological definitions of women.

In Western societies, negative stereotypes have been attached to women past childbearing years, and to the physiological processes associated with menopause (cessation of menstruation). Research indicates that the subjective experience of menopause depends on societal attitudes. Furthermore, cross-cultural research suggests what some Western women have revealed in recent literature, that the quality of our lives often improves in our middle and postmenopausal years. In most societies, women on average live longer than men.

Beliefs about women's sexuality are not rooted in biological facts; they are often contradictory and vary culturally and historically. Laboratory research on female sexual response indicates little difference between females and males. This research has undermined heterosexist and androcentric beliefs by showing that, at least physiologically, a woman's achievement of orgasm does not require sexual intercourse with a man; the source of stimulation is irrelevant.

Most research on human sexuality has been androcentric and phallocentric, ignoring women's own preferences. Research on lesbian sexuality reinforces recent research on women's sexuality in general, showing similarities in preference for romance, intimacy, and less "goal-oriented" sexual expression.

In general, research on human sexuality has rested on faulty assumptions. Human sexuality cannot be isolated from its social, cultural, and situational context.

Discussion Questions

1. People generally view scientists as being objective and scientific findings as being factual. As a result, it is frequently assumed that scientific definitions of "women" and social science studies of gender roles are free from sexist biases. Do you think this is accurate? Defend your answer.
2. The "polarity between the sexes" implies that females and males are "opposites." Given what you have learned in this chapter, does this seem a reasonable concept? Explain.
3. If the biological events that accompany such phenomena as menstruation, pregnancy, childbirth, lactation, and menopause are documentable, why is it reasonable to say that these events reflect cultural attitudes? How do these attitudes reflect biological experience? What experiences from your own life relate to this discussion?
4. How have scientific explanations affected sexual behavior and expectations? How have sexual beliefs and behavior affected scientific explanations about human sexuality?
5. Based on the biological information you have learned, construct a theory of the superiority of women.

Recommended Readings

Boston Women's Health Book Collective. *The New Our Bodies, Ourselves.* New York: Simon & Schuster, rev. ed., 1992. This informative book, written by a women's health collective, is a revised and expanded edition of a book first published in 1976. Topics include medical and women's self health care, violence against women, health hazards, relationships and sexuality, anatomy and physiology, control of fertility, sexually transmitted diseases, childbearing, aging and women, and the medical system. The contents are clearly written and have a personal touch. An excellent reference book for the nonscientist to keep close at hand.

Doress, Paula Brown, Diana Laskin Siegal, and The Midlife and Older Women Book Project. *Ourselves, Growing Older.* New York: Simon & Schuster, 1987. This book, written in cooperation with the Boston Women's Health Book Collective, focuses on the health and living concerns of middle-aged and older women. Taking a positive approach to the quality of life as we age, this book addresses such topics as facilitating aging well, sexuality, relationships, childbearing in midlife, menopause, work and retirement, money matters, caregiving, and medical problems. It is informative, realistic, and encouraging.

Jacobus, Mary, Evelyn Fox Keller, and Sally Shuttleworth, editors. *Body/Politics: Women and the Discourses of Science.* This series of essays addresses the intersection of literary, social, and scientific discourses on the female body. Drawing from a wide array of disciplines, the book looks at the relationships between science and the feminine body and examines their political and social implications.

Tiefer, Leonore. *Sex Is Not a Natural Act and Other Essays.* Boulder, Co.: Westview Press, 1994. This collection of essays from the author's popular and professional writings and lectures explores the social construction of sex and sexuality. Covering a range of topics, such as the history, scientific study, marketing, and medicalization of sexuality; popular discourse and writings on sexuality; and the politics of sexuality, this book is a provocative challenge to our assumptions about the "essentialism" of human sexuality.

References

Adams, D. B., Gold, A. R., and Burt, A. D. "Cycles of Sexual Desire." *New England Journal of Medicine* 299 (1978):21.

Angier, Natalie. "Biologists Hot on Track of Gene for Femaleness." *New York Times*, C1,5, August 30, 1993.

Ballinger, C. B., Browning, M.C.K., and Smith, A.H.W. "Hormone Profiles and Psychological Symptoms in Perimenopausal Women." *Maturitas* (1987):235–51.

Bart, Pauline B. "Depression in Middle-aged Women." In *Women in Sexist Society: Studies in Power and Powerlessness*, edited by Vivian Gornick and Barbara Moran. New York: Basic Books, 1971.

Boston Women's Health Book Collective. *The New Our Bodies, Ourselves.* New York: Simon & Schuster, rev. ed., 1992.

Brooks-Gunn, J., and Furstenberg, F. F. "Adolescent Sexual Behavior." *American Psychologist* 44 (1989):249–57.

Brown, J. K., and Kerns, V., editors. *In Her Prime: A New View of Middle Aged Women.* South Hadley, Mass.: Bergin and Garvey, 1985.

Clunis, Dana M., and Green, G. Dorsey. *Lesbian Couples.* Seattle: Seal Press, 1988.

Cole, Ellen, and Rothblum, Ester. Commentary on "Sexuality and the Midlife Woman." *Psychology of Woman Quarterly* 14 (1990):509–12.

Datan, F. "Aging into Transitions: Cross-cultural Perspectives on Women at Midlife." In *The Meaning of Menopause: Historical, Medical and Clinical Perspectives*, edited by Ruth Formanek. Hillsdale, N.J.: Analytic Press, 1990.

Digby, Anne. "Women's Biological Straightjacket." In *Sexuality and Subordination: Interdisciplinary Studies of Gender in the Nineteenth Century*, edited by Susan Mendus and Jane Randall. New York: Routledge, 1989.

Eisner, H., and Kelly, L. "Attitudes of Women Toward the Menopause." Presented at the American Gerontological Society meeting. San Diego, Calif., 1980.

Faderman, Lillian. *Surpassing the Love of Men: Romantic Friendship and Love Between Women from the Renaissance to the Present.* New York: Morrow, 1981.

Flint, Marsha. "The Menopause: Reward or Punishment?" *Psychosomatics* 16 (1975):161–63.

Formanek, Ruth. "Continuity and Change and 'the Change of Life.' Premodern Views of the Menopause." In *The Meaning of Menopause: Historical, Medical and Clinical Perspectives*, edited by Ruth Formanek. Hillsdale, N.J.: Analytic Press, 1990.

Golub, Sharon, ed. *Menarche.* Lexington, Mass.: Heath, 1983.

Grau, Lois, and Susser, Ida, editors. *Women in the Later Years.* New York: Harrington Park Press, 1989.

Greene, J. G. "Psychosocial Influences and Life Events at the Time of the Menopause." In

The Meaning of Menopause: Historical, Medical and Clinical Perspectives, edited by Ruth Formanek. Hillsdale, N.J.: Analytic Press, 1990.

Greene, J. G., and Cooke, D. J. "Life Stress and Symptoms at the Climaterium." *British Journal of Psychiatry* 136 (1980):485–91.

Greer, Germaine. *The Change: Women, Agency, and the Menopause.* New York: Knopf, 1992.

Griffen, Joyce. "A Cross-cultural Investigation of Behavioral Changes at Menopause." In *Psychology of Women,* edited by Juanita Williams. New York: Norton, 1979.

Haraway, Donna. *Primate Visions: Gender, Race, and Nature in the World of Modern Science.* New York and London: Routledge, 1989.

Heisel, Marcel A. "Older Women in Developing Countries." In *Women in the Later Years,* edited by Lois Grau and Ida Susser. New York: Harrington Park Press, 1989.

Hite, Shere. *The Hite Report.* New York: Macmillan, 1976.

Hubbard, Ruth, Henifen, Mary Sue, and Fried, Barbara, editors. *Biological Woman—the Convenient Myth: A Collection of Essays and a Comprehensive Bibliography.* Cambridge Mass.: Schenkman, 1982.

Jacklin, Carol. "Female and Male: Issues of Gender." *American Psychologist* 44 (1989):127–33.

Jalland, Pat. *Women, Marriage and Politics 1860–1914.* Oxford: Clarendon Press, 1986.

Jay, K., and Young, A. *The Gay Report.* New York: Summit, 1977.

Kaplan, Helen Singer. *Disorders of Desire.* New York: Simon & Schuster, 1979.

Keller, Evelyn Fox. *Reflections on Gender and Science.* New Haven: Yale University, 1985.

Kinsey, Alfred, Pomeroy, Wardell, Martin, Clyde E., and Gebhard, Paul H. *Sexual Behavior in the Human Female.* Philadelphia: Saunders, 1953.

Laws, Judith Long, and Schwartz, Pepper. *Sexual Scripts: The Social Construction of Female Sexuality.* Springfield, Ill.: Dryden, 1977.

Leiblum, Sandra. "Sexuality and the Midlife Woman." *Psychology of Women Quarterly* 14 (1990):495–508.

Leiblum, Sandra, and Swartzman, L. "Women's

Attitudes toward the Menopause: An Update." *Maturitas* 8 (1986):47–56.

Longino, Helen, and Doell, R. "Body, Bias and Behavior: A Comparative Analysis of Reasoning in Two Areas of Biological Science." In *Sex and Scientific Inquiry,* edited by S. Harding and J. F. O'Barr. Chicago: University of Chicago Press, 1987.

Luce, G. G. *Biological Rhythms in Psychiatry and Medicine.* Chevy Chase, Md.: U.S. Department of Health, Education, and Welfare, 1970.

Malinowski, Bronislaw. *The Sexual Life of Savages.* London: Routledge, 1932.

Marshall, D. F. "Too much in Mangaia." *Psychology Today* 4 (1971):43–44.

Masters, William H., and Johnson, Virginia E. *Human Sexual Response.* Boston: Little, Brown, 1966.

McFarlane, Jessica M., and Williams, Tannis M. "Placing Premenstrual Syndrome in Perspective." *Psychology of Women Quarterly* 18 (1994):339–74.

McFarlane, J., McKinlay, S., and Brambilla, D. "Health Status and Utilization Behavior Associated with Menopause." *American Journal of Epidemiology* 125 (1987):110–25.

McFarlane, J., Martin, C. L., and Williams, T. M. "Mood Fluctuations: Women Versus Men and Menstrual Versus Other Cycles." *Psychology of Women Quarterly* 12 (1988):201–24.

McKinlay, J., McKinlay, S., and Brambilla, D. "The Relative Contribution of Endocrine Changes and Social Circumstances of Depression in Mid-aged Women." *Journal of Health and Social Behavior* 28 (1987):345–63.

Mitchell, Valory, and Helson, Ravenna. "Women's Prime of Life: Is It the 50's?" *Psychology of Women Quarterly* 14 (1990):451–70.

Money, John, and Ehrhardt, Anke. *Man and Woman, Boy and Girl.* Baltimore: Johns Hopkins University Press, 1972.

Moos, R. H. "Typology of Menstrual Cycle Symptoms." *American Journal of Obstetrics and Gynecology* 103 (1969):265–68.

Morokoff, Patricia J. "Sexuality in Perimenopausal and Postmenopausal Women." *Psychology of Women Quarterly* 12 (1988):489–512.

Paige, Karen. "Women Learn to Sing the Menstrual Blues." *Psychology Today* 7 (1973):41–46.

Parlee, Mary. "Stereotypic Beliefs about Menstruation: A Methodological Note on the Moos Menstrual Distress Questionnaire and Some New Data." *Psychosomatic Medicine* 36 (1974):229–40.

Parlee, Mary. "Psychological Aspects of Menstruation, Childbirth and Menopause: An Overview with Suggestions for Further Research." In *Psychology of Women: Future Directions of Research*, edited by Julia Sherman and Florence Denmark. New York: Psychological Dimensions, 1978.

Ramey, Estelle. "Men's Cycles (They Have Them Too You Know)." *Ms.* Preview Edition (1972):8–14.

Rice, S. "Sexuality and Intimacy for Aging Women: A Changing Perspective." In *Women as They Age: Challenge, Opportunity, and Triumph*, edited by J. D. Garner and S. O. Mercer. New York: Haworth Press, 1989.

Rierdan, J. "Variation in the Experience of Menarche as a Function of Preparedness." In *Menarche*, edited by Sharon Golub. Lexington, Mass.: Heath, 1983.

Robinson, Paul. *The Modernization of Sex: Havelock Ellis, Alfred Kinsey, William Masters and Virginia Johnson.* New York: Harper & Row, 1976.

Rodin, Judith, and Ickovics, Jeannette R. "Women's Health: Review and Research Agenda as We Approach the 21st Century." *American Psychologist* 45:9 (1990):1018–34.

Sherfey, Mary Jane. *The Nature and Evolution of Female Sexuality.* New York: Random House, 1972.

Showalter, Elaine, and Showalter, English. "Victorian Women and Menstruation." In *Suffer and Be Still: Women in the Victorian Age*, edited by Martha Vicinus. Bloomington and London: Indiana University Press, 1972.

Sissley, E., and Harris, G. *The Joy of Lesbian Sex.* New York: Simon & Schuster, 1977.

Sommer, B. "Stress and Menstrual Distress." *Journal of Human Stress* 4 (1978):5–10, 41–47.

Tiefer, Leonore. "Social Constructionism and the Study of Human Sexuality." In *Sex and Gender*, edited by P. Shaver and C. Hendrick. Newbury Park, Calif.: Sage Publications, 1987.

Todd, Judith, Friedman, Ariella, and Kariuki, Priscella W. "Women Growing Stronger with Age: The Effect of Status in the United States and Kenya." *Psychology of Women Quarterly* 14 (1990):567–78.

Travis, Cheryl. *Women and Health Psychology: Biomedical Issues.* Englewood Cliffs, N.J.: Prentice-Hall, 1988.

Vida, Ginny, editor. *Our Right To Love.* Englewood Cliffs, N.J.: Prentice-Hall, 1978.

Weideger, Paula. *Menstruation and Menopause: Their Physiology and Psychology, the Myth and the Reality.* New York: Dell, 1977.

chapter 4

Women's Personalities

Is There a Female Personality?

What Are Women Like?

Dimensions of Variability among Women

Explanations for Differences between Women and Men

Biological Approaches

Psychodynamic Theories

Cognitive-Developmental Theory

Social Learning Theory

Gender Schema Theory

Social Interactions and Gender Roles

The "Politics of Gender" and Sexism

The Process of Socialization

The Development of a "Female Personality"

Lesbian Psychologies

Older Women

At one time it was considered a compliment for a woman to be told "You think like a man," or "You're not like other women." In contrast, for it to be said of a man that "he thinks like a woman" was (and probably still is) an insult. Today we shudder at such statements, for we recognize their implicit sexism, and we no longer believe that thinking or acting "like a man" is necessarily desirable. We may even question whether there is such a thing as thinking like a woman or man. The statements are, nonetheless, curious. What thinking processes, verbal comments, or behavior could prompt such a "compliment" or "insult"? What images or associations are stimulated in the mind of the receiver? Such statements as these are evidence of a cultural stereotype of the feminine and masculine and blatantly reflect the values attached. Are these stereotypes valid? How can we understand their existence?

Is There a Female Personality?

Is there a specifically "female" way of thinking? Do women as a group possess certain behavioral characteristics that distinguish us from men as a group? These questions have been explored for generations. In this chapter, we look into the ways in which women's personalities, motivations, and behavior have been characterized and explained by men and by feminist writers who have developed quite different perspectives on the subject of women's psychological makeup.

What Are Women Like?

By "personality" we mean an individual's characteristic pattern of thinking, feeling, and acting. Personality refers to organized, learned, and relatively stable global patterns of behavior. Characterizations of women's psychological traits in our society have a specific history, class origin, and cultural context. Yet stereotyped notions about women are frequently viewed as universal and are applied to all women. These generalizations are rooted in the popular belief that female behavioral and personality characteristics are a consequence of biological functions (see Chapter 3). Yet these ideas about women are indeed class- and culture-bound. For example, the stereotype of women as delicate and in need of protection has never applied to women domestic workers (see **Sex and Temperament**).

Stereotypes of Femininity.

What are little boys made of?
Frogs and snails and puppy dog tails
That's what little boys are made of.

What are little girls made of?
Sugar and spice and everything nice
That's what little girls are made of.

As the above children's rhyme indicates, we begin gender stereotyping very young and create rhymes, stories, and the like that actively teach these expectations to children.

In the 1950s, sociologist Talcott Parsons analyzed the American family structure and concluded that in middle-class families,

> the most fundamental difference between the sexes in personality types is that, relative to the total culture as a whole, the masculine personality tends more to the predominance of goal-oriented interests, needs and functions, presumably in whatever social system both sexes are involved, while the feminine personality tends more to the primacy of expressive interests, needs and functions. We would expect, by and large, that other things being equal, men would assume more tech-

nical, executive and "judicial" roles, women more supportive, integrative and "tension-managing" roles. (Parsons and Bales, 1955: 100)

Parsons's dichotomy of female-male behavior in the family set the tone for many subsequent analyses of gender roles and established a framework for the stereotype of the "middle-class suburban family," with members playing traditional roles, as the social ideal.

Women and men have been stereotyped in American society according to a broad range of psychological characteristics. A sample of these traits and the values placed on them appears in Table 4.1. The topic of stereotyping is taken up in more detail in Chapter 5.

Biases in Data Collection. Stereotypes are not very useful for characterizing the real women that are studied by researchers. Empirical research that tries to measure psychological and behav-

"Some Living American Woman Artists/Last Supper" (1972) by Mary Beth Edelson is a celebration of the diverse personalities of women artists. Throughout history, women have had almost no chance for recognition as individual painters, and very limited opportunities for serious and sustained work in any of the arts. The center figure is Georgia O'Keeffe. To her left is Louise Nevelson. On her far left is Yoko Ono. Edelson is at the bottom, one square away from the right corner. (Offset poster courtesy of the artist)

Sex and Temperament

We have now considered in detail the approved personalities of each sex among three primitive peoples. We found the Arapesh—both men and women—displaying a personality that, out of our historically limited preoccupation, we would call maternal in its parental aspects, and feminine in its sexual aspects. We found men, as well as women, trained to be cooperative, unaggressive, responsive to the needs and demands of others. We found no idea that sex was a powerful driving force either for men or for women. In marked contrast to these attitudes, we found among the Mundugumor that both men and women developed as ruthless, aggressive, positively sexed individuals, with the maternal cherishing aspects of personality at a minimum. Both men and women approximated to a personality type that we in our culture would find only in an undisciplined and very violent male. Neither the Arapesh nor the Mundugumor profit by a contrast between the sexes. . . . In the third tribe, the Tchambuli, we found a genuine reversal of the sex-attitudes of our own culture with the woman the dominant, impersonal, managing partner, the man the less responsible and the emotionally dependent person. These three situations suggest, then, a very definite conclusion. If those temperamental attitudes which we have traditionally regarded as feminine—such as passivity, responsiveness, and a willingness to cherish children—can so easily be set up as the masculine pattern in one tribe, and in another be outlawed for the majority of women as well as for the majority of men, we no longer have any basis for regarding such aspects of behavior as sex-linked. And this conclusion becomes even stronger when we consider the actual reversal in Tchambuli of the position of dominance of the two sexes. . . .

. . . Only to the impact of the whole of the integrated culture upon the growing child can we lay the formation of the contrasting types. There is no other explanation. . . . We are forced to conclude that human nature is almost unbelievably malleable, responding accurately and contrastingly to contrasting cultural conditions. The differences between individuals who are members of different cultures, like the differences between individuals within a culture are almost entirely to be laid to differences in conditioning, especially during early childhood, and the form of this conditioning is culturally determined. Standardized personality differences between the sexes are of this order, cultural creations to which each generation, male and female, is trained to conform.

(Mead, 1935:279–80)

© Margaret Mead, 1935. Reprinted by permission.

ioral characteristics along a scale is based on direct observation of representative samples of populations. However, such research, objective as it may attempt to be, also contains many biases. Most systematic observations in Western countries of hypothetical differences between females and males involve white, middle-class people, both as observers and as subjects. The labels the researchers use to classify behavior may reflect their own biases, as when they label nurturing or passivity as "feminine." Furthermore, the context of observation influences the results. Women might, for example, behave one way at home, another way at school or work, and still another way in a laboratory situation, and the effects of these environments may differ for women and men. The observer may unwit-

Table 4.1 Typical and Desirable Characteristics: Differences in Ratings of Male Versus Female Targets

Typical man > woman	Typical woman > man
Independent	Emotional
Aggressive*	Grateful
Not excitable in minor crises*	Home-oriented
Skilled in business	Strong conscience
Mechanical aptitude*	Kind*
Outspoken	Cries easily*
Acts as leader*	Creative
Self-confident	Understanding
Takes a stand	Considerate
Ambitious	Devotes self to others
Not easily influenced	Needs approval
Dominant*	Gentle*
Active	Aware of others' feelings
Knows ways of world	Excitable in a major crisis
Loud	Expresses tender feelings*
Interested in sex	Enjoys art and music
Makes decisions easily	Doesn't hide emotions
Doesn't give up easily	Tactful
Stands up under pressure	Feelings hurt
Not timid	Helpful to others
Good at sports*	Neat*
Likes math and science	Religious
Competitive*	Likes children
Adventurous	Warm to others
Sees self running show	Need for security
Outgoing	
Intellectual	
Feels superior	
Forward	

NOTE: In items marked *, gender differences were considered desirable as well as typical.
Source: Adapted from T. L. Ruble (1983). Sex stereotypes: Issues of change in the 1970s. *Sex Roles* 397–402.

tingly influence the subjects' behavior. If the person administering a psychological test behaves one way toward female subjects and another way toward males—say, by smiling more often at women, or speaking more abruptly to men—then the results may reflect the differential treatment of the subjects. Finally, research reporting gender differences is more likely to be published than research failing to find differences and there is a strong tendency to magnify gender differences even

when the evidence is questionable. As a result, there is considerable potential for confusion about the results of empirical research on personality and behavioral differences between women and men (see Unger, 1990).

An example of gender bias in research is well demonstrated by the research on moral development. American psychologist Lawrence Kohlberg (1964; 1969) hypothesized a three-stage theory of moral development. Kohlberg found that females (and males of color) did not reach as high a level of moral reasoning on his scale as white males. However, Kohlberg used only white, middle-class males in devising his scale, eliminating females because they did not behave as he predicted. Thus, he formulated a theory and used to validate his theory a select sample who behaved as he predicted they would, concluding that those who behaved differently were not as morally developed.

Carol Gilligan, a student of Kohlberg, challenged his work (1982). Testing both females and males, she concluded that there are two parallel paths of moral development. One emphasizes principles of justice and individuals' rights and the other focuses on caring, relationships, and reciprocity among people. Gilligan found that boys seem to favor the former and girls the latter but that both can reason in both ways.

Gilligan's research has been subject to scrutiny and debate. Some have pointed out that the particular moral dilemma may determine the favored response and that factors, such as education, are more powerful predictors of reasoning about moral dilemmas than is gender (e.g., Colby and Damon, 1983; Ford and Lowery, 1986). It has also been suggested that patterns in moral reasoning reflect gender differences in power and dominant-subordinate positions (Hare-Mustin and Maracek, 1988; Tronto, 1993). What is more, ethnic diversity continues to receive little attention although it has been suggested that there is greater gender similarity and a favoring of the care ethic among both female and male African Americans (e.g., Collins, 1989). Though difficulties have been found with Gilligan's research, it has greatly exposed the kind of gender bias that can and does occur in psychological research and theory (compare discussion, Chapter 2).

What the Researchers Report. Research on gender differences in behavior and traits provide little substantiation for most presumed differences. Table 4.2 presents a summary of the research findings about hypothetical gender differences. Even where differences do exist, the differences refer to group averages, and the overlap between groups is considerable. What is more, the research suggests that these differences are amenable to change and often vary depending on the circumstances. Thus, what differences do seem to appear are never consistently found, which undermines the validity of stereotypic characterizations.

Dimensions of Variability among Women

Characterizations and caricatures of women vary by culture and class. The personalities of female aristocrats is not expected to be like those of female servants. Stereotypes also differentiate women and men of different ethnic origins. African American women have been characterized as strong, dominant, and nurturing; Latina women as emotional, nurturing, and passionate; Jewish women as aggressive, dominant, and intellectual; and so forth. Because of this variation, different explanations are given for different "types" of women. "Female psychology" also varies by age. The characteristics of little girls are not the same as those of elderly women. Thus, general characterizations of female personality and emotions must take into account factors associated with life experiences, changing biological states, and social context.

From the feminist viewpoint, among the most important dimensions of variability are those that occur among individuals of the same sex and within the same individual at different times. It is such dimensions as these that, for women, have been most neglected, and that most directly challenge previous assumptions about women and explanations grounded in earlier male-dominated theory. Chapter 5 discusses stereotypes and the interaction of race, ethnicity, and class.

Explanations for Differences between Women and Men

While researchers can document differences between women and men (within the limits and contexts of particular studies), theories attempt to explain such differences. Theories of gender differences in behavior and traits differ in a number of ways. Some theories attribute gender-related behavior to "nature," that is, biology (our bodies). Others explain it as a result of "nurture," that is, socialization—how we have learned to behave as a result of being raised female or male.

A second factor that distinguishes among theories requires us to understand the distinction between sex, gender identity, and gender roles. "Sex" is a biological label. Societies identify children as female or male at birth based on some anatomical criteria (see Chapter 3). Gender identity refers to a psychological sense of ourselves as female or male as internalized from our culture. Gender roles are the behaviors or traits that societies assign to individuals because they have been labeled female or male. Theories differ on the relationship they posit exists between gender identity and gender roles, with some viewing personality traits as something we "are," while others see traits as a function of a given context, and, thus, as being something we "do." The theories that follow deal with these issues.

Table 4.2 Summary of Research Findings about Hypothetical Gender Differences

Cognitive

Intellectual aptitude: No difference
Memory: No difference
Verbal skills: Essentially no difference, although girls show a slight edge on some tasks.
Quantitative skills: No difference before high school; males show an edge in problem-solving tasks and in the incidence of math genius.
Visual-spatial abilities: Males perform somewhat better, especially if tasks involve rapid mental rotation of images.
Cognitive styles: No difference in analytic or computer abilities. Possible difference in style preferences, with males preferring an autonomous and females a connected style.
Creativity: Unclear. Females sometimes have an edge.

Personality and Temperament

Personality: Girls describe themselves as more people-oriented, males as more instrumental and power-oriented.
Temperament: Unclear. Females may be more timid.

Communication Patterns

Verbal: Males dominate conversations; females listen, qualify, and self-disclose more. Situational and sex-typing factors are important.
Nonverbal: Males dominate after childhood; females are more expressive and more sensitive to nonverbal cues. Situational, cultural, and sex-typing factors are important.

Prosocial Behaviors

Affiliation: Females show greater interest by adolescence.
Empathy: Unclear. Females express more interest in others' feelings. Situational and sex-typing factors important.
Nurturance Unclear. Females more likely to be in nurturant roles.
Altruism: Unclear. Females express more concern, but males are more likely to help strangers. Situational factors important.
Morality: Unclear. Females may be more concerned about the feelings of others.

Power-Related Behaviors

Aggressiveness: Males tend to be more physically aggressive.
Assertiveness: Unclear. Situational and sex-typing factors important.
Dominance: Dominance appears more important to males. Definitional, sex-typing, and situational factors important.
Competitiveness: Males tend to be more competitive. Situational and sex-typing factors important.
Achievement: No difference in motivation. Definitional, sex-typing, and situational factors important.
Noncompliance-nonconformity: Males tend to be less compliant and conforming. Situational factors important.

From *Gender: Stereotypes and Roles*, p. 101, by Susan A. Basow. Copyright © 1992 Wadsworth, Inc. Reprinted by permission of Brooks/Cole Publishing Company, Inc., Pacific Grove, Calif. 93950.

Biological Approaches

Attempts to attribute behavioral and personality differences to biological causes have concentrated on the influence of prenatal hormones on the system, brain lateralization (the side of the brain that dominates when performing a task), and different characteristics associated with the sex chromosomes (XX vs XY) and reproductive hormones (estrogen and androgens) on the mature adult. Because females and males have different experiences as well as some physiological differences it is virtually impossible to separate the two to determine the role of biology in behavior and emotions. As such, much research has de-

Margaret Mead (1901–1978) was perhaps the most influential and widely read anthropologist of our time. Her field work among different societies in the South Pacific illustrated the great diversity one can find in the cultural definition and shaping of gender roles and personalities. This very diversity, in her view, indicated that what is thought to be "feminine" and "masculine" is culturally, not biologically, determined. (American Museum of Natural History)

pended on animal studies and people born with gender-atypical genitals due to prenatal hormonal exposure (see Chapter 3). Even with the latter group, differences may well be a result of the individuals' atypical social status and not physiology, and research on nonhuman species does not easily generalize to humans.

One extensive review of the literature (Hood et al., 1987) concludes that there is little support for the belief that personality and behavioral differences between females and males can be attributed to biological factors. Differences, when found, are small and amenable to environmental influences. Female and male brains are considerably more similar

than dissimilar. The brain continues to develop after birth and the accumulated effects of different experiences could produce slight differences in brain development. In short, differential social and psychological experiences are confounding factors in the study of biological determinates of gender differences.

The one area of gender differences in behavior in which hormonal differences have been strongly implicated is males' greater physical aggression than females' (Jacklin, 1989). Most of this support, however, is based on animal studies that suggest a relationship between testosterone and aggression. Interestingly, there is also evidence that providing a monkey with an opportunity to dominate increased his testosterone levels (Rose et al., 1972). Such research suggests that not only is there a relationship between a hormone and aggressive behavior (at least in monkeys), but that such behavior can affect the production of the hormone as well. While human males are more likely to behave aggressively than females, such differences are not consistently found (Eagly and Steffen, 1986). As Katz et al. (1993) point out, "it is not only the accuracy of a documented difference but also the interpretation and the power of the interpreter that can be potentially damaging" (p. 261) (see **The Power of Interpretation**).

Psychodynamic Theories

According to psychodynamic theories, females and males develop different personality structures as a result of early-childhood experiences with their caretakers and identification with the same-sex parent. This personality is rooted in the unconscious, begins early in life, and is internalized, thus, stable across different situations. To psychodynamic theorists, girls and boys develop distinct "gender identities" as female or male. These identities are intrapsychic and their behavioral expressions simply follow as a result of our identity.

Traditional Psychoanalytic Theory. Traditional psychodynamic theory, *psychoanalytic theory*, was founded by Viennese neurologist Sigmund Freud (1856–1939). Freud became intrigued by the number of patients he saw whose symptoms appeared to be the result of sexual conflicts and repressions. Based on case studies of these patients, he developed a theory of personality development called "psychosexual development." According to Freud, sexual drives underlie all personality development.

Freudian theory stipulates that the significant turning point in the formation of gender identity occurs about the age of three. Before this time, sensual pleasure has been centered on oral gratification—sucking for milk at the bottle or at the breast of the mother or wet nurse. Experiences in this *oral* stage influence the child's attitudes about the gratification of needs, and the development of a sense of trust. As the child grows, the anal area and anal functions become a source of sensual pleasure. This stage is termed *anal* and is characterized by issues of retention and elimination, toilet-training, and a sense of autonomy, self-control, and control over the environment.

The anal stage is followed by the *phallic* stage, where the sexual organs become the source of pleasure. It is at this stage, according to Freud, that girls notice that boys and men

---

The Power of Interpretation

Take the case of hormonal differences between men and women. Women's apparently greater hormonal variability has been used to buttress charges of emotional instability. Of course, men are also affected by hormones, and one former President of the American Psychological Association suggested that antitestosterone pills be taken by male leaders to reduce war (Clark, 1971). If men were more hormonally variable rather than women, however, it would probably be argued that because they were more flexible and more in touch with themselves and their social environment, they were thus better suited by "nature" to fill important leadership positions.

(Katz et al., 1993:261)

have a penis, a source of pleasure that is larger (and presumably more pleasurable) than our own clitoris. According to Freud, this recognition leads girls to develop a sense of inferiority and the desire for a penis, a wish he labeled "penis envy." At the same time, boys notice that girls and women do not have penises, and this leads boys to suspect that girls' penises were somehow denied or taken from them. Freud concluded that this produces anxiety in boys that they too will lose their principal source of pleasure, the penis. Freud called this anxiety the *castration complex.* He argued that girls blame our "inferior anatomy" (lack of a penis) on our mothers. We turn our affections toward our father, hoping to get the desired object (a penis) or a substitute (a baby) from him. We later learn that we cannot possess our father either, and must replace him with another man to provide gratification. Furthermore, to gain gratification through a relationship with a man, we must give up active sexual stimulation (clitoral masturbation) and turn to passive gratification (vaginal intercourse).

Boys, by contrast, desire to marry their mothers and replace their fathers but fear that their fathers will retaliate for this desire by castrating them. A resolution of this *Oedipal conflict*[1] is generally achieved by relinquishing the mother as love object, while identifying with the father. This identification with the father removes a boy from the realm of competitor, thus reducing the castration fears. As a result of this identification with the father, the boy develops a "male" identity and internalizes parental moral standards.

Girls identify with our mothers. According to Freud, girls do so reluctantly because this identification does not help obtain the

wished-for penis. Our own moral standards are weaker and less developed than those of boys because they do not evolve in response to castration fears but in order to counteract the shame of having been castrated. Because internalization of moral standards is essential to maturity, girls are seen as having more difficulty maturing than boys.

Thus, according to Freudian theory, gender identity and the foundation for all later personality development is established within the first six years of life and is indirectly derived from anatomy. "Anatomy is destiny," according to Freud (1925).

In her two-volume discussion of the psychology of women (once a standard reference on the subject), Helene Deutsch, who had been a student and colleague of Freud, proposed that the triad of passivity, masochism, and narcissism is a natural concomitant of female biology (1944, 1945). Deutsch suggests that because girls do not possess an "active" sexual organ, our "active" impulses must be inhibited and transformed into passive aims. Deutsch defines female passivity as "receptive readiness." As a consequence of our anatomy, women are naturally suited to be "acted upon" rather than to take action, and the reward for passivity is love. Some degree of masochism, according to Deutsch's formulation, is an adaptive attitude for the female gender, whose biological functions of childbirth and menstruation are infused with both pleasure and pain. While the psychologically healthy woman is not masochistic to the point of self-destruction in her relationships with men, she is willing to renounce her own needs to obtain love. Narcissism, for women, serves the necessary psychic function of balancing out what might otherwise be an unhealthy tendency toward masochism.

Psychoanalytic Dissidents: Karen Horney and Clara Thompson. Psychoanalysts Karen Horney (pronounced

---

[1]Named after the Greek myth about Oedipus, who unwittingly killed his father and married his mother.

Horn-eye) and Clara Thompson both diverged from the classical Freudian theory of female psychology, elaborating on the cultural constraints that contribute to the formation of the "feminine" personality. Karen Horney (1885–1952) differed radically with the interpretation of female masochism propounded by Deutsch (1939). Horney did not see masochism as an inevitable accompaniment to female biological functions. Masochism represents, in Horney's formulation, an attempt to achieve personal safety and satisfaction by appearing inconspicuous and dependent. Weakness and suffering provide a vehicle for controlling others. She examined the cultural factors that nourish masochistic attitudes in women: women's economic, and hence emotional, dependency on men; society's emphasis on women's inherent weakness and delicacy; the barriers that block women's expansiveness and sexuality; and, finally, the ideology permeating our culture that dictates that a woman's purpose in life centers around the concerns of family, husband, and children. Horney suggested that these factors can explain masochistic tendencies in women without requiring any reference to anatomical determinants.

The "overvaluation of love" that Horney observed in normal as well as neurotic women of her time and class is a consequence of our economic and social dependency, which limited our direct access to security and prestige. The vicarious aspect of women's status and accomplishments can explain why women may seem to be more afraid of losing love than are men. It is not necessary to attribute this to the symbolic desire for a penis.

Thus, Horney's explanation of "feminine psychology" suggests that social change might be able to remedy traits deemed undesirable. If socialization and work practices were changed to permit the development of women's sexuality and independence, the female personality would be different. This view is in stark contrast to those who attribute "femininity" to penis envy and biological makeup.

Clara Thompson (1893–1958) took issue with the assumption that the discovery of the penis is invariably a psychic trauma for the girl; yet she agreed that it may function this way if the lack of a penis is associated with lower status and fewer privileges within the family—and, historically, this has generally been the case (Thompson, 1942, 1943).

Rather than attributing the adolescent female's renunciation of the "active" role in life to the resolution of penis envy, Thompson attributed it to external social pressures. Insofar as the requirements of a culture are unchangeable or unchanging, it may be a more positive adaptation for the female to find pleasure in pain and self-sacrifice than to reject the conventional life of a woman altogether and refuse to marry and bear children.

Freudian theory characterized women as less capable of moral integrity than men. Supposedly our superegos are weaker because we cannot fully resolve our identity. This conclusion was based on the observation that women's judgments seemed to be based on feelings of hostility and affection and that many women merely repeated the views and opinions of the men who were nearest and most important. Thompson suggested that this is a function of the status characteristic of females and males rather than of women's failure to develop strong internal standards of right and wrong, pointing out that people in subordinate positions may try to get along with authority figures by espousing similar interests and beliefs. Social psychological research on "integration" behavior provides empirical evidence for just such a proposition (Jones, 1964). Irrespective of gender, people who are dependent and relatively powerless are more likely to conform in their opinions than those who are immune from the sanctions of others. Thus, differences between women's and men's status and power appears to be a more

Karen Horney (1885–1952) published a major feminist critique of Freudian psychoanalysis and women in her 1926 paper "The Flight from Womanhood." She pointed out that the masculinist mode of thought represented by the psychoanalysts of her day was not surprising given the male domination of all institutions. Thus both social reality and theoretical constructs were based on male views of the inferiority of women. She attributed this male perspective to a deep envy of the primacy of women in reproduction. (Association for the Advancement of Psychoanalysis of the Karen Horney Psychoanalytic Institute and Center)

reasonable explanation for Freud's observations.

Criticisms of Freud's Theory. One group of critics is inclined to dismiss the basic assumptions that underlie Freudian theory because the events are largely unconscious developments and they cannot be observed directly. They offer alternative hypotheses for explaining the development of gender roles and identities. A second group of critics (including even a number of Freud's students) attack not the psychoanalytic approach but Freud's specific formulation of female development. In *Psychoanalysis and Feminism* (1974), Juliet Mitchell views Freudian theory in a cultural context, taking the position that psychoanalytic theory is an analysis of a patriarchal society—not a recommendation for one. Similarly, Dorothy Dinnerstein, a psychologist who has written about the development of gender roles, incorporated much Freudian thought into her work:

> I am disturbed . . . by the sexual bigotry that is built into the Freudian perspective. But I am disinclined to let the presence of the bigotry deflect my attention from the key to a way out of our gender predicament that Freud, in a sense absent-mindedly, provides. Feminists' preoccupation with Freud's patriarchal bias, with his failure to jump with alacrity right out of his male Victorian skin, seems to me wildly ungrateful. The conceptual tool that he has put into our hands is a revolutionary one. (Dinnerstein, 1976:xi)

The aspect of Freudian theory most criticized by feminists is his emphasis on penis envy and his view that our lives must be determined by our anatomy. Many critics have pointed out that women have anatomical features and capacities that men lack and may well envy. Karen Horney, for example, believed that the wish for a penis in girls may be no more significant than the frequently observed wish in boys for breasts and the ability to give birth to a child. Indeed, she suggests that this male envy of women is at the root of misogyny and, as a result of male power in societies, gives rise to male oppression of females (1922/1973). Research suggests that males in many societies experience feelings of breast and womb envy (Mead, 1949; Zalk, 1980, 1987).

"Modern" feminist psychoanalysis has rejected Freud's basic premise of biological/sexual determinism, which implies that female and male personality traits are "inevitable" and universal. It places development within the context of relationships with others and sees a sense of self (identity) as emerging in the context of a culture that assigns different roles and status based on gender. These theories recognize two points: (1) the androcentric bias of Freud's theories in which the penis (its presence or absence) forms the core of gender identity and personality and females are devalued such that our unique biological capacities are trivialized; and (2) that gender development exists within a cultural context and cannot be separated from it. Thus, while Freudian theory postulates that gender roles reflect gendered personalities that are the inevitable outcome of anatomical differences, more recent feminist theories postulate that biological differences take on their meaning as a consequence of different gender roles.

Alternative Feminist Psychodynamic Explanations. Attempts to understand female personality development within a psychoanalytic or psychodynamic framework have led many theorists to explore the mother-daughter relationship and the differential impact on girls and boys of being raised by a female figure. These writers focus not on genitals but on the impact on early identity formation of having a same-sex or other sex caretaker. It may be that the fact that the female child is cared for and raised primarily by a parent or a parent-surrogate of the same sex engenders feelings and conflicts that differ from those elicited in the mother-son relationship. Flax, for example, suggested that mothers "do not seem to have as clear a sense of physical boundaries between themselves and their girl children as do mothers of boys" (1978:174).

Chodorow (1978) discussed the effect that predominantly female parenting has on the establishment of the boy's gender identity. In order for him to develop his appropriate gender role, the boy must break away from the female-dominated world from which he emerges. The devaluation of femininity and female activities may represent the male's attempt to differentiate himself from that feminine world. According to Chodorow, males have an easier time establishing autonomy than females, but a less stable gender identity and less access to feelings of empathy, nurturance, and dependency, which are a reminder of their early identification with their mothers. Indeed, males do demonstrate a greater concern with maintaining gender-role distinctions than do women (Silvern and Katz, 1986). Because females initially identify with a same-sex caretaker, they have less trouble establishing a positive gender identity but more difficulty developing feelings of autonomy than males. Chodorow suggests that family relations that emphasize male dominance and female caretaking result in a perpetuation of gender roles and female oppression and inhibit healthy development in females and males. She suggests equal parenting as a solution. Contemporary psychoanalysts have suggested that fear and envy of women and female sexuality may underlie negative attitudes toward women and may be traced back to these early mother-son relations.

Traditional psychodynamic theorists stress the importance of separation from the mother and the establishment of an independent, autonomous identity as the hallmark of mental health and necessary to obtaining mature, intimate, and trusting relationships (Erikson, 1963). Within this perspective, women have been viewed as at a disadvantage. Jean Baker Miller (1984) and her colleagues at The Stone Center at Wellesley College challenge this perspective. They suggest that relatedness is the central goal of development and that it is only within the context of relatedness that autonomy can develop. Miller's self-in-relation theory proposes that it is the reciprocal give-and-take relationship between the caretaker and the child that forms the core "self" and that this reciprocal relationship is the precursor of empathy, nurturance, and connecting with others. Miller notes that females are more likely to have these experiences than are males and that as a result women possess a greater capacity for emotional connectedness, empathy, and intimacy and that this relational self is a core self structure for females, and a strength.

While feminist psychodynamic theories share with traditional psychoanalytic theories the belief that individuals form a core gender identity based on early-childhood experiences, they reject the Freudian premise that "anatomy is destiny" and instead look at the cultural context within which girls and boys grow up and the impact of the context on the development of gender identities. Thus, while these theories are based primarily on Western families, their theories can better accommodate cultural diversity and can also be considered under the category of socialization theories.

Cognitive-Developmental Theory

Other schools of psychological thought offer alternative explanations for the development of female and male gender identities and roles. External pressures to conform to gender-appropriate behavior are augmented by an internal need to fulfill one's learned gender identity (Kohlberg, 1966; Kohlberg and Ullian, 1974). Cognitive psychologists are interested in the ways in which people organize and understand their perceptions of physical and social reality and how these perceptions change at different developmental stages. They have suggested that at age two, girls and boys begin to learn gender categories based on experiences with representatives of each gender, although they are not initially aware of anatomical distinctions or conceive them to be unchangeable characteristics. Once children have classified themselves as female or male and recognize that their gender does not change (at about age five), they are motivated to approximate to the best of their ability the social definitions of this identity. In the case of female children, the motivation to fulfill our gender identity presses us toward the ideal of femininity (as socially defined), independent of externally mediated rewards or punishments for attaining such a goal. This explanation for gender-role acquisition may account for the fact that often girls and boys will conform to stereotypic gender roles even when their parents or other socializing agents do not differentially reinforce feminine and masculine behavior in them (Kohlberg and Zigler, 1967).

Social Learning Theory

Social learning theory associates gender-role conformity with the external reinforcements (rewards and punishments) that people receive for behaving in particular ways. This theory minimizes the role of stable "personality" traits existing independently of external forces. It holds that we learn both "female" and "male" behavior by observing others. However, the behavior we *perform* is a function of whether it is rewarded ("you're a good girl") or punished ("nice girls don't do that!"). Social learning theorist and experimental psychologist Albert Bandura (1965) presents research evidence suggesting that when rein-

forcements for behavior are changed—for example, when women are rewarded rather than punished for engaging in so-called masculine activities—behavior changes accordingly. Bandura suggests that the introduction of rewards for cross-sex behavior will enable girls and boys to expand their behavioral repertoires with little difficulty.

Cognitive theory of gender-role development focuses on the internal motivations of females and males to excel at the roles in which they find they have been classified, while the social learning theorists emphasize the role of external pressures imposed on the developing girl and boy. Both cognitive and social learning theories stress the acquisition of personality traits within a social context, and not as inherent in the individual.

Gender Schema Theory

Sandra Bem (1981, 1983, 1985) proposes a "gender schema theory," which attempts to incorporate cognitive, childrearing, and cultural factors in explaining the development of gender identity and roles. All people have ways of organizing information. We have mental categories that are a network of associations, and in order to understand or make sense of information, we try to place it into the categories that form a kind of blueprint in our mind. We call these *schema*, which not only are descriptive categories but also consist of associations and assumptions. For example, our schema for "teacher" and "student" is not simply "one who teaches" and "one who learns," but involves all kinds of associations about authority, judgment, power, expertise, interdependence, and the like.

One of the most culturally salient categories in which people are grouped is gender, and the development of gender schema begins early in childhood. Children begin early to learn to categorize people by gender and develop a gender schema that incorporates cultural gender roles, norms, attributes, and definitions of "feminine" and "masculine." Bem proposes that our gender schemas become part of our self-concept. "As children learn the contents of the society's gender schema, they learn which attributes are to be linked with their own sex and, hence, with themselves. This does not simply entail learning where each sex is supposed to stand on each dimension or attribute—that boys are to be strong and girls weak, for example—but involves the deeper lesson that the dimensions themselves are differentially applicable to the two sexes" (Bem, 1981:355). According to Bem, people fall on a continuum from having more to having less well developed gender schema. There is evidence to support her suggestion that the more developed our gender schema the more gender typed our self-concept and behavior, and, alternatively, people who are less gender typed have less developed gender schema (Bem, 1985; Frable and Bem, 1985; Bigler and Liben, 1990; Liben and Signorella, 1987). Thus, Bem does not consider gender typing as inevitable but suggests that raising children in gender-aschematic home and school environments, in which "sex" refers only to anatomy, results in less gender typed behavior or expectations.

Social Interactions and Gender Roles

The above theories attempt to explain how individuals develop gender identities and the relationship between gender identity and gender roles. Other theories place greater emphasis on social roles, and rather than view gender-typed behaviors as primarily a function of internalized gender identities, understand them as an outcome of gender-differentiated role assignments and expectations and the unequal distribution of power between females and males. These theories hold that gender-typed personality traits or behaviors are, at least in part, behavioral displays that are shaped or a result of social demands, interactions, or oppression, rather than necessarily represent internal or stable characteristics.

Alice Eagly (1987), for example, explains gender-typed behaviors as compliance to gender-role expectations. Her social-role theory suggests that women and men demonstrate different traits because the family and occupation roles they are assigned require these different behaviors. Thus, women are communal because of our roles in the family as caretakers and nurturers and men more agentic because of their roles in the workplace. Although roles may be changing in much of the world, even in the United States, women and men continue to assume different family and workplace responsibilities and roles (Eccles and Hoffman, 1984; Ruble, 1988).

Authors Candace West and Don Zimmerman (1987) present a thoughtful argument for conceiving of gender as a verb rather than a noun. In other words, they view gender as something we *do*, not as something we *are*, and that each of us *does* gender through our dress, speech, behavior, and interactions with others (see **Doing Gender**). Other researchers have presented a model that explains the display of gender-typed behavior rather than its acquisition. They propose that the enactment of gender takes place within the context of social interactions, is highly flexible, and is context dependent (Deaux and Major, 1987). In other words, gender-related behaviors are an outcome of the individual's self-perception, emitted expectation of an other, and the context of ongoing social interactions.

The "Politics of Gender" and Sexism

The politics of gender refers to the unequal status and distribution of power between women and men (Unger, 1978) and how that reality translates into gender-related behav-

Doing Gender

When we view gender as an accomplishment, an achieved property of situated conduct, our attention shifts from matters internal to the individual and focuses on interactional and, ultimately, institutional arenas. In one sense, of course, it is individuals who "do" gender. But it is a situated doing, carried out in the virtual or real presence of others who are presumed to be oriented to its production. Rather than as a property of individuals, we conceive of gender as an emergent feature of social situations: both as an outcome of and a rationale for various social arrangements and as a means of legitimating one of the most fundamental divisions of society. . . .

To elaborate our proposal, we suggest at the outset that important but often overlooked distinctions be observed among sex, sex category, and gender. Sex is a determination made through the application of socially agreed upon biological criteria for classifying persons as females or males. . . . Placement in a sex category is achieved through application of the sex criteria, but in everyday life, categorization is established and sustained by the socially re-quired identificatory displays that proclaim one's membership in one or the other category. In this sense, one's sex category presumes one's sex and stands as proxy for it in many situations, but sex and sex category can vary independently; that is, it is possible to claim membership in a sex category even when the sex criteria are lacking. Gender, in contrast, is the activity of managing situated conduct in light of normative conceptions of attitudes and activities appropriate for one's sex category. Gender activities emerge from and bolster claims to membership in a sex category.

. . . doing gender also renders the social arrangements based on sex category accountable as normal and natural, that is, legitimate ways of organizing social life. Differences between men and women that are created by this process can then be portrayed as fundamental and enduring dispositions. . . . Thus if, in doing gender, men are also doing dominance and women are doing deference . . . the resultant social order, which supposedly reflects "natural differences," is a powerful reinforcer and legitimator of hierarchical arrangements.

(West and Zimmerman, 1987:126–27; 146)

iors and traits. Many feminist researchers have drawn parallels between the behavior of women in social settings and that of low-status individuals. Henley (1977), for example, found that when females relate to males, and males in subordinate positions to those in dominant positions, they touch less, smile more, make less frequent eye contact, and are more tentative. Other researchers have also found parallels between the behaviors of women and men and that of low- and high-status people (Lott, 1987a; Hall and Halber-stadt, 1986; Kollock et al., 1985; Carli, 1990). Men take up more public space and talk more and interrupt more than women in mixed groups (Henley, 1977; West and Zimmerman, 1983).

Miller (1976) suggests that women's per-sonality styles are a result of their subordinate position in society. The dominant group de-fines the roles and the standards of "normal-ity" for the subordinate group. In our society, the ideal standard for women, the subordinate group, is "submissiveness, passivity, docility, dependency, lack of initiative, inability to act, to decide and to think . . . qualities more char-acteristic of children than adults. . . . If sub-ordinates adopt these characteristics they are considered well-adjusted" (Miller, 1976:7). Miller suggests that many women internalize this definition of inferiority.

The implications of male dominance on women's lives may be a direct and powerful influence on gender-related behaviors. MacKinnon (1987), for example, suggests that women behave differently from men because they grow up and live under the constant threat of physical violence and sexual exploitation. Many more women are subject to physical and sexual assault than men (e.g., battering, rape, sexual harassment) (Finkelhor, 1984; Gelles, 1987; Strickland, 1988; Gutek, 1985). It is understandable that we may behave in ways that minimize a challenge to male dominance and the possibility of being victimized (Zalk, 1987).

Having discussed the premise of the importance of the cultural context, we turn now to the process of socialization—how cultures socialize females and males differently.

The Process of Socialization

Margaret Mead (1901–1978), an anthropologist and pioneer in research on the cultural and social context of personality development, began with the question: Are there universals of personality development? She empirically tested propositions about universals by comparing people in different cultural settings. Her first study addressed the question of whether adolescence is necessarily fraught with tension and conflict as it seemed to be in her own society. Studying adolescent girls in American Samoa, Mead concluded that adolescence was a very relaxed, comfortable period of life in that society. She argued that it was the socialization of human development that shaped its form, rather than any biologically determined universals (1928). Later, investigating the relationship between gender and personality, she compared several other South Pacific societies with her own and discovered that what we think of as "feminine" and "masculine" are culturally determined traits, not inherent in biological difference (1949; see Chapter 3).

Socialization theories focus attention on the social context of learning, with an interest in the messages a child receives from others in the social environment—and how these messages are conveyed. For example, if girls are systematically discouraged from playing with mechanical toys, and from fixing them ourselves, while boys are encouraged to do so, this might account for differences in the experience of competency in mechanical areas between girls and boys. Observation would provide support for the hypothesis that the lower self-judged competence in mechanical ability of girls results from what we are taught about our abilities (Denmark, 1977).

The Development of a "Female Personality"

Historical and Cultural Variation. A variety of theorists have had a great deal to say about the development of a feminine personality, stage by stage. We should keep in mind that their statements are based mostly on observations of twentieth-century Western society and are limited to the white middle class. They do not take account of the enormous historical and cultural variation that in fact exists. Western cultures tend to place a rather strong emphasis on individuation (the perception of one's self as a separate and unique entity). In many respects, psychological maturity is defined in terms of individuation, particularly by psychologists. But such an emphasis is not necessarily universal. Others may define maturity in different terms. Thus, many of the observations we will be discussing must be viewed with the understanding that they reflect certain cultural values and conceptions of the nature of childhood.

All societies teach their young culturally prescribed gender roles. Parents and peers are powerful socializing agents but gender expectations are communicated in many different ways. Television, school, books, clothing, toys, even fairy tales all operate as socializing agents.

Psychologists still know little about cultural diversity in the experience of girlhood and adolescence. The evidence we do have suggests that the experience of growing up in different cultures is quite varied. North American middle-class society kept girls close to home, supervised our activities closely, and trained us early in the tasks of household work and child care. Samoan girls grew up in a social environment that was very relaxed about sex. Thus Samoan girls did not have the same types of anxieties about sex that American middle-class girls seemed to have. To take another example, Joyce Ladner's study of African American girlhood in America (1971) suggests that unlike white middle-class girls, African American girls in urban ghetto environments develop emotional stability, strength, and self-reliance early in life in order to cope with harsh conditions. Unfortunately, research on American females of color has been limited, and plagued with biases and unfounded assumptions (Dill, 1979).

Parents' Attitudes and Treatment. The first words spoken about an infant who has just been born usually are: "It's a girl" or "It's a boy" and, almost immediately, concepts and expectations related to gender affect our behavior toward the infant. Within the first twenty-four hours after birth, parents attribute gender stereotypic traits to their infants, viewing boys as firmer and stronger and girls as softer and finer (Rubin et al., 1974). Parents hold different expectations for daughters and sons throughout their childhood. Sons are expected to be more active and daughters more emotional (Antill, 1987), and sons are expected to perform better in math and science than daughters (Eccles, 1989). Research by

Money and Ehrhardt (1972) on changes in gender assignments of infants born with ambiguous genitals dramatically illustrates the impact of gender labeling on parental behavior; even small children altered their behavior toward siblings whose gender label was changed. Another study (Seavey et al., 1975) shows how one can demonstrate the effects of gender labeling on the treatment of infants on an experimental basis. Adults who were told that a three-month-old baby was a girl were more likely to engage in one sort of treatment (such as playing with a doll) than they were when told that this same baby was a boy. It appears that the process of gender socialization begins with the label "girl" or "boy." Some examples of how this operates follow.

From the earliest age, mothers look at and talk to female infants more than male infants. Differences have been observed in the ways in which mothers hold sons and daughters, and in patterns of physical contact and proximity (Lewis, 1972). Males are expected to be more independent than females and less fragile, and they are restricted less and allowed more freedom to explore the environment (Aberle and Naegle, 1952; Lewis, 1972). Gender-role socialization of children, however, differs according to culture and social role realities. The socialization of African American children, for example, occurs less along gender stereotypes as prescribed by the larger society. Both females and males are encouraged toward independence, employment, and child care (Bardwell et al., 1986; Hale-Benson, 1986).

Parental socialization continues throughout childhood. Parents respond differently to girls' and boys' moods, displays of anger, and aggressive behavior (Condry and Ross, 1985; Fivush, 1989; Troncik and Cohn, 1989). They even talk to sons and daughters differently (Fagot, 1974; Weitzman et al., 1985). Activities assigned at home follow gender-role expectations such that girls are more likely to be assigned domestic chores (e.g., cooking) and boys maintenance chores (e.g., taking out the garbage) (Burns and Homel, 1989; Goodnow, 1988; McHale et al., 1990). This pattern is more exaggerated among people in lower economic classes and increases from childhood to adolescence.

Parental socialization extends to their encouragement of particular activities, the use of certain toys, and their choice of clothing and room decor for their youngsters. For example, by age two, girls are already being socialized into nurturing activities (doll play), while the exposure to toy vehicles encourages motor activity in boys (Liss, 1983; O'Brien and Huston, 1985b).

Parents often discourage children from engaging in other-gender activities and toy play and reinforce gender-appropriate activities. This is more pronounced with sons than with daughters (Antill, 1987; Fagot, 1978; Lytton and Romney, 1991). Fathers are usually more concerned with their children's conformity to gender-appropriate behavior than mothers. They view their children in more gender stereotypic ways and are more likely to interact with their daughters and sons in ways that encourage gender-appropriate behavior and toy playing than are mothers. This is particularly true with sons (Jacklin et al., 1984). Thus, it is not surprising that boys show stronger gender-typed preferences than girls and that this increases for boys with age while girls become more flexible in the toys and activities they engage in (Katz and Boswell, 1986).

What are the effects of adult behavior on children? Do differences in treatment of girl and boy infants have any clear impact on the children's behavior or on their later lives? While we can only speculate on the long-term effects of the differential treatment of children, the research suggests that it influences gender behavior in children and adolescents. In a study with one-year-olds, for example, researchers found that caretakers attended more

to assertive behavior in boys and to verbal behavior in girls. Although girls and boys did not differ in the behavior initially, they did ten months later (Fagot et al., 1985). Many studies have found that children demonstrate gender-stereotyped behavior and toy preferences by eighteen to twenty-four months (Huston, 1985; O'Brien and Huston, 1985a; Perry et al., 1984; Caldera et al., 1989). It is not surprising, given the propensity of parents to encourage gender-appropriate activities in their children.

The gender-role attitudes and expectations of parents do seem to have a direct link to children's gender-role conformity and self-esteem. For example, mothers who believe that boys have greater aptitude for math than girls tend to have daughters who have lower confidence in their math abilities even when they obtain good grades in their math courses (Eccles, 1989; Eccles and Jacobs, 1986). Parents with nontraditional gender attitudes encourage less stereotypic behavior in their children, and sons tend to hold less traditional gender attitudes if their fathers do (Antill, 1987; Weisner and Wilson-Mitchell, 1990). Women are more likely to perceive women's roles as involving satisfaction and freedom of choice if their mothers are employed than if they are not (Baruch and Barnett, 1986). Lesbian mothers hold more egalitarian views about daughters and sons than do heterosexual mothers and are more likely to encourage daughters in nontraditional role expectations (Hill, 1988).

Beyond the Family. Most children in the Western world and many throughout the world spend a large portion of their time in school. The structure of schools, teachers' behavior, and peer group pressure are all powerful gender socializing agents, and this is true from the preschool years through post-secondary education.

Both peers and teachers reward gender-appropriate behavior and punish gender-inappropriate behavior (Fagot, 1985). Peer pressure to conform to gender-typed behavior is strong from preschool through adolescence, and children who engage in more traditional gender-role activities are more socially acceptable to peers than those who do not (Fagot, 1984; Martin, 1989). The terms *sissy* and *tomboy*, derogatory labels children apply to boys who favor girls' activities and girls who engage in boys' activities, respectively, serve to pressure peers toward gender-role conformity. Not surprisingly, given the greater status of males in our society, a sissy is viewed considerably more negatively than a tomboy (Martin, 1990).

Gender segregation, that is, girls grouping with girls and boys grouping with boys, begins in the preschool years and increases through adolescence. While children prefer same-gender playmates, teachers encourage this by dividing their classes by gender, for example, when they have them line up. Same-gender grouping seems to be an outcome of the differential status of females and males in societies, and males are particularly intent on dissociating themselves from females in societies where the higher status and better treatment of men is most blatant (Whiting and Edwards, 1988). It may be, as well, that girls find playing and working in mixed-gender groups a negative experience (Maccoby and Jacklin, 1987).

It appears that the give-and-take between girls and boys favors boys in group interactions. For example, girls offer help to both girls and boys, while boys rarely offer help to girls (Lockheed, 1985). As a result of gender segregation, girls and boys grow up in different subcultures and the subcultures support the process of gender socialization.

The role of peer groups in gender socialization intensifies in the adolescent years (Canter and Ageton, 1984). In mixed-gender teenage groups, boys dominate interactions. Although this pattern was found among Af-

rican American and white teenagers, it was less intense among African Americans (Filardo, 1991). This is consistent with the evidence suggesting that African Americans hold less polarized gender-role stereotypes and have more egalitarian child-rearing practices (Lewis, 1975). Research also suggests that gender-related behavior differs in racially mixed as opposed to racially homogeneous groups, reflecting the interaction of gender and race in the display of gender-role behavior. One study found the gender status differential between females and males less strong among African American children when grouped with white children (Grant, 1985).

Even the instructional materials used in school depict females and males differently. From elementary school through college, males dominate the curricula and the textbooks (Ferree and Hall, 1990; Schau and Scott, 1984). The material presented continues to depict sexist attitudes and beliefs, thus disseminating stereotypes.

It has been well documented that teachers treat females and males differently, although the implications of this are less clear (see Wilkinson and Marrett, 1985). Since we have been socialized differently, we bring different behavior and expectations to the classroom. Teachers both respond to our behavior and treat us in ways that reinforce gender distinctions. As compared to boys, girls receive less attention and praise from teachers; request less help; and are less dominant in class (Epperson, 1988). Boys are encouraged more to engage in "academic" behavior and girls in social compliance (Fagot, 1984; Gold et al., 1987). Even at the college level, teachers pay more attention to male students than to female students (Sadker and Sadker, 1986). Interestingly, while the gender of the teacher does not seem to make a difference in treatment of girls and boys at the elementary or secondary level, in colleges, female teachers as compared to male teachers appear to be more positive toward female students and encourage a more participatory classroom (Crawford and MacLeod, 1990; Statham et al., 1991).

Many variables shape a teacher's behavior toward children. Recent research has demonstrated that both the behavior of the teacher as well as the behavior of the child vary as an interaction of gender, race, and age (see Wilkinson and Marrett, 1985). For example, teachers seem to have lower expectations for African American males (Ross and Jackson, 1991). Eccles (1989) suggests that the greater attention and encouragement teachers give to white boys promotes better mathematical skills (Table 4.3).

Even the recreation we engage in, the news we read, the entertainment we seek serve as agents of gender socialization. Television, movies, magazines, newspapers, advertisements, commercials, all perpetuate gender stereotypes.

Cultural Diversity in America. There are similarities and differences among ethnic and racial groups. Among Asian American women, for example, the split between the "ideal" woman and man has traditionally been quite extreme (Fujitomi and Wong, 1976). Asian women have been taught from birth that we are subservient to men and inferior to them in all valued areas. While Asian cultures encourage affiliation, altruism, adaptiveness, and timidity for women and men, women are particularly discouraged from acquiring such traits as activism, independence, and competitiveness (Chow, 1987). We must be submissive, passive, and demure (see **We, the Dangerous**): "Since the image of the passive, demure Asian woman is pervasive the struggle for a positive self-identity is difficult. Within the Asian community, the family supports the development of the male's personality and aspirations, while the sister is discouraged from forming any sense of high self-esteem and individuality" (Fujitomi and Wong, 1976:236). Al-

Table 4.3 Summary of Major Barriers to, and Facilitators of, Women's Career Development

Barriers	Facilitators
Environmental	
Gender role stereotypes	Working mother
Occupational stereotypes	Supportive father
Gender bias in education	Highly educated parents
Barriers in higher education	Girls' schools/Women's colleges
Lack of role models	Female models
The null environment*	Proactive encouragement
Gender-biased career counseling	Androgynous upbringing
	Work experience
Individual (Socialized)	
Family-career conflict	Late marriage or single
Math avoidance	No or few children
Low self-esteem	High self-esteem
Low self-efficacy expectations	Strong academic self-concept
Attributing failure to ability	Instrumentality
Low expectancies for success	Androgyny

Adapted from: Betz, in Denmark, ed., *Psychology of Women: A Handbook of Issues and Theories* (Greenwood Press, Westport, CT, 1993), p. 637. Reprinted with permission.
Null environment is an environment that neither encourages nor discourages individuals (Freeman, 1989).

though attitudes about family roles are much less traditional among Asian American women today, Asian American males are far more reluctant to make such changes.

The socialization of African American women is quite different from that of the Asian American or European American women. African American women and men in the United States do not perceive any differences in the way they were socialized to

We, the Dangerous

I swore
it would not devour me
I swore
it would not humble me
I swore
it would not break me.

    And they commanded we dwell in the desert
    Our children be spawn of barbed wire and barracks

We, closer to the earth,
squat, short thighed,
knowing the dust better.

    And they would have us make the garden
    Rake the grass to soothe their feet

We, akin to the jungle,
plotting with the snake,
tails shedding in civilized America.

    And they would have us skin their fish
    deft hands like blades / sliding back flesh / bloodless

We, who awake in the river
Ocean's child
Whale eater.

    And they would have us strange scented women,
    Round shouldered / strong and yellow / like the moon
    to pull the thread to the cloth
    to loosen their backs massaged in myth

We, who fill the secret bed,
the sweat shops
the launderies.

    And they would dress up in napalm,
    Skin shred to clothe the earth,
    Bodies filling pock marked fields.
    Dead fish bloating our harbors.

We, the dangerous,
Dwelling in the ocean.
Akin to the jungle.
Close to the earth.

    Hiroshima
    Vietnam
    Tule Lake

And yet we were not devoured.
And yet we were not humbled
And yet we are not broken.

(Mirikitani, 1978)

achievement and are less prone to gender stereotyping than are white children (Bardwell et al., 1986; Turner and Turner, 1971). Large discrepancies in power and status between girls and boys are more infrequent among African American children than white children, due to the combined influence of the upbringing of African American girls, which promotes competence and decisiveness, and the relative absence of gender stereotyping.

In a study of African American preschoolers, the elimination of conventional roles in childrearing was also found to predict higher achievement (Carr and Mednick, 1988). The "ideal" woman as described by African American women and men is more independent than is the "ideal" woman described by white women and men (Crovitz and Steinmann, 1980).

Psychologist Virginia O'Leary notes that

according to the commonly held female stereotype, women are (or should be) weak, passive, dependent, and submissive.... [S]tereotypically feminine traits are valued less than stereotypically masculine ones. However, these stereotypically feminine traits do not reflect accurately those characteristics that are most highly valued in Black women within the Black community— strength, independence, and resourcefulness.

As a member of a minority group, the Black woman has had to assume a central role in the economic structure of her community. Forced to compete in the economic marketplace, often in the role of sole provider of financial resources for her family, the Black woman adopted behaviors and attitudes characteristically assumed to be "masculine." Submission, passivity, and dependence were for many Black women dysfunctionally related to the reality of their lives and roles. (1977: 136)

African American females and males tend to exhibit more similar gender stereotypes in terms of competency and passivity than those evidenced by white females and males (Smith and Midlarsky, 1985).

In this country, there are fewer economic opportunities for African Americans than for whites, and, historically, those jobs that have been available have often been thought to be more suited for women than men. African American women are preferred as employees over their male counterparts. Two-thirds of African Americans who occupy professional positions are women and this often leads to resentment, which in turn creates tension and stress in female-male relationships (Bell, 1989).

In line with our less traditional gender roles, African American women appear to be more aware of sex discrimination and more supportive of women's rights in the workplace and politics. In a racist and sexist society, African American women, as well as all women of color, are in the position of what Frances Beal referred to as "double jeopardy" (1970). They live not only in a society that devalues women but one that devalues people of color as well (Almquist, 1989).

More African American women than white women are heads of households. The socialization of African American girls is a preparation for these realities of adult life. This is particularly true among those living in poverty. Ladner (1971) points out that poor African American girls are given a great deal of responsibility and independence at a young age and are likelier to spend more time in peer groups without adult supervision at a younger age than are white counterparts. Ladner contends that these girls are socialized into womanhood by the age of eight.

In reviews of the research on the work patterns and gender roles of African American women, Janice Porter Gump (1972, 1975, 1978) also notes that African American girls grow up with the expectation of working; it is an integral and accepted part of African American identity. Although many African American women's attitudes about marriage, children, and gender roles are traditional, work and motherhood are not seen as incompatible. According to Gump, intelligent, competent African American women are more attractive and less threatening to African American men than are similar white women to white men. African American women express greater feelings of competence and self-confidence than white women.

There is evidence that the Latino culture, in contrast to the African American community, relies upon strict gender roles that serve as deterrents to women who want to venture outside of traditional gender boundaries and hinder the development of characteristics such as assertiveness and independence. Recent research indicates that Latinas also face economic hardship because of our dual minority status; however, we suffer from even more unyielding gender-role guidelines and limitations than white or African American women. Consequently, we are subjected to barriers on all fronts—pay discrimination, and criticism by family members for breaching traditional gender roles by participating in the workforce. Furthermore, Chicanas are wary of the larger Hispanic community's perception of college-educated, career-oriented women as elitist and threatening to their male counterparts, another discouraging factor (Gonzales, 1988).

These issues take their toll on our mental health. In a study assessing the impact of marital inequality on symptoms of depression, researchers found that the more housework is unequally divided the more household strain is experienced among both Latina and non-Latina whites, and that household strain contributed to depression. However, housework inequalities were much more characteristic of Latinos than whites and, as a result, Latinas displayed a greater amount of household strain resulting from our assumption of the majority of responsibility for household tasks (Golding, 1990).

When we speak of women of color in the United States, we often divide the designation into such broad categories as African American, Hispanic, or Asian. These categories themselves, however, represent a range of ethnic and cultural backgrounds. African American women in the United States may hear family stories about Africa, slavery, or life on the Caribbean islands; Latinas may identify as Chicanas, Puerto Ricans, or South Americans; and women with Asian roots may come from widely divergent cultural contexts. Native Americans, while representing less than one percent of the United States population, come from Indian nations with diverse languages, values, and life-styles. Some value women and men equally, such as the Klamath of western North America, and others devalue the work of women (LaFromboise et al., 1990). What is more, such factors as social class and education influence the experiences of women of color. And recent immigrants or the children of immigrants will have different experiences than those with a longer history in the United States.

Consequently, generalizations about the experiences that shaped the personalities of women of color, as well as the personalities themselves—as is the case for white women—are apt to be inaccurate for many individuals. What many of us who identify as women of color do have in common is the experience of discrimination and the pressure to reconcile family culture and values with those imposed on us by the particular kind of Western culture that predominates where we live. Chicanas, for example, have roots in a Mexican Indian heritage. Historically, Mexican Indian women had a responsible role in the social, religious, and economic life of the community (Nieto-Gomez, 1976; Anzaldúa, 1987). With the arrival of a colonizing Spanish culture and the Catholic Church, the opposed concepts of good woman–bad woman took over. The Spanish "lady," representing a different set of traditional roles, became the new ideal, and the place of Mexican Indian women was diminished and denigrated within that culture (see **The Socialization of Las Chicanas**).

The divergent pulls of personal heritage and the new dominant culture impose additional stresses and conflicts on women of color in the United States, who must struggle to maintain roots while establishing an individual identity. In doing this, women confront not only the inherent sexism of our cultures but the racism as well. The importance of this struggle cannot be overestimated (see **The Bridge Poem**). As Cherríe Moraga writes in *This Bridge Called My Back*, "I think: what is my responsibility to my roots—both white and brown, Spanish speaking and English? I am a woman with a foot in both worlds; and I refuse the split" (Moraga, 1981:34).

Lesbian Psychologies

Is there such a thing as a "lesbian personality"? Stereotypes about lesbians and gay men are numerous and almost always negative. Lesbians are thought to be less attractive and extroverted than heterosexual women (Dew, 1985). We are often thought to be "man-haters," inadequate women, suffering from a traumatic sexual experience, or socially and psychologically maladjusted. Research does not indicate greater pathology among lesbians than among heterosexual women. It also does not suggest greater adjustment problems among our children (Garnets and Kimmel, 1991; Patterson, 1994). And there is remarkable similarity between lesbian, gay, and heterosexual couples in the processes that regulate satisfaction in relationships (Kurdek, 1994).

Terms like *butch* and *dyke* can be crude and hostile labels when used to imply that lesbians are more like men than women or that we want to be men. These are unfounded stereotypes and assumptions. Sexual orientation is independent of biological gender or gender identity or roles. The sexual politics of such references and beliefs are evident by the fact that these labels are often applied to women who fail to conform to traditional gender

---

The Socialization of Las Chicanas

Marianisma is the veneration of the Virgin Mary. . . . Through the Virgin Mary, the Chicana begins to experience a vicarious martyrdom in order to accept and prepare herself for her own oppressive reality. . . . To be a slave, a servant, woman cannot be assertive, independent and self defining. . . . She is conditioned to believe it is natural to be in a dependent psychological condition as well as dependent economically. The absolute role for women is not to do for themselves but to yield to the wishes of others. . . . Her needs and desires are in the charge of others—the patron, her family, her father, her boyfriend, her husband, her God. She is told to act for others and to wait for others to act for her. . . .

The basis for La Mujer Buena, the good, respectable woman in La Casa Grande, was the upper class Spanish woman whose role was to stay home. . . . The concept of Marianisma reinforced this Spanish role as a positive ideal for everyone to follow. . . .

. . . Marianisma convinced the woman to endure the injustices against her.

(Nieto-Gomez, 1976:228–33)

The Bridge Poem

I've had enough
I'm sick of seeing and touching
Both sides of things
Sick of being the damn bridge for everybody
Nobody
Can talk to anybody
Without me
Right?
I explain my mother to my father my father to my little sister
My little sister to my brother my brother to the white feminists
The white feminists to the Black church folks the Black church folks
To the ex-hippies the ex-hippies to the Black separatists the
Black separatists to the artists the artists to the parents of my friends . . .
Then
I've got to explain myself
To everybody
I do more translating
Than the Gawdamn U.N.
Forget it
I'm sick of it
I'm sick of filling in your gaps
Sick of being your insurance against
The isolation of your self-imposed limitations
Sick of being the crazy at your holiday dinners
Sick of being the odd one at your Sunday Brunches
Sick of being the sole Black friend to 34 individual white folks
Find another connection to the rest of the world
Find something else to make you legitimate
Find some other way to be political and hip.

roles, without any knowledge of our sexual orientation. It reflects the fear aroused when confronting women who do not conform to societal gender role dictates and serves as a mechanism to attempt to maintain the status quo. As Garnets and Kimmel point out, "Lesbians may be perceived as having greater power than heterosexual women because they live independently of men, and do not depend on men for sexual, emotional, or financial support" (1991:149). In fact, lesbians have been increasingly adopting and adapting these orig-

inally negative labels as positive symbols of independence and difference.

A question that is continually posed is, "Why are some people lesbians or gays?" One might as well ask, "Why are some people heterosexual?" While the psychological theories cited above offer different theoretical answers to these questions, little is known about the origins of sexual orientation. One of the problems that arises in attempting to arrive at a greater understanding of sexual orientation is the assumption that it is a bipolar dichotomy,

I will not be the bridge to your womanhood
Your manhood
Your human-ness
I'm sick of reminding you not to
Close off too tight for too long
I'm sick of mediating with your worst self
On behalf of your better selves
I am sick
Of having to remind you
To breathe
Before you suffocate
Your own fool self
Forget it
Stretch or drown
Evolve or die
The bridge I must be
Is the bridge to my own power
I must translate
My own fears
Mediate
My own weaknesses
I must be the bridge to nowhere
But my true self
And then
I will be useful

Donna Kate Rushin, 1981:xxi–xxii

This poem originally appeared in a slightly different version in *This Bridge Called My Back: Writings by Radical Women of Color*, edited by Cherríe Moraga and Gloria Anzaldúa. © 1981 Donna Kate Rushin. Reprinted by permission.

that is, we are either lesbians/gays or heterosexuals. Bisexuals, as a category, have added little to dislodge this position, and researchers frequently group bisexuals in the homosexual category (Garnets and Kimmel, 1991). Additionally, the almost exclusive focus on sexual acts ignores the distinctions between such things as life-style, attraction, fantasies, and identification. We may be "heterosexual" in one of these areas and "homosexual" in another. Garnets and Kimmel prefer the terms *homophilia* and *heterophilia* because they emphasize love (*philia*) and suggest that these are two parallel continuums in the individual and that we may be high in one and low in the other, high in both, or low in both. They conclude that "a complex set of factors interact, varying from individual to individual, to produce lesbian and gay adults. Likewise, the gay male and lesbian community is diverse and multiethnic and differs by gender, socioeconomic status, and few generalizations apply across cultural borders" (1991:174). Additionally, sexual orientation is not always stable. It may change over the life span. Biological, cultural, historical, and psychosocial factors influence our sexuality.

Nonetheless, lesbians (and gay men) do have different experiences than heterosexual women (and men). These are, however, more an outcome of than a contributor to being a lesbian. Lesbian and gay sexual orientation is generally established during adolescence (Table 4.4). However, we are early socialized within a culture that expects us to adhere to traditional gender roles. As women we are taught to attract and please men and aspire to wifehood and motherhood. Many lesbians want to be mothers and many are. But even as mothers, we are still defying assigned gender roles by becoming *lesbian* mothers. Thus, when we discover our attraction to women, we are aware that we deviate from societal prescriptions. We are also exposed to cultural stereotypes, fears, and rejection of our lesbianism. We stand the risk of internalizing this

Table 4.4 Modal Ages for Milestones of Lesbian and Gay Male Identity Development

Identity Development	*Age (in years)*	
	Lesbians	*Gay Men*
Initial awareness of same-gender affectional-erotic feelings	14–16	12–13
Initial same-gender sexual experience	20–22	14–15
Self-identification as lesbian or gay	21–23	19–21
Initial same-gender sexual relationship	20–24	21–24
Positive gay or lesbian identity	24–29	22–26

By Linda Garnets and Douglas Kimmel in *Psychological Perspectives on Human Diversity in America* (ed. J. D. Goodchild). Copyright © 1991 by the American Psychological Association. Adapted by permission.

homophobia and feeling ashamed and self-rejecting (Margolies et al., 1987).

Even those of us who do not internalize societal attitudes toward lesbians are still confronted with institutional and personal hostility toward us for our sexual orientation. We may be subject to hate crimes, victimization, and verbal abuse, all factors that have negative consequences to our mental health (Garnets et al., 1990; Herek, 1991). Even heterosexuals who are not overtly hostile often have stereotyped attitudes and treat us differently by avoiding contact or judging us negatively (see, for example, Kite, 1994; Rothblum, 1994; Herek, 1994). As a result, we may choose to "pass" as heterosexuals (Greene, 1994a). We may be afraid to "*come out*" to family for fear of their disappointment, rejection, and loss of support; we may avoid acknowledging our sexual orientation to friends for fear of rejection and misunderstanding; and we may hide our lesbianism at work and in the neighborhood for fear of job and housing discrimination.

Passing may be practical in that there is overt and subtle discrimination against lesbians and gays. However, *passing* puts up a barrier to intimacy and closeness between us and others, causing feelings of isolation and making it more difficult to identify a community of other lesbians for support and emotional relationships. We must pretend to be different than we are, and this can create personal identity conflicts (Greene, 1994a). "Coming out," that is, accepting a lesbian or gay male identity and revealing it to others, is related to psychological adjustment. Lesbians and gays with a positive homosexual identity have fewer depressive, neurotic, and anxious symptoms and higher self-esteem than do those with a less positive identity (Savin-Williams, 1989).

While white lesbians confront both sexism and heterosexism in our daily lives, lesbians of color face what Beverly Greene calls "triple jeopardy"—sexism, racism, and homophobia.

(1994b:391). "Just as the experience of sexism is 'colored' by the lens of race and ethnicity for women of color, so is the experience of heterosexism similarly filtered for lesbian women of color" (1994b:395). The particular meaning and value of family, gender roles, and community held by a cultural and ethnic group are imposed upon one's attitudes and responses to lesbianism. For racially oppressed groups, lesbianism may seem like a betrayal of our ethnic community. Among African Americans and Native Americans, for example, reproductive sexuality may be viewed as contributing to the survival of a group subject to racist genocide attempts (Kanuha, 1990).

Immigrant lesbians may be more dependent on their families and local ethnic community because of separation from our homelands, family members, and friends. We will have difficulty identifying lesbian communities as well as lesbians within our ethnic groups. In some ethnic minority groups, such as Asian American and Latino, lesbians may be "invisible" because of the rigidly held traditional gender role beliefs (Chan, 1989, 1992; Espin, 1987).

Beverly Greene notes:

> For lesbian women of color, like their heterosexual counterparts, family is regarded as the primary social unit and a major source of emotional and material support. Family and ethnic community, for women of color, serves an additional and important function as a refuge and buffer against the racism in the dominant culture. Separation and rejection by family and community of lesbian members is felt keenly and many women will not jeopardize their connections to them for alliances in the broader lesbian community or by divulging the fact that they are lesbian. These observations were true for Latina, African American/Caribbean, Asian American, Indian/South Asian and American Indian/Native lesbians. (1994b:391)

In spite of the negative attitudes held by the dominant culture, lesbians and gay men have adopted strategies to cope with oppression and to manage their lives and differences from the mainstream. Lesbian communities provide support and encourage a positive group and individual identity. We generally form a positive sense of self and self-esteem (Garnets and Kimmel, 1991). As a result of the feminist movement, which challenged traditional ideas about sexuality and gender, lesbianism became more visible and, increasingly, is being viewed not as abnormal but as *normatively different* (Brown, 1989).

As lesbians we are a diverse group. While we may be grouped into a category based on some limited criteria of sexuality, we are as different from one another as are heterosexual women. Lesbians have more in common with heterosexual women than they do with gay men. Some lesbians adhere to rather traditional roles and beliefs, while others explore nontraditional options. Nonetheless, our rejection of a heterosexual life-style encourages experimenting with more androgynous gender role behaviors, developing greater independence, and pursuing occupational options. Our relationships are more equal in power, decision making, and role responsibilities (see Garnets and Kimmel, 1991). The growing activism and visibility of lesbian and gay groups draws attention to our political presence and to the abuse of our civil liberties.

Older Women

Why are so many women more concerned with signs of aging than men? As this chapter and the preceding chapters have indicated, much of the theorizing we have criticized about women's personalities and behavior has been based on the assumption of biological determinism. With the loss of our reproductive and active parenting roles, Western cultures devalue our worth, an attitude which is not universal. Along with this social attitude, stereotypes of the older woman abound. We are viewed as asexual, hypochondriacal, dependent, intrusive, and, generally, in negative terms. In contrast, men are often perceived as more appealing with age (see Lott, 1987b). Sontag (1979) refers to this discrepancy as the "double standard of aging." In the United States and elsewhere, elderly women are devalued considerably more than elderly men, who gain status from experience and, perhaps, power. For women, however, the value of youth and physical attractiveness, as well as the emphasis on reproductive functioning, diminishes the respect and value granted older women. This is not universal, however. In many cultures, older women are respected, viewed as wise, consulted on community and family decisions, and allowed to participate in events barred for younger women (Grambs, 1989; Brown and Kerns, 1985).

On television older women are, with rare exceptions, shown negatively, or more often ignored. Our mood changes are attributed to what has popularly been referred to as "change of life." We may be condemned or tolerated for this change in body chemistry. Undoubtedly, negative social responses have an effect on our emotional state, but interviews with and research on older women reveal the gross distortions of the stereotypes. (See Etaugh, 1993, for a review of the literature.)

Aging may be as difficult for individuals as growing to adulthood often is, but personal responses to the process by women are usually the result of a complex set of circumstances: our physical health, our social realities, and our sense of psychological well-being. In each case, the messages we receive from our culture and those with whom we interact can make a significant difference. It is a matter of whether aging comes to mean the shutting down of possibilities or new and different opportunities for self-expression.

In fact, many older women experience the

benefits of increased self-confidence that is tied to the emotional and economic independence that comes along with paid employment. Life for many women continues to be exciting and fulfilling after the age of forty, fifty, sixty, and seventy years. These women often undertake new interests and endeavors. They may be involved more intensely in social interactions or in a number of community interests (see Lott, 1987b).

Menopausal depression refers to stress and depression women may experience during menopause. The empty nest syndrome refers to stress and depression experienced by a mother (or father, for that matter) when children grow up and leave the home, no longer requiring care. Some women do suffer emotional distress during menopause (see Chapters 3 and 12). Several psychologists have attributed this to our failure to fully accept our "feminine" role, claiming that women who do accept this role have less difficulty (Benedek, 1952; Deutsch, 1945). Others attribute depression in older women to the loss of the child-caring role—the "empty-nest syndrome" (Lowenthal, 1975). Research findings, however, throw considerable doubt on both these conclusions. Studies with menopausal and postmenopausal women indicate that most women do not view menopause as a stressful or even a very important event in our lives (Black and Hill, 1984; McKinley and Jeffries, 1974; Neugarten and Datan, 1974). Lott (1987b) quotes Rossi (1980) that "contrary to assumptions . . . menopause is rarely a crisis to women. There is more dread in the anticipation than difficulty in the experience; and, far from being upset at the loss of an important biological function, most women feel relief to have it behind them."

In fact, despite some of the discomforts of aging experienced by some older women, middle and old-age years can be more productive, invigorating, and exciting than the early-adulthood years. Often, once children are out of the home, many women find time to redefine their personal identities and to uncover abilities and strengths they had never developed. Some researchers have concluded that women in their later years have an increased sense of well-being (Brown and Kerns, 1985). Middle-aged and older women, provided that they are economically stable and in good health, report looking forward to satisfying experiences provided by work, sociability, travel, and study.

Research also provides little support for the idea that the "empty nest" causes distress in women. Indeed, research suggests that once children have left the home marital happiness increases and women experience less depression than those whose children remain at home (Anderson et al., 1983; Antonucci et al., 1980; Campbell, 1981; Radloff, 1975, 1980). In her research on depression in older hospitalized women, Pauline Bart (1971) found that women who embrace the traditional feminine role and norms are more prone to depressive reactions when their children leave. Bart concludes that the difficulty some women have during menopause results from an overinvestment in our families and the lack of alternative identities. Other research suggests that women who have developed few extrafamilial activities and interests and whose lives have been extremely child-centered are more likely to experience distress at the departure of children (Lehr, 1984).

In a cross-cultural study of women's behavioral changes at menopause, Joyce Griffen notes that in some cultures there are no associated behavioral changes; in others, postmenopausal women are granted special privileges and status; and in still others, there are negative attitudes toward menopause and associated emotional conflicts. After reviewing the literature on these cultures, Griffen suggests that "the magnitude of symptoms associated with menopause is positively correlated with the paucity of roles (or of availability of demeaning roles only) available to the postmenopausal woman" (1979:493). A study of

American women whose children had grown found the women optimistic about the years ahead. Many were pursuing new or second careers, going back to school, and trying out new endeavors. They were enjoying their newfound freedom and feeling positive about themselves (*New York Times*, 1980).

Widowhood is one of the stresses women are likely to experience in the later years. Loneliness is one of the greatest difficulties widows confront. However, this is less problematic for women who have social and familial support and social contact with friends and neighbors (Lopata et al., 1982; Rook, 1984; McGloshen and O'Bryant, 1988; Peplau et al., 1982). Research suggests that men have more difficulty dealing with the loss of their spouse than women (Stroebe and Stroebe, 1983). This may be because women are more effective in maintaining social networks. Women's acclimation to spousal loss is noteworthy in light of the fact that widowhood most often carries with it the additional burden of economic distress, which is less the case for men.

Women and men do change later in life, often becoming more alike. Research indicates that both women and men become more androgynous, demonstrating both "feminine" and "masculine" psychological characteristics. Women in the United States and other societies display more independence and assertive behavior and men demonstrate more nurturance and feelings of affiliation (Gutman, 1975, 1977). Increasing numbers of writers are depicting older women not as looking backward toward youth, but as changing, developing people who are perceiving and coping with situations in the present and planning for the future.

Summary

Women tend to be characterized by certain stereotyped psychological traits not shared by men or aspired to by them. Although views on women's traits are formulated within a certain historical and cultural context, these traits are thought of as universal, resulting from a woman's biological role. Much of the research into female and male differences is affected by the biases of the researchers. Nonetheless, there is little research substantiation for most presumed differences. When differences are found, they vary among women and within the same woman at different times and in different contexts.

Biological differences, psychodynamic theories, and socialization practices have all been used to explain why women and men differ. Strictly biological explanations refer to genetically derived factors, such as hormones, which may influence behavior and emotions.

According to psychodynamic theories, females and males develop different personality structures as a result of early-childhood experiences with their caretakers and identification with the same-sex parent. Traditional psychodynamic theory, psychoanalytic theory, founded by Sigmund Freud, proposes that sexual drives start playing a key role in gender personality development at age three. Freud attributed many developmental consequences, including a sense of inferiority, to girls' "penis envy." Males, in contrast, were said to struggle with "castration anxiety."

Freud's theories have been criticized both within and outside of psychodynamic schools of thought. Psychoanalysts Karen Horney and Clara Thompson stressed the role of socialcultural factors, such as economic and social dependency on men, in the development of a female personality and suggest that men's envy of women may account for misogyny and the oppression of women. Feminist psychodynamic explanations, such as the self-in-relations theory proposed by Jean Baker Miller or Nancy Chodorow's analysis of the impact of female caretakers on gender role development, offer alternative perspectives on female development.

Cognitive-developmental theory holds that girls and boys feel internal needs as well as external pressure to conform to a gender-appropriate identity and roles. Social learning theory gives greater weight to external factors, such as the reward of gender-appropriate behavior and the punishment of cross-gender behavior.

Sandra Bem proposes a "gender schema theory," which incorporates cognitive, child-rearing, and cultural factors in explaining the development of gender identity and roles. Other theories place greater emphasis on social roles, and explain gender-typed behavior as primarily a function of gender-differentiated role assignments and expectations and the unequal distribution of power between females and males.

All societies teach their young culturally prescribed gender roles. Parents and peers are powerful socializing agents, but gender expectations are communicated in many different ways. Television, school, books, clothing, toys, even fairy tales, all operate as socializing agents. Parents, particularly fathers, encourage different behaviors in girls and boys. Teachers have different expectations and responses to female and male students from the preschool through the postsecondary levels.

The experience of growing up in different cultures is varied. Even within the United States, socialization experiences differ among ethnic and cultural groups. Women of color in the United States confront a "double jeopardy"—racism and sexism—and these experiences contribute to their socialization.

Lesbians are subject to a range of hostile and unsubstantiated stereotypes. Lesbians are exposed to homophobic and heterosexist beliefs and discrimination and struggle with the consequences of openly acknowledging their sexual orientation. The lesbian and gay rights movements, the women's movement, and the visibility of lesbian social communities have facilitated the development of a positive lesbian identity, which is related to more positive mental health. Lesbians, freed from expectations of emotional and social dependency on men, are freer to explore nontraditional roles. Lesbian couples are more likely to have role equality in their relationships.

In Western cultures older women are devalued because of the emphasis placed on women's reproductive roles and physical attractiveness. There are many negative stereotypes about older women, such as asexuality, hypochondria, and menopausal depression. The experience of the older years is a result of many factors, including health, financial status, and support systems. For many older women, the later years are a time of increased self-confidence and new interests and activities. Both women and men tend to become more androgynous in the later years. In many cultures, older women are respected, viewed as wise, and consulted on community and family decisions.

Discussion Questions

1. List three differences between girls/women and boys/men that have been reported in research. These can be differences in personality, skills, or conduct. What kinds of contrasting explanations can you give for them? Which do you find most convincing, and why?
2. Most psychological theory tends to focus attention on the formation of personality in the younger years. What questions should be explored with regard to mature women?
3. Theories of personality development offer different explanations for gender identity and gender roles. What experiences did you have as a child that shaped your gender role behaviors and attitudes? Explain these from two or three different theoretical positions. Are they consistent with the research on gender role socialization or do they contradict it?
4. Review some popular children's fairy tales or stories, such as "Cinderella," "Jack and the Bean Stalk," and "Sleeping Beauty," and discuss how girls and boys are portrayed. How might these operate to socialize girls' and boys' attitudes and behaviors? Similarly, analyze the depiction of females and males in popular television programs. Give particular attention to the gender, ethnicity, class, and age of the characters. Are heterosexist assumptions apparent in the show?

Recommended Readings

Chodorow, Nancy. *The Reproduction of Mothering: Psychoanalysis and the Sociology of Gender.* Berkeley: University of California Press, 1978. Employing psychoanalytic principles, Chodorow develops an original thesis showing how the traditional family structure, in which women have the primary responsibility for child care and nurturing, shapes female (and male) development and results in the generational reproduction of gender roles.

Cole, Johnnetta, editor. *All American Women. Lines That Divide, Ties That Bind.* New York: The Free Press, 1986. While many bonds unite women in a sisterhood, varied political, economic, and social circumstances introduce a great diversity among women of different races, ethnicities, religions, classes, and sexualities.

Dangarembga, Tsi-tsi. *Nervous Condition.* London: Woman's Press, 1988. A deeply felt novel about the impact of sexism on the socialization of women, and of colonialism on two female cousins living in Zimbabwe (formerly Rhodesia) before the liberation.

Tannen, Deborah. *You Just Don't Understand: Women and Men in Conversation.* New York:

Ballantine Books, 1990. According to the author's argument, girls and boys grow up speaking different languages; women use a language of connection and closeness, while men speak in terms of social status and impersonal subjects.

Unger, Rhoda, and Crawford, Mary. *Women & Gender: A Feminist Psychology*. New York: McGraw-Hill, 1992. This comprehensive text applies a feminist theoretical framework to the psychology of gender. It is attentive to issues of diversity and thorough in its exploration of the issues, research, or perspectives in the field.

References

Aberle, David F., and Naegle, Kasper D. "Middle-Class Father's Occupational Role and Attitudes toward Children." *American Journal of Orthopsychiatry* 22 (1952):366–78.

Almquist, E. M. "The Experiences of Minority Women in the United States." In *Women: A Feminist Perspective*. 4th ed., edited by J. Freeman. Palo Alto, Calif.: Mayfield, 1989.

Anderson, S., Russell, C., and Schumm, W. "Perceived Marital Quality and Family Life Cycle Categories: A Further Analysis." *Journal of Marriage and the Family* 45 (1983):127–38.

Antill, J. K. "Parents' Beliefs and Values about Sex Roles, Sex Differences, and Sexuality: Their Sources and Implications." In *Sex and Gender* edited by P. Shaver and C. Hendrick. Newbury Park, Calif.: Sage, 1987.

Antonucci, T., Tamir, L. M., and Dubnoff, S. "Mental Health across the Family Life Cycle." In *Life Course: Integrative Theories and Exemplary Populations*, edited by K. W. Back. American Association for the Advancement of Science Selected Symposium No. 41. Boulder, Co.: Westview, 1980.

Anzaldúa, Gloria. *Borderlands/La Frontera: The New Mestiza*. San Francisco: Aunt Lute Books, 1987.

Bandura, Albert. "Influence of Models' Reinforcement Contingencies on the Acquisition of Imitative Responses." *Journal of Personality and Social Psychology* 1 (1965):589–95.

Bardwell, Jill R., Cochran, Samuel W., and Walker, Sharon. "Relationship of Parental Education, Race, and Gender to Sex Role Stereotyping in Five-Year-Old Kindergarteners." *Sex Roles* 15 (1986):275–81.

Bart, Pauline B. "Depression in Middle-Aged Women." In *Women in Sexist Society: Studies in Power and Powerlessness*, edited by Vivian Gornick and Barbara Moran. New York: Basic Books, 1971.

Baruch, Grace K., and Barnett, Rosalind C. "Fathers' Participation in Family Work and Children's Sex-Role Attitudes." *Child Development* 57 (1986):1210–23.

Basow, Susan A. *Gender Stereotypes and Roles*. 3rd ed. Pacific Grove, Calif.: Brooks/Cole, 1992.

Beal, Frances. "Double Jeopardy: To Be Black and Female." In *The Black Women*, edited by Toni Cade. New York: Mentor, 1970.

Bell, Derrick. "The Effects of Affirmative Action on Male-Female Relationships among African Americans." *Sex-Roles* 21 (1989):13–24.

Bem, Sandra L. "Gender Schema Theory: A Cognitive Account of Sex Typing." *Psychological Review* 88 (1981):354–64.

———. "Gender Schema Theory and its Implications for Child Development: Raising Gender-Aschematic Children in a Gender-Schematic Society." *Signs* 8 (1983):598–616.

———. "Androgyny and Gender Schema Theory: A Conceptual and Empirical Integration." In *Nebraska Symposium on Motivation, 1984: Psychology and Gender*, edited by T. B. Sonderegger. Lincoln: University of Nebraska Press, 1985.

Benedek, Therese. *Psychosexual Functions in Women*. New York: Ronald, 1952.

Betz, Nancy. "Women's Career Development." In *Psychology of Women: A Handbook of Issues and Theories*, edited by Florence L. Denmark and Michele A. Paludi. Westport, Conn.: Greenwood Press, 1993.

Bigler, R. S., and Liben, Lynn S. "The Role of Attitudes and Interventions in Gender-Schematic Processing." *Child Development* 61 (1990):1440–52.

Black, S. M., and Hill, C. E. "The Psychological Well-being of Women in their Middle Years." *Psychology of Women Quarterly* 8 (1984):282–92.

Broverman, Inge K., Vogel, Susan R., Broverman, Donald M., Clarkson, Frank E., and Rosenkrantz, Paul S. "Sex-Role Stereotypes: A Current Appraisal." *Journal of Social Issues* 28 (1972):59–78.

Brown, J. K., and Kerns, V., editors. *In Her Prime: A New View of Middle-Aged Women.* South Hadley, Mass.: Anchor Press, 1985.

Brown, Laura S. "New Voices, New Visions: Toward a Lesbian/Gay Paradigm for Psychology." *Psychology of Women* 13 (1989):445–58.

Bulkin, Elly. "Kissing/Against the Light: A Look at Lesbian Poetry." In *Lesbian Studies: Present and Past*, edited by Margaret Cruikshank. New York: Feminist Press, 1982.

Burns, A., and Homel, R. "Gender Division of Tasks by Parents and their Children." *Psychology of Women Quarterly* 13 (1989):113–25.

Caldera, Y. M., Huston, A. C., and O'Brien, M. "Social Interactions and Play Patterns of Parents and Toddlers with Feminine, Masculine, and Neutral Toys." *Child Development* 60 (1989):70–76.

Campbell, A. *The Sense of Well-Being in America.* New York: McGraw-Hill, 1981.

Canter, R. J., and Ageton, S. S. "The Epidemiology of Adolescent Sex-Role Attitudes." *Sex Roles* 11 (1984):657–76.

Carli, L. L. "Gender, Language, and Influence." *Journal of Personality and Social Psychology* 59 (1990):941–51.

Carr, Peggy G., and Mednick, Martha T. "Sex Role Socialization and the Development of Achievement Motivation in Black Preschool Children." *Sex Roles* 18 (1988):169–80.

Chan, C. S. "Issues of Identity Development among Asian American Lesbians and Gay Men." *Journal of Counseling and Development* 68:1 (1989):16–20.

———. "Cultural Considerations in Counseling Asian American Lesbians and Gay Men." In *Counseling Gay Men and Lesbians*, edited by S. Dworkin and F. Gutierrez. Alexandria, Va.: American Association for Counseling and Development, 1992.

Chodorow, Nancy. *The Reproduction of Mothering: Psychoanalysis and the Sociology of Gender.* Berkeley: University of California Press, 1978.

Chow, E. N. "The Influence of Role Identity and Occupational Attainment on the Psychological Well-being of Asian-American Women." *Psychology of Women Quarterly* 11 (1987):69–81.

Clark, Kenneth B. "Pathos of Power: A Psychological Perspective." *American Psychologist* 26 (1971):1047–57.

Colby, A., and Damon, W. "Listening to a Different Voice: A review of Gilligan's *In a different voice.*" *Merrill-Palmer Quarterly* 29 (1983):473–81.

Collins, Patricia Hill (1989). "The Social Construction of Black Feminist Thought." *Signs* 14 (1989):745–73.

Condry, J. C., and Ross, D. F. "Sex and Aggression: The Influence of Gender Label on the Perception of Aggression in Children." *Child Development* 56 (1985):225–33.

Crawford, Mary, and MacLeod, M. "Gender in the College Classroom: An Assessment of the 'Chilly Climate for Women.'" *Sex Roles* 23 (1990):101–22.

Crovitz, Elaine, and Steinmann, Anne. "A Decade Later: Black-White Attitudes Toward Women's Familial Roles." *Psychology of Women* 5 (1980):170–76.

Deaux, Kay, and Major, Brenda. "Putting Gender into Context: An Interactive Model of Gender-Related Behavior." *Psychological Review* 94 (1987):369–89.

Denmark, Florence L. "What Sigmund Freud Didn't Know About Women." Convocation Address, St. Olaf's College, Northfield, Minn. January 1977.

Denmark, Florence L., and Paludi, Michele A., editors. *Psychology of Women: A Handbook of Issues and Theories.* Westport, Conn.: Greenwood Press, 1993.

Deutsch, Helene. *The Psychology of Women.* vols. 1 and 2. New York: Grune & Stratton, 1944, 1945.

Dew, M. A. "The Effects of Attitudes on Inferences of Homosexuality and Perceived Physical Attractiveness in Women." *Sex Roles,* 12(1985):143–55.

Dill, Bonnie T. "The Dialectics of Black Womanhood." *Signs* 4 (1979):543–55.

Dinnerstein, Dorothy. *The Mermaid and the Minotaur.* New York: Harper & Row, 1976.

Eagly, Alice H. *Sex Differences in Social Behavior: A Social-Role Interpretation.* Hillsdale, N.J.: Erlbaum, 1987.

Eagly, Alice H., and Steffen, V. J. "Gender and Aggressive behavior: A Meta-Analytic Review of the Social Psychological Literature." *Psychological Bulletin* 100 (1986):309–30.

Eccles, Jacqueline S. "Bringing Young Women to Math and Science." In *Gender and Thought: Psychological Perspectives,* edited by M. Crawford and M. Gentry. New York: Springer-Verlag, 1989.

Eccles, Jacqueline S., and Hoffman, Lois W. "Socialization and the Maintenance of a Sex Segregated Labor Market." In *Research in Child Development and Social Policy* vol. 1, edited by H. W. Stevenson and A. E. Siegel. Chicago: University of Chicago Press, 1984.

Eccles, Jacqueline S., and Jacobs, J. E. "Social Forces Shape Math Attitudes and Performance." *Signs* 11:21 (1986):367–80.

Epperson, S. E. "Studies Link Subtle Sex Bias in School with Women's Behavior in the Workplace." *Wall Street Journal* (Sept. 16, 1988):27.

Erikson, Erik. *Childhood and Society.* New York: Norton, 1963.

Espin, Oliva. "Issues of Identity in the Psychology of Latina Lesbians." In *Lesbian Psychologies: Exploration and Challenges,* edited by Boston Lesbian Psychologies Collective. Urbana: University of Illinois Press, 1987.

Etaugh, Claire. "Women in the Middle and Later Years." In *Psychology of Women: A Handbook of Issues and Theories,* edited by F. L. Denmark and M. A. Paludi. Westport, Conn.: Greenwood Press, 1993.

Fagot, Beverly I. "Sex Differences in Toddlers' Behavior and Parental Reaction." *Developmental Psychology* 10 (1974):554–58.

———. "The Influence of Sex of Child on Parental Reactions to Toddler Children." *Child Development* 49 (1978):459–65.

———. "Teacher and Peer Reactions to Boys' and Girls' Play Styles." *Sex Roles* 11 (1984):691–762.

———. "A Cautionary Note: Parents' Socialization of Boys and Girls." *Sex Roles* 12 (1985):471–76.

Fagot, Beverly I., Hagan, R., Leinback, M. D., and Kronsberg, S. "Differential Reactions to Assertive and Communicative Acts of Toddler Boys and Girls." *Child Development* 56 (1985):1499–1505.

Ferree, M. M., and Hall, E. J. "Visual Images of American Society: Gender and Race in Introductory Sociology Textbooks." *Gender & Society* 4 (1990):500–533.

Filardo, Emily K. "A Comparison of the Cooperative Problem-Solving Task Interactions of Black and White Children in Mixed-Sex, Same-Ethnicity Groups." Ann Arbor, Michigan: U.M.I. Dissertation Information Service (Ph.D. Dissertation, City University of New York), 1991.

Finkelhor, D. *Child Sexual Abuse.* New York: Free Press, 1984.

Fivush, R. (1989). "Exploring Sex Differences in the Emotional Content of Mother-Child Conversations about the Past." *Sex Roles* 20 (1989):675–91.

Flax, Jane. "The Conflict between Nurturance and Autonomy in Mother-Daughter Relationships and Within Feminism." *Feminist Studies* 4 (1978):171–89.

Fliegel, Zenia. "Half a Century Later: Current Status of Freud's Controversial Views of Women." Paper presented at the American Psychological Association Conference, Montreal, Canada, 1980.

Ford, M. R., and Lowery, C. R. "Gender Differences in Moral Reasoning: A Comparison of the Use of Justice and Care Orientations." *Journal of Personality and Social Psychology* 50 (1986):777–83.

Frable, Debra E. S., and Bem, Sandra L. "If you're Gender-Schematic, All Members of the Opposite Sex Look Alike." *Journal of Personality and Social Psychology* 47 (1985):182–92.

Freeman, Jo. "How To Discriminate against Women Without Really Trying." In *Women: A Feminist Perspective.* 4th ed., edited by J. Freeman. Palo Alto, Calif.: Mayfield, 1989.

Freud, Sigmund. "Some Psychological Consequences of the Anatomical Distinction between the Sexes." *International Journal of Psychoanalysis* 8 (1925):133–43.

Fujitomi, Irene, and Wong, Diane. "The New Asian-American Woman." In *Female Psychology: The Emerging Self,* edited by Sue Cox. Chicago: Science Research Associates, 1976.

Garnets, Linda, Herek, Gregory M., and Levy, B. "Violence and Victimization of Lesbians and Gay Men: Mental Health Consequences." *Journal of Interpersonal Violence* 5 (1990):366–83.

Garnets, Linda, and Kimmel, Douglas. "Lesbian and Gay Male Dimensions in the Psychological Study of Human Diversity." In *Psychological Perspectives on Human Diversity in America,* edited by J. Goodchilds. Washington, D.C.: American Psychological Association, 1991.

Gelles, Richard J. *Family Violence.* Beverly Hills, Calif.: Sage, 1987.

Gilligan, Carol. *In a Different Voice.* Cambridge, Mass.: Harvard University Press, 1982 (Republished in 1993 with a new preface.)

Gold, D., Crombie, G., and Noble, S. "Relations between Teachers' Judgments of Girls' and Boys' Compliance and Intellectual Competence." *Sex Roles* 16 (1987):351–58.

Golding, Jacqueline M. "Division of Household Labor, Strain, and Depressive Symptoms among Mexican American and Non-Hispanic Whites." *Psychology of Women Quarterly* 14:1 (1990):103–18.

Gonzales, J. T. "Dilemmas of the High-Achieving Chicano: The Double-Bind Factor in Male-Female Relationships." *Sex Roles* 18 (1988):367–80.

Goodnow, J. J. "Children's Household Work: Its Nature and Functions." *Psychological Bulletin* 103 (1988):5–26.

Grambs, J. D. *Women Over Forty: Visions and Realities.* rev. ed. New York: Springer, 1989.

Grant, L. "Race-Gender Status, Classroom Interaction, and Children's Socialization in Elementary School." In *Gender Influences in Classroom Interaction,* edited by L. C. Wilkinson and C. B. Marrett. New York: Academic Press, 1985.

Greene, Beth, and Russo, Nancy F. "Work and Family Roles: Selected Issues." In *Psychology of Women: A Handbook of Issues and Theories,* edited by F. L. Denmark and M. A. Paludi. Westport, CT: Greenwood Press, 1993.

Greene, Beverly L. "Lesbian and Gay Sexual Orientations: Implications for Clinical Training, Practice, and Research." In *Lesbian and Gay Psychology: Theory, Research, and Clinical Applications,* edited by B. Greene and G. M. Herek. Thousand Oaks, Calif.: Sage, 1994.

———. "Lesbian Women of Color: Triple Jeopardy." In *Women of Color and Mental Health,* edited by L. Comas-Diaz and B. Greene. New York: Guilford Press, 1994.

Griffen, Joyce. "A Cross-Cultural Investigation of Behavioral Changes at Menopause." Reprinted in *Psychology of Women,* edited by Juanita Williams. New York: Norton, 1979.

Gump, Janice. "A Comparative Analysis of Black and White Women's Sex Role Attitudes." *Journal of Consulting and Clinical Psychology* 43 (1975):858–63.

———. "Sex-Role Attitudes and Psychological Well-Being." *Journal of Social Issues* 28 (1972):79–92.

———. "Reality and Myth: Employment and Sex Role Ideology in Black Women." In *The Psychology of Women: Future Directions of Research,* edited by Julia Sherman and Florence Denmark. New York: Psychological Dimension, 1978.

Gutek, Barbara. *Sex and the Workplace.* San Francisco: Jossey-Bass, 1985.

Gutman, D. L. "Parenthood, Key to Comparative Study of the Life Cycle." In *Life Span Development Psychology: Normative Life Crisis*, edited by N. Data and L. Ginsberg. New York: Academic Press, 1975.

————. "The Cross-Cultural Perspective: Notes Toward a Comparative Psychology of Aging." In *Handbook of the Psychology of Aging*, edited by J. E. Birren and K. W. Schaie. New York: Van Nostrand Reinhold, 1977.

Hale-Benson, J. E. *Black Children: Their Roots, Culture, and Learning Styles*. rev. ed. Provo, Utah: Brigham Young University Press, 1986.

Hall, Judith A., and Halberstadt, A. G. "Smiling and Gazing." In *The Psychology of Gender: Advances through Meta-analysis*, edited by J. A. Hyde and M. Linn. Baltimore, Md.: Johns Hopkins, 1986.

Hare-Mustin, Rachel T., and Marecek, Jeanne. "The Meaning of Difference: Gender Theory, Postmodernism, and Psychology." *American Psychologist* 43 (1988):455–64.

Henley, Nancy, M. *Body Politics: Power, Sex, and Nonverbal Communication*. Englewood Cliffs, N.J.: Prentice-Hall, 1977.

Herek, Gregory M. "Assessing Heterosexuals' Attitudes toward Lesbians and Gay Men: A Review of Empirical Research with the ATLG Scale." In *Lesbian and Gay Psychology: Theory, Research, and Clinical Applications*, edited by B. Greene and G. M. Herek. Thousand Oaks, Calif.: Sage, 1994.

————. "Stigma, Prejudice, and Violence against Lesbians and Gay Men." In *Homosexuality: Research Findings for Public Policy*, edited by J. C. Gonriorek and J. D. Weinrich. Newbury Park, Calif.: Sage, 1991.

Hill, M. "Child-rearing Attitudes of Black Lesbian Mothers." In *Lesbian Psychologies: Explorations and Challenges*, edited by Boston Lesbian Psychologies Collective. Urbana: University of Illinois Press, 1988.

Hood, K. E., Draper, P., Crockett, L. J. and Petersen, A. C. "The Ontogeny and Phylogeny of Sex Differences in Development: A Biopsychosocial Synthesis." In *Current Conceptions of Sex Roles and Sex Typing: Theory*

and Research, edited by D. B. Carter. New York: Praeger, 1987.

Horney, Karen. "The Flight from Womanhood." *International Journal of Psychoanalysis* 7(1926):324–339.

————. *New Ways in Psychoanalysis*. New York: Norton, 1939.

————. "On the Genesis of the Castration Complex in Women." In *Psychoanalysis and Women*, edited by Jean Baker Miller. New York: Brunner/Mazel, 1973. (Original work published in 1922.)

Huston, Althea C. "The Development of Sex-Typing: Themes from Recent Research." *Developmental Reviews* 5 (1985):1–17.

Jacklin, Carol N. (1989). "Female and Male: Issues of Gender." *American Psychologist* 44:2 (1989):127–33.

Jacklin, Carol N., DiPietro, J. A. and Maccoby, Eleanor E. "Sex-typing Behavior and Sex-typing Pressure in Child/Parent Interaction." *Archives of Sexual Behavior* 13:5 (1984):413–25.

Jones, E. E. *Ingratiation: A Social Psychological Analysis*. New York: Appleton-Century-Crofts, 1964.

Kanuha, Val. "Compounding the Triple Jeopardy: Battering in Lesbian of Color Relationships." *Women & Therapy* 9:1/2 (1990):169–83.

Katz, Phyllis A., Boggiano, Ann, and Silvern, Louise. "Theories of Female Personality." In *Psychology of Women: A Handbook of Issues and Theories*, edited by F. L. Denmark and M. A. Paludi. Westport, Conn.: Greenwood Press, 1993.

Katz, Phyllis A., and Boswell, S. "Flexibility and Traditionality in Children's Gender Roles." *Genetic, Social, and General Psychology Monographs* 112 (1986):103–47.

Kite, Mary E. "When Perceptions Meet Reality: Individual Differences in Reactions to Lesbian and Gay Men." In *Lesbian and Gay Psychology: Theory, Research, and Clinical Applications*, edited by B. Greene and G. M. Herek. Thousand Oaks, Calif.: Sage, 1994.

Kohlberg, Lawrence. "The Development of Moral Character and Ideology." In *Review of Child*

Development Research, vol. 1, edited by M. Hoffman and L. Hoffman. New York: Russell Sage, 1964.

———. "A Cognitive-Developmental Analysis of Children's Sex-Role Concepts and Attitudes." In *The Development of Sex Differences*, edited by E. E. Maccoby. Stanford, Calif.: Stanford University Press, 1966.

———. *Stages in the Development of Moral Thought and Action*. New York: Holt, Rinehart, and Winston, 1969.

Kohlberg, Lawrence, and Ullian, D. Z. "Stages in the Development of Psychosexual Concepts and Attitudes." In *Sex Differences in Behavior*, edited by R. C. Friedman, R. M. Richard, and R. L. Vande Wiele. New York: Wiley, 1974.

Kohlberg, Lawrence, and Zigler, Edward. "The Impact of Cognitive Maturity on the Development of Sex-Role Attitudes in the Years 4–8." *Genetic Psychology Monographs* 75 (1967):89–165.

Kollock, P., Blumstein, P., and Schwartz, P. "Sex and Power in Interaction: Conversational Privileges and Duties." *American Sociological Review* 50 (1985):34–46.

Kurdek, Lawrence A. "The Nature and Correlates of Relationship Quality in Gay, Lesbian, and Heterosexual Cohabiting Couples: A Test of the Individual Difference, Interdependence, and Discrepancy Models." In *Lesbian and Gay Psychology: Theory, Research, and Clinical Applications*, edited by B. Greene and G. M. Herek. Thousand Oaks, Calif.: Sage, 1994.

Ladner, Joyce. *Tomorrow's Tomorrow: The Black Woman*. New York: Doubleday, 1971.

LaFromboise, Theresa D., Heyle, Anneliese M., and Ozer, Emily J. "Changing and Diverse Roles of Women in American Indian Cultures." *Sex Roles* 22 (1990):455–76.

Lehr, W. "The Role of Women in the Family Generation Context." In *Intergenerational Relationships*, edited by V. Garms-Homolova, E. M. Hoerning, and D. Schaeffer. Lewiston, NY: C. J. Hogrefe, 1984.

Lewis, D. K. "The Black Family: Socialization and Sex Roles." *Phylon* 36: 3 (1975):221–27.

Lewis, Michael. "Parents and Children: Sex Role Development." *The School Review* 80 (1972):229–40.

Liben, Lynn S., and Signorella, Margaret L., editors. *Children's Gender Schemata*. San Francisco: Jossey-Bass, 1987.

Liss, Marcia B. *Social and Cognitive Skills: Sex Roles and Children's Play*. New York: Academic Press, 1983.

Lockheed, Marlaine E. "Sex and Social Influence: A Meta-Analysis Guided by Theory." In *Status, Relations, and Rewards*, edited by J. Berger and M. Zeldich. San Francisco: Jossey-Bass, 1985.

Lopata, H. Z., Heinemann, G. D., and Baum, J. "Loneliness: Antecedents and Coping Strategies in the Lives of Widows." In *Loneliness*, edited by L. A. Peplau and D. Perlman. New York: Wiley, 1982.

Lott, Bernice L. "Sexist Discrimination as Distancing Behavior: I. A Laboratory Demonstration." *Psychology of Women Quarterly* 13 (1987a):341–55.

———. *Women's Lives: Themes and Variations in Gender Learning*. Monterey, Calif.: Brooks/Cole, 1987b.

Lowenthal, Marjorie F. "Psychosocial Variations Across the Adult Life Course: Frontier for Research and Policy." *The Gerontologist* 15 (1975):6–12.

Lytton, H., and Romney, D. M. "Parents' Differential Socialization of Boys and Girls: A Meta-Analysis." *Psychological Bulletin* 109 (1991):267–96.

Maccoby, Eleanor E., and Jacklin, Carol N. "Gender Segregation in Childhood." In *Advances in Child Development and Behavior*. vol. 20, edited by H. W. Reese. New York: Academic Press, 1987.

MacKinnon, Catherine A. *Feminism Unmodified: Discourses on Life and Law*. Cambridge, Mass.: Harvard University Press, 1987.

Malson, M. R. "Black Women's Sex Roles: The Social Context for a New Ideology." *Journal of Social Issues* 39:3 (1983):101–13.

Margolies, Liz, Becker, Martha, and Jackson-Brewer, Karla. "Internalized Homophobia: Identifying and Treating the Oppressor

Within." In *Lesbian Psychologies: Exploration & Challenges;* edited by Boston Lesbian Psychologies Collective. Urbana: University of Illinois Press, 1987.

Martin, Carol L. "Children's Use of Gender-Related Information in Making Social Judgments." *Developmental Psychology* 25 (1989):80–88.

———. "Attitudes and Expectations about Children with Nontraditional and Traditional Gender Roles." *Sex Roles* 22 (1990):151–65.

McGloshen, T. H., and O'Bryant, S. L. "The Psychological Well-being of Older, Recent Widows." *Psychology of Women Quarterly* 12 (1988):99–116.

McHale, S. M., Bartko, W. T., Crouter, A. C., and Perry-Jenkins, M. "Children's Housework and Psychosocial Functioning: The Mediating Effects of Parents' Sex-Role Behaviors and Attitudes." *Child Development* 61 (1990):1413–26.

McKinley, S. M., and Jeffreys, M. "The Menopausal Syndrome." *British Journal of Preventive and Social Medicine* 28 (1974):108–15.

Mead, Margaret. *Coming of Age in Samoa.* 1928. New York: Morrow, 1971.

———. *Sex and Temperament in Three Primitive Societies.* New York: Morrow, 1935.

———. *Male and Female.* New York: Dell, 1949.

Miller, Jean Baker. "The Development of Women's Sense of Self." *Work in progress,* No. 12. Wellesley, Mass.: Stone Center Working Paper series, 1984.

———. *Toward a New Psychology of Women.* Boston: Beacon Press, 1986 (Originally published in 1976).

Mirikitani, Janice. "We, the Dangerous." In *Awake in the River, Poetry and Prose.* San Francisco: Isthmus Press, 1978.

Mitchell, Juliet. *Psychoanalysis and Feminism.* New York: Random House, 1974.

Money, John, and Ehrhardt, Anke. A. *Man and Woman, Boy and Girl.* Baltimore: John Hopkins University Press, 1972.

Moraga, Cherríe. "La Guera." In *This Bridge Called My Back,* edited by Cherríe Moraga and Gloria Anzaldúa. Watertown, Mass.: Persephone Press, 1981.

Neugarten, B. L., and Datan, Nancy. "The Middle Years." In *American Handbook of Psychiatry.* vol. 1, 2nd ed. Edited by S. Arieti. New York: Basic Books, 1974.

New York Times. "A New Start for Women at Midlife." December 7, 1980.

Nieto-Gomez, Anna. "Heritage of La Hembra." In *Female Psychology: The Emerging Self,* edited by Sue Cox. Chicago: Science Research Associates, 1976.

O'Brien, M., and Huston, Althea C. "Development of Sex-Typed Play in Toddlers." *Developmental Psychology* 21 (1985a):866–71.

———. "Activity Level and Sex Stereotyped Toy Choice in Toddler Boys and Girls." *Journal of Genetic Psychology* 146 (1985b):527–34.

O'Leary, Virginia. *Toward Understanding Women.* Belmont, Calif.: Brooks/Cole, 1977.

Parsons, Talcott. "The Social Structure of the Family." In *The Family: Its Function and Destiny,* edited by R. N. Ashen. rev. ed. New York: Harper, 1959.

Parsons, Talcott, and Bales, Robert. *Family Socialization and Interaction Process.* New York: Free Press, 1955.

Patterson, Charlotte J. "Children of the Lesbian Baby Boom: Behavioral Adjustment, Self-Concepts, and Sex Role Identity." In *Lesbian and Gay Psychology: Theory, Research, and Clinical Applications,* edited by B. Greene and G. M. Herek. Thousand Oaks, Calif.: Sage, 1994.

Peplau, Letitia A., Bikson, T. K., Rook, K. S., and Goodchilds, J. D. "Being Old and Living Alone." In *Loneliness,* edited by L. A. Peplau and D. Perlman. New York: Wiley, 1982.

Perry, D. G., White, A. J., and Perry, L. C. "Does Early Sex-Typing Result from Children's Attempts to Match their Behavior to Sex Role Stereotypes?" *Child Development* 55 (1984):2114–21.

Radloff, Lenore S. "Depression and the Empty Nest." *Sex Roles* 6 (1980):775–82.

———. "Sex Differences in Depression: The Effects of Occupation and Marital Status." *Sex Roles* 1 (1975):249–65.

Reid, Pamela T., and Paludi, Michele A. "Developmental Psychology of Women: Conception to Adolescence." In *Psychology of Women: A Handbook of Issues and Theories*, edited by F. L. Denmark and M. A. Paludi. Westport, Conn.: Greenwood Press, 1993.

Rich, Adrienne. *Poems: Selected and New 1950–1974*. New York: Norton, 1975.

Rook, K. S. "The Negative Side of Social Interaction: Impact on Psychological Well-being." *Journal of Personality and Social Psychology* 46 (1984):1097–1108.

Rose, R. M., Gordon, T. P., and Berstein, I. S. "Plasma Testosterone Levels in the Male Rhesus: Influences of Sexual and Social Stimuli." *Science* 178 (1972):643–45.

Ross, S. I., and Jackson, J. M. "Teachers' Expectations for Black Males' and Black Females' Academic Achievement." *Personality and Social Psychology Bulletin* 17 (1991):78–82.

Rossi, Alice S. "Aging and Parenthood in the Middle Years." In *Life-Span Development and Behavior*. vol. 3, edited by P. B. Baltes and O. G. Brim, Jr. New York: Academic Press, 1980.

Rothblum, Esther D. "Lesbian and Physical Appearance: Which Model Applies?" In *Lesbian and Gay Psychology: Theory, Research, and Clinical Applications*, edited by B. Greene and G. M. Herek. Thousand Oaks, Calif.: Sage, 1994.

Rubin, J. S., Provenzano, F. J., and Luria, Z. "The Eye of the Beholder: Parents' Views on Sex of Newborns." *American Journal of Orthopsychiatry* (1974):353–63.

Ruble, D. N. "Sex-Role Development." In *Developmental Psychology: An Advanced Textbook*, edited by M. H. Bornstein and M. E. Lamb. Hillsdale, N.J.: Erlbaum, 1988.

Ruble, Thomas L. "Sex Stereotypes: Issues of Change in the 1970s." *Sex Roles* 9 (1983):397–402.

Rushin, Donna K. "The Bridge Poem." In *This Bridge Called My Back*, edited by Cherríe Moraga and Gloria Anzaldúa. Watertown, Mass.: Persephone Press, 1981.

Sadker, M., and Sadker, D. "Sexism in the Classroom: From Grade School to Graduate School." *Phi Delta Kappan* (March 1986):512–13.

Savin-Williams. "Coming Out to Parents and Self-Esteem among Gay and Lesbian Youth." *Journal of Homosexuality* 18 (1989):1–35.

Schau, C. G., and Scott, K. P. "Impact of Gender Characteristics of Instructional Materials: An Integration of the Research Literature." *Journal of Educational Psychology* 76 (1984):183–93.

Seavey, Carol A., Katz, Phyllis A., and Zalk, Sue R. "Baby X: The Effect of Gender Labels on Adult Responses to Infants." *Sex Roles* I (1975):103–9.

Silvern, Louise, and Katz, Phyllis A. "Gender Roles and Adjustment in Elementary-School Children: A Multidimensional Approach." *Sex Roles* 14 (3/4) (1986):181–202.

Smith, Patricia A., and Midlarsky, Elizabeth. "Empirically Derived Conceptions of Femaleness and Maleness: A Current View." *Sex Roles* 12 (1985):313–28.

Sontag, S. "The Double Standard of Aging." In *Psychology of Women: Selected Readings*, edited by J. H. Williams. New York: Norton, 1979.

Statham, A., Richardson, L., and Cook, J. A. *Gender and University Teaching: A Negotiated Difference*. Albany: State University of New York, 1991.

Strickland, Bonnie R. "Sex-Related Differences in Health and Illness." *Psychology of Women Quarterly* 12 (1988):381–99.

Stroebe, M. S., and Stroebe, W. (1983). "Who Suffers More: Sex Differences in Health Risks of the Widowed." *Psychological Bulletin* 93 (1983):279–301.

Thompson, Clara. "Cultural Pressures in the Psychology of Women." *Psychiatry* 5 (1942):331–39.

———. "Penis Envy in Women." *Psychiatry* 6 (1943):123–25.

Troncik, E. Z., and Cohn, J. F. "Infant-Mother Face-to-Face Interaction: Age and Gender Differences in Coordination and the Occurrence of Miscoordination." *Child Development* 60 (1989):85–92.

Tronto, Joan. *Moral Boundaries: A Political Argument for an Ethic of Care*. New York: Routledge, 1993.

Turner, Castellano B., and Turner, Barbara F. "Perception of the Occupational Opportunity Structure, Socialization to Achievement and Career Orientation as Related to Sex and Race." Paper presented at the American Psychological Association annual conference, Washington, D.C., 1971.

Unger, Rhoda. "Imperfect Reflections of Reality: Psychology Constructs Gender." In *Making A Difference: Psychology and the Construction of Gender*, edited by Hare-Mustin, Rachel and Marecek, Jeanne. New Haven: Yale University Press, 1990.

———. "The Politics of Gender: A Review of Relevant Literature." In *Psychology of Women: Future Directions of Research*, edited by J. Sherman and F. Denmark. New York: Psychological Dimensions, 1978.

Weisner, T. S., and Wilson-Mitchell, J. E. "Nonconventional Family Life-Styles and Sex Typing in 6-Year-Olds." *Child Development* 61 (1990):1915–33.

Weitzman, N., Birns, B., and Friend, R. "Traditional and Nontraditional Mothers' Communication with their Daughters and Sons." *Child Development* 56 (1985):894–98.

West, Candace, and Zimmerman, Don H. "Small Insults: A Study of Interruptions in Conversations between Unacquainted Persons." In *Language, Gender and Society*, edited by B. Thorne, C. Kramarae, and N. Henley. Rowley, Mass.: Newbury House, 1983.

———. "Doing Gender." *Gender and Society* 1:2 (1987):125–51.

Whiting, B. B., and Edwards, C. P. *Children of Different Worlds: The Formation of Social Behavior*. Cambridge Mass.: Harvard University Press, 1988.

Wilkinson, Louise C., and Marrett, C. B., eds. *Gender Influences in Classroom Interaction*. New York: Academic Press, 1985.

Zalk, Sue R. "The Re-emergence of Psychosexual Conflicts in Expectant Fathers." In *Pregnancy, Birthing, and Bonding*, edited by Barbara Blum. New York: Human Science Press, 1980.

———. "Women's Dilemma: Both Envied and Subjugated." Paper presented at the Third International Interdisciplinary Congress on Women, Trinity College, Dublin, Ireland, 1987.

Social Roles: Gender, Race, and Class

Small children, aged three and four years, play out some of the principal roles in their societies in make-believe games. "I'll be the mommy, you be the daddy," for playing "house," or "teacher" and "student," for a "school" game, or "doctor" and "nurse," and so on. Children playing these games have learned to associate a set of appropriate kinds of behavior with named social positions; more often than not, they also associate these roles not only with hierarchical positions of authority and subordination but also with gender. "Mommy" is a feminine role, and "daddy" is a masculine one. While they know that there is scope for individual creativity in acting out roles, each role is "scripted," constrained by expectations and patterned to mesh with the corresponding roles of others. Children are often eager to try out these roles in play; they are learning to conduct themselves according to social roles they have observed.

Social Roles and the Individual

The ways that human beings interact with one another are shaped by the roles they play vis-à-vis one another. A role consists of a set of rules or guidelines for conduct by an individual in relation to others. These rules or guidelines set the basis for what an individual play-ing a role is expected or required to do and what is not expected or is forbidden. All socially prescribed conduct is organized in terms of roles. Roles may be familial (mother, daughter) or occupational (plumber, teacher, salesperson, office manager), or relate to some other social context (citizen, religious figure, hostess).

The Determinants of Role Assignment

Gender. Individuals are assigned to play specific roles by the societies in which they live and work. In most societies, most of the roles we play are assigned to us on the basis not of our own choice but on the basis of supposed attributes we possess by virtue of membership in some social category or another. For example, women are assigned the roles of "wife" and "mother" (however these are defined by society) by virtue of their being female. In most cases, being female means being expected eventually to take on the roles of being wife and mother; girls are generally taught these roles as part of their upbringing. In most societies, for most of human history, women have not been given the option of rejecting these roles or opting for a change in how they are defined.

What roles one is expected to fill in society generally depend on gender and, in more

From an early age, girls work longer and have less leisure than boys. Here a girl in Colombia, South America, carries firewood. (*Save the Children.* Photo by Andy Mollo)

complex societies, ethnicity or race and class. Which roles one is forbidden to fill or discouraged from filling also depend on these social categories. In most societies, a woman is forbidden to play the role of husband, simply because she is socially classified as female. This classification, and other social restrictions, also make it less likely that she will play other roles, such as judge or ruler or chief executive officer of a corporation.

Any one person may play a multiplicity of roles in a lifetime, often changing roles as she or he matures or otherwise changes social position. Thus, a woman may be a daughter at the outset of her life—and retain this role (in changing form) all her life, but also take on the roles of sister, wife, mother, and grandmother as well. Each of these roles has its guidelines or behavioral requirements and re-

strictions, sometimes conflicting with one another. In complex societies, many other roles may be piled on to these: a sister, wife, and mother may also be an office manager, a community representative, a church officer. She may also at times be a hostess, a complainant in a court case, a volunteer health worker, and, if she has time, a lover. Some of these roles, in some societies or at some times, have been deemed mutually exclusive. Being a wife and mother, for example, have been considered in some societies in some social classes as excluding, as appropriate roles, wage-earning and social leadership; being a husband and father, on the other hand, have not been deemed as conflicting with such roles.

The roles to which people are assigned on the basis of such attributes as gender and age are associated with social status. Social status is an expression of our rights and entitlements with regard to one another, our social standing in a hierarchy of social positions. We play certain roles because of the status to which we are assigned, and we are assigned to a status because of the value that society places on our roles. Our status is reflected in the privileges that society bestows on us or deprives us of. Being a chief executive officer of a large corporation, for example, is a high-status occupation in the United States and entitles the person who plays this role to a high salary, which in turn brings with it the likelihood that the role player will be able to own a large, comfortable residence, take luxurious vacations, and employ workers to perform a variety of domestic tasks. Being a domestic worker, by contrast, is a low-status occupation that entitles the person playing this role to a low salary, which denies the role player the opportunity to own a large, comfortable home, take luxurious vacations, or employ anyone at all. Because of other role assignments and their statuses, it is more likely that the chief executive officer will be a man than a woman, and more likely that the domestic worker will be a woman than a man.

Race and Class. However, gender and age are not the sole determinants of who becomes a chief and who becomes a servant. In complex societies, other social categorizations intersect with gender and age to determine which roles are open to and expected of individuals and which are denied or discouraged. Most common among these restricting categorizations are class, "race," caste, ethnicity, and religious affiliation, and these often intersect.

Generally, these categorizations are hierarchically arranged, so that membership in such a group entitles one or denies one entitlement to filling roles of one social status or another—that is, the social categories are the basis of discrimination. Membership in a dominant group tends to entitle one to as-

sumption of certain privileged roles that are denied to members of a subordinate group, while freeing one from undesirable roles that are assigned to members of the subordinate group. Thus, the person holding the position of chief executive officer of a corporation is not only likely to be male, but in the United States is also likely to be white; his domestic employee, on the other hand, is likely to be a woman of color.

However, and this is a very important point, if the chief executive officer is a white male, his wife is also likely to be white; even though she is female, she is likely to experience the privileges of his high status by virtue of being his wife, despite the fact that her femaleness and role as wife make it unlikely that she herself will be a chief executive officer in his corporation. Her membership in the category of "white people" makes it more likely that she will play the role of the wife of a chief executive officer than will a woman of color. (Of course, only a very few white women play this role and, conversely, some women of color play it as well—we are speaking here only of probabilities.)

Postmodern Perspectives. Such differences resulting from the assignment of roles and status to members of society on the basis of attributes other than gender add major complexities to our understanding of the social meaning of gender itself. Is it possible to generalize about gender attributes and experiences across class, ethnic, racial, religious, and other social categories? How different are the roles we play, our perceptions of the world, our experiences? What are the implications of our differences for our understanding of women's circumstances now and through history?

Postmodernist perspectives in feminist theory draw our attention to the importance of difference (Tong, 1989; see Chapter 2 of this textbook). Proponents of a postmodern feminist view, such as French writer Julia Kristeva, argue that there is no "essential woman," but rather a multiplicity of experiences that reflect the greatly diverse positions women have held by virtue of attributes other than gender. To be a French lesbian feminist of the intellectual elite in Paris of 1993 is quite a different experience from that of a rural Ugandan landless mother of six, for example. To make a generalization that would comprehend the two *as women* would be fairly meaningless.

While feminist theorists have deplored the misrepresentation of women in literary and scholarly works because the majority of writing about women has been done by men, postmodernist scholars also point out that in recent years most of the writing about women has been done by women who are more like French lesbian urban intellectuals than rural Ugandan landless mothers. Consequently, the argument goes, the lens through which women are seen and portrayed is still likely to be distorted, until we recognize the importance that *difference* of experience makes for understanding what is actually going on.

The most extreme version of this argument would claim that we can only see the world through our own experience, but cannot, and should not (because it is presumptuous) attempt to generalize about the experience of all women (or men). Carried to its logical conclusions, this would suggest that we can only understand, only write about, ourselves as individuals. A more moderate view would hold that we *can* attempt to understand others but need to learn from *them* how they understand themselves rather than interpret their experiences for them.

In this chapter, we explore the different roles women have been assigned by virtue of being women, and how these roles have varied with other social attributes, such as membership in specific racial, ethnic, class, and other social categories. In examining these social roles, we attempt to pay close attention to the descriptions of the experience of being placed in these categories by members of these groups wherever possible. In recent years, feminist scholars have devoted a great deal of attention to discovering ways to describe the interplay among social categorizations as they affect women's self-image and self-esteem as well as the way they link into systems of discrimination and inequality (for example: Brewer, 1989, 1991; Carby, 1985; Cole, 1986; Davis, 1981; Dill, 1983; Eisenstein and Jardine, 1980; Frye, 1983; Hammonds, 1986; Haraway, 1989; hooks, 1982; Hull et al., 1982; Joseph and Lewis, 1981; Lorde, 1984; Lugones and Spelman, 1983; Minh-ha, 1987; Okazawa-Rey et al., 1986; and Spelman, 1988).

Social Roles and Social Stereotypes

Stereotyping prevents us from seeing people. Stereotyping means reacting to people on the basis of our expectations of what they are like, without actually knowing them as individuals. Negative stereotypes are usually caricatures, broad characterizations that emphasize a negative valuation of gender, race, class, and other labels. Stock characters based on such assumptions include the "dumb blonde," the "lazy black," the "scheming Jew," the "aggressive dyke," and the "nagging mother-in-law." The expectations people have, based on common stereotypes, are reflected in day-to-day interactions. United States Supreme Court Associate Justice Sandra Day O'Connor has remarked that when she first went job hunting, the personnel offices of the legal firms she approached assumed she was seeking a job in the secretarial pool, rather than a position as a lawyer.

The Social Construction of Gender

According to current usage, "sex" refers to biological distinction related to reproductive organs, whereas "gender" refers to social roles and characteristics assigned on the basis of presumed sexual difference. In the biological sense, a "woman" ordinarily is a person whose chromosomes (see Chapter 3), internal and external sexual organs, and hormonal chemistry mesh in such a way as to warrant the label "female" at birth. The biological "woman" is a human being generally capable in various phases of life of menstruating, gestating, and lactating, though physical appearance (breasts, external genitalia) is commonly used for assignment of a person to the biological category "woman." The rich variety of social arrangements that exist in the world, however, suggests that biological sex alone cannot explain the differing gender roles assigned in

Storekeepers in Egypt. Women from poorer economic classes have always worked, at home and outside, all over the world. Contrary to established conventions, especially in some Muslim countries, that "a woman's place is at home," these three women have installed a small enterprise, a grocery store, an activity more often perceived to be in the domain of men. (CARE)

these societies. Beyond a biological core, a "woman" in the social sense is a great many other things, depending on the society in which she finds herself. In this sense, a "woman" is a social construct.

Even though many women never marry, bear children, or nurse them, we are socially defined by our capacity to do so and by the *social expectation* that this capacity is a basic characteristic of our existence. What this means, of course, varies from context to context. In some West African societies, a wife and mother was traditionally expected to provide food for herself and her children by gardening her own land; in some Middle Eastern Islamic societies, by contrast, women of childbearing age were required to live in such seclusion that farming for themselves was out of the question.

Social definitions of "women" include many physical, psychological, and behavioral characteristics, the sum of which, for any society, represents the gender label "woman" for that group. Since every society makes a gender assignment at birth, an infant is immediately heir to all these social expectations. Essential to the construction of gender is the notion of polarity: There are only two genders (with some rare cultural exceptions) and each is the "opposite" of the other. Thus, boys and girls, men and women, are each defined in terms of what the other is not.

Socialization of children consists of introducing them to the rules or norms of behav-

Woman spinning and weaving. From this early fourteenth-century book illustration we have a sense of the ages-old assignment to women in the Western world for the care of such domestic needs as the clothing of the family. Other cultures, as in many of the countries of North Africa, may assign to men the tasks of sewing, tailoring, and clothing making. (MS Cod. gall. 16 folio 20x, Bayerische Staatsbibliothek, Munich)

ior, the social expectations by which they can make sense of how others act toward them and how they should, in turn, behave. The extent to which women and men conform, even partially, to the stereotypes of gender-appropriate behavior depends in part upon their successful socialization, the degree to which they have internalized the cultural pressures to conform.

The social structure, which defines gender-appropriate behavior, is composed of a pattern of values, beliefs, and customs *embedded in a specific material way of life*. As these variables change through time, the social norms within societies also change. The social roles and behavior of women in any society represent some measure of change over past time. Yet, there can be a lag between changes of behavior and changes of values or expectations. For example, since World War II in the United States, white middle-class mothers of ever-younger children have increasingly held jobs outside the home, yet continue to experience cultural "norms" that create daily stress. We may feel guilty about leaving our children in the care of strangers, and may daily confront a community that still does not accommodate working mothers. Only a few years ago, parents in Shaker Heights, Ohio, held public demonstrations to oblige the school board to accommodate children who could not go home for lunch every day, where they were

Young girls planting trees in Niger, Africa: Another example of the way gender assignment of jobs changes with culture, class, and race. (CARE)

sent on the assumption that their mothers would be there to feed them. Meetings of the parent-teachers association continued to be held at 9:00 A.M., however, on the assumption that mothers would be available to attend. On the other hand, employers also have not recognized the parental responsibilities of workers. Parental leave is a recent and far from universal phenomenon (see Chapter 13), and accommodations are rarely made for the long period after infancy when parents are still expected to be available to take children to pediatricians and dentists and to attend parent-teacher conferences. The less status the job, the more difficult it may be to make such arrangements.

Whether or not we are wives or mothers, women who pursue jobs or activities whose pattern of behavior has traditionally been defined by men experience daily conflict between the male-defined norms of that activity and the social roles expected of us as women. Being "women" automatically sets boundaries on our range of acceptable behavior and activity, creating tension for those who seek to combine different sets of roles traditionally divided along gender lines.

As women we experience social restrictions regarding education, choice of work, mobility, forms of cultural expression, and political participation. We also face social controls over our health and whether we may—or must—have children. These social controls limit our choices from the moment of our birth and affect the range of our individual autonomy and self-expression. They govern our social reali-

---

The Social Construction of Gender

Gender is a socially imposed division of the sexes. It is a product of the social relations of sexuality. Kinship systems rest upon marriage. They therefore transform males and females into "men" and "women," each an incomplete half which can only find wholeness when united with the other. Men and women are, of course, different. But they are not as different as day and night, earth and sky, yin and yang, life and death. In fact, from the standpoint of nature, men and women are closer to each other than either is to anything else—for instance, mountains, kangaroos, or coconut palms. The idea that men and women are more different from one another than either is from anything else must come from somewhere other than nature. Furthermore, although there is an average difference between males and females on a variety of traits, the range of variation of those traits shows considerable overlap. There will always be some women who are taller than some men, for instance, even though men are on the average taller than women. But the idea that men and women are two mutually exclusive categories must arise out of something other than a nonexistent "natural" opposition. Far from being an expression of natural differences, exclusive gender identity is the suppression of natural similarities. It requires repression: in men, of whatever is the local version of "feminine" traits; in women, of the local definition of "masculine" traits. The division of the sexes has the effect of repressing some of the personality characteristics of virtually everyone, men and women. The same social system which oppresses women in its relations of exchange, oppresses everyone in its insistence upon a rigid division of personality.
(Rubin, 1975:179–80)

ties as women. We take our reality from a variety of identities—culturally imposed and individually claimed—connected with the various social constructions we call "gender," "race," "ethnicity," and "class," as well as our age, our religion, our personal sexual orientation, and the physical abilities and disabilities we may have had from birth or may have developed thereafter. Our decisions to accept or resist particular social assignments or to give priority to one or another of them at different times depend on circumstances, political needs, and strategies for making change. The multiplicity of social expectations attached to the gender label "woman" from birth exposes us to all the positive and negative assumptions, and the resulting stereotypes, that we will have to deal with in forming an image of ourselves—for ourselves and for others.

Race

"Race," like sex and gender, is a social construct, and one that has differed over historical time and place. Although the term assumes the inheritance of biological characteristics that determine either conduct or capability as well as identifiable physical characteristics (nose shape, eye form, skin color, stature), the relationship between racial labels and biological reality is generally weak at best. The term has often been used to designate what we might otherwise call "ethnic," or "religious," or "national" categories ("the Irish race" or "the Jewish race" or "the French race"), which include people of a broad range of physical characteristics. "Race" has also been used for presumed biological groups ("Asians," "Pacific Islanders," or "African Americans"), whose genetic roots are extremely diverse and combined with those of other, presumably separate groups. The assignment of a racial label to a group of people, in other words, is in the biological sense, fairly

arbitrary, and has its roots in society rather than in biological reality.

In the United States, this arbitrariness becomes particularly clear when we attempt to define, for official purposes, what it means to be "Native American," "African American," "Asian American," or "Hispanic American." We must ask, how many of our ancestors, in what proportions, and how far back do we trace them, to determine into which category we may, or must, place ourselves. In the case of Native Americans, we may need to seek documentation that a single grandparent was a member of a certain tribe or nation, to be entitled to membership in that group. Until recently, having a single African American great-grandparent was sufficient to place a descendant in the category "African American." For many Latinas and Latinos in the United States, having a Hispanic surname is both necessary and sufficient to place one in the official category "Hispanic," whatever its advantages or disadvantages; like members of the other racial categories, people carrying the label "Hispanic" may have light or dark hair, round or almond-shaped eyes, and darker or lighter skin.

Race (now that we have established its arbitrariness as a term, we will drop the quotation marks) is a social construction that has developed in order to serve social purposes. Context is critical to consciousness, and consciousness takes its meaning from history.

The condition of slavery, for example, which circumscribed the experience of African Americans for over a century, has taken its toll on the lives of some four generations and shaped indelibly the consciousness of those who descended from them. The conditions of social and economic life experienced by freed slaves after 1865, the hierarchies of a rural, sharecropping world, and the harsh conditions of employment that confronted those who migrated to urban areas of the South and North of the United States, created the cir-

The Complexities of Labeling

Not all Third World women are "women of color"—if by this concept we mean exclusively "nonwhite." I am only one example. And not all women of color are really Third World—if this term is only used in reference to underdeveloped or developing societies (especially those not allied with any superpower). Clearly then it would be difficult to justify referring to Japanese women, who are women of color, as Third World women. Yet, if we extend the concept of Third World to include internally "colonized" racial and ethnic minority groups in this country, so many different kinds of groups could be conceivably included that the crucial issue of social and institutional racism and its historic tie to slavery in the United States could get diluted, lost in the shuffle. . . .

I don't know what to think anymore. Things begin to get even more complicated when I begin to consider that many of us who identify as "Third World" or "women of color," have grown up as or are fast becoming "middle-class" and highly educated, and therefore more privileged than many of our white, poor and working-class sisters.

(Quintanales, 1983:151)

cumstances that continue to shape race consciousness among both African Americans and those with whom they interact.

To be an African American woman in a northeastern city in the United States today means confronting a set of cultural prejudices. And yet an African American woman in this context who is a recent immigrant from the Caribbean has a different set of historical and personal roots to bring to her identification with race than those whose forebears migrated north two or three generations ago (Jones, 1985). A white woman growing up in the South (Pratt, 1984) may have a different consciousness of race from one who grows up in Maine or Minnesota, although modern mass media have tended to obscure these differences. She will certainly have a different consciousness of being "white" from an Italian woman who comes to live in the United States (de Lauretis, 1986). An Asian American woman, depending upon her country of origin and circumstances of her parents' or grandparents' migration to the United States, similarly has varying personal understandings of

race; the perceptions of the world of a Vietnamese bride brought to the United States by her American soldier-husband in 1968 may be expected to be different from a second-generation Chinese American woman. Consciousness of difference as a part of coming of age in America is explored by Chinese American authors Maxine Hong Kingston in *The Woman Warrior* (1976) and Amy Tan in *The Joy Luck Club* (1989) and *The Kitchen God's Wife* (1991). Paule Marshal's *Brown Girl, Brown Stones* (1981) is a classic story of growing up West Indian in Brooklyn with a consciousness of race, gender, and class.

Ethnicity

Just as "race" as a classificatory system is fairly arbitrary, the difference between "race" and "ethnicity" is also fairly arbitrary. The distinctions of ethnicity are subtler; ethnic identity generally refers to a constellation of cultural traits, sometimes (especially in the past) termed "nationality." Ethnically aware groups themselves have a history that changes over time (Mullings, 1978). There is a great variety of ethnicity among African Americans, Native North American Indians, Asian Americans, Latinas/Latinos, as well as groups today designated as "white."

In fact, most people designated on official forms as "white" in the United States actually think of themselves as "Irish," or "Armenian," or "Norwegian" or "Greek" or "Cajun" or "Jewish" or a mixture of two or more ethnicities, depending on the ethnic origins of their parents. Major American cities have neighborhoods designated not as "white" but in ethnic terms—like "Polish" or "Italian" (often called "little Italy"). "White" becomes a racial-ethnic category only in dualistic opposition to "people of color," and an identity imposed in some sense from outside the group. It is a category that often obscures what is felt by its members to be their own identity as differentiated by other significant categories of ethnicity. "White," in other words, covers at least as diverse an ethnic conglomeration as the term "Latina/Latino," a label used in the United States for a heterogeneous group that includes Puerto Ricans, Mexicans, Cubans, Colombians, and Dominicans, among many others. Thus, just as the case with women designated as "white," and "Asian American," and "African American," it is difficult simply to generalize about the experiences and identity of women designated as "Latinas." There has also developed a movement among students, especially in California, to claim with pride their mixed heritage, as African Americans and Chicanas or Chicanas and Native Americans or Asian Americans and African Americans. They want recognition for their mixed identities, and have protested official designation as one or another group. The experiences of growing up within these dual and sometimes triple cultural inheritances make clear the problem of trying to generalize on the basis of labels.

Understanding Contextual Difference

The dualistic thinking of earlier years of Women's Studies and the women's movement—"women" and "men" as single meaningful categories—has given way to greater complexity of analysis and greater appreciation of diversity. In part, this new effort arises from intellectual critiques that include "deconstructionist" theories that demand that we reexamine our use of the concept "woman" (see above and Chapter 2). In part, the change is inspired by political forces within the women's movement and within the world itself, which have precipitated this shift in understanding. Current feminist thought acknowledges that, as in the past, the dominant discourse of any society sends out powerful messages about the *ideals* of "femininity" and "womanhood." Such ideologies have set up archetypes of beauty and behavior that not only do not conform to the historical experience of many within the dominant group but also exclude absolutely the realities of oppressed women who are exploited by the power of the dominant group. This has never been expressed more clearly than in Sojourner Truth's classic statement, "Ain't I a Woman?" She demonstrates that the dominant culture's description of frail womanhood could not be applied to the reality of her life as an African American former slave, nor was it intended to. She laid claim to her own womanhood in terms of her experiences (White, 1985).

An understanding of difference begins with an examination of the specific context in which difference operates and how differences change over time, place, and circumstances. Histories of slavery and lynching for African Americans, genocide for Native North American Indians, and military conquest for Mexican Americans and Puerto Ricans, for example, serve as contexts for understanding these groups. As Deborah K. King reminds us, how-

"Ain't I a Woman?"

Sojourner Truth (1795–1883) was born a slave in New York State and freed in 1827 when all slaves in that state were emancipated. She became a domestic worker. She then became an evangelist and, in her late forties, an active abolitionist. In 1851, at a women's rights convention in Ohio, she spoke out against male delegates who warned women that we were going beyond our true natures when we wished to participate in the world of men.

That man over there says that women need to be helped into carriages and lifted over ditches, and to have the best place everywhere. Nobody ever helps me into carriages or over mud-puddles, or gives me any best place! And ain't I a woman? Look at me! I have ploughed and planted, and gathered into barns, and no man could head me! And ain't I a woman? I could work as much and eat as much as a man—when I could get it—and bear the lash as well! And ain't I a woman? I have borne thirteen children, and seen most all sold off to slavery, and when I cried out with my mother's grief, none but Jesus heard me! And ain't I a woman?

(Schneir, 1972:94–95)

ever, understanding the overall experience of a group has not specifically told us of the nature of women's experiences within the group, "the physical abuse, social discrimination, and cultural denigration suffered by women" (King, 1988:45). We need to seek in the histories of racial and ethnic groups the gendered meaning of their experiences to ask: What did these circumstances mean for social roles?

For example, after slavery, African American women assumed powerful leadership roles within their communities, founding schools and churches, organizing unions, and establishing commercial enterprises. We also played leading roles in struggles for racial justice: women such as Harriet Tubman who organized an underground railway for runaway slaves before the Civil War; Ida Wells Barnett who led an antilynching crusade in the early twentieth century; Rosa Parks, who precipitated the antisegregation Montgomery bus boycott in 1955; and Fannie Lou Hamer and Ella Baker who played pivotal roles in the 1960s civil rights movement. Nineteenth-century writers like Anna Julia Cooper and

Frances Watkins Harper and more recent twentieth-century writers such as Paule Marshall, Audre Lorde, and Angela Davis have sought to define broad educational and political roles for African American womanhood. An understanding of the roles these particular women have played in American history requires an understanding of the context in which they have acted, spoken, and written (Collins, 1986, 1991).

Our roles in society depend not only on traits attributed to us, but *on the way we claim an identity*, and that in turn depends on the social, economic, political, and historical contexts of our lives. Racial and ethnic groups have histories, and the extent to which we are aware of them determines how much we claim from them in asserting our identities. When we try to understand how diverse women claim our own histories, we have to learn both about those histories and the experience of the women who lived them. A virtual explosion of literature by women since the 1970s—novels, autobiographical accounts, analyses of our heritages—and rediscovery and republication of earlier literature have supplied the voices of some of these women.

One very striking example of the emergence of a substantial literature illustrating our differences is by and about Native North American Indian women. The peoples represented in this literature are enormously diverse, from the Arctic North to the Southern woodlands, from the deserts of the Southwest to the urban concentrations of both coasts. The quality of life described varies immensely in its texture, reflecting local environments and significant historical differences of custom and belief and aesthetic. Even so, common themes are derived from certain common experiences of oppression, specifically those related to the experiences of conquest, decimation, dislocation, adjustment, and resistance (Allen, 1989). One common theme is the problem of remembering and holding on to the traditions—knowledge, belief, ritual—of the past, in the face of the loss of hundreds of thousands of people to war and disease with the coming of European conquerors and colonists. Stories are told of how Native American women secretly sustain traditions and lovingly pass them on, one generation to the next. A second, related theme is that of the abduction of children, forced to live in boarding schools to learn "European" religion and cultural values, humiliated out of speaking their own languages and observing their own religious practices. Separation, loss of parents and children, loneliness of isolation from one's kin are central themes of this literature. Yet another important theme is resistance, not only through insistent memory of customs, but through recounting the actual history of struggle, those who fought back. Finally, it is important to understand the continuity, the ties between pre-Conquest, post-Conquest, and the present. Paula Gunn Allen's anthology *Spider Woman's Granddaughters* (1989) illustrates these themes.

Like the experiences of Native North American Indian women, those of Asian American women are extremely diverse: Histories and homelands and experiences in the United States are very far from uniform. *Making Waves: An Anthology of Writings by and about Asian American Women* (Mazumdar, 1989) suggests great diversity in selections about women of Chinese, Japanese, Philippine, Indian, Korean, Southeast Asian, and other Asian American origins. The experiences recounted make us aware of the differences between those who came long ago and those who arrived more recently; those who lived in cities and those who went to rural areas; those who were poor and worked as migrant farmworkers or urban garment workers, and those who were the well-educated daughters of professional men. Common themes, however, emerge here as well; the daughter of immigrants balancing between two cultures, so beautifully captured by Maxine Hong Kingston and Amy Tan, is a theme that ties together much of the Asian American women's literature, but recalls that of other immigrant women as well.

Class, Ethnicity, and Gender

A social class is a group sharing the same social or economic status. Generally speaking, racial, ethnic, and class divisions reinforce one another in complex, stratified societies. That is, ethnicity and race, depending on the historical and regional context, often become stereotyped signs of class position.

The economic roles played by various ethnic/racial groups have a major impact on the social roles of the women of these groups. Their economic and social roles are closely tied with those of the men of their groups, but not identical with them. For example, in the United States, high rates of unemployment for African American men persisted once they began to leave impoverished Southern farms

Daughters Balancing between Two Cultures

"Wah!" cried the mother upon seeing the mirrored armoire in the master suite of her daughter's new condominium. "You cannot put mirrors at the foot of the bed. All your marriage happiness will bounce back and turn the opposite way."

"Well, that's the only place it fits, so that's where it stays," said the daughter, irritated that her mother saw bad omens in everything. She had heard these warnings all her life.

The mother frowned, reaching into her twice-used Macy's bag. "Hunh, lucky I can fix it for you, then." And she pulled out the gilt-edged mirror she had bought at the Price Club last week. It was her housewarming present. She leaned it against the headboard, on top of the two pillows.

"You hang it here," said the mother, pointing to the wall above. "This mirror sees that mirror—*haule!*—multiply your peach-blossom luck."

"What is peach-blossom luck?"

The mother smiled, mischief in her eyes. "It is in here," she said, pointing to the mirror. "Look inside. Tell me, am I not right? In this mirror is my future grandchild, already sitting on my lap next spring."

And the daughter looked—and *haule!* There it was: her own reflection looking back at her.

(Tan, 1989, 147)

at the turn of the twentieth century; this in turn meant that among African American women, who had become urban wage earners somewhat earlier, married women continued to need to hold wage-paying jobs more often than the majority of married white women (Jones, 1985). In increasingly urbanized America, African American women had greater access to wage jobs, albeit low-paying domestic and service ones, than did African American men. These facts have implications for gender relations in African American families.

The issue of class at times divides racial and ethnic groups and genders, but class and race or ethnicity often correspond. We see this, for example, in the case of Chicana/Chicano workers' movements. Patricia Zavella's (1987) study of the organization of Chicana cannery workers in Northern California illustrates some of the conflicts women experience as members simultaneously of a subordinate eth-nic group, class, and gender. The dominant labor union tacitly complies with ethnic discrimination while claiming to represent all workers. The most subordinate workers of all are Chicanas and Chicanos, with women, as only seasonal workers, at the bottom of the hierarchy. To resist ethnic discrimination, the Chicanos have sought to break away from the establishment union, the Teamsters, an action that implies class disunity. But the Chicanos' alternative, the United Farm Workers Union, appears insensitive to the women's concerns. The concerns of their husbands and the women's own cultural image of ourselves as primarily responsible for family care militate against justice for Chicanas in the workplace. Women in the cannery are also divided by race: Anglo women are more privileged in the workplace than Chicanas. The formation of a separatist Chicana women's movement within both the unionization movement and the Chicano unity movement is a case in which separatism and coalition building, rather than the simpler "unity" with previously masked difference and injustice, gained women justice and needed improvements.

Rationalization and Resistance

Subordinate groups learn to rationalize their position in terms promulgated by dominant groups under the guise of "natural" subordination and dominance. We can understand the characteristics and actions of members of dominant and subordinate groups in terms of this rationalization, and of resistance to it. That is, group members come to define themselves in terms of the superiority or inferiority ascribed to them by others and themselves, and they act on these ascriptions, or they resist them in various ways. This process is applied to many of the characteristics that combine to make up the social person in a complex society: age, gender, race, religion, abilities, and sexual orientation. Negative stereotypes that develop to rationalize power relations persist despite their obvious contradictions with reality. The notion that women are the "weaker sex" contradicts evidence of women's abilities to engage in hard physical labor, endure great pain, and live longer than men.

What societal function does stereotyping serve? It is easier to exploit people if you think they are inferior; easier too, if *they* think they are inferior. Stereotypes distance people and position them hierarchically.

> We learn in childhood that such things as sex and race bring differences in power and privilege, and that these are acceptable. This idea that difference justifies domination is deeply embedded in society and defended as natural . . . as women who have challenged the so-called naturalness of male supremacy, feminists must also question it in other areas of domination. (Bunch, 1987:150)

Fear and distrust contribute to the maintenance of the privileges of the powerful. Negative stereotypes lower the self-esteem of their targets. Even "positive" stereotypes, such as the belief that Asian Americans are especially gifted in mathematics and the sciences, may serve to lower the self-esteem of those who cannot live up to the stereotype.

The internalization of these images helps to perpetuate the social order that promotes them. Resistance, in the form of alternative interpretations and reverse stereotyping, undermines the power structure by encouraging opposite action or thinking. The Black Power movement of the 1960s was such an effort at resistance. With the slogan "Black Is Beautiful," this movement affected the self-image, and power to resist negative stereotypes, of many African Americans at the time. Looking back, Claudette Williams, a West Indian woman who emigrated to Britain, writes, "Black consciousness enabled me to make the connection between class and racism . . . : why we acquire the worst housing, education, and health care, why we are targeted for racial abuse and assaults" (Williams, 1988:155). Finding a voice, a new sense of identity, has never been uncomplicated, for resistance to social control and oppression of one kind suggest the way other kinds function around us as well.

Like racial, ethnic, and class stereotypes, those that apply to gender promote subordination. Women may be in triple jeopardy, being oppressed on the basis of gender, race or ethnicity, and class. As a result of being discriminated against and excluded because of both our race and our class, a woman may readily come to accept society's attribution of inferiority because of our gender. Negative stereotypes of age, religion, sexual orientation, and being differently abled, all compound this process of oppression.

The Complexities of Identity, Voice, and Oppressions

The arrival of the Black Panther movement and the Black consciousness era offered me the necessary knowledge and confidence to survive. . . . Black power taught me to value myself and others like me in a way I had not experienced before. "Black Is Beautiful," "Be Proud To Be Black" carried their unique message to my heart.

I was presented with a history, people and struggle of which I was a part; and I found out that there was much beauty and pride in being a Black woman. I was able to recognize the significance of pressing my hair, and bleaching my skin. While consciously I did not want to be white, everything I had learned and was surrounded by told me that to be white was "good," but here for the first time in my life were other Black people addressing "me" and my personal doubts and inadequacies. I was being told not to be ashamed or afraid of what, and who I am.

. . . Black consciousness enabled me to make the connection between class and racism . . . why we acquire the worst housing, education and health care, why we are targeted for racial abuse and assaults. . . . However, with political enlightenment came contradictions that became very antagonistic with women's demands for autonomous groups.

The "brothers" took it hard. They saw autonomy as a threat to male leadership and male egos. Gender oppression was reduced to sexuality, and lesbianism became a weapon to deter women from organizing independently.

(Williams, 1988:152, 155–56)

Dominant Discourses/Muted Groups

One way of understanding how the power of those who dominate society works to maintain stereotypes of gender, race, ethnicity, class and the like is to consider the concept of "muted groups." According to this explanation, which takes its core from the ideas of the Italian Marxist philosopher Antonio Gramsci, every society has a dominant ideology that describes all social behavior (Cocks, 1989). That dominant discourse shapes thinking about social norms and expectations, supplies the vocabulary used to describes these social relations, and reflects the image of reality held by the dominant group in society. Women in oppressed groups, whose sense of ourselves and the dominant group may differ radically from the stereotyped versions offered by the dominant group, may lack the language to express—or even an adequate vocabulary by

which to conceptualize—that difference. Or, finding voice, we may adopt the prudent course of not airing our differences beyond our own subgroup to avoid the consequences of antagonizing those with power. Or we may not wish to air the gender differences within our oppressed group in public, as tending to seem disloyal or unsupportive of the group as a whole. As a way of talking about how those with less power are sometimes "muted," anthropologists have worked out the notion in terms of gender. The theory of "muted groups" has provided one explanation for why in the past male anthropologists and male-trained female anthropologists accepted information supplied by the men of the societies they were studying concerning the activities of women, failing to question the women of those societies about our reasons for our actions (Ardener, 1975).

Edwin Ardener concluded that the dominant male perceptions (both the European, white, middle-class male anthropologist and the indigenous, local male) provided a model of the world whose existence and pervasiveness impeded the creation of alternate models. Women, raised in a world where the dominant model of reality is male-created, may characteristically be less articulate because we must express ourselves through the dominant, male-oriented discourse. The dominant discourse does not offer a way of expressing a wholly different perspective. When we are trained in academic disciplines, like anthropology or sociology, whose theoretical models correspond to a male perception of reality, we find it exceedingly difficult to find the conceptual frameworks and vocabulary to express our own perceptions of reality (Smith, 1974).

An achievement of the first two decades of the modern women's movement is the feminist critique of those privileged white male-defined concepts framing our academic disciplines. As a result, we now understand how much the dominant discourses monopolize the forms of self-expression available to all subordinated groups in a society. Just as gender is always shaped by and is a part of race, ethnicity, and class, so self-expression takes its shape from these same categories. Women, again, may be doubly "muted," both within the expressive medium of our subordinate ethnic and class grouping, and as members of the subordinate gender.

Constraints on Choice and Self-Realization

The process of conforming to the dominant images of ourselves occurs through constraints on our choices; through the ways we are educated into our social roles and the limited access we have to the resources by which to shape what we can do and how. Individuals and groups in subordinated positions are oppressed by the force of the dominant culture, and in the end, this process places real limits on self-realization. As women in previously silenced groups begin to speak, we better understand the effects of subordination and oppression (Hurtado, 1989; see Chapter 11).

We must note that in addition to the oppressed, oppressors also experience negative effects of oppression. In a project carried out in the Netherlands (Pheterson, 1990), small groups of women met over a period of five months, each organized around issues such as racism, anti-Semitism, and homophobia. The women in these groups found that oppression and domination are experienced

> as a mutually reinforcing web of insecurities and rigidities . . . [and] the psychological consequences are surprisingly alike . . . the fear of violence one feels as a victim of oppression reinforces the fear of revenge she feels as an agent of oppression. The isolation resulting from feelings of inferiority reinforces the isolation resulting from feelings of superiority. The guilt felt for dominating others likewise reinforces the guilt felt for one's own victimization. (Pheterson, 1990:45)

As individuals within an oppressed group, we tend to accept the stereotypes of ourselves formulated by the dominant group in society, setting up a pattern of low self-esteem and isolation. This *internalized oppression*, Pheterson concludes, "is likely to consist of self-hatred, self-concealment, fear of violence and feelings of inferiority, resignation, isolation, powerlessness, and gratefulness for being allowed to survive" (Pheterson, 1990:35). Those in the dominant group in society use this mechanism to control those dominated by fostering in us a self-image that conforms to the oppressor's negative stereotype of us. *Internalized domination*, on the other hand, imposes its own self-constraints by creating stereotypes that deny the humanity of others, and one's own. Degradation of others leads to feelings of superiority and self-righteousness, but often at

Veils and *chadors*. Ranging widely in style depending on the particular Muslim society, layers of cloth—highly decorated or exceedingly plain—cover all but the eyes of women who daily live with a reminder of the constraints that their culture places on their activities. Veils and *chadors* may still be worn by older women in a household where younger Muslim women have begun to adopt Western clothing styles. The decorated veil covers the face of a mother in a nomadic tribe in Egypt. (Photo of veil by George Holton, courtesy of UNICEF)

the cost of feelings of guilt, fear, and a denial of reality.

There is a considerable correlation in U.S. society between being African American, Latina, Asian American, or Native North American Indian and being poor. Poverty means limited access to all the resources of society, not just its wealth, but housing, health care, and education as well. For example, a survey in 1987 indicated that while white women's wages had reached 67.5 percent of parity with white men, wages earned by African American women had reached only 61.3 percent, and the pay of women in groups labeled "Hispanic" had barely reached 54.8 percent (Hurtado, 1989). Staying in high school and getting college degrees is more difficult for women of color. Asian American women tend to split into two groups: those with a high level of education, who nonetheless tend to find only clerical and administrative support jobs, and those with little education at all who are seamstresses in garment factories or assembly workers in the electronics industry. The pattern of education at the high school level affects, in turn, the pattern of participation in college and graduate school, which has obvious consequences for access to material resources, economic mobility, choice of career, and self-realization.

There are precedents, however, for forming groups whose members can help one another resist this pattern of low achievement and low self-esteem. Within such groups, women develop a self-consciousness that provides us with the strength to resist the dominant stereotypes that denigrate us and helps us mobilize for change. Women caught within patterns of poverty have learned how to work together successfully to aid ourselves, our children, and our neighborhoods, as Barbara Omolade has demonstrated in her work on African American single mothers (Omolade, 1986). African American women have a tradition of community and church activism. As Patricia Hill Collins reminds us, there is a rich African American oral tradition among women as storytellers, which we bring to our roles as mothers, teachers, musicians, and preachers. The exchange of ideas and tactics for action that emerge from this daily life and contact with others form a base of power that

---

The Psychology of Racism in White Feminists

The fact is, white wimmin are oppressed; they have been "colonized" by white boys, just as third world people have. Even when white wimmin "belonged" to white boys they had no reality. They belonged as objects, and were treated as such. (As someone else has noted, the original model for colonization was the treatment of white wimmin.) Nobody has yet sufficiently researched or documented the collective psychology of oppressed white wimmin. So consider this as a thesis: they know. And so do I. The reality of their situation is the real pits. . . . The cause of racism in white feminists is their bizarre oppression (and suppression). . . . In other words, their elitism and narrowminded rigidity are defense mechanisms . . . they are threatened by anyone different from them in race, politics, mannerisms, or clothing. It's partly a means of self-protection but that does not excuse it. Feminism either addresses itself to all wimmin, or it becomes even more so just another elitist, prurient white organization, defeating its own purposes.

(davenport, 1983:88–89)

many different groups of women can bring to self-identity, group consciousness, and methods of resistance (Gilkes, 1992; Collins, 1986, 1991).

Unionization of workers has involved various kinds of class-based alliances, whether the unions have been formed around specific skills or around working together in a specific industry or organization. The history of unionization in the United States has included both broad-based outreach that incorporated white women and African American women and men and narrowly constituted groups that excluded all but a small group of similarly skilled white men. In both cases, organizations of workers have called into being powerful organizations of employers that exploited popular fears about the radical and subversive goals of organized workers. As unionization increased the diversity of its base, the image of union membership has gradually changed since the Depression years of the 1930s. In the process, the self-image and self-esteem of those who were unionized grew stronger. We have already examined a case of the strengthening of women workers' material position through the formation of a separatist Chicana cannery workers' union.

Commonalities of Experience

Johnnetta Cole has commented, "Among the things which bind women together are the assumptions about the way women think and behave, the myths—indeed the stereotypes—about what is common to all women" (Cole, 1986:2). The myths about women as madonnas or temptresses (see Chapter 1), assumptions about women's irrationality and otherness (see Chapter 2), claims and warnings about women's bodies (see Chapter 3), and assertions about women's personalities (see Chapter 4) all form part of a system of stereotypes about women that relate to social expectations—in diverse contexts—of our sub-

ordinate and supporting roles in society. As often, we as women are bound by our common assumptions about those to whom we are subordinate or for whom we are supportive, men as a group. We can identify the supportive and supporting roles women are commonly assigned and regularly play in relationship to men, but we must allow for the diversity women experience due to culture and class, ethnicity, and race.

For example, many wives perform hostess duties on behalf of their husbands and their husbands' careers or social positions. How this is done, however, greatly differs from class to class, from country to country, from culture to culture, yet in each case the men are spared the expense of their time and energy for this function (Ostrander, 1984). Similarly, women usually undertake to arrange social relationships in general and kinship relationships in particular, releasing men from this obligation, the forms varying enormously, depending upon the social group. Women even undertake to oil the social wheels of impersonal work organizations with seasonal celebrations of holidays and birthdays, thereby indirectly aiding our employers in maintaining social harmony within the workplace (Leonardo, 1987).

Family Roles

Commonalities among women have to do with our family roles as daughters, wives, and mothers. Whatever the particular arrangements are, due to race, ethnicity, culture, religion, or even time in history, we experience the roles of daughter in connection with parental figures to whom we owe duties of obedience and loyalty, and for whom we may experience tenderness and love. We may also, as daughters, feel bonds of love and bonds of jealousy toward siblings, depending upon circumstances, and bonds of responsibility depending upon age relationship. Whatever our

---

How We Differ: What We Have in Common

It is a general principle of feminist inquiry to be sceptical about any account of human relations that fails to mention gender or to consider the possible effects of gender differences; for in a world in which there is sexism, obscuring the workings of gender is likely to involve— whether intentionally or not—obscuring the workings of sexism. We thus ought to be sceptical about any account of gender relations that fails to mention race and class or to consider the possible effects of race and class differences on gender: for in a world in which there is racism and classism, obscuring the working of race and class is likely to involve—whether intentionally or not—obscuring the workings of racism and classism.

. . . If I am justified in thinking that what it means for me to be a woman must be exactly the same as what it means for you to be a woman (since we are both women), I needn't bother to find out anything from you or about you in order to find out what it means for you to be a woman: I can simply deduce what it means from my own case. On the other hand, if the meaning of what we apparently have in common (being women) depends in some ways on the meaning of what we don't have in common (for example, our different racial or class identities), then far from distracting us from the issue of gender, attention to race and class in facts helps us to understand gender. In this sense it is only if we pay attention to how we differ that we come to an understanding of what we have in common.

(Spelman, 1988:111–13)

---

fate, to marry or not, to stay at home or not, as we grow in years our obligations toward our families are maintained at some level; and as women we more often find ourselves directly responsible for providing care to elderly parents than do our brothers.

If we marry, whoever we are, we undertake a new set of obligations that sometimes involves a husband alone, sometimes extends to relationships with a new kin group, and for some of us includes quite specific duties to our parents-in-law. In some instances, we might be a co-wife, which means we have new obligations to other wives as well. In terms of commonalities, marriage around the world generally means household responsibilities, social obligations, and a new status derived from our husband's social position.

Commonalities also occur if we become mothers. Motherhood may have many differ-

ent meanings in many different contexts, but in general it brings responsibility for the continued nurture and health of a new life and must be undertaken in addition to any and all other obligations and responsibilities of living and working. Women's arrangements throughout the world to cope with this unceasing obligation yield common experiences among us.

Alternative Roles. Where choice was possible, some women have always chosen not to marry. Single women have become nuns in the Christian and Buddhist worlds; we have devoted ourselves to caring for others outside the family, to traveling through the world, to living alone, together with other women in groups, or as couples in loving relationships. For those of us for whom these are preferred choices, different kinds of commonalities exist.

Society and Social Control

When we look at the various ways in which we enter into relationships in society as a whole, in terms of religion, education, health, work, and politics, we see common patterns at work that cut across our differences and diversity as women.

The more formal and institutionalized the religious system we belong to—the large-scale religions of the world—the more there are formal rules and regulations that place men in control and keep women in subordinate and supportive roles. The less formal the religious structures—the small sects and spiritual groups—the more likely women will play a leadership role.

In terms of education, women around the world usually have less access to literacy and formal means of learning than men. In consequence, where formal learning provides channels to advancement, achievement, and power, far fewer individual women than men will acquire positions of leadership and importance in societies. Where women have achieved access to formal education, we will more likely be found, as in the case of employment, in gender-segregated specialties; the humanities and literature rather than the sciences; in the sciences, biology rather than physics; in medicine, pediatrics rather than surgery. Only where learning is not highly valued or where it takes place in informal ways will women be found acquiring it in any numbers, as in the early Middle Ages in Europe (when nuns were more learned than lay men) or in oral tradition societies (where lore is conveyed by word of mouth within families and age groups segregated by sex).

Women's health has largely been in our own hands until the last century, when modern professionalization of medicine has both impersonalized treatment and made assumptions about the "diseased" state of women's bodies (Brack, 1979; Jordanova, 1989). In the process, a medicalized health system has taken over women's bodies and our health in the name of modern science, and the natural function of childbirth has been subjected to forms of mechanical monitoring and regimentation. Adequacy of health care still depends on access to resources, and women commonly have fewer resources. Everywhere women are centrally concerned about reproductive rights. Our views may differ widely as to birth control and abortion, but it is not a matter over which we are generally indifferent. The issue of sterilization, at least if it is not a choice, is a bitter one.

In terms of work, women commonly supply unpaid household labor, either manual or managerial. In addition, if we work for pay, we tend to work in gender-segregated sectors of the economy—such as the clerical, teaching, and nursing fields—and to receive less wages than men in comparable jobs. If married we commonly have responsibility for our household and children in addition to any paid work we do. In the United States, this situation is complicated by race and ethnicity, and the wage differential between women and men is less for people of color (Cole, 1986). Those few women who have begun to reach the top of middle management jobs in corporations have found a "glass ceiling" that makes it difficult to break through to top corporate positions. The problem identified some decades ago, that work patterns in offices and factories are usually based on the expectation that a man will be doing the job—and will have a female support system at home taking care of household, clothing, food, children, and social responsibilities generally—has not fundamentally altered. Women who work for pay outside the home find ourselves still burdened by home care, and discussions of flexitime, shared jobs, and part-time work have made no real change in the expectations of employers, especially in terms of white collar jobs. Women in rural areas around the world, depending on the nature of the plant and animal life, often share the same concerns about planting and harvesting, animal care and dairying, and coping with seasonal changes and unexpected turns in the weather. Negotiating what we do and how direct our return is for our work is part of every rural woman's daily concern.

Politics has become a broad term for women, beginning with the recognition that the "personal is political." Though politics continues to refer to the processes of government, where women are still relatively few and far between at the higher levels, it also refers widely to the systematic oppression of women. Certainly the Senate Judiciary Committee Hearings on the confirmation of Clarence Thomas as Associate Justice of the United States Supreme Court in the fall of 1991, at which Anita Hill accused the candidate of sexual harassment on the job, made clear to a wide spectrum of the country the linkage between the personal and the political. As a result a larger number of women than ever before decided to enter the senatorial and congressional political races in the fall of 1992. The Hill-Thomas hearings also occasioned an ongoing discussion with the African American community about the issues of racial solidarity and gender equity (Morrison, 1992; Fraser, 1992). Women have been "political" without being in formal "politics" for a long time, in the United States and other countries. In the United States, we have taken leadership roles in community affairs, from churches to school boards to planning boards. At the turn of the twentieth century, social feminists in the Progressive movement led the fight for child labor laws, workmen's compensation, safety inspection laws, and limits on the workday for women. Women have created Peace parties in many countries throughout the world, worked for nuclear dis-

armament, protested as mothers and grandmothers, and contributed to the analysis of the power structures of both domestic and international policies (Enloe, 1988; Femenia, 1987; Morgen and Bookman, 1986; Torres, 1991).

If politics refers to the exercise of power, it also refers to the system of keeping groups powerless through laws that abet the social control of women. Social control through sexual violence, sexual exploitation, and sexual harassment makes women victims, and women have begun to fight back. Physical violence, rape, wife and child battering, incest, have been found to exist far more commonly than ever acknowledged in the past. Sexual exploitation of women from advertising to pornography to prostitution keeps women feeling physically vulnerable and more readily subject to social control as to what we do, where we do it, and how we do it. As Johnnetta Cole has put it, "These various assaults against women are best characterized not as sexual acts but as acts of violence which dramatically signal women's powerlessness" (Cole, 1986:26).

The Heterosexual Prescription

In a similar way, the presumption that all women must become wives and mothers and care for husbands, homes, and children to prove our adulthood is an important method of social control. It is a basic social script that women learn in childhood. Remaining single and taking care of elderly parents has always been one lesser alternative, as has remaining single for other reasons. Some 10 percent to 20 percent of women through time in the Western world have remained single. But we were usually looked down upon and pitied as leading a "lesser" life. Those who choose to live with other women because we love them have always existed, but only since the late nineteenth century have we been called "lesbians," after the island of Lesbos where the poet Sappho lived in the sixth century B.C.E. As was expected of an upper-class woman in Archaic Greece, Sappho was married and apparently had a daughter, but her erotic and emotional life was centered on women. She wrote poetry extolling the beauties of young women and telling of her sadness when they left the island, presumably to marry men in distant cities (Pomeroy, 1975). Those who fear and dislike the independence of thought implied in feminist analysis sometimes use the term "lesbian" interchangeably with "feminist," but feminists, like all women, come in many shapes, sizes, races, ethnicities, classes, and sexual orientations.

Lesbians today continue to find it painful to deal with parental reproaches, employer discrimination, and public disparagement, but lesbian groups have joined for self-help and companionship. Lesbians have formed coalitions with gay men on political issues locally and nationally, and some have successfully achieved legal rights to child custody and adopted children. Yet the world continues to be organized around heterosexist assumptions that actively control lesbians' behavior.

Adrienne Rich made a now classic analysis of what she called "The Heterosexual Prescription," based on eight characteristics of male power identified by the anthropologist Kathleen Gough. In this analysis she cites examples of how each of these kinds of power have been used by men to enforce heterosexuality on women to convince us that marriage, and sexual orientation toward men, are "inevitable, even if unsatisfying or oppressive components" of our lives (Rich, 1980:640).

The Social Construction of Human Beings

Overcoming the perpetuation of gender oppression will require more than new languages, new analysis, and new theories. A vast array of changes in social practice and thought are required. Consider the reactions of people to a young adult dressed and groomed in such a way that it is not possible to tell whether the person is female or male. Responses may vary from discomfort or anxiety to intense curiosity or great disgust. But why do people feel compelled to place human beings immediately into the social category "woman" or "man"? Are all our responses to people so fixed that we do not know how to react to a person without definite gender? Since gender as we know it implies social placement, which in turn implies a pattern of dominance and subordination, does our unease at an indefinite gender suggest that we are socialized to accept others *only* in such terms? Can we respond to people simply as other human beings?

Difference without Hierarchy

The answer at this time in history is no. Our need to identify the gender of any human being stems from the thorough duality of the thought system that underpins our social construction of reality. Yet humans have more in common with one another, as Gayle Rubin (1975) pointed out in her now classic article, "Traffic in Women," than we have with any other living thing in the universe. If gender assignment to nurturing roles were less rigid—if all children grew up expecting to nurture the next generation—it might be less necessary to emphasize differences between two genders (see Chapter 8). The concept of a human continuum, *difference without hierarchy*, in which personality and preference (rather than assigned gender) led to a rich variety of possibilities for the performance of social—and family—roles, would help us think in terms of "human beings" rather than "women" and "men." To do so would widen our range of human choice enormously. Such possibilities would begin to address the problem of unequal access created by sexism, and

Heterosexuality as a Political Institution

Characteristics of male power include: *the power of men*

1. *to deny women* [our own] *sexuality*
   [by means of clitoridectomy and infibulation; chastity belts; punishment, including death, for female adultery; punishment, including death, for lesbian sexuality; psychoanalytic denial of the clitoris; strictures against masturbation; denial of maternal and postmeno-pausal sensuality; unnecessary hysterectomy; pseudolesbian images in media and litera-ture; closing of archives and destruction of documents relating to lesbian existence];

2. *or to force it* [male sexuality] *upon them*
   [by means of rape (including marital rape) and wife beating; father-daughter, brother-sister incest; the socialization of women to feel that male sexual "drive" amounts to a right; idealization of heterosexual romance in art, literature, media, advertising, etc.; child marriage; arranged marriage; prostitution; the harem; psychoanalytic doctrines of frigidity and vaginal orgasm; pornographic depictions of women responding pleasurably to sexual violence and humiliation (a subliminal message being that sadistic heterosexuality is more "normal" than sensuality between women)];

3. *to command or exploit their labor to control their produce*
   [by means of the institutions of marriage and motherhood as unpaid production; the horizontal segregation of women in paid employment; the decoy of the upwardly mobile token woman; male control of abortion, contraception, and childbirth; enforced steriliza-tion; pimping; female infanticide, which robs mothers of daughters and contributes to generalized devaluation of women];

4. *to control or rob them of their children*
   [by means of father-right and "legal kidnapping"; enforced sterilization; systematized infanticide; seizure of children from lesbian mothers by the courts; the malpractice of

would help us find ways of ending other kinds of human oppression as well (Young, 1990).

Summary

From earliest ages, children try out social roles according to the gendered social rules they have observed concerning what is re-quired and what is forbidden. Roles may relate to family, work, or some other social context. Women are generally assigned wife and mother roles. Gender often determines which social roles people will play, or be forbidden to play. The roles people are assigned on the basis of gender and age are associated with so-cial status. In complex societies, class, race, caste, ethnicity, and religious affiliation often intersect with these social categories to estab-lish hierarchies of groups, membership in which affects the likelihood of various roles individuals play in a particular society.

Postmodern perspectives in feminist theory draw our attention to the importance of dif-ferences among "women," making generali-zations difficult. This chapter explores the dif-ferent roles women have been assigned and how these roles have varied with other social attributes, such as racial, ethnic, class, and other social categories. When we stereotype people, we react to them on the basis of our expectations rather than our knowledge of them as individuals. Negative stereotypes are male obstetrics; use of the mother as "token torturer" in genital mutilation or in binding the daughter's feet (or mind) to fit her for marriage];

5. *to confine them physically and prevent their movement*
   [by means of rape as terrorism, keeping women off the streets; purdah; foot-binding; atrophying of women's athletic capabilities; haute couture, "feminine" dress codes; the veil; sexual harassment on the streets; horizontal segregation of women in employment; prescription for "full-time" mothering; enforced economic dependence of wives];

6. *to use them as objects in male transactions*
   [use of women as "gifts"; bride-price; pimping; arranged marriage; use of women as entertainers to facilitate male deals, e.g., wife-hostess, cocktail waitress required to dress for male sexual titillation, call girls, "bunnies," geisha, *kisaeng* prostitutes, secretaries];

7. *to cramp their creativeness*
   [witch persecutions as campaigns against midwives and female healers and as pogroms against independent, "unassimilated" women; definition of male pursuits as more valuable than female within any culture, so that cultural values become embodiment of male subjectivity; restriction of female self-fulfillment to marriage and motherhood; sexual exploitation of women by male artists and teachers; the social and economic disruption of women's creative aspirations; erasure of female tradition]; and

8. *to withhold from them large areas of the society's knowledge and cultural attainments*
   [by means of noneducation of females (60% of the world's illiterates are women); the "Great Silence" regarding women and particularly lesbian existence in history and culture; sex-role stereotyping which deflects women from science, technology, and other "masculine" pursuits; male social/professional bonding which excludes women; discrimination against women in the professions].

(Rich, 1980:638–40)

usually caricatures, emphasizing a negative valuation of gender, race, class, and other labels.

At birth, the label "biological woman" is commonly based on anatomy: The social construction of the gender "woman" is then based on the social expectations of societies and may differ. Essential to the construct, however, is the notion that there are only two genders and that each gender is what the other is not. Socialization introduces children to the rules or norms of behavior of a particular society, and gender-appropriate behavior. Social norms are embedded in specific material ways of life, which change over time, sometimes creating a gap between norms and needs, as in the case of working mothers and social expectations of motherhood roles based on nonworking mothers. We take our identities from a variety of culturally imposed and individually claimed social constructions: gender, race, ethnicity, religion, class, age, sexual orientation, and physical abilities.

"Race" is a social construct, too. The term assumes biological characteristics, but the genetic roots of groups so identified are both diverse and often mixed with other groups. *Hispanic*, for example, merely refers to a Hispanic surname and covers a wide range of physical appearance. What is important is that

Identity Beyond Labels—Beyond Negative Stereotypes

MINNIE BRUCE PRATT: If I have come to the point of consciousness where I have begun to understand that I am entrapped as a woman, not just by the sexual fear of the men of my group, but also by their racial and religious terrors; if I have begun to understand that when they condemn me as a lesbian and a free woman for being "dirty," "unholy," "perverted," "immoral," it is a judgment that has been called down on people of color and Jews throughout history by the men of my culture, as they have shifted their justification for hatred according to their desires of the moment; if I have begun to understand something of the deep connection between my oppression and that of other folks, what is it that keeps me from acting, sometimes even from speaking out, against anti-Semitism and racism? . . .

As I try to strip away the layers of deceit that I have been taught, it is not hard to be afraid that these are like wrappings of a shroud and that what I will ultimately come to in myself is a disintegrating, rotting *nothing*: that the values that I have at my core, from my culture, will only be those of negativity, exclusion, fear, death. And my feeling *is* based in the reality that the group identity of my culture has been defined, often, not by positive qualities, but by negative characteristics: by the *absence of:* "no dogs, Negroes, or Jews"; we have gotten our jobs, bought our houses, borne and educated our children by the negatives: no niggers, no kikes, no wops, no dagos, no spics, no A-rabs, no gooks, no queers. . . .

> "Identity: Skin Blood Heart" by Minnie Bruce Pratt. From *Yours in Struggle: Three Feminist Perspectives on Anti-Semitism and Racism.* Copyright © 1984 by Elly Bulkin, Minnie Bruce Pratt, and Barbara Smith. Firebrand Books, Ithaca, N.Y.

BARBARA SMITH: Relationships between Black and Jewish women are the very opposite of simple. Our attempts to make personal/political connections virtually guarantee our being thrust between "the rock" of our own people's suspicion and disapproval and "the hard place" of the other group's antagonism and distrust. It is a lot easier to categorize people, to push them into little nastily-labeled boxes, than time and again to deal with them directly, to make distinctions between the stereotype and the substance of who and what they are. It's little wonder that so often both Black and Jewish women first label and then dismiss each other. All of us resort to this tactic when the impact of our different histories, cultures, classes, and skins backs us up against the wall and we do not have the courage or the desire to examine what, if anything, of value lies between us. . . . We are certainly damaged people. The question is, finally, do we use that damage, that first-hand knowledge of oppression, to recognize each other, to do what work we can together? Or do we use it to destroy?

> "Between a Rock and a Hard Place" by Barbara Smith. From *Yours in Struggle: Three Feminist Perspectives on Anti-Semitism and Racism.* Copyright © 1984 by Elly Bulkin, Minnie Bruce Pratt, and Barbara Smith. Firebrand Books, Ithaca, N.Y.

the context of the use of the label is critical to the consciousness of its meaning, and that both contexts and meanings have changed through time. Ethnicity similarly refers to a social construct that developed over time, and sometimes refers to what in the past was called nationality. African Americans, Native North American Indians, Asian Americans, Latinas/Latinos, and whites all are divided ethnically.

We can begin to understand difference only when we examine the specific context in which it operates over time, place, and circumstances. Our roles in society depend not only on what is attributed to us but what we lay claim to as our identity. Native North American Indian women, though representing diverse groups and diverse experiences, find identity in common themes of oppression related to conquest, decimation, dislocation, adjustment, and resistance. Similarly, the many groups who make up Asian American women, who differ from each other in striking ways, still have common themes as daughters of immigrants balancing between two cultures.

Ethnicity and race often become stereotyped signs of class position. Class can divide groups or provide a unifying factor. Subordinate groups learn to rationalize their position in terms of negative stereotypes that suggest that subordination to another, dominant, group is "natural." This hierarchical thinking maintains the privileges of the powerful and lowers the self-esteem of their targets, perpetuating the social order that promotes the relationship. Resistance, like the Black Power movement of the 1960s, fought back against the negative stereotypes. Oppressed groups find it difficult to express their own versions of themselves, however; they are "muted" by the dominant discourse. Women, raised in a world where the dominant reality is male-created, may characteristically be less articulate; training in academic disciplines is learning to view the world conceptually through male models of society. The achievement of the modern women's movement is to find self-expression, to overcome "mutedness," and to a create models reflecting women's experiences.

Conforming to dominant images of ourselves constrains our choices. Internalized oppression fosters the negative self-images that reinforce negative stereotypes. Poverty comes from having limited access to the material resources of society. Negative self-images abet the process of keeping women of oppressed groups out of educational channels that would increase their mobility, career choice, and self-realization. But even within poor groups of women, there have been successful attempts to provide mutual self-help, to resist society's negative stereotypes, and to create a positive self-identity. The spread of unionization, with an increasingly diverse membership, has provided one means for strengthening workers' material positions.

Women have experiences in common that cross many of the lines that divide them. These commonalities have to do with their family roles. Some women have always chosen alternatives, however, despite the assumption that all women must become wives and mothers and care for husbands, homes, and children. Women who love other women have always existed, though the term *lesbian* dates only to a century ago. Lesbians have to face work and legal discrimination, public disparagement, and sometimes outright violence. To overcome gender oppression, we need to transform society to give everyone the chance to develop whatever potential we have without negative stereotypes, without patterns of hierarchical dominance, without all the problems of unequal access created by sexism. But only by being aware of these issues can we begin.

Discussion Questions

1. How do we learn to take the roles society expects of us because of our gender? How does this relate to the biological factors introduced in Chapter 3 and the philosophical issues about "women's nature" in Chapter 2?

2. In order to see how differently societies can shape the roles assigned to women, read about women in a society very different from your own—another racial or ethnic group, another country, another time period. What kinds of works, talents, and personality characteristics are assigned to

Chief Wilma P. Mankiller, the first woman to lead the Cherokee nation, is acclaimed for her authority and guidance. She was only 38 years old when appointed *chief* in 1985. She was elected in 1987, and re-elected in 1991; she retired in 1995. In her own words, "You don't have to have a title or a position to be effective." (Quoted in *The New York Times*, April 6, 1994)

women in these situations, and how do they differ from your own experience? How would you account for the difference?

3. If race and ethnicity, like gender, are social constructions, how can we account for the intensity with which individuals identify with them, on the one hand, and the highly negative stereotypes that may surround them, on the other? How are these constructs used to structure hierarchical status and constrain access to resources? How does gender factor into these identities?

4. If society teaches negative stereotypes to members of oppressed groups, how can members of such groups support each other and recapture self-esteem?

5. What specific projects in your area, your campus, or your city would benefit from coalition building among diverse groups of women? How would you go about convincing these groups that it was in their interest to act together?

Recommended Readings

Albrecht, Lisa, and Brewer, Rose M. *Bridges of Power: Women's Multicultural Alliances.* Philadelphia, Santa Cruz, and Gabiola, BC: New Society Publishers, 1990. An important contribution to the key questions raised by women's multicultural alliances, from the problems of diversity and coalition building to women's leadership and power within and across diverse groups. The essays discuss critical ground concerning personal interactions between women of different backgrounds and socially claimed identities, what causes conflict, what encourages cooperation, what constitutes risks worth taking, and how creativity functions to liberate such efforts.

Spider Woman's Granddaughters: Traditional Tales and Contemporary Writing by Native American Women, edited with an introduction by Paula Gunn Allen. Boston: Beacon Press, 1989. For insights into the themes of despair and hope and concerns about heritage and the need to keep struggling for justice, there is no better place to start. The grandmother spider, according to Cherokee legend, brought intelligence and experience to people; the tales and stories about past and present lives in this book bring to the reader a recognition of the enormous diversity behind the label Native American woman.

Anzaldúa, Gloria. *Borderlands/La Frontera: The New Mestiza.* San Francisco: Aunt Lute Books, 1987. A wonderful example of how the personal is political. By telling her own story, Anzaldúa tells also the history of the American Southwest and the Mexican, African American, Anglo, and Native American cultures that converged and clashed within it. The product of mixed cultures, she experiences alienation and a yearning for roots and connection. Her "borderlands" are her world of life and poetry, where diversity comes together.

Baca Zinn, Maxine, and Dill, Bonnie Thornton, editors. *Women of Color in U.S. Society.* Philadelphia: Temple University Press, 1994. These essays examine the ways gender, race, and class operate in the lives of African Americans, Latinas, Asian Americans, and Native Americans. The authors raise questions about resistance, agency, and cultural practices that are challenged by and that challenge U.S. social institutions.

Collins, Patricia Hill. *Black Feminist Thought.* New York: Routledge, 1991. Collins provides us with a road map for the ways African American women have used our lives and experiences to forge feminist thought about ourselves, our social relations with men, our communities, our children, and our work. She points out that the tradition for such thinking goes back into the nineteenth century and today forms a coherent framework for analysis.

Making Waves: An Anthology of Writings By and About Asian American Women, edited by Asian Women United of California. Boston: Beacon Press, 1989. The first anthology of writings by and about Asian Americans from a women-centered perspective, with a comprehensive introduction by Sucheta Mazumdar. In poems, letters, short stories, and essays, the volume deals with the immigration experience: the impact of World War II on Asian American lives: issues of work (from garment work to professional occupations); generational relationships; identity issues (including mixed marriages and lesbians); sexual exploitation; and organizing for change. In this last section, the issues of political movements, unionization, women's movements, and taking part—as self-conscious Asian Americans—in activism brings us back to the issues raised in Albrecht and Brewer above.

References

Acosta-Belen, Edna, and Sjostrom, Barbara, editors. *The Hispanic Experience in the United States: Contemporary Issues and Perspectives.* New York: Praeger, 1988.

Albrecht, Lisa, and Brewer, Rose. "Bridges of Power: Women's Multicultural Alliances for Social Change." In *Bridges of Power: Women's Multicultural Alliances*, edited by Lisa Albrecht and Rose M. Brewer. Philadelphia, Santa Cruz, and Gabiola, BC: New Society Publishers, 1990.

Allen, Paula Gunn. "Deep Purple." In *Spider Woman's Granddaughters: Traditional Tales and Contemporary Writing by Native American Women*, edited with an introduction by Paula Gunn Allen. Boston: Beacon Press, 1989.

Alperin, Davida J. "Social Diversity and the Necessity of Alliances: *A Developing Feminist Perspective.*" In *Bridges of Power: Women's Multicultural Alliances*, edited by Lisa Albrecht and Rose M. Brewer. Philadelphia,

Santa Cruz, and Gabiola, BC: New Society Publishers, 1990.

Anzaldúa, Gloria. *Borderlands/La Frontera: The New Mestiza.* San Francisco: Spinsters/Aunt Lute, 1987.

———: "Bridge, Drawbridge, Sandbar or Island: Lesbians-of-color Hacienda Alianzas." In *Bridges of Power: Women's Multicultural Alliances*, edited by Lisa Albrecht and Rose M. Brewer. Philadelphia, Santa Cruz, and Gabiola, BC: New Society Publishers, 1990.

Ardener, Edwin. "Belief and the Problem of Women." In *Perceiving Women*, edited by Shirley Ardener. London: Dent, 1975.

Brack, Datha Clapper. "Displaced—The Midwife by the Male Physician." In *Women Looking at Biology Looking at Women*, edited by Ruth Hubbard, Mary Sue Henifen, and Barbara Fried. Cambridge, Mass.: Schenckman, 1979.

Brewer, Rose. "Black Women and Feminist Sociology: The Emerging Perspective." *The American Sociologist* 20(1) (Spring 1989):57–70.

———. "Gender, Class and the Woman's Movement: The Role of Black Feminist Intellectuals." In *The Third Wave: Feminist Perspectives on Racism*, edited by Norma Alcaron, Lisa Albrecht, Jacqui Alexander, Sharon Day, and Mab Segrest. New York: Kitchen Table: Women of Color Press, 1991.

Bulkin, Elly. "Hard Ground: Jewish Identity, Racism, and Anti-Semitism." In *Yours in Struggle: Three Feminist Perspectives on Anti-Semitism and Racism*, edited by Elly Bulkin, Minnie Bruce Pratt, and Barbara Smith. New York: Kitchen Table: Women of Color Press, 1984.

Bunch, Charlotte. *Passionate Politics: Feminist Theory in Action.* New York: St. Martin's Press, 1987.

Burnham, Linda. "Has Poverty Been Feminized in America?" *Black Scholar* 16:2 (March/April 1985):14–24.

Carby, Hazel V. " 'On the Threshold of Woman's Era': Lynching, Empire, and Sexuality in Black Feminist Theory." In *"Race," Writing, and Difference*, edited by Henry Louis

Gates, Jr. Chicago: University of Chicago Press, 1985.

Chai, Alice Yun. "Toward a Holistic Paradigm for Asian American Women's Studies: A Synthesis of Feminist Scholarship and Women of Color's Feminist Politics." *Women's Studies International Forum* 8:1 (1985):59–66.

Cocks, Joan. *The Oppositional Imagination: Feminism, Critique and Political Theory*. London and New York: Routledge, 1989.

Cole, Johnnetta B. "Commonalities and Differences." In *All American Women: Lines that Divide, Ties that Bind*, edited by Johnnetta B. Cole. New York: Free Press, 1986.

Collins, Patricia Hill. "Learning from the Outsider Within. The Sociological Significance of Black Feminist Thought." *Social Problems* 33:6 (1986):14–32.

———. *Black Feminist Thought*. New York: Routledge, 1991.

davenport, doris. "The Pathology of Racism: A Conversation with Third World Wimmin." In *This Bridge Called My Back: Writings by Radical Women of Color*, edited by Cherríe Moraga and Gloria Anzaldúa. New York: Kitchen Table: Women of Color Press, 1983.

Davis, Angela. *Women, Race and Class*. New York: Vintage Books, 1981.

De Lauretis, Teresa. "Feminist Studies/Critical Studies: Issues, Terms, and Contexts." In *Feminist Studies/Critical Studies*, edited by Teresa de Lauretis. Bloomington: Indiana University Press, 1986.

Di Leonardo, Micaela. "The Female World of Cards and Holidays: Women, Families, and the Work of Kinship," *Signs* 12:3 (Spring 1987):440–53.

Dill, Bonnie Thornton. "Race, Class, and Gender: Prospects for an All-Inclusive Sisterhood." *Feminist Studies* 9:1 (1983):131–48.

Eisenstein, Hester, and Jardine, Alice, editors. *The Future of Difference*. New Brunswick, N.J.: Rutgers University Press, 1980.

Enloe, Cynthia. *Beaches, Bananas, and Bases: Making Feminist Sense of International Politics*. Berkeley: University of California Press, 1988.

Femenia, Nora Amalia. "Argentina's Mothers of Plaza de Mayo: The Mourning Process from Junta to Democracy," *Feminist Studies* 13:1 (1987):9–18.

Fraser, Nancy. "Sex, Lies, and the Public Sphere: Some Reflections on the Confirmation of Clarence Thomas." *Critical Inquiry* 18 (Spring 1992):595–612.

Frye, Marilyn. *The Politics of Reality*. Trumansburg, N.Y.: Crossing Press, 1983.

Gilkes, Cheryl Townsend. "A Case Study: Race-Ethnicity, Class, and African American Women: Exploring the Community Connection." In *Revolutions in Knowledge: Feminism in the Social Sciences*, edited by Sue Rosenberg Zalk and Janice Gordon-Kelter. Boulder, Co.: Westview Press, 1992.

Hammonds, Evelynn. "Race, Sex, AIDS: The Construction of the 'Other.'" *Radical America* 20:6 (1986):28–36.

Haraway, Donna. *Primate Visions: Gender, Race and Nature in the World of Modern Science*. New York: Routledge, 1989.

hooks, bell. *Ain't I a Woman? Black Women and Feminism*. Boston: South End Press, 1982.

———. *Feminist Theory: From Margin to Center*. Boston: South End Press, 1984.

Horno-Delgado, Asunción, Ortega, Eliana, Scott, Nina M., and Sternbach, Nancy Saporta, editors. *Breaking Boundaries: Latina Writings and Critical Readings*. Amherst: University of Massachusetts, 1989.

Hull, Gloria, Scott, Patricia, and Smith, Barbara, editors. *All the Women Are White, All the Blacks Are Men. But Some of Us Are Brave*. New York: Feminist Press, 1982.

Hurtado, Aida. "Relating to Privilege: Seduction and Rejection in the Subordination of White Women and Women of Color." *Signs: Journal of Women in Culture and Society* 11:4 (1989):833–55.

Jones, Jacqueline. *Labor of Love, Labor of Sorrow: Black Women, Work and the Family, From Slavery to the Present*. New York: Basic Books, 1985.

Jordanova, Ludmilla. *Sexual Visions, Images of Gender in Science and Medicine between the Eigh-*

teenth and Twentieth Centuries. New York and London: Harvester Wheatsheaf, 1989.

Joseph, Gloria, and Lewis, Jill. *Common Differences: Conflicts in Black and White Perspectives.* Garden City, N.Y.: Doubleday/Anchor, 1981.

King, Deborah K. "Multiple Jeopardy, Multiple Consciousness: The Context of a Black Feminist Ideology." *Signs: Journal of Women in Culture and Society* 14:1 (Autumn 1988):42–72.

Kingston, Maxine Hong. *China Men.* New York: Knopf, 1980.

———. *The Woman Warrior.* New York: Knopf, 1976.

Lorde, Audre. *Sister Outsider.* Trumansburg, N.Y.: The Crossing Press, 1984.

Lugones, Maria C., and Spelman, Elizabeth. "Have We Got a Theory for You! Feminist Theory, Cultural Imperialism and the Demand for 'The Woman's Voice.' " *Women's Studies International Forum* 6:6 (1983):573–81.

Marshall, Paule. *Brown Girl, Brown Stones.* New York: The Feminist Press, 1981.

Mazumdar, Sucheta. "General Introduction: A Woman-Centered Perspective on Asian American History." In *Making Waves: An Anthology of Writings By and About Asian American Women,* edited by Asian Women United by California. Boston: Beacon Press, 1989.

Minh-ha, Trinh. "Difference: A Special Third World Women Issue." *Feminist Review* 25 (1987):5–22.

Moraga, Cherríe, and Gloria Anzaldúa, editors. *This Bridge Called My Back: Writings by Radical Women of Color.* New York: Kitchen Table: Women of Color Press, 1981, 1983.

Morgen, Sandra, and Bookman, Ann. "Introductory Essay." In *Women and the Politics of Empowerment,* edited by Ann Bookman and Sandra Morgen. Philadelphia: Temple University Press, 1986.

Morrison, Toni, editor. *Race-ing Justice, En-gendering Power: Essays on Anita Hill, Clarence Thomas, and the Construction of Social Reality.* New York: Pantheon, 1992.

Mullings, Leith. "Ethnicity and Stratification in the Urban United States." In *Papers in Anthropology and Linguistics,* edited by May Ebihara and Rosamund Gianutsos.´ New York: New York Academy of Sciences, 1978.

Musil, Caryn McTighe. "Foreword." In *Bridges of Power: Women's Multicultural Alliances,* edited by Lisa Albrecht and Rose M. Brewer. Philadelphia, Santa Cruz, and Gabiola, BC: New Society Publishers, 1990.

Okazawa-Rey, Margo, Robinson, Tracy, and Ward, Janie Victoria. "Black Women and the Politics of Skin Color and Hair." *Women's Studies Quarterly* 14:1/2 (Spring/Summer) (1986):13–14.

Omolade, Barbara. *It's a Family Affair: The Real Lives of Black Single Mothers.* New York: Kitchen Table: Women of Color Press, 1986.

Ostrander, Susan. *Women of the Upper Class.* Philadelphia: Temple University Press, 1984.

Palmer, Phyllis Marynick. "White Women/Black Women: The Dualism of Female Identity and Experiences in the United States." *Feminist Studies* 9:1 (Spring 1983):151–70.

Pheterson, Gail. "Alliances Between Women: *Overcoming Internalized Oppression and Internalized Domination.*" In *Bridges of Power: Women's Multicultural Alliances,* edited by Lisa Albrecht and Rose M. Brewer. Philadelphia, Santa Cruz, and Gabiola, BC: New Society Publishers, 1990.

Pomeroy, Sarah B. *Goddesses, Whores, Wives, and Slaves: Women in Classical Antiquity.* New York: Schocken, 1975.

Pratt, Minnie Bruce. "Identity: Skin Blood Heart." In *Yours in Struggle: Three Feminist Perspectives on Anti-Semitism and Racism,* edited by Elly Bulkin, Minnie Bruce Pratt, and Barbara Smith. New York: Kitchen Table: Women of Color Press, 1984.

Quintanales, Martha. "I Paid Very Hard for My Immigrant Ignorance." In *This Bridge Called My Back: Writings by Radical Women of Color,* edited by Cherrie Moraga and Gloria Anzaldúa. New York: Kitchen Table: Women of Color Press, 1983:151.

Rich, Adrienne. "Compulsory Heterosexuality and Lesbian Experience." *Signs* 5 (1980):631–60. Anthologized in Catharine Simpson and Ethel Person, editors. *Women—Sex and Sex-*

uality. Chicago: University of Chicago Press, 1980.

Rubin, Gayle. "The Traffic in Women: Notes on the Political Economy of Sex." In *Toward an Anthropology of Women*, edited by Rayna Rapp Reiter. New York: Monthly Review Press, 1975.

Schneir, Miriam, editor. *Feminism: The Essential Historical Writings*. New York: Vintage, 1972.

Smith, Barbara. "Between a Rock and a Hard Place: Relationships between Black and Jewish Women. In *Yours in Struggle: Three Feminist Perspectives on Anti-Semitism and Racism*, edited by Elly Bulkin, Minnie Bruce Pratt, and Barbara Smith. Brooklyn, N.Y.: Long Haul Press, 1984.

Smith, Dorothy E. "Women's Perspective as a Radical Critique of Sociology." *Sociological Inquiry* 44 (1974):7–13.

Spelman, Elizabeth V. *Inessential Woman: Problems of Exclusion in Feminist Thought*. Boston: Beacon Press, 1988.

Tan, Amy. *The Joy Luck Club*. New York: Putnam, 1989.

———. *The Kitchen God's Wife*. New York: Putnam, 1991.

Terborg-Penn, Rosalyn. "Discrimination Against Afro-American Women in the Women's Movement, 1830–1920." In *The Black Woman Cross-Culturally*, edited by Filomina Steady. Cambridge, Mass.: Schenkman, 1981.

———. "Discontented Black Feminists: Prelude and Postscript to the Passage of the Nineteenth Amendment." In *Decades of Discon-tent: The Women's Movement, 1920–1940*, edited, with an introduction and a new foreword, by Lois Scharf and Joan M. Jensen. Boston: Northeastern University Press, 1987.

Tong, Rosemarie. *Feminist Thought: A Comprehensive Introduction*. Boulder and San Francisco: Westview Press, 1989.

Torres, Lourdes. "The Construction of Self in U.S. Latina Autobiographies." In *Third World Women and the Politics of Feminism*, edited by Chandra Talpade Mohanty, Ann Russo, and Lourdes Torres. Bloomington: Indiana University Press, 1991.

Washington, Mary Helen. "Introduction: 'The Darkened Eye Restored': Notes Toward a Literary History of Black Women." *Invented Lives: Narratives of Black Women 1860–1960*. New York: Anchor Press, 1987.

White, Deborah Gray. *Arn't I a Woman?: Female Slaves in the Plantation South*. New York: Norton, 1985.

Williams, Claudette. "Gall . . . You Come from Foreign." In *Charting the Journey: Writings by Black and Third World Women*, edited by Shabnam Grewal, Jackie Kay, Liliane Landor, Gail Lewis, and Pratibha Parmar. London: Sheba Feminist Publishers, 1988.

Young, Iris Marion. *Throwing Like a Girl and Other Essays in Feminist Philosophy and Social Theory*. Bloomington: Indiana University Press, 1990.

Zavella, Patricia. *Women's Work & Chicano Families: Cannery Workers of the Santa Clara Valley*. Ithaca and London: Cornell University Press, 1987.

Part *II*

The Family Circle

Introduction

Images of families in the popular media—television, films, magazines—inform us about acceptable and unacceptable family forms and ways to play roles within them. In the United States, traditional nuclear families such as Bill Cosby's "Huxtable Family" have long been a staple of prime-time television, but for the past two decades we have also seen accepting, though sometimes idealized, depictions of families headed by single mothers, single fathers, and families composed of combinations of relatives incorporating grandparents, uncles and aunts, and nephews, nieces, or cousins. We have also become increasingly aware of cross-cultural differences in family organization and roles.

Popular depictions have challenged earlier assumptions that, for example, married mothers ideally always stay at home to engage in full-time domestic work for their families, or even that mothers need or wish to have husbands to share in the raising of their children. However, such depictions have at times provoked criticism and controversy. Former Vice President Dan Quayle, for example, criticized the presentation of a television character, "Murphy Brown," a woman with a successful professional career, who chose, on discovering that she was pregnant, not to marry, but to

have and raise her baby by herself. The Vice President felt that making such a choice seem like an acceptable, even attractive option for some women constituted a challenge to "traditional family values"—which indeed it did. The television program's rebuttal to his criticism, that there are many kinds of families in America, underlined the fact that issues related to family structures and roles are issues of power, responsibility, and rights. In other words, the issues are *political*.

Daughterhood, sisterhood, wifehood, and motherhood are socially defined roles women play in a family context. Our understanding of these roles is shaped from the earliest childhood experience. It can be argued that all our roles in society are governed by family role expectations. In a sense, this is not at all surprising. Families, however structured and realized, are extremely important organizing units for all known societies, from the pre-industrial hunter-gatherers and cultivators to the highly urban industrial (and, some say, postindustrial) nations. In all these societies, families tend to be assigned the organization of childrearing, marriage, and various aspects of domestic life. However, in many societies, the family and its domestic concerns mark out the confines of women's worlds, while men, though also tied to families, are not confined entirely within them. In many societies in the past and present, women have been defined largely in terms of family role assignments, while men have been defined in other ways as well.

We have learned through the study of history and through cross-cultural comparison that sentiments and activities ascribed to women's family roles are variable; hence we cannot assume that they are simply "natural," but are socially shaped. Society may tell us that daughters are "naturally" obedient, sisters competitive, mothers loving of their children, wives dependent on their husbands, and we may indeed conform to these social expectations because we have been taught to do so. But as we examine family interactions in times and places other than our own, we see that there are many diverse ways to fulfill family expectations.

To understand our family roles and how they have shaped us, we need to understand both social expectations and the scope for variation in our choices in how we fulfill prescribed roles. We need to take into account, as well, the conflicts that may arise between our different assigned family roles and between those roles and others that may be assigned to us—or to which we may aspire.

Women have sometimes seen the family as too constricting, too limited, for the fulfillment of their aspirations. At times, we have had the option of developing alternative ways of organizing ourselves at the household or domestic level, of fulfilling our assigned roles, or even of replacing households and families with other social forms. This section will examine ways that women have redefined our family roles and redefined our families.

The family circle can be seen as a warm, enfolding, supportive center to our lives, or it can be viewed as a small confining cage that we long to escape. Many women have experienced both kinds of feeling toward families at different times in our lives.

Daughters and Sisters

The tie between daughters and sisters in our natal families lasts beyond our girlhoods. Eventually, most women leave home, marry, and become mothers. Male viewpoints in the study of family history or comparative kinship structures have tended to emphasize the role change to wife and mother and to draw attention away from our permanent attachments to our parents and siblings. These relationships, however, constitute the formative experience of our lives, and they continue in some form or another until our deaths.

No amount of legal sleight-of-hand can disguise the permanency of these links. To begin with, there is an enduring genetic legacy that ties us as daughters, and in turn our children, to the family of our birth. The strengths and weaknesses that women carry in our genes are transmitted to the next generation. No change of name or status can affect that transmission. Even death, accident, or a parental decision to put a child up for adoption cannot sever that tie.

In addition, our girlhood experiences mold us socially. From our natal, adoptive, or foster families, we derive our notions about human relationships. Families share small mannerisms, private jokes and recipes, and customary ways of doing tasks that tie them together as a group. Families also assign different roles to different members based largely on sex, age, and birth order. These early role designations continue to affect people throughout their lives. Both biological and psychological differences have been used by society to set sisters and brothers apart. Parental expectations differentiate between one sibling and another. Out of the politics and emotional currents that are played out in girlhood, the woman emerges. Our first role in life is as daughter/ sister. In many ways, it is also our last.

Daughter in the Family

The conception and birth of a child is usually a welcome event in the history of a family. Sometimes, however, it is inconvenient or even disastrous. The physical survival of the mother and older children, especially an un-weaned child, might be threatened by the arrival of another child. Where contraceptive and abortive methods are unknown, unavailable, or undependable, the only "choice" may be infanticide. Even in societies with forms of birth control available, infanticide has been practiced.

Those readers who believe that there is a "maternal instinct" that naturally causes mothers to protect our children must wonder what could prompt us to kill them instead. Inability to care for a child, particularly if it is "illegitimate" or if the other parent or other members of the society are not available for assistance, may be a motive. Where infanticide is a socially recognized option, it may be the father alone who makes the decision, and it may be the midwife or another party who carried it out. Historians and anthropologists have not documented the emotions of mothers in the face of such directives. Indeed, remarkably little has been said or recorded about so widespread a phenomenon.

Female Infanticide

In 1 B.C.E., a husband in Alexandria wrote to his wife in the Egyptian countryside: "I beg you and urge you . . . if by chance you bear a child—if it is a boy, let it be; if it is a girl, cast it out" (Hunt and Edgar, 1932). Until recent times, female infanticide has been the only method of population control that enables the responsible parties to make decisions on the basis of sex. The Greeks abandoned many more girls to die than boys, and the Romans had a law requiring fathers to raise all healthy sons but only one daughter (Pomeroy, 1975). In medieval Christian society, where church law strictly forbade infanticide, there is evidence that it was carried on quite extensively. Girls were the most common victims of "accidents" where women claim to have "overlaid" (smothered) children at night. When foundling homes were established, as in Florence in the fourteenth century, the records provide incontrovertible evidence that parents discarded many more females than males (Trexler, 1973).

Today it is possible to perform tests in early pregnancy to discover the sex of the fetus. In China the preference for sons persists even in the post-Liberation period. In the 1980s, state policies to increase agricultural production and limit population growth had a detrimental effect on the value of women. To meet these goals, many families resorted to past practices of both female infanticide and the abortion of fetuses identified as female (Honig and Hershatter, 1988). In the United States, more couples still prefer to have a son than a daughter, particularly if it is the first child (Jaccoma and Denmark, 1974; Williamson, 1976), and statistics show that many couples tend to continue having children until they have a son. Then they stop. There is virtually no society that positively prefers girl babies to boys.

Where infanticide has not been practiced, we would imagine that the genetic advantages of girls (discussed in Chapter 3) would result in our making up slightly more than half of the adult population. Often this is not the case. Why in many societies do more girls than boys die in infancy and early childhood (Dickemann, 1979)? One answer seems to be that male children get better treatment. If one child is systematically allotted less food, neglected during illnesses, and overworked or abused physically, that child is more likely to die. In many families, when protein has been scarce, women have customarily stinted ourselves and our daughters in favor of the husband and sons. This has prejudiced the daughters' chances of survival and helped to socialize those who survived to play the same role later in their own households. The neglect of daughters is masked almost everywhere by the assertion that girls do not require as much food as boys. This belief might account for more discrepancy in the size and physical strength of girls and boys than is generally acknowledged.

The Value of Daughters

The selective destruction of female babies by individual families throughout history would not have been possible unless society as a whole condoned it. Why the murder of female children should be a method of population control, why it took so long to develop effective and safe contraceptives, why these contraceptives, though available, are often not

used, and why so many people display a preference for sons over daughters are questions
that all who study women must ask. Many of
the answers must lie in the social patterns that
define women's place and our value to the society at large.

One theory that has received much publicity matches female infanticide with the high
valuation of males in societies engaged in
chronic warfare. If men are the warriors, sons
must be raised and "masculine" qualities
stressed. Because investment in daughters de-
tracts from investment in sons, daughters are
sacrificed. The evidence supporting this argument shows systematic correlation between
female infanticide, chronic warfare, and male
supremacist cultural values (Divale and Harris, 1978).

Another theory rests on speculations concerning the marital strategies of individual

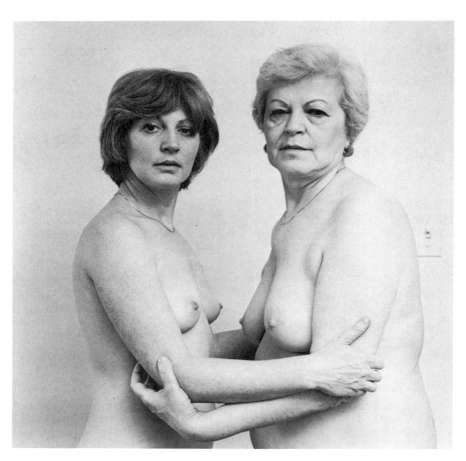

The younger woman is the photographer, who is seeking in her own way here to establish both the identity and separateness of herself and her mother.
Struck by the similarities of face and feature, she is aware at the same time that each represents a different generation, a different stage in the life cycle,
and an ongoing relationship at different stages in their own lives. (Photo of Niki Berg)

families. Where the potential marital pool is known and limited, parents may sacrifice daughters for whom there are no possibilities of a profitable future settlement (Coleman, 1976). In many societies, brides must be accompanied by wealth when we leave our fathers' houses. In others, daughters represent potential wealth that will be paid our parents in return for us (see Chapter 7). Clearly these economic prospects play an important role in the family's decision making.

These decisions seem to be based on men's values about the aggregation of wealth, political alliances, and the relative importance of warriors versus mothers. Decisions that favor women seem to exist only in the realm of fantasy. Ancient Greek myths about Amazons tell of women warriors who preferred girl babies to boys. According to the legend, sons were maimed or killed or immediately sent to their fathers. Feminists have adopted this myth about strong women but have modified its ugly features. In *The Female Man* (1975), Joanna Russ created a fictional utopia where women live without men and have only girls. Reproduction is accomplished by the merging of ova, and children are raised communally.

Daughters' Work. Some daughters, even when mature, are retained by parents to perform daughters' work and do not marry. The care and services of a daughter are often very highly esteemed even when they are not a dire necessity. It is not uncommon for a father to refuse to give his daughter in marriage because he wishes to reserve her services for himself, particularly if he is widowed and does not wish to remarry. If he does agree to part with his daughter, he may often demand much bride wealth in compensation for the loss.

Daughters serve as old-age security, and we are generally expected to provide our parents with a home, personal care when needed, affection, and other emotional supports. Sons are also liable for the same responsibilities, but all too often they limit their contributions to cash or manage to escape altogether. It is an old saying among the Turks that only a daughter can be relied upon on a dark day. The son will defect to his wife's family when he is most needed. There is also a saying in the Western world that "a son's a son till he gets him a wife/A daughter's a daughter the whole of her life."

Daughters have a certain intrinsic value in that we represent the reproducers of the next generation. If there is to be a future generation, women must be raised to produce it. The universal taboos against the mating of members of the immediate family make it necessary to procure a daughter-in-law for the production of grandchildren. The most common way in which a family gets a daughter-in-law is in exchange for a daughter. Indeed, some societies operate on a fairly rigid one-to-one basis: The even exchange of cousins, for example, is seen as the right and normal way of pairing off young people. Thus daughters are valuable directly or indirectly in that we represent chips in the bargains that make up the composition of society.

Girls occupy an important position within our natal families on the basis of the work we perform. Women are usually assigned a specific series of tasks considered to be beneath the attention of men. But these tasks must be done, and in most households daughters are trained to care for younger siblings and to assist in food preparation and other domestic chores. We fetch water and firewood, feed chickens, go to the market, wash clothes, help with the dairying, and undertake income-producing tasks like lacemaking. All this work may go unnoticed by a girl's father or brothers until it is left undone, but they depend on it nonetheless. The value mothers place on the help of daughters can hardly be overestimated.

Families without daughters or girls to perform daughters' work often adopt us or bring girls in from other sources. Many girls abandoned by parents or exposed to die have been adopted in this informal manner. A warm relationship can develop, and the unwanted daughter may come to occupy a valued and secure place in the new home. In the ancient world, girls were also raised as slaves and often trained as prostitutes by the men and women who owned brothels.

In the contemporary world, the value of daughters' work to families and societies is most evident in a 1988 U.S. House of Representatives report pointing out that the average American woman is likely to spend eighteen years looking after elderly parents and in-laws in addition to seventeen years of child-rearing. Regardless of our racial, ethnic, and class background, many of us assume our dependent-adult caring responsibilities willingly. However, this work is not shared by brothers and husbands. Hence, while some of us may not choose the "mother track," we retain for the most part the "daughter track." With so many women in the paid workforce today, the strains of eldercare on personal and professional life can be so extensive that many of us must make major alterations in our lives (*Newsweek*, July 16, 1990).

Young women, then, start our lives on the basis of a series of considerations about our future worth to the family. We then enter into a political system in which parents, sisters, and brothers all figure in a series of shifting alliances and antagonisms. We struggle for identity and material advantage within a pattern imposed by chance and social convention.

Naming the Daughter

The names given us at birth are sometimes the most powerful indicators of our value and place in the family and social scheme. Because the process of naming is profoundly political, we can learn much about the status of women in different societies by understanding the naming patterns.

A name designates the sex of a child. The more emphasis a society places on the difference between girls and boys, the more carefully it will distinguish their names. Medieval Europeans usually got through life with a single name, which often repeated the father's name or embroidered on it, such as Charles, Charlotte, or Charlene. When named for fathers, daughters were given a close feminine form of his name: John/Joan; Robert/Roberta.

Boys are almost never given names that signify girls, but the reverse can occur, perhaps reflecting the greater worth attached to male associations. Indeed, many names originally assigned to men, such as Evelyn, Beverly, and Shirley, have become incontrovertibly female by virtue of such transfers. Sons are frequently named for their fathers. Daughters are far

---

Buying Daughters in Traditional China

Among the sellers with their ropes, cages, and water tanks were the sellers of little girls. . . . There were fathers and mothers selling their daughters, whom they pushed forward and then pulled back again. . . . My mother would not buy from parents, crying and clutching. . . . My mother would buy her slave from a professional whose little girls stood neatly in a row and bowed together when a customer looked them over.

        (Kingston, 1976:93) Reprinted by permission of Alfred A. Knopf, Inc.

more rarely named for our mothers (although one popular Western name, Eleanor, was first bestowed on the twelfth-century heiress of Aquitaine to celebrate the memory of her mother, Anor; thus she was named Ali-anor, the other Anor).

Custom may reserve the privilege of naming sons for fathers and give mothers the right to select names for daughters. Mothers often seek to express pleasure in having daughters or to transfer desirable qualities through a name like Joy, Linda ("beautiful" in Spanish), or Miranda ("marvelous"). Mothers frequently name daughters for admired objects such as flowers or jewels or for a character in a movie or novel. Sometimes mothers may even signal private dreams in the name of a girl. Among medieval Jews living in Islamic Cairo, infant girls bore names like Nasr ("victory") or Sitt-al-Jami ("she who rules over everybody") (Goitein, 1978).

The importance of children for the continuity of a lineage is reflected in the use of *patronymics* (fathers' names). For example, the ancient Romans did not give their daughters individual names at all. A daughter was automatically called by the feminine form of the father's name. Thus, all the daughters of a Claudius were called Claudia and referred to informally in numerical order: Claudia prima, Claudia secunda, Claudia tertulla (the little third). In some areas, patronymics continued into modern times. The heroine of a Scandinavian novel by Nobel Prize winner Sigrid Undset (1882–1949), set in the fourteenth century, was called Kristin Lavransdatter (daughter of Lavrans). Similarly, the heroine of Tolstoy's novel (published in 1875–1877) was named Anna Arkadyevna (daughter of Arkady) Karenina (wife of Karenin). The use of patronymics in the United States has commonly rigidified into a permanent family name (such as Jackson or Richardson). But it is rare to find in modern times a perpetuation of the old system of using matronymics where

the mother may have been the better known or wealthier of the parental couple (Maryson or Margaretson) (Herlihy, 1976). African American slaves in the American South named sons for their fathers in an effort to retain family ties despite the common breakup of the conjugal unit through sale (Gutman, 1977).

Other forms of family names developed extensively in Europe from about the ninth century on as the practice of bestowing "Christian" names became popular. The frequent use of John, Mary, and other saints' names often made the addition of some other name a necessity for identification. Names associated with a parent, a profession, or a geographical location gradually hardened into the "family" name bestowed alike on daughters and sons at birth. These names reflect the perpetuation of a male lineage since they are derived from the father's name, profession, or place of birth.

In the modern Western world a daughter's surname generally changes at the time of marriage. Women have reported feelings of a loss of identity when they suddenly stop using their own names and become, instead, Mrs. ————. A woman's married name designates a position rather than a person, and a first Mrs. ———— may be replaced by a second or third with the same name (see Chapter 7).

Traditionally in Korea, Confucian custom deemed female status too low even for married women to be permitted to use the family name of their husbands. In contrast, Burma, probably the most egalitarian Asian society with a Buddhist tradition and a matrilineal past, did not have a family name system but gave both females and males their own individual names, which they retained after marriage (Matsui, 1987).

In Spanish-speaking societies, women often retain our father's names by adding them (with *y*) to the husbands' names. Among noble families, it is often possible to trace a whole genealogical history by a recitation of the full name of an individual. In other societies, children will often perpetuate the name of their mother's family as a middle name.

Many American couples today experiment with combining both names as a family name, or women may keep our names when we marry, as we are legally entitled to do. It is still most common for American children to have the surnames of their fathers, but it is perfectly possible to register the children under other names, alternating the names of mother and father with each child, for example, according to the sex of the child. In a society where the names of women prevailed as often as the names of men, whatever loss of identity resulted from the losing of one's name would be shared by women and men equally. Some women reject the surnames of both fathers and husbands and choose our own, as did, for instance, artist Judy Chicago (see Chapter 1).

Family Relationships: Parents

From the moment girls are born and named, we are started on a track that will take us through our whole lives. Our parents react to us in ways prescribed by social convention or by their own emotional preferences. We are handled and dressed and trained to fulfill a role in the family as daughters. Our siblings shape our personalities by assigning us an individual role among themselves.

Daughters and Mothers

Children experience the mother as the first "other" and a daughter's sense of self must be forged out of that opposition. But since the mothering person is nearly always a woman, daughters tend also to experience stronger feelings of identity with the mother than do sons (Chodorow, 1978). The first task of individuation that we as daughters must undertake is the discovery of the ego boundaries between ourselves and our mothers. All children have the task of separating psychologically from their mothers, of discovering where one ends and the other begins. This is more difficult for girls, as we will discuss later.

The developmental task is made even harder if mothers see daughters as a reflection of ourselves as children. In relatively simple societies where girls grow into women looking forward to a predictable life, and women's and men's roles are distinctly defined, this is probably not a matter for distress and does not seem to create a great deal of tension between generations. Mothers act easily as role models and guides for young women. In complex societies, however, particularly those that reward a highly developed sense of individualism, daughters may suffer much confusion in separating ourselves from our mothers, as is suggested by the title of Nancy Friday's *My Mother/My Self: The Daughter's Search for Identity* (1977).

Very often, mothers tend to inhibit the development of this separate sense of identity. First, we expect our daughters to remain at home more often than we expect it of our sons. Nursery schools, for example, receive far more applications for boys than for girls. This may indicate that parents are more willing to pay for a boy's education and set higher expectations for his future achievements. But it may also reflect a more universal pattern in which the boy is sent out into the world at a relatively early age to shape himself for his predicted adult role (Lewis, 1972). Second, girls are generally expected to help our mothers with "women's work" around the home even after we have started school. A daughter is often shaped into a "little mother" and taught nurturing skills. Mothers may mold daughters in our own images, or we may consciously set out to create daughters who will not repeat our experiences but will live out a life that some ill fate snatched from us.

Whatever confusion and tension that may occur between mothers and daughters, rela-

African-American daughters often experience mother relationships with grandmothers and with aunts as well as with mothers. Here the hairdo, as well as the face and the tightly clasped hands, suggests the closeness of this relationship. (Photo by Niki Berg)

tionships generally become closer and mutu-ally interdependent at two key points in our lives: first, after daughters marry and become mothers; and second, when mothers become frail and our roles begin to reverse (Fischer, 1986).

In urban areas where families can live close together, the clustering of daughters within the neighborhood of our mothers' homes is common, and by no means accidental. Indeed, the marked ethnic character of many urban neighborhoods in the United States often re-

"Mother and Child" (c. 1905) by Mary Cassatt (1845–1926) uses the mirror motif, which often symbolizes the way women at all ages seek to find our identity by searching in a reflecting glass. We look in a mirror as we look in other's eyes to find out what it will tell us about who we are. (National Gallery of Art, Washington, D.C. Chester Dale Collection)

Mothers and Daughters

They perpetuate themselves
one comes out of the other
like a set of Russian dolls.

Each is programmed to pass on
her methods to the daughter
who in turn becomes a mother.

They learn to cry and get
their way and finally to say
"I did it all for you."

When they are old and can't
be mended they're either burnt
or laid in boxes in the dark.

Russian Dolls. (Photo by Richard Zalk)

Sometimes their sons are sad.
Their daughters go away and weep
real tears for themselves.

(Feaver, 1980) Reprinted by permission.

sults from the efforts of daughters and mothers to keep families in close proximity.

These "pseudomatrilineal" arrangements bear the mixture of anxiety, tension, and love that the natal family itself offers to the young girls. The support and affection enjoyed by young daughters in our maternal homes may be extended to our married lives, but only if husbands tolerate it and usually at the price of conflict with the interests of the married couple.

The poet Honor Moore has recounted her fears of failure and insanity growing from too close a sense of identity with her grandmother Margarett, a painter who unaccountably ceased to paint in middle age, and her mother, who unaccountably delayed the beginning of her writing career until the same age and then died before she could develop her talent.

But mothers may also be the strongest allies in helping daughters to realize our dreams. In *Sido* (1930, 1953), the French author Colette wrote of the encouragement she received as a child in her mother's house. The leader of the militant British suffrage movement, Emmeline Pankhurst (1858–1928), raised her daughters to lead independent and creative lives. Sylvia Pankhurst first chose an artistic career and then became the socialist leader of working-class women. Christabel Pankhurst also became a leader in the fight for women's rights. Adela Pankhurst emigrated to Australia, where she became a social reformer.

Given the hostile social environment facing women of color, many African American mothers have purposely raised daughters to be independent and able to enhance our capacity to survive (Joseph, 1984; Ladner, 1971). Joseph also writes of the respect and affection of daughters for our mothers and mother sur-

My Grandmother Who Painted

I write about Margarett to find out, concretely, for myself. That silence, that unused canvas, thwarted passion and talent passed down a matrilineage to me. My mother has nine children, survives a near-fatal automobile accident, a nervous breakdown to put herself first, to commit herself to writing. She publishes one book, but in two more years, at fifty, she dies of cancer. Talent. And failure. Failure to hold, failure to focus, failure to hold the focus to the hot place so the transformation can occur, carry you out of self, so what you create may support, steady, nurture and protect you.

(Moore, 1980:52) Permission granted by the Julian Bach Literary Agency, Inc.

rogates in recognition of the obstacles our mothers confront. It is grandmothers who often become surrogate mothers, especially when the biological mother is young and continues to live at home. Sometimes, to permit biological parents to carve out a better life, children are sent away to be raised by grandmothers.

The literary critic Mary Helen Washington acknowledges the persistent image of the strong black mother and dedicates her anthology, *Black-Eyed Susans: Classic Stories by and about Black Women* (1975), "to the fine black women who brought me up." Yet she also perceives the theme of mother-daughter conflict in the literature of black women. The mothers are pragmatic and conservative while the daughters are idealistic and reject "the good life" as defined by those mothers. According to Washington, "the conflict is not only personal but historical. And the resolution of the conflict can be discovered only as one comes to terms with history" (Washington, 1975).

Mother-daughter relations are further complicated in multicultural and multiracial societies such as the United States where there is tension and ambivalence over strategies of racial or ethnic maintenance and cultural assimilation. What kind of a personal identity does one develop as a mother or daughter of color? What are our relations with our ethnic communities and the dominant culture? The theme of mother-daughter conflict within an ethnic community underlies much of American ethnic literature. For example, Paule Marshall (1981) writes in *Brown Girl, Brownstones* of growing up female and Barbadian in Brooklyn. In *The Joy Luck Club* (1989) and the film by that name, Amy Tan described the different historical experiences and expectations of four Chinese American women and our Chinese mothers. In assessing Chicana poetry, Marta Sanchez (1985) discusses the "double ambivalence" borne by Mexican American women in our struggles against racism in the United States and sexism from within and without the community and the significance of mothers, grandmothers, and mother surrogates as role models.

The ability of daughters to define and redefine ourselves can be evidence of assertiveness and strength. But it can also betray the absence of a sense of a fixed inner core. A common motif in the work of women artists is the mirror in which women search for ourselves and beautify our bodies. In her painting of a mother and daughter, Mary Cassatt portrays a mother who is helping her daughter find the image of herself in a mirror. Women's art is commonly haunted by the fear that a woman will look into the glass and see noth-

I Know Why the Caged Bird Sings

When I was three and Bailey four, we had arrived in the musty little town, wearing tags on our wrists which instructed—"To whom It May Concern"—that we were Marguerite and Bailey Johnson Jr., from Long Beach, California, en route to Stamps, Arkansas, c/o Mrs. Annie Henderson. . . .

Years later I discovered that the United States has been crossed thousands of times by frightened Black children traveling alone to their newly affluent parents in Northern cities, or back to grandmothers in Southern towns when the urban North reneged on its economic promises. . . .

We lived with our grandmother and uncle in the rear of the Store (it was always spoken of with a capital *s*) which she had owned some twenty five years. . . .

To describe my mother would be to write about a hurricane in its perfect power. . . . My mother's beauty literally assailed me. Her red lips (Momma said it was a sin to wear lipstick) split to show even white teeth and her fresh-butter color looked see-through clean. . . . I knew immediately why she had sent me away. She was too beautiful to have children. I had never seen a woman as pretty as she who was called "Mother." Bailey on his part fell instantly and forever in love. I saw his eyes shining like hers; he had forgotten the loneliness and the nights when we had cried together because we were "unwanted children." He had never left her warm side or shared the icy wind of solitude with me. She was his Mother Dear and I resigned myself to his condition.

(Angelou, 1969:29–30) Reprinted by permission.

ing; it is "an allegory of nonidentity . . . fear of desertion, of dependence upon an insufficiently integrated self" (Peterson and Wilson, 1976:4). The double female image is another common theme, for we frequently view ourselves as part of a mother-daughter dyad. Young women frequently find that our struggles to break away from the pattern of our mothers' lives tangle us ever more deeply in a mesh of invisible threads. Daughters who have grown up, married, and become mothers in turn may still be haunted by the nagging voices of our mothers telling us how to do everything, setting standards of perfection that we can never reach. This is an irritating experience if the voices come to us daily over the telephone or in person. It is even more maddening if the maternal voice has been internalized in the daughters' sense of permanent inadequacy.

Some daughters react with rage to our mothers' dependency. Others react against our mothers' independence. The Clytemnestra/Electra antipathy has not yet been solved in the relations of women across the generation gap.

Daughters and Fathers

Our relationships with our fathers can be fraught with tension and instability. Daughters often find ourselves in league with our mothers against the foreign male element represented by our fathers. On other occasions, our hunger for the approval of our fathers makes us vulnerable indeed to the subtle training they give us on how to become attractive and socially desirable women in maturity.

Fathers who want to bring their daughters up as "little women" will actively discourage

Three generations of mothers and daughters. As daughters and mothers our lives are deeply enmeshed. As years pass, we find ourselves closer to older generations of women and seek out their companionship as well as reconciling earlier differences. (Photo by Hope Wurmfeld, from *Mothers and Daughters* series)

our efforts to break out of the conventional restrictions of our feminine role. They will compliment us on pretty clothing and beguiling ways. They will frown on us if we are messy or "tomboyish." They will let us know that straightforward competition will not earn paternal respect. When Elizabeth Cady Stanton (1815–1902) won a first-place Latin award in school to compensate her father for the son he had lost, her father sighed heavily, "You should have been a boy" (Stanton, 1971:23). Only after years of marriage and motherhood, conforming to the roles so clearly marked out for her, did Stanton finally return to the ambitions of her youth, pursuing a career as a writer and feminist agitator.

Fathers may encourage their daughters to reject our mothers and love them alone. Freud came to believe that when his female patients talked of incest with their fathers, they were revealing wishes rather than reporting facts. But today in clinics, hospitals, and psychiatric centers, incest between father and daughter is a frequently reported infraction of the general taboo against sexual intercourse among close relatives. Sexual abuse of females is also perpetrated by uncles, stepfathers, brothers, cousins, and grandfathers. Very little is known about the occurrence of mother-daughter and sister-sister incest. Mother-son incest is apparently rare (Russell, 1986).

The effects of father-daughter incest are manifold. Research indicates it often leaves deep and lasting trauma. The experience may drive girls away from home as runaways or into a premature and unwanted marriage or pregnancy to escape abuse; or to a destiny of drug addiction and prostitution. Even if abused girls remain at home and the relationship runs its course, we may be haunted by anxiety attacks, adult sexual dysfunctions, and difficulties in social relationships. When fathers use force to rape their daughters, step-daughters, foster daughters, or even the daughters of women with whom they live, the physical and psychic traumas are magnified. Even when a more subtle and seductive approach is taken, father-daughter incest or its semblance is a cruel relationship of power and dominance between unequals (Russell, 1986).

The experience may be made even worse for the daughters if it becomes public knowledge. To prevent this, mothers and daughters may engage in a conspiracy of silence lest the offending fathers be imprisoned and their wages lost to the family. They may also fear the removal of the daughter to a hostile or at least unfamiliar environment. If daughters seek help, we may be made responsible for the dissolution of the family, punished for "misbehavior," and loaded down with a misplaced burden of guilt that may emotionally cripple us forever. If daughters become mothers of our fathers' children, the damage to all concerned may be extraordinary.

Fathers can, of course, be very supportive. Many prominent women have noted with gratitude the approval of their fathers in helping them to a career beyond the domestic sphere. In many cases, however valuable the emotional support of mothers to aspiring daughters, the sheer material support that the

---

Male Parenting

It is precisely *because* he cannot carry the baby in his belly or give it milk from his bosom that the human father—with his capacity to imagine being what he is not, doing what he cannot, seeing what is gone or not yet here or out of sight—feels an especially vivid urge to use his other, more singularly human, capacities to nurture the baby. To him the neonate is not the small, writhing and squeaking, special-smelling lump of flesh that it is for the tomcat. It is a daughter or a son, a being started with his own seed whose long, mysterious gestation in the dark inside of another person he has typically been thinking about—often with impatience and jealousy—for many months; a being whose resemblance to his dead grandparents he is excited to notice, whose future as a companionable child and supportive adult and maker of grandchildren he anticipates, whose bodily growth and steady stream of ordinary achievements will soon be flooding him with joyful pride.

So far, men have had to act on this urge mainly in indirect ways. . . .

It is now for the first time possible for us to rearrange the structure of our primary-group life so that men can act directly, rather than indirectly, on this specifically male and human urge of theirs, *this impulse to affirm and tighten by cultural inventions their unsatisfactorily loose mammalian connection with children.* They need leeway to work out ways of making their actual . . . contact with the very young as intimate as woman's. And with the very young, actual contact is the bodily contact that keeps them clean, fed, tranquil, safe, rested, and mentally stimulated. "As intimate," obviously, does not mean qualitatively identical. It is precisely the irreducible qualitative *difference* between motherhood and fatherhood—the physical difference, as it is reflected and reworked in the parents' thoughts and feelings—that gives men's passion for babies its own special male edge, its characteristic paternal flavor.

(Dinnerstein, 1976:80–81)

From *The Mermaid and the Minotaur* by Dorothy Dinnerstein.
Reprinted by permission of Harper Collins Publishers, Inc.

father commands can make the difference in determining our fates. Marie Sklodowska (1867–1934) began her scientific career under the instruction of her father, a professor of physics in Warsaw. Without his assistance, it is doubtful that she would ever have been sent to study in Paris, have married Pierre Curie, and used his laboratory facilities in her discovery of radium. Maria Mitchell, the astronomer from Nantucket, began by spending many hours with her father gazing at stars through his telescope. In 1847, she discovered the comet that is named for her. And research into the lives and careers of a group of women who were among the few to hold top management positions in American business and industry in the early 1970s revealed a distinct pattern. The women were generally firstborn or only children, and all had a close father-daughter relationship in which the daughters were given strong support to pursue their interests (Hennig and Jardim, 1976).

The relationships of women with our fathers have not received much attention in recent feminist literature. At present, it appears that domineering fathers may provoke reactions in their daughters that release our feminist impulses and creative potential. But it is also true that the fathers of many feminists and women artists, scientists, and other creative women were sympathetic and actually involved in the rearing of their daughters. What we can say with confidence is that equal participation by both parents, where possible, will often provide children with the best chances of finding helpful role models, and with the support necessary to develop and cultivate their talents.

Sisters: Sibling Relationships

The most common means of discriminating among siblings is age-ranking. In some ways, age-ranking is a simple and inescapable result of the facts of nature. The firstborn child will tend to be given more responsibility for the care of younger children and given leadership in the organization of family chores. The older child will generally go to school first and break the path in obtaining privileges, such as an extended bedtime, from the parents. In addition, of course, many societies reserve very specific privileges for older children. For example, the upper ranks of English society as well as feudal Japan long held to a tradition of passing the family wealth and property to the oldest male offspring. Parents also discouraged younger daughters from marrying until an older sister was settled. Folklore and fairy tales are often dominated by the plight of the younger children obliged to make their way in a hostile world controlled by their elders.

Age-ranking tends to impose personality characteristics on the children. An older child will very often emerge as the more aggressive, achievement-oriented, responsible member of the family. A younger child is likely to feel cheated; she or he is outfitted with hand-me-down clothes and toys and is constantly treated as an inferior in the games and conversations of older siblings. But younger children may also emerge as more insouciant, carefree personalities, the darlings of parents and older siblings (Sutton-Smith and Rosenberg, 1970; Leman, 1985).

A fictional illustration of the interaction of age-ranked siblings that conforms to the findings of modern psychologists can be found in *Little Women* by Louisa May Alcott (1823–1888), which first appeared in 1873. In the book, four sisters struggle to help their mother make ends meet while their father is away at war. Their life experiences shape their parts in the family scenario. Meg, the oldest, is the "little mother," the somewhat strait-laced, responsible leader of the flock. Her seriousness and occupation of the adult role leave the next sister, Jo, free to occupy the part of tomboy, mischief maker, and, eventually, liberated woman. The third sister, Beth, is the family saint whose peacemaking role continues even after her pathetic death. Amy is the family beauty whose childish vanity and self-centeredness are a cause of concern for her censorious older sisters. A similar assortment of role assignments can be seen among the Bennet girls in the 1813 novel of English sisterhood, *Pride and Prejudice*, by Jane Austen (1775–1867).

The dynamics established in childhood among siblings may last throughout life. Many people feel that the sense of place or role developed in childhood may never be overcome. Younger siblings never lose the sense of following in the footsteps of older children. The labeling imposed by parents, rivalry between siblings, and reactions against family roles sometimes influence young adults into certain career paths and life goals. Even late into life, jealousy of one another and rivalry for the attention of parents who may long since have died can mark the relationship.

Siblings can be sources of strength as well as conflict. In a period of widespread divorce, many individuals find relationships with sisters and brothers a core of stability in lives that are otherwise gravely troubled. Continuing and successful sibling relationships appear to have wider effects in heightening women's sense of security and in improving our social skills in the wider community.

Sisters as Opposites and Companions

The Bible provides us with two examples of sisters who reflect and complement one another: Leah and Rachel in the Old Testament and Martha and Mary in the New. Leah was the older, maternal sister, while Rachel, young and long childless, was the well-beloved sister for whom Jacob was willing to work for fourteen long years. Martha was the careful, domestic sister engaged in making Jesus and his companions comfortable in her house. Mary was the intellectual, visionary sister who cast aside her domestic responsibilities in order to listen to Jesus' teaching. Such polarizations between sisters can be interpreted as two sides of a single personality as well as two possible choices in life.

Despite our occasional rivalries and jealousies, even tantrums, sisters have loving and affectionate bondings as well. Swapping of clothes, boyfriends, advice, and support often overshadow hostility. We play against one another in lifelong dialogue. This was dramatically expressed by Jessamyn West in her memoir *The Woman Said Yes* (1976), a record of her sister's bout with cancer in which the author assisted her first with home care and finally with a peaceful death. In the course of the long ordeal, the sisters spent the nights reliving their youth together, comparing and reconciling the differences in their experiences.

Older sisters provide models and assistance to younger ones. Traditionally, one of the roles of married sisters is to chaperone younger sisters at social gatherings and to use our husbands' contacts to look for husbands for our sisters. We may also provide a home for younger sisters or brothers who leave the family home for a new location. Thus, older sisters may emigrate to a city, marry or become established in jobs, and provide a base for following siblings who come looking for similar opportunities.

In old age, the original bonds may reassert themselves. Divorced, widowed, and maiden sisters often come at last to shared households.

Sister-Brother Relations

Age-ranking is often nullified by sex-ranking. All too frequently, the privileges and importance that a girl might expect as the oldest child are brutally canceled by the appearance of a brother. Many feminists received the first jolt of awareness of "woman's place" when we suddenly realized that the leadership role was destined for a new baby by right of his gender alone (Shaarawi, 1987). Throughout the early years, girls and boys are almost always routed along different tracks. This is often formalized by the practice of special initiation ceremonies for boys alone. A young girl attending a *brith* (a Jewish circumcision ceremony) was told not to be distressed at the baby's discomfort. "For," said her aunt, "it is a small price to pay for being a man." In some societies, boys are "breeched" or otherwise endowed with the garb of a man at an early age, while girls have traditionally never changed our mode of dress to signify womanhood.

In a horticultural community in Kenya, girls aged five to seven may spend half their time doing chores, while boys of the same age spend only 15 percent of their time at work and never do woman's work unless there is no sister available to help the mother (Ember, 1973). Among the Hopi, men teach boys to weave cloth and women teach girls to weave baskets. In the United States, even though it is the law that both girls and boys must go to school, girls tend to be steered into different and less educationally valued subjects and different extracurricular activities, on the basis of gender (see Chapter 11).

In all too many families, the achievements and talents of sisters may be subordinated to the ambitions of brothers. In the nineteenth century, for example, poet Dorothy Wordsworth devoted her life to the care of her poet brother, William. The talents of Charlotte, Anne, and Emily Brontë far overshadowed those of their brother, Branwell, but they were able to gain recognition only by publishing their novels under male pseudonyms. In one of America's preeminent political families, the Kennedys, it has been the brothers and their male offspring rather than the Kennedy women who have garnered the most family support in the pursuit of their aspirations.

Sisters may resent the preference that our families show to our brothers. We may resent their freedom, education, friends, and the favored treatment they receive at home. Resentments of this kind may open deep gulfs between sisters and brothers and may be reflected in our relationships with our spouses and our own children.

Age-ranking still plays a role in establishing the relationships between sister and brother. Older sisters may well be forced to give precedence to our brothers in the family strategies, but we may also be cast in the role of "mothers" to them, establishing a burden that may last throughout life. On the other side, older brothers tend to play the masculine role toward their sisters, taking a protective and even bullying tone with them. They become stronger and more confident as they grow older, while we may find ourselves restricted by limitations and a suffocating protection that deprives us of the confidence that can come only from the experience of success. Even older sisters may come to appear fragile and in need of protection. Often societies impose this role on young men whether they like it or not. "A man's honor lies between his sister's legs" is a common saying throughout the Mediterranean world. Young men are thus encouraged to police the behavior of their sisters and personally to avenge any infringement of the customary male code of honor by both the sisters and their chosen lovers. In some societies, the brothers take an active role in arranging their sisters' marriages, even if the fathers are still alive, on the understanding that it is they who will have to live longest with the proposed brothers-in-law.

Inheritance

Women who leave our natal families to take up our mature lives carry with us the emotional legacies of sibling and parental interaction. But we also have a more formal legacy defined through custom, law, and social institutions. The family is the recognized unit that bestows status, class, property rights, privilege, or position upon its members, whether biological or adopted. The determination of legitimacy is the first social characteristic that girls derive from our families. If the sexual relationships of our parents have followed a prescribed pattern of propriety, or if they have fulfilled a socially approved set of rituals governing formal adoption, daughters will usually be legitimately established—or confined—in that social place that our parents occupied before us.

The inheritance of social *status* may include legacies from both parents. Women may derive our citizenship in a modern state from either mother or father or both, depending on the laws set by the state. Jews, for example, inherit Jewish affiliation through the mother's line, and therefore the right to claim Israeli citizenship. In the United States, illegitimate children of a woman citizen inherit the mother's position. Often lower status or dependent status (slavery, serfdom, or noncitizenship) comes through the mother. Thus, in the American South, the children of slave women were born slaves, even if fathered by a man who became the president of the United States (as has been asserted in the case of Thomas Jefferson).

Sex is an important factor affecting inheritance among sisters and brothers. *Patrilineal* societies pass authority, property, and descent directly through the male line from father to son. *Matrilineal* societies sometimes pass authority and property through males, but descent passes through females; sometimes productive property passes from mothers to daughters. While matrilineal societies, such as the Native American Navajo and Iroquois and the African Bemba, tend to confer greater authority upon women than do patrilineal societies, observers have noted that these societies have a less rigid system of authority in general. Where extensive trade or manufacturing ex-

ists, matrilineal systems appear to vanish and even patrilineal systems are modified in favor of a *bilateral* system, allowing a child to inherit from both parents.

In capitalist societies, patterns of inheritance of property and position favor sons over daughters. In Japan, a household head without children would adopt a boy to be raised as the successor to manage economic matters, inherit property, and worship the ancestors. Or, in the case of having only daughters, the household head would adopt a son-in-law as his successor, who would also assume the head's surname (Yanagisako, 1985). Even in the simplest societies, where personal property is restricted to a few effects that are buried with their possessor, the inheritance of parental skills or privileges will generally be apportioned according to a child's sex. And in socialist societies, which typically aimed to reduce disparities of private property, it remained possible to inherit status or position informally. There, too, it was fairly clear that discrimination favored the male.

Commonly, a system that allows the passage of property to and through women is accompanied by the development of class and caste hierarchies with strict rules for controlling individual heirs, particularly females. Generally, women are admitted to the inheritance of our fathers and/or brothers only when strong measures exist to control our marriages and our sex lives in general. These societies are careful to enforce adultery laws against women, to link "honor" with virginity before marriage and fidelity after, and to endow fathers and brothers with strong coercive powers over the female members of their families (Goody, 1977).

Many societies have had laws that restricted the leaving of property. These laws may recognize *primogeniture* (the passage of the patrimony to the firstborn son), *entail* (the strict line of succession to property, usually through the oldest related male), and *coverture* (husband's complete control over his wife's property). The more wealthy and productive a society has been, the more likely that a social hierarchy of class has formed that has caused women to lose position in a variety of ways.

The Sisterhood of Women

Our identities are formed by our relationships with our parents and siblings in the natal family. These identities are shaped by the tension of closeness and conflict and informed by the ideals of womanhood that the family accepts from the larger community. In this way, we receive two levels of self-consciousness from our childhood: our sense of womanliness and our sense of individuality. Our ability to accept our own identities with self-confidence in our mature life is largely dependent on the feelings that we have developed about other women.

Psychotherapist and political theorist Jane Flax (1980) sees a connection between the development of the feminine personality and a patriarchal society that devalues women. She implies that only a radical transformation of society can bring about changes in family relationships that now undermine the confidence of women and our sense of solidarity with one another. Flax, like Chodorow, notes that the mother functions as the first love object for all her children. Daughters, according to Flax, must suppress our desire for the mother and transfer our sexual feelings to the more powerful father, as society is currently organized. Failure to make the transfer results, as with sons, in a failure to achieve individual autonomy. Yet the identification with the father as an autonomous person, in comparison with the mother, creates a conflict within women about our own identity. As daughters, we are trained to turn to the father as a source of autonomous identification, but we are also taught that we can never experience his autonomy except in a substantially vicarious manner.

The sibling situation often contributes an external conflict in a woman's development. Siblings of both sexes, of course, experience rivalry and competition with one another, but the rivalry is more intense and has more permanent consequences when both rivals are women. Sisters are set to rival one another as well as our mothers for the love and attention of our fathers. Brothers are able to diffuse this rivalry in later life by choosing from a wide range of competitive possibilities, but these possibilities have generally been severely restricted among women.

According to Flax (1978), the rejection of the mother is responsible for the antifeminism of adult women. In such women, the turn to the father results in the effective heterosexual orientation that Freud saw as essential to maturity. But it leaves a legacy of rage and contempt for the mother, which in turn scars daughters as we attempt to work out our own adjustments to life's ordeals/experiences. Nor can we turn to our sisters for support and comfort in the battle, because their own maturity has too often depended on rivalry. Heterosexuality based on contempt for mothers and hatred of sisters alienates women; and such alienation is reinforced, according to this analysis, by susceptibility to threats that the "penalty" for not winning the struggle for autonomy will be "frigidity" or "homosexuality."

One of the challenges that women's studies must meet in the attempt to redefine women from the center of our own experiences is to expose the power relationships that endorse such threats and then to reconstruct womanhood as a positive experience. A heterosexuality based on the rejection of mothers and sisters is an identity based on self-denigration and dependency. What kinds of people will women be when we can form our identities from a dual model of mother and father? We will certainly be less role-ridden when we choose to turn from the daughter to the mother role in life. Such a resolution to our conflict—the liberation of our mothers as payment for the liberation of ourselves—might bring all women to an experience of the underlying, universal sisterhood of women.

Many feminists believe that the struggles that now mark the relationships between daughters and mothers are a consequence of inflexible family sex and gender roles and the oppression of women. The differences observable among sisters in the same family point the way to possibilities for future change. The early slogan of women's liberation, "Sisterhood is powerful," sought to establish the bonds between women that male-oriented kinship and political structures have so often obscured. Through the agency of consciousness-raising, many women began painfully to reexamine the real histories of our lives to see how we had been damaged in our individual integrity and alienated from our sister women by false myths and oppositions. Most difficult of all, perhaps, is the effort to reach past the long and painful barriers of age and experience and see our mothers at last as full members in the sisterhood of women. It is a task that all women must undertake to reach full appreciation of our own selves.

We must also reach out across our differences of race, class, and nationality without ignoring them. Every woman is the daughter of another woman. Every mother is a daughter. All women are sisters.

Summary

Virtually no society expresses a preference for girl babies over boy babies. In some societies, the first decision to be made on the birth of daughters is whether we are to live at all. Female infanticide is a way of controlling the population on the basis of sex. In general, girl babies receive less careful treatment than boy babies, thus reducing the girls' chances for survival.

The devaluation of daughters has its roots in the low worth and value placed on woman's place in society at large. Warriors, for example, tend to be more highly valued than mothers. But daughters do provide valuable services to the family. We can be relied on more than sons to take care of our parents in their old age. We help to carry out the household tasks. Daughters also have intrinsic value in that we represent the reproducers of the next generation.

The names given to daughters indicate our place in the social scheme. Most societies are careful to distinguish the sex of the child by the name. Most surnames perpetuate the male lineage, reflecting a name, profession, or place of birth. In general, women have changed our surnames on marriage, but many women today keep our own names.

Daughters tend to identify with our mothers. Gender identity is thereby made easy, but the task of developing our own individuality becomes complicated. Mothers may inhibit this development by expecting daughters to be at home more than sons and to help with "women's work." In this way, daughters are socialized into accepting an established role model.

Mother-daughter relationships may be marked by conflict, especially in the case of daughters who want to break away from the patterns of the mothers' lives or who resent maternal dependency.

A close and supportive father-daughter relationship can enhance our self-worth and educational and occupational achievements. Sometimes our relationships with fathers are tense and unstable. Girls often desire paternal approval, which makes us vulnerable to the training fathers give us to become socially desirable women. Father-daughter incest is the most commonly reported type of incest and may cause lasting trauma.

Families commonly discriminate among siblings on the basis of age-ranking. The first-born child enjoys certain responsibilities and privileges denied to later-born children. Certain personality characteristics, which have consequences in later life, also go with our birth order.

Sisters are both opposites and companions. We may be rivals for our parents' affection, but we also have close bonds with one another. Older sisters often provide role models and assistance for younger sisters.

Sex-ranking may nullify age-ranking. The rights and privileges of the oldest child may be canceled if that child is a girl and a brother is born. Sisters and brothers are further differentiated by division of labor in the house. Our talents and ambitions are often subordinated to those of our brothers.

Age-ranking helps establish the type of relationship a sister and brother have. Older sisters are often cast in the role of "mother" to younger brothers, and older brothers play the role of protector of younger sisters.

The inheritance women can claim is qualified by custom and law. We inherit legitimacy and social status from our parents. Sex often determines legal inherited rights. Most societies favor sons over daughters in the inheritance of property and position. Even where rights may descend from either parent to any of the children, inheritance for women is often curtailed by custom or law.

Women who develop an autonomous self-image by transferring identity from the mother to the father often suffer a conflict about our identity as women. This is complicated by sibling rivalry. Antifeminism in adult women may stem from this rejection of the mother and hatred of the sister. Women need to examine our life histories for sources of alienation from the sisterhood of women.

Discussion Questions

1. Draw a chart illustrating naming patterns of all the members of your extended family. What conclusions can you draw?

2. What changes occurred in your own relationships to your mother and father as you were growing up?

3. Describe your relationships with your sisters and brothers. Are they satisfactory? If you could, how would you change them?

4. Inheritance practices usually favor boys and perpetuate class differences. Give examples from your own experience.

5. Write a brief essay on the slogan, defending or refuting the premise: "Sisterhood is powerful" or "Sisterhood is global."

Recommended Readings

Davidson, Cathy N., and Broner, E. M., editors. *The Lost Tradition: Mothers and Daughters in Literature*. New York: Frederick Ungar, 1980. An exploration of the theme of mothers and daughters in literature, including the myths of ancient Greece, nineteenth- and twentieth-century writers, and the works of women of color. The book includes an excellent bibliography.

Glenn, Susan A. *Daughters of the Shtetl: Life and Labor in the Immigrant Generation*. Ithaca and London: Cornell University Press, 1990. Jewish daughters' experiences in the late nineteenth and early twentieth centuries as immigrants in the American garment industry and union movement. These daughters played a unique historical role in negotiating domestic and social roles, transforming their sense of female worth, and seeking self-esteem through political involvement.

Joseph, Gloria I., and Lewis, Jill. *Common Differences: Conflicts in Black and White Feminist Perspectives*. Garden City, N.Y.: Doubleday, 1981. Section two of this book contains two chapters that deal with the authors' perspectives on growing up as a black daughter and a white daughter, the "messages" about life that mothers convey to their daughters, and the feminist issues involved in mother-daughter relations.

Owen, Ursula, editor. *Fathers: Reflections by Daughters*. London: Virago, 1983. A collection of memoirs, stories, and poems describing father-daughter relationships through daughters' eyes. Among the authors included are Cora Kaplan, Doris Lessing, Grace Paley, and Adrienne Rich.

Tan, Amy. *The Joy Luck Club*. New York: Putnam, 1989. A novel of four Chinese women reared in China, and their relations with their Chinese American daughters.

Woolf, Virginia. *The Three Guineas*. 1938. New York: Harcourt, Brace, 1966. As an "educated gentleman's" daughter, Woolf presents a critique of the educated fathers and brothers who monopolize the ruling structures of the state, its government, educational establishments, and professions to the exclusion of daughters and sisters. Her footnotes present a feminist history of the English women of her class from the nineteenth century to her own day.

References

Alcott, Louisa M. *Little Women*. 1873. New York: Western, 1977.

Angelou, Maya. *I Know Why the Caged Bird Sings*. New York: Bantam, 1969.

Austen, Jane. *Pride and Prejudice*. 1813. Reprint. New York: Dell, 1959.

Chodorow, Nancy. *The Reproduction of Mothering: Psychoanalysis and the Sociology of Gender*. Berkeley: University of California Press, 1978.

Coleman, Emily. "Infanticide in the Early Middle Ages." In *Women in Medieval Society*, edited by Susan Mosher Stuard. Philadelphia: University of Pennsylvania Press, 1976.

Colette, Sidonie-Gabrielle. *My Mother's House and Sido*. 1930. Translated by Una Vincenzo and Enid McLead. New York: Farrar, Straus, and Giroux, 1953.

Dickemann, M. "Female Infanticide, Reproductive Strategies, and Social Stratification: A Preliminary Model." In *Evolutionary Biology and Social Behavior: An Anthropological Perspective*, edited by Napoleon Chagnon and William Irons. Duxbury, Maine: Duxbury, 1979.

Dinnerstein, Dorothy. *The Mermaid and the Minotaur: Sexual Arrangements and Human Malaise*. New York: Harper & Row, 1976.

Divale, William, and Harris, Marvin. "Population, Warfare, and the Male Supremacist Complex." *American Anthropologist* 78 (1978):521–38.

Ember, Carol. "Feminine Task Assignment and Social Behavior of Boys." *Ethos* 2 (1973):424–39.

Feaver, Vicki. "Mothers and Daughters." *Times Literary Supplement*, February 29, 1980.

Fischer, Lucy. *Linked Lives*. New York: Harper & Row, 1986.

Flax, Jane. "The Conflict Between Nurturance and Autonomy in Mother-Daughter Relationships and Within Feminism." *Feminist Studies* 4 (1978):178–89.

———. "Mother-Daughter Relationships: Psychodynamics, Politics and Philosophy." In *The Future of Difference*, edited by Hester Eisenstein and Alice Jardine. Boston: Hall, 1980.

Friday, Nancy. *My Mother/My Self: The Daughter's Search for Identity*. New York: Dell, 1978.

Goitein, Solomon D. *A Mediterranean Society, the Jewish Communities of the Arab World as Portrayed in the Documents of the Cairo Geniza*. vol. 3. *The Family*. Berkeley: University of California Press, 1978.

Goody, Jack. *Production and Reproduction*. Cambridge: Cambridge University Press, 1977.

Gutman, Herbert. *The Black Family in Slavery and Freedom, 1750–1925*. New York: Vintage, 1977.

Hennig, Margaret, and Jardin, Anne. *The Managerial Woman*. New York: Pocket Books, 1976.

Herlihy, David. "Land, Family, and Women in Continental Europe, 701–1200." In *Women in Medieval Society*, edited by Susan Mosher Stuard. Philadelphia: University of Pennsylvania Press, 1976.

Honig, Emily, and Hershatter, Gail. *Personal Voices:*

Chinese Women in the 1980's. Stanford, Calif.: Stanford University Press, 1988.

Hunt, A. S., and Edgar, C. C. *Select Papyri I: Non-Literary Papyri, Private Affairs.* No. 105. Cambridge, Mass.: Harvard University Press, 1932.

Jaccoma, Gail, and Denmark, Florence. "Boys or Girls: The Hows and Whys." Master's thesis, Hunter College. 1974.

Joseph, Gloria. "Black Mothers and Daughters: Their Roles and Functions in American Society." In *Common Differences: Conflicts in Black White Feminist Perspectives,* edited by Gloria Joseph and Jill Lewis. Garden City, N.Y.: Doubleday, 1981.

———. "Black Mothers and Daughters: Traditional and New Populations." *SAGE* 1 (Fall), 1984.

Kingston, Maxine Hong. *The Woman Warrior.* New York: Knopf, 1976.

Ladner, Joyce. *Tomorrow's Tomorrow The Black Woman.* Garden City, N.Y.: Doubleday, 1971.

Leman, Kevin. *The Birth Order Book.* Old Tappan, N.J.: Fleming H. Revell Co., 1985.

Lewis, Michael. "Parents and Children: Sex-Role Development." *School Review* 80 (1972):229–40.

Marshall, Paule. *Brown Girl, Brownstones.* Old Westbury, N.Y.: Feminist Press, 1981.

Matsui, Yayori. *Women's Asia.* London: Zed, 1987.

Moore, Honor. "My Grandmother Who Painted." In *The Writer on Her Work,* edited by Janet Sternberg. New York: Norton, 1980.

Newsweek. "Trading Places." July 16, 1990:48–54.

Petersen, Karen, and Wilson, J. J. *Women Artists: Recognition and Reappraisal from the Early Middle Ages to the Twentieth Century.* New York: Harper Colophon, 1976.

Pomeroy, Sarah B. *Goddesses, Whores, Wives, and Slaves: Women in Classical Antiquity.* New York: Schocken, 1975.

Russ, Joanna. *The Female Man.* New York: Bantam, 1975.

Russell, Diana E. *The Secret Trauma: Incest in the Lives of Girls and Women.* New York: Basic Books, 1986.

Sanchez, Marta Ester. *Contemporary Chicana Poetry.* Berkeley: University of California Press, 1985.

Shaarawi, Huda. *Harem Years: The Memoirs of an Egyptian Feminist (1879–1924).* Translated, edited and introduced by Margot Badran. New York: The Feminist Press, 1987.

Stanton, Elizabeth Cady. *Eighty Years and More.* 1898. Reprint. New York: Schocken, 1971.

Sutton-Smith, Brian, and Rosenberg, Benjamin G. *The Sibling.* New York: Holt, Rinehart, & Winston, 1970.

Tan, Amy. *The Joy Luck Club.* New York: Putnam, 1989.

Trexler, Richard. "The Foundlings of Florence, 1395–1455." *History of Childhood Quarterly: The Journal of Psychohistory I* (1973):259–84.

Washington, Mary Helen. *Black-Eyed Susans: Classic Stories by and about Black Women.* Garden City, N.Y.: Doubleday, 1975.

West, Jessamyn. *The Woman Said Yes.* New York: Harcourt, Brace, 1976.

Williamson, Nancy E. "Sex Preferences, Sex Control and the Status of Women." *Signs I* (1976):847–62.

Yanagisako, Sylvia Junko. *Transforming the Past: Tradition and Kinship among Japanese Americans.* Stanford: Stanford University Press, 1985.

Wives

Kathleen Gerson (1987) poses two questions fundamental to a feminist consideration of marriage: "What tensions and contradictions develop when hierarchical power relations are intertwined with sexual intimacy and emotional attachment? What strategies of adjustment make it possible for heterosexual commitment to coexist with power inequality?" (p. 115). The authors of this book began by considering our own personal perspectives on marriage. We discovered that we had all been wives at least once in our lives (and some of us more than once). Our experiences, whether or not we were involved in stable, "happy" marriages, led us to take a uniformly critical stance on this institution, to regard it as an instrument of social oppression. But many feminists have tried to envision other ways of being "married" than the more oppressive conventions of the past. To see where we might go, and how far that is, we must look at where we have come from. That is the subject of this chapter.

Why Marriage?

Our cultural traditions stress the importance of the family that consists of mother, father, and children. Our daily experience, from what we see in commercial advertisements to the books we read, including the Bible, praise marriage as it is seen as the basis of the family. In fact, 91 percent of American women do marry; although 51 percent of women divorce, most remarry. Let us ask ourselves: Why do we want to marry? The young and romantic among us may answer, "For love! of course." A cursory analysis of "love" may explain many of the answers that would be given by the more experienced (older?) to the main question: Love (and marriage) means companionship with a person to whom we feel close, and sharing a home; it means wanting to have a sexual relationship with someone in whom we place our trust, and marriage may extend the security of emotional and sexual intimacy with one person. With our beloved we may want to have children, and being married guarantees a "father" or legitimacy to our children. Although not expressed as a component of "love," economic cooperation or "division of labor" between spouses is often cited as one of the founding reasons for marriage. Finally, our society expects us, women, to be married; therefore, we seek social approval by marrying. All the above reasons are indeed related to "home" and, therefore, to "family." Emotionally and culturally, we want to belong to a family; if it happens to be a loving one based on marriage, our dreams seem to have come true. Let us now take a closer look at marriage and the causes for the existence of the heterosexual institution called marriage.

As far as we know, marriage, the joining of a woman and a man in a socially recognized union, is universal: It exists in all societies (though it has been banned among some subgroups such as celibate religious communities). Almost universally, marriage necessarily implies sexual intimacy between the couple; usually, but not always, this union involves co-residence and some kind of mutual economic responsibility; also, with rare exceptions, marriage is used to legitimize children resulting from the union.

What purposes does marriage serve? Some social scientists regard the social functions of female-male bonding as providing an answer.

Various species of mammals and birds have stable mating patterns. One study (Ember and Ember, 1979) related this bonding to the inability of females of these species to feed themselves and their dependent young, hence bonding could be explained as a means of ensuring male participation in care of their offspring.

In almost every society, human marriage often takes place for the explicit purpose of rearing children. Males in general, it is speculated, cannot be relied upon to cooperate in the care of offspring unless they are certain that these offspring are their own (Wilson, 1975). This accounts, according to some explanations, for the imposition of tight social constraints on the sexual relations of wives. Where inheritance through the male line is practiced, marriage legitimates a wife's children's claim to their father's property, titles, rights, or group membership. The investment is made in the male line only; thus, the marriage is to augment the father's interests. Some societies approve of female-female marriages under particular conditions. In these cases, one woman assumes the legal and social roles of husband and father, while the spouse acts as wife and mother (O'Brien, 1977).

Do women *need* men to help us rear our children? This depends, of course, on the circumstances. If society denies us the kinds of jobs that pay enough to enable us to support ourselves and our children, or if society denies us the training and education we need to obtain such jobs—and also discriminates against children born "out of wedlock" at the same time it provides no means of avoiding pregnancy—a woman may well *need* a husband. But these facts do not always apply. Among a number of West African societies, for example, women are expected to provide family subsistence and have the means (resources and training) to do so. During wars, many societies undergo long periods in which most of the men are absent and nonproductive, and women manage to support ourselves and our children. And yet, marriage persists and prevails in these societies as well. Why?

In our own society today, large numbers of women with children manage without the help of husbands who abandoned us or whom we have divorced. Generally speaking, women and children do fare better materially (economically) when a husband contributes, and this contribution is a primary motive for most women's marrying (Price-Bonham et al., 1983). Men stand to gain material benefits from their female partners as well as a legal and moral claim on the children they have *legally* fathered. Recently there have been court cases where fathers have made claims on the fetus.

Minimizing Male Rivalry and Cementing Male Alliances

Various other social functions have been attributed to marriage. It has been suggested, for example, that marriage reduces rivalry between males over women by assigning women to individual men; social rules enforce (with greater or lesser effectiveness) men's agreements to avoid sexual relations with one another's wives (Ember and Ember, 1993:168).

Marriage has also served in many societies as an institutional means of forming or cementing political alliances between groups of men. That is, men offer their sisters and daughters to one another as part of a formal "mutual aid" agreement. In societies where warfare is rife, "marry out or be killed out" may be the only options available (Tylor, 1889). Marriage has regularly been used through history by royal families to create alliances, and it has been used by other families to protect and extend property and to develop allies of various kinds. The politics of marital exchange of women, however, is largely male business, although women, particularly older women, often participate in making the arrangements. The institution of marriage when used as a political device clearly reduces women to objects of exchange (Levi-Strauss, 1969).

Reducing Competition between Women and Men

The institution of marriage has generally been characterized by two complementary but unequal roles: wife and husband. Each role is assigned its own sphere of rights and obligations, activities, and patterns of behavior. By separating the social functions assigned to adults on the basis of a marital contract between a wife and a husband, society tends to eliminate competition between women and men for the same social rewards. Wives' duties to care for home and children tend to reduce or eliminate our ability to compete for prestige or influence over public decisions of the sorts assigned to men. That leaves to men the competition for public power. Domestic maintenance roles assigned to wives also provide for continuity in the care of males from childhood through adulthood: Wives take over where mothers leave off. Thus, husbands are—in principle—free to take responsible public roles (engage in warfare or politics) even after they have had children, while wives are tied to domestic duties even before we have given birth. Japanese women writers of fiction often take up the theme of women who have forfeited their chances of becoming a career women to marriage. Yamamoto Michiko (b. 1936) is one of them. She was encouraged by her family to write poetry, and later fiction. Since her marriage she has lived in Australia and in Seattle where her husband was transferred. Her stories give a glimpse of the hidden frustration, guilt, and boredom of housewives, and deal with women living in foreign countries; and she focuses on women whose lives seem to maintain a precarious balance between sanity and insanity (Tanaka and Hanson, 1982). Yamamoto's stories speak for

---

The Christian View of Monogamy

And [Jesus] answered and said Have ye not read, that he which made them at the beginning made them male and female, and said, For this cause shall a man leave father and mother and shall cleave to his wife: and the twain shall be one flesh? Wherefore they are no more twain, but one flesh. What therefore God hath joined together, let not man put asunder. . . . Whosoever shall put away his wife, except it be for fornication, and shall marry another, committeth adultery: and who marrieth her which is put away doth commit adultery.

(Matthew 19:4–6;9)
The New Testament. Authorized (King James) Version

millions of women of all nationalities who leave their natal homes to follow their husbands to strange lands, and lead lives of loneliness and longing. Wives who are daily engaged in work that goes beyond household duties undertake that work as an additional, not a substitute, burden (see Chapters 13 and 14; Hochschild, 1989).

The institution of marriage and the role of "wife" are intimately connected with the subordination of women in society in general. It is the constraints on women to engage freely in various social activities, whether in sexual intercourse, economic exchanges, politics, or war, that make us "dependent" on men, that oblige us to become "wives." By marrying, women enter into contracts by which we gain protection from sexual molestation by men other than our husbands (and lose our freedom to engage in sexual relationships with other men should we so choose); we gain a right to our husbands' economic support (and undertake an obligation to provide for their domestic support and comfort); and we gain a claim on their possessions and rights for our children (and accept their right to control and dispose of a family's material wealth as they wish). On balance, it would appear that husbands gain much more than wives. They not only gain domestic servants, sexual compan-

ions, and producers of children but also political assets and instruments for acquiring allies.

Not all marriages are glum and terminally doomed. Many women enjoy being married; we find love and satisfaction in our marriages, our spouses are supportive and affectionate. Fiction of women writers can reflect well-disposed unions. Harriet Doerr (born in 1910 and received her B. A. from Stanford University in 1977) wrote of a mutually loving and developing marriage in her award-winning first novel, *Stones for Ibarra* (1978). Here, she portrays the life of Richard and Sara Everton, who have come to the small Mexican village of Ibarra to reopen a copper mine abandoned by Richard's grandfather fifty years before. They remain as the only foreigners in Ibarra, and adapt themselves to a growing love as much as to their surroundings. It is a touching and eloquent story.

Personal Reasons

Generally, however, women share some personal motivations in getting married. First, young women often find that "adult" status can only be achieved (or recognized) through marriage. That is, it is only when we are wives that we are seen as entitled to having homes of our own, the benefits of motherhood, and

---

Monogamous Marriage as Economic Exploitation

The first class opposition that appears in history coincides with the development of the antagonism between man and woman in monogamous marriage, and the first class oppression with that of the female sex by the male. Monogamy was a great historical step forward; nevertheless, together with slavery and private wealth, it opens the period that has lasted until today in which every step forward is also relatively a step backward, in which prosperity and development for some is won through the misery and frustration of others. It is the cellular form of civilized society in which the nature of the oppositions and contradictions fully active in that society can already be studied.

(Engels, 1884, 1972:129)

some degree of control over matters falling into "women's domain." Second, many women seek social and financial security and success through marriage. Most young women believe (and rightly so, under present conditions) that we will have higher status and a more satisfactory social life—in conventional terms—if we secure the "right" husband. Third, there are stigmas attached to "singleness" for women. Ekaterina Alexandrova (1984) says that a Soviet woman without the stamp "married" on her official documents feels incomplete. Finally, women are motivated by a desire for emotional intimacy as well as sexual intimacy. Traditionally, societies have not condoned this outside of the institution of marriage. Many women need the commitment of marriage to feel truly intimate with our mates.

It seems to us that the various theories that have been put forth to explain marriage fail to address the emotional and psychological reasons that motivate women and men to marry. A commitment to build a life together fulfills many personal needs; and marriage takes on importance to many women and men as a symbol of that commitment. What we are analyzing here, however, is not the bonding of two individuals and the rewards that may bring, but the institution of marriage and the role of wifehood. Indeed, the social roles and expectations for wife and husband may impede the mutuality of the bonds.

There is, further, an implication of *passivity* that fails to accord with what we have begun to learn about women's history, and certainly what we know about women's lives today. Women have been constrained by the role of "wife," but we also have interpreted that role in active ways. We have acted as economic and psychological partners despite legal definitions to the contrary; we have even taken the leading part in some relationships. Because we cannot yet recapture the past in the detail that would allow us to make better generalizations,

we can only note that systematic subordination of women in the role of "wife" most closely describes what we do know and await further research to tell us more

Selecting a Mate

Most women grow up expecting to become wives. The only question is, therefore, whose wife? Social customs narrow the range of alternatives even when, ideally, we are presumed to make the choice ourselves. In many societies, the families of prospective brides and grooms play active roles in making choices for them.

Society Chooses

Every society has a set of prescriptions and constraints governing the selection of mates among its members. Almost universally, a woman's choice is limited to men. Furthermore, most societies practice some degree of formal or informal *endogamy* (marrying "within"), that is, a woman's prospective mate should come from her own ethnic, racial, religious, educational, and/or class background. In some cases, a custom of endogamy may be enforced by informal sanctions, such as social disapproval of marriage to an "outsider" or refusal of family and friends to accept a husband or wife from the "wrong" class. Sometimes religious or legal prohibitions enforce endogamy. For example, both a priest and a rabbi may refuse to perform a marriage between a Catholic and a Jew. In Egypt, the law forbids a Muslim woman to marry a non-Muslim (but no such ban is imposed on men). South Africa by law forbade interracial marriage, as did many of our own Southern states until 1967.

No society allows pairing to take place within relationships classed as incestuous. Sometimes this prohibition includes first cousins; sometimes the circle of prohibited

Marriage in English Common Law

By marriage, the husband and wife are one person in law; that is, the very being or legal existence of the woman is suspended during the marriage, or at least is incorporated and consolidated into that of the husband; under whose wing, protection, and cover, she performs everything. . . . Upon this principle, of an union of person in husband and wife, depend almost all the legal rights, duties and disabilities that either of them acquire by the marriage. . . . A man cannot grant anything to his wife, or enter into covenant with her, for the grant would be to suppose her separate existence. . . . The husband is bound to provide his wife with necessaries by law, as much as himself: and if she contracts debts for them, he is obliged to pay them; but for anything besides necessaries he is not chargeable. . . . If the wife be indebted before marriage, the husband is bound afterward to pay the debt; for he has adopted her and her circumstances together. . . .

These are the chief legal effects of marriage during the coverture; upon which we may observe that even the disabilities, which the wife lies under, are for the most part intended for her protection and benefit. So great a favorite is the female sex of the laws of England.

(William Blackstone [1723–1780], *Commentaries on the Laws of England*, in *Beard*, 1946:89)

mates is even wider. For example, in the early Middle Ages, the European incest prohibition came to include in-laws, on the Christian principle that marriage makes two people one flesh. (see **The Christian View of Monogamy**.) Yet other rules of *exogamy*, or "marrying out," apply in many societies, where people must find mates from a different lineage, clan, or village.

Among the women who "married out" are those who came to the United States as "war brides." During and after World War II alone, nearly one million foreign brides of American servicemen, the majority of whom were from Europe, came to the United States (Shukert and Scibetta, 1989). Asian American and American servicemen also returned from the Pacific Theater with Chinese, Filipino, and Japanese wives. More recently, Filipino, Korean, Vietnamese, and Thai women have married American men and settled in the United States. Although many of the interracially married wives of U.S. servicemen have enjoyed stable, happy marriages, serious prob-

lems, including domestic abuse, have also been reported. Loneliness and homesickness are relatively common complaints, especially because language and cultural adjustment difficulties are compounded by social isolation on scattered military bases (Kim and Otani, 1983).

As a result of endogamous and exogamous rules, the available choices for mates may be few indeed. In a small, rural society, it may be difficult to find a suitable mate, not to mention an attractive or compatible one. But such strict rules and the problems they create tend to break down somewhat in large, complex, urban situations, where young people encounter a wider range of choices. However, even in a society as presumably open, mobile, and large as our own, we feel the pressure of customary constraints. Surely we are all familiar with cases of "inappropriate" marriages, where sisters or friends have married outside of the religion or ethnic group or even age group, and encountered social disapproval. Whether we subscribe consciously to such rules or not, most of us do marry within the "right" social categories: someone not too closely related, but from the same social and often even the same geographical background.

Families Choose

In most societies, women's marriages are a matter of concern to our relatives, particularly when they involve complex negotiations and economic settlement such as bride price and dowry. In Hindu society, "of all the duties of parenthood, arranging proper marriages for one's children probably weighs heaviest" (Nyrop, 1986:242). Sometimes the partners of the future marriage are consulted, and occasionally some allowance is made for real repugnance on the part of one or another party, or for some "unforgivable" breach (such as the girl's loss of virginity). But parental or familial interests are primary, and young women (and young men) may be subjected to intense persuasion and even physical coercion to bend us to the judgments of our elders. Where "arranged marriage" is customary (and this is very widespread), young women and men generally are informed of the arrangement after it has been made and cannot be easily undone. The preferences of the prospective couple are not thought to be relevant.

In some societies, marriage arrangements are helped along by intermediaries or professional matchmakers. The matchmaker may initiate the entire arrangement by undertaking to find a suitable mate for an individual from the broker's pool of clients. This is vividly illustrated in Sholem Aleichem's story "Tevye the Milkman," on which was based the play *Fiddler on the Roof.* Although everyone in the Russian *shtetl* (Jewish village) knows everyone else, it is unseemly for families to approach one another directly. Rather, the groom or his family goes to the matchmaker for help in approaching a young woman's parents concerning the delicate issue of the daughter's marriage.

Matchmaking may even be carried on over long distances. During the late nineteenth and early twentieth century, scores of Asian women came to the United States, including Hawaii, to marry men they had never met. These were "mail-order" or "picture" brides whose descriptions were solicited by Asian immigrants who had entered America and Hawaii as laborers. Lacking the funds to return home to secure a wife, according to the custom, go-betweens provided photographs of eligible women to the immigrant bachelors and also sent pictures of the men to prospective brides. Chinese, Japanese, and Korean picture brides often were encouraged by tales of wealth and plenty overseas. Some women were disappointed in our husbands (looking much older and less handsome than the photograph) and in the harsh conditions under which we toiled. Others worked hard at home and outside, often also doing housekeeping services for unmarried men of the community. As wives in our own homes, we were relatively independent to raise our children free from the dominance of a husband's family. Working outside the house also allowed some economic freedom (Kim and Otani, 1983).

The marriages that were contracted across the Pacific Ocean between two "strangers" are examples of "endogamous" marriage: alliance of two people, and perhaps of their families, within the same ethnic/racial group. Contemporary dating services perform an analogous function for young "singles" in many American cities, using computers and video equipment to bring "suitable" people together, with (they claim) a minimum of embarrassment or chance of disappointment.

Use of an intermediary also minimizes the risk of conflict in resolving different expectations and protects the dignity of both parties from the humiliation of a "jilt" or the damage of a breach-of-promise suit. Traditional intermediaries or matchmakers sometimes help families to negotiate customary marriage settlements—gifts of goods, money, or land between the families of the bride and groom that are part of the marital agreement.

Marriage settlements have several rationales. They are sometimes viewed as compensation to the bride's family for the loss of the woman's labor (bride price) or, conversely, as compensation to the groom's family for assuming responsibility for the bride's support (dowry). Sometimes they are seen as a deterrent to divorce—the groom is reluctant to return the dowry, or the bride's parents are reluctant to return the bride price, on which the marriage is contingent, so the families pressure the couple to work things out. Finally, the goods, money, or land may be used as capital to start a new household for the couple.

The financial, legal, and political aspects of marriage agreements tend to be drawn up by men, often with the assistance of male agents or lawyers or male-aligned female matchmakers. But it is rare that a girl's mother does not also participate in the arrangement of the daughter's future. For example, Lawrence Rosen observed a Moroccan father in the process of closing a contract with another chieftain. Veiled and discreet, not venturing beyond the modest bounds set by Islam, the mother undertook to interject herself into the negotiation. In effect, the husband took over the responsibility for securing a sound financial and political settlement, while the mother raised her voice for the personal preference and satisfaction of the daughter. After a lengthy and convoluted conversation, a negotiated compromise finally determined the ultimate choice of the son-in-law (Rosen, 1978).

Dowry in India

In the early 1980's women's groups, lawyers, jurists and others began to speak out about the phenomena of "bride burning" and "dowry murders" and the probably related increase in the number of presumed suicides by young married women. The murders—committed by the young woman's mother-in-law, husband, and other in-laws and staged to look like accidental burning—most frequently occur when the postwedding dowry payments are not as great as the in-laws anticipated or when the woman fails to produce a son. (To return the woman to her family, if they would accept her, would require the repayment of the dowry already paid.) An article in the *Washington Post* reported that in 1983, in New Delhi alone, almost 700 women died in circumstances that social workers described as probable murders. Jurists and other observers stated that this was more than twice the number of similar incidents in 1977. Competent authorities informed Clairborne that the number of actual murders was probably higher and the practice is becoming increasingly common, at least in part because the perpetrators are only rarely charged and convicted. The suicides—some of which may in fact be murders and most of which are by immolation, the most common form of suicide by Hindus—presumably are carried out by young women who can no longer tolerate the physical and psychological abuse to which they are subjected yet who are too shamed or fearful to seek the assistance of their families.

(Nyrop, 1986:248–249)

The text of the *ketuba,* or standard Jewish marriage contract, dates to the second century B.C.E. and is written in Aramaic. Jewish law requires that every Jewish bride be given one. It assures the married woman that her husband will take care of her, provide for and cherish her, and specifies the financial support due to her if he dies or divorces her. The one shown here was prepared for Susan Lees, one of the authors of this text, by her parents.

Women Choose

In most traditional societies, women did not have the choice of whether, when, or whom to marry. In modern, complex, urban societies for women of legal age, it is ideally the reverse. As we have seen, however, complete freedom of choice is something of an illusion. Society in general, and families in particular, apply subtle (and often not-so-subtle) pressures to induce us to marry and to constrain the kinds

of husbands we choose. But even within the constraints of class, religion, ethnicity, race, and similar considerations, a choice must be made. How do we choose?

Historically an acceptable alternative to marriage for a woman has been joining a convent, taking the vows of poverty, chastity, and obedience in religious communities. As mentioned in Chapter 10, on religion, women choose to become sisters or nuns "not only as a response to a call from God, but as a refuge

Frida Kahlo, *My Grandparents, My parents, and I (Family Tree):* (1936) Oil and tempera on metal panel, 12½ × 13 ¼". The Museum of Modern Art, New York. Gift of Allan Roos, M.D., and B. Mathieu Roos. Photograph © 1994 The Museum of Modern Art, New York. Kahlo was a painter who considered herself a Mexican although she was born to an Indian-Spanish mother and a German-Jewish father. She was brought up in Mexico. Through most of her life she was ravaged by sickness and in her last years was confined to bed. She married the Mexican muralist Diego Rivera, whom she later divorced. In this painting, after establishing the relationship between herself and her elders, thus identifying her lineage, Kahlo added the portrait of her husband and the child she hoped for but never had. She positioned herself as a wife linking generations and families.

from heterosexuality, Catholic marriage, and exhausting motherhood" (Curb and Manahan, 1985:xx). If a nun then falls in love with another nun and discovers her sexuality, both must leave, a decision that may be made with anguish. If being a nun seems to deny the "natural instincts" of a woman, such as being sexual, having children, and so on, lesbian nuns strike society equally as going against "nature." Let us consider reasons that might have contributed to a woman's choice of religious vocation: to escape marriage, to receive an education, and a preference to live in a community of women (ibid.). We can begin to see the intensity of sexuality that may occur when a sister discovers homosexual feelings in herself while being cloistered in a community of women. Denial of flesh and senses may come to a halt when communion and communication between lovers are established, and the sisters leave the cloister for their own reality. Then, if they choose, they can form their own household.

The popular Western belief is that marriage should be made for love. Romantic love has often been viewed as the antithesis of family loyalty. At the end of the sixteenth century, Shakespeare captured this sentiment in *Romeo and Juliet*. A modern musical adaptation of this dramatic tale, Leonard Bernstein's *West Side Story*, expresses the same tragic tension between two kinds of bonds. Julia Kristeva (1975) argues that in the contemporary People's Republic of China, the state has promoted the idea of marriage for love in order to dismantle the traditional (anticommunist) patriarchal family.

Carol Stack (1974) tells the story of Ruby, a black woman, who lived in an American urban ghetto. Here, a woman's relatives expected constant favors from one another, often at the expense of her responsibilities (real or imagined) to her husband and her home. To safeguard her projected marriage, Ruby knew she would have to move with her husband to another town. But she hesitated and finally returned to her kin network because she feared the loss of strength and support she herself received from them.

Widespread acceptance of the idea of love *before* marriage and as the primary basis of choice of partners is a rather recent phenomenon. Less than a hundred years ago, the desire of women to love whom we pleased appeared as a sort of rebellion against fate.

Emma Goldman, an American anarchist leader and proponent of free love, expressed this attitude in the following description of a scene from her adolescence in early-twentieth-century tsarist Russia: "I had protested [the marriage arranged by her father], begging to be permitted to continue my studies. In his frenzy, he threw my French grammar into the fire, shouting: 'Girls do not have to learn much! All a Jewish daughter needs to know is how to prepare gefilte fish, cut noodles fine, and give a man plenty of children.' I would not listen to his schemes; I wanted to study, to know life, to travel. Besides, I would never marry for anything but love, I stoutly maintained" (Goldman, 1970:12).

For many women, the quest for freedom of choice in making a marriage may well lead us back into the maze of cultural demands and social pressures from which we had sought escape. As young women, we have often spent our time grooming ourselves as well as being groomed by our parents to fit the description of the "ideal" wife. We study what men want and like. We try to conform as closely as possible to the conflicting images that guide us and that are to be found in the contemporary period in the pages of magazines, in motion pictures, or in television advertising. The contradictions and conflicts that beset a married white American woman's life are even greater for Latinas. The stereotypes held about Hispanics are the images of the "macho" man who is oppressive and the submissive woman. The stereotypes are reinforced by cultural behavior. Despite the widespread belief that "most men are undependable and are not to be trusted," being with a man is an important source of a Latin woman's sense of worth, and women are often told to be submissive and subservient to men in order to "have a man." On the other hand, many Latinas rely upon each other for our personal and practical needs. "Empty-nest syndrome" is mitigated among Latinas who retain important roles, status, and power even after our daughters and sons are married. Older women gain respect and attention in the family and wider community. Sons, in particular, continue to respect their mothers, even when they are abusive to other women (Espin, 1986). Latinas, perhaps more than other groups of American women, experience a "unique combination of

Inside the illustration:

SPRING/72 PREVIEW ISSUE $1.50

Ms.™

THE NEW MAGAZINE FOR WOMEN

Gloria Steinem On Sisterhood

Letty Pogrebin On Raising Kids Without Sex Roles

Sylvia Plath's Last Major Work

Women Tell The Truth About Their Abortions

Jane O'Reilly on The Housewife's Moment of Truth

Ms. magazine has raised women's consciousness about our world and brought feminist thinking to hundreds of thousands of women. Here an early *Ms.* cover illustration, for spring 1972, graphically captured the sense of unending tasks and occupations expected of wives. (Courtesy of *Ms.*)

power and powerlessness which is characteristic of the culture" (Espin, 1984:155).

A woman as a *wife* faces a dilemma in any
culture, anywhere in the world; she expects
and may find happiness; but unfortunately the
role is accompanied by emotional and physical
burdens that sometimes prove too strenuous
for the marriage. Separation, abandonment,
or divorce may end an unhappy and unre-
warding marriage.

Marrying

A marriage may take years in the making.
Family negotiations may be lengthy and subject to many changes. The couple may spend
years in courtship, particularly if the union is
subject to economic or social barriers. They
may try out a period of premarital cohabita-
tion. In some societies, a marriage is not considered complete until a child is born.

Types of Marriage

In our society, a woman may have only one
legal husband at a time. *Monogamy* is the most
common form of marriage in any class or society. This form of marriage contributed
greatly to the Western tendency to emphasize
the ideal of individual preference in mating.

Polygamy (marrying more than one spouse)
is illegal for both women and men in the
United States. In a few societies, a woman may
be wed to more than one husband, a system
called *polyandry*. The best-known cases usually
involve brothers sharing a limited number of
women among themselves, as in landed families in Tibet or in ancient Britain, as a device
to avoid or delay the breakup of estates
through equal inheritance among sons.

Polygyny, where women share husbands
with one or more other wives, is a relatively
more common cultural institution. However,
while it may be an ideal form of marriage

among some peoples, usually only a small,
wealthy minority actually achieve polygynous
households. For men, there are a number of
advantages in polygyny. In many African societies, for example, where women are important producers of wealth, a man can increase
his income and social standing by acquiring
several wives. Furthermore, where marriage is
used to create political alliances, multiple
marriages can extend the range of a man's allies. Thus, it has been customary in many
Asian, African, and Middle Eastern societies
for the aristocracy, particularly the royal families, to consolidate alliances with both equals
and followers by multiple marriages. The
royal family of Saudi Arabia today provides a
good example (Cole, 1977).

The advantages of polygyny for women are
not so readily apparent, although we shall discuss some later in the chapter. In some cases,
wives resist the taking of a second wife (for
example, Ba, 1981). In their daughters' marriage contracts, many Muslims include a
promise from the husband not to marry a second wife. However, where *sororal* polygyny
(two or more sisters marrying one man) is
practiced, wives may welcome the company
and help of sisters as co-wives. *Levirate* marriage, in which a woman must marry a dead
husband's brother, may be viewed as a form
of protection for women, as illustrated in the
biblical story of Ruth. According to the Bab-
ylonian Talmud, a dead man's eldest brother
(or next of kin), even if married already, is
obliged to marry the widow. From the male
perspective, the purpose is to provide the dead
man officially with children to carry on his
name in Israel. From the female perspective,
such a marriage maintains a woman's status in
society. Thus, Ruth, with the help of her
mother-in-law, Naomi, was able to call upon
her dead husband's kinsman, Boas, to marry
her. In Israel today, and among all orthodox
Jews, widows without sons must obtain a rab-

binical divorce (*get*) from our late husbands' brothers or nearest male kin before we can remarry.

While officially sanctioned, polygyny tends to be limited to the wealthy; unofficial polygyny is nonetheless sometimes practiced among the poor in modern, urban societies. Juan Sanchez, described by Oscar Lewis (1969), simultaneously supported three common-law wives and their children by him in different neighborhoods of Mexico City. It took years for them to learn about one another's existence.

The average age at the time of marriage is increasing worldwide, especially in economically advanced developing countries (United Nations, 1987). Older brides have more opportunity for personal choices and the emotional maturity to make that choice. To some extent, this maturity helps balance the influence of the particular desires of the bridegroom. In modern Egypt, young men desiring to be supported or to find lodging have advertised publicly to find employed or widowed women as wives. In polygynous situations, a young man may often wish to start with an older woman to delay the responsibilities of fatherhood and provide an experienced woman to direct the younger wives he expects to add to the household. Khadijah, the first wife of the prophet Muhammed (570–632), was over forty when she married him (he was about twenty-five). A later wife, Aisha, was so young (eight to nine) that she went to her husband's house with her dolls (Walther, 1981).

The Rite of Passage

For women, the first marriage has traditionally been the most significant rite of passage in life. The wedding ceremony has not only marked the community's recognition of the establishment of a new union but has also symbolized the passage of woman from girlhood to womanhood. With this change of status may come new modes of behavior and dress and acquisition of a new home, new relatives, and new responsibilities. In modern Western society, a woman's identity shift from the premarital to the married state is so complete that it is traditionally marked by an entire change of name: Miss Mary Smith becomes Mrs. George Jones. These profound changes of status and identity upon marriage for a woman have no parallel for a man, although men also participate in the marital rite of passage. Thanks to women's struggle in gaining our rights since the 1970s more women have chosen to retain our names after marriage. Some of us have added the spouse's name attached with a hyphen. In Europe, married career/professional women began to keep their names much earlier.

Because a wedding signifies such an important and far-reaching change in the status of women, the ceremonies that are central to the wedding ritual are often rich in religious and social symbolism. Some societies dramatize a new wife's relationships to a husband by a ritual capture of the bride. Eskimos cheer enthusiastically when brides put up really convincing struggles against ardent grooms before finally submitting to being carried away to the new home (Freuchen, 1961). The custom of having the groom carry the bride over the threshold of the new home has been interpreted as a holdover from earlier bride-capture rituals. In this case, it is not customary for the bride to display any resistance!

In some societies, the centerpiece of the marriage is the symbolic surrender of authority over a woman by the bride's family to the groom. In traditional American weddings, for example, the father (or his equivalent) "gives away the bride." The wedding may also contain a symbol of the couple's consent, as in joining of hands or the lifting of the veil, enabling the couple to see and accept each other for the first time. The bride and groom exchange vows and seal the ceremony with a ring and a kiss. An exchange of rings originally signified the exchange of property previously negotiated in the contract. In this century, it is rapidly becoming recognized as a symbol of the equal nature of the couple's commitment. In modern nations, the final seal is the pronouncement that the state recognizes the couple as "husband and wife." If they want to separate after that, they will have to go to court and get a release.

Weddings are rarely a private matter between bride and groom. Not only the state but kin and community participate in the legitimizing of a union. Thus, elopements entail both defiance of the couple's (or at least the bride's) parents and denial of a communal celebration. Wedding celebrations usually involve elaborate feasting to mark the event. Those who participate directly, and even friends and relatives from far away, are expected to join in the ritual formation of a new union by contributing gifts, as well as the bride's trousseau. In this way, the wedding becomes an opportunity for a whole community to demonstrate various relationships to the bride and groom, to vie for prestige, and to enjoy a fine show. Generally, the higher the status of the couple, the more spectacular the performance becomes. Modern urban civilization has not altered this point, as the wedding of Great Britain's Prince Charles and Lady Diana in 1981 reminded us.

Virginity and Marriage

Most societies expect brides to enter the first marriage as virgins. An unmarried girl who is not a virgin is considered "damaged goods." For example, the contemporary women of Bangladesh who were raped by invading soldiers were considered "impure" and were expelled from their homes. These violated women found themselves living together, unable to be absorbed back into their own villages and "unfit" to become wives of the young men in the village (Brownmiller, 1975).

Sometimes the exclusive rights to sexual access that marriage confers on men have been taken so seriously that any damage to unmarried girls' virginity could bring the death penalty on the seducers, and on ourselves if we had cooperated. Until the twelfth century, the legal definition of rape in European law codes was the abduction of another man's sexual property. Unless the injured party (father, brother, husband, or other male guardian) agreed to receive compensation, as he usually did, the death penalty could be imposed on the rapist.

Yet not *every* society has demanded virginity of its brides. In Samoa, a period of sexual freedom and experimentation is viewed as a natural part of life for young girls. It is our happy time, which we generally seek to prolong before taking up the burdens of wifehood (Mead, 1928). Increasingly, in the United States, there is a greater acceptance of premarital sex contending with the continued strong sentiment of those who are adamant that a "nice" girl will "save herself" for her husband.

Although virginity is hardly an issue in a marriage contract in the United States or Western Europe, the "sexual revolution" of the 1960s is on the wane. Today women are more reluctant to have casual sex or multiple sex partners. The horror and undiscriminating reality of AIDS is the principal cause of our changing attitudes toward sex outside marriage, or rather, outside a long-term monogamous union. Some conservative elements in our society might try to take advantage of the presence of sexually transmitted diseases and curb the freedom of choice for us. While keeping in mind that our lives, our bodies, are our responsibility, and nobody else's business, we have to weigh the possible consequences of a sexual encounter: it may mean life or death for us.

Once a woman and man are married, they are expected to engage in sexual intercourse sooner or later. Often when a bride is extraordinarily young, the groom will be encouraged to wait. Still, contemporary reports in India, where child marriage is fairly common, provide extensive testimony to the physical damage done to child brides (India, 1974; Forbes, 1979). There have been strong legislative attempts in that country to correct so oppressive a marital system.

The Marital Household

In many societies, the transition from the status of daughterhood to one of wifehood entitles women to "homes of our own." In theory, the status of wife or "woman of the house" entails a set of rights to make certain decisions for the family that conventionally fall under a woman's domain, and a set of obligations that are conventionally assigned to wives. Most of these rights and obligations concern the day-to-day pattern of domestic life, the furnishing of the home, and the feeding and care of its occupants.

The ideal of one married woman in the household is associated with the ideal of the *nuclear family household.* A nuclear family consists simply of a married couple and the immature offspring. In some societies, such as prerevolutionary China, the ideal was not the nuclear family but the *extended family household,* usually representing at least two generations. Typically, an extended family household will have a married couple, one or more of the couple's married offspring, and unmarried children. The status of wives in an extended family household will depend in part on our seniority, in part on how many other wives there are, and in part on whether we have children, particularly male heirs. Thus, women who share households with our mother-in-law or our husbands' older brothers' wives may find that we have very few decision-making rights and a lion's share of domestic responsibilities. Older women whose sons have brought wives into the household may be delighted to be unburdened from domestic tasks that can now be assigned

---

The Wifely Obligations of American Slave Women

The ex-slave narratives make abundantly clear that women had responsibilities for what has traditionally been seen as women's work. There is no evidence, for example, that men engaged in spinning, a job that occupied much of the women's time in the evenings. More typical of the life of the ordinary slave woman is the description by the former slave Henry Baker: ". . . de wimmin plowed jes lack de men. On Wednesday night dey had tuh wash en aftuh de washed dey had tuh cook suppah. De nex' mornin' dey would get up wide de men en dey had tah cook breafus 'fore dey went tuh de fiel' en had tuh cook dinner (the noon meal) at de same time en take hit wid' em." Even husbands in cross-owner marriages, who saw their wives only on weekends, did not do their own laundry. A white man living in Georgia described how, on Saturday night, the roads were . . . filled with men on their way to the "wife house," each pedestrian or horseman bearing his bag of soiled clothes.

(Farnham, 1987:79–80)

to the daughter-in-law, while the mother-in-law assumes the position of manager.

Wives' positions in our homes are affected not only by whether or not we share the home with other married women but also by how the women are related to us. The nuclear family is usually *neolocal:* The newly married couple set up housekeeping on their own and form a new establishment. Many societies, however, like the traditional Chinese, are *virilocal:* The couple take up residence with or near the husband's relatives. This is likely to be the case in patrilineal societies, where rights and property are inherited in the male line. In societies that adhere to a virilocal residence pattern, new brides must operate as aliens in a strange territory, learning new family customs and accommodating to the caprices of new people. We may be hedged in by a variety of traditional constraints that keep us in our place. For example, in some Islamic groups, as among the traditional Chinese, a new daughter-in-law is not addressed by name for over a year, being called simply "son's wife." Among the Turkmen of northeastern Iran, new brides are returned to fathers' households, and the period of "spouse avoidance" starts. This period lasts one to three years during which bride and groom may visit one another if it can be done secretly (Irons, 1975).

An alternative to virolocal residence, found in some matrilineal societies such as the Hopi and Navajo in the United States, is *uxorilocal* (sometimes termed *matrilocal*) residence: The couple resides with the wife's family. This is likely to occur where rights and property are inherited through women. In uxorilocal residence, a core group of women, mothers and daughters, remain together throughout life, while the husbands come to join us. Generally, wives seem to have more power and autonomy in these situations, and greater ease in dissolving unsatisfactory marriages, than in vi-

---

Housework and Marriage I: Who Does How Much?

[Various studies of time spent] demonstrate the patriarchal benefits reaped in housework. First, the vast majority of time spent on housework is spent by the wife, about 70 percent on the average, with both the husband and the children providing about 15 percent on average. Second, the wife is largely responsible for child care. The wife takes on the excess burden of housework in those families where there are very young or very many children; the husband's contribution to housework remains about the same whatever the family size or age of the youngest child. It is the wife who, with respect to housework at least, does all the adjusting to the family life cycle. Third, the woman who also works for wages . . . finds that her husband spends very little more time on housework than the husband whose wife is not a wage worker. Fourth, the wife spends perhaps eight hours per week additional housework on account of her husband. And fifth, the wife spends, on average, a minimum of forty hours a week maintaining the house and husband if she does not work for wages and a minimum of thirty hours per week if she does.

Moreover, while we might expect the receipt of patriarchal benefits to vary according to class, race, and ethnicity, the limited data we have relating to socioeconomic status or race indicate that time spent on housework by wives is not very sensitive to such differences.

(Hartman, 1981:3)

Housework and Marriage II: What Do We Expect?

The underlying issue for individual spouses is equity and fairness in distribution of costs and rewards within the relationship. With a majority of wives employed in the United States, a new definition of an equitable marital role bargain is emerging that suggests that men should take a more active role in housekeeping and child care. Yet, sharing the responsibilities for housework, parenting, and nurturing others is difficult when tradition has delegated those tasks solely to women.

[In a study of 489 married couples, in which 69 percent of the wives had jobs outside the home, the authors found that] irrespective of the family role in question, over two-thirds of the couples had similar expectations. However, for roles traditionally thought the wife's, 84 percent agree that child care should be shared, but only 38 percent agree that housework should be. Almost as many couples, 36 percent, agree that housework should be the wife's responsibility. For the roles traditionally assigned to husbands, 69 percent agree that the management of money should be shared, but only 24 percent agree that earning it should be. Almost twice as many—43 percent—agree that earning money is the husband's responsibility.

[Comparisons of partners' expectations about the division of family roles show] first, spouses misperceive their partners' expectations fairly often. In five out of the nine comparisons, over 40 percent inaccurately perceive their partners' expectations. In two of these comparisons—wife's perceptions of husband's attitude about her working and who should manage money—the majority were incorrect. Second, husbands perceive their spouses' expectations more accurately than their wives perceive theirs. . . .

Third, inaccurate perceptions about housekeeping and child care roles occur most often because husbands are less traditional and wives more traditional than their partners expect . . . inaccuracies in perceptions of expectations for roles traditionally assigned to men occur most often because husbands are more traditional and wives less traditional than their partners expect. . . .

Fifty-eight percent of husbands say housework should be shared; yet, except for two tasks listed . . . not more than a third of the husbands either share or do regular household tasks, even by their own estimate. Thirty-three percent of the husbands report they shop for food, and 43 percent wash dishes. Note that the percentages of wives who see their husbands doing or sharing these tasks is lower than the percentages of husbands who see themselves doing them. . . . Across the board, both husbands and wives see themselves participating more than their spouses see themselves participating. Husbands are especially more likely to see tasks as shared, while wives see themselves with major responsibility.

(Hiller and Philliber, 1986:3)

rilocal situations. This authority probably relates both to our greater degree of control over productive property in these societies and to the support we have from living with our own female kin.

Family Politics

Although marriage may lay the basis for a new household, wives rarely establish homes in isolation. As we have already noted, we may

Housework and Marriage III: What Do We Want?

[Based on a study of young adult working class and middle class women] commitment to being a housewife or to another career, and related attitudes to dependence upon or independence from mates, depend in large part on their own personal histories taken in social context. The principal determinants were a combination of past career opportunities and past relationships with men.

"Domestically oriented" women (full-time housewives) had established traditional marriages. Over 60 percent had begun with non-domestic aspirations, yet became traditional over time. How? First, commitment to their husbands meant that their husbands' jobs took priority over their own career opportunities. Second, their husbands were able to sustain comfortable standards of living on one income. Third, the vast majority had themselves encountered blocked mobility at work. Finally, they were subject to pressures to bear and rear children.

By contrast, "non-domestic" women experienced unstable or dissatisfying heterosexual partnerships. Their experience led them to be self-reliant through work rather than depend on men. Sometimes this was precipitated by failure of men in their lives to meet support expectations. Although two-thirds of this group of women began with domestic aspirations, commitment to work by necessity turned out to offer an unexpected source of support and rewards; three fourths experienced expanded work opportunities which promoted non-traditional orientations toward work, parenthood, and men.

Domestically oriented women found themselves in the unenviable position of defending the legitimacy and viability of the domestic option against the incursions of social change. Behaviorally and ideologically, they supported traditional male privileges and obligations and struggled to keep men economically responsible. They were happy to provide homemaking services in return and, indeed, excluded men from domestic duties, which they wished to preserve for themselves. They thus became unwittingly involved in a defense of a way of life once considered sacrosanct but increasingly devalued and insecure.

Domestic women thus supported and reproduced a strict sexual division of labor in breadwinning and caretaking responsibilities. They carefully subordinated work commitments to family commitments; they looked to husbands to provide the economic support that made their domesticity possible; and, given limited options in the paid labor force, they had little or no desire to trade places with their husbands. . . .

[Women committed to childlessness] were, however, the opposite of their domestic counterparts. Instead of opting for domesticity, they chose childlessness as the only acceptable response to a set of structural arrangements that relieves men of child-rearing responsibility (beyond breadwinning) and a set of beliefs that pits the interests of the work-committed mother against the interests of the child. . . .

Those women who decided to combine work and motherhood found male partners who both wanted children and supported female partners' work careers. These women were thus better positioned to ease the cross-pressures of their situations by bringing men into the job of parenting and demanding greater equality in their private lives. Their husbands' dependence on economic contributions coupled with their husbands' desires to become fathers gave work-committed women the power to change the sexual division of labor at home. This situation also led them to change their beliefs about men's, women's, and children's natural needs and abilities.

(Gerson, 1987; 115–130)

live with in-laws or with a husband's other wives, or we may find ourselves—as is increasingly the case in our own society—with a husband's children by a former marriage as well as with our own. Our relationships with these various people may be those of cooperation or competition, warm friendship, or grudging tolerance.

Living with in-laws may pose special complexities for women. In Muslim Bosnia, for example, the parents of each spouse become "instant" relatives when offspring marry (Lockwood, 1975). The in-laws, or *kuma*, are considered closer to each other than to blood kin. The strategic advantages for wives in this position may be manifold. We find ourselves in a union backed and aided by two kin groups. We have enlarged our circle of friends and relatives as well as our visiting network. We have acquired two sets of supporters to play against one another or to aid us against our husbands if that is necessary. On the other hand, we have doubled the disadvantages as well. Because of the importance placed on the interaction between the parents and the married couple, we find ourselves being "managed" by both sides. Two sets of parents and two sets of siblings give us well-meant advice and expect willing cooperation (Peristiany, 1976).

Women who share a house with women to whom we are not related, whether our mothers-in-law, sisters-in-law who are married to our husbands' brothers, or co-wives in a polygynous marriage, may find ourselves at a disadvantage. We lack privacy, if it is important to us, and we must share the domestic territory that is commonly considered women's domain, including the cooking area. Even if the co-wives and children occupy separate apartments or huts, emotional strains such as jealousy, personality conflicts, rivalry, and unpleasantness among the children of different mothers may occur. A poignant contemporary tale of the emotional hurt (and material

harm) caused to an older Muslim wife in Senegal when her husband takes a second, younger wife, is told in *So Long a Letter*, by Mariama Bâ (1981). In some Muslim societies where polygyny is lawful but rarely practiced, taking another wife remains a threat that husbands can use to exercise control over their wives.

However, there may be some advantages for a woman in polygyny. In a society that consistently segregates and isolates women from public life, polygyny provides a domestic society within which there is companionship, cooperation, and emotional support. A Western observer has detailed this comfortable domestic life for a harem in a small Iraqi village (Fernea, 1958). There the co-wives not only cooperated happily in household tasks and child care but made up the core of a wider society of women who spent many hours "roof-hopping" to visit one another, smoking and chatting in the harem out of sight of the men in the main square.

Where co-wives live together, women may be ranked according to preestablished custom or by the personality or authority of individual women. Commonly, first wives are the oldest and most respected because of age and experience in household matters. If we can consolidate this authority, we may become the equivalent of mothers-in-law in controlling the younger wives. We can withdraw from actual housework and assume the task of manager. But we may have to play a subordinate role to a more favored sexual partner of the husband (Hsu, 1949). In other instances, the honor of being "first wife" is given to women who bear the first son, whether or not we were the first wives. In Ottoman Turkey, the sultana who gave birth to the first male child, the successor to the throne, was granted the highest honors and bore the title "head woman." The possibilities for manipulation and political maneuver among co-wives and among children in a polygynous community are varied and sometimes dangerous if the stakes include the eventual power that will accrue to the mother of the heir (Makhlouf-Obermeyer, 1979).

While the politics of polygynous households may seem remote and exotic to the American reader, complex family rivalries and struggles for power in the context of divorce and remarriage are probably more familiar. About 32 percent of all marriages in the United States today are remarriages, and about 13 percent of the nation's children under the age of eighteen are in reconstituted families (Chilman, 1983). Many women find that we are tied in many-stranded relationships with our husbands' former wives, our own former husbands, or our former husbands' new wives, in ongoing mutual decisions and interactions regarding children, income, and property. While the various parties to these complex relationships may come to mutual and supportive arrangements, struggles between new and old spouses, or between children of a former marriage and a new spouse, often create major difficulties for a wife.

Extramarital Affairs

Whether or not we have married for love, many wives have found romance outside of marriage. In the twelfth century, the Countess Ermengarde of Narbonne was reputed to have declared that love could not exist within marriage: Since most women of her day married, she clearly meant that women must seek love from men other than our husbands. However, traditionally adulterous wives (and sometimes our partners) have been subjected to terrible penalties, such as starvation, burning at the stake, or mutilation. As in other sexual codes, there is a double standard regarding adultery. For men, it is equally "immoral," but it rarely has been punished by such severe measures.

Wives may seek affairs to fulfill some of the emotional and sexual needs not satisfied in the marriage. Sexual and emotional intimacy that is free from the constraints of marital roles, obligations, and mutual dependency may provide some women with gratifications they cannot find with husbands. An affair may provide a woman with a remedy for neglect, boredom, or loneliness, or may give a sense of excitement or feeling of desirability. Gustave Flaubert's *Madame Bovary*, first published in 1854, illustrates a woman's search for fulfillment and self-definition through adultery.

Like many a fictional adulteress, Emma Bovary ended her life in suicide. The real tragedy of adultery for women, however, has more often been the threat of an unwanted pregnancy. Before the days of reasonably safe birth control, pregnancy was a likely outcome of any sexual relationship, and an adulterous woman was thus faced with a high risk of discovery.

Today, this risk has lessened, though partly replaced by fear of sexually transmitted diseases (see Chapter 12). And although not necessarily overtly condoned, extramarital affairs for women have probably become more common. Shere Hite (1987) reported that some 70 percent of the women married over five years, in her survey of 2,000 women, had extramarital affairs. This figure is higher than most other reports and sparked outraged disbelief from some of her critics. Whether her survey indicates a likely trend of increase that will continue is another matter.

Wives who discover that our husbands have engaged in affairs may under some circumstances have no choice but to tolerate the situation. But we may also feel hurt, humiliated, rejected, and betrayed—as might our husbands if the positions were reversed. It is generally understood in the marriage contract that sexual relations are the exclusive reserve of the partners in marriage; by law and custom, wife and husband are "entitled" to feel possessive toward one another. It is true that many women, and even some men, have taken a more tolerant view toward a woman's extramarital sex in recent times.

Sexual relations within marriage reflect the gender roles and related sexual attitudes in any society. If a social system were based on gender equality and positive attitudes about sex and sexual choice, gender relations within as well as outside marriage would be different. Whether the existence of gender equality would diminish the need to find love outside marriage, if that institution actually continued, we will never know. Sexual possessiveness is part of gender attitudes and female-male relationships now embedded in our social structures. Changes in those structures would result in changed expectations about marriage and the issues as they have been discussed here would no longer concern us.

Of course, between any two marriage partners, sexual relations may not be a microcosm of unequal gender relationships in society. For some couples sex may offer a respite from daily battles to survive and to achieve, the only private time wife and husband have in a day to share thoughts and intimacies. Lovemaking for such a couple may be an expression of these mutual feelings and may provide a moment when both can respond to physical needs that transcend social roles.

Divorce

The failure of our society to deal with the precipitous increase in the divorce rate and its negative economic consequences for women and children is the primary factor in what has been referred to as "the feminization of poverty." The U. S. Bureau of Census tells us that between 1962 and 1981, the annual number of divorces tripled; the divorce ratio (number of divorced persons per 1,000 married persons

living with their spouses) increased from 47 in 1970 to 100 in 1980 to 128 in 1985 (U.S. Bureau of Census, 1987). The male divorce ratio in 1986 (106 per 1,000) was lower than that of women (157 per 1,000) because divorced men remarry more than do divorced women. There is variability among ethnic groups: for whites, the divorce ratio in 1986 was 124 per 1,000, for African Americans it was 248 per 1,000, and for Latinos/Latinas it was 139 per 1,000 (U.S. Department of Commerce, 1987).

Most of the U.S. families living in poverty are female-headed families, and the 1985 census data indicate that 69 percent of all single mothers are either divorced or separated. "Divorce is a primary contributor to the increase in the number of impoverished women" (Arendell, 1987:122). In part this impoverishment has to do with gender roles in marriage. While women are married, we contribute domestic labor, and if we work outside the home, our income contribution comes to, on the average, only 22 percent of the total family income as of the mid-1980s (Arendell, 1987). When we are divorced, we lose access to the financial resources that were available to us through our husbands, and as a consequence of this and the fact that we are usually left with our children, our standards of living decline, while our former husbands' tend to rise. We tend to have less to spend on food, recreation, clothing, and housing, yet our needs are higher. "The total family incomes of most divorced women and their children is less than 50 percent of their family incomes prior to divorce, yet the custodial parent needs approximately 80 percent of the income prior to divorce to maintain the family's standard of living" (Arendell, 1987:124). Because we continue to be discriminated against in the job market, and because we continue to bear major responsibility for the care of our children, our chances of economic recovery from divorce are slender. In fact, our possibilities of recovery are directly related to the extent to which we have become, as wives, regular labor force participants. Since the chances of our becoming divorced are fairly high (one study projected that 40 percent of all marriages of persons born in the 1970s will end in divorce (Glick and Norton, 1977), our economic futures will often depend more on our own job situations than those of our husbands. "More than three fourths of divorced mothers with custody of their children are employed; 88 percent, full time. Divorced mothers constitute the largest proportion of employed women" (Arendell, 1987:129).

While the law requires our former husbands to pay child support in most cases, less than half pay anything at all, only a small proportion pay what the court has ordered them to pay, and what the courts call for is almost never enough to pay the actual costs. From the figures given above, it is clear that the most economically oppressed ethnic groups in this country are those experiencing the most severe negative economic effects of divorce. However, economic setbacks may be faced by these groups differently. "While both Black and White mothers reported significantly large decreases in income [following divorce], Black mothers perceived themselves as experiencing significantly less distress than White mothers. . . . Black mothers reported greater social supports and were more likely to view religion as a factor helping to integrate them into the community" (Price-Bonham et al., 1983).

Women initiate most divorces in the United States. A recent report compiled by the National Center for Health Statistics, a division of the Department of Health and Human Services, noted that women filed 61.5 percent of the divorce petitions acted on in 1986, and men filed 32.6 percent. The remaining petitions were filed jointly. More telling figures are that women with children filed 65.7 percent of divorce petitions (*New York Times*, June 15, 1989). According to Barbara Foley Wilson, a statistician at the Center, traditionally women have predominated in filing divorce petitions. Hite (1987) found in her survey of 2,000 women that 91 percent of divorces were initiated by women who cited loneliness and emotional isolation within the marriage. Of the divorced women, 71 percent of every age and economic status expressed relief and well-being, and only 24 percent had mixed feelings after divorce.

Divorced women in general are left in worse economic conditions than when we were married; often we have dependent children for whom we care, frequently without the financial and emotional help of the absentee father. Yet it is significant that although women suffer these economic consequences of a divorce, we still pursue divorce because we find our emotional state more important than our financial one.

In comparison with the majority of other societies, however, in the United States it is relatively easy to marry and difficult, although not as difficult as in the past, to get divorced. To marry, a couple of legal age need do no more than register, have a blood test (in most states), exchange brief vows in the presence of an official and a witness, and pay a very small fee. Waiting time is usually about three days, often less. No parental consent is needed (once the participants have reached legal majority), nor any promise of family support. To get divorced, on the other hand, couples usually require lawyers, legal documents, a court hearing (or several), and often a considerable amount of time, even when both parties are in agreement. If the couple disagree about the terms of the divorce, as is likely to be the case when the marriage has dissolved in discord and there are children and property rights in dispute, the legal cost of settlement can be immense, while the costs in time and personal agony may be incalculable. The issue of the burdens borne by children in divorce is usu-

Domestic Abuse

From a sample of 3520 couples representative of the general population in 1985, 4.4 percent of wives reported one or more physical attacks of severe violence by their spouse over the past year, and 11.3 percent reported acts of minor violence.

At one point in time in their married lives, 25 to 50 percent of wives are physically assaulted by their husbands.

A psychologist specializing in helping abuse victims has estimated that 50 percent of all women will be battering victims at some point in their lives.

Wife-beating, occurring once every 18 seconds, is estimated by the FBI to be the most frequently occurring crime in the country.

Sixteen percent of college students reported their parents had been physically violent toward one another within the past year.

In 3 percent of divorce actions, husbands mentioned the wife's physical abuse as a reason for seeking a divorce; 37 percent of wives in divorce actions mentioned their husband's physical abuse as a reason.

Seven percent of the respondents to a newspaper survey reported experiencing marital rape. In another study, 12 percent of the married women in a San Francisco study reported being the victim of some form of forced sex in marriage.

(Zinn and Eitzen, 1987:314)

ally a matter of profound concern to parents, as well as to the courts and other involved parties.

While these costs may deter some individuals from seeking a divorce, the penalties of an incompatible marriage are deemed by many to be far greater. Reasons for divorce vary and often are not mutual for the couple in question. In addition to personal incompatibility, common grounds in our society and most others are infidelity, mistreatment, economic problems, sexual problems, abandonment, and premarital misrepresentations about such things as desire for children. In 75 percent of the societies in one anthropologist's sample, women and men had approximately equal rights to initiate divorce on these various grounds, while in only 15 percent did men enjoy superior rights. In 10 percent, women had superior rights. In a matrilocal so-

ciety such as the Iroquois, wives can divorce husbands by dumping their belongings outside the door (Murdock, 1950). Divorce is sometimes equally simple for women and men in certain patrilocal, even patriarchal, societies such as the Mongols. Islamic law, which is based on the Koran, permits a man to repudiate a wife without giving a reason or going to court. The interpretation of the Holy Scriptures has varied in different times and places. In many Muslim countries today, the divorce law has been modified; in Turkey, a woman can initiate divorce. On the other hand, the men in some Muslim groups like the Bakhtiari of Iran and Pathan of Afghanistan prefer killing their wives because they view divorce as shameful, as admitting that they have failed to bring a wife to "her knees" (Lindholm and Lindholm, 1979).

The larger number of societies disapprove

of divorce, and Western society is no exception—as testified by the many legal obstacles to divorce in the laws of both church and state. While laws, rules, customs, and attitudes toward divorce have changed in the West over the centuries, it is undeniable that social stigma against it remain to this day. There are people who experience a sense of personal failure (or attach personal blame to partners) when their marriages fail. They, and outsiders, are likely to feel that marital failure is due to their own inadequacy rather than to problems inherent in the institution of marriage. It is worth pondering that while the divorce rate is high, the remarriage rate is also high (Laws and Schwartz, 1977). The partners may change, but the institution, embedded in the structure of society, endures.

The process of getting divorced can exacerbate the pain of marital failure. Divorce laws in some states require evidence of misbehavior ("cruelty," for example) or inadequacy, even when both parties agree that neither was "at fault." Rights to alimony may depend not only on the husband's ability to pay and the wife's need for support but also on the wife's fidelity. If women have committed adultery, we may have no right to support. Thus, court-mediated settlements involve accusations and denials, recriminations and bitter counter-recriminations. Although the establishment of "no-fault" divorce options in some states has eased the process for some couples, disagreements over serious issues such as child custody remain very painful for many. To the extent that women are dependent on our husbands economically, socially, and psychologically, divorce is a terrifying situation.

But release from an outgrown or unworkable marriage, no matter how painful the process, can be a step toward liberation for women. As a result of divorce, some women have discovered a "new lease on life." Once free of the emotional burden of a miserable marriage, we have returned to school or to previously abandoned careers or have taken up new ones with renewed energy. The theme of a woman's growth and liberation consequent to divorce has been explored in a number of contemporary novels. Once the bitter period of initial separation is over, some women can even look back on former marriages fondly, as happy and constructive periods of our lives. Anthropologist Margaret Mead, in her own view, had three successful marriages (Mead, 1972).

Widowhood

Because women in developed societies have a greater life expectancy than men, we stand a good chance of ending our lives as widows. One-third to one-half of all elderly populations are widowed, and three out of four of the oldest old women are widowed. While less than 10 percent of the Japanese elderly live alone, in most industrially developed countries, the elderly are increasingly likely to live alone. In the United States, half of all women over seventy-five lived alone in 1985, while the figures are much lower for men of this age; elderly women are also more likely to be widowed than married. "Elderly women greatly outnumber elderly men in most countries of the world" (Torrey et al., 1987:21).

In some societies, the social structure tends to make women young widows but inhibits our chances to remarry. It is not uncommon for widows to be permanently ensconced in the houses of our in-laws, who possess and control the dowry and the chances of remarriage. Widowed women may be victims of the ill-disguised hostility of in-laws. A most extreme example of this treatment is exemplified in the case of young Indian widows, who are permanently left in the houses of in-laws, barred from remarriage, and treated as pariahs who (according to the laws of Karma) probably caused the death of the husband by some evil committed in a previous life, if not in this one. Traditionally, the women's only recourse

Marriage and Career: Two Options

The Two-Person Career: Hanna Papanek (1973) draws our attention to professional careers that make "formal and informal institutional demands on both members of a married couple of whom only the man is employed by the institution." Wives of men who are (or aspire to be) executives in corporations, or politicians, sometimes doctors, and, traditionally, professors, are regarded by the institutions employing their husbands as requiring certain qualifications (which bear on their husbands' career opportunities), certain duties, such as business entertainment, and certain responsibilities, such as loyalty to the employing institution. Two-person careers are serious obstacles to the career aspirations women have developed in recent times; the resignation by Elizabeth Dole from a Cabinet position as Secretary of Transportation in order to devote herself to her husband's (unsuccessful) campaign for nomination by the Republican Party for president in 1988 is a clear illustration. Even in careers that do not require two persons, geographical mobility may play an important role in elevating the husband's career at the expense of the wife's; if the company relocates the husband, the wife is likely to interrupt her own career to follow him.

(Papanek, 1973)

Commuter Marriage: An alternative solution some couples have found to the problem of geographical mobility is to live apart while sustaining the marriage through periodic visits. Naomi Gerstel and Harriet Gross (1983) found that although there were some financial gains to sustaining two careers in this way, the financial costs were even greater; they conclude that the arrangement to commute must be explained in terms of a dual commitment to career and marriage. Couples who live apart (at least part of the time) have varied sorts of arrangements for getting together. The most successful commuter marriages were those that were already well established, and that did not require prolonged separations of irregular duration. Couples who got together every weekend experienced less strain than those who did not, due to job demands or distance. The advantages of commuting were that wives could pursue their own careers, and, on a daily basis, some wives found relief from family pressures, which gave them more freedom to concentrate on their work, without interruption.

Careers that separate couples are not entirely new. For example, men in navy and merchant marine careers leave their wives ashore for many months of the year, and in the past, sometimes did so for years. Gerstel and Gross found that in contemporary merchant marine families, wives seem to develop two alternating patterns of life, one when the husband is home, and the other when he is away (nine months of the year). While he is away, the wife will develop her own, autonomous existence; when the husband returns, many wives find it difficult to readjust to expectations of dependency and "togetherness."

(Gerstel and Gross, 1983)

was to volunteer for *suttee*, self-immolation on the husband's funeral pyre (Stein, 1978).

Social ostracism is the common way to rid society of women who no longer fit into the structure. Young widows who escape from the control of elders and resist taking new hus-

bands threaten a system designed to limit women's choices as well as the self-esteem of men in the community. We also threaten the security of the other women in the community because we are seen as a danger to their own marriages. This potential multiple threat to social structures explains, in part, the excessive pressure and hostility that is applied to young widows in Greece and southern Italy (Cornelisen, 1969). We are socially shunned and abused unless we capitulate and remarry. In early European society, widows who found ourselves outside the protection of a related male often found ourselves outside the law altogether, with no protection against rape, theft, or other abuses.

Nonetheless, a husband's death does not end a woman's life. Tomioka Taeko (b. 1935), a Japanese poet and fiction writer, encapsulates the state of widowhood in her story "Family in Hell," in these words: "After all what is it they say? When a man's left a widower the maggots start to crawl, but when a woman's left a widow flowers come out in bloom!" (Tanaka and Hanson, 1982:176). Widowhood may have advantages for some women, especially where we have been protected by both religious and secular law from being obligated to marry a second time. Where women are economically secure, no one can interfere with us. Our increased maturity and independence enhance our chances of choosing a mate to our own liking or remaining single and actively independent. Financial security is all-important in determining the fate of widows; without it, we may quickly fall into the category of objects of charity.

Feminist Options

Is there a feminist argument in favor of marriage? Most feminists who discuss the institution favorably argue for a redefinition that emphasizes and reinforces equality between partners. Given a social environment in which pairing of mates is the norm, these writers believe that there is considerable scope for

---

John Stuart Mill on Marriage as Friendship

When each of two persons, instead of being a nothing, is a something; when they are attached to one another, and are not too much unlike to begin with; the constant partaking in the same things, assisted by their sympathy, draws out the latent capacities of each for being interested in the things which were at first interesting only to the other; and works a gradual assimilation of the tastes and characters to one another, partly by the insensible modification of each, but more by a real enriching of the two natures, each acquiring the tastes and capacities of the other in addition to its own. This often happens between two friends of the same sex, who are much associated in their daily life: and it would be a common, if not the commonest, case in marriage, did not the totally different bringing-up of the two sexes make it next to an impossibility to form a really well-assorted union. Were this remedied, whatever differences there might still be in individual tastes, there would at least be, as a general rule, complete unity and unanimity as to the great objects of life. When the two persons both care for great objects, and are a help and encouragement to each other in whatever regards these, the minor matters on which their tastes may differ are not all-important to them; and there is a foundation for solid friendship, of an enduring character, more likely than anything else to make it, through the whole of life, a greater pleasure to each to give pleasure to the other, than to receive it.

(Mill, 1869, 1970:233)

molding marital agreements according to principles of equality and fairness. Some of the efforts that have been made in this direction are discussed in Chapter 9. But as for the more conventional concepts of "wifehood," there seems little that can be said in their defense. To be sure, most feminists argue for a woman's freedom of choice, and perhaps many of us would freely choose to subordinate our own interests to those of our husbands as conventional "wifehood" would imply. Others believe our best interests lie in the role of wife. But it is at least equally likely that this "choice" is governed by those role expectations in life that most women have been socialized to accept.

Feminist utopian literature seems generally to argue against the institution of marriage. While some utopias, like Marge Piercy's Mattapoisett in *Woman on the Edge of Time* (1976), allow scope for mutually gratifying stable bonding between women and men (as well as same-sex couples), the form of the union is open, flexible, and highly individualized. The role of "wife" has no place in feminist utopian literature.

But utopias are imaginary, and we live in a world where compromises must be made. Many women choose to enter into the legal commitment of a marriage, and for those who want to marry, there are feminist options. Some of the literature on this subject has concentrated on the ideal of egalitarian marriage. Most feminists support the ideal of shared household work, more equitable treatment in divorce, and a fair division of parental and economic responsibilities. Some also argue for the revival of the explicit marriage contract; yet others have made a case for cash payments for housework and other services within the household. Yet other options for family life, such as lesbian households or communes, are explored in Chapter 9. Today's economic and social climate, in which many women earn our own incomes and have choices concerning whether and when to have children, favors experimentation with new forms of commitment and family life.

Summary

The institution of marriage and the existence of the complementary roles of "wife" and "husband" are often explained in terms of their social functions. The most common rationales are those related to reproduction: Marriage obligates a man to assist a woman in rearing their children and, by requiring the wife's sexual fidelity, reassures him that it is his own offspring that he supports. An alternative perspective on this issue suggests that marriage confers upon a man a right of access to and control over a woman's children but does not necessarily guarantee his support. A second rationale for marriage is that it minimizes male rivalry over sexual access to women and provides an important means of forming or cementing alliances between men. In this view, women are reduced to objects of exchange between men. A third perspective suggests that marriage reduces competition between women and men by assigning to each distinctive, nonoverlapping roles in life.

None of these explanations addresses the personal motivations of individuals in marriage. These are variable and include emotional and psychological reasons as well as social and economic ones.

The selection of marital partners is generally conditioned by social constraints and family goals as well as personal preferences. Social customs and laws delimit the circle from which prospective marital partners can be chosen. Rules of exogamy forbid us to marry anyone too closely related, while rules of endogamy enforce marriage within certain social boundaries such as our own religious, ethnic, or racial group. Families also traditionally restrict choices, particularly where marriage is arranged by parents and kin for prospective couples. Families tend to search for unions that are advantageous to themselves, though they may take the couple's preferences into account as well. Modern societies permit considerably more latitude for personal choice than traditional ones.

Marriage takes many forms. Some societies encourage arrangements whereby women may have more than one husband (polyandry), but this is rare by comparison with those societies in which women ideally share our husbands with one or more other wives (polygyny). Regardless of ideals, however, monogamy, marriage to a single partner, is far more common in any society, than polygamy, marriage to more than one mate at a time.

A woman may be formally "married" at any stage of life, but most women's first marriages—except in Western societies—take place when they are between fifteen and eighteen years old. Our first wedding is an important rite of passage in which we assume a new, adult identity with new rights and obligations. The wedding ceremony is often replete with symbolic gestures representing a major shift in a woman's social place.

Marital households are as variable in form as are marriages themselves. A couple may reside in a separate domestic establishment or may join other couples, parents, or siblings of the bride or groom. Just where the bride fits in depends on whether we start out alone, with our own kin, with our husband's kin, or with his other wives.

With reference to extramarital affairs, society tends to hold a double standard, as in many other matters; women tend to be more constrained, and to be more severely penalized for adultery. However, extramarital affairs have long had their attractions for women, despite the risks; in the United States today, about one out of four women reports having had such affairs.

Nearly every society, while expecting marriage to have some degree of stability, also rec-

ognizes grounds for divorce. In most, women and men have roughly equal rights to terminate a marriage. The divorce rate in the United States is not unusually high, compared to that in non-Western societies. What is universal is the disparity between the ease with which couples in the United States can marry and the difficulties encountered in getting divorced. Divorce tends to be costly, time-consuming, and painful. However, despite the legal, social, and emotional costs, many women have found it an important step toward liberation.

For social or demographic reasons, women stand a very high chance of being widowed. In some societies, the experience of widowhood can be made extremely bitter by systematic constraints, ostracism, or persecution.

Feminist writers have, on the whole, been critical of traditional marital institutions, and many have suggested new options for marital arrangements. In addition to arguing for greater latitude of choice about whether, when, and whom to marry, the greatest concern has been for ways to build equality into the marital agreement. Some of these options are explored in Chapter 9.

Discussion Questions

1. Marriage is an institution that is found in all known human societies. Why do you think this is so? What explanations have been offered for the institution of marriage? Do you find any of them convincing? Why?

2. Do you think that the social position and roles of wives have changed through time? Select a specific case and describe what changed and how it changed. What brought about the change?

3. Make a list of the weekly services performed by a wife for a household with which you are familiar. How do these services compare with those rendered by the husband in this household?

4. Do you think a woman is better off married or single? What conditions argue in favor of marriage for a woman, and what against?

5. What, in your view, would be an ideal form of marriage? What kinds of social conditions would be necessary for this kind of marriage to be possible?

Recommended Readings

Bâ, Mariama. *So Long a Letter.* Translated by Modupé Bodé-Thomas. London: Heinemann, 1981. First published in French in 1980, this long "letter" from a recently widowed Senegalese school teacher to her girlhood friend is a story of marriage and polygamy in modern, urban Africa. It is a short, deeply moving narrative.

Chopin, Kate. *The Awakening.* 1899. Reprint. New York: Avon, 1972. A novel about a young wife who fell in love and attempted to extricate herself from an oppressive marriage.

Hartman, Mary S. *Victorian Murderesses: A True History of Respectable French and English Women Accused of Unspeakable Crimes.* New York: Schocken, 1977. A social historian's study of middle-class women who vented frustrations by murdering relatives, lovers, and, in one case, a pupil, as seen in the context of the struggle for domestic power.

Hochschild, Arlie, with Machung, Anne. *The Second Shift.* New York: Avon Books, 1989. A groundbreaking study that examines why wives who work outside the home continue to be responsible for the bulk of household chores, how couples arrive at these arrangements, and why women stand for them.

Rubin, Lillian. *Worlds of Pain.* New York: Basic Books, 1976. A well-written study of working-class wives in California by a noted sociologist.

Seifer, Nancy, editor. *"Nobody Speaks for Me!" Self-Portraits of American Working Class Women.* New York: Simon & Schuster, 1976. All the women who speak for themselves in this anthology are married; the diverse backgrounds of these ten women who speak for themselves include Irish, Norwegian, and German. They live in every section of the United States, in cities, suburbs, small towns, and rural areas.

References

Alexandrova, Ekaterina. "Why Soviet Women Want to Get Married." In *Women and Russia: Feminist Writings from the Soviet Union,* edited by Tatyana Mamonova. Boston: Beacon Press, 1984.

Arendell, Terry. "Women and the Economics of Divorce in the Contemporary United States." *Signs* 13:1 (1987).

Bâ, Mariama. *So Long a Letter.* Translated by Modupé Bodé-Thomas. London: Heinemann, 1981.

Brownmiller, Susan. *Against Our Will: Men, Women, and Rape.* New York: Simon & Schuster, 1975.

Chilman, Catherine. "Remarriage and Stepfamilies: Research Results and Implications." In *Contemporary Families and Alternative Lifestyles,* edited by Eleanor Macklin and Roger Rubin. Beverly Hills: Sage, 1983.

Cole, Donald P. "The Household, Marriage and Family Life Among the Al Murrah Nomads of Saudi Arabia." In *Arab Society in Transition,* edited by Saad Eddin Ibrahim and Nicholas S. Hopkins. Cairo: American University in Cairo Press, 1977.

Cornelison, Ann. *Torregreca: Life, Death, Miracles.* Boston: Little, Brown, 1969.

Curb, Rosemary, and Manahan, Nancy, editors. *Lesbian Nuns: Breaking Silence.* New York: Warner Books, 1985.

Doerr, Harriet. *Stones for Ibarra.* New York: Penguin Books, 1978.

Ember, Carol, and Ember, Melvin. *Cultural Anthropology,* 7th edition. Englewood Cliffs, N.J.: Prentice-Hall, 1993.

Ember, Melvin, and Ember, Carol R. "Male-Female Bonding: A Cross-Species Study of Mammals and Birds." *Behavior Science Research* 14 (1979):37–56.

Engels, Friedrich. *The Origin of the Family, Private Property, and the State.* 1884. Translated by Alec West, 1942. Edited by Eleanor Burke Leacock. New York: International Publishers, 1972.

Espin, Oliva M. "Cultural and Historical Influences on Sexuality in Hispanic/Latin Women: Implications for Psycho-Therapy." In *Pleasure and Danger: Exploring Female Sexuality*, edited by C. Vance. Boston: Routledge and Kegan Paul, 1984.

————. Reprinted in *All American Women: Lines that Divide, Ties that Bind*, edited by J. B. Cole. New York: Free Press, 1986.

Farnum, Christie. "Sapphire? The Issue of Dominance in the Slave Family, 1830–1865." In *"To Toil the Livelong Day": America's Women at Work, 1780–1980*, edited by Carol Groneman and Mary Beth Norton. Ithaca, N.Y.: Cornell University Press, 1987.

Fernea, Elizabeth. *The Guests of the Sheik.* Garden City: N.Y.: Doubleday, 1958.

Flaubert, Gustave. *Madame Bovary.* 1854. Translated by Mildred Marmur. New York: New American Library, 1964.

Forbes, Geraldine. "Women and Modernity: The Issue of Child Marriage in India." *Women's Studies International Quarterly* 2 (1979):407–19.

Freuchen, Peter. *Book of the Eskimos.* New York: Matson, 1961.

Gerson, Kathleen. "What do Women Want from Men?" In *Changing Men: New Directions in Research on Men and Masculinity*, edited by Michael Kimmel. Newbury Park, Calif.: Sage Publications, 1987.

Gerstel, Naomi, and Gross, Harriet. "Commuter Marriage: Couples Who Live Apart." In *Contemporary Families and Alternative Lifestyles*, edited by Eleanor Macklin and Roger Rubin. Beverly Hills: Sage, 1983.

Glick, P. C., and Norton, A. J. "Marrying, Divorcing, and Living Together in the U.S. Today." *Population Bulletin* 32:5. Washington, D.C.: Population Reference Bureau, 1977.

Goldman, Emma. *Living My Life.* 1931. Reprint. New York: Dover, 1970.

Hartman, Heidi. "The Family as Locus of Gender, Class, and Political Struggle: The Example of Housework." *Signs* 6:3(1981).

Hiller, Dana, and Philliber, William. "The Division of Labor in Contemporary Marriage: Expectations, Perceptions, and Performance." *Social Problems* 33:(1986).

Hite, Shere. *Women and Love: A Cultural Revolution in Progress.* New York: Knopf, 1987.

Hochschild, Arlie, with Machung, Anne. *The Second Shift.* New York: Avon Books, 1989.

Hsu, Francis L. K. *Under the Ancestor's Shadow.* London: Routledge & Kegan Paul, 1949.

India (Republic), Department of Publication. *Towards Equality.* Report of Committee on the Status of Women. Delhi: Controller of Publications, Civil Lines, 1974.

Irons, William. *The Yomut Turkmen: A Study of Social Organization Among a Central Asian Turkic-Speaking Population.* Ann Arbor: University of Michigan, 1975.

Kim, Elaine H., with Otani, Janice. *With Silk Wings; Asian Women in America.* San Francisco: Asian Women United of California, 1983.

Kimmel, Michael, editor. *Changing Men: New Directions in Research on Men and Masculinity.* Newbury Park, Calif.: Sage Publications, 1987.

Kristeva, Julia. "On the Women of China." Translated by E. C. Kennedy. *Signs* 1:1 (1975).

Laws, Judith Long, and Schwartz, Pepper. *Sexual Scripts.* Hinsdale, Ill.: Dryden, 1977.

Levi-Strauss, Claude. 1949. *The Elementary Structures of Kinship.* 1949. Translated by James H. Bell and John R. von Starmer. Boston; Beacon, 1969.

Lewis, Oscar. *A Death in the Sanchez Family.* New York: Random House, 1969.

Lindholm, Charles, and Lindholm, Charry. "Marriage as Warfare." *Natural History* 88 (1979):11–21.

Lockwood, William. *European Moslems.* New York: Academic Press, 1975.

Macklin, Eleanor, and Rubin, Roger, editors. *Contemporary Families and Alternative Lifestyles.* Beverly Hills: Sage, 1983.

Makhlouf-Obermeyer, Carla. *Changing Veils: A Study of Women in North Yemen.* Austin: University of Texas Press, 1979.

Mamonova, Tatyana. *Women and Russia: Feminist Writings from the Soviet Union.* Boston; Beacon Press, 1984.

Mead, Margaret. *Blackberry Winter.* New York: Morrow, 1972.

———. *Coming of Age in Samoa.* New York: Morrow, 1928.

Mill, John Stuart. "On the Subjection of Women." In John Stuart Mill and Harriet Taylor Mill, *Essays on Sex Equality* (1869), edited by Alice S. Rossi. Chicago: University of Chicago Press, 1970.

Murdock, George P. "Family Stability in Non-European Cultures." *Annals of the American Academy of Political and Social Science* 272 (1950):175–201.

Nyrop, Richard. *India, A Country Study.* Washington D.C.: American University Foreign Area Studies, 1986.

O'Brien, Denise. "Female Husbands in Southern Bantu Societies." In *Sexual Stratification: A Cross-Cultural View,* edited by Alice Schlegal. New York: Columbia University Press, 1977.

Papanek, Hanna. "Men, Women, and Work: Reflections on the Two-Person Career." In *Changing Women in a Changing Society,* edited by Joan Huber. Chicago: University of Chicago Press, 1973.

Peristiany, Jean G. *Mediterranean Family Structures.* Cambridge: Cambridge University Press, 1976.

Piercy, Marge. *Woman on the Edge of Time.* New York: Knopf, 1976.

Price-Bonham, Sharon, Wright, David, and Pittman, Joe. "Divorce: A Frequent 'Alternative' in the 1970's." In *Contemporary Families and Alternative Lifestyles,* edited by Eleanor Macklin and Roger Rubin. Beverly Hills: Sage, 1983.

Rosen, Lawrence. "The Negotiations of Reality: Male-Female Relations in Safrou, Morocco." In *Women in the Muslim World,* edited by Lois Beck and Nikki Keddie. Cambridge, Mass.: Harvard University Press, 1978.

Shukert, Elfrieda Berthiaume, and Scibetta, Barbara Smith. *War Brides of World War II.* New York: Penguin Books, 1989.

Stack, Carol. *All Our Kin.* New York: Harper & Row, 1974.

Stein, Dorothy K. "Women to Burn: Suttee as a Normative Institution." *Signs* 4 (1978):253–78.

Tanaka, Yukiko, and Hanson, Elizabeth, translators and editors. *This Kind of Woman: Ten Stories by Japanese Women Writers, 1960–1976.* New York: Perigree Books, 1982.

Torrey, Barbara, Kinsella, Kevin, and Taeuber, Cynthia. "An Aging World." International Population Reports Series P-95, No. 78. Washington D.C.: U.S. Department of Commerce, 1987.

Tylor, E. B. "On a Method of Investigating the Development of Institutions, Applied to Laws of Marriage and Descent." *Journal of the Royal Anthropological Institute* 18 (1889):245–69.

United Nations. Fertility Behavior in the Context of Development. New York: United Nations, 1987.

United States Bureau of Census. Current Population Reports, Series P-23, No. 150. Profile of the United States: 1984–85. Washington, D.C.: U.S. Government Printing Office, 1987.

United States Department of Commerce. "Marital Status and Living Arrangements: March, 1986." Current Population Reports, Population Characteristics, Series P-20, No. 418, 1987.

United States Department of Health and Human Services. Vital and Health Statistics. "Duration of Marriage Before Divorce." Series 21, No. 38. Washington, D.C.: U.S. Government Printing Office, July 1981.

———. "National Estimates of Marriage Dissolution and Survivorship." Series B, No. 19. Washington D.C.: U.S. Government Printing Office, November 1980.

Walther, Wiebke. *Women in Islam.* Montclair, N.J.: Schram, 1981.

Wilson, Edward O. *Sociobiology.* Cambridge, Mass.: Belknap Press of Harvard University, 1975.

Zinn, Maxine Baca, and Eitzen, D. Stanley. *Diversity in American Families.* New York: Harper & Row, 1987.

Motherhood

Motherhood is a central issue to women everywhere: whether we are, intend to be, or intend not to be mothers ourselves. We are all daughters of mothers. For some women, motherhood is a source of immense pleasure and pride; for others, of conflict and pain. Many feel that it is women's very capacity to become mothers that has been used as a rationale for the unjust and harmful social constraints placed on us. Furthermore, many people believe that society has institutionalized motherhood in such a way as to make the experience of it often degrading, debilitating, and painful, to the detriment of everyone—women, children, and men.

Until recently, few women were able to choose not to be mothers. Now the question is not only whether women must become mothers but whether we must make a choice between motherhood and a career. Shouldn't we be able to choose both?

Despite the centrality of mothering in human experience, it has received remarkably little attention. Because motherhood is often taken so much for granted as a biological "fact," we will begin with an examination of the ways that society has institutionalized women's reproductive role. We will then take a close look at the ways that culture shapes even those events that appear to be most directly associated with biology: pregnancy, childbirth, and lactation. Next, we will address two political issues associated with motherhood: support systems by the family and by society in general, and the control over whether, when, and how a woman becomes a mother. We will look at the ways that motherhood has been depicted in art, literature, and the popular media. This should help us understand how ideas about motherhood are reflected in and shaped by social processes. Finally, we will consider how appropriate attention to mothering might change fundamental conceptions about human thought and society.

Parental Behavior: Instinct and Culture

All organisms come from other organisms. In this sense, all organisms have "parents." Sexual reproduction involves a differentiation of reproductive functions, in that some organisms contribute ova and some contribute sperm, but we do not think of all sexually reproducing organisms as "mothers" and "fathers." Many plants, for example, have female and male reproductive functions, but we do not speak of "mother" and "father" plants. Contributing an egg, then, is not sufficient (or even necessary) to make a female a mother.

It is usually only where parents contribute some care after birth that the terms *mother* and *father* seem to apply. But organisms do not invariably differentiate parental care after birth according to the sex of the parent, or in any particular way. Among many bird species, for example, female and male parents share equally in nest building, egg hatching, and feeding and protection of the young. Even among mammals, whose female members lactate (produce milk), there is considerable variability in parental roles. The male marmoset, which is a primate like ourselves, carries and protects his young; he brings them to the female from time to time to be nursed.

How do we account for parental behavior? When we observe it in birds and fish, or dogs and cats, we assume that their activities are "instinctive." By this we mean to say that their nervous systems are so programmed by genetic inheritance that, given a healthy organism and an adequate environment (proper stimuli), a parent will automatically behave in certain ways (responses). Parents who are not programmed this way will not produce viable offspring, while those who are ensure that their offspring will themselves carry the same program. The females will perform reproductive roles assigned in their species to females, and the same is true for the males.

When we consider more complex animals, particularly primates like ourselves, we begin to question the applicability of the notion of "instinct." We discover that sexually differentiated parental roles are not simple biological "givens." Laboratory experiments with female rhesus monkeys, for example, show that when they are reared in isolation, with no opportunity to observe or experience rhesus maternal behavior, they do not instinctively display maternal behavior toward their own young. Furthermore, normally reared male rhesus monkeys who are placed with rhesus infants in the absence of mature females do display "maternal" behavior. We can conclude from these studies and others that for complex organisms, like monkeys, maternal behavior must be learned, and that its expression by females or males depends on their experience and social conditions. (For an overview, see Liebowitz, 1978.)

If this is true of monkeys, is there any reason to believe it is not true of humans? While it is unlikely that any informed person would deny that learning and circumstances play a role in shaping maternal behavior, it is often assumed that the behavior of human mothers toward our children is somehow "natural" or instinctive, and that women are more biologically predisposed to perform this behavior than men. Is there such a thing as "maternal instinct" in humans, and is it present only in women? The emotional and developmental need of children for "mothering" is most likely one of the progenitors of the role of "mother." But must humans who "mother" be female? No.

Of course, humans do have some relatively simple "instincts," which we call *reflexes*. We are innately "programmed" to blink our eyes when a foreign object enters or threatens to enter. Women who breast-feed experience the "let-down" reflex (involuntary ejection of milk) in response to the sensation of the infant's sucking. But this type of simple reflex is not what people usually mean when they refer to "maternal instinct."

It can be argued that humans have innate predispositions for complex and varied sorts of behavior; however, genetic inheritance provides the general pattern, not the details, of such behavior. Humans are innately predisposed to learn to speak, if we are not handicapped and have a proper environment; but *which* language we learn depends on what we have had the opportunity to hear. Do similar sorts of general innate predispositions underlie the parental behavior of either sex? There is no evidence that this is the case, although researchers have been looking into the matter (Rossi, 1977).

Interest in the question of what does shape

Maternal behavior is culturally variable. The San of the Kalahari Desert in southern Africa carry their infants and nurse them for several years. Here, a San woman relaxing with her child is depicted in a 1931 bronze sculpture by Malvina Hoffman (1887–1966). (*Mother and Child.* © Field Museum of Natural History)

maternal behavior has only served to under-line the extent of our ignorance of what maternal behavior is. We know little, for example, about the extent of human variability in parental behavior patterns, although we do know from anthropological and historical evidence that they are, indeed, quite variable. We know little about paternal behavior, perhaps because of the cultural bias of researchers, which leads them to believe that fathers play a less important role in early childhood. Likewise, the bias that holds that motherhood comes "naturally" to women has prevented research into what women actually feel about assuming maternal roles (Denmark, 1978). Toni Morrison's powerful novel *Beloved* portrays the devastating conflict of an escaped slave who loves her baby daughter so much she kills her to prevent the child's recapture and return to slavery (Morrison, 1987). Of course, "nature" can neither explain nor predict such human actions.

Another area of ignorance is the role that infants play in shaping parental behavior. Human parents, like birds and monkeys, respond in ways evoked by the behavior of their offspring. A number of researchers have indicated that early parent-infant interactions affect the quality of later interactions.

In addition to the obvious influence of learning and of environmental and circumstantial conditions, we should consider the possible impact of the experience of pregnancy, childbirth, and breast-feeding on the differentiation of female and male parental roles. While maternal behavior is variable, the fact that women usually carry our offspring in our bodies for nine months, give birth to them, and then often hold them close to feed them (the breast) for months, even years, afterward, while fathers do not, is likely to have some influence on general differences between maternal and paternal roles. But what are the implications, if any, of these differences? We do not know.

Motherhood: Ideology and Reality

The stereotypical view that motherhood "comes naturally" to women may have no basis in fact, but it does have an influence on women's feelings and attitudes. Many cultures regard motherhood as a major source of fulfillment and satisfaction for women and disapprove of negative attitudes toward childbearing and childrearing. Despite cultural biases, increasing numbers of women the world over have begun to express feelings of ambiguity, dissatisfaction, fear, resentment, inadequacy, and anger about these experiences.

Some cultures set such high standards and expectations, and so strongly oppose dissent, that feelings of incompetence and frustration would appear inevitable. As Betty Friedan revealed in *The Feminine Mystique* (1963), middle-class American society during the 1950s seemed to carry this to an extreme. Mothers are assumed to love our children infinitely and unreservedly, to be glad to devote ourselves completely to our role, and to want to be with our children at all times. Such idealization evoked disappointment and anxiety in many women, particularly given the social context in which we engaged in mothering. Isolated in nuclear families in suburban communities built in response to the postwar "baby boom," women were encouraged to have many children in rapid succession but were denied practical help from husbands, kin, or the public, in the form of day care. We had virtually no outlet in the form of other employment, intellectual activity, or social purpose. Raising children was our "job" in life. Because we accepted this definition of motherhood as "natural," we could only attribute any dissatisfaction we might have felt to personal inadequacy.

This idea of motherhood as a "job," akin to other jobs like being a doctor or plumber or salesperson, is a relatively recent innovation, limited to classes of Western cultures sufficiently affluent to keep women out of the wage labor force. Note that the above applies to the economically able. However, in most cultures, women have worked at various productive tasks while looking after children. In any case, motherhood is not a "job" in that there is no pay.

The consequences of the belief that motherhood is, or ought to be, a full-time job are far-reaching for women, children, and whole families (Bernard, 1974). Many women who attempt to live up to this ideal are highly restricted in our activities and become isolated from the adult world. We focus all our emotions, aspirations, and energies on childrearing, far more than most children need. If we do go out to work for wages, leaving our children in the care of others, or alone if we must, we feel guilty, and this guilt is magnified by the censure of others. If we do not go out to work, when our children grow up we may suddenly find we have nothing to "do," no purpose in life. Women's life expectancy has risen so dramatically in modern times that the "empty nest" years of life now exceed the number of years spent in childrearing.

Children raised by full-time mothers may learn independence late in life, since their mothers devote so much attention to filling their needs. Or they may feel resentment at being "smothered." Before technology took productive work out of the home, women and men could be both workers and parents. Children benefited from exposure to the work activities of their parents and by participating in them.

Because "mothering" as a job is assigned to women, fathers may be excluded (or exclude themselves) from an active role in childrearing. Most important, perhaps, is the asymmetry introduced into female-male relationships resulting from economic asymmetry. Mothers who do not or cannot work at paying jobs must depend on men who are their husbands or lovers or on some such support as welfare or charity. This dependency may often contribute to the paternalistic attitudes of men toward women, and to women's own insecure feelings. Women who are or intend to be full-time mothers may find that our identities become submerged in the identities of our husbands and children. Many popular novels written by women in recent years, such as Marilyn French's *The Women's Room* and Sue Miller's *The Good Mother*, explore the problems of the full-time mother who is finding independence and sexual fulfillment. These two novels reflect the experience of white middle-class women in particular. Poor women or highly trained women who work full-time outside the home have had a different experience from mothers who stay at home. Generally, working women leave our children in the care of surrogate "mothers"— a grandmother, an aunt, a hired babysitter, or a nurse. Maya Angelou, in her autobiographical book *I Know Why the Caged Bird Sings* (1969), writes about the relationships of a young girl with her glamorous but elusive mother and the grandmother who cares for her through most of childhood.

Are oppressive conditions the inevitable consequence of motherhood? Some feminist writers see the roots of women's oppression in our reproductive function (Firestone, 1970). Because only women can bear children, men, who are excluded from this creativity, try to create everything else and deny women access to their world (de Beauvoir, 1953). Other feminist writers argue that it is not motherhood itself, but the way that society has institutionalized it that oppresses women, children, and men (Rich, 1976). Charlotte Perkins Gilman's 1915 fantasy novel *Herland* (1979) depicts a world in which motherhood is gratifying but not oppressive, a world in which motherhood does not preclude other forms of creativity and achievement. This world, however, has no men. But other feminists see motherhood as the possible source of the most fundamental pride and power in women; they ask that society be reshaped from the point of view of mothers so that it respects first of all the well-being of children and thus of those who care for them (Trebilcot, 1984).

We need not turn to the imagination to see alternative forms of motherhood and different notions of what it ought to be. Motherhood as an institution has been variable through time, and it changes from place to place. The behavior, attitudes, and feelings that different cultures attribute to or expect from mothers change with different social conditions (Mead, 1962). Demography, technology, economic conditions, and family form are all variables that affect the institution of motherhood. But perhaps the most significant is the variable relationship between women and men. Many feminists believe that more equitable relationships between women and men can, and will, lead to forms of motherhood that are more rewarding to all concerned.

In America today, as in other countries, diverse forms of family life have emerged that have important repercussions for the institution of motherhood (Bernard, 1974). Lesbian couples, extended families, communes, stepfamilies, and single-parent households provide contexts that radically challenge conventional ideas of motherhood. Even within the once standard nuclear family, mothers' roles have shown considerable change. Increasingly, with the rise in divorce and remarriage, many of us are called upon to be mother, not just to our own children, if we have any, but also the children of our new spouses. Stepmothering requires us to mother children who may resent our presence and our efforts to "mother" (Smith, 1990). The number of working mothers of small children has dramatically increased (see Chapter 13), and more and more fathers are participating in childrearing for both practical and ideological reasons. And studies show that the "dual-career family," which is beginning to be the norm, is not only better for women, but for children as well, especially if adequate social supports are available (Rubin, 1984; Shreve, 1987).

The Assignment of Mothering to Women: Whose Interest Does It Serve?

A woman's biological contributions to reproduction, though costly in time, energy, and risk, are of relatively short duration compared to the social role of motherhood, which lasts decades. But even the brief time span of pregnancy, childbirth, and breast-feeding involves a major commitment on the part of the woman who undertakes biological motherhood. If we spend most of our time with children, we are excluded from many public activities. Through our association with small children, mothers tend to be belittled by others as typically engaged in the trivial repetitive tasks of domestic life. Rearing children is very hard work, and usually it is mothers who have borne the primary responsibility for this indispensable contribution to society.

Why do women want to become mothers? Women learn from early childhood that we ought to want children, that motherhood is venerated, and that adult status is sure to be achieved with motherhood. We may also come to believe that motherhood will bring us security by attaching us more closely to our husbands or our families through our children. Thus, motherhood may be a way of seeking social approval and acceptance. Unless in religious orders, women in the past who did not have children were generally pitied and stigmatized, and sometimes even thought to be cursed.

"Childless" women have been burned as witches, persecuted as lesbians, have been refused the right to adopt children because they were unmarried. They have been seen as em-

Women's Mothering

The early experience of being cared for by a woman produces a fundamental structure of expectations in women and men concerning mothers' lack of separate interests from their infants and total concern for their infants' welfare. Daughters grow up identifying with these mothers, about whom they have such expectations. This set of expectations is generalized to the assumption that women naturally take care of children of all ages and the belief that women's "maternal" qualities can and should be extended to the nonmothering work that they do. All these results of women's mothering have ensured that women will mother infants and will take continuing responsibility for children.

The reproduction of women's mothering is the basis for the reproduction of women's location and responsibilities in the domestic sphere. . . . That women mother is a fundamental organizational feature of the sex-gender system: It is basic to the sexual division of labor and generates a psychology and ideology of male dominance as well as an ideology about women's capacities and nature. . . .

Women's mothering also reproduces the family as it is constituted in male-dominant society . . . it produces men who react to, fear, and act superior to women, and who put most of their energies into the nonfamilial work world and do not parent . . . it produces women who turn their energies toward nurturing and caring for children—in turn reproducing the sexual and familial division of labor in which women mother. . . .

. . . Women in their domestic role as houseworkers reconstitute themselves physically on a daily basis and reproduce themselves as mothers, emotionally and psychologically, in the next generation. They thus contribute to the perpetuation of their own social roles and position in the hierarchy of gender.

(Chodorow, 1978:208–9)

bodiments of the great threat to male hegemony: the woman who is not tied to the family, who is disloyal to the law of heterosexual pairing and bearing. . . .

The "unchilded" woman, if such a term makes any sense, is still affected by centuries-long attitudes—on the part of both women and men—towards the birthing, child-rearing function of women. Any woman who believes that the institution of motherhood has nothing to do with *her* is closing her eyes to crucial aspects of her situation. (Rich, 1976:251–52)

There are many external pressures on women to have and rear children. There are also very real pleasures: acts of nurturing—cuddling, loving, playing with children, tending to their needs—are a delight to many peo-ple, and not only mothers. The sacrifices a mother makes, such as staying up all night to care for a sick child or interrupting work to listen to a child's troubles, are burdens often gladly undertaken out of love and do not require external forces to explain them. We might even ask if it is fair to men to exclude them from maternal pleasures. (Chodorow's work offers an explanation: boys, too, want to mother.) But by and large the assignment of long-term child care responsibilities to mothers rather than to fathers has left men free to acquire economic, political, and social power, which can and often has been used against women (Trebilcot, 1984).

Some writers have pointed out that the unpaid work of mothers serves capitalism: Mothers produce the next generation of workers and service the current generation for free (Dalla Costa, 1972). The fact that mothers and others see women's primary job as childbearing helps to justify low levels of job training, high levels of unemployment, and low pay for women. Thus women form a pool of cheap labor. In socialist societies, the provision of maternity leave, day care, and family allowances helps to mitigate the costs of motherhood to women and to spread them more evenly, though leadership roles are still largely held by men. Capitalist societies, especially the United States, have resisted the reduction of the imbalance in the costs of motherhood. Few companies allow flexible work hours so that both parents can work and share child care responsibilities, nor do they commonly provide day care for children of working parents.

It may be the exclusion of men from motherhood and their consequent fear, envy, and mystification of it that accounts for the peculiar behavior of men toward women (see Chapters 1 and 2). Is this what underlies the oppression of women, not motherhood itself?

The Cultural Shaping of Biological Events

Attitudes toward Pregnancy

Our emotional state, attitudes, and reactions to our social environment can all influence the way we experience any physiological process. How women experience pregnancy, for example, will depend in part on whether the pregnancy was wanted or unwanted, planned or unplanned. It will also depend on the social support system we have, our attitudes toward motherhood, perhaps our relationship with our own parents, and perhaps with the father of the expected child. And it will depend on whether this is our first pregnancy, on the nature of our previous experiences, on our expectations.

Pregnant women must adjust simulta-neously to both physiological changes (in hormones and body shape and weight) and changes in self-perception. These adjustments will be affected by often dramatic changes in other people's reactions to us. If our pregnancies are received with social approval, as when we are eagerly expected to produce heirs, we may get flattering extra attention at this time. If our cultures define pregnancy as a vulnerable, fragile, or even polluting state, we may feel anxious, isolated, or undesirable. In our society, it has been shown that men's attitudes toward pregnant women are often filled with conflict. Not infrequently, men living with pregnant women feel competitive and will become particularly active in producing something creative themselves (Bittman and Zalk, 1978). Some men feel not only envy but rage; the "battered wife syndrome" may start with pregnancy.

Most societies have sets of rules and beliefs that dictate how a woman ought to feel and act during pregnancy. Depictions of pregnant women in painting and sculpture are found as far back as early antiquity, probably the paleolithic era. Current interpretations suggest that they represent the notion of fertility, and that pregnancy was a desirable, even venerated state.

In many societies, pregnancy involves numerous taboos such as prohibitions on certain food, or on attending certain rituals or viewing certain events. These taboos are generally interpreted as existing for the protection of the unborn child. The mother's experiences and feelings during pregnancy are thought to affect the health, even the sex, of the child as well as the relative ease or difficulty of childbirth.

In the middle and upper classes of European society, pregnant women were once secluded from public life; it was thought improper for us to be seen in the pregnant state. Pregnant women couldn't teach children. Earlier in this century in the United States,

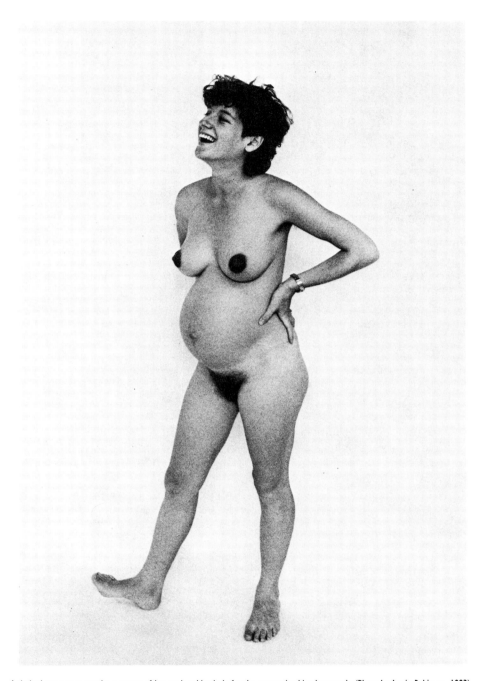

A desired pregnancy may be a source of joy, as it evidently is for the woman in this photograph. (Photo by Jamie Robinson, 1982)

obstetricians advised pregnant women to avoid a variety of activities, including bathing, physical exercise, and sexual intercourse. Today, however, healthy pregnant women in the United States are encouraged to engage in all activities until the last few weeks before childbirth.

Taboos and proscriptions may also apply to the male parent. The Arapesh, for example, believe that the sperm contributes to the fetus's growth; thus, the parents are expected to engage in frequent sexual intercourse so the father can supply the necessary material for his child's formation during pregnancy (Mead, 1963). Such social beliefs have no obvious relation to the strict biological facts of pregnancy, but they can affect its course through influencing the pregnant woman's emotional and physical state.

There is speculation that modern science will soon have the capacity to eliminate pregnancy altogether. It is now possible to produce fertilization of the ovum in a dish; will it be long before a fetus can be brought to term in an artificial womb? Science fiction (like Marge Piercy's *Woman on the Edge of Time*, 1976) has long considered the possible implications of such a development. Would it help to equalize female-male relations by producing a more balanced parenthood? Much will depend on who controls the technology.

Childbirth: A Cultural or a Natural Event?

Today most American women give birth in hospitals, where the process is monitored and controlled by medical professionals (see Chapter 12). Increasing numbers of women, however, have taken an interest in home birth. Many believe that there is something "unnatural" about hospital births and are looking to older traditions to provide a more "natural" model.

For humans, there is really no such thing as "natural childbirth." Every society has beliefs that provide the basis for expectations, attitudes, and practices that shape this event. It is culture that informs women and other participants at birth about what should be done, who should do it, and how. Our culture relies on medical practitioners to intervene in childbirth. Many societies take a more positive and relaxed attitude than our own, allowing women more scope for personal preferences in birthing (Jordan, 1978), although this is not invariably the case.

Typical American birth procedures are unusual in a number of respects. Women in hospitals generally give birth lying on our backs (for the convenience of the obstetrician), but more common delivery positions elsewhere in the world are kneeling, sitting, and squatting. There is ample evidence that these positions facilitate delivery. Hospitals rarely allow friends and relatives to attend births, as they get in the way of the hospital staff; if anyone is admitted, it is likely to be the father of the child. But elsewhere, birthing women are attended by female kin and neighbors as well as midwives; rarely are strangers admitted. Husbands often play a key role, whether in direct assistance to the birthing woman or indirectly, through prescribed rituals. By contrast, American fathers have typically had fairly little to do, and the key roles have been played by strangers, though the participation of fathers in the birth process is increasing.

Finally, hospital births suggest that birthing should be viewed as a medical event, with associations of illness. Other societies vary greatly in their attitudes, ranging from beliefs that childbirth is dangerous or defiling to beliefs that it is a blessed achievement. Where childbirth is considered a normal and positive event, it appears that women experience less trouble and pain than elsewhere (Newton and Newton, 1972). It is worthwhile considering whether the experience shapes the attitude or the attitude shapes the experience.

Childbirth, then, is an event shaped by culture. More important, for our purposes, it is an event heavily influenced by more general social attitudes toward women, attitudes that have a significant political component. The history of the "natural childbirth" movement illustrates this.

Judith Triestman (1979), an anthropologist and trained midwife, places the rise of the natural childbirth movement in the framework of social concerns about decreases in rates of childbearing. Toward the end of the nineteenth century in England, the birth rate began to decline, and more and more single middle-class women went to work outside the home. At the turn of the century, the Boer War made many public figures aware of the poor health of the lower classes and conscious of the fact that the healthier middle classes were producing fewer potential soldiers than the lower classes. This alarm increased with the enormous death toll among young men during World War I. Nonetheless, the women of the middle classes showed no inclination to reverse the declining birth rate.

There was a parallel concern about birth rates during the latter part of the nineteenth century in the United States. Concern was expressed that the white middle class would soon be swamped by the poor, particularly by blacks and the large number of immigrants from eastern and southern Europe who were entering the country. Birth control for the middle class was viewed by such alarmed and racist observers as race suicide. Middle-class white women were exhorted to have more babies to preserve their race and even "civilization," which was equated with white middle-class culture (ibid.; Gordon, 1976).

To encourage middle-class women to have babies, men in politics and the clergy tended to glorify motherhood: It was a woman's duty to have babies. While in earlier times such spokesmen counseled resignation to the pain of childbirth, "Eve's curse" (see Chapter 1), medical experts now sought to reassure

women. Pain could be eliminated with ether or with other drugs. At the same time, childbirth itself was promoted as "naturally" desired by women, an exalted state that should not be missed.

The two messages were contradictory. The early form of the natural childbirth movement, started by Grantly Dick-Read in England, resolved the contradiction. Dick-Read believed that the pain of childbirth was merely the result of culturally induced fear; if women were not afraid, they would not feel pain. He opposed the use of anesthesia, which he thought denied women the supreme joy of the childbirth experience.

The idea of natural childbirth was transformed by French and Russian physicians between the 1930s and the 1950s. Both countries suffered tremendous population losses in the First and Second World Wars, giving them impetus to encourage higher birth rates. In the Soviet Union, ideas about behavior conditioning led to a new approach to childbirth. "Prepared childbirth" involved mental concentration so women could control our awareness of contractions as pain before we experienced them. We would learn how to recognize "stages" of labor, how to interpret these levels of sensation, and how to concentrate on different methods of breathing to manage our responses to each stage. A French doctor who was sympathetic to such ideas eagerly adopted the approach. This was Dr. Fernand Lamaze, whose name is commonly associated with prepared childbirth in the United States.

In America, the Lamaze method was popularized by several authors, particularly Marjorie Karmel, who in *Thank You, Dr. Lamaze* (1965) wrote a testimonial to its effectiveness, and Elizabeth Bing, who wrote an instructional manual, *Six Practical Lessons for Easier Childbirth*, during the 1960s. It began very much as a liberal middle-class phenomenon and to a great extent remains so.

In effect, then, there is nothing particularly "natural" about "natural childbirth," despite its emphasis on avoidance of anesthesia. The very concept of natural childbirth has changed as cultural and social needs have changed. Today it is leading to yet new developments. Triestman (1979) points out that many American women first learned about the importance of self-determination and the role of the larger social context in our private lives through our experiences in the natural childbirth movement. Group sessions in prepared childbirth encouraged us to speak to one another and to publicize our experiences. The increased awareness that resulted from the movement led to greater demands for individual, private control of childbirth and a gradual drift away from the ritualized dogma once taught in prepared childbirth classes. The current resistance by many women to standard hospital routines and the growing popularity of home births, or birthing in those hospitals where midwives assist, are two manifestations of these new trends.

Breast-Feeding: Attitudes and Choices

Political and cultural factors also affect breast-feeding practices. These factors shape both the biological aspects of lactation and the treatment and welfare of babies. Women who are supported by our social environment are more successful at breast-feeding, for stress and distractions can interfere with a mother's production of milk. If mothers can afford a reasonable substitute, such as a safe and nutritious formula, and our infants can tolerate such a replacement, the children generally suffer no deleterious consequences. But many women throughout the world cannot afford an adequate substitute, with the result that children suffer from malnutrition and other illnesses.

Most women at most times in most parts of the world have had no choice: Breast-feeding was the only way to nourish infants. Work did not interfere with breast-feeding: Mothers simply brought our infants with us wherever we went. There was considerable variation in style, however. In some societies, like that of the Kalahari Desert dwellers, babies were nursed all day at short intervals of less than an hour apart. American mothers today are sometimes advised to schedule nursing at intervals of two to four hours. In many societies, children are nursed for three or four years; most American breast-fed babies are weaned some time during the first year of life.

Substitutes for breast-feeding do have a long history. In the Athens of Pericles, in imperial Rome, in France during the reign of Louis XIV, and in early eighteenth-century England, wealthy women had an option other than nursing: the use of wet nurses, who breast-fed other women's infants. Poor and urban working women in Europe also used wet nurses at various times, and in the nineteenth century, there were attempts at bottle-feeding.

In this century, however, it was women from the prosperous middle class who first led the way in giving up breast-feeding and then later reversed the trend by taking it up again. At the turn of the century, 90 percent of American mothers breast-fed. By midcentury, the number had dropped to 12 percent. But in 1966, it had risen again to 20 percent, and that upward trend has continued (McCary, 1973). Similar patterns were found in Europe (Newton, 1968). Among poor women, the decline in breast-feeding came later and has not reversed itself. And in the low-income nations of the world, the decline in breast-feeding has begun more recently and is continuing.

When breast-feeding first declined in the United States, infant mortality rates went up. Concerned health care officials here and in Europe waged campaigns to encourage women to breast-feed (Brack, 1975). While it is difficult to reconstruct all the factors that

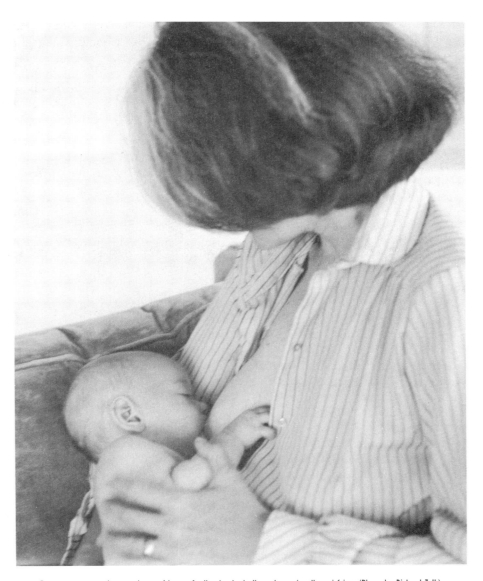

For some women, the experience of breast-feeding is physically and emotionally satisfying. (Photo by Richard Zalk)

led to the decline at that time, it is not so difficult to see what is happening in today's less-developed nations. Ambitious advertising by baby-formula companies encourages women to switch to bottle-feeding, which we then may be unable to afford to keep up at adequate levels. These companies supply free samples to new mothers and promote the idea that their formulas are better for the babies' health. Countercampaigns to encourage breast-feeding do not include the establishment of places for mothers to nurse in public or at work. Poor women are especially vulnerable to commercial sales propaganda for formula because we often must work out of the home for wages. Frequently we are forced to dilute the formulas to make them go further, which deprives our children of nutrition and may introduce contaminated water into their diet. In the meantime, we have lost the ability to breast-feed.

Women receive all sorts of conflicting messages regarding breast-feeding. On the one hand, American mothers may be told that our own milk is best for our babies. On the other hand, our culture shuns nursing in public and sometimes treats the nursing mother as a social outcast. Furthermore, American women are taught to think of our breasts in erotic terms; husbands have even expressed resentment and jealousy at having to share their wives' breasts with a new infant (Bittman and Zalk, 1978). There is some evidence that less autonomous women, who feel less in control of our lives and more subordinate to men, are less likely to want to breast-feed than more autonomous women (Brack, 1975), but even autonomous women usually cannot bring our babies to work, or nurse them in a restaurant, and middle-of-the-night feedings can wear out the strongest of women. Someone else in the family can give the baby a bottle, but not a lactating breast.

Some women resent the idea of being tied down to a nursing schedule or feel that breast-feeding is uncomfortable and exhausting. Others find the experience sensually and emotionally gratifying. Should it not be possible for women to make a choice concerning breast-feeding, as well as childbirth, not on the basis of stereotypes and cultural strictures, but to suit our own personal beliefs, desires, and circumstances?

Mothers and Others: Support Systems

Motherhood is a social institution both in the sense that it is a creation of society and in the sense that it normally is a collective effort. Bringing up a child usually involves some degree of cooperation between mothers and other people. These others can be the fathers of our children, our own parents, our siblings, our other children, and our friends and neighbors, or fellow citizens. Some of the roles that these others play may be socially prescribed; some vary with personal preference and individual circumstances.

The Western industrialized world, particularly its middle class, emphasizes the nuclear family, mobility, and domestic privacy. As a result, mothers of young children are often subject to extreme isolation, especially if we live in the suburbs. Isolated motherhood can be an alienating experience for women, and our own alienation can lead to emotional problems for our children (Bernard, 1974). Women who are single parents, whether through choice or as a result of divorce, desertion, or widowhood, may experience isolation similar to that of the suburban married mother as a result of similar social conditions.

However, such isolation is neither typical of other parts of the world nor historically characteristic of motherhood. Far more often, mothers of young children receive practical and emotional support from various sources, including fathers, other women, and the community at large.

Fathers

As Margaret Mead pointed out in *Male and Female* (1962), human fatherhood is culturally variable, but it is also universal. That is, every known human society has "some set of permanent arrangements by which males assist females in caring for children while they are young." In some societies, such as the Arapesh, mentioned earlier, the father's nurturing role is believed to begin during his wife's pregnancy. In some societies, fathers undergo a ritual version of childbirth, called *couvade*, where they imitate (and sometimes claim to feel) the pains of labor and childbirth, and later observe a variety of postpartum taboos. In other societies, fathers are kept at a distance until their children are older, but they contribute to the material support of children and mothers.

In addition to the considerable cultural variation in the kinds of support fathers are expected to give, there is also considerable personal variability. Many fathers in the United States today, for example, play a much greater role in the daily care of their small children than fathers normally did a generation ago, though getting fathers to make an equal contribution to child care is still a distant goal for most women. The trend toward greater participation of fathers suggests that the ideal of equality in parenting is not just a utopian dream, but studies show progress toward it to have been modest so far. At the same time, fathers living apart from their children contribute little to their support, and this neglect is evident regardless of income. Overall, the total monetary contribution that American fathers make to support their children not living with them averages only 2 to 5 percent of their income (Bergmann, 1981).

Women's Networks

Most American mothers get some support from the fathers of our young children. Many may feel the lack of support from other women. Traditionally, female support networks, primarily kin, were extremely important to mothers. This continues to be the case among many black families in the United States today, particularly those who live in poverty (Stack, 1974; Collins, 1990). In many societies, mothers of young children could turn to our own mothers, to our sisters and other kin, and to our female friends. Though this network of women did little to loosen the grip of gender roles, it helped us care and also helped us to learn *how* to be mothers. Our female support network might provide us with advice, sympathy, and emotional support or just necessary adult companionship. Today, it is not uncommon for mothers of young children in the suburbs and the cities to form networks of similar women to take the place of the traditional female support systems to which we no longer have access.

Community Support

Unlike kin-based support systems, institutionalized community support in the form of day care is a fairly recent phenomenon. In some countries, institutionalized group support for childrearing is an ideological issue. The traditional private nuclear family, for example, may be frowned on as antithetical to social changes favored by some governments.

Institutionalized day care may be as much a practical as an ideological issue, although the two are closely related. That is, if most adult members of society, including mothers of young children, are to be employed outside the home, regardless of the "approved" family form, children must be cared for by people other than mothers. In many industrialized

Fathers are nurturers too. Given the opportunity, many men enjoy caring and loving roles. Feminists have encouraged the idea of equal parenting as beneficial for both generations. (Photo by Jean Shapiro)

countries other than our own, including capitalist ones, day care tends to provided on a systematic basis. The United States in the 1990s stands almost alone among industrialized societies in having a very limited national family policy with regard to such social supports as family allowances, mandatory parental leaves, and child care facilities (Sidel, *Women & Children Last*, 1986).

As child care moves from the private family sector to the public sector, questions about the rights and responsibilities of mothers, and of others toward mothers, are fought increasingly in the political arena. Mothers who do not share in a man's earnings often fall, with their children, into poverty. Divorce is the strongest predictor that children and their mothers will be poor. One in three of all households headed by a woman in the United States was poor in 1984, compared to one in eleven with a male householder. The impoverishment of women and their families results from women's low wages and the inadequacy of social supports for mothers (Gelpi, 1986).

Choice and Control

Feminists have long protested against the traditional denial to women of rights to control our own bodies and lives. Recent developments and new legal decisions have brought to light past abuses of women's rights and possible directions of future change.

Whether, When, and How Often to Become a Mother

It is sometimes hard to remember that reliable birth control is a very recent phenomenon. In the past, the question was rarely whether or not to become a mother at all, but rather how often and at what intervals. Too many children too close together caused problems for women and our families, particularly where resources were scarce. In some societies, an extended ban on postpartum intercourse, or on intercourse while women were still breastfeeding our last infants, contributed to spacing pregnancies. Societies have had a variety of practices for abortion of unwanted pregnancies, although these may have been relatively ineffective or quite harmful. In some cases, women resorted to infanticide as a more or less acceptable way of limiting the number of children.

Only in this century has considerable effort gone into the development of safe and effective contraceptive devices. The majority of these devices are for women's use, not men's. To the extent that there is risk or discomfort involved, it is largely women who bear the burden. On the other hand, to the extent that there is choice of and responsibility for birth control, these devices emphasize the woman's role.

Despite the imbalance in responsibility assigned to women and men for having or not having babies, there has been a history of legal obstacles to our own reproduction. In England, the first laws banning abortion altogether were passed in 1803; the Catholic Church banned abortion for its communicants in 1869. In the United States, abortion up until "quickening," or the second trimester of pregnancy, was legal in most states until the middle of the nineteenth century. After the Civil War, many states outlawed abortion entirely. In 1873, as part of a new restrictive attitude toward sexual expression ("social purity"), the federal government passed the Comstock Law, which banned distribution of pornography, methods of abortion, and all means of preventing conception (Gordon, 1976).

Efforts to open birth control clinics in Europe and the United States in the late nineteenth and early twentieth centuries were met with strong state and church opposition. The depression of the 1930s, when economic conditions discouraged large families, resulted in the loosening of restrictions on birth control in the United States. By 1940 every state except Massachusetts and Connecticut had legalized the dissemination of contraceptive information. Family planning clinics, some publicly funded, began to be established. In 1964 the Supreme Court held that an individual's right of privacy encompasses the right to make decisions on whether to conceive children and, therefore, to have unrestricted access to contraception. Elsewhere in the world, some countries that are predominantly Catholic still outlaw use of contraceptive devices, while other countries, concerned about severe poverty in the midst of a rapidly expanding population, have made it official policy to encourage contraception, as in the case of India and of the People's Republic of China, or to restrict by means of serious financial and other disincentives the number of children couples may have.

In order to make a choice, women need not only legal backing and access to technical devices but full knowledge and awareness of the options. Social conditions have not fostered an atmosphere conducive to real choices. Rather, women have usually been pressured to become mothers from early childhood on. Traditionally, men could divorce women for barrenness; women who depended on husbands for economic support and protection had no choice but to try to become mothers. For many teenage girls living in poverty, having a child seems like a chance for happiness and self-esteem, though many become pregnant out of ignorance.

Today, many women ask themselves whether they want a child (Klepfisz, 1977). We have become aware of the options available to us and are making choices with regard to birth control and reproductive technology. But questions about the rights of others remain. Should such rights be granted to a pregnant woman's parents if the woman is a minor and unable to support a child? The U.S. Supreme Court said no to both these questions

in 1964, but such issues continue to be debated. The continuing contest over abortion rights in the United States is the focus of a struggle over the meanings to be attached to motherhood and women's lives. Women on both sides of this struggle often claim that a concern for nurturance motivates our stands (Ginsburg, 1987).

Because it is women who undergo the burdens of pregnancy and who give birth to children, it seems appropriate to place the right to determine control over childbearing in our hands. But others are often unwilling to accord such power to women.

Much attention has recently been paid to surrogate motherhood, where a woman is inseminated with a man's sperm and gives birth to a child to be raised by the man and his wife, or where a fertilized egg is implanted in the womb of a woman who will carry the embryo to birth for the genetic parents. Feminists have been concerned about the likelihood of exploitation, as poor women may be induced, for a fee, to have children for the rich. The courts wrestling with the issues can hold that the surrogate mother be permitted to change her mind about giving up her child; without assurance that surrogacy contracts will be valid, the practice may remain rare.

There is, at present, almost no help from public sources for infertile women who cannot pay the high fees demanded for the new birth technologies. And infertility is often the result of restricted options, such as for parental leave and child care, which require women to delay having children until it may be too late. Infertility is also often caused by workplace and environmental hazards that should be controlled (Thom, 1988).

Control over Children

While women in the past were obligated, for the most part, to bear children if we could, the extent to which we had control over our chil-

Surrogacy: A Consensus

Rights of the Mother Upheld in Settlement

The Michigan court action this week in the first legal challenge to a law making it a crime to arrange a contract with a surrogate mother may mark an emerging consensus on the legal status of such arrangements. Dozens of states have been grappling with the surrogacy issue in the aftermath of the Baby M case, a highly publicized and emotionally wrenching battle between a surrogate mother and the man who contracted for her to bear his child. The New Jersey Supreme Court earlier this year said the contract was unenforceable and restored the surrogate mother's parental rights, but the father retained custody of the child.

Michigan, the home base of the lawyer who arranged the contract that led to the birth of Baby M, was the first state to pass a law making it a felony to arrange a surrogacy contract.

The law, which went into effect Sept. 1, was immediately challenged, and many legal experts expected the litigation to turn into a test case on the legality of surrogacy. . . .

"This is a reasonable compromise," said Martha Field, a family law professor at Harvard Law School, who has written a book on surrogacy. "It seems to me almost self-evident," she said, "that the contract isn't enforceable, that the mother has the right to change her mind, just like a mother who is giving up her baby for adoption.

A Balance of Rights

"But given the reality that women can choose to do this, and the history that shows it is not a good idea to tell women what to do with their bodies, I don't think it makes sense to outlaw it completely," Professor Field said. . . .

Noel Keane, the lawyer who arranged the birth of Baby M and more than 200 other babies, said the decision will have no effect on his practice.

"This goes along with everything that's in our agreements now," Mr. Keane said. "I don't have to change anything, because we don't make the payment contingent on the mother giving up her parental rights. This is not baby selling; it's women providing a service, and we treat these agreements as payment for services." . . .

However, Jeremy Rifkin, chairman of the National Coalition Against Surrogacy, said that the Michigan decision will put Mr. Keane and others like him out of business—or behind bars.

"These are really contracts to sell a baby, and the judge is going to look at the intent even if the words of the contract say that it's a payment for the women's gestational services," Mr. Rifkin said.

(*New York Times*, September 22, 1988.
© 1988 by the New York Times Company. Reprinted by permission.)

dren once they were born was variable. Patriarchal societies have often viewed children legally as well as by custom as the "possession" of their father and his kin group, and these relatives have determined how children should be raised, taught, married, and employed. Often this kin group was not formally obligated to consult or even inform the children's mother about decisions that had been made for them. If we left our husbands, we were often obliged to leave our children as well. This was true in Victorian England, for example, until the 1850s, when laws made it possible for women to claim physical custody over children under seven years old. In the United States the issue has been dealt with on a state-by-state, case-by-case basis. In the twentieth century, women were generally able to win legal custody; courts in the United States ruled, until recently, that mothers should have custody of our children if our marriages ended in divorce. In recent years, some states have made custody decisions that reflect a changing view of the best interests of the child. A father who wants custody no longer has to show that the mother is morally unfit to have custody (mentally ill, alcoholic, "immoral") but only has to argue why his custody may be better for the children. Judges now exercise greater authority over what the "best interests" of the child or children require. The women's movement and concurrent rethinking of parental roles have led more fathers to seek physical and legal custody of their children, and more judges have awarded them such custody. Another recent development is the increasing number of cases in which parents agree to have joint custody of children.

Lesbian mothers have generally not fared well in the courts. Some judges have held that a woman who is a lesbian is by definition an unfit mother, and have flatly denied custody. Other judges have held that custody requests by lesbian mothers must be examined case by case, in some instances deciding that it is in the best interest of the children for the mother to have custody. The tendency in the courts has been to remain intolerant of nonheterosexual preferences and to grant custody to lesbian mothers only on condition that we not live openly in a lesbian relationship. Yet there is no indication that children of lesbian mothers fare less well than children of heterosexual mothers.

Poor women often find our rights to our children denied by the courts in the United States. Laws, designed to protect children, ironically have been used as weapons against poor (and frequently minority) women who have not in fact neglected our children. In many instances, mothers have been charged with neglect of children because of the condition of our homes (too crowded, too dirty) or because a social worker disapproves of our methods of childrearing (often stemming from a different cultural background). Occasionally, children are taken from the mother and adopted by someone else, permanently cutting off all ties with the mother. Poor women are often unable to fight the actions because of inadequate legal help.

Questions about our rights to keep and make decisions for our own children are sometimes related to our financial responsibility and that of others. Traditionally, the father has the primary responsibility for the economic support of children, but it falls on the mother if the father fails to provide for his children. If mothers are to be legally responsible for the economic support of our children, how are we to get the means to provide it? This brings us to the issue of work and motherhood.

Working for Wages

Although a recent phenomenon, the ideal of full-time motherhood has become so strong that it affects everyone, including poor women who have always worked for wages when it was possible. Women of all classes feel social pressure to keep out of the workplace and stay in the home when we have young children.

These pressures are augmented by additional conflicts. One is the desire on the part of many mothers of very young children not to be separated from them for long hours. For many women, this is a special time of our children's lives, which we cherish and enjoy. We want to be present during the day, to teach our children and watch them grow.

And yet economic realities often conflict with social ideals and personal preferences. Today vast numbers of mothers of young children must work for wages to help support our families. Many are single parents. Others live with the children's fathers or with other adults but need at least two incomes to get by. And still others feel that despite the attractions of spending time with our children, we cannot afford to take time out from our careers or education. All women who must be away from home face major obstacles, as do those who simply prefer to continue working without major interruption as well as to have children, to have, that is, options comparable to those men have routinely had. Two of the obstacles women face in the workplace will be considered here: job discrimination and lack of day care options.

It is not unusual to find job discrimination against mothers, even where discrimination against women in general is not so apparent or clear-cut. Women commonly report losing our jobs when we become pregnant, although this is now illegal discrimination. As yet, few women in the United States get paid maternity leave. In some jobs, women who have babies are obliged to take leave without pay whether or not we want it. Many women who wish to return to our jobs after time out for childbearing find those jobs filled by someone else and employers unwilling to take us back.

The most serious problem for working mothers in America today is day care for our young children. As we have noted, many industrialized countries provide government or industry-sponsored day care and family allowances. Trained caretakers look after children as a matter of course while mothers are at work. In the United States, federal, state, and local-level organizations have made some ef-

forts to establish day care centers, but these are rare and limited. Community-led cooperatives provide an option for some mothers, while others resort to private day care centers at a fairly high cost. And day care run as a business, for profit, often fails to be guided by the values most important to mothers: what is best for our children.

Those who can afford full-time employees to tend to children at home often find that few qualified people are interested in doing this kind of domestic work. Some mothers are fortunate in having close relatives, often our own mothers, available and willing to look after the children while we work, but grandmothers are increasingly involved, as well, in our own work.

The shortage of acceptable day care options in the United States hurts children most of all. Sometimes mothers have no choice but to place our children in substandard facilities, or we are obliged to give up or refuse employment, to go on welfare, and to subsist on a marginal income at best. Failure to provide adequate day care facilities discriminates against women, keeps us weak and dependent, perpetuates general inequality, and shortchanges children.

Making real choices, not only about whether and when to become a mother, but also *how*, such as how much time to spend with children, and what to do with them during that time, depends in part on having the right and opportunity to choose to work, or not to work, for wages. This issue, like birth control, is very much affected by public policy. Public welfare policy has fostered the traditional arrangement in which mothers stay home to care for our children. If we have no other means of support, we are usually entitled to receive welfare payments, at a subsistence level while our children are young. Some states have introduced "workfare" provisions, requiring the mothers of school-age children to work for these payments; other states allow mothers to supplement welfare payments by working and provide work-related expense money and child care payments to help us. But mothers who accept welfare payments are usually made to feel guilty, rather than to feel entitled to an allowance for the mothering work they do. And welfare payments are notoriously inadequate for bringing up children with dignity.

Women are becoming increasingly aware that motherhood is a political issue, involving power relationships and political action. While this has been the case all along, it has been difficult for many people to see the connection because motherhood has generally been regarded as a private, personal, and family matter. Many of the central political issues concerning motherhood are now being fought in courts and legislatures in the United States. For example, should women share control over our reproductive capacity? How much of a role, if any, should others than the mother play in raising children? Who should accept responsibility for providing basic necessities for the next generation of citizens: the parent(s) only or the whole society also?

The feminist theorist Mary O'Brien argues in an important book that women's emerging control over reproduction and our consciousness of this constitute what Hegel called "a world historical event" (O'Brien, 1981). Achieving such revolutionary change can be expected to involve conflict and pain, but the prospect is promising indeed.

Images of Motherhood

As a symbol, motherhood conveys a wide variety of meanings, ranging from patriotism to sexual virtue. Images of mothers, depicted in myth, art, and literature, are often of central importance in teaching women and men their respective roles in society. And yet there has been surprisingly little investigation of the symbolic aspects of motherhood, particularly in historic times and in cultures other than our own. We will draw from the more recent Western heritage to provide some examples of the treatment of motherhood in art, literature, and commercial media.

Perspectives: Who Creates the Image?

Images project and convey the ideas of their creators. The creators of imagery of mothers have been predominantly people looking at motherhood from a child's point of view, rarely from a mother's. Why do we rarely see motherhood from the perspective of mothers ourselves? One reason is obvious: Most of the professional image makers (such as writers and artists) have been men. When a male artist or writer depicts motherhood, he draws from his experience as a son or other observer of mothers. In addition, mothers are usually very busy people, with little privacy, time, or freedom to paint or write (Olsen, 1978). Still, there have been women artists and writers who were also mothers; why have we written so little about our experiences of motherhood? Poet Adrienne Rich sees this as a consequence of the social devaluation of women and our experiences. Motherhood has been so trivialized and stereotyped that even artists and writers who are mothers have not valued our experiences as worthy of literary or artistic attention. "Once in a while someone used to ask me, 'Don't you ever write poems about your children?' The male poets of my generation did write poems about their children— especially their daughters. For me poetry was where I lived as no one's mother, where I existed as myself" (Rich, 1976).

Daughters' explorations of our relationships with our mothers are a relatively new phenomenon in Western literature. The relationships of sons with their mothers have received considerably more attention. To illustrate, we can examine two powerful Greek

The Bonds between Mother and Child

The close intimacy between a mother and her children finds a different expression according to the sex of the child. A mother with her daughters is on terms almost of camaraderie as together they tackle the heavy domestic responsibilities of their sex. Between mother and son, because of the opposition of their sexes, there is some abruptness, especially during those years when the son is trying compulsively to behave in a masculine manner. But their relationship is none the less close, unconditional acceptance of her son and his deeds by the mother, protective concern on the part of the son for his mother. To take in vain the name of a man's mother is to offer him the worst possible insult. The bond between mother and son is indestructible. She gave him life; in him she fulfills herself and transcends the moral inferiority of her sex. Although a mother is more in the company of her daughters, it is the sons who are closest to her heart. They are her pride and the significant achievement of her life. . . .

The final stage of a woman's life is the period between the marriage of her eldest son and her death. She now gains a new freedom both from the authority of her husband, who retires about this time, and from the restrictions of social convention. She goes freely into shops to make small purchases for the family and may stop to pass the time of day with unrelated men she meets. With a young bride to do the heavy work about the hut she at last finds a respite from constant drudgery, and her sons treat her with a new-found respect as the mistress of the extended family. Such an old woman should have a kind heart and treat the wives of her sons with firmness but justice. She is their moral guide and practical adviser, to whom they turn in difficulty or doubt. At childbirth she is the midwife who delivers their children and gives them comfort and courage.

(Campbell, 1964:168, 290)

myths that appear in poetry created by men more than twenty-five hundred years ago. The two stories deal with extreme forms of sons' feelings toward their mothers. One son loves his mother too much, the other too little. The "loving son" is Oedipus. Without knowing who his natural parents were, he murdered his father and subsequently married his mother and had four children by her. When he discovers that he has committed incest and patricide, he is tortured by guilt and blinds himself. The son who is deficient in love is Orestes. To avenge his father, Orestes murders his mother (his father's assassin). He, like Oedipus, is tormented by a guilty conscience. The gods then invent the first court

of law to try the case of matricide. Two great Olympian gods declare that a father is more truly a parent than a mother, and Orestes is acquitted. The myths illustrate a more general theme: Sons must dissociate themselves from their mothers and identify with their fathers, or pay an enormous penalty.

Male authors of the twentieth century, heavily influenced by Freudian theories, write in a similar vein of the destructiveness of their mothers' seductive and engulfing love, of conflicts of interest between growing sons and overpowering mothers. This literature depicts mothers as emasculating and possessive, dangerous and antithetical to adult maleness. Only by overpowering the mother can the son

Separation and Autonomy

I closed my eyes and breathed evenly, but she could tell I wasn't asleep.

"This is terrible ghost country, where a human being works her life away," she said. "Even the ghosts work, no time for acrobatics. I have not stopped working since the day the ship landed. I was on my feet the moment the babies were out. In China I never even had to hang up my own clothes. I shouldn't have left, but your father couldn't have supported you without me. I'm the one with the big muscles."

"If you hadn't left, there wouldn't have been a me for you two to support. Mama, I'm sleepy. Do you mind letting me sleep? I do not believe in old age. I do not believe in getting tired." . . .

. . . "There's only one thing that I really want anymore. I want you here, not wandering like a ghost from Romany. I want every one of you living here together. When you're all home, all six of you with your children and husbands and wives, there are twenty or thirty people in this house. Then I'm happy. And your father is happy. Whichever room I walk into overflows with my relatives, grandsons, sons-in-law. I can't turn around without touching somebody. That's the way a house should be." Her eyes are big, inconsolable. . . .

The gods pay her and my father back for leaving their parents. My grandmother wrote letters pleading for them to come home, and they ignored her. Now they know how she felt.

"When I'm away from here," I had to tell her, "I don't get sick. . . . I've found some places in this country that are ghostfree. And I think I belong there, where I don't catch colds or use my hospitalization insurance. Here I'm sick so often, I can barely work. I can't help it, Mama."

She yawned. "It's better, then, for you to stay away. The weather in California must not agree with you. You can come for visits." She got up and turned off the light. "Of course, you must go, Little Dog."

A weight lifted from me. The quilts must be filling with air. The world is somehow lighter. She has not called me that endearment for years—a name to fool the gods. I am really a Dragon, as she is a Dragon, both of us born in dragon years. I am practically a first daughter of a first daughter.

"Good night, Little Dog."

"Good night, Mother."

She sends me on my way, working always and now old, dreaming the dreams about shrinking babies and the sky covered with airplanes and a Chinatown bigger than the ones here.

(Kingston, 1976:122, 126–27)

free himself of infantilism and go forth into the civilized world of adult men. As a metaphor, the assertion of manhood by overthrowing the control of a once-powerful mother is similar to the social charter myths discussed in Chapter 5.

"The Happy Mother": Painting as Propaganda

Depictions of mothers, fathers, and children in paintings have a long history in the Western world, but the nonreligious image of the mother in blissful ecstasy as the center of domestic life was an innovation in French art in the eighteenth century (Duncan, 1973). This image, first exemplified by Greuze's painting *The Beloved Mother* (1765), portrays marriage and domestic life as a major source of happiness, not simply as a legal and economic structure. The new emphasis on personal happiness and the elevation of maternity to an exalted state challenged earlier assumptions about marriage, families, and children. The new style in art represented a shift in attitudes that accompanied economic and social changes in the eighteenth century.

It was during this period that modern bourgeois culture began to take shape. Growing numbers of people could achieve social mobility through their own personal efforts in the commercial and professional world. Heredity had less to do than before with one's success in life, and the environment of the home for educating and forming children took on increasing importance.

The contrast between public and private life came to be emphasized as economic enterprise moved out of the home and into the marketplace. The home was seen as a haven of warmth and comfort, in contrast to the harsh competitiveness of the business world. The home was a place of protection and a place to be protected. Women were responsible for making the home a warm and happy place as well as for the health and welfare of our children. It was assumed that motherhood itself was natural for women and that we derived great pleasure and fulfillment from devoting ourselves to the tasks of childrearing and homemaking. Though many mothers and children would subsequently be forced to work for pitiful wages in horrendous conditions as the Western world industrialized, the image that was held up for aspiration was that of woman as joyful guardian of the peaceful home.

The eighteenth-century paintings convey a clear moral message. They teach women and men that women should be ecstatically happy in the home making babies. They say that men's responsibility is to help women find happiness by keeping their wives at home with plenty of children. And they suggest that for women to feel or wish otherwise is unnatural. This early form of media propaganda was exemplified on a more massive scale in the women's magazines, advertising, movies, and television programs of the 1950s and '60s. It can often still be recognized today.

"Ethnic Mothers" and Social Mobility

The United States, a nation comprised largely of immigrants, has displayed an enduring fascination with ethnicity. The literature of the twentieth century is replete with ethnic and racial stereotypes. Among these stereotypes, two female figures are particularly striking as peculiarly American phenomena: the "Jewish mother" and the "black mother." Both are familiar to Americans through literature, movies, and television; the stereotypes depicted in the public media have also been the object of study in the scholarly literature of sociology and psychology.

The stereotypic Jewish mother in literature has undergone dramatic changes that correspond to changes in the Jewish family itself in American society during the century. As the family and its social position have changed, the image of the Jewish mother has shifted from an object of veneration to an object of ridicule (Bienstock, 1979).

The first depictions of the American Jewish family, Bienstock argues, were written by men whose parents immigrated from Eastern Europe from the 1880s to the 1920s. In the "old country," Jewish families had often (though not always) lived in *shtetls* (small villages and towns) dominated by their cultural traditions. The roles of wife and husband were clearly defined: Wives were responsible for the material welfare of families, and husbands were, ideally, pious scholars. While men studied and

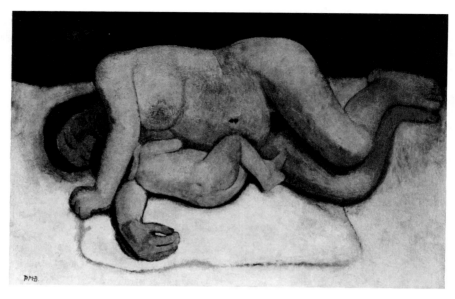

How do mothers see themselves? In her painting *Mother and Child* (1907), Paula Mondersohn-Becker (1876–1907) portrayed the sensual intimacy of which some mothers speak when they examine their personal experience of motherhood. (Nationalgalerie, Berlin [loaned by Staatliche Museeum Preussischer Kulturbesitz, Berlin])

prayed, women might run small businesses to support the family.

In the New World, the system of roles and status underwent a change. Immigrant families, poorer than ever, continued to rely on the strong and practical housewife for material support, but the prestige of the pious scholar was left behind; the husband and father, often seen as unfit for the hard labor of the sweat-shop, suffered a great loss of dignity and self-esteem. Sons depicted Jewish mothers of this period as supporters of traditional values and respect for the father and as self-sacrificing protectors of the children.

Gradually, Bienstock continues, the situation of the family changed. Mothers, caught between cultural traditions and the practical changes in our lives, served as mediators be-tween husbands and children. The children began to make their way in the New World by adopting new, materialistic values, with their mothers' encouragement. The image of the fathers began to fade; they were depicted as weak, as outsiders, while the mothers be-came the de facto heads of families, adjusting to necessary changes as we went along. We became increasingly ambitious for our chil-dren, pushing them toward upward mobility through education. The children measured their achievements by our yardsticks.

By the end of the 1930s and into the 1940s, Jewish sons began to question the perceived materialistic goals of their mothers, and to rebel. Their liberal bias led them to reject the crass materialism of American life as well as the traditions of their fathers. Their mothers came to represent all that was wrong with the past and the present. The mothers were now blamed for stunting the sons' emotional growth by overbearing protectiveness and overweening social ambition. As the sons became more integrated into American society, they became more ashamed of their ethnic and lower-class origins. Their mothers came to represent for them this shameful past, even though the sons had achieved their positions in the American cultural establishment largely through their mothers' efforts to help them obtain education.

By the 1960s, Bienstock concludes, the image of the pushy Jewish mother had become ubiquitous in American literature and the popular media. She had at once become a comic figure and an object of alarm. Freudian theory suggested to these writers that their emotional problems stemmed from their early erotic relationships with their mothers; development required breaking away. The Jewish son saw in his mother the primary obstacle to his own maturity and freedom. Turning her into a comic figure was a way of reducing her imagined power. In effect, it was also a way of belittling the past, of denying its value and importance.

In an era of rapid social change, when people felt uneasy about undefined roles for women and men, the problem of the Jewish son and his mother held a message comprehensible to a broad range of Americans who could identify with the hostility and anxiety of the uprooted, upwardly mobile son. Although mothers were the immediate targets of the sons' rage, we represented much more. We stood for virtually every social inhibition, every anxiety-provoking element of the past. Recognition of the pain of the American experience was made tolerable through ridicule.

The black experience in America was very different from the Jewish one, and yet there are elements of similarity. Like the Jewish mother, the black mother has been stereo-typed. In this case, we address the stereotype promoted by some black authors, not the "black mammy" stereotype familiar from American movies and novels like *Gone with the Wind*. This stereotype had its roots in the slave experience, which, like the experience of immigration, evoked extreme strength and endurance from mothers to protect families.

After slavery, black families were faced with economic survival in America. Racial prejudice virtually barred social mobility for blacks and denied job opportunities in nearly every sphere. Those jobs that were open to men paid very little and offered no security. To feed their children, women were obliged to work at low-paying menial tasks.

While black men suffered low esteem and humiliation in American society, black women struggled to keep our families together morally and physically. Black mothers, like Jewish mothers, were seen as the moral backbones of our homes. And, like Jewish mothers, the idealized black mothers "pushed" our children upward, emphasizing education and achievement in our ambition for their future.

The image of the strong, supportive, and protective black mother grew along with an image of a weak, ineffective black father. Sociological literature refers frequently to the "matrilocal household" as if it were the product of slavery or the African heritage; in fact, where it exists, it is part of a survival strategy, an adjustment to contemporary conditions (Stack, 1974; Collins, 1990). The image promoted by literature and popular media is that of a strong mother figure and a weak or absent father figure. As the family becomes more involved with the mainstream of American life, mothers are more and more mediators between past and present. We are depicted as the source of our children's strength. But, already subjected to one attack in *The Negro Family* (Moynihan, 1965), the image of the black mother may suffer a fate similar to that of the Jewish mother. From an object of respect and sentimental reverence, we may become increasingly an object of anxiety and ridicule. On the other hand, the strong feminist voices of our black daughters may prevent that fate.

Motherhood and the Media

An idea of motherhood is "sold" to us along with a variety of commercial products in the public media. Magazine advertising and television commercials are blatant in the image that they convey of how motherhood "ought to be." Those who advertise their products are also supporting the magazine stories and television programs that sell a life-style in which the products are likely to be used; the message in these stories and programs is more indirect, and perhaps even more effective as a result.

Television programs do not feature women as much as men; only 20 percent to 40 percent of all figures on television are women. Women appear more in comedies than in any other form of television program. Two out of three women on television are depicted as wives, while few men are depicted as married. Most women on television are represented as incompetent. We nearly always fall into the categories of sex object, housewife, or mother. Twice as many women as men are shown with children. Seventy-five percent of the advertisements that show women have us in either the kitchen or the bathroom (Tuchman, 1978).

Since television is a domestic medium, a family pastime, it should not be surprising that we find motherhood portrayed so frequently on TV. The image of the television mother has changed over the past twenty years or so, but it continues to represent a stereotype. One of the early images was that of the series "I Remember Mama," a sentimental reconstruction of immigrant Swedish family life in San Francisco based on memoirs written by a

daughter. That mother was gentle, comforting, a moral force, and a hardworking housewife. For the most part, however, the mother image of the 1950s on television was typically a much weaker figure. Mothers did very little, had few significant anxieties or functions, and were always neat, well-dressed, calm, and eminently middle-class and suburban. We had no jobs, made no major decisions, and showed few emotions. We were sexless and characterless. By the 1970s, however, several stronger images began to appear. There were some "ethnic" mothers, including black, Jewish, and Italian women. Some were "liberated" women; some were even divorced. A number of these mothers did voice opinions, have jobs, and display emotions and anxieties about serious problems. But with few exceptions, the characters were unrealistic idealizations playing out exaggerated roles—now as "feminists." Always, these "mothers" achieved a superiority in whatever role they portrayed that the average mother could not attain. Modern television mothers may be "hip," with lives of our own—work, outside interests, sex lives—but rarely do we grow or change. Idealized, we are again trivialized.

Magazines intended explicitly for parents demonstrate most fully what the image of motherhood means in the popular media. Motherhood is marketable; magazine stories and features, like the advertisements that support them, create "needs" by spelling out the requisites of mothering. We learn that the tasks of parenting are still mainly the responsibility of the mother; virtually all the visual images show women with children. The few men depicted are "experts," primarily obstetricians and pediatricians. The "experts" are rarely women ourselves. Mothers are shown as dependent on these experts for constant advice on the most trivial matters. Although the articles purport to be reassuring, they in fact merely emphasize the mothers' helplessness.

What Is American Mothers, Inc.?

We are an organization working to preserve American family values. At a time when the return of family values has become a national priority, American Mothers, Inc., responds with educational, cultural, and spiritual programs for mothers of all ages.

The organization honors mothers and publicizes, promotes, and stimulates observance of Mothers Day. Each year to more fully recognize Mother's Day, a National Mother of the year is selected from the 50 State Mothers, the District of Columbia, and Puerto Rico. The first National Mother of the Year was selected in 1935.

The stories and articles address such issues as how to select your child's blocks and what to do about thumb sucking. Although it is frequently suggested that it is normal for mothers to have jobs outside the home, we are not depicted at work. Rather, we are shown attending to our babies' comfort; mother is, above all, a source of physical comfort and protection. The mother is expected to purchase a vast array of lotions, powders, toys, furniture, and gadgets. One company even packages a "breast-feeding kit" with all sorts of equipment for women who may have thought that we were fully equipped by nature.

Do these magazines serve the interests of their readers? By fostering feelings of personal inadequacy and dependency, they serve the interests of the commercial enterprises that sell products and of the medical profession on which mothers now depend for expert advice. The trivial nature of many of the issues the magazines explore means a waste of time to mothers. Yet these magazines claim a readership of over a million each month.

If the public image of motherhood reflects women's social position in general, we must conclude that despite considerable changes in our economic roles during the past generation, little has changed in our social roles. Parenting is not generally assumed to be the equal responsibility of both women and men. Women are still assumed to be mentally inferior, and our vulnerability as childbearers and childraisers continues to be exploited.

Mothers Speak Out

The women's movement has encouraged awareness and self-expression by mothers on the contradictions and conflicts of our experience. Some of this self-expression has taken the form of autobiographical literature. We find such writings as Phyllis Chesler's diary of her first year of motherhood, *With Child* (1979); Jane Lazarre's autobiographical book, *The Mother Knot* (1976); and Adrienne Rich's treatise on motherhood, *Of Woman Born* (1976), which combines autobiography with search for meaning.

And feminist theorists are exploring the implications of the central but neglected human experience constituted by mothering (Trebilcot, 1984). Sara Ruddick, for instance, examines the distinctive thinking involved in the practice of mothering. It is characterized by its interests in the child's preservation, growth, and acceptable development, and it is oriented toward the peaceful solution of conflict (Ruddick, 1980)

Carriages and Strollers

My first words as I came from under the ether after I had my son were, "I think I made a mistake." Unfortunately, since then, and one more child later, I've had very little reason to change my mind. This is not to say that children cannot be lovable. It's not them, it's all the foolishness that goes on in the name of them. From the beginning, motherhood took on the complexion of a farce.

To begin with, aside from the indignity of being trussed up like some sort of sacrificial pig in order to be delivered, there was the matter of nursing. I chose to brew my own rather than to spend the next few months encumbered by a slew of rattling bottles. At first the hospital staff were rather sweet and condescending about it. They'd bring me the baby, say something like, "Aren't you a good little mother," and then whip those bed curtains around to screen me from my roommate as if a little infant fellatio was the very least that was going to happen inside my hutch. . . .

I may be more upsettable than most, but during the years I was involved with carriages and strollers and wagons and tricycles, I was always getting bugged. Why wasn't there, even in the children's section of a department store, a high chair so you could deposit your child and spend your money in some sort of comfort? Why did it have to be a major struggle to get a stroller or a shopping cart across a street; would it cost so much to rake the curbs? And why did the entrance to the playground offer the steepest curb of all? Small enough problems, but enough to clue in to the fact that the last people anyone in charge of planning the city is concerned with are mothers and children.

(Clark, 1970:63–64)

Summary

Parental roles among humans do not develop by instinct but are primarily learned. We actually know very little about what constitutes maternal behavior. We know even less about paternal behavior and the effect of children on parental behavior.

In American society today, woman's attitudes and feelings are shaped by the prevailing view that motherhood "comes naturally" to us and that it is our full-time job. Women who try to live up to this ideal often experience anxiety, frustration, and isolation. Society institutionalizes motherhood so that it oppresses women, men, and children. More equitable relationship with men may lead to more rewarding forms of motherhood.

Many women welcome motherhood. We have been taught from childhood to expect it, and the pleasures of mothering are very real. However, mothers also serve the interests of business by producing and servicing workers, without pay, and by socializing the next generation, who will become a pool of cheap labor. Women also serve military interests by providing soldiers. Some observers speculate that the exclusion of men from motherhood is a source of men's oppression of women.

Many writers conclude that it is impossible to live up to the standards that have been set for mothers. Ideal mothers love children perfectly; real mothers feel ambivalence toward our children—love, to be sure, but also frustration, resentment, and anger. And real mothers are whole persons, not one-dimensional readers of a social script. Mothers have complicated lives, with all sorts of pressures and interests, which include—but are not completely subsumed by—our children. Conflicts result from the isolated positions many mothers are placed in by society. Emotional problems that might be irritating but manageable often become overwhelming when women consider how inadequate are our sources of social support.

While society claims to value motherhood, in reality it discounts the activities and ideas of mothers and fails to organize itself in ways conducive to the well-being of children and their caretakers. Mothering is interpreted as a "natural" activity of mere reproduction and repetition.

As women come to see motherhood "from the inside" we can see it as a tremendously active and positive force (Rich, 1976; Held, 1987). We can demand that society be reorganized so that the enormously valuable activity of human mothering be accorded the support and esteem it deserves. Rather than being a source of weakness, motherhood can be seen as the source of the greatest power human beings possess: the power to create new human persons.

The way women experience the biological events of pregnancy, childbirth, and breastfeeding varies with personal circumstances and social environment. Sometimes the cultural shaping of these events has a political component, as when natural childbirth was promoted as a means of encouraging women to have more babies at a time of low birth rates.

Mothers have need of the practical and emotional support of others, but the nature and extent of that support differs from one society to another. In many societies, fathers play an active role from pregnancy onward; in others, fathers have little to do with child-rearing. Traditionally, female support net-

works, especially kin, have been important to mothers. Many countries today provide support to mothers in the form of institutionalized day care.

Feminists argue that women should decide for ourselves whether, when, and how often to become mothers. The choice of and responsibility for birth control tends to be given to women, although a number of legal obstacles have been thrown in our way through the years. In the past, when a marriage ended, women were obligated to yield custody of children to fathers, but in this century we have usually been given legal custody. Today, judges are more likely to award custody on the basis of specific circumstances in accordance with their view of the best interests of the child. Lesbian and poor women often have difficulty keeping our children.

Images of mothers in the past have usually been produced by sons. Comments by daughters have been a relatively recent phenomenon. Mothers have often been too busy to create, or have thought our experiences too trivial to record. Two females figures commonly portrayed in stereotypical ways in literature are the Jewish mother and the black mother.

In the eighteenth century, art began to portray the "happy mother" in scenes of domestic bliss. This theme coincided with the beginnings of modern bourgeois culture, with its emphasis on the warm and happy home in contrast to the harsh workplace.

Popular magazines and TV programs, commercials, and advertisements often portray women as either home-bound or sex objects. Magazines directed to parents emphasize women's helplessness and capitalize on our desire to be "good" mothers; some magazines promote the image of the "supermom."

Mothers today are writing about our experiences in order to revise the image of model motherhood that has made so many women feel inadequate or guilty. We are attempting to portray mothers not as stereotypes but as whole persons who lead rich and complicated lives. And we are asking how society should be restructured to be truly hospitable to children and their creators.

Discussion Questions

1. List some of the sources from which an American woman learns how to be a mother.
2. Discuss the impact of advertising and technology on the mother-child relationship.
3. Considering economic, social, and biological factors, discuss the optimum age for a contemporary woman in a specified culture to begin bearing children.
4. What happens to mothers when our children leave the "nest"? Discuss the physical and psychological effects of the "empty nest" on a woman whose whole identity has been as mother (review Chapter 4).
5. How would you define the role of grandmother and mother-in-law (hers and his)?
6. The "good and nurturing mother" and the "terrible mother" are important mythic figures. Find examples from literature and popular fiction, films, and folk tales to represent the devaluation and simultaneous exaltation of mothers.

Recommended Readings

Colette, Sidonie-Gabrielle. *My Mother's House and Sido.* 1930. Translated by Una Vincenzo and Enid McLeod. New York: Farrar, Straus, and Giroux, 1953. This book by the distinguished French writer is her loving reminiscence of her own mother and a search for beneficent influences she had on Colette's early life. The author depicts the warm, rich atmosphere of the rural home where she grew up—a product, she claims, of her mother's creation.

Kingston, Maxine Hong. *The Woman Warrior.* New York: Knopf, 1976. A Chinese American woman's depiction of her maternal forebears in China and America. Kingston writes vividly of her mother's life as a doctor in China and as an immigrant in the New World. We are provided with an unusual view of mother-daughter relationships in a highly patriarchal cultural setting.

Lazarre, Jane. *The Mother Knot.* New York: Dell, 1976. An autobiographical account of a mother living in contemporary New York. It explores her conflicting feelings about maternity, her child, and her husband. So rarely have women written about ourselves as mothers that books such as this one can be considered a unique product of the contemporary women's movement, which has encouraged women like Lazarre to speak out on such personal and intimate matters.

Rich, Adrienne. *Of Woman Born: Motherhood as Experience and Institution.* New York: Norton, 1976. An examination of motherhood as a social institution and the way that it has evolved from antiquity to the present. The author shows how relationships between women and men are reflected in the institution of motherhood and how concepts related to this institution change with changes in women's status. Rich, a feminist and poet, draws from her own experience as well as the scholarly literature.

Rothman, Barbara Katz. *Recreating Motherhood. Ideology and Technology in a Patriarchal Society.* New York: Norton, 1989. A critical, impassioned analysis of the effect of patriarchy, capitalism, and reproductive technology on mothers, fetuses, and newborns. Some feminists will sympathize, but not necessarily concur, with Rothman's views on these controversial issues.

Trebilcot, Joyce, editor. *Mothering. Essays in Feminist Theory.* Totowa, N.J.: Rowman & Allanheld, 1984. A collection of essays exploring the meanings and implications of mothering, and discussing how the ways in which mothering has been organized have been oppressive to women.

References

Angelou, Maya. *I Know Why the Caged Bird Sings.* New York: Knopf, 1969.

Beauvoir, Simone de. *The Second Sex.* 1949. Translated by H. M. Parshley. New York: Knopf, 1953.

Bergmann, Barbara. "The Economic Support of 'Fatherless' Children." In *Income Support: Conceptual and Policy Issues,* edited by Peter G. Brown et al. Totowa, N.J.: Rowman & Littlefield, 1981.

Bernard, Jessie. *The Future of Motherhood.* New York: Dial, 1974.

Bienstock, Beverly Gray. "The Changing Image of the American Jewish Mother." In *Changing Images of the Family,* edited by Virginia Tufte and Barbara Myerhoff. New Haven: Yale University Press, 1979.

Bing, Elisabeth. *Six Practical Lessons for an Easier Childbirth.* New York: Bantam, 1969.

Bittmann, Sam, and Zalk, Sue Rosenberg. *Expectant Fathers.* New York: Dutton, 1978.

Brack, Datha Clapper. "Social Forces, Feminism, and Breast Feeding." *Nursing Outlook* 23 (1975):556–61.

Campbell, J. K. *Honour, Family, and Patronage. A Study of Institutions and Moral Values in a Greek Mountain Community.* Oxford: Oxford University Press, 1964.

Chesler, Phyllis. *With Child: A Diary of Motherhood.* New York: Crowell, 1979.

Chodorow, Nancy. *The Reproduction of Mothering: Psychoanalysis and the Sociology of Gender.* Berkeley: University of California Press, 1978.

Clark, Joanna. "Motherhood." In *The Black Woman,* edited by Toni Cade. New York: New American Library, 1970.

Collins, Patricia Hill. *Black Feminist Thought, Knowledge, Consciousness, and the Politics of Empowerment.* Boston: Unwin Hyman, 1990.

Dalla Costa, Mariarosa. *The Power of Women and the Subversion of the Community.* Bristol: Falling Wall Press, 1972.

Denmark, Florence. "Psychological Adjustments to Motherhood." In *Psychological Aspects of Gynecology and Obstetrics,* edited by B. B. Wolman. Oradell, N.J.: Medical Economics, 1978.

Duncan, Carol. "Happy Mothers and Other New Ideas in French Art." *Art Bulletin* (December 1973):570–83.

Firestone, Shulamith. *The Dialectic of Sex.* New York: Morrow, 1970.

Friedan, Betty. *The Feminine Mystique.* New York: Dell, 1963.

Gelpi, Barbara C. et al. *Women and Poverty.* Chicago: University of Chicago Press, 1986.

Gilman, Charlotte Perkins. *Herland.* 1915. Reprint. New York: Pantheon, 1979.

Ginsburg, Faye. "Procreation Stories: Reproduction, Nurturance, and Procreation in Life Narratives of Abortion Activists." *American Ethnologist* 14 (1987):623–36.

Gordon, Linda. *Woman's Body, Woman's Right: A Social History of Birth Control in America.* New York: Grossman, 1976.

Held, Virginia, "Non-contractual Society. A Feminist View." *Canadian Journal of Philosophy* (Suppl) 13 (1987):111–37.

Jordan, Brigitte. *Birth in Four Cultures.* New York: Eden, 1978.

Karmel, Marjorie. *Thank You, Dr. Lamaze.* New York: Dolphin, 1965.

Kingston, Maxine Hong. *The Woman Warrior.* New York: Knopf, 1976.

Klepfisz, Irena. "Women Without Children/ Women Without Families/Women Alone." *Conditions: Two* (1977):72–84.

Lazarre, Jane. *The Mother Knot.* New York: McGraw-Hill, 1976.

Liebowitz, Lila. *Females, Males, Families: A Biosocial Approach.* New York: Holt, Rinehart, & Winston, 1978.

McCary, James L. *Human Sexuality.* 2nd ed. New York: Van Nostrand, 1973.

Mead, Margaret. *Male and Female.* Middlesex: Penguin Books, 1962.

———. *Sex and Temperament in Three Primitive Societies.* New York: Morrow, 1963.

Miller, Sue. *The Good Mother.* New York: Harper & Row, 1986.

Morrison, Toni. *Beloved.* New York: Knopf, 1987.

Moynihan, Daniel P. *The Negro Family: The Case for National Action.* Washington, D.C.: U.S. Department of Labor, Office of Policy Planning and Research, 1965.

Newton, Niles. "Breast Feeding." *Psychology Today* 2 (1968):34, 68–70.

Newton, Niles, and Newton, Michael. "Childbirth in Cross-Cultural Perspective." In *Modern Perspectives in Psycho-Obstetrics,* edited by J. G. Howells. New York: Mazel, 1972.

O'Brien, Mary. *The Politics of Reproduction.* London: Routledge, 1981.

Olsen, Tillie. *Silences.* New York: Delacorte, 1978.

Piercy, Marge. *Woman on the Edge of Time.* New York: Knopf, 1976.

Reed, Adrienne. *Of Woman Born: Motherhood as Experience and Institution.* New York: Norton, 1976.

Rossi, Alice. "A Biosocial Perspective on Parenting." *Daedalus* 106 (1977):1–31.

Rubin, Nancy. *The Mother Mirror. How a Generation of Women Is Changing Motherhood in America.* New York: Putnam, 1984.

Ruddick, Sara. "Maternal Thinking." *Feminist Studies* 6 (1980):342–67.

Sanger, Margaret. *Motherhood to Bondage.* New York: Bantam, 1928.

Shreve, Anita. *Remaking Motherhood. How Working Mothers Are Shaping Our Children's Future.* New York: Viking, 1987.

Sidel, Ruth. *Women and Children Last: The Plight of Poor Women in Affluent America.* New York: Viking, 1986.

Smith, Donna. *Stepmothering.* New York: St. Martin's Press, 1990.

Stack, Carol. *All Our Kin.* New York: Harper & Row, 1974.

Thom, Mary. "Dilemmas of the New Birth Technologies." *Ms.* (May 1988).

Trebilcot, Joyce, editor. *Mothering. Essays in Feminist Theory.* Totowa, N.J.: Rowman & Allanheld, 1984.

Triestman, Judith. "Natural Childbirth: A Millenarian Movement." Thesis, Master of Science in Nursing. New Haven: Yale University School of Nursing, 1979.

Tuchman, Gaye. "The Symbolic Annihilation of Women by the Mass Media." In *Hearth and Home: Images of Women in the Mass Media,* edited by Gaye Tuchman, Arleen K. Daniels, and James Benet. New York: Oxford University Press, 1978.

Choosing Alternatives

Women's lives are in the process of changing dramatically around the world, though the change is more rapid and deeper in some countries and among some groups than in others. At present, gender roles are in flux, and both what women expect and what is expected of us are often unclear. But even when social roles have been more stable, there have usually been alternatives that could be chosen; social change has often depended more on the relative numbers choosing a standard role or an alternative than on totally new roles being invented.

At present, women are increasingly choosing to live as we decide to, rather than conforming to preestablished and prevailing gender roles. Sometimes this requires devising new patterns of behavior, but even when we do what seems most unprecedented, we can learn from previous alternative patterns that some women have chosen.

Every society has some kind of conventional pattern of family life, a cultural norm for the expected behavior between people defined by society as "kin." The term *scripts* is sometimes used to refer to the behavior and feelings ascribed to culturally defined roles (Laws and Schwartz, 1977). Thus the scripts for daughter, wife, and mother inform women (as actors) of how we are expected to perform in society. We learn our scripts as we become socialized; that is, as we grow up we learn how we are supposed to act and feel in the various positions we are expected to hold during our lives. But what happens if a person does not feel comfortable, happy, or competent in following the standard script? Most societies, for example, expect adult women to be wives to men and the culture tells us what the script "wife" entails. But some women may not wish to become wives, or having become wives, may wish to get out of marriage, or may wish to play a wifely role that differs from societal conventions. For such conditions, a society may provide alternative scripts. Our society has developed such scripts as "single career woman," and "divorcée" to prescribe conduct for adult women who are not wives. New scripts, being written for patterns that once were more rare but now are common or have taken on new meaning, are the "dual career" marriage, "working mother," and "lesbian parent" (Hertz, 1986; Gilbert, 1988).

This chapter is about institutionalized or "scripted" alternatives to conventional family life. Such alternatives are deviations from a standard pattern, but they differ from personal or individual deviation, which is "unscripted." Anyone who occupies a social role, whether standard or alternative, may deviate in some way or another from the script; perhaps we all do. This kind of deviation may cause the individual to feel insecure, alienated, isolated, or even inferior.

For example, it has been in the script for married women in many societies to feel happy, proud, and fulfilled when we became pregnant. But particular married women may have felt very unhappy about our pregnancies. Because such feelings were not in the script, we may have believed there was something "wrong" with us. We may have experienced guilt or shame, have hidden our misgivings, or sought professional counseling. Even though many, and perhaps the majority, of women may have felt at least ambivalence about our pregnancies, if this feeling was unscripted, it may have been considered a deviation rather than an alternative.

Women who develop alternative scripts often start out as deviators as a result of failing to follow a typical script. We may later discover that one or another untypical pattern suits us better, and can be thought of as a chosen alternative rather than a deviation. Men often discover that an alternative shaped by women is one that they also support (Brod, 1987; Jardine and Smith, 1987). When large numbers of people turn to alternative scripts, the alternative may become the new social norm or standard script.

Whether or not women succeed in alternative roles depends on many things. First, as we shall see, many idealistic and adventurous efforts in alternative living arrangements have failed or been deflected from their original intentions because the participants did not achieve an independent source of economic support. Second, we may find that our intentions run counter to the wishes of others, to whose wills we must submit. If the alternative arrangement was designed by men, or even by women and men, for purposes other than the provision of a satisfying life for women, it may prove to be even more oppressive for us than the traditional life it seeks to replace (Abramovitz, 1988). Finally, the new scripts may be fully satisfying in a variety of ways but so shaped that they can be only a temporary refuge from the ongoing demands of a woman's life.

The scripted alternatives to conventional family roles and lives are extremely diverse. This chapter is concerned mainly with the options that women have shaped for ourselves, with ways of living that we have chosen, or designed, or dreamed of—although in many cases the outcomes were influenced by external forces. In this chapter, we begin with considerations of different types of communities of women—religious, educative, work-oriented, and supportive. We then turn to nonconventional communities of women and men, both utopian dreams of communal organization and actual experiments in communal life. We will then look at families that retain some features of conventional family life but whose members have reshaped roles by choice. These include role reversals, egalitarian households, families of women, and single-parent households. Finally, we consider the lives of women who choose to be on our own.

Communities of Women

Many of women's choices have been realized when we have grouped together to form women's communities. In the absence of men, we have been able to do work otherwise denied us. Free from the service required of wives and mothers, we have been able to develop careers and skills requiring our full attention. Finally, communities of women sharing common values and interests have provided valuable moral support and companionship, a support many women need when embarking on new ventures in a sometimes hostile environment.

Religious Communities

Buddhist and Christian orders of nuns have enabled sizable numbers of women to live outside the boundaries of the family circle. Christian convents go back to the fourth and fifth centuries in the Mediterranean area and, like the churches to which they are attached, have had a complex and varied history. Buddhism also has a long history of monasticism for women, with a parallel geographical extent in Asia and a comparable complexity (Falk, 1980).

In certain forms, both Buddhism and Christianity are turned intensely toward an otherworldly vision. This attitude provides the basis for monasticism. However, both Buddhism and Christianity as male-dominated institutions have distrusted women who aspired to a monastic life. Eight provisions were added to the basic rule of the Sangha to ensure the Buddhist nuns would continue to be subordinated to the male monks. Similarly, Christian nuns were placed under a severe rule in the fifth century by Caesarius of Arles, who wrote the first rule for nuns in the West at the request of his sister Caesaria. Nuns were never to come out from behind convent walls, and all necessary business with the outside world was to be done through the intermediacy of male monks (Bolton, 1976).

Modern Maryknoll Sisters, no longer wearing the traditional habits of nuns, work with women in communities in Latin America, Asia, and Africa. Discussing the problems of these far-flung areas, nuns report that, freed from the clothing that once signified their separateness as a group, religious women are able to make better contact with the people among whom they labor. (Maryknoll Sisters)

In writing regulations for female convents, Caesarius and his successors were aware of the difficulties nuns would encounter in being self-supporting. Accordingly, he prohibited the admission of nuns who could not provide a "dowry" sufficient for self-support in the communal life. Medieval annals tell of women whose genuine longing for the celibate religious life was frustrated by an inability to supply the needed dowry. Some women lamented the unwillingness of families to relieve us from the duty to marry and bear children. In the hope of gaining release from these secular pressures to marry, some women fled from home, went disguised as men, or even disfigured ourselves to become less marriageable (McNamara, 1976).

Despite these frustrations, the convents of Europe provided an arena in which many women not only realized religious aspirations but also found scope for economic, political, and intellectual talents. The convent provided women with opportunities to exercise abilities in administration, handiwork, learning, and spiritual exploration that we could not use outside those walls. Not everyone praised our successes. Nuns were regularly threatened with the dissolution of our convents. We were the butt of salacious jokes and stories that often led to serious vilification. In the past, nuns who ventured out even to perform acts of charity, which were in fact much-needed social services, were criticized and disciplined. Convents were perpetuated only through the constant persistence of women seeking an extrafamilial way of life. The willingness of these beleaguered women to contend with such systematic opposition is eloquent testimony of our desire to find a different way of life. Renunciation of sexuality was not too high a price for the many women of every rank and condition who chose this alternative.

During the religious crises of sixteenth- and seventeenth-century Europe, nuns were able to overcome the restrictions of strict cloistering, and to expand teaching, charitable, and nursing activities. The nun of early modern times stood out as a public model for generations of European women seeking a respectable alternative to conventional duty to home and hearth.

Today, convent life takes many different forms; women who are nuns vary widely in work, dress, and social relationships. What we have in common are a dedication to spiritual life (though this may take many forms), a decision not to marry or engage in any sexual relationships, and a commitment to a community of like-minded women organized in convents and orders.

Noncontemplative orders are extremely variable in their patterns of life. Members of these orders may be committed to teaching or nursing (the two most common kinds of work), helping the poor, providing shelter for orphans or unwed mothers, working with drug addicts, or fighting for human rights. Like the members of contemplative orders (those dedicated to prayer), women in these orders generally take vows of poverty, chastity, and obedience. Many women in religious orders continue to observe traditional, sometimes highly stylized, patterns of prayer, dress, and daily ritual, while others lead lives whose outward pattern seems little different from many secular women who are single.

By renouncing intimate personal ties, women who become nuns hope to come closer to God. The family in particular is seen as a distraction to the concentration on devotion (Bernstein, 1976). While the rewards of this sacrifice are primarily spiritual, they have a practical quality as well. By renouncing family obligations, nuns are able to follow careers, whether in prayer or in some sort of social service work. By submitting to set rituals of daily routine and to formalized patterns of dress and conduct, nuns are freed from the constant need to make trivial decisions. And sacrificing control over material possessions results in freedom from economic anxiety. In addition, for many women the companionship and support of like-minded women is an attraction.

Many church officials today recognize the costs of the sacrifices convent life entails. Modern orders often permit fulfillment of some human inclinations (such as permitting friendship or personal expression in clothing). The costs of sexual continence are also more widely recognized, although today, as in the past, those who wish to marry must leave the convent life.

With the wider availability of other alternatives and a decline in the authority of organized religion, many nuns today leave orders while relatively few women decide to join. As a consequence, convent life as a significant alternative has declined (Bernstein, 1976). One component of dissatisfaction with convent life has been resistance by women to the rule of men (see Chapter 10). The Catholic Church is still dominated by men who see women as subordinate by necessity. The church has taken a few steps to give convent women greater participation in the governance of religious life, but it lags far behind the secular community in responding to women's demands for equality.

History shows that women did gain considerable power through convent life in such periods as thirteenth- and fourteenth-century England and tenth-century Germany. It is possible, therefore, that the impact of the contemporary women's movement will once again allow women in religious life to come into positions of power and authority in the church. Perhaps, as some believe, new forms of religious communities will attract women who no longer find the traditional forms acceptable.

Educative Communities

Convents have traditionally housed schools for girls, and many modern women's institu-tions have been based on that model. Numerous women have enjoyed a brief intermission from the traditional roles of the female life cycle in single-sex schools, both as students and as teachers. The first known example was created by Sappho in ancient Greece.

Sappho's legacy consists of but a handful of beautiful broken lines of poetry—hardly a sufficient basis from which to draw any but the most tentative conclusions. But in them a fleeting world glimmers—a world of girlhood that existed two centuries before the misogynistic social system we identify with classical Athens. What comes through in her poetry is the memory of a golden moment in life between childhood and marriage when the young women of the island of Lesbos were released from the family circle into one another's company. Sappho's lyrics express the love they felt for one another and their sorrow over the permanent parting that marriage entailed for those who left the island never to return.

Another world of female bonding in nineteenth-century America is revealed to us through the letters and diaries of women separated from one another by marriage (Smith-Rosenberg, 1975). The same sense of shared emotions and of love and sorrow was depicted by Charlotte Brontë in the early sections of *Jane Eyre*, first published in 1847, which described the love and caring that linked Jane with the dying Helen Burns during their terrible days in Lowood Academy. Rosamund Lehman's *Dusty Answer* (1927) explores the emotional ties and explicit lesbian experience of a pair of young women in an English school.

A continuum exists for women that includes the short-term sharing of emotions, longer-lived close relationships characterized by care and tenderness, and an emotional commitment that may include the sexual expression of love. All women have experienced these feelings, but until recently such relationships have been ignored by society or thought not

Sappho, fragment 94

... and I honestly wish I were dead.
Weeping heavily, she left me,
and said, "Our anguish, Sappho,
is terribly deep—
I am really leaving you against my will."
And I answered her with this:
"Go, be happy—and
remember me—for you know
how I have cherished you,
and if you doubt it, let me call to mind for you
.... the beauty we shared,
the times when you would wrap around yourself,
beside me/a profusion of garlands,/
of violets and roses, woven together ...
and thick-plaited, sweet-smelling wreaths,
fashioned of blossoms,
you hung at your soft throat ...
... and when you had anointed ...
with rich and regal scents,
upon the soft bed you would fulfill your desire
for the lovely ...
and no one ... nor a holy ...
.... that we were absent from ...
nor a grove ...
... sound ...

(Sappho, 1966:43)

to exist: If they were discernible, they were condemned outright.

As a women's community, the boarding school or women's college is but a temporary release from the men's world in which women will function for most of our lives. These experiences provide women with an opportunity to study, excel, and develop skills and goals without the pressures and restrictions inherent in settings dominated by men.

School experiences often bear fruit in lifelong relationships, such as those delineated by Mary McCarthy in *The Group* ([1963], 1972). The range of leadership roles possible in single-sex education has created advocates for

such experiences, and we explore their views in Chapter 11.

Laboring Communities

Many women, by necessity or choice, have attempted to become self-supporting outside a family circle. Social pressure in the form of low wages, abuse of unprotected women, and, sometimes, outright coercion has often led working women to organize on a collective basis. In medieval Belgium, for example, unmarried women, including widows, formed quasi-religious communities based on the idea of collective housekeeping and economic enterprise. The religious element in these *beguine* organizations ensured their social respectability and enabled members to claim the protection of local ecclesiastical authorities. Nevertheless, women met with hostility and even violence from the guildsmen who would neither admit us to the craft "brotherhoods" nor allow us to compete by working for lower wages or longer hours (McDonnell, 1976). In nineteenth-century France, "secular convents" of women, working as free-lance textile manufacturers, were also attacked for competing successfully with men (Donzelot, 1979). Indeed, it may be that the growing emphasis on family roles as the only proper career for women who were not servants during this period was, at some level, a social reaction to the threat that industrialization (with the potential of wage earnings for large numbers of women) posed to the male-controlled family.

Parallel instances of female working communities are documented in Asia. In Canton, the center of the Chinese silk industry in the nineteenth century, the "purity" of unmarried women was thought to act favorably on the development of silkworms. Consequently, the women silk workers of Canton were customarily housed for a finite period between childhood and marriage in "women's houses." These houses grew into real communities of women, often welcoming and protecting married women who had fled from unhappy homes. Many sought to continue lifelong residence in the women's houses, and women found it possible to avoid unwelcome marriages, occasionally in favor of lesbian relationships. A few of the houses even forged a series of fictive kinship relationships to provide ancestral altars that would care for the members' ghosts after death (Topley, 1975). The depression that hit the silk industry late in the century destroyed this way of life, but a number of the residents flocked to the rapidly growing city of Hong Kong to take up

domestic service. These women were conspicuous among the servants of the city for unusual energy in forming working women's associations for mutual aid and protection from exploitation (Sankar, 1978).

Industrialization in the nineteenth century brought to Western Europe and the United States a major social shift away from the organization of production by the individual artisan to factories and machines owned by industrial capitalists. A feature of early factory communities was the careful supervision and control of unmarried girls and young women who had left home to work in the mills.

The most famous experiment of a protected mill community was located in Lowell, Massachusetts, in the 1820s. Rural New England girls and young women were recruited into the textile factories by the lure of a new model of industrial life. For two decades, the famous "Lowell girls" were reported on by Charles Dickens and other enthusiastic writers who contrasted neat, highly respectable, well-tended Yankee mill girls with the ragged and filthy appearance of mill workers in England. These new industrial paragons lived in company boardinghouses, where morals as well as physical needs were carefully monitored. "On the corporation," as it was put, the women enjoyed the benefits of urban life; lectures and other culturally enriching events were scheduled in the few leisure hours. Several young women produced a magazine, *The Lowell Offering*, a few being sufficiently inspired to go on to more rewarding careers (Eisler, 1977). Lucy Larcom (1824–1893), who worked in the factories for ten years from the age of eleven, remembered the experience as a great opportunity. After the freedom and autonomy she experienced there, she never married but went on to become a teacher, writer, and editor. Reflecting in later years, she concluded that it was "one of the privileges of my youth that I was permitted to grow up among those active, interesting girls, whose lives were not mere echoes of other lives but had principle and purpose distinctly their own" (Brownlee and Brownlee, 1976).

The Lowell experiment, however, lasted less than two decades and was not to be repeated. For most women, the experience of the factory system was not an idyll but a nightmare of hard labor, tuberculosis, and, not infrequently, sexual exploitation. But the point is that for some women in England and New England, industrialization made possible a new image as well as a new kind of role. Women need not marry; we need not be mothers.

The new image emerging at this time, the "working girl," grew slowly out of the new industrial life of the mill towns. She was a spunky, bright, enterprising, earnest person. She worked hard and, in legend, seemed never to have been depressed at her failure to rise above a certain level of success. In this she lagged behind Horatio Alger's heroes, who usually ended up marrying the boss's daughter. Yet, for women who had been deprived of any image of autonomous life, whose only escape to unpaid but respectable status doing domestic tasks as wives was low-paid, low-status employment as servants, working in a factory for wages was a real, attractive alternative.

Support Networks

With the growth of the nation state and industrialization, the confines of the family were broken down for various groups of people; women emerged as breadwinners, social reformers, and even political revolutionaries. Our personal lives have been greatly misrepresented by traditional modes of writing history. The marital difficulties and conflicts experienced by active women like Elizabeth Cady Stanton, reformer and suffragist, or Eleanor Roosevelt have been examined in great detail, as have relatively happy unions such as those of the poets Elizabeth Barrett

(1806–1861) and Robert Browning, and Lucy Stone (1818–1893), a feminist social reformer, and Henry Blackwell, brother of the first American woman physician. Even such unorthodox heterosexual arrangements as those of the women who chose the literary names of George Eliot (1819–1880) and George Sand (1804–1876) have been widely discussed by their biographers. But the affective relationships of these women with members of their own sex have barely been noticed at all. Moreover, women who had no known heterosexual connections have been traditionally treated as though we lived alone and were utterly unloved.

In reality, these women often had the love and support of networks of female colleagues, companions, and often lovers (Faderman, 1981). At Hull House, the social reformer Jane Addams (1860–1935) enjoyed the support of a community of women who gave her the love and loyalty she needed to continue her work. The same kind of network is now known to have existed for Eleanor Roosevelt, who has previously been depicted as a lonely woman, permanently scarred by the infidelity of her famous husband (Lash, 1982; Cook, 1992). Contemporary feminists have uncovered evidence of these past communities, even as we seek to build new networks to strengthen us in our present struggles. One writer observes that "the power of communities of independent women, and of the love between individual women, expressed not only sensually but in a range of ways, is part of the history that has been taken from us by heterosexual culture. To recognize this history is to recognize our own personal forces of energy and courage and the power to change" (Cook, 1979).

Support networks to accomplish the tasks of mothering are well illustrated by practices among African American women in the United States. Patricia Hill Collins describes the networks of "othermothers"—grandmothers, sisters, aunts, cousins, and "fictive kin," who have traditionally assisted blood-mothers in raising children. The institution of African American motherhood has included sharing responsibility among many women for one another's children so that families could survive (Collins, 1990).

In her novel *The House of the Spirits*, Isabel Allende describes a period in a Latin American country when suspected opponents of a tyrannical regime were arrested and tortured and often killed. She writes of the women in a prison whose comforting hands and voices of encouragement enabled a young victim of such terror and rape to live through her ordeal.

The workings of networks of women supporting women have often been overlooked, but have provided needed means for women to confront and sometimes to break out of oppressive conditions.

Utopian and Experimental Communities

Some women and men have envisioned communities that alter the structure of the conventional family, which they view as an impediment to the development of human potential. Philosophers over time have imagined whole societies that are founded on new domestic principles, sometimes eliminating marriage, sometimes the individual control by parents of their offspring, sometimes both. The general idea has usually been that such societies would produce more altruistic individuals and would provide the context for greater fulfillment of human potential, often for both women and men. Not all utopian visions have sought to abolish or alter the family, of course; but in this section we consider only those that did suggest alternatives to prevailing family forms.

During the nineteenth century, a large number of experimental communities, some religious, some secular, attempted to make utopia real. Each tried to put into practice its ideas of reforming institutions of marriage and childrearing—and most communities foundered in the process. A few of today's experimental communities are derived directly from a utopian text; others, usually known as *communes*, may result from an unplanned process of trial and error. Still others, such as the kibbutz in Israel, combine explicit social phi-

---

Feminist Family Circles

In the years since my divorce, I seem to have created a new extended family that consists not only of my own children but also friends on whom I can always depend for a bed and a loving ear. Although I live alone in my little house in Sag Harbor, my family stretches from California to Cambridge. And there is an authentic note of family reunion as we who founded N.O.W. a generation ago reconvene for the Assembly on the Future of the Family, our sons and daughters at our sides, our hands extended to men. As our children grow up and leave home, as more of us struggle with the problems of husbands' strokes and heart attacks, and our own illnesses and loneliness, we admit our needs and vulnerabilities to each other. We get love and support from this family that was knit together in our battle for equality. The movement itself has become "family," and now we call each other long distance just to say "hello" as families do.

(Friedan, 1979:102)

losophy and practical modification. So far, none have approached the Christian convent in longevity, geographical scope, or popularity. Are altruism and fulfillment of human potential more difficult to achieve when women and men live together? Or when children are born and raised within the community? What seem to be the elements of success—and failure—for these alternatives to family life?

Utopian Literature

The most frequently cited utopian writer of antiquity is the Greek philosopher Plato. His *Republic*, written in the fourth century B.C.E., is perhaps the prototype of antifamily utopias. He imagined a state governed by an elite group, the "guardians," in which women and men participate on equal terms. Women and men are given the same education; the curriculum is based on that followed by the upper-class male in Athenian society. Reproduction is carefully regulated. At certain times of the year, women and men of prime reproductive capacity are brought together to mate. When children are born, they are taken from the mother and put under the supervision of special caretakers who can be either women or men. Mothers are brought to the nursery to breast-feed at random and are prevented from knowing which of the infants is ours. Women, thus freed from child care and other domestic duties, can join the men in the job of governing and defending the republic. Parents, freed of feelings of favoritism for their own children, feel concern and affection for all the society's children. Plato's utopia has been regarded as androgynous. However, Plato's proposals can also be viewed as an attempt to reduce the biological differences between women and men, and to turn women into men, as much as possible.

While many utopian writers took a dim view of marriage and parental control over children, their ways of solving the problems were far less innovative than their suggestions for dealing with government or property. Perhaps this has to do with the fact that they were all men; there are no known utopias written by women before the twentieth century (Lane, 1979). Since marriage and childrearing were not as central to their lives as they were to women's, men devoted attention to things they believed were more important.

A number of modern utopias have been conceived by women. Ladyland is a utopia described by the Bengali author Rokeya Sakhawat Hossain in her book *Sultana's Dream*, which was written in the early 1900s. It is a place in which the private and public roles of women and men have been reversed. Women were able to take control over Ladyland after men proved themselves incapable of defending the country through conventional warfare. On the verge of a total defeat, the queen of Ladyland requested that all men go into seclusion and allow the women to fight the enemy. Rather than use military force (a male task), the women of Ladyland, who have spent their time developing technology and science, conquer the invading army by directing intense solar power rays at them. After having been removed from public life, the men are forever relegated to seclusion and the women take over all public social and political functions. Women rule in Ladyland, not through the traditional male manner of domination and oppression, but through more cooperative means. Women use power judiciously. The laws of Ladyland require that its citizens love one another and be truthful, and law-breakers are not put to death but are asked to leave the country. Women work with nature to extract the sun's energy for use in cooking and locomotion and the water from clouds for agricultural needs. As a result of a less exploitative approach to nature, catastrophes such as drought and floods have been eliminated. All domestic chores, formerly done by women, are now carried out by men. It is the men who cook, clean, and garden. These chores are viewed as simple; however, female inventions in science and technology have turned them into simple but pleasant tasks.

The restrictions on women's access to men so prevalent in Hossain's native Bengal have been eliminated in her utopia; here females can interact with more men. And when females and males couple to have children, it is the men who have the task of raising them. It is curious, and perhaps contradictory, that while women view men as having low morals and as not good for doing much in Ladyland, men are deemed qualified to raise children. Her approach to the problem of childrearing and childbearing does not resemble the approach of other feminist utopian writers who eliminate men altogether from feminist utopian societies. Men are seen as being incapable of doing certain tasks such as embroidery that require patience. Because males are viewed as being dangerous and have been eliminated from the public arena, both crime and sin are absent. It is also interesting to note that there is a consistency in the domestic and foreign policies of the women of Ladyland in that there is no trade conducted with other countries if the women in those countries are oppressed.

Other utopias we consider challenge the institution of marriage and the practices of childrearing; in both cases, the solution has a "technical" as well as a social component.

Herland, a utopia described by Charlotte Perkins Gilman in the early 1900s, solves the problem of the family (and all other social problems, apparently) through the simple device of eliminating men from society altogether. Here, women have found a way to conceive children by means of parthenogenesis (nonsexual reproduction by a single parent). Motherhood is a venerated achievement. All of society, in fact, is oriented toward nurturance. Besides caring for offspring, the inhabitants of Herland are engaged in all the arts of growing and cultivation. Life is pre-

dominantly rural, and women tend gardens, fields, and forest. Domestic lives are simple and austere, but the surroundings are lush and bountiful. As a conservation measure, the inhabitants have given up raising animals and eating meat. The women are cooperative, noncompetitive, strong, and healthy, but are also gentle, nonviolent, and self-controlled. This is a society of mothers and women who see ourselves as potential mothers and do not ever have to be wives.

Mouth-of-Mattapoisett, a utopia placed in the future, has been fashioned by Marge Piercy in *Woman on the Edge of Time* (1976). Unlike Gilman's utopia, it includes men as well as women. Like Herland, it is a community oriented toward nurturance and mothering. It begins with an androgynous conceptualization of humanity. Language does not distinguish female from male, either by pronouns or by names of individuals. People form domestic groups solely to raise children to puberty. Such groups include three adults (in any combination of sexes), with no person economically dependent on the others. The three join together for the express purpose of nurturing a child.

Children are conceived and born outside the womb, in test tubes or tanks, and cared for by specialists. The children are raised in nurseries but maintain a special relationship with the three parents. All three (whether women or men) are "mothers." Men may choose to receive hormones to enable them to breastfeed. Thus motherhood need not be denied to anyone merely on the basis of sex. However, the physical burden of childbearing falls on no one person, nor is childrearing a private affair. Special nurses tend babies, and children live separately from "mothers" for life. Puberty is celebrated as a crucial rite of passage that effectively separates adolescents from the primary emotional bonds with the early comothers and encourages full autonomy. Piercy suggests that the solution to the problem of harmony between the sexes and between generations lies in reducing gender distinctions and generational privileges by removing the exclusivity of personal relationships. Instead, the emphasis is on bonding temporarily and freely, without long-term possessiveness. She poses for women the question of whether, when the mother-child bonds are relaxed, we gain in freedom as much as we lose in strong emotional ties.

While people's lives in this society are not austere, the emphasis is on conservation and ecological balance rather than consumption and exploitation. Technology is geared toward security and cautious use, not bounty. Perhaps more important, individuals, although encouraged to serve community interests in some ways, are also encouraged to fulfill personal potential, whether through artistic, scholarly, or other creative endeavors. Individualism is fostered to the benefit of community life. The education of children and the economic activities of adults are designed so as not to inhibit the free expression of individuality.

Thus utopian ideals, inasmuch as they are directed to family life, tend to see the oppression of women as a consequence of our roles as wives (not as mothers, necessarily), and the development of selfishness and competitiveness as a consequence of possessiveness by parents toward children and spouses toward one another. The remedies envisioned are radical in the extreme, suggesting paradoxically that perhaps the biology of reproduction itself is at fault, after all. The question of biological determination becomes all the more serious when we turn to the efforts people have made to put utopian ideas into practice.

Experimental Communities

Nineteenth-Century Utopian Experiments. Perhaps because of the opportunities offered by the frontier, the dislocations caused by industrialization, or yet other reasons, utopia became more than a literary exercise in nineteenth-century Amer-

ica. Hundreds of utopian or "intentional" communities were founded. A number of these experiments lasted a generation and some even lasted several generations; most, however, failed in a few short years. Many experimented with alternative forms of family life because they saw families as divisive, detracting from community loyalties. Others saw families as the source of human, particularly women's, oppression. Yet others saw families as arbitrarily limiting *human* potentiality, particularly in sexual expression. When communities failed, it is not always clear whether failure was due to the social experiments themselves, to economics, or to external pressures. In any case, the formation of an intentional community, with special rules and regulations applied to personal conduct, inevitably meant intervention in family life.

The most direct and common form of intervention in the nineteenth century was the imposition of celibacy. Some utopian communities imposed celibacy for economic reasons; others, such as the Shakers, required it for theological reasons. The Shakers, founded by Ann Lee, also preached women's equality. Celibacy reordered the priorities of community members, establishing the interests of the community over those of the individual (Muncy, 1973).

A number of communities permitted, even condoned, familism (retention of personal ties between wife and husband, parents and children) but intervened in family *functions* such as food preparation and dining. The Mormons were an example of a religious utopian movement that for half a century was familistic and also preached *polygyny*. Apparently the women of the community resisted polygyny at the outset, and even subsequently, but on the whole believed the sacrifices being made in this world would be rewarded in the next (Muncy, 1973).

There were experimental communities that frowned on marriage but approved of sex. Some of these communities advocated "free love," and among these most were anarchists in general philosophy; members believed that no arbitrary rules or governmental structure should control people's lives. Other communities engaged in nonstandard sexual practices under the control and leadership of a single charismatic individual whose philosophy had religious overtones. The most famous and long-lived of these was Oneida, settled by the Perfectionists under the leadership of John Humphrey Noyes. The Perfectionists practiced "complex marriage," in which each member was formally married to every other member of the opposite sex; exclusive attachments between couples were forbidden. Each member had her or his own room. Members were encouraged to engage in sexual intercourse with a variety of partners, but sexual relations were monitored by a committee of elders. The leaders initiated the young, both girls and boys.

Noyes preached separation between sexuality and reproduction. For twenty years, sex for reproduction was prohibited; birth control was the responsibility of the men, who were enjoined to avoid ejaculation. Female orgasm was the ultimate objective of every sexual encounter, and failure was deemed to be the fault of the male partner. After twenty years the community engaged in a ten-year eugenics experiment (selective mating to improve the race or species), controlled by a committee that selected couples to mate and bear offspring. More women than men volunteered for the experiment (Carden, 1969; Muncy, 1973).

In 1869, Noyes required the young women of Oneida to take an oath that stressed that in decisions about who should bear children, women belonged not to ourselves, but to God and, secondarily, to Noyes, God's representative. They agreed "that we have no rights or personal feelings in regard to child-bearing which in the least degree oppose or embarrass him in the choice of scientific combinations.

That we will put aside all envy, childishness, and self-seeking and rejoice with those who are chosen candidates; that we will if necessary become martyrs to science . . . 'living sacrifices' to God and true Communism" (Kern, 1979:184–85).

As a result of eugenic planning, some fifty-eight children were born in the decade following 1869. The children were raised by a group of specialists, consisting of fifteen women and three men. Mothers could visit offspring but were discouraged from forming exclusive attachments (Muncy, 1973).

These young women of the 1870s willingly consented to an experiment in breaking down the exclusivity of families. But the next generation of women at Oneida reconsidered support of the "scientific" selection of parents. Some were reluctant to renounce all rights to motherhood, and others desired to retain control over children. The community began to flounder when these women rejected male definitions of women's proper communitarian roles and demanded autonomy within the more traditional nuclear family (Kern, 1979).

The positions taken by the experimental communities on women's rights varied. On the whole, the rights of women were greater in the celibate communities, while in the familistic communities our status resembled women's traditional status in the wider society. The Mormons ignored women's rights. The reformists, the economic cooperatives, and the anarchists all championed women's rights and tried to establish equality. But the societies that sought equality tended to fail and to be strongly resisted by the women. Why? A frequently cited cause is friction between the mothers and the rest of the community over control of children. A look at more recent experiments may help provide tentative answers.

Twentieth-Century Intentional Communities. The intentional communities of the present show an even greater range of variability than in the past. They are found all over the world. As in the past, many are religious; others are purely secular groups, linked by political beliefs, moral principles, and at times economic necessity. Some are rural, some urban. Some are communistic, some anarchistic, some joined together under the influence of a charismatic leader. In those cases where celibacy is not the rule, the problem of what to do about marriage and children often becomes the undoing of the commune (Kanter, 1973).

There are communes where children simply are not welcome. Other communes, however, welcome women with children. Some see an advantage in the income children can provide by means of government welfare payments. (Few communes run economically successful ventures, and many depend on outside subsidies.) In the less organized, more anarchist communes, responsibility for raising the children is either not delegated or extremely diffuse. Children might even be treated as adults, left to themselves as much as possible. There are communities that give considerable thought to raising children, as for example, Twin Oaks, a community based on B. F. Skinner's *Walden II* (1962), which places a high priority on methods of childrearing. Such communities appear to be in the minority, however; surprisingly few studies have been done of mother-child relationships in communes (Bernard, 1975).

The Israeli kibbutz has long been viewed as a success in the tradition of communes based on socialist ideals of equality and shared effort. Since 1909, the kibbutz has explored the communal alternative, providing collectivized "domestic" services for its members (food preparation, clothing maintenance, health care, child care) in return for their labor in communal enterprises, which are primarily rural but may include some industrial production. The ideology of women's equality with men and the subordination of private family interests to those of the collective have been fundamental to the kibbutz movement throughout its history. Women, married or single, are classed as independent autonomous members of the community, with full voting rights in its organization and full economic rights in its collective resources (Spiro, 1980).

Observations of conditions in these kibbutz communities, however, show that women participate less than men in governing and supervising and often follow separate educational careers. Traditional gender distinctions emerge. Women engage overwhelmingly in service work, clothing care, cooking, and child care, while men tend to be employed mainly in farming and industry. Kibbutz women have long argued, unsuccessfully, that labor-intensive cultivation in which women could participate while remaining close to the children's quarters was preferable to heavy-machine, large-scale crops. The men of the kibbutz, however, have preferred the larger return from mechanized farming and have outvoted the women. Faced with the choice of a long day's absence or domestic labors, women have not elected to abandon our children completely. Instead, in recent years, women have shown an increasing inclination to return to a strong family life, centering on our relationships with our children. Asked to lead lives according to men's priorities, kibbutz women have apparently rejected those parts that do not satisfy our own preferences.

On the whole, men have elaborated communal ideology in the past. Even where women's equality has been part of that ideology, women's roles have in fact closely resembled those of women in the rest of the world. Women bear the major burdens of child care and domestic upkeep and tend to be socially subordinate to men. As in the last century, women in modern communes have expressed dissatisfaction with the tendency to exploit our labor and with the inadequacy of arrangements for the care of children.

A recent development has been the emergence of women's communes—that is, women's communes that are not convents. The *New Women's Times* describes rural communes open to women and children in a number of states. For example, in Oregon,

> OWL Farm is a beautiful 150 acres in a protected valley with a relatively moderate climate. She is probably the only women's land which is "owned" by *all* women. She belongs to you and me and is there for our use anytime, now or in the future. In the warm weather there are usually enough women around to help raise the $360.00 per month mortgage payments—not much considering there's a well-built two story log house, a "children's house," a "quiet house," several tipis, a barn, a good well with running water in the main house, plenty of open fields for farming and timberlands for wood. (*New Women's Times*, 1980)

But women's communes often have difficulty in raising the funds necessary for survival.

People are motivated to join communes for a variety of reasons. Almost invariably, however, there is dissatisfaction with standard family life. Some people are motivated to join communes to help establish a new morality; some desire to gain greater intimacy with others, to relieve the loneliness and isolation of our particular nuclear families. Whatever the motives, people usually discover that group living involves unanticipated problems whether they be economic support, domestic upkeep, or personal conflicts over sexual relations or childrearing. Many of the problems of communal life are identical with those of standard families; the disagreements that undermine the unity and survival of communes are those that lead to the breakup of conventional families as well. This suggests that it is not just the structure of families or communal living that is "at fault" but problems people have in relations with others in general: problems of role expectations, attitudes, self-expression, and learning to cooperate, listen, and tolerate.

But experimental communities have the further problem of potential conflict with the wider community. Like convents in the past, experimental communities that have not become part of the establishment are targets of suspicion, criticism, and efforts at outside control, especially when sexual practices deviate from the social norm.

Criticisms of Experimental Alternatives

Persecution suggests that many in the dominant society view the existence of alternatives as threatening. The failure of most communes to survive may be seen as partially, if not largely, due to lack of general social support. But Alice S. Rossi suggests that the experiments with new forms of family life fail because of inadequate provision for the expression of biologically rooted sex differences, particularly in regard to childrearing. According to Rossi, the experiments show us that there are limits to the extent to which we can (short of biological intervention) successfully modify the social roles of parents, particularly mothers (Rossi, 1977).

Rossi criticizes the literature on family alternatives (and alternative practices themselves) for overemphasizing adult sexual relationships rather than considering the implications of these relationships for parenting. Ego, indulgence, immediate gratification, and catering to male preferences for variety in sexual partnerhood all occur at the expense of children's needs. She cites studies that document the stressful childhood of children raised in communes, particularly urban ones. "Just as the sexual script, so the parenting script in the new family sociology seems to be modeled on what has been a male pattern of relating to children, in which men turn their fathering on and off to suit themselves or their appointments for business or sexual pleasure. . . . It is not at all clear what the gains will be for either women or children in this version of human liberation" (ibid.:16).

Rossi suggests that both our biological and our cultural heritage link mating and parenting more closely for females than males, and she believes "that the mother-infant relationship will continue to have greater emotional depth than the father-infant relationship" (ibid.:18). Only the extensive training of men will help to "close the gap produced by the physiological experience of pregnancy, birth and nursing" (ibid.). Few experimental noncelibate alternatives to family life have endured long enough to provide a test of Alice Rossi's arguments. However, we need not postulate a biological base to the attachment mothers feel for our children to understand the conflicts that can occur when we are separated from the nurturing of our offspring.

Utopian models for social life, generally designed by men, do not make much allowance for the desires of women to associate closely with our own children: Many utopias seek actively to intervene in maternal attachment, seeing it as a source of evil or distraction from community commitment. History, indeed, does seem to indicate that mother-child attachments may undermine community commitments and frequently cause conflict in real experimental communities. But we know of no noncelibate experimental communities designed or led by women in the past, and as yet we know little about how those that exist today are working out. Present studies suggest that if children are to be reared, no experimental communal alternative to the family designed by men has been more satisfactory *to women* than some family form.

It is only in women's utopian fantasies that we see possible alternatives acceptable to women. *Herland* and *Woman on the Edge of Time* give motherhood its due and emphasize this attachment. These ideal forms do not provide a practical model for the present, but they do express values that are not allowed to flourish in sexist societies. We do not find conventional nuclear families in women's utopian fantasies, but rather a variety of flexible social arrangements. Nor do we find exclusive attachments, but scope for many loving, supportive relationships between individuals. These fantasies do not picture a separation between parents and very young children (although responsibilities for child care tend to be communalized); if separation occurs, it happens later in life. Motherhood rarely is seen as a threat to these utopias; instead, it is depicted as a beneficial and rewarding experience to be shared more widely (Pearson, 1977). While the prerequisites for these utopian fantasies are often remote or impossible events (parthenogenesis, cataclysms that eliminate men), it is possible that less radical changes could bring us closer to the values they express. Let us consider, for example, some alterations of conventional family form that have been tried.

Alternative Family and Household Forms

What used to be thought of as the "ideal" family in our society—one that lives in a household consisting of a father as sole wage earner, a mother as full-time housewife, and one or more dependent children—is a statistical minority. While all societies, like ours, have an "ideal" form of family that occupies a household, a large proportion, perhaps even the vast majority, of living arrangements do not actually conform to the ideal.

We often fail to understand how social norms differ from social realities. A *social norm* is what most people in a society say and believe is right and proper; what people *do* might be quite different. In fact, every society has some alternatives to the normative or ideal family and household pattern. In a number of African societies, for example, the ideal family is represented by a polygynous household. But to acquire wives, men must pay the kin a bride price, and most men cannot afford to pay for more than one wife. Thus, while the social norm may be a polygynous household, the statistical norm is often a monogamous one.

Our impression that people in tribal and peasant societies have no choice but to live in heterosexual households is reinforced by the emphasis often given to the economic basis of marriage. The basic division of labor in simple societies is by sex and age. Because each sex contributes something essential to the survival of the other, individuals presumably have no choice but to marry. In fact, the apparent universality of economic interdependence of women and men is as illusory as the apparent uniformity of household structure: Both represent postulated rather than real situations. Not only do all societies have individuals who fail or choose not to achieve the norm, but many, if not most, societies have institutionalized alternative social scripts.

Role Reversals

Among the best-known types of "exotic customs" widely found in tribal societies is the provision of institutionalized means of crossing gender roles. A typical example is that of "women marriage" among the Igbo of Southeast Nigeria. Women may marry other women by paying a bride price. This Igbo institution provides an opportunity for women who have skills and economic resources to operate as men do, within socially sanctioned patterns (Uchendu, 1965). The option to cross gender roles has been documented as available for men as well. A well-known case is that of the *berdaches* of the Cheyenne, men who adopt the clothing and behavior of women and become "wives" of other men (Hoebel, 1960).

Gender-role reversal in Western society is not as institutionalized as it is in these indigenous Western African and North American examples, but it does occur. It provides a comic theme in the popular media, but also a serious option for many couples who feel their talents lie in areas usually assigned to the opposite gender. Thus, we find men who wish to be "house husbands" taking on full responsibility for homemaking and child care, financially supported by working wives. Participants in this alternative have grown more numerous in recent years as associations between kinds of work or activity and gender become less rigid.

Egalitarian Households

Feminists are beginning to define the family in new ways that will give more autonomy and genuine support to its individual members (Thorne, 1982). We have embarked, with considerable energy, on a redefinition of marriage (see Chapter 7).

A historical precedent was set in 1855, when Lucy Stone married Henry Blackwell after a long and determined resistance to his suit. The pair signed a contract, which was a manifesto criticizing and abjuring the legal authority of husbands, their conjugal rights to sex on demand, the female duty of constant childbearing, and the obliteration of the wife's personality by the imposition of the husband's name. This marriage resulted in a forty-year partnership in pursuit of women's rights (Rossi, 1964).

The example of Lucy Stone had immediate repercussions. Followers across the country, "Stonerites," refused to change our names on marriage and demanded similar contracts. This example influences women today who are experimenting with ways to decrease the oppressive features of traditional marriage. Many women and men are developing new arrangements for the sharing of domestic, economic, and social responsibilities (Libby and Whitehurst, 1977).

Three fathers, taking care of their children, meet in an art gallery. In egalitarian families, tasks such as child care are shared. Assuming gender roles for which we have not been trained may be hard at first; these fathers seem to be willing, if a little awkward, to learn a new role. (Photo by Richard Zalk)

Such arrangements, which may be called *egalitarian households*, involve equal sharing by adults of the work and rewards of both family life and opportunities outside the home. This sharing means that both partners contribute to the economic and physical maintenance of the home and both have the opportunity and the responsibility to pursue other interests. Both need not perform the same tasks or do all these things simultaneously; each may take turns at completing educational programs or starting new jobs or caring for young children, but in terms of contribution and responsibility, there must be true parity (Held, 1979; Okin, 1989).

Truly egalitarian marriages are still excep-

tions. More often, when women join the workforce, we are not relieved of our household work and responsibilities by a parallel shift of roles by men. Instead, women who hold outside jobs tend to work a "double shift"—one at work and one at home (see Chapter 13). However, most young women in the United States at least aspire to have egalitarian marriages, and increasing numbers are approaching that ideal.

Families of Women

Women have long been accustomed to setting up housekeeping together. It is the customary social solution for women who from some accident of fate find ourselves outside the traditional family circle. The arrangement has often been viewed either as transient or unfortunate. When young women share a household, we are considered to be marking premarital time until our real domesticity begins. Older women have commonly been classed as "spinsters." Both never-married and formerly married women have been scorned as second-class citizens making the best of our manless state. The idea of a happy, stable, enduring relationship between women, especially lesbians, is alien to conventional views. To admit that such relationships can be very satisfactory would threaten the notion that men and marriage are essential to women's fulfillment.

Only with the emergence of lesbian consciousness in the context of the modern feminist movement has the concept of lesbian families gained clarity. Women increasingly insist that we have the freedom to define ourselves. The law defines a family in terms of blood relationships and heterosexual marriage, shared property, and the legitimation of children. Individual women may consider ourselves families, however, if we feel that we are experiencing the commitments of emotion, property, and time that warrant the label (Rothblum and Brehony, 1993).

Laws are made by people, and people can change the laws. In recent years the traditional legal definitions of families have been challenged by "palimony" suits (payment to one member of a couple whose members have lived together without legally binding marriage) and by the development of homosexual marriage ceremonies. Contracts and wills have also been used to separate the property commitment of individuals to one another from the overall legal framework of marriage and family.

The recognition of lesbian families has been helped by the slowly growing success with which lesbians have defended rights to the custody of children. This has been a long struggle. In current legal practice, the "good of the child" has been used by judges to separate children from lesbian mothers because of the social attitudes about lesbianism that judges have shared (Lewin, 1981). Mothers who wish to be free of oppressive marriages do not by any means also want to abandon our children. Women who choose lesbian relationships may not lose the desire to have children or maternal affection for children we already have. Poet Adrienne Rich (1980), a highly articulate lesbian mother, has exposed the stereotypical thinking that has caused even the most "enlightened" to imagine that the categories of lesbian and mother are mutually exclusive. The late Audre Lorde, also a poet, was concerned with racial as well as sexual labeling and argued that black children of lesbian mothers have a special awareness "because they learn, very early, that oppression comes in many different forms having nothing to do with their own worth" (Lorde, 1979).

Single-Parent Households and Other Arrangements

Increasing numbers of women are separating the function of motherhood from the function of wife. Many of these are divorced women who may or may not have chosen to become the heads of single parent households, and many are mothers who have never married.

If women are to bring up children in an atmosphere in which we are free to make decisions to suit our own temperaments, economic autonomy is vital. Our ability to support ourselves and our children plays a large role in our freedom to ignore those who do not approve of our choices. Unfortunately, in the United States these choices are limited by an economic system that provides fewer social services and less social support for human needs than almost any other advanced industrial economy (Edelman, 1987; and see Chapter 13).

Single mothers and married mothers face similar problems in childrearing. In addition, single mothers face the emotional stresses of unstable relationships, unwelcome social pressures, and loneliness. Nonetheless, many unmarried women have chosen to raise children.

Among African American women in the United States there is some discussion of "sharing" husbands, given the shortage of suitable marriageable black men. The aim may be to build on the African tradition of polygamy without perpetuating the ways in which polygamy has traditionally upheld male dominance. Some women doubt this can be done, but others are willing to experiment (Edwards, 1991).

Choosing Not to Mother

Motherhood is not the only family form available to women. Today, increasing numbers of women choose to live with other women as couples without having children. Whereas once women achieved adult status primarily by becoming mothers, now many other roles define adult status for us. Careers, avocational interests, and community activities provide rewards, personal gratification, and a sense of identity. Some women feel that children would substantially hinder our pursuit of these commitments and undermine our goals. In the past, couples without children were pitied; childlessness was seen as an unfortunate fate. Today, especially in the West, the choice not to have children is increasingly accepted as valid (Trebilcot, 1984).

Women on Our Own

Many women have decided to marry later than our mothers did, if at all. Some women may choose never to marry, and growing numbers may choose to dissolve the marriages we make. With improved medical knowledge and a rising life expectancy, a growing number

of healthy, active widows are also joining the ranks of single women in our society. The possibility of economic independence or at least a greater number of life choices brought young women in the 1960s to attend college in larger numbers than ever before. The demand for affirmative action, which grew out of the civil rights movement of the same decade, also brought women without college educations new opportunities in various well-paid sectors formerly closed to us, such as business, management, and the construction industry. In 1980, for the first time, the numbers of women in colleges and some professional schools were equal to and, in some cases, surpassed the numbers of men. One source of this increase is the large number of women over thirty who are now returning to complete or supplement the education abandoned earlier for marriage.

With all these changes, the need to marry for economic security has seemed less compelling to women. The first requirement for women's emancipation, and for a greater range of choices, is an independent source of income. "Five hundred pounds and a room of one's own" was the formula supplied by Virginia Woolf in 1929 (1957).

Nowadays women are viewed less and less as either accessories to men or, if single, social rejects. The title *Ms.*, which has growing acceptance, helps to obliterate the emphasis society once placed on a woman's marital status. Unmarried women have been found to have higher intelligence, more education, and greater occupational success than married counterparts. This relationship is not found with men; successful men are more likely to marry than successful women (Spreitzer and Riley, 1974). It is clear that permanent or intermittent singlehood has emerged as a workable alternative to marriage or long-term coupling. It is no longer regarded as a mistake, an accident, or a tragedy. There is not only a real increase in the numbers of women who choose to be unmarried but also a revision of our social perceptions of this state. We are liberating ourselves from the traditional scripts.

Sexual Freedom

Being single, women are able to choose whether or not to have sexual relations. Throughout history, for religious or personal reasons, some women have preferred to live without sexual relations, either temporarily or permanently. Indeed, a number of active feminists in the past, particularly when "conjugal duties" produced large families, maintained that women could do very well without sex. Such was the view, for example, of Elizabeth Cady Stanton, herself a mother of five and an important figure in the nineteenth-century suffrage movement (Rossi, 1973).

However, most women wish to have sex. We wish to enter into free and loving relationships with persons of our choice. With few serious restrictions, men have always enjoyed a considerable measure of sexual freedom, but it has rarely been granted to women. We have most commonly been confined to the bonds of heterosexual marriages.

The freedom to love cannot be achieved until it is accompanied by freedom from the fear of involuntary maternity. Whether or not we have sufficient financial independence to support children on our own, the threat of unwanted children is a fearsome barrier to our enjoyment of our sexuality. No revolution has been more important in the liberation of women from the old patriarchal family circle than the development of birth control devices. Perhaps no revolution has been more persistently and more violently contested. For well over a hundred years, the opponents of women's reproductive rights have been fighting back. Earlier in this century, they sought by law even to withhold knowledge of the existence of choice from women. In our own time,

such opponents continue to seek by law to withhold the exercise of such choice, focusing on abortion rights.

With the availability of more reliable modes of contraception in the 1960s and the legalization of abortion throughout the 1970s, women have felt less constraint in expressing our emotions and desires and have sought greater sexual satisfaction. Some women, delighted with the opportunity to enjoy the bodies of men in relationships that entailed no commitments, joined Erica Jong in celebrating "the zipless fuck," the expression she used to refer to this experience (1973). For others, the "free love" advocated in the sexual revolution of the 1960s all too often turned into an exercise in realizing male sexual fantasies. Some women discovered that "sexual liberation" meant only freedom for men to enjoy the bodies of women (Ehrenreich, 1984). For us, a more genuine sexual liberation has meant the confidence to say no without fear of offending men on whom we were, or might have to be, dependent. And it has meant the possibility that the relations we would enter into, whether short-term or long-term, would be genuinely voluntary.

Some women have discovered the possibilities of lesbian love. It is only recently that substantial numbers of women have been willing to comment publicly on this sexual preference. Few have had the courage of Gertrude Stein (1874–1946), who lived as she wished, disdaining public opinion. For too many, the tragic experience of lesbians depicted by Radclyffe Hall in her The Well of Loneliness (1926, 1975) represented the truth.

For these reasons, lesbians of the contemporary period represent a new development (Kennedy and Davis, 1993). Lesbian writers now express more fully than in the past the full range of lesbian experience. Some writers define lesbians as women who make other women the primary center of our emotional, social, and erotic lives, regardless of the details

Virginia Woolf (1882–1941), a British novelist, critic, essayist, and publisher (she founded the Hogarth Press with her husband, Leonard, in 1917), and member of the Bloomsbury Group. She wrote witty and biting essays exposing the restrictive conditions that existed in England, even for upper-class women like herself. (See *A Room of One's Own* [1929/1957]).

Loving women. Until recently, lesbians remained hidden from history and the contemporary record. Today women not only exhibit their love for one another openly, they also celebrate that love in prose, poetry, and graphic art. (Photo by Joel Cohen)

of our sexual relationships (Cook, 1979; Roth-blum and Brehony, 1993). These definitions are derived from women's own experiences and feelings about lesbianism, not from men's fantasies and images.

Ultimately, the significant question is, Who are the label makers? The threat of being labeled "unfeminine" has long confined women to socially approved roles. Blanche Cook (1979) argues that the idea of a lesbian, not as an absolute sexual category but as an acceptable self-image of women who love women, is enormously useful. So long as women who form bonds with one another, be they professional, social, domestic, or sexual, react to the label of lesbian as though it were a slur against which we must defend ourselves, the accusation will force us back into the rigid molds of conventional family.

A major achievement of a new feminist consciousness today is renewed interest in and care for women by other women. Too long has the male image of women as competitors for men's favors separated and divided us. Loving women, caring about women, and being interested in women's lives all exist along a continuum that is characterized by support and concern, not competition and jealousy. Women's sympathy for one another is a new source of strength.

Notes of Caution

Freedom to find love outside of marriage and the family and the opportunity to be self-supporting are prerequisites to the choice of singlehood. Otherwise, most women would not find being single desirable or even feasible. We have emphasized the changing circumstances that have made the option of not marrying more attractive to more women today. Some notes of caution must be added. First, this option is not available to the vast majority of women in the world, whose societies do not readily condone singlehood and continue to censure the independent and autonomous woman. In most of the world, women are still expected to fall under the protection and control of a family. Second, most women do not earn enough money to live comfortable lives. Today, in the United States, where job opportunities for women have increased during the past century, women working full-time and year-round still earn only about two-thirds of what men earn (see Chapter 13). The majority of poor people are women and children. Thus, being single by choice still entails considerable sacrifice, both social and economic.

The search for personal autonomy may be difficult and costly even for women with economic means. Pressures to marry and have children continue to be great. It takes considerable psychic and emotional strength to resist such pressures, which, in fact, most women have internalized from childhood.

Summary

Socially scripted options have historically been available to women who wished to live outside the conventional family circle. These choices presented possibilities for roles other than those of the conventional daughter, wife, and mother. From the perspective of history, we can see that women have increasingly impressed our own wishes upon the design of alternative roles and family organizations.

Communal arrangements provided some of the earliest options for women to leave the family circle. The best documented of these are the religious communities of women, the convents of Christianity and Buddhism. Although convent life relieved members of the domestic constraints of marriage and motherhood, control by external male authorities tended to diminish women's autonomy.

Women have also spent intermittent periods living in single-sex educative communities, such as boarding schools and women's colleges. Some women have by necessity or choice joined other women in a laboring community. This kind of life gave rise to the role of "working girl." Finally, women have long enjoyed the support of other women in informal networks.

Philosophers have from ancient times depicted utopian communities for women and men that alter or abolish conventional family life. In the nineteenth and twentieth centuries, communal experiments appeared. All too often, these communities were oriented toward fulfillment of men's utopian ideals, without taking women's wishes and perspectives into account. Consequently, women members tended to be dissatisfied with our roles. If we compare these experiments with women's literary utopias, we see that women view the ideal society differently from men. Women's utopias emphasize a reduction or elimination of gender-role distinctions and maintain a continuous respect for parent-child bonding.

Communal arrangements are only one form of alternative to the conventional family. Women and men may reverse roles or share equally in family tasks. Women may choose to live with men on our own terms, or to couple with other women. We may decide to live as single parents, or to marry and not have children.

Free choices are increasingly possible to contemporary women with good jobs. Many of these women are choosing to live independently and to maintain relationships of our own choosing. In this role, we are aided by the fact that birth control has separated the maternal function of women from our sexual enjoyment and search for emotional fulfillment.

For women who choose to live outside the conventional family, the ability to command a sufficient income is essential. Another prerequisite is social independence. Women who have attempted to live outside "respectable" social boundaries have often experienced se-

vere disapproval and even physical abuse. One of the most powerful constraints on women's freedom of choice has been our own internalization of conventional societal values.

Discussion Questions

1. In what ways is (was) your family "nonconventional"?
2. If you could write your own script for your role in the family, what would it be? What would be the roles of others in your family?
3. What are the risks of writing your own script?
4. Discuss your own utopia: Are there "families" in it? How are they organized?
5. Which of the alternatives presented here appeals to you the most? Why? Which appeals the least? Why? What options might you choose that have not been mentioned?
6. Do you belong to a "women's network"? What kind of network would be most helpful to you now? Explain.

Recommended Readings

Allende, Isabel. *The House of the Spirits.* Translated by Magda Bogin. New York: Bantam, 1986. A novel that offers examples of women supporting women over several generations of Latin American extended families.

Bulkin, Elly, editor. *Lesbian Literature.* New York: Persephone, 1981. Writings by lesbians about their family relationships, love relationships, "coming out," and getting along.

Faderman, Lillian. *Surpassing the Love of Men: Romantic Friendship and Love between Women from the Renaissance to the Present.* New York: Morrow, 1981. A historical exploration of romantic friendship between women. With or without sexual expression, such choices were alternatives to social expectations for women.

French, Marilyn. *The War against Women.* New York: Simon & Schuster, 1992. Why alternatives are still so badly needed for women around the world.

Lorde, Audre. *Zami: A New Spelling of My Name.* Freedom, CA: The Crossing Press, 1982. Lorde calls her work a "biomythography." In this powerful (fictional) autobiography Lorde traces the issues that surround being a black woman in white America and a lesbian in a homophobic society, raising questions about social, sexual, and immigrant identities and marginalities.

References

Abramovitz, Mimi. *Regulating the Lives of Women: Social Welfare Policy from Colonial Times to the Present.* Boston: South End Press, 1988.

Allende, Isabel. *The House of the Spirits.* Translated by Magda Bogin. New York: Bantam, 1986.

Bernard, Jessie. *The Future of Motherhood.* New York: Penguin, 1975.

Bernini, Marie Louise. *Journey through Utopia.* London: Routledge & Kegan Paul, 1950.

Bernstein, Marcia. *The Nuns.* New York: Bantam, 1976.

Bolton, Brenda. "Mulieres Sanctar." In *Women in Medieval Society,* edited by Susan Stuard. Philadelphia: University of Pennsylvania Press, 1976.

Brod, Harry, editor. *The Making of Masculinities. The New Men's Studies.* Boston: Allen & Unwin, 1987.

Brontë, Charlotte. *Jane Eyre.* 1847. Reprint. New York: Oxford University Press, 1980.

Brownlee, W. Elliot, and Brownlee, Mary M. *Women in the American Economy.* New Haven: Yale University Press, 1976.

Carden, Maren Lockwood. *Oneida: Utopian Community to Modern Corporation.* Baltimore: Johns Hopkins Press, 1969.

Collins, Patricia Hill. *Black Feminist Thought, Knowledge, Consciousness, and the Politics of Empowerment.* Boston: Unwin Hyman, 1990.

Cook, Blanche W. *Women and Support Networks.* New York: Out and Out Books, 1979.

———. *Eleanor Roosevelt. vol. 1, 1884–1933.* New York: Viking, 1992.

Donzelot, Jacques. *The Policing of Families.* Translated by Robert Hurley. New York: Pantheon, 1979.

Edelman, Marian Wright. *Families in Peril: An Agenda for Social Change.* Cambridge: Harvard University Press, 1987.

Edwards, Audrey. "You, Me and He." *Essence* (February 1991):59–64, 108–10.

Ehrenreich, Barbara. *The Hearts of Men: American Dreams and the Flight from Commitment.* New York: Doubleday, 1984.

Eisler, Benita, editor. *The Lowell Offering: Writings by New England Mill Women.* New York: Harper & Row, 1977.

Faderman, Lillian. *Surpassing the Love of Men: Romantic Friendship and Love between Women from the Renaissance to the Present.* New York: Morrow, 1981.

Falk, Nancy Auer. "The Case of the Vanishing Nuns: Fruits of Ambivalence in Ancient Indian Buddhism." In *Unspoken Worlds,* edited by N. A. Falk and Reta Gross. New York: Harper & Row, 1980.

French, Marilyn. *The Women's Room.* New York: Summit, 1977.

Friedan, Betty. "Feminism Takes a New Turn." *New York Times Sunday Magazine* (November 18, 1979):40.

Gilbert, Lucia A. *Sharing It All: The Rewards and Struggles of Two-Career Families.* New York: Plenum, 1988.

Gilman, Charlotte Perkins. *Herland.* 1915. New York: Pantheon, 1979.

Hall, Radclyffe. *The Well of Loneliness.* 1928. New York: Pocket Books, 1975.

Held, Virginia. "The Equal Obligations of Mothers and Fathers." In *Having Children: Philosophical and Legal Reflections on Parenthood,* edited by Onora O'Neill and William Ruddick. New York: Oxford University Press, 1979.

Hertz, Rosanna. *More Equal Than Others. Women and Men in Dual-Career Marriages.* Berkeley: University of California Press, 1986.

Hochschild, Arlie Russell. *The Second Shift: Working Parents and the Revolution at Home.* New York: Viking, 1987.

Hoebel, E. Adamson. *The Cheyennes: Indians of the Great Plains.* New York: Holt, Rinehart, & Winston, 1960.

Hossain, Rokeya Sakhawat. *Sultana's Dream.* New York: The Feminist Press at The City University of New York, 1988.

Jaffe, Rona. *The Best of Everything.* 1958. New York: Avon, 1976.

Jardine, Alice, and Smith, Paul, editors. *Men in Feminism.* Routledge Chapman and Hall, 1987.

Jong, Erica. *Fear of Flying.* New York: Holt, Rinehart, & Winston, 1973.

Kanter, Rosabeth Moss, ed. *Communes: Creating and Managing the Collective Life.* New York: Harper & Row, 1973.

Kennedy, Elizabeth Lapovsky, and Davis, Madeline D. *Boots of Leather, Slippers of Gold: The History of a Lesbian Community.* New York and London: Routledge Press, 1993.

Kern, Louis J. "Ideology and Reality: Sexuality and Women's Status in the Oneida Community." *Radical History Review* 20 (1979):180–205.

Klepfisz, Irena. "Women Without Children/Women Without Families/Women Alone." *Conditions: Two* (1977):72–84.

Lane, Ann. "Introduction." In Charlotte Perkins Gilman, *Herland.* New York: Pantheon, 1979.

Lash, Joseph. *Love, Eleanor. Eleanor Roosevelt and Her Friends.* Garden City, N.Y.: Doubleday, 1982.

Laws, Judith Lang, and Schwartz, Pepper. *Sexual Scripts: The Social Construction of Female Sexuality.* New York: Dryden, 1977.

Lehman, Rosamund. *Dusty Answer.* 1927. New York: Harcourt, Brace, Jovanovich, 1975.

Lewin, Ellen. "Lesbianism and Motherhood: Implications for Child Custody." *Human Organization* 40 (1981):6–14.

Libby, Roger, and Whitehurst, Robert, editors. *Marriage and Alternatives: Exploring Intimate Relationships.* Glenview, Ill.: Scott, Foresman, 1977.

Lorde, Audre. "Man Child: A Black Lesbian Feminist's Response, Not Only of a Relationship, but of Relating." *Conditions: Four* (1979):30–36.

McCarthy, Mary. *The Group.* 1963. New York: New American Library, 1972.

McDonnell, Ernest. *Beguines and Beghards.* New York: Octagon, 1976.

McNamara, Joann. "Sexual Equality and the Cult of Virginity in Early Christian Thought." *Feminist Studies* 3 (1976):145–58

Muncy, Raymond L. *Sex and Marriage in Utopian Communities in 19th Century America.* Bloomington: Indiana University Press, 1973.

New Women's Times, February 1–14, 1982.

Okin, Susan Moller. *Justice, Gender, and the Family.* New York: Basic Books, 1989.

Pearson, Carol. "Women's Fantasies and Feminist Utopias." *Frontiers* 2 (1977):50–61.

Piercy, Marge. *Woman on the Edge of Time.* New York: Knopf, 1976.

Rich, Adrienne. "Compulsory Heterosexuality and Lesbian Existence." *Signs* 5 (1980):631–60.

Rossi, Alice. "Equality Between the Sexes: An Immodest Proposal." *Daedalus* 93(1964):607–652.

Rossi, Alice. "A Biosocial Perspective on Parenting." *Daedalus* 106 (1977):1–31.

Rothblum, Esther D., and Brehony, Kathleen. *Boston Marriages: Romantic but Asexual Relationships among Contemporary Lesbians.* Amherst, Mass.: University of Massachusetts Press, 1993.

Sankar, Andrea. "Female Domestic Service in Hong Kong." *Michigan Occasional Papers in Women's Studies* 9 (1978):51–62.

Sappho. *The Poems of Sappho.* Translated by Suzy Q-Groden. Indianapolis: Bobbs-Merrill, 1966.

Skinner, B. F. *Walden II.* New York: Macmillan, 1962.

Smith-Rosenberg, Carroll. "The Female World of Love and Ritual: Relations between Women in Nineteenth Century America." *Signs* 1 (1975):1–29.

Spiro, Melford E. *Gender and Culture: Kibbutz Women Revisited.* New York: Schocken Books, 1980.

Spreitzer, E., and Riley, L. E. "Factors Associated with Singlehood." *Journal of Marriage and Family* 36 (1974):533–42.

Thorne, Barrie, editor. *Rethinking the Family.* New York: Longmans, 1982.

Topley, Marjorie. "Marriage Resistance in Rural Kwangtung." In *Women in Chinese Society,* edited by Margory Wold and Roxanne Wilke. Stanford: Stanford University Press, 1975.

Trebilcot, Joyce, editor. *Mothering. Essays in Feminist Theory.* Totowa, N.J.: Rowman & Allanheld, 1984.

Uchendu, Victor. *The Igbo of Southeast Nigeria.* New York: Holt, Rinehart & Winston, 1965.

Woolf, Virginia. *A Room of One's Own.* 1929. Reprint. New York: Harcourt, Brace, 1957.

Part *III*

Women in Society

Introduction

The earlier sections of this book have explored various ways women have been defined by others, the roles we have been assigned in the family, and the alternative living arrangements we have chosen. This final section will deal with our relationship to what has been called the "public" sphere. In it we explore the contributions of women to the fields of religion, education, health, work, and political power, and offer suggestions for future directions of women's actions.

Women have always participated in the world beyond the family circle, but often our contributions and efforts have been undervalued or ignored. For many people, the threat of feminism has been the growing power of women in the public domain and the redefinition of our roles in what has been misleadingly called the "private" domain.

Religion has been a continuing force in the lives of many women. Religions prescribe human behavior and provide models for human aspiration. Women have often been viewed only as saints or sinners. Many women through the years have chosen a "religious life" as an acceptable alternative to secular life and marriage. We have not only been involved as worshipers and followers, but we have also taken leadership roles, ranging from curers to clergy.

Feminists involved in religions and religious life have reinterpreted theological doctrines and questioned the sexist bias of the language and cultural practices in which religious dogmas are framed. Feminists today also seek a religious expression for self-affirming beliefs in womanhood.

Education stimulates us to ask questions and search for answers. Too often, those who do not have the advantage of an education do not learn how to question the nature of our environment and experience. In many parts of the world, parents without the necessary resources choose not to educate their daughters, but just their sons. Women's education can be a controversial issue. Will it provoke us to challenge the status quo? What is appropriate for women to learn? Access to certain fields often requires specific educational preparation. In the past, women were not permitted to obtain instruction in the male-dominated professions of the ministry, law, and medicine. Women today are challenging long-held beliefs about our lack of ability for scholarship. In our research, our scholarly questions differ from the traditional approaches of the past and are adding to the knowledge base about both women and men.

Standards for the health of women have very often been based solely on our reproductive roles. The norms for women's physical and emotional health have usually been defined by men. Women have not been encouraged to be responsible for our own well-being, especially as men have controlled the field of women's health care. When we rebelled against our assigned roles and asserted ourselves, the health care system labeled us "sick."

Health and medical care have become major political means for controlling the activities of women. Who should be able to make decisions about women's bodies is a controversial national and international issue. Similarly, contraception and sterilization are significant political issues. The international women's health movement has begun to challenge antiquated notions of women's health care issues.

Work has usually been devalued when labeled "women's work." Much of the work done by women has been interwoven with the traditional roles of housewife and mother. Within the context of the household, women have rarely, if ever, been paid or given credit for our work. With the advent of industrialization and modernization, much of the work formerly done by women in the home was transformed into activities increasingly performed outside the home for wages—for example, spinning, sewing, education of the young, and care of the sick. Some of the traditional areas of women's work were taken over by men in factories, schools, and hospitals. When done by men, the status of the work and the pay received for it rose. In the industrialized world, technology continues to change the nature of work, and more women are seeking a place in the paid labor force than ever before—as well as demanding respect for those tasks that we have traditionally performed.

The growing numbers of women and mothers in the workforce has led to demands for changes in the workplace and the family to accommodate women's needs. Child care facilities, flexible working hours, and parental leave have been implemented by employers and governments in response to the influx of women into the workforce.

Politics and the power to change society are crucial to women's lives. Where there is power, there are means for exerting social control. Those who wield power are not quick to redistribute or relinquish this advantage. In societies where particular characteristics are ascribed to groups of people by virtue of race, religion, ethnic origin, or gender, it has been difficult for the oppressed group to gain sufficient power to alter the status quo. This pattern can be seen in women's struggles for our political rights.

The struggle for women's political power has become international. Through international conferencing, women from different countries come together to share their common experiences and work together to improve women's lives. Despite the differences that separate women, the women's movement and feminism are global phenomena.

Should women strive to reform the existing social system, or will nothing less than its major restructuring be necessary? Different women have different political objectives. Women do not make up a homogeneous group, but we can and do support one another in realizing a variety of shared goals.

chapter 10

Women and Religion

Radicals and reformers the world over have perceived organized religion as a bastion of conservatism. Religion seems to represent stability; it derives legitimacy from ancient tradition and custom and lends support to the preservation of old familiar patterns of belief and behavior. Many active feminists who hope to bring about radical change are often directly opposed to religious beliefs, organizations, and practices. Yet, feminist leadership has also come from within religious institutions: Some feminists cherish aspects of our religious experience and beliefs. Such women are struggling to reform repressive customs and legislation.

In a religious society, a change in religious institutions is a necessary aspect of a change in social consciousness, in the social perception of what is right and good. A revision in the social order requires examination and criticism of its bases in ideas and belief, and the introduction of new elements of thought and faith. This is what feminist activism in religion often aims at.

This chapter considers religious beliefs, mainly of the traditional varieties, in their social context: how they affect the roles of women and values concerning women. We look at constructs of the supernatural world— such as gods, spirits, saints, and ghosts—and the ways these relate to the social realities of gender distinctions. We consider the value

systems supported by religious beliefs and the ways that these systems have exerted social controls on women. And we see how women are struggling to change religion.

Religious Beliefs

People everywhere throughout history have believed that there exists something beyond our perceived material surroundings. This "something," which we may refer to as the supernatural, has variously been described as a cosmic design governing the world, as a realm of spirits or forces of nature that control our lives, or as a great power that is anthropomorphized (endowed with human qualities to make it more comprehensible for ordinary mortals). However it is conceived, the supernatural is thought to have a power beyond our own. It inspires and awes. For many people, the supernatural serves as an ultimate point of reference on "right" or "wrong" behavior. Religion is often of great importance to an understanding of any society. What people believe about the supernatural is reflected in the ways that they order their social relationships.

The Organization of Religion

We do not know how the first religions were formed, but archaeological evidence suggests that even in the earliest religions documented, there were what are now termed *shamans*, persons with special skills in communicating with what was thought to be the supernatural world to bring about desired events in our world (Malefijt, 1968). There have always been some individuals with special knowledge, learning, or understanding who have interpreted their views of the supernatural to others in society. They tell people what is required of them to follow right principles of behavior. But in simple societies, and often in new religions or the religions of the very poor and the oppressed, these specialists are like ordinary people in most other ways. Women or men, they have to do what others do to earn a living, and they influence others by example and guidance, not by force.

As societies become more complex and the division of labor more elaborate, formal institutions, including religious institutions, are established to deal with matters that specifically fall within their domains. Institutions develop, staffed by priestesses and priests, theologians and teachers, persons who are socially recognized as religious "authorities." Such organizations usually determine which ideas are acceptable and which must be rejected (sometimes classed as *heresy*). They codify (write down) the ethical regulations designed to control the actions of individuals within the society and sometimes enforce control by threatening divine sanctions for misbehavior. In many societies, there is no clear-cut division between the organizations that govern religion and those that rule secular affairs. Where there is such a separation, religious organizations generally have considerable influence on secular institutions anyway. For example, voters in the United States may be influenced by the official views of their churches, and American presidents may consult with religious leaders on sensitive social issues.

The organization of religious institutions usually reflects the organization of society at large. In a complex and hierarchical society, dominant religious institutions are complex and hierarchical as well. In societies that deny leadership roles to women and to all men of color, such roles will also frequently be denied these groups in religious institutions. Currents of change and rebellion against the status quo are manifested in challenges to the structure of religious institutions. The organization of a new religion often expresses the dissatisfaction its adherents feel about the established social order.

The Religious Experience of Women

Today's contemporary feminists, like our sisters in the past, realize that most of the organized religions that have dominated the historical and modern world have been profoundly sexist. They have not only denied women a place in leadership but have promulgated ideas that devalue women in general (see Chapters 1 and 2). Why, then, are women in great numbers the world over devoted members of religions?

Women's personal experiences of religion suggest that we see and feel something beyond and apart from the negative messages that male clergy, ritual, and teaching convey. Women often make aspects of religion that are underplayed by the male hierarchy the essence of our own belief. For example, many Christian women have concentrated on Mary, or on Christ as healer and nurturer, or on a loving, benevolent, even maternal God (Bynum, 1982). For Phillis Wheatley, a totally committed Congregationalist, Christianity was the inspiration of some of her most lyrical poetry.

While the major religions have produced formal codes, the great masses of their adherents have developed their own versions of belief and practice. Catholic women are everywhere excluded from the clerical hierarchy of "Catholicism." In belief and practice, rural

Phillis Wheatley: Thoughts on the Works of Providence

Phillis Wheatley (1753–1784) was brought from Senegal to Boston at about the age of seven. Like her owners, John and Susanna Wheatley, she became an ardent Congregationalist. Her poems were published in England in 1773.

Arise, my soul, on wings enraptur'd, rise
To praise the monarch of the earth and skies
Creation smiles in various beauty gay,
While day to night and night succeeds to day;
That *Wisdom* which attends *Jehovah's* ways,
Shines most conspicuous in the solar rays;
Without them, destitute of heat and light,
This world would be the reign of endless night;
In their excess how would our race complain,
Abhorring life! how hate its length'ned chain!
From air adust what num'rous ills would rise!
What dire contagion taint the burning skies;
What pestilential vapours, fraught with death,
Would rise, and overspread the lands beneath!
Hail, smiling morn, that from the orient main
Ascending dost adorn the heav'nly plain!
So rich, so various are thy beauteous dies,
That spread through all the circuit of the skies,
That, full of thee, my soul in rapture soars,
And they great God, the cause of all adores
Infinite *Love* where'er we turn our eyes
Appears: this ev'ry creature's wants supplies;
This most is heard in *Nature's* constant voice,
This makes the morn, and this the eve rejoice;
This bids the fost'ring rains and dews descend
To nourish all, to serve one gen'ral end.
The good of man: yet man ungrateful pays
But little homage, and but little praise.
To him, whose works array'd with mercy shine.
What songs should rise, how constant, how divine!

Shields, John C., editor. *The Collected Works of Phillis Wheatley.*
The Schomburg Library of Nineteenth-Century Black Women Writers,
Henry Louis Gates, Jr., editor. New York: Oxford University Press, 1988, p. 43.

Italian Catholic women may well resemble rural Mexican or Irish or Peruvian Catholic women more closely than we do the urban Roman priest. In some respects, rural Catholic women may have in common certain religious attitudes and interests with rural Islamic and Hindu sisters that neither shares with the men who dominate their systems of codified knowledge. The "popular" versions of religions of the world have often provided a scope for women's activities denied us by the male governing elite in the formalized versions of these religions. For the majority of religious women in the past, this standing appears to have been enough. For a few, as we shall see, it was not; and today numbers of women are demanding an equal place, "at the top."

Some feminists are attempting to discover more about ancient religions that had goddesses as well as gods, priestesses and priests, and strong female imagery (Christ, 1979; 1987).

These religions are now obscured by time and male renderings of history. Peggy Sanday (1981), an anthropologist, hypothesizes that societies that undergo considerable stress from natural or social pressures come to view nature as threatening and to depend for survival on the aggressive acts of men. According to Sanday, these societies tend to view women as dangerous and threatening and tend to worship male deities. They are more concerned with war and destruction than with fertility. Not only are female deities irrelevant to their predominant interest, but they appear to undermine these interests.

In contrast, societies that see nature as beneficent, depend on agriculture, and are centrally concerned with fertility tend to accord women great ritual power and worship female deities. However, all ancient societies that we know about were concerned with fertility. Like our information about other early religions, our knowledge of the position of women

among the Israelites is androcentric. Biblical historian Phyllis Bird argues that historical sources and scholarly interpretations that focus on the activities of males must be understood to be telling only half the story, for the Israelite religion was the religion of women and men. The Hebrew Bible focuses on the national rituals, assemblies of men, pilgrimages, and the liturgical calendar based on men's agricultural production. But, because of the sexual division of labor, women's religious activities were connected with the domestic sphere or were carried out at local shrines. We were exempted from participation in religious practices that would have conflicted with our responsibilities to our families. Cross-cultural studies indicate that we probably engaged in devotions at home, in the company of other women, but these activities were either unknown to men or deemed unworthy of recording. Bird points out that Israelite religion was no different from other religions of the ancient Near East in granting leadership roles to women like Miriam, Deborah, and Hannah, but in restricting supreme priestly authority to men (Bird, 1989).

Origin Myths

Most religions provide a creation myth, which tells of what are thought to be the first humans and how they came to be. The creation myth subscribed to by Jews, Christians, and Muslims, the story of Adam and Eve, is much more, of course, than a tale of the first humans. Like other people's creation myths, it provides a "charter" and a "plan" for relations between people and the supernatural, between women and men, and between humans and nature. We have already discussed some of the implications for women of the Adam and Eve myth in Chapter 1. A myth that tells of the descent of the Iroquois nation from females was recorded by Father Louis Hennepin, a missionary working in New France, 1679–80.

The Varied Creation Stories of Native Americans

The Cherokee say they came from Corn Mother, or Selu, who cut open her breast so that corn could spring forth, giving life to the people. For the Tewa Pueblo people, the first mothers were known as Blue Corn Woman, the summer mother, and White Corn Maiden, the winter mother. The Iroquois believe that they were born into this world from the mud on the back of the Earth, known as Grandmother Turtle. The essentials of life—corn, beans, and squash—were given to them by the Three Sisters. The Iroquois refer to the Three Sisters when giving thanks for food in everyday prayers. The Apache believe that they are descendants of Child of the Water, who was kept safe by his mother, White-Painted Woman, so that he could slay all the monsters and make the world safe for the Apache people. . . . For the Sioux, White Buffalo Calf Woman gave the people the gift of the Pipe, and thus a gift of Truth.

Rayna Green, *Women in American Indian Society* (1992):21

[According to the Western Apache creation myth,] "There was a time when White Painted Woman lived all alone" . . .

> Longing for children, she slept with the Sun and not long after gave birth to Slayer of Monsters, the foremost culture hero. Four days later, White Painted Woman became pregnant by water and gave birth to Born-of-the-Water (also known as Child-of-the-Water). As Slayer of Monsters and Child-of-the-Water). As Slayer of Monsters and Child-of-the-Water matured, White Painted Woman instructed them on how to live. Then they left home and, following her advice, rid the earth of most of its evil. White Painted Woman never became old. When she reached an advanced age, she walked toward the east. After a while, she saw herself coming toward herself. When she came together, there was only one, the young one. Then she was like a young girl all over again. . . .

Quoted in H. Henrietta Stockel,
Women of the Apache Nation: Voices of Truth (1991):5

Females in the Supernatural World

Most forms of religious belief include some conceptualization of a supernatural world that is inhabited by forces with superhuman qualities. These saints, ghosts, and spirits of various sorts are often considered more approachable, and more interested in "ordinary" people, than are the great deities of their religions. Although the formal traditions of Judaism, Christianity, and Islam are monotheistic (believing in a single divinity), the "folk" or "popular" versions of these religious traditions have always included belief in lesser supernatural forces.

Immortal Women: Souls, Saints, and Ghosts. The question of what happens to the soul after death is a critical one. Many people believe that the soul persists, to occupy a place in the supernatural world or to return to life in another body. The latter, called *reincarnation,* as represented in Hinduism and Buddhism, involves belief in an ascending scale of perfection that an individual can climb or descend, through successive lifetimes, depending on how virtuously each life was lived. Individuals are destined to be reborn again and again, to endure the pain of existence, until they reach the pinnacle of perfection, after which they are released. The most virtuous life is one devoted to study, meditation, and unconcern about worldly things (like marriage, children, wealth, and comfort, even eating and sleeping). But women are very unlikely to have the opportunity to pursue a life of study and meditation in Hindu and Buddhist societies. "In Hindu mythology, women came to symbolize the eternal struggle that men must wage between materiality and spirit. Kali (the Goddess) symbolizes the womb, connected with rebirth and consequent illusion and entanglement in the world (Hoch-Smith and Spring, 1978; Mookerjee, 1988).

Christianity and Islam teach direct individual immortality, with the soul experiencing punishment or reward in accordance with the virtues and vices of a single lifetime. These religions strongly espouse the idea that souls are essentially without sex, and that salvation is open to both women and men. Some souls, because of unusual virtue, become saints. They continue to provide blessings for the living who appeal to them. Fiorenza (1979) argues that "the lives of the saints provide a variety of role models for Christian women. What is more important is that they teach that women, like men, have to follow their vocation from God even if this means that they have to go frontally against the ingrained cultural mores and images of women" (ibid.:140).

Many religions believe in the existence of ghosts as opposed to immortal souls. A ghost is someone whose spirit outlasts the physical body for some period. Ghosts are thought to be capable of beneficence, particularly as protectors of their survivors in the family. But if maltreated or forgotten, they are also believed capable of vengeance. Bad luck, sickness, nightmares, and even psychic persecution are often blamed on ghosts. Ghosts differ from saints in that they are interested in their own families and they require appeasement and respect, not veneration (Harrell, 1986).

The family is usually regarded as the proper channel for the satisfaction and control of the dead. This is true of ancestors as well as ghosts. In most ancestor-worshiping societies, however, women do not fare very well in receiving the worship of descendants. In such societies, the significant ancestors usually are male and require male descendants for their worship. The male ancestors of wives, however, are not worshiped by husbands and sons. In the ancestor cults of China, only the mothers of sons are included on the family altars of husbands (Jordan, 1972). In many modern cults, the spirits of women are considered weaker than those of men and not entitled to worship as ancestors (Lewis, 1971).

Despite, or perhaps because of, the poor position of women as ancestors, we figure extensively as ghosts. For example, in a study of a Taiwanese village, a high proportion of the ghosts that were thought to regularly disturb the villagers were divined to be the spirits of women demanding a place on a family altar. These spirits were generally women who had died before being received into a husband's family or whose marital histories featured some irregularity that left them stranded between family altars (Jordan, 1972).

Goddesses. Many people believe that the supernatural world consists of elevated regions inhabited by deities of wider sway than spirits, saints, and ghosts. This cosmos is generally perceived to be inhabited by a number of divine persons paired and grouped in relationships not unlike those found on earth. The Hindu Shiva and Devi, for example, are regarded as the primeval twofold personalization of the Absolute.

The goddess, like the unfettered woman of male fantasies, is often envisaged as a threatening and terrible being. This is the case with the Inuit goddess Sedna. In Hindu mythology, the goddess is dark Kali (see Chapter 1), whose orgiastic dancing brings death and destruction on the world. But when she submits to her husband, Shiva, the goddess becomes beneficent, and her energy is harnessed for good by the rational principle of maleness. In the countryside, however, peasants in the nineteenth century prayed to Kali alone as the good mother: "Though the mother beats the child, . . . the child cries mother, mother, and clings still tighter to her garment. True I cannot see thee, yet I am not a lost child. I still cry mother, mother. All the miseries that I have suffered and I am suffering, I know, O mother, to be your mercy alone" (Eliot, 1962 II:287–88). Tamed and controlled, a goddess may become a great and well-loved figure, worthy of the worship of men as well as women.

Buddhism has sometimes been called an atheistic religion because in its most sophisticated vision of the cosmos, all personality and individual attributes are wholly dissolved into divine unity, Nirvana. However, the religion provides focus for worshipers in figures of Bodhisattvas, personages whose perfection has freed them from mortal life but who choose to remain in a personalized existence in order to be accessible to the appeals of the struggling faithful. The greatest and most popular of all is Avalokitesvara, the Bodhisattva of compassion, who appears as a goddess in one manifestation. Avalokitesvara originated in India but is worshiped in Tibet as Tara, in China as Gaunyin, in Japan as Kwannon, and by other names throughout the Orient. Guanyin is the very quintessence of the compassion of the Buddha. Pregnant women turn to her for help, and she cooperates with mediums seeking communication with ancestors or ghosts.

In the great polytheistic religions of later antiquity, goddesses appear with a variety of powers and attributes. They are patronesses of cities (Athena), of marriage (Hera), and sex (Aphrodite). They are in charge of agriculture (Demeter) and human fertility (Artemis). Isis was an amalgam of female deities of the Mediterranean world, gathering their attributes, powers, and myths into her own cult. She also controlled powers usually attributed to male divinities. She began as a local Egyptian god-dess associated with the cult of Osiris who was both her brother and husband. By Hellenistic times, when the Greeks ruled Egypt, her cult was one of the most popular in the ancient world, promising immortality to its adherents. Women were active participants in the cult of Isis as priestesses, members of religious societies, and donors. However, male participants far outnumbered females, and the chief priesthoods were held by men (Pomeroy, 1975).

In the sixth century B.C.E., Jews returning to the Holy Land from their exile in Babylon enforced their belief in one male divinity, outlawing the worship of all other gods and goddesses. When European pagans became Christians, they turned their backs on the gods and goddesses of the Greek and Roman worlds, reducing them to hollow idols. Some second-century Christians favored endowing the Holy Ghost with a feminine persona, but this impulse was rejected, and all three persons of the Christian Trinity became male or without gender. In the seventh century, the Muslims in their turn rejected the goddesses of their ancient Arabian tribes in favor of the one (male) god.

For most ordinary worshipers, however, monotheistic religions have not entirely excluded the old female deity. For example, the Christians exalted the memory and attributes of Mary, "mother of God (Jesus)," in direct proportion as God himself became increasingly patriarchal (Fiorenza, 1979, 1983). In many respects, Mary seems hardly distinguishable from the great goddesses of the ancient world whom she supplanted. A stranger unacquainted with the formal theology of Catholicism would not hesitate to advance the idea that the great cathedrals and shrines were devoted to the worship of a great goddess (Mâle, 1949).

The Gender of God

Some feminists feel that the social position of women can be enhanced by the worship of a

Isis announces her divine powers and titles in this second-century Greek document found in Asia Minor. This document is a copy of a text from Memphis, Egypt.

The Praises of Isis

Demetrios, the son of Artemidoros, who is also (called) Thraseas, a Magnesian / from (Magnesia on the) Maeander, an offering in fulfillment of a vow to Isis. / he transcribed the following from the stele in Memphis which / stands by the temple of hephaistos:1 I am Isis, // the tyrant 2 of every land; and I was educated by / Hermes, 3 and together with Hermes I invented letters, both the hieroglyphic / and the demotic, in order that the same script should not be used / to write everything. I imposed laws on men, / and the laws which I laid down no one may change. // I am the eldest daughter of Kronos. 4 I am the wi/fe and sister of King Osiris. I am she who discovered (the cultivation of) grain / for men. 5 I am the mother of King Horos. / I am she who rises in the Dog Star. 6 I / am she who is called goddess by women. By me the city of Bubastis 7 // was built. I separated earth from sky. / I designated the paths of the stars. The sun and the moon's / course I laid out. I invented navigation. / I caused the just to be strong. Woman and man I / brought together. For woman I determined that in the tenth month she shall deliver a baby into // the light. I ordained that parents be cherished by their children. / For parents who are cruelly treated / I imposed retribution. / Together with (my) brother Osiris I stopped cannibal/ism. I revealed initiations to men. // I taught (men) to honor the images of the gods. I / established precincts for the gods. The governments of tyrants / I suppressed. I stopped murders. I / compelled women to be loved by men. I / caused the just to be stronger than gold and silver. // I ordained that the true be considered beautiful. / I invented marriage contracts. Languages / I assigned to Greeks and barbarians. I caused the honorable and the shameful / to be distinguished by Nature. 8 I / caused nothing to be more fearful than an oath. He who unjustly / / plotted against others I gave into the hands of his vic/tim. On those who commit unjust acts / I imposed retribution. I ordained that suppliants be pitied. / I honor those who justly defend themselves. / With me the just prevails. Of rivers and winds // and the sea am I mistress. No one becomes famous / without my knowledge. I am the mistress of war. Of the thunder/bolt am I mistress. I calm and stir up the sea. / I am in the rays of the sun. I sit beside the / course of the sun. Whatever I decide, this also is accomplished. // For me everything is right. I free those who are in bonds. I / am the mistress of sailing. The navigable I make unnavigable when/ever I choose. I established the boundaries of cities. / I am she who is called Thesmophoros. 9 The island from the *dep/ths* I brought up into the light. I // conquer Fate. Fate heeds me. / Hail Egypt who reared me.

The Synagogue by Sabina von Steinbach, dating to the early thirteenth century, is one of the sculptures on the south portal of the Strasbourg Cathedral. Little recognition has been given so far to the role of women like von Steinbach as cathedral builders. (Musées de la Ville de Strasbourg)

goddess, and that belief in a female deity would give religion more usefulness and meaning. This position has been taken by such leading theologians and feminists as Mary Daly (1973), Carol Christ (1979, 1989), and Naomi Goldenberg (1979). They believe that the image of the deity we worship is important to our understanding and appreciation of ourselves. In patriarchal religions, divinity is male; hence, men see an image of themselves in the divine, while women are denied this identification with divinity.

The goddess symbol that is being created for the contemporary woman is, for some, an inspiring reaction to the repression of patriarchal monotheistic religions. The goddess symbol means above all "an affirmation of the legitimacy and beneficence of female power." The goddess is not limited to the female symbolism of good and evil as represented by Mary and Eve but is (1) "divine female, a personification who can be invoked in prayer and ritual; (2) the Goddess is symbol of the life, death, and rebirth energy in nature and culture, in personal and communal life; and (3) the Goddess is symbol of the affirmation of the legitimacy and beauty of female power" (Christ, 1979:278). She is very much like Isis. Female spiritual leaders, such as Starhawk, have prophesied the dawning of a new religion: feminist witchcraft. Witchcraft is the first modern theistic religion to conceive of its deity, the Goddess, mainly as an internal set of images and attitudes (Goldenberg, 1979). Most modern witches use the Old English term *wicca*, meaning "wise woman." Witches use a goddess concept to give women positive self-images in all stages of life: maiden, mother, and crone (Goldenberg, 1979). The wicca are developing rituals and designing ceremonies around the symbolism of womanhood. The woman god appears at all stages and situations in a positive light, shedding the demeaning attributes that patriarchal religions have given to her. According to modern proponents of feminist witchcraft, the image of woman elevated in the symbolism of the goddess will have a positive effect on real women (Starhawk, 1979).

Starhawk, founder of two covens in San Francisco, California, is a licensed minister of the covenant of the Goddess, a legally recognized church. She suggests that patriarchal or monotheistic religions that assert laws of heaven "have brought us to a point at which our chances of destroying ourselves and poisoning the biosphere seem much greater than our chances of preserving life into the future" (Starhawk, 1979: 416). Therefore, she says, the evolving Goddess religions, "include regarding divinity as imminent: in the world, not outside the world, as manifest in nature and in human beings, human needs and desires" (ibid.). And we consider ourselves "as a true part of the fabric of life" and of nature; and thus, we wish to preserve and conserve life (ibid.:417). For that reason, making choices about preserving life become ethical choices. Then, you will ask, how about our stand about abortion? For the point of view of Starhawk, and we believe, of many other feminists, see **Starhawk's Views on Abortion**).

Mythologists have sometimes argued that the rule of a great goddess in the early periods of human civilization was reflected on earth by a matriarchy (see Stone, 1979, for arguments in favor of this belief). In periods for which we have historical documentation, cults and sects that accorded the deity a female nature, in part or in whole, accorded women an active position in religious practices concerning the deity. The six Vestal Virgins who were devoted to the cult of Vesta in ancient Rome were respected and provided with special honors by their social peers, but they were subject to the authority of the Pontifex Maximus (chief priest). Although the few women selected to serve as priestesses for such cults might have enjoyed a higher status than secular women, it has not been possible to estab-

The "Venus" of Willendorf, as this prehistoric figurine has been called, is taken as a prototype of the neolithic goddesses. Faceless, with an elaborate headdress and exaggerated breasts, thighs, and buttocks, she has been interpreted as a fertility goddess. This figurine, carved from stone, sometime between 25,000 B.C.E. and 20,000 B.C.E., is only 4⅜ inches high. Others, also small, were made in ivory, clay, and other materials. Their actual purposes are not known. (Austrian Institute)

Starhawk's Views on Abortion

The issue that comes to mind here is abortion. While the so-called "right-to-life" movement tries to pose this question as one involving the rights of fetuses, Goddess religion recognizes that to value life as an untempered absolute is ridiculous—it is to maintain the right of every cancer cell to reproduce blindly, of every sperm and every egg to unite a new embryo, of every flea and cockroach to populate the world endlessly. Life is interwoven in a dance of death, the limiting factor that sustains the possibility of new life. The predator is as necessary to an ecological balance as the prey—because it is the richness and diversity of the interplay between species that manifests the Goddess.

Human life is valuable and sacred when it is the freely given gift of the Mother—through the human mother. To bear new life is a grave responsibility, requiring a deep commitment— one which no one can force on another. To coerce a woman by force or fear or guilt or law or economic pressure to bear an unwanted child is the height of immorality. It denies her right to exercise her own sacred will and conscience, robs her of her humanity, and dishonors the Goddess manifest in her being. The concern of the antiabortion forces is not truly with the preservation of life, it is with punishment for sexuality. If they were genuinely concerned with life, they would be protesting the spraying of our forests and fields with pesticides known to cause birth defects. They would be working to shut down nuclear power plants and dismantle nuclear weapons, to avert the threat of widespread genetic damage which may plague *wanted* children for generations to come—if there are generations to come.

(Starhawk, 1979:420)

lish any necessary correlation between the worship of goddesses and the status of women in ancient societies (Pomeroy, 1984). Nevertheless, the presence of a goddess or quasi-goddess in a religious system has the psychological value of providing women with a role model and an object for supplication. On the other hand, such figures can be employed as models to confine the ambitions of women.

Some gods are thought to incite enthusiastic female worship and appear to prefer female devotees. Dionysus, Krishna, and Jesus have all been particularly venerated by women. Dionysus liberated some of the frustrated and confined women of ancient Greece periodically with ecstatic experiences of dancing and frenzied activity. Krishna, who is often represented as a baby, is associated with a sect of female worshipers who call themselves "Mothers of God" (Freeman, 1980). As young men, all three gods are represented as attractive and loving of women, posing in their lives as our protectors. They continue to attract the warm affection of women in their apotheosized state.

The position of goddesses in polytheistic societies varies widely, as did the positions of women in ancient Egypt, Athens, and Rome. Similarly, there is such wide variation in the position of women in monotheistic societies that it becomes difficult to generalize about the influence of women's roles on beliefs about the gender of God and vice versa. Not everyone is convinced, then, that we need a female deity to improve the status and position of women in our society, or that belief in such a deity would support that goal.

Religion and Social Controls

Religion provides more than the imagery by which we can conceptualize the supernatural world. It provides a basis for a code of ethics to govern human conduct. In highly organized religions, clergy and other specialists interpret and sometimes enforce a code of ethics grounded in religious belief. But all religious systems have some means for exerting control over human conduct.

Family Cults and Controls

As the kinship/family group lies at the base of society, so does it lie at the social base of religion. In addition, however, community codes and ceremonies strengthen the authority of the kinship groups, usually the authority of the head of the family, and train each generation's successors, whether female or male offspring.

Life-Cycle Rituals. As we have already seen, the family provides the framework within which women are confined and socialized. Public performance of rituals during the life cycle, for example at puberty, marriage, and death, enhance the power of the family, the relationships considered proper for its members, and the control of those individuals in accordance with the decorum of the community. In traditional Greek society from antiquity to the present, death rituals have been almost entirely the responsibility of women. Of course, women in such a society have always been freer than men to show their emotions. In addition, because a woman's self-definition is exclusively as a member of a family, she may actually feel the loss more deeply. In Greece women bathe the corpse, wear black to announce their mourning, and, in some areas, make daily hour-long visits to the grave for five years. They tend the grave as they had tended the family member when alive, bring-

ing flowers, scrubbing the grave, lighting candles and lamps so the dead can see. When they visit the grave they believe they are keeping the dead company and perpetuate their roles as wife or mother, not saying, "I am going to visit my son's grave," but rather, "I am going to visit my son" (Danforth, 1982). For men, life-cycle rituals are usually occasions that help to define and enhance their potency and social power as they advance toward full adult membership in the community. The major life-cycle rituals for Jewish males, for example, are the *brith millah*, the circumcision ritual of eight-day-old infant boys, which provides them with a physical identity as Jews, and the *bar mitzvah*, the ritual of first participation in adult study and prayer, which marks the entry of a thirteen-year-old boy into the community of adults. For infant girls, there is no equivalent of the *brith*, but for Conservative and Reform Jews there is a girls' equivalent to the *bar mitzvah*, a *bat mitzvah*. Unlike the *bar mitzvah*, the *bat mitzvah* is not essential to girls' membership in the Jewish community, nor does it mark our "coming of age" in the traditional sense.

In patriarchal, patrilineal societies, the most important life-cycle ritual or rite of passage for women is likely to be the wedding ceremony. This marks the major transition from our families of birth to our husbands' families. Since divorce for women may be difficult or even impossible in such societies, women are likely to undergo this ceremony only once. It may last for days, preceded by months of preparation and preliminary rituals. In Western societies, weddings have traditionally spotlighted the bride. They are our one and only major ritual role. Neither menarche nor childbirth (unless it is the birth of a royal son and heir) are accompanied by equivalent attention.

This is not the case in several matrilineal societies. Marriage does not substantially alter women's social position, since we remain in our own matrilineage for life. If there is a major life cycle ritual, it is likely to be associated with menarche, when we become of reproductive age, ready to contribute new members of the matrilineage. A good example is the *chisungu* ceremony of the matrilineal Bemba, a large and complex society of Zimbabwe. Periodically, all the girls of a district whose first menstruation has occurred since the last *chisungu* participate in the month-long ceremony. The initiates are honored by the whole community; the women sing and dance before these girls, and parents, fiancés, and prospective in-laws contribute to the expenses of the ceremonial feasting.

During the complex ceremony of initiation, the Bemba girls pass through several role changes, beginning with separation and seclusion, physical degradation (such as being prohibited from bathing), and testing for strength and courage. The ritual ends with reentry and renewal. After initiation, the girls are believed to be protected from any ill effects of menstruation, prepared for marriage and reproduction, related to other women in a new, more intimate way, and newly knowledgeable about the role requirements of women (Richards, 1956).

Female circumcision (removal of the clitoris and/or labia minora) is prevalent in East Africa, particularly in the Muslim nations of Sudan and Egypt, and in Christian Ethiopia. It is also found in West Africa. Feminists within these countries as well as elsewhere have condemned this genital mutilation of women as an odious and oppressive custom. Unlike the circumcision of boys, it is not dignified with religious prescription. Instead of being a mark of honor, it is intended to keep women from becoming sexually active before marriage and from enjoying our sexuality when married. African American novelist Alice Walker has explored this issue (1992).

Feminist critics of Western religious systems have favored the establishment of a meaningful life-cycle ritual for women in connection with menarche. Theologian Penelope Washbourne believes that such a ritual would help young women deal with our ambivalent feelings about menstruation and achieve our new adult identities.

> Experiencing menstruation creatively is of immense importance, for it lays the foundation for resolving the next life crises which have to do with personal selfhood and expressing sensuality to others. A woman will be unable to experience menstruation gracefully unless the family and community provide a context within which the graceful and demonic elements of life crisis may be expressed and her new identity as a woman is celebrated. Perhaps in a time of secular culture it is the role of the immediate family and friends to provide that context in a ritual and symbolic form, since it is from them that a woman learns her sense of what is ultimately valuable in the first place. (Washbourne, 1979:257)

Sexual Controls. For women, life-cycle rituals are often constraining. They are intended to control and inhibit our power and remind us of the limits of our expectations. At puberty in most cultures, the freedom we might have enjoyed as little girls is sharply curtailed. We may be told that we are unclean and must learn to control the possible ill effects of our polluted nature. At the same time, we may be schooled in the hard facts of our vulnerability, both to public censure and physical attack. The leaders of every major literate religion in the world have produced literature against the sexuality of women. Representatives of the major religious hierarchies have continually urged women to contain ourselves within the narrow limits of our homes and the narrower limits of female modesty and decorum, threatening us with both earthly and eternal punishments for the sins of our "nature."

The most effective method of controlling the dangers represented by women's sexuality is to ensure that we are kept under the authority of our male kin. Patriarchal religions offer a chief (or only) god as role model for the father of the family. At puberty, men are proclaimed mature and ready to undertake public responsibilities. Many societies begin a process of weakening the control of the father over his son at this point to free the son for service in the greater community. Women, however, are not released from our fathers' power; rather, fathers are given the right to hand us over to the power of a husband. This right to "give" a daughter in marriage has been, until recently, the sovereign right of the father. Even in Christian societies that defended the individual's right of consent to marriage, the economic dependency of daughters usually made us subject to paternal authority.

Religious laws in patriarchal societies often protect men from the "dangers" of pollution inherent in close proximity to women during our menstrual periods. In the Koran, the sacred book of Islam, men are ordered to sepa-rate themselves from their wives until we have taken the ritual bath at the end of the menstrual period (Delaney et al., 1976). The same religious proscription on sexual relations between husband and wife applies to Orthodox Jews. Such laws reinforce women's own fears about menstruation and undermine our self-esteem by labeling us as periodically "unclean."

The codes of most religions urge husbands to use their authority prudently. They warn of the damage that may be caused to a family by the despair of unhappy women. They remind men of the blessings of a home cared for by a contented wife. But while men are subjected to moral suasion, women are subjected to physical coercion. The Koran instructs husbands on how to ensure the right behavior in their wives: "Say to the believers, that they cast down their eyes and guard their private parts; that is purer for them" (XXIV:30) (Ar-berry, 1955). Nearly every written religious code is based on double-standard morality. Christianity, whose rhetoric consistently

In the first communion ceremony, little girls traditionally dress up with finery suggestive of bridal rituals. (Photo by Jean Shapiro)

states that what is not allowed to women is not allowed to men either, has never made wide practical application of the rule.

Protection of Women

Religious laws generally offer some protection to the obedient weakling. While they justify authority and preach obedience, they also restrain human authority in the name of a higher power and teach men the limits on their insubordinate will.

In this spirit, Jewish, Christian, and Islamic laws are concerned with the economic responsibilities of men toward their wives and daughters. The rights of women to dowries, inheritance, and other economic protections are spelled out carefully. Arbitrary divorce is discouraged, and polygyny is regulated to ensure the rights of co-wives. Catholic canon law sanctifies the consensual basis of marriage and protects wives from repudiation by husbands. It defines rape as a crime of violence against women and denies men the right to kill their wives. All the "peoples of the Book" are urged to protect and support widows and orphans and to treat moral and observant women with respect and kindness.

Within that framework, religion acts to establish and enforce the norms of family life. Sexual relationships between wife and husband resulting in the birth of children are universally viewed as divinely ordained. Deviation from that pattern is sometimes considered immoral and sometimes violently punished. Christianity and Buddhism, which were initially relatively antipathetic to sexual activity and procreation, gradually modified and shifted their positions. By the seventh century A.D., the exclusivity of the monastic route to salvation for the Buddhists had given way to the growing popularity of Mahayana, a variant of Buddhism emphasizing the values of marriage, sexual and parental love, and familial virtue. This route was considered particularly appropriate for women.

Public Cults and Controls

Outside the religious activities of the family, most societies engage in a wider set of ceremonies, celebrations, and rituals devoted to the deities worshiped in the community. These require the services of a professional and trained clergy who enjoy the accoutrements of public art and architecture, conduct time-consuming and often occult rituals (sometimes in a language unknown to the laity), and make use of an extensive tradition of myth and law to enforce their social authority.

Women as Worshipers. Nearly all religions encourage, indeed command, the active participation of women as worshipers. But even as worshipers, we are subjected to a variety of restrictions. Lay participation in the performance of rituals is usually restricted to men.

Nowadays, except in Orthodox Judaism, Jewish women are counted in the *minyan*, the quorum of ten required for the conduct of certain services. Until very recently, there were no female altar servers in Roman Catholic churches. And yet, any traveler in a Catholic country must be struck by the idea of the church as "woman's space." It may be dominated by an all-male hierarchy, but every day the women spend hours there in devotion and conversation with one another. Even from the earliest times, Christian moralists have complained about women's habit of using the church as a social center. Similarly, the shrines of Sufi saints are centers where Islamic women meet daily for rest and relaxation and to confide in the sympathetic saint (Fernea and Fernea, 1972). Underneath the restrictive and apparently prohibitive structure of the great religions is the elusive, often undocumented world of women.

Popular Religions. On the fringes of the "established religions" are hosts of *syncretistic* religions, each of which combines elements from a variety of others. They flourish today as they have throughout history. For the sake of simplicity, we shall restrict our discussion to a small sample of groups found in the Americas today. However, the findings of historians and anthropologists bear ample witness to the presence of similar "popular" religions throughout the world.

Many syncretistic religions have spun off from Catholicism. The black leaders of the ancestor religions of the Caribbean see no contradiction between their beliefs and Catholicism. Indeed, they maintain that the one is not possible without the other (Simpson, 1978). Women outnumber men four to one in these religions and are the principal dancers in the Shango and Big Drum sects. Similarly, the women of Haiti dominate the popular religions there, even though we are excluded from men's groups in that society.

A study of black religious sects in America has shown that contrary to dominant belief, these women believers are not salvation-oriented (Simpson, 1978). In these sects, we can therefore afford to be indifferent to the sacraments in such cults as Vodun, to continue to speak of ourselves as Catholic and never question church dogmas, because we are, like so many rebellious "Catholics" the world over, anticlerical.

In North America, where the dominant form of Christianity has generally been Protestant, Mambo and other African cults have been syncretized to particular sects, principally variants of Baptist (Simpson, 1978). In these groups, women often emerge as preachers and leaders. Women are also prominent among the Quakers and other nonhierarchical dissenting sects. Women assume much more important places in both leadership and participation in dissenting and popular religions, than in established ones, whether or not we see ourselves as opponents to established authority. In the United States women comprise 75 to 90 percent of the participants in the activities of black churches. In some denominations of the Sanctified Church women are equal to men. In the Pentecostal Assemblies

of the World, women may offer communion and perform marriages. Even in the denominations that prohibit the ordination of women, they exercise a powerful influence through Women's Departments. Women's economic contribution and role in education and community work are essential to the survival of these churches, and women's expression of spirituality is likewise central to their theology.

Women as Religious Leaders

Only rarely do women enjoy the authority of clergy, and when we do our range of activities is usually restricted. The most highly organized religions welcome women clergy the least. Thus, in Catholicism, the clergy has not only been restricted to men but only to celibate men since the eleventh century. Eastern Christianity (the Greek and Russian Orthodox churches) allows women to marry priests but not to be ordained ourselves. Only very recently have a number of women been ordained in some of the larger, institutionalized Protestant churches.

Women tend to emerge as ministers in sects that do not control their clergy and that depend on genuine spontaneous religious emotion, as opposed to a weighty establishment supported by endowments and state cooperation. Thus, the loosely organized pentecostal or evangelical sects are frequently ministered by women.

Women have customarily been kept from the rabbinate. Since Jewish girls are not required by religious law to study the Scriptures and sacred texts as boys are, it has only been the exceptional Jewish woman who has qualified, in the past, for the specialized learning of the rabbi. However, Judaism, like Protestant Christianity, lacks a single central hierarchy, so it allows for a proliferation of congregations of varying opinions on matters of administration and discipline. In Conservative and Reform Judaism, the predominant forms in the United States, female rabbis are now ordained. Islam, like Judaism, has no formal clergy and no "church" hierarchy. Professional mullahs and ayatollahs in the Shiite branch along with other teachers and prayer leaders serve many of the functions of clergy, such as officiating at marriage and funeral rites and interpreting customary law. Women are not numbered among these revered individuals. The conventions of purdah (segregation of women) and veiling severely restrict Muslim women from participating in services and prayers with men, not to mention leading them. These same conventions have in some places given rise to a class of female mullahs whose job is to minister to women, to teach the rudiments of the Koran, and to conduct rituals with women at home.

Shamans

Women excel at ritual and spiritual services connected with nurturance and healing. In folk traditions around the world, both in the countryside and in the cities, women have served our communities as curers and midwives. These traditional arts are generally thought to have a supernatural or spiritual component as well as a practical one. Both illness and childbirth are widely viewed as spiritually dangerous states. Curers, generally termed *shamans*, are active in societies where it is believed that illness—or certain types of illness—is caused by supernatural agency. Both curers and midwives are thought to have esoteric knowledge about how to fend off or appease threatening supernatural beings. Traditional curers of this sort need not be exclusively female, but they often are, and midwifery almost everywhere is a women's profession.

To cure an illness, the shaman often enters a trance state, during which she (or he) communicates with the spirit world for assistance in the restoration of health. For example, in parts of southern Mexico, people believe that a traumatic experience of some sort may cause the victim's soul to leave the body, where it is snatched by an underground spirit, Nahual. As a result, the victim experiences sleeplessness, headaches, and general malaise. To cure this illness, the victim must obtain the services of a shaman, who knows how to speak to the spirit and convince it to release the victim's soul. Family members, neighbors, and even passersby witness and participate in the curing ceremony. They listen sympathetically to the victim's recounting of the terrible experience and support the curer as, together, they vanquish fear and evil.

The curer, the midwife, and the medium (who puts her clients in touch with departed souls) all have a nurturing, supportive relationship to clients, unlike the often nonpersonal and authoritarian relationships that male physicians and priests tend to have with those who come to them for help. Yet curers, midwives, and mediums can be professionals too, often devoting years of training to such careers (Hoch-Smith and Spring, 1978).

Among American Indians, women as shamans perform healings, hunting ceremonies, and create artifacts, such as baskets, ornaments, talismans. They officiate at burials, births, child namings, and menstrual and pregnancy rituals. The shamans perform these rites through dancing and chanting, as well as songs they sing and stories they tell. Native American Indian women writers reflect in fiction and poetry the woman shaman's connection to the spirit world (Allen, 1988). One such work is a novel, *The Woman Who Owned the Shadows* by Paula Gunn Allen (1983), and another is *Ceremony* by Leslie Marmon Silko (1977).

Women play these spiritual roles in vastly different sorts of societies, from South Africa to north Florida, from Southeast Asia to Latin America. Some feminist authors have deplored the loss of these roles among the middle class and wealthy women of the Western world as the healing professions have been

One of the consequences of the modern women's liberation movement has been the assertion by women of leadership roles in large-scale religions.
(Opposite top) The Rev. Ellen Barrett, first declared lesbian ordained an Episcopal priest, January 10, 1977. (Photo by Bettye Lane)
(Opposite bottom) Sally Priesand, the first woman to be ordained a rabbi, June 2, 1972. (Photo by Terry H. Layman)
(Above) The Rev. Pauli Murray, first black woman ordained an Episcopal priest, January 8, 1977. (Photo by Susan Mullally Weil)

"Without a husband I shall live happily"

According to folk tales dating to the early seventeenth century, the Nisan Shaman was a young widow who dutifully took care of her mother-in-law and her domestic duties. But she had a far-reaching reputation for her ability to communicate with the dead and bring them back to life. She had a lover who assisted her in her seances. On one ghostly journey, she met her deceased husband who begged her for resurrection. She refused, saying:

"Without a husband
I shall live happily.
Without a man
I shall live proudly.
Among mother's relatives
I shall live enjoyably.
Facing the years
I shall live cheerfully.
Without children
I shall live on.
Without a family
I shall live lovingly.
Pursuing my own youth,
I shall live as a guest."

(Durrant, 1979:345–46)

From "The Nishan Shaman Caught in Cultural Contradictions" by Stephen Durrant, *Signs* (1979). Copyright © 1979 by The University of Chicago Press. Reprinted by permission of The University of Chicago Press.

---

gradually taken over by men (Ehrenreich and English, 1979). Herbalists, midwives, and other sorts of woman healers have often been classed with fraudulent mediums by professional clergy and professional male healers, whose reasons for doing so may involve a defense of their professional (and male) monopoly.

Missionaries and Martyrs

The great religions of the world, distinguished by monumental places of worship, professional clergy, written literature, and a large following, reflect the institutionalized worlds of men. But the great religions started as popular religions, often as sects of rebels against a greater system, as the Christians within the Roman Empire, or the Buddhists in India. They have all known periods of danger and persecution; they have all entered into periods of struggle to win recognition for themselves. During these times, women often played significant roles.

Where the role of a missionary is dangerous and the reward often death, women have found favorable conditions for the expression of our zeal and spirit of adventure. Women were welcomed into the original Buddhist fellowships for our missionary contributions but were later restricted as the religion became established and more secure (Carmody, 1979).

Women have enjoyed a long and honorable history in Christian missions. The Samaritan woman whom Jesus sent to spread news of his coming among her people might be called the first of all Christian missionaries. In the conversion of Europe, Christian queens opened the way for priests and monks by marrying pagan kings and converting them; the most famous of these was Clotilda, wife of Clovis, King of the Franks at the beginning of the sixth century A.D. Modern Christian missionary women tend to fall under the control and supervision of men: Catholic nuns by supervisory priests and Protestant missionaries by husbands, male relatives, or male mission heads.

If women are welcomed by churches as missionaries, how much more welcome we are when a religion is in need of martyrs. Every religion that seeks converts has produced its martyrs, and all too often the blood and mutilation of women have seemed to constitute the most persuasive testimony of faith. Such instances are traditionally held up to Catholic girls, for example, as part of our religious education.

Religious Rebels

In the early centuries of Christianity, women were active in heretical movements such as Montanism and Gnosticism. As historian Jo Ann McNamara explains, our participation in these movements arose from social rather than intellectual motives. Women saw in early Christianity a vehicle for liberation, for activity on a broader scale than was offered by the traditional homebound destiny. Some of us rebelled against versions of Christianity that imposed restrictions on women (McNamara, 1983).

In the major religious rebellions in Europe in the sixteenth century, Protestant churches freed themselves from the authority of the pope and his orthodox establishment. In the process, women again took an active part as defenders and preachers of both new and old religions. But Catholics and Protestants alike were alarmed by the apparent assumption on the part of women that the new conditions would offer us a broader field of activity. Both acted to put an end to the threat. Catholic women like Angela Medici and Mary Ward who thought the time was ripe for a more active public role for nuns were severely disciplined. Protestant women like Anne Askew were executed for thinking that the priesthood of all believers urged by Luther and his contemporaries included women (Dickens, 1964).

The late medieval period in Europe had also been a time of great social upheaval. From the fifteenth century on, women were perceived to be behaving in a variety of eccentric and unconventional ways. An outstanding example from the early fifteenth century was Joan of Arc, who led troops of French soldiers against the invading English armies. The English burned her at the stake as a heretic and witch, but the French supported her memory as a martyr, and she was finally canonized by the Catholic church.

Historians have recently been attempting to reinterpret the great witch-hunt in Western Europe in the light of work of anthropologists on witchcraft in other cultures. The accused witches in eastern England, southwestern Germany, and Switzerland, for example, seem to have been the same sort of women accused in Africa and elsewhere outside Europe: old women, deprived of the protection of husbands or sons, living on the risky margins of society. These were the women who irritated and angered neighbors with efforts to gain assistance and ill-tempered cursing of the ungenerous.

Another theory, advanced by Margaret Murray (1967) and made popular recently by some modern feminists, is that there really was a witch religion to which large numbers of common people, including Joan of Arc, subscribed. Although much of Murray's evidence has not withstood scholarly scrutiny, we do know that under the apparently monolithic facade of the medieval church, there was a world of popular religion. Wise women de-

The Trial of Joan of Arc

Joan of Arc, at the instigation of "voices" sent by God, took up arms against the English occupation of France. Her military victories against the English began the process of ultimate French victory in the Hundred Years War. She was captured by the English and tried. Her prosecutors dwelt particularly on her insistence on wearing male clothing:

"Your have said that, by God's command, you have continually worn man's dress, . . . that you have also worn your hair short, cut *en rond* [a "bowl" cut] above your ears, with nothing left that could show you to be a woman; and that on many occasions you received the Body of our Lord dressed in this fashion, although you have been frequently admonished to leave it off, which you have refused to do, saying that you would rather die than leave it off, save by God's command. And you said further that if you were still so dressed and with the king and those of his party, it would be one of the greatest blessings for the kingdom of France; and you have said that not for anything would you take an oath not to wear this dress or carry arms; and concerning all these matters you have said that you did well, and obediently to God's command."

(Scott, 1968:156) Reprinted by permission.

voted to healing and prophesying flourished, not unlike the female curers and shamans found in Catholic countries in Latin America today. The popular religion of the Middle Ages was full of vestiges of paganism, rituals, incantations, herbalism, and magic, both beneficial and malevolent. The medieval church systematically dealt with that religion in a successful manner. The harmless and beneficial practices of the country people were "Christianized"; for example, incantations to old goddesses were retained with the names of Christian saints substituted. The demons of Hell were reduced to mischief makers of limited intelligence and minimal power.

Another set of theories associates witchcraft with heresy. In this view, the sixteenth-century belief in demon worshipers, and witch churches with covens, sabbaths, "black masses," and other paraphernalia of witchcraft developed as a result of the mentality of the Spanish Inquisition and the fear of women that the Protestant Reformation awoke.

There may indeed have been witch cults. One or two such groups have been uncovered.

The women may have been religious visionaries or sexual nonconformists, antisocial rebels of one sort or another. These witches may have been women who had seized upon the illusion of religious and moral freedom that the Reformation seemed to offer, only to learn that the leaders of the new churches were no more welcoming than had been those of the old.

Religion and Individual Fulfillment

We have seen that while women have made many dramatic and effective accommodations to the restraints placed on us by organized religion our participation is often viewed by men as a marginal activity. Religion is simply one of the most universal and distinctive of human activities, and women are human in every way. We are subject to all the multiplicity of impulses, emotions, and inquiries that lead men to faith. In this sense, religion is necessary to many women for reasons of pure individual satisfaction.

Some women, particularly in patriarchal monotheistic religions, seek individual fulfill-

A Moroccan Story

One day two old ladies decided to invoke the Devil and persuade him to part with some of his magic secrets. So they pretended to quarrel, for it is well known that the devil appears whenever there is a dispute. "I am sure that the Devil must be dead," said one old woman. "And I am sure that he is not; what makes you say such a silly thing?" retorted the other, and they went on arguing furiously. The Devil was very flattered to be the subject of their argument and he decided to make himself visible. "Indeed, I am very much alive—here I am!" he said, appearing before the two old ladies. "How can we be sure that you are really the Devil?" asked one shrewdly. "You must prove it to us by doing something extraordinary. Let's see you squeeze yourself into a sugar bowl," added the other. "Easy!" said the Devil and he slipped into the bowl. As soon as he was inside the old ladies put the lid on and held it down firmly. "Let me out and I will do you a good turn," begged the Devil. "How can you do that, Father of Evil?" demanded the old women. "I shall teach you how to dominate men," he replied, and so he did. And that is why witches are feared everywhere to this day, especially by men.

(Epton, 1958:44) Reprinted by permission.

ment in a greater union with God by means of a life of prayer and meditation. These women seem to compensate for our exclusion from the religious hierarchy and our ignorance of occult languages and rituals by developing a more personal, idiosyncratic approach to religion.

One Yemenite Jewish woman said her mother never suffered from not learning Hebrew: "My mother says what she wants to God." Similarly, the Muslim saint Leila Mimouna, illiterate like most of her sisters, said, "Mimouna knows God and God knows Mimouna" (Fernea and Bezirgan, 1977:197). Barred from the study of theology even after Protestantism had made the Scriptures available in the languages of its adherents, women used the vehicle of the novel, poetry, or the popular hymn to make religious statements. See, for example, the poetry of Phillis Wheatley.

Mysticism

Mysticism is the most personal and individualistic expression of religion. The mystic en-gages in intense self-examination and simultaneous rejection of the perceived world in which she or he lives, and moves through the state of pain and disorientation to an altered state of consciousness, a sense of liberation and illumination of the cosmos that release her or his confidence, energy, and creativity. Women mystics have sometimes become authors and painters, the founders of female orders, and prophets (Bynum, 1982). In the formal religions of men, women mystics have become saints, exalted into the realms beyond gender.

The rhetoric of mysticism is the rhetoric of romantic love, sometimes in its most intense sexual form. Mystics with a biblical background frequently express the intensity of their experience in the language of the Song of Songs, a section of the Hebrew Scriptures which, as noted in Chapter 1, some authorities have speculated may have been written by a woman. The Bride's cry, "Oh, I am sick with love!" describes the sense that both female and male mystics have that some higher power has ravished them from their senses. This is rhetoric that comes easily to the pens of women mystics and even authors of devotional literature. Mysticism is the one area of religion where women have been unequivocally considered to be equal to men.

Possession

The popular religions of the poor, marginal, and alienated make their mystics the visionaries of ecstasy cults and the mediums of "possession" sects. The possessed woman may be regarded as holy or as unclean, depending on circumstances. Possessed women may become shamans; or we may be thought to be diseased by an infesting spirit whose purpose is malicious, a spirit that is an enemy of the recognized deities of the group. Women who are thus possessed often have reason to complain of our circumstances in the first place. We are frequently the victims of an exogamous marital situation, vulnerable to hostile charges of witchcraft when misfortune strikes any member of our husbands' kin, as well as vulnerable to repudiation, isolation, and lack of support.

Possession has been found, sometimes in mass outbreaks, among women in every area of the world. Possession tends to afflict alienated people who are responding to the strains of oppression. It is an experience that is guaranteed to gain attention for a discontented woman. And it provides a vehicle for revenge against an oppressive husband, co-wife, mother-in-law, or, in the case of nuns, father confessor (Simpson, 1978).

Possession serves a variety of purposes for the possessed. First of all, it frees women from the guilt associated with rebellion and also from responsibility for antisocial behavior. We can say and do things that would never be permitted if we were in control of ourselves. Where the religious structure is not too rigid or highly controlled, possession gives women access to real cultic power. Many of the possessed women are believed to gain sufficient

control over spirits to have the ability to work healing magic, divination, or other powerful spells. Such women are particularly useful in curing similarly afflicted women. For many women, possession, like mysticism, has proven to be the first stage of a liberating experience that culminated in a more active life of social service and reform (Simpson, 1978).

The male establishment tends carefully to control possessed behavior. The mechanics of exorcism, for example, often involve much physical abuse of the possessed women (to guard against faking). The saint is never far from accusations of malicious witchcraft or heresy. Like Joan of Arc, saints will be allowed to obey "voices" only up to the point where established authorities are not discomfited. But the dominating powers are generally willing to allow some latitude to these strong spirits to avert a more general social disruption. Thus female cults, like some of the more expressive churches organized by black prophets in America, are often on the edge between the socially acceptable role of releasing strong emotions and the socially unacceptable role of revolution.

In modern countries where religion is effectively separated from the state, women enjoy a fairly wide opportunity to participate in religious sects of our own devising. Women who have been excluded from positions of active leadership in more formal religions have been welcomed into spiritualist and pentecostal sects that emphasize the individual experience of grace above the organized ministry. The testimony of grace is an experience invaluable to many women. Amanda Smith, a young African American woman who was a former slave, testified at a camp meeting that the experience of grace freed her from reticence, her fear of whites, and her fear of men and enabled her to begin preaching and speaking of her own experience with confidence (Hardesty et al., 1979).

American Women and Religion

The formal separation between church and state in the United States has not prevented special forms of dialogue between religious organizations and the government. Religious groups committed to major social reforms have spearheaded important political and legal changes; other religious groups, more conservative in orientation, have provided focal points for resistance and reaction. It has been largely through our participation in religious groups, rather than in government itself, that women have had a strong voice in political processes. In particular, feminism, with its call for women's rights and its role in other legislative reforms (most notably abolition of slavery and suffrage), has had a significant impact on the history of religion in America.

Leadership by Women

Protestant Denominations. Women emerged as religious leaders and reformers early in American history, in the notoriously intolerant context of colonial New England. Anne Hutchinson, a Puritan woman of Massachusetts Bay Colony, was banished for her refusal to stop preaching her doctrine of salvation by grace alone. In 1638, she was driven out of Massachusetts with her husband and children and was excommunicated from the Puritan community in Boston. She led her followers to Rhode Island, where she helped to establish a new colony and pursued her evangelical ministry. Finally, she migrated yet again to Long Island, New York, where she and her family were killed by Indians. Her friend Mary Dyer, who supported her throughout her trials in Massachusetts, died on the gallows in 1660 for defending the Quakers who had begun to preach in the colony, and for refusing to accept banishment (Dunn, 1979).

The Quakers, or Society of Friends, believed in the equality of all people, including the equality of women and men. They op-

posed settlement on lands claimed by Indians and particularly opposed the institution of slavery. Despite the hostility of the colonies to Quakerism, the movement spread. Nearly half the Quaker missionaries were women, mostly traveling without husbands, and often with other women. They continued to travel and do missionary work through the seventeenth century (Dunn, 1979). In these early years, while numbers of women's "meetings" (congregations) were established, there was some difference of opinion on how strong they should be or even how legitimate they were. Some women's meetings deferred to men; others were quite assertive of their autonomy and conducted their own affairs. When permanent meetinghouses were built, it became common to construct a building to house both women and men, who sat on separate sides. A partition down the center was open for worship but closed for the conduct of their separate business (ibid.).

Quaker women's experience in the organization of religious meetings provided training in the public arena that few women of colonial or postcolonial times had an opportunity to gain. The "Friends" became accustomed to public speaking, to creating organizational structures, and to feeling equal to others. Quakers were disproportionately represented among American women abolitionists, feminists, and suffragists (Dunn, 1979). The Grimke sisters and Lucretia Coffin Mott (1793–1880) are among the most famous of these women in the nineteenth century.

Although Lucretia Mott grew up as a Quaker, she held her own convictions on social reforms, not limited by the views of more traditional Quakers. For example, she was a radical abolitionist, whereas many Quakers preferred gradual emancipation. Mott's reformist views particularly influenced and shaped the abolitionist and feminist movements in America. The formation of her views dates from the time when she attended the world Anti-Slavery Convention in London in 1840, together with Elizabeth Cady Stanton. At the opening of the convention, the question of seating the American women delegates arose. After a long debate, the effort to seat them failed, and Mott and Stanton were relegated to sit behind a bar and curtain and thus forbidden to voice their opinions (Buhle and Buhle, 1978). When Mott and Stanton returned to America, they brought a firm objective: to continue to work for both abolition of African American slavery and an end to women's inferior property and family rights. Eight years later, under their leadership, the "Women's Rights Convention" took place in July 1848 at Seneca Falls, New York (see Chapter 15). The convention is considered the official beginning of the women's rights movement in the United States (it is now the site of a national museum).

The United Society of Believers in Christ's Second Appearing, better known as the Shakers, was founded and led in colonial America by Ann Lee (1736–1784). The Shakers believe that the "Godhead is defined in four persons—Father, Son, Holy Mother Wisdom and Daughter" (Zikmund, 1979:209). They live a communal life and practice celibacy. Few practitioners are left.

Christian Science, a late-nineteenth-century sectarian religion, also supported women's rights. Its founder, Mary Baker Eddy (1821–1910), believed and preached that God is both masculine and feminine. She frequently referred to God in her writings as Father-Mother God. Christian Science has a very successful and extensive establishment today, including its widely read newspaper, the *Christian Science Monitor*, published in Boston, and free reading rooms in towns and cities throughout the world.

Seventh-Day Adventism, an evangelical religion, was guided by Ellen Harmon White (1827–1915) from its beginning in Battle Creek, Michigan, in 1860 (Zikmund, 1979). She emphasized temperance, education, and health, particularly in diet. Her hegemony over Adventism lasted fifty years and was responsible for much of its influence and growth.

Many other American women, black and white, rose to prominence and leadership in evangelical and revivalist movements in the nineteenth and twentieth centuries (Gilkes, 1985). Today, Holiness denominations "have a higher percentage of ordained women than does their mother church, the United Methodist Church" (Hardesty et al., 1979:240). Like Quakerism, the evangelical and revivalist movements have been a training ground for women activists, providing us with unique opportunities for public speaking and group organizing. Religious activity was practically the only important extrafamilial activity permitted to most women in the nineteenth and much of the twentieth century. Reform-oriented women had to work through the church, and sectarian religions offered us precisely this opportunity. The initial entry of women into reformist movements through evangelical religion served women in good stead during later periods when we entered nonsectarian public arenas as well.

Jewish Denominations. American Jewish women contribute to religious life as professionals and through domestic activities; the latter role reaches back beyond the Jews' arrival in America through a long history. The heart of Judaism since the diaspora (exile from the Holy Land) has been the ritual of hearth and home. Of major importance to Jewish self-definition is *kashruth*, or purity, particularly of diet. It is the responsibility of religious Jewish women to keep kitchens "kosher," to see that meat and milk are not mixed, that the family consumes no "unclean" foods such as pork or shellfish or improperly butchered meats. We prepare the festive foods for holidays and most particularly for the celebration of the Sabbath. The conduct of Jewish life is completely dependent on women's perpetuation of religious traditions in the home.

In 1988, Conservative Judaism moved women to the focal point by declaring that the home was the center of Jewish religious life. Various Jewish women's groups, particularly charity organizations, provide an arena for major public activities. Prominent among these is Hadassah, founded in 1912 by an American woman, Henrietta Szold (1860–1945). In 1893, Hannah Greenbaum Solomon initiated the formation of the National Council of Jewish Women, dedicated to education, social reform, and issues concerning women. These organizations and others like them provide vehicles for women to learn how to organize, how to manage money, and how to raise funds; they raise and distribute millions of dollars in the causes they espouse.

Catholicism. Catholic women, in contrast to Jewish women, have had the option of following a "vocation" in religion by becoming nuns. As nuns, American women have played a number of influential roles in American life, particularly in education and nursing.

Today, nuns may be women in street clothes who may or may not wear symbolic head scarves and crosses. We are no longer found only in the shadows of a cloister but also in public places. Since medieval times, nuns have held professional responsibilities in education and in attending the sick and elderly, but today we are also found in executive positions, managing self-supporting philanthropic or educational institutions and projects.

The decision to join a convent and become a nun may be prompted by expectations for the future that have nothing to do with religion: For a poor Catholic girl convent life means moving to another class with privileges that she may not have access to if she remained in secular life. She might be seeking an orderly and secure life where education is offered, friendship of sisters is promised, and marriage and children are prohibited. Organized religions do offer spiritual security, and above all, ethical and moral codes that are time-tested. Choices to be made are ours, and we should be free to follow our sincere beliefs.

The dedication of nuns to education, health care, and social welfare is well illustrated in the life of Mother Elizabeth Bayley Seton (1774–1821) and the order of Sisters of Charity that she founded. In 1975, Mother Seton was canonized as the first American-born saint. It was she who founded the first sisterhood in the United States and the first Catholic free school in America, in Emmitsburg, Maryland. She governed her religious community and administered her school through many early hardships. At the time of her death, Mother Seton's Emmitsburg community numbered fifty sisters. Now six branches claim her as their founder and have remained independent North American groups.

In following Christian beliefs, Native American women of the Americas often find themselves at conflict: Some of their ancestral traditions are at opposite ends of the monotheistic/patriarchal scriptures of Judeo-Christianity. The scholar Paula Gunn Allen, who herself is part Indian, asserts, "Traditional tribal lifestyles are more often gynocratic than not, and they are never patriarchal" (Allen, 1988:2). You can begin to judge the basic conflicts that arose when Indians were gradually converted into Christianity by missionaries and conquerors. The work of Mary Tall-Mountain (Athabascan) demonstrates "(the) difficult and uneasy alliance between the pagan awareness that characterized tribal thought and the less earthy, more judgmental view of medieval Christianity" (ibid.:172). TallMountain is a devout Roman Catholic, and her poetry reveals the conflict between her faith and her tribal awareness (TallMountain, 1981).

Feminist Contributions to Religious Change

Religious change comes from many different sources and in many different forms. The spokeswoman for the numerous sectarian branches of American religion mentioned here all sought changes in established practice and belief. Elizabeth Cady Stanton, one of the presidents of the National Woman Suffrage Association and cofounder in 1868 with Susan B. Anthony of the radical magazine *The Revolution*, went further than most of her coworkers and even today's feminists in confronting the sexist language of the Scriptures. Maintaining that the Bible contributed to the low self-image of women, she attempted twice to organize a group to write commentaries on passages from the Old and New Testaments dealing with women. Eventually, between 1895 and 1898, she succeeded in publishing *The Woman's Bible*, parts I and II, and an appendix.

This work is the result of Stanton's belief that the language and interpretations of passages dealing with women in the Bible were a major source of women's inferior status because we turned to the Bible so much for comfort and inspiration. She maintained that the language of the Scriptures had to be rendered in such a way that it would not center only on man, nor celebrate man as the superior creation, nor allow man to dominate women. Certain passages in the Bible, Stanton believed, could be interpreted to conform to women's experiences as humans, as well as men's experiences.

Her attempts were not well received by the majority of suffragists, and the National American Woman Suffrage Association disclaimed any official connection with *The Woman's Bible* in 1895. The organization feared a backlash from society at large on purely religious issues, a reaction that could have halted the political and social changes sought. The decision was based on the view that it was possible to separate political and secular issues from religious ones. Stanton, on the other hand, saw the traditions of religious belief as an important cause of women's subordination. Nowadays, some biblical historians feel that Elizabeth Cady Stanton expressed unacceptable anti-Jewish views in *The Woman's Bible*. They caution against belief in unsubstantiated theories about the history of the Israelites, which result in blaming Judaism for patriarchy (Plaskow, 1979; Bird 1987).

In addition to changing the language of devotion, feminists in the United States have also been developing new versions of traditional rituals. We are taking out the sexist bases of general rituals and adding new rituals for women to complement those specifically intended for men. For example, some Jewish women have written a complement to the boy's *brith* to bring our daughters into the covenant (Plaskow, 1979). Aviva Cantor (1979) has composed a woman's *haggadah*, a version of the Jewish Passover text that traditionally celebrates freedom from slavery and oppression, while others have developed Sabbath prayers for women (Janowitz and Wenig, 1979).

For some religious feminists, the old traditions are insufficient, even when revised. Some call for a menstrual ritual to be performed for girls at the time of menarche. Zsuzsanna Budapest writes of a "self-blessing ritual," derived from oral tradition and feminist beliefs, to be performed by all women in private (1979:269). Budapest also writes "of witchcraft in its modern form—of the ways in which contemporary women could free themselves from internalized male values and learn to cherish their own bodies, thoughts, and wishes" (Goldenberg, 1979:95). Others offer language and earthly images for the "transformation of our culture away from the patriarchal death cults and toward the love of life, of nature, of the female principle" (Starhawk, 1979:268).

Summary

Religion and society affect each other. As societies become more complex and hierarchal, so do their religious institutions. In societies that deny leadership roles to women, religious institutions do so too. Religious beliefs about what is "good behavior" influence societies.

Despite our devalued status in religion, women have been active participants in religions throughout history. Many of us focus on certain aspects of religion (such as the healing Christ or the Virgin Mary) that appeal to our concerns and evolve from our beliefs and practices. "Popular" versions of traditional religions often provide scope for women's activities.

Some ancient religions included goddess worship and gave priestesses status. The origin myths of many of the major religions support the dominant religious and social roles of men.

Most religions have conceptions of supernatural beings, and females are featured among them. These beings may be souls, saints, ghosts, and goddesses. The goddess is often envisaged as a threatening being who is tamed and controlled by being linked to a male god. As monotheism entered religious belief, the goddesses of ancient religions were dropped in favor of a single male God. Some feminists believe that worship of a female God would enhance women's social position.

Religious codes serve to govern human conduct and exert social controls. Life-cycle rituals for men enhance their power and status in the community, but the wedding ceremony, the most important ritual for women in patrilineal societies, serves only to shift control over us from the father to the husband.

Religious leaders in many societies attempt to control female sexuality by urging us to stay within the home and to be modest and decorous. Many religious laws require women and men to be separate during the menstrual period. Religious codes also protect women and promote family life and procreation.

In public worship, women are subject to a number of controls. We are frequently prohibited from lay participation in rituals and sometimes segregated from men. Even so, it is women who spend the most hours of devotion in the church.

The most highly organized religions are least welcoming to women as clergy. Many women find that we can play far more active roles in the religions that are on the fringes of or in conflict with "established" religion. Often we emerge as preachers or leaders of these sects.

Women excel at ritual and spiritual services connected with nurturance and healing. That is why so many women are numbered among the shamans, or curers, of societies. Women have also served our religions as missionaries and as martyrs.

Women have been active as rebels in religious movements, probably because we have often seen rebellion as the only means of winning more liberation for ourselves. During the Reformation, women heretics were frequently accused of being witches. Some women have found fulfillment in religions through an individual idiosyncratic approach. Mysticism and possession by spirits are both highly personal expressions of religion.

Women, especially Quakers, were among the early religious leaders and reformers in American history. In the nineteenth century, women had important parts to play in the founding and organization of the Shakers, Christian Science, Seventh-Day Adventism, and a number of evangelical movements. Jewish women have been responsible for maintaining religious traditions in the home and are active in the public arena by means of various Jewish women's groups. American nuns have played influential roles in education and nursing in the United States.

Feminists have contributed to religious change. In the last century, Elizabeth Cady Stanton wrote a commentary on the Bible, *The Woman's Bible*, while feminists today are developing new versions of traditional rituals and adding new rituals for women as well.

Lucretia Mott, a renowned Philadelphia Quaker preacher and abolitionist, attended the 1840 London Anti-Slavery Convention and preached in a Unitarian Church in London to a mixed audience, a rare event at the time. Mott also helped in planning the first women's rights convention at Seneca Falls, New York, in 1848. (The Sophia Smith Collection [Women's History Archive], Smith College, Northampton, Mass. 01063)

Invocation to the Goddess

Queen of the night
Queen of the moon
Queen of the stars
Queen of the horns
Queen of the earth
Bring to us the child of light.

Night sky rider
Silver shining one
Lady of wild things
Silver wheel
North star
Circle
Crescent
Moon-bright
Singer
Changer!
Teach us!

See with our eyes
Hear with our ears
Breathe with our nostrils
Kiss with our lips,
Touch with our hands,
Be here now!

From *Changing of the Gods: Feminism and the End of Traditional Religions* by Naomi Goldenberg.
Copyright © 1979 by Naomi Goldenberg. Reprinted by permission of Beacon Press.

Discussion Questions

1. Nearly everyone receives some religious education—in the home, in school, in church, in the community at large—on both a conscious and an unconscious level. What do you think you learned about relations between women and men from this background? What were the sources of what you learned (the Bible, ritual, prayer, and the like)?

2. In various times and places, women have emerged as important religious leaders. Select one you have heard of from ancient times, the recent past, or the present. Tell about her life, her accomplishments, her beliefs, and her influence.

3. Does the gender of God matter to you? Why or why not? What have been the arguments offered on both sides of this issue?

4. Study some of the representations of Isis, Diana, the Virgin Mary, and Avalokitesvara (Guanyin or Kwannon). What do these images have in common? What type of convictions do you think they reflect?

Recommended Readings

Christ, Carol P. *Laughter of Aphrodite: Reflections on a Journey to the Goddess*. San Francisco and New York, Harper & Row, 1987. Reflections on the spiritual and intellectual journey of a feminist theologian through her first encounters with graduate studies on the holocaust to her questioning of male religious language to her exploration of the goddess tradition.

Fiorenza, Elizabeth Schussler. *In Memory of Her: A Feminist Theological Reconstruction of Christian Origins*. New York: Crossroad, 1983. A reconstruction of women's role in early Christianity, providing new models of historical interpretation and a revised Christian spirituality for women and men.

Kraemer, Ross Shephard. *Her Share of the Blessings: Women's Religions among Pagans, Jews, and Christians in the Greco-Roman World*. New York: Oxford University Press, 1992. The first comprehensive view of the religious life of women in classical antiquity, including women's activities as religious leaders.

Mernissi, Fatima. *Dreams of Trespass. Tales of a Harem Girlhood*. Reading, Mass.: Addison-Wesley, 1994. The author, a sociologist, describes her girlhood in a harem in Morocco in the 1940s, where women constantly dreamed of trespassing and staged theatrical performances in which they impersonated famous Arab feminist leaders.

Plaskow, Judith, and Christ, Carol P., editors. *Weaving the Visions: New Patterns in Feminist Spirituality*. San Francisco and New York: Harper & Row, 1989. A sequel to *Womanspirit Rising*, these essays attempt to reconceptualize central religious categories through the experiences and voices of white, black, Chicana, Asian American, and Native American feminists.

Ruether, Rosemary, and McLaughlin, Eleanor, editors. *Women of Spirit: Female Leadership in the Jewish and Christian Traditions*. New York: Simon & Schuster, 1979. A collection of original essays on women's religious leadership with an emphasis on historical developments in Europe and America.

References

Allen, Paula Gunn. *The Sacred Hoop: Recovering the Feminine in American Indian Traditions*. Boston: Beacon Press, 1986, 1988.

_____. *The Woman Who Owned the Shadows*. San Francisco: Spinsters, Ink, 1983.

Arberry, A. J. *The Koran Interpreted*. New York: Macmillan, 1955.

Berger, Pamela. *The Goddess Obscured. Transformation of the Grain Protectress from Goddess to Saint*. Boston: Beacon Press, 1985. (Mother Goddess of Vegetation from neolithic to contemporary folk songs.)

Bird, Phyllis. "Women's Religion in Ancient Israel." In *Women's Earliest Records: From Ancient Egypt and Western Asia*, edited by Barbara S. Lesko. Atlanta: Scholars Press, 1989.

Budapest, Zsuzsanna E. "Self-Blessing Ritual." In *Womanspirit Rising: A Feminist Reader in Religion*, edited by Carol P. Christ and Judith Plaskow. San Francisco: Harper & Row, 1979.

Buhle, MariJo, and Buhle, Paul, editors. *The Concise History of Woman Suffrage: Selections from the Classic Work of Stanton, Anthony, Gage, and Harper*. Urbana, Ill.: University of Illinois Press, 1978.

Burstein, Stanley M. *The Hellenistic Age from the Battle of Ipsos to the Death of Kleopatra VII*. Cambridge, Eng.: Cambridge University Press, 1985.

Bynum, Caroline Walker. *Jesus as Mother: Studies in the Spirituality of the High Middle Ages*. Berkeley and Los Angeles: University of California Press, 1982.

Cantor, Aviva. "Jewish Women's Haggadah." In *Womanspirit Rising*, edited by Carol P. Christ and Judith Plaskow. San Francisco: Harper & Row, 1979.

Carmody, Denise. *Women and World Religions.* Nashville, Tenn.: Abingdon, 1979.

Carson, Anne, *Feminist Spirituality and the Feminist Divine. An Annotated Bibliography.* Trumansburg, N.Y.: Crossing Press, 1986.

Christ, Carol P. "Why Women Need the Goddess: Phenomenological, Psychological, and Political Reflections." In *Womanspirit Rising,* edited by Carol Christ and Judith Plaskow. San Francisco: Harper & Row, 1979.

_____. *Laughter of Aphrodite: Reflections on a Journey to the Goddess.* San Francisco and New York: Harper & Row, 1987.

Clark, Elizabeth, and Richardson, Herbert, editors. "The Malleus Maleficarum: The Woman as Witch." In *Women and Religion: A Feminist Sourcebook of Christian Thought.* New York: Harper & Row, 1977.

Daly, Mary. *Beyond God the Father: Toward a Philosophy of Women's Liberation.* Boston: Beacon, 1973.

Danforth, Loring. *The Death Rituals of Rural Greece.* Princeton: Princeton University Press, 1982.

Delaney, Janice, Lupton, Mary J., and Toth, Emily, eds. *The Curse: A Cultural History of Menstruation.* New York: New American Library, 1976.

Dickens, A. G. *The English Reformation.* New York: Schocken, 1964.

Downing, Christine. *The Goddess: Mythological Images of the Feminine.* New York: Crossroad, 1988.

Dunn, Mary Maples. "Woman of Light." In *Women of America: A History,* edited by Carol Ruth Berkin and Mary Beth Norton. Boston: Houghton Mifflin, 1979.

Durrant, Stephen. "The Nisan Shaman Caught in Cultural Contradictions." *Signs* (1979):338–47.

Ehrenreich, Barbara, and English, Deidre. *For Her Own Good; 150 Years of the Experts' Advice to Women.* Garden City, N.Y.: Doubleday, 1979.

Eliot, Charles. *Hinduism and Buddhism.* vol. II. London: Routledge & Kegan Paul, 1962.

Engelsman, Joan Chamberlain. *The Feminist Dimension of the Divine.* Wilmette, Ill.: Chiron Publications, 1979, 1987.

Epton, Nina. *Saints and Sorcerers.* London: Cassell, 1958.

Fernea, Elizabeth W., and Bezirgan, Basima Q., eds. *Middle Eastern Muslim Women Speak.* Austin: University of Texas Press, 1977.

Fernea, Robert A., and Fernea, Elizabeth W. "Variation in Religious Observance Among Islamic Women." In *Scholars, Saints, and Sufis,* edited by Nikki R. Keddie. Berkeley: University of California Press, 1972.

Fiorenza, Elisabeth Schussler. "Word, Spirit, and Power: Women in Early Christian Communities." In *Women of Spirit,* edited by Rosemary Ruether and Eleanor McLaughlin, New York: Simon & Schuster, 1979.

_____. *In Memory of Her: A Feminist Theological Reconstruction of Christian Origins.* New York: Crossroad, 1983.

Freeman, James M. "The Ladies of Lord Krishna." In *Unspoken Worlds,* edited by Nancy Falk and Rita Gross, New York: Harper & Row, 1980.

Gilkes, Cheryl Townsend. " 'Together and in Harness': Women's Traditions in the Sanctified Church." *Signs* 10 (1985):687–99.

Goldenberg, Naomi. *Changing of the Gods: Feminism and the End of Traditional Religions.* Boston: Beacon, 1979.

Green, Rayna. *Women in American Indian Society.* New York and Philadelphia: Chelsea House, 1992.

Hardesty, Nancy, Dayton, Lucille Sider, and Dayton, Conald. "Women in the Holiness Movement: Feminism in the Evangelical Tradition." In *Women of Spirit,* edited by Rosemary Ruether and Eleanor McLaughlin. New York: Simon & Schuster, 1979.

Harrell, Steven. "Men, Women, and Ghosts in Taiwanese Folk Religion." In *Gender and Religion: On the Complexity of Symbols,* edited by Caroline Walker Bynum, Steven Harrell, and Paula Richman. Boston: Beacon Press, 1986.

Hoch-Smith, Judith, and Spring, Anita. *Women in Ritual and Symbolic Roles.* New York: Plenum, 1978.

Janowitz, Naomi, and Wenig, Maggie. "Sabbath Prayers for Women." In *Womanspirit Ris-*

ing, edited by Carol Christ and Judith Plaskow. San Francisco: Harper & Row, 1979.

Jordan, David K. *Gods, Ghosts, and Ancestors.* Berkeley: University of California Press, 1972.

Lewis, I. M. *Ecstatic Religion: An Anthropological Study of Spirit Possession and Shamanism.* Harmondsworth (England): Penguin, 1971.

Mâle, G. *The Gothic Image: Religious Art in the Thirteenth Century.* Translated by Dora Nussey. New York: Harper & Row, 1949.

Malefijt, AnnMarie. *Religion and Culture.* New York: Macmillan, 1968.

McNamara, Jo Ann. *A New Song: Celibate Women in the First Three Christian Centuries.* New York: Haworth, 1983.

Monter, E. William. "The Pedestal and Stake: Courtly Love and Witchcraft." In *Becoming Visible: Women in European History*, edited by Renate Bridenthal and Claudia Koonz. Boston: Houghton Mifflin, 1977.

Mookerjee, Ajit. *Kali: The Feminine Force.* New York: Destiny Books, 1988.

Murray, Margaret. *The Witch in Western Europe.* Oxford: Clarendon, 1967.

Plaskow, Judith. "Bringing a Daughter into the Covenant." In *Womanspirit Rising*, edited by Carol Christ and Judith Plaskow. San Francisco: Harper & Row, 1979.

Pomeroy, Sarah B. *Goddesses, Whores, Wives, and Slaves.* New York: Schocken, 1975.

———. *Women in Hellenistic Egypt: From Alexander to Cleopatra.* New York: Schocken Books, 1984.

Richards, Audrey. *Chisungo.* London: Faber & Faber, 1956.

Ruether, Rosemary Radford. "Motherearth and the Megamachine." In *Womanspirit Rising*, edited by Carol Christ and Judith Plaskow. San Francisco: Harper & Row, 1980.

Sanday, Peggy. *Female Power, Male Dominance.* Cambridge: Cambridge University Press, 1981.

Scott, W. S., editor and translator. *Trial of Joan of Arc.* London: Folio Society, 1968.

Silko, Leslie Marmon. *Ceremony.* New York: Penguin Books, 1977.

Simpson, George E. *Black Religions in the New World.* New York: Columbia University Press, 1978.

Stanton, Elizabeth Cady. *The Woman's Bible.* 1895–1898. Reprint. Parts I, II, and Appendix. Arno, 1972.

Starhawk. "Witchcraft and Women's Culture." In *Womanspirit Rising*, edited by Carol Christ and Judith Plaskow. San Francisco: Harper & Row, 1979.

Starhawk. *The Spiral Dance, a Rebirth of the Ancient Religion of the Great Goddess (Rituals, Invocations, Exercises, Magic)*, San Francisco: Harper & Row, 1973.

Starhawk. "Ethics and Justice in Goddess Religion." In *The Politics of Women's Spirituality. Essays on the Rise of Spiritual Power within the Feminist Movement*, edited by Charlene Spretnak. Garden City, N.Y.: Anchor/Doubleday, 1979.

Stockel, H. Henrietta. *Women of the Apache Nation: Voices of Truth.* Reno and Las Vegas: University of Nevada Press, 1991.

Stone, Merlin. "When God Was a Woman." In *Womanspirit Rising*, edited by Carol P. Christ and Judith Plaskow. San Francisco and New York: Harper & Row, 1979.

TallMountain, Mary. "There Is No Word for Goodbye." *Blue Cloud Quarterly* (Marvin, S.D., 1981).

Umansky, Ellen M. "Women in Judaism: From the Reform Movement to Contemporary Religious Feminism." In *Women of Spirit*, edited by Rosemary Ruether and Eleanor McLaughlin. New York: Simon & Schuster, 1979.

Walker, Alice. *Possessing the Secret of Joy.* New York: Harcourt Brace Jovanovich, 1992.

Washbourne, Penelope. "Becoming a Woman: Menstruation as Spiritual Challenge." In *Womanspirit Rising*, edited by Carol Christ and Judith Plaskow. San Francisco: Harper & Row, 1979.

Zikmund, Barbara Brown. "The Feminist Thrust of Sectarian Christianity." In *Women of Spirit*, edited by Rosemary Ruether and Eleanor McLaughlin. New York: Simon & Schuster, 1979.

Zimmer, Heinrich. *Myths and Symbols in Indian Art and Civilization.* Princeton: Princeton University Press, 1978.

Women and Education

One morning in May 1853, the home of Mary Douglass in Norfolk, Virginia, was raided. She was tried, found guilty, and sentenced to one month in prison for violating a state law: teaching reading and writing to black children. A former slaveowner herself, she was aware that it was against the law to provide instruction to slave children; she did not know it was also illegal to teach free black children (Hellerstein et al., 1981).

Why should it have been a transgression against the rules laid down by men in the Virginia legislature to teach African American children to read and write? Why should the dominant group in any society fear education in the hands of an oppressed subgroup? Does literacy bring power? UNESCO defines literacy as "the ability to read and write a sentence in daily life" with understanding (Seager and Olson, 1986:112). Few places today remain totally untouched by economic and technological change; yet literacy, which is a first step toward reshaping individual lives and enabling people to participate fully in modern society, has a lower rate for women than among men throughout the world.

Women comprise nearly two-thirds of the world's illiterates! In 1985, there were 597 million illiterate women as compared with 352 million illiterate men. Illiteracy rates have been dropping worldwide, yet because of limited educational resources and, in some cases, population growth, the number of illiterate girls and women has increased, particularly in developing countries and rural areas (United Nations, 1991). Hidden from view, even in the industrialized world, is the number of functional illiterates, those with only basic reading and writing skills. Within the United States, these figures are currently as high as 16 percent for whites, 44 percent for blacks, and 56 percent for Hispanics, with women making up 60 percent of the total (Seager and Olson, 1986). We must conclude that even where access to education is easiest, it is still more difficult for women than for men to acquire education. This gender-specific pattern is uniform. Why should this be so?

This chapter investigates the difficulties women faced in achieving literacy and obtaining *formal education*, i.e., schooling. It discusses how women participated in bringing about a modern revolution in our education. It also considers the way women's educational choices continue to be limited and how women's studies has begun to challenge subject matter and disciplines. We start with the view that literacy and education are potentially liberating, and conclude that women's studies has become a powerful liberating force for women today and has begun to transform

A classroom in an elementary school for girls in the Philippines, operated by Catholic nuns. This temporary structure was built with the aid of parents. Education for girls, at least at this level, is considered an important community priority. (Courtesy of the United Nations)

knowledge, scholarship, and social institutions.

Women's Knowledge, Women's Literacy, Women's Place

Women always had a great store of knowledge about our immediate world that we taught our daughters and our daughter's daughters. From earliest times, we actively participated in the nonformal educational process by generating and transmitting knowledge. We taught ourselves and other women how to find, prepare, and preserve food. We formed the first pots for cooking. We developed the art of cultivation and learned how to domesticate and use animals. We sheared the wool from sheep, spun it, and wove it into cloth; milked animals and turned the milk into dairy products; designed, built, and carried tents;

learned to make and keep fires going; taught ourselves the lore of herbs and the arts of healing; and organized the secrets of birthing, the tasks of child care, and the rituals of dying and mourning the dead. Women worked out the ways of barter and exchange and organized market life and long-distance trade.

Women's knowledge has been of direct benefit to our families and our communities. To the extent that women organized and cared for the needs of daily life, men were able to devote more of their time to the generation of other knowledge. For example, men were probably responsible for the early development of pictographs and alphabets upon which the written word has been built. From the first, power over the word was important, and the elite male groups who monopolized this power played a significant role in the development of societies. Through time, however, women have struggled to achieve equal access to literacy and formal education.

What role does formal education play in our lives? Does it liberate by offering women new opportunities? Does it oppress by simply reflecting societal values and reinforcing inequality? Or can it serve as an instrument for transforming society (Kelly and Elliot, 1982)?

Formal Education in the Past

Access to formal education through time and across the globe has been a privilege provided for young males from wealthy and high-status backgrounds. Opportunity for women is a very recent phenomenon and is still largely dependent on family and societal needs.

The Ancient World

In the ancient Greek world, athletics, music, and reading were formal educational requirements for young males destined to become full members of the citizen class. Occasionally, young upper-class Athenian girls were taught to read and write by tutors hired for their brothers. After marriage, the educational training of girls was organized by husbands, who were typically fifteen to twenty years older. No formal education existed for lower-class or slave women.

In the late sixth century B.C.E., the famous poet Sappho, who lived on the island Lesbos, is thought to have taught a few select young maidens (Hallett, 1979; Snyder, 1991). And the philosopher Pythagoras was known to have had women disciples. By the fourth century B.C.E., there were women who studied and practiced poetry, music, and painting as well as philosophy as professions (Cole, 1981; Pomeroy, 1975; Wider, 1986). Women learned medicine in classes taught by physicians and even wrote gynecological texts (Pomeroy, 1977). But these cases were rare.

During those years when Roman sons acquired formal education, daughters prepared for marriage. However, Romans of the propertied classes considered it desirable for their daughters to read Latin and Greek literature, play the lyre, and know how to dance (Pomeroy, 1975; Snyder, 1989).

In the late fourth century A.D. in Egypt, Hypatia, the daughter of a learned father, received an education in mathematics and philosophy that allowed her to teach at the University of Alexandria. She wrote a treatise on astronomy and invented instruments for studying the stars, distilling water, and measuring the specific gravity of liquids (Osen, 1974; Wider, 1986).

The Middle Ages

Property, wealth, and family position could open opportunities for formal education for women. This was true for women in the Middle Ages in Japan as well as in Europe. Aristocratic women in the Heian period (794–1185) led restricted lives but excelled in aesthetics and politics and produced the major literary works of the day. Among these were Sei-Shonagon, a tenth-century chronicler of Japanese court life, and Lady Murasaki Shikibu, who lived at the Japanese royal court in the eleventh century and wrote the *Tale of Genji*, the world's earliest novel and one of the most notable. Lady Murasaki, like other educated women of her time, wrote in Japanese rather than Chinese, the language taught to learned men. Never formally taught Chinese, she did acquire knowledge of it by listening in on her brothers' lessons (Jayawardena, 1986).

In Europe, Emperor Charlemagne's daughters and sons were taught by royal tutors in the late eighth and early ninth centuries. Education was more typically acquired in the West in Christian monasteries and convents. At first young women were the main beneficiaries of such education; for many centuries it was thought more important for elite young men to learn how to use the sword and engage in field sports than to read. Scholarship was left to the clergy and to the women placed by families in convent schools as a safe harbor until marriage. As a result, outside the church there were probably more literate women than men in Europe from the ninth to the twelfth centuries, although many more learned to read than to write (Lucas, 1983).

The intellectual activities of a few famous learned women during these years included Latin plays by Hroswitha, a tenth-century nun of Gandersheim, Saxony (Germany); the poems of eleventh-century women troubadours in Provence; and mystical writings by the Abbess Hildegard of Bingen in the twelfth century. Equally famous were Héloïse—renowned for her learning even before Abelard became her tutor—and Marie de France, who wrote short verse tales (*lais*) in twelfth-century France (Ferante, 1980; Thiébaux, 1994). By the thirteenth century, formal education in Europe came to be dominated by the universities, where admission was restricted to men being trained in theology, law, and medicine. Nonetheless, women did achieve some recognition in medicine, for we know of one female physician who attended King Louis IX of France, who reigned in the thirteenth century (Osen, 1974).

Renaissance Humanism and Early Modern Europe

In the fourteenth and fifteenth centuries in Italy, a trend toward humanistic ideas and secular learning placed a value on cultivated women, which encouraged the aristocracy to allow their daughters to participate in higher education. In practice, however, after a period of adolescent study when young women were free to pursue knowledge at leisure, the truly learned woman was faced with an absolute choice—either marriage and abandonment of these studies or withdrawal from the ordinary social world to a convent or a solitary, book-lined cell (King, 1980).

These learned women of Italy composed letters, delivered orations, and wrote dialogues and treatises and poems, all in the style of the scholarly male humanists of the day. Although praised extravagantly, we were never actually received as equals into the company of learned men, nor given any opportunities to enter the learned professions. Male admirers likened educated women to Amazons, by which they meant unnatural women, or monsters. Real women were those who wanted love, marriage, and motherhood, for which the active intellectual life must be put aside. One exception was Christine de Pizan (1365–1431). Brought from Italy to the French court by her physician father, she supported herself as a young widow with children by writing lyric poetry, courtly romances, and tracts on moral conduct and public matters. She was commissioned by the brother of King Charles V to write a history of his reign (Davis, 1980). She also wrote *The Book of the City of Ladies* in 1405 in praise of famous women of legend and history (Pizan, 1982).

By the sixteenth century in Europe, education for women became more common in the upper classes. Royal and noble families educated both their daughters and sons. Yet the views of women's education as expressed by Juan Luis Vives, who was brought by Catherine of Aragon to England after her marriage to King Henry VIII to tutor their daughter Mary, the future queen, emphasized ladylike conduct and theological readings. Young women were expected to be humble, virtuous, and silent (Kaufman, 1978).

Nonetheless, there were more learned women in sixteenth-century Europe than in any earlier period. Two powerful women rulers in this period, Catherine de Medici in France and Elizabeth I in England, were well-educated humanist scholars, reading works in their original languages, especially the ancient texts surviving from the Greek and Roman world.

The Protestant reformers of the sixteenth century placed an emphasis on reading the New Testament, recommending education of this sort for girls as well as boys. Yet they too believed that women should confine ourselves to our own homes and keep silent in public, lest we spread "false opinions." Despite these dominant attitudes, some female scholars did teach outside the family and the court circles. However, families of wealth and position emphasized training cultivated daughters, not learned scholars.

The invention of printing in the late fifteenth century and the development of the book trade in the sixteenth century were accompanied by a remarkable increase in literacy and learning among men, including those engaged in skilled artisan crafts as well as men of rank and wealth. For women, however, the revolution in literacy was of lesser magnitude. Village schools were often built for boys only, and if girls were admitted, we were not taught Latin because this would have introduced us to "immoral" and "pagan" writers.

Similarly, larger educational institutions in growing cities were also for boys only. Women of the wealthier classes might be tutored privately, but only a few had the courage or determination to become serious scholars. Historian Natalie Davis (1975) finds that few women in the French countryside in the sixteenth century even knew the alphabet, while male artisans in towns exhibited far greater literacy than their wives. It was left to the convent to educate a small number of elite women in religious instruction and some elements of reading, writing, and arithmetic. As before, more serious studies had to be pursued privately (Lee, 1975).

In seventeenth-century Paris, there was a flowering of literary salons organized by fashionable aristocratic women wealthy enough to obtain private education. Although hampered by class assumptions, French feminists began to challenge the double standard in education and the existing social hierarchy, arguing that only those whose moral worth merited it should be called noble. They questioned the authority of tradition, custom, and religion in defining the conventional roles for women and advocated wider nondomestic roles for women of rank (Lougee, 1976). The collected letters of Madame de Sevigné, numbering over a thousand, offer a vast amount of information about women's lives in the aristocratic circles at court and in the countryside of seventeenth-century France.

The negative reaction to these feminists was a protest against the ways in which women, by our intermarriage between the classes and our social leadership, were challenging the position of the old aristocracy. The conservatives among the old nobility announced that women must be taught to remain in our "proper" spheres, invisible to the world. Those who saw a link between feminist writings and unwelcome social change in the seventeenth century put a renewed emphasis on circumscribing women's education.

The Traditional Goals of Women's Education Debated

From the seventeenth century on, the "proper" education for women was a topic of serious discussion. In France, a special school at Saint-Cyr was established under the supervision of Madame de Maintenon (1635–1719), an official mistress of King Louis XIV, with a curriculum influenced by the writings of Abbé Fénelon. His *Education for Girls*, appearing in 1687, sought to ensure that a woman remain confined to household concerns and wifely duties and not aspire "above her fortune and condition" (Lougee, 1976:182–87). Such an

Shakespeare's Sister

[Let us suppose] that Shakespeare had a wonderfully gifted sister, called Judith. . . . Shakespeare himself went, very probably—his mother was an heiress—to the grammar school, where he may have learnt Latin—Ovid, Virgil and Horace—and the elements of grammar and logic. . . . [He went] to seek his fortune in London. . . . Very soon he got work in the theatre, became a successful actor, and lived at the hub of the universe, meeting everybody, knowing everybody, practising his art on the boards, exercising his wits in the streets, and even getting access to the palace of the queen. Meanwhile his extraordinarily gifted sister, let us suppose, remained at home. She was as adventurous, as imaginative, as agog to see the world as he was. But she was not sent to school. She had no chance of learning grammar and logic, let alone of reading Horace and Virgil. She picked up a book now and then, one of her brother's perhaps, and read a few pages. But then her parents came in and told her to mend the stockings or mind the stew and not moon about with books and papers. They would have spoken sharply but kindly, for they were substantial people who knew the conditions of life for a woman and loved their daughter—indeed, more likely than not she was the apple of her father's eye. Perhaps she scribbled some pages up in an apple loft on the sly, but was careful to hide them or set fire to them. Soon . . . she was to be betrothed to the son of a neighboring wool-stapler. She cried out that marriage was hateful to her, and for that she was severely beaten by her father. . . . She . . . let herself down by a rope one summer's night and took the road to London. She was not seventeen. . . . She stood at the stage door; she wanted to act, she said. Men laughed in her face. . . . no woman . . . could possibly be an actress. . . . She could get no training in her craft. Could she even seek her dinner in a tavern or roam the streets at midnight? . . . At last the actor-manager took pity on her; she found herself with child by that gentleman and so—who shall measure the heat and violence of the poet's heart then caught and tangled in a woman's body?—killed herself one winter's night and lies buried at some cross-roads where the omnibuses now stop.

(Woolf, 1929, 1957:80–84)

Excerpt from *A Room of One's Own* by Virginia Woolf. Copyright 1929 by Harcourt Brace & Company and renewed 1957 by Leonard Woolf.
Reprinted by permission of the publisher.

education was not meant to expand our intellects, but to restrain and direct us to the "proper" sphere of womanhood within its class context and to prepare us as young girls to submit graciously to a fate of dependency on others for our welfare (Stock, 1978). Saint-Cyr became a model for eighteenth-century French convents, which educated the daughters of various segments of the aristocracy and middle classes (Lee, 1975).

Across the channel in England, the first woman to write a treatise on the education of women was Bathsua Makin (1608–1675?), with *An Essay to Revive the Ancient Education of Gentlewomen* in 1673. English plays of the late seventeenth century suggest the nature of what must have been an ongoing debate, deploring as they do by their plots the dangers to society posed by rebellious daughters, emancipated wives, and "she-philosophers," "all rebels against male authority" (Kinnaird, 1979:53). What was caricatured on stage did characterize some of the books and pamphlet literature of the day. For example, Hannah Woolley (1627–1670), a schoolmistress and writer of books on cookery and household management, began her 1675 advice book, *The Gentlewoman's Companion*, with a diatribe on the right of women to a better education. And Aphra Behn (1640–1689; see Chapter 1), the first woman dramatist writing in English, who supported herself by writing over twenty plays between 1670 and 1689, was accused of "bawdiness" because she used the same sexually explicit language as male playwrights of her day (Mahl and Koon, 1977). Her novel, *Oroonoko*, introduces a West African prince enslaved in Surinam in the New World (South America), raising issues of slavery and the slave trade which become increasingly important in Englishwomen's texts in the next century and a half (Ferguson, 1985; Hobby, 1988).

As Saint-Cyr was becoming established in France, Mary Astell in England was calling for a true institution of higher learning for women in her *Serious Proposal to the Ladies for the Advancement of Their True and Greatest Interest* in 1694. Dismissing all conventional arguments about women's inferior intellects, she took the radical position that God had given the same intellectual potential to all human beings, poor and rich, female and male. As to claims men made for their superiority, she wrote with heavy irony: "Have not all the great Actions that have been perform'd in the World been done by Men? . . . Their vast Minds lay Kingdoms waste, no Bounds or Measures can be prescrib'd to their Desires. . . . They make Worlds and ruin them, form Systems of universal Nature and dispute eternally about them" (Kinnaird, 1979:63).

Astell insisted that only serious education could fortify women enough to aid us in building strong and happy marriages and rearing our children properly. Although she preached women's duties, not women's rights, her plan for a "Female Monastery" was aimed at realizing women's full potential as thinking persons (Hill, 1986).

Another feminist of the period, Eliza Haywood (1690?–1756), worked as a novelist, playwright, and publisher of *The Female Spectator* from 1722 to 1746. This was the first magazine published by and for women; written largely by Haywood herself, it dealt with

---

Seventeenth-Century English Feminism

The right Education of the Female Sex, as it is in a manner everywhere neglected, so it ought to be generally lamented. Most in this depraved later Age think a Woman learned and wise enough if she can distinguish her Husbands Bed from anothers. Certainly Mans Soul cannot boast of a more sublime Original than ours, they had equally their efflux from the same eternal Immensity, and [are] therefore capable of the same improvement by good Education. Vain man is apt to think we were merely intended for the Worlds propagation, and to keep its humane inhabitants sweet and clean; but by their leaves, had we the same Literature, he would find our brains as fruitful as our bodies. Hence I am induced to believe, we are debar'd from the knowledge of humane learning lest our pregnant Wits should rival the towering conceits of our insulting Lords and Masters.

(Hannah Woolley in Kinnaird, 1979:53)

questions of female education, literature, the arts, and philosophy. For example, she wrote in the 1740s:

> [I]t is entirely owing to a narrow Education that we either give our Husbands room to find fault with our Conduct, or that we have Leisure to pry too scrutinously into theirs:—
> . . . O but, say they, Learning puts the Sexes too much on an Equality, it would destroy that implicit Obedience which it is necessary the Woman should pay to our Commands:— If once they have the capacity of arguing with us, where would be our Authority! (Mahl and Koon, 1977:234–35)

Like Paris, London in the eighteenth century had salons at which some of the intellectual women of English society, called *bluestockings*, mingled with literary men of the day. Nevertheless, for every woman like Astell who called for the development of women's reason to make us better wives and mothers, there were men and women who emphasized that girls should be taught patient submissiveness to male authority. The most articulate spokesperson for this view was the "radical" French philosopher Jean-Jacques Rousseau.

In his treatise on the ideal education for a young man, *Emile* (1762), Rousseau takes up the psychological, moral, and social consequences that must follow from the physical distinctions between the sexes, concluding that "by nature" women have been intended to obey men. Thus, the same philosopher who proclaimed in *The Social Contract* (1762) that might never makes right, and that human beings should only obey governments to which they consent, failed to extend this view to women's relations with men. In *Emile*, the education of Sophie was designed to make her completely submissive to her future husband. The proper study of women, according to Rousseau, was men, whose traits and disposi-

tions we must observe in order to bend easily to them and for whose pleasure we were in fact created (Keohane, 1980).

The first feminist response to Rousseau came from Catharine Macaulay, a historian whose eight-volume *History of England* appeared between 1763 and 1783. In her *Letters on Education* (1790), she asserted the need for women and men to understand each other better. Coeducation was her solution. If both sexes shared the same curriculum and the same physical exercises, women would learn alongside men to develop our intellectual and physical powers. As educated members of the state, women would then undertake our share of its political responsibilities (Boos, 1976).

Another response to Rousseau came from Mary Wollstonecraft, a writer who had supported herself from the age of nineteen as a lady's companion, needleworker, governess, schoolmistress, journalist, and translator. By 1786 she had written her first book, *Thoughts on Education of Daughters*. In it she deplored the useless "accomplishments" that society thought appropriate to the education of young women. Self-educated like many other intellectual women in the past, and inspired by Catharine Macaulay's views and the revolutionary developments in France, Wollstonecraft wrote her passionately felt *Vindication of the Rights of Woman* in 1792. She attacked the conservative views that promoted ignorance in young women in order to keep us innocent. She attacked Rousseau, pointing out scathingly that since Sophie's reasoning powers were left uncultivated, she would make a very poor mother for Emile's children. Wollstonecraft also advocated coeducation, insisting that young women must receive an education that would enable us to be rational, competent, and independent (see Chapter 2). She did not ignore the reality that the majority of women would become wives and mothers; instead, she claimed most earnestly that we could fulfill those roles best if we learned first to respect ourselves as individuals (Ferguson and Todd, 1984; Sapiro, 1974, 1992).

The debate over traditional goals of education for women was not limited to European societies in this same period. In China, for example, while Confucian ideology maintained a system of male dominance and separate public and private spheres for men and women, there were scholar-officials who advocated education for women, although sometimes with qualifications. Lu K'un, in 1590, encouraged women to gain practical expertise, such as medical knowledge, but was anxious lest women of the upper class should forget our proper role. Ch'en Hung-mou (1696–1771), who wrote a book for the education of women before Mary Wollstonecraft, argued that all people were educable and that women should not be neglected, no matter what their rank in society. That during the seventeenth and eighteenth centuries in many parts of China and other Asian societies women were writers, artists, and poets reveals that the reality of women's lives differed somewhat from the expressed ideal of subordination within the confines of the household (Jayawardena, 1986).

The Modern Educational Revolution

In the two hundred years since Wollstonecraft "debated" with Rousseau over the proper education of women, people's beliefs have undergone a true revolution. Gradually, the view that the modern state has an obligation to offer at least elementary education to all its citizens has gained influence in much of the world. But how much education and for what purposes are the subject of continued debate. The same social conventions that hindered the acquisition of learning by women in earlier centuries still limit our educational opportunities. Even in countries offering high levels of education to women, the problem of

defining educational goals for women today remains fiercely controversial.

As in earlier centuries, our struggle since 1800 to achieve an ever higher level of education has been led by women who simply refused to accept the view that we are intellectually inferior. Such women in the nineteenth century sought to prove that women could excel in the educational curriculum pursued by men; more recently, we have emphasized the need for women's search for self-knowledge and self-definition. Like our learned sisters before us, women involved in educational reform have been caught in the dominant society's gender definitions. By this measurement, if women succeed in our intellectual pursuits, we are no longer "true women." To define ourselves, therefore, means working to change broad social definitions of gender, gender roles, and the values assigned to being born female.

The Achievement of Elementary and Secondary Education in the United States

In colonial America, the simple rudiments of education—reading, writing, and arithmetic—were often supplied in "dame schools" run by women for girls and boys. But formal education for women beyond the most elementary level was considered inappropriate, dangerous, and unsettling to women's domestic duties.

Studies on literacy through the colonial period conclude that while male literacy rates may have been as high as 80 percent by the late eighteenth century, women's rates were as low as 45 percent (Cott, 1977). Abigail Adams (1744–1818) felt it necessary to remind her husband, John, who would become the second president of the United States, of the neglect of female education that characterized their young country: "If we mean to have heroes, statesmen, and philosophers, we should have learned women" (ibid.:106). Yet when

Young Women Plucking the Fruits of Knowledge and Science (1892) by Mary Cassatt is the center panel of the mural *Modern Woman,* painted for the Woman's Building of the World Columbian Exhibition held in Chicago in 1893. Cassatt's imagery captures the idea that women have had to take the initiative to gather the fruit of the tree of knowledge for ourselves and the generations of women to come. (Chicago Historical Society)

the Young Ladies' Academy of Philadelphia opened its doors in 1787, its curriculum excluded what was standard for young men, classical languages and advanced mathematics.

Wollstonecraft's *Vindication of the Rights of Women* was reprinted in Philadelphia soon after its English publication and followed by a *Memoir* of her life by her husband, William Godwin. He revealed that she had lived with a prior lover and himself before marrying him and had had an illegitimate daughter previously before dying in giving birth to her second daughter. This personal history labeled Wollstonecraft as a social and political radical and made her views about educating women unacceptable. The prevailing opinion in the early American republic was that a proper education for women made us virtuous examples for our brothers, husbands, and sons and true mothers of future heroes and statesmen (Kerber, 1974, 1980).

After the American Revolution, a small number of boys' academies were opened to girls, but it was the custom to teach us separately, either in different spaces or at different times. In the early decades of the nineteenth century, a number of all-female academies opened. Emma Willard proposed in 1819 that the New York State legislature sponsor a publicly supported female seminary to help meet the increasing need for teachers. Women, she said, were "natural teachers of the young," and it was easy to hire us at lower wages than were paid men (Cott, 1977:117–21). Unable to enlist public financial support, Willard established her own private female seminary in Troy, New York, in 1821.

Emma Willard's views were important in reshaping education throughout the new nation. Her message to each class of young women over the next three decades was the same: Women can study any academic subject we choose; we should prepare ourselves to be self-supporting in a profession; and marriage for women is not an end in itself. Graduates of Troy Female Seminary formed a network committed to the education of women and to the professionalization of teaching (Scott, 1979). Similar networks were formed by Catharine Beecher (1800–1878) in her Hartford Female Seminary and Mary Lyon (1797–1849) at Mount Holyoke (Solomon, 1985).

The argument that a developing nation required an educated people gradually led a number of Northern states to provide free public elementary education by the mid-nineteenth century. To meet the growing demand for teachers as attractive alternative careers became available to the traditional schoolmaster, young women turned to this occupation and agreed to far lower wages. By 1870, of the more than 200,000 teachers in American public elementary and secondary schools, over one-half were women. Catharine Beecher encouraged the graduates of her Hart-

ford Female Seminary to seek posts in the West where we would be needed (Kaufman, 1984). Most elementary school teachers were the products of the public or "common" schools, and only gradually did we begin to attend teacher-training or "normal" schools.

Down to the 1880s, women were increasingly employed as teachers, consistently underpaid, and generally praised for our dedication to the profession. Late in the century, a reversal of attitudes developed. Because most women teachers eventually followed the conventional expectations of the day and got married, criticism was raised against training us in public normal schools in return for just a few years' service. In addition, critics complained that American boys were being "feminized" by their exclusive exposure to female teachers. Women were accused of failing to provide that adequate "manly" role model needed by older boys. The dearth of male teachers now came to be seen as a grave peril, and women were accused of driving men from

---

Equal Pay for Women Teachers, 1853

In 1853, Susan B. Anthony, a teacher and leader in the nineteenth-century women's rights movement, attended an education convention at Rochester, New York. She listened to long discussions of the low prestige in which the teaching profession was held, compared to the law, medicine, and the ministry. The discussion was conducted entirely by men, "the thousand women crowding that hall could not vote on the question," nor did they venture to speak. After asking to be heard, and waiting for a further half-hour discussion on whether her request would be granted, she spoke:

"It seems to me, gentlemen, that none of you quite comprehend the cause of the disrespect of which you complain. Do you not see that so long as society says a woman is incompetent to be a lawyer, minister, or doctor, but has ample ability to be a teacher, that every man of you who chooses this profession tacitly acknowledges that he has no more brains than a woman? And this, too, is the reason that teaching is a less lucrative profession, as here men must compete with the cheap labor of women. Would you exalt your profession, exalt those who labor with you. Would you make it more lucrative, increase the salaries of the women engaged in the noble work of educating our future Presidents, Senators, and Congressmen."

(Lerner, 1977:234–36)

the profession because we accepted such low wages. One critic, steeped in gender stereotypes, claimed that the long-range effect of the feminization of the teaching profession was "a feminized manhood, emotional, illogical, non-combative against public evils. . . . Men think in terms of steamships, railways, battleships, war, finance, in a word, the greatest energies of the world, which the woman's mind never, in a practical way, really concerns itself with, nor can it do so" (Woody, 1966, I:512).

What if a woman married but wanted to keep teaching? Many school boards at the turn of the century decided it was improper to employ married women teachers. It was thought that wives should be supported by husbands and leave employment opportunities to the unmarried. As passed by the New York City school board, the only exceptions to such a rule could be wives whose husbands were mentally or physically unable to earn a living or who had been deserted (ibid.). This New York City regulation was revoked in 1920, but women teachers continued to experience discrimination throughout the country. Women teachers were expected to conform to social ideals in private as well as in public and adhere to rules about our appearance and behavior *outside* the classroom. Yet while teaching was in many ways an extension of our domestic sphere, it also contributed to the growth of feminism by providing opportunities for women to develop a collective identity, networks, and organizing skills (Schwager, 1987).

The revolution in secondary school instruction in the United States took place in the second half of the nineteenth century. Although the first public high schools for girls were founded in Worcester, Massachusetts, in 1824, and in New York City and Boston soon thereafter, only gradually did such institutions become graded schools whose curriculum was taught at levels above those of elementary

schools. Although many public high schools remained gender-segregated, the pattern by the end of the nineteenth century was coeducation. Girl students outnumbered boys in attendance and in the number who graduated by a ratio of three to two (Woody, II:1966). Some reasons have been suggested for this differential. Families who could afford it sent boys to private schools. In rural areas, boys were kept out of school during peak cultivation and harvesting seasons, while girls were sent to school because the time left each day still allowed us to do our domestic chores. In the cities, poorer families expected boys to leave school as soon as possible to add to the family income, while school was seen as a place that kept girls out of trouble.

The high numbers of educated women in the latter part of the nineteenth century created a new supply of workers for the developing clerical and sales opportunities opening up in business offices and department stores (see Chapter 13). However, whether we were white, African American, Native American, or immigrant girls, those who argued for our need to be educated were not concerned to prepare us for careers or to develop our talents, but to make us conform to dominant ideals about the kind of wives, mothers, and homemakers that would better serve our husbands and provide for the future generations of the nation (Hansot and Tyack, 1988; Trennert, 1994).

The Education of African American Women in the United States

The states in which slavery continued to exist in the first half of the nineteenth century, as noted earlier, legislated against the provision of education of African Americans, free or enslaved. Free African Americans before the end of slavery sought education outside the South; afterward, freed slaves turned to education in great numbers in search of opportunities for personal and community advancement. African American women were in the forefront of such activities.

After the Civil War, most African Americans in the South received only elementary-level education in schools established by mission societies and the Freedmen's Bureau, set up by Congress in 1865. Typically, white males were supervisors and upper-level teachers, while the lower levels were taught by white women from the North and a few educated black women. African American women teachers fared the worst, being assigned to remote schools and segregated housing and sometimes whipped, raped, and even killed (Ihle, 1986:I).

Despite the intimidation and lack of resources (school funding in the South was the poorest in the nation), many African American women persevered and established schools to fill the gap left by the Freedmen's Bureau, which was disbanded in 1870. Lucy Craft Laney graduated from the first class of Atlanta University in 1873 and in 1886 opened Haines Normal and Industrial Institute in Augusta, Georgia, a state that did not provide public high schools for blacks. Her school was unique in offering liberal arts courses at a time when educators in the South viewed vocational training as sufficient education for African Americans. Laney was also to influence future school founders: Janie Porter Barrett, Mary McLeod Bethune, and Charlotte Hawkins Brown (Giddings, 1984).

By the end of the nineteenth century, black schoolchildren were taught largely by African American women teachers. Teaching had become for black women the highest-paid and most prestigious position. Up until World War I, domestic service remained the only other alternative. But teaching was also an economic necessity, as few African American women could afford not to work. However, as with white women teachers, employment was restricted to unmarried women, and black women earned less than men and whites (Ihle, 1986:I).

African American women sought to use our acquired skills to further the race and uplift the masses. Throughout the end of the nineteenth century and the first two decades of the twentieth century, we also debated the educational philosophies of Booker T. Washington and W. E. B. Du Bois as to which was more appropriate for the advancement of the black community. Washington, principal of Tuskegee Institute, advocated industrial education as the only realistic approach for economic survival. Du Bois, who taught economics and history at Atlanta University, argued that only an academic program of liberal arts studies could produce the kind of African American leadership required for a rapidly changing economy. Industrial education for blacks was also favored by a segregationist racist society, for it provided the necessary menial labor for the American economy while severely restricting blacks from opportunities for social mobility. For African American women this meant being educated in domestic science—sewing, laundering, cooking—with a heavy emphasis on moral virtues and good work habits. But while African American women could find employment as teachers or domestics and worked out of economic necessity, they lived in a dominant society that viewed work outside the home as temporary or secondary to the needs of husbands and children (Ihle, 1986).

Nonetheless, many African American women strived for and obtained an academic education and founded private black schools with a mixed curriculum of practical skills, liberal arts, and character building. Anna Julia Cooper (1858–1964) made the education of black girls her special concern. Born a slave, she was freed at the time of the Civil War and began teaching at the age of nineteen. Married and widowed within a span of two years, she went to Oberlin College and earned her degree in 1884. She taught in Washington, D.C., and called for the establishment of higher education for black women and men. (See **Anna Cooper on the Higher Education of Women.**) When she retired as a schoolteacher, she went to Paris in 1924 and earned a Ph.D. in Latin (Loewenberg and Bogin, 1976).

The Education of Immigrant Women in the United States

Prior to the Civil War, schooling for the general population was relatively limited. Immigrant girls and boys were taught reading, writing, and arithmetic alongside native-born children. With industrialization, urbanization, and the arrival of East Asian immigrants to Hawaii and the Pacific Coast states after the 1840s and eastern and southern Europeans to midwestern and northeastern cities during the 1880s to 1920s, the educational system was radically transformed.

The public school system was also expanded to "Americanize" or assimilate immigrants and to prepare them for proper places in an industrial economy. As immigrant women, we were taught skills and habits for the workplace, including hygiene and patriotism, as well as the English language, Protestant values, and Anglo-Saxon culture. Newcomers were often blamed for urban problems, such as diseases, alcohol abuse, poverty, and crime. Thus schools were also expected to solve these social ills (Seller, 1981).

On the other hand, immigrant communities also relied on the American educational system to provide greater opportunities for their children. While seeking acculturation through formal education, ethnic groups sought at the same time to preserve their own languages and customs, sometimes through setting up their own institutions. Immigrant school programs were held after American public school hours or on weekends. Occasionally, immigrant communities established their own separate, often religious-based school systems as an alternative to the public school (Seller, 1977).

Anna Cooper on the Higher Education of Women

In the very first year of our century, the year 1801, there appeared in Paris a book . . . entitled "Shall Woman Learn the Alphabet?" The book proposes a law prohibiting the alphabet to women, and quotes authorities weighty and various, to prove that the woman who knows the alphabet has already lost part of her womanliness. The author declares that women can use the alphabet only as Moliere predicted they would, in spelling out the verb amo; . . . while Sappho, Aspasia, Madame de Maintenon, and Madame de Stael could read altogether too well for their good; finally if women were once permitted to read Sophocles and work with logarithms, or to nibble at any side of the apple of knowledge, there would be an end forever to their sewing on buttons and embroidering slippers.

. . . Now I claim that it is the prevalence of Higher Education among women, the making it a common everyday affair for women to reason and think and express their thought, the training and stimulus which enable and encourage women to administer to the world the bread it needs as well as the sugar it cries for . . . that has given symmetry and completeness to the world's agencies.

(B. J. Loewenberg and R. Bogin, eds., 1976:318–19, 321)

As immigrant women we had to meet the expectations of the dominant U.S. society as well as those of our own ethnic communities, and we struggled to overcome the gender restrictions of both cultures. Access to formal education denied to us in our home countries because of tradition or colonialism and lack of family resources was made more readily available through the American public school system. For example, born in Prussia and raised by Polish parents, Marie Zakrzeska (1829–1902) embodied the determination of an immigrant woman of the nineteenth century to become educated and to fulfill higher aspirations. She ignored her father's pleas to marry and followed her midwife mother's example and studied midwifery and medicine. After Royal Hospital Charite in Berlin refused her a permanent position and a medical degree, Zakrzeska emigrated to the United States in 1853. She eventually obtained a medical degree and became an advocate for medical and nursing education, the abolition of slavery, and women's rights (Seller, 1981). Thus educational opportunities for new social and economic roles were possible.

Most women in the United States—native-born and immigrant—had a different experience from Zakrzeska. Even educators and reformers, in the first half of the twentieth century, considered the home to be our proper place. Women who worked outside the home, especially immigrant women, were viewed as the cause of many social problems. By working for low wages, becoming too independent, and potentially becoming involved in "irregular" sexual lives, we were said to weaken traditional family life. Thus women's education of the day, but especially for immigrant women, emphasized "domestic arts" in an effort to keep us at home. And, as the industrial economy turned toward mass production of goods, our proper role was recast as that of consumer homemaker (ibid.).

Work and family responsibilities, however, left few immigrant women with the time for formal education. It was our daughters who were "Americanized" in the schools, and some grew up to be writers who recorded their experiences (Litoff and McDonnell, 1994). Some were joyful at the new worlds opened to them. Mary Antin, a Jewish immigrant, author of *The Promised Land*, published in 1912, recalled her delight at her academic progress and of how proud she was to carry books home every day (Hoffman, 1981; Sellers, 1981). Japanese American Monica Sone, in her autobiography, *Nisei Daughter*, compared her modest behavior conditioned by the formality and politeness of afternoon Japanese school, which her parents insisted that she attend, with her public school in Seattle where she was a "jumping, screaming, roustabout Yankee" in the years prior to World War II (Sone, 1979:22). Other immigrant girls recalled school years with personal pain, remembering the ridicule of having different dress, language, and food habits and of being treated as socially inferior (Gibson and Ogbu, 1991).

Most immigrant girls obtained only elementary education in the years prior to World War II. Unlike African American and native-born girls, who generally completed more years of schooling than male counterparts, immigrant girls more frequently than our brothers left school early to take care of younger siblings or to work and earn a small wage for the household. Immigrant families tended to use what few resources they had to support boys rather than girls to obtain an education. Higher education for women was also viewed as a detriment rather than an asset, since marriage was our ultimate goal. For immigrant girls growing up in a new culture, women teachers were one of our few role models. With the additional encouragement of our mothers who desired more for us, many im-

Elizabeth Loza Newby's Choice and Dilemma

Late one afternoon, within a week following my graduation from high school, Mother greeted me at the door. . . . The note said that I was the recipient of a one-thousand dollar scholarship for college. . . . At last I was being given the opportunity to escape from my dreary migrant existence.

. . . While most of my classmates were destined to go to institutions of higher learning, I considered myself fortunate just to complete high school. My sense of accomplishment, which my mother shared, is beyond expression in words. . . . We knew it was going to be difficult to tell Dad. . . . He was furious! . . . He continued his tirade and gave me the longest lecture I had ever heard on the evils of college and the terrible nature of career women. . . . Mom and I sat in grave silence until his tirade ended. . . . He could not understand why I could not accept the traditional life-style of the typical Mexican migrant girl. . . . Dad did not speak to me the rest of the week.

[The day before she was to leave for college, her father finally spoke and], my world came crashing down all around me, leaving me drained and speechless. He continued: "I have decided that you can give up all these foolish ideas about college and have the love and protection of your family, or you can go ahead with your foolish plans to enter college. But the minute you walk out our door, consider it closed to you forever."

. . . After Dad had left, Mom came in to comfort me. . . . "Elizabeth I know this is a difficult decision you have to make, but I want you to think about this: Don't let emotion and 'old country' traditions hinder your future. You *are* and *always will be* my daughter. Your father can never take that away from me. I want you to go and take advantage of this wonderful opportunity. Make us all proud. Your father is slow to change, but give him time and pray for him. Please go with my blessing."

With great reluctance I left home that last Monday of August 1966. It was the most difficult decision I had ever had to make, for I knew full well the consequences of being disowned. That day was a turning point in my life in that my family ties and relationships could never be the same again—I had lost my father forever. I was frightened and lonely as I boarded the bus for college, and my heart was heavy for Mom and the family. . . . I cried most of the way to Texas, thinking about the family which I had lost. . . .

(Newby, 1977: Chapter 3)

migrant girls, past and present, continued to use the educational system to widen our opportunities (ibid.). Some choices were conflicted ones for both daughters and mothers. For Mexican-born Elizabeth Loza Newby, from a family of migrant workers, the rejection of a marriage arranged by her father and her decision to go to college resulted in independence at a high price, the loss of family ties.

The Struggle for Higher Education in the United States

Relatively little resistance accompanied the establishment of coeducational public elementary schools and all-female and coeducational high schools in the United States. The real struggle took place over the issue of higher education, which was identified with the male professions of college teaching, the ministry, the law, and medicine. The establishment of colleges for women, the attempts to gain entry into all-male universities, and the struggle to gain theological, legal, and medical degrees began in the second half of the nineteenth century.

The success of women's colleges depended to a large extent on the compromises made by their organizers, administrators, and students. For the freedom to follow the male-defined curriculum, women's colleges committed themselves to maintaining a high level of feminine decorum, what sociologist Sara Delamont has called "double conformity." This "double conformity" concerned the strict adherence on the part of both educators and the educated to two sets of rigid standards: those of ladylike behavior at all times *and* those of the dominant male cultural and educational system (Delamont, 1978a).

The pattern for such a compromise was set in the experience of women who entered men's colleges in the first half of the nineteenth century. These colleges were reluctant to admit women because college education was considered training for a profession, and the professions, particularly the ministry, were viewed as men's occupations. Thus the notion of allowing women to attend was contrary to the domestic ideology of separate spheres. Four years after its founding, Oberlin College, in 1837, was the first in the country to accept women for its collegiate program. Of state universities, only Iowa admitted women from the beginning, starting with four out of eighty-nine students in 1855. The decline in university enrollments during the Civil War led a number of other schools to admit women. By 1870, eight state universities were open to women, but many were enrolled only in separate "female departments" (Newcomer, 1959).

Oberlin's policies illustrate the prevailing attitudes toward higher education for women. Oberlin was established to train men to the ministry, especially for the newly opened West. Its "Ladies' Department" offered a similar course of study to the regular collegiate program, but did not require Latin, Greek, or higher mathematics. Young women made up one-third to one-half of the student body, mixed freely with young men in classrooms, at meals, and on social occasions, and were excluded only from the religious functions of men. However, a study of the first four decades at Oberlin reveals that despite the appearance of coeducation, women were admitted primarily for the well-being of male students, to provide the future clergy with suitable wives who were cultivated, discreet, religious, and good, prudent housekeepers. Women students were expected to wash and repair the clothing of the "leading sex," care for men's rooms, take charge of dining hall tasks, and serve as models of manners and refinement, while helping to counteract men's "morbid fantasies" about us (Hogeland, 1972–1973).

When Lucy Stone (1818–1893), later a leader in the American women's rights movement, entered Oberlin in 1837, she and three other young women were permitted to take the regular four-year collegiate course after completing the preparatory one of equal length in the Ladies' Department. Even when she was admitted to classes with men, she was not allowed to engage in debates or read her own essays in class. When she graduated, she refused to write the commencement address that was hers by right of intellectual achievement because the college would not let her read it at the ceremony (Harris, 1978; Lerner, 1977).

Her classmate Antoinette Brown (1825–1921) announced upon graduation that she wished to become a minister, to the horror of her teachers and her parents. Although she was admitted to the Oberlin Theological School as an "exception," and parts of her dissertation—a critique of the writings of St.

Paul on the subject of women—were published in the *Oberlin Quarterly*, the college authorities refused to give her a student's license to preach. In 1850, the college also refused to confer on her the divinity degree she had earned. When she did achieve ordination in 1853 in a Congregational church in New York State, she became the first woman to be ordained a minister in the United States (Harris, 1978).

By 1870 the results of the efforts to achieve higher education for women were meager. Some three thousand women were studying for a liberal arts degree, twenty-two hundred of them in women's colleges. Although about forty private coeducational institutions were "open" to women, the number of women in their collegiate departments was not over six hundred. The number of women in the eight state universities that admitted women was some two hundred (Newcomer, 1959). Coeducation was virtually nonexistent in the East.

The move to establish separate, private women's colleges contributed to the founding of Smith and Wellesley in 1875, Bryn Mawr in 1885, and Radcliffe College in 1893. In addition, Mary Lyon's Mount Holyoke became a college in 1888 (Horowitz, 1993). The lack of funds for black higher education in general discouraged the creation of separate colleges (often called seminaries in the South) for African American women. The exceptions—Miner Teachers College, Spelman College, and Bennett College—were established with the assistance of white Northern philanthropists and missionary associations (Ihle, 1986:III, IV).

A renewed resistance to the idea of higher education for women occurred during the 1870s. Dr. Edward Clarke, until 1872 a professor of medicine at Harvard University, was keenly aware that women were not only demanding higher education but "knocking loudly at the door of medicine." In 1873 he published *Sex in Education; or, A Fair Chance for the Girls*, a best-seller on both sides of the Atlantic. Dr. Clarke argued that women experienced a sudden spurt of growth at puberty, during which our reproductive systems developed. If anything happened to interfere with this development, the entire system was threatened. If, for example, our nervous energies were expended elsewhere, rather than concentrated upon the reproductive system, we would not become normal, healthy young women but would suffer physical deterioration, accompanied by menstrual disorders, constant headaches, and even hysteria. Thus higher education threatened women with "monstrous brains and puny bodies; abnormally active cerebration and abnormally weak digestion; flowing thought and constipated bowels" (Burstyn, 1973; Walsh, 1977:119, 124–26).

The influence of Clarke's challenge must be gauged by the debate that continued through the next thirty years. One of the first public replies, *The Question of Rest for Women During Menstruation* (1876) by Dr. Mary Putnam Jacobi, challenged the scientific grounds of his observations. Using questionnaires and health tests of a sample of young women, some of whom were studying medicine, she found that those of us who maintained normal work patterns suffered less menstrual discomfort than those who did not (Walsh, 1977).

Most female college graduates gravitated to the socially acceptable positions of teacher and librarian (Garrison, 1979). The more adventurous created new professions for women such as the settlement-house worker in the slums of major cities. Three-fifths of all settlement-house workers between 1889 and 1914 were women, and nine-tenths of these women were college graduates. This social reform movement provided two important opportunities for women who had been to college. The first was the residence itself, which allowed us to continue the close peer group

Jane Addams surrounded by settlement house children. As a young woman college graduate in the 1880s, Addams sought a way of putting her higher education to work. At age 29, after a visit to Toynbee Hall in London, the first settlement house in the world, she established Hull House in Chicago, the first settlement house in the United States. She maintained a connection with Hull House the rest of her life. (University of Illinois Library at Chicago Circle Campus, Jane Addams Memorial Collection)

relationships that had characterized our college years, and the second was the sense of mission it gave us, a sense of doing the world's work. College-educated women saw in settlement house work both adventure and an opportunity to demonstrate our "refinement, taste, travel, and culture" and to act as mediators between the idle rich and the working poor (Rousmaniere, 1970). It was also a profession that gained respectability because it fit so well with the values of "nurturance, sympathy, domestic management and self-sacrifice" that society identified with the condition of being a woman (Harris, 1978:118).

It has also been suggested that the women who graduated from women's colleges before and after 1910 differed significantly in the number who married, had children, had oc-cupations, and went to graduate school. Analyzing the alumnae rosters of Bryn Mawr and Wellesley colleges, one study finds that among the group who graduated before 1910, far fewer married; those who did marry had fewer children; and far more took jobs than in the later group. The conclusion is that larger numbers of women among the first generations of graduates chose to remain unmarried and to achieve independence by pursuing careers, but that in the longer run, college "did not permanently change the domesticity cult which prescribed a role of subservice and dedication to the home and family for women" (Wein, 1974:45; Frankfort, 1977).

To some extent, this conclusion is borne out by the development of domestic science and home economics as a professional move-

A domestic science class early in the twentieth century. Such classes became a standard part of the public school curriculum for girls, based on the assumption that since all women would undertake household responsibilities, they should be trained to carry them out efficiently. (Photo by Jacob A. Riis. Jacob A. Riis Collection, Museum of the City of New York)

ment, both within and outside colleges, early in the twentieth century. Women who pioneered the new home economics field were academic women whose careers had begun as challenges to male professional preserves. For example, Ellen Swallow Richards became the first woman to earn a B.S. degree at the Massachusetts Institute of Technology, in chemistry. Although MIT allowed her to do graduate work, it refused to grant her a Ph.D. because she was a woman. She married an MIT professor and established her own women's laboratory to train women scientists, contributing her own money to keep it in operation (Harris, 1978). Shut out from a scientific career as it would have been pursued by a man, Richards pioneered the application of modern science to cooking, nutrition, sanitation, and hygiene. She developed courses in these areas and organized the American Home Economics Association in 1908 (ibid.).

By 1927, domestic science and home economics courses or majors were available in over 650 colleges and normal schools (Walsh, 1977). At Cornell University, the first women to achieve faculty status were professors of home economics, Martha Van Rensselaer and Flora Rose. Even so, when they were appointed in 1911 they were also advised not to attend faculty meetings until some of the opposition to appointing women to faculty rank subsided (Conable, 1977).

The Education of Women in the Third World

European imperialism and colonialism after 1500 imposed in varying degrees Western institutions and practices in Asia, Africa, the Caribbean, and Latin America and transformed existing traditional ones. The results for the education of women were mixed. On the one hand, the colonial experience provided some

Elizabeth Blackwell (1821–1910). The first woman in the United States to earn a medical degree. Blackwell founded an Infirmary for Women and Children in New York in 1857 to provide a clinic where women who wished to become doctors might train. The difficulties women faced in obtaining medical training led Blackwell to found a women's medical college in 1868. (New York Academy of Medicine Library)

women with the opportunity for formal education for the first time with the introduction of missionary schools for girls. In the eighteenth and nineteenth centuries, modern schools were established in the colonies for girls as well as boys. Indigenous institutions of higher education were introduced in many colonies to train colonial professionals and political leaders. The most privileged colonial subjects, including a few women, also studied at elite institutions and church-related schools in Europe or the United States by late in the nineteenth century. Such opportunities, as in India, enabled some women to become teachers, nurses, midwives, doctors, and lawyers (Jayawardena, 1986).

Elsewhere, colonial governments simply neglected educational services as in the Portuguese African territories of Angola, Guinea-Bissau, and Mozambique (Lindsay, 1980). In the Belgian Congo, present-day Zaire, sex discrimination in enrollment and curriculum was legal, resulting in one of the lowest educational attainment rates for women in the

Third World (Yates, 1982). Such policies contributed to major shortages of trained personnel in a multitude of fields after independence. In these situations, it was women who were most likely to be deprived and to suffer a declining status when our lack of access to formal educational institutions had served to further marginalize us from the modern sector and to downgrade our historical political and economic contributions to society (Lindsay, 1980; Yates, 1982).

Western colonialism brought not only political and economic domination but also concepts of racial and cultural hierarchy. The belief that European races and cultures were superior had a tremendous impact on how colonized peoples began to view themselves and their societies. Indigenous elites began to

Girls tending vegetable garden in the Philippines. Education of children may take many aspects. It can be in a "shop" class in secondary schooling in the United States where girls as well as boys participate in craft activities, or in team sports, like soccer. In economically developing countries like the Philippines, young girls receive instruction, in addition to traditional subjects, in such basic skills as raising crops. (CARE)

redefine traditional concepts, including that of modernity and womanhood. For male leaders from the upper classes and the intelligentsia who identified with their colonial masters and sought to reform their traditional societies to more closely resemble those of the West, the emancipation and education of women became a critical factor.

Educated women, as in the West, were seen as essential to a modern society; but our education was likewise narrowly defined. Women did not study the same curriculum as men. Nor were the same educational opportunities made available to poor women. Influenced in part by missionary schools with Christian values of the nuclear family, men as heads of households, and women as the prime upholders of virtue and goodness, the colonial and emergent nationalist leadership sought to replicate nineteenth-century European codes of conduct for women in the Third World. As Kumari Jayawardena has summarized: "The objectives of the reformers were thus twofold: to establish in their countries a system of stable, monogamous nuclear families with educated and employable women such as was associated with capitalist development and bourgeois ideology; and yet to ensure that women would retain a position of traditional subordination within the family" (Jayawardena, 1986:15).

Hence the content and nature of our education was to prepare us to be supportive wives and mothers within a patriarchal nuclear family system to facilitate the advancement of male elites in the colonial system, which also was differentiated by color and caste. In the British Caribbean, for example, lower-class black boys and girls attended coeducational schools, but studied different subjects that prepared females to be domestic servants and males to be artisans. Divisions by color, class, and sex were further reinforced in the curriculum at the secondary level. Upper-class white males were educated for the professions and senior positions in the colonial administration, and middle-class males, many of whom were of mixed black and white backgrounds and called "colored" or "mulattoes," received training for the civil service and commercial life. Middle-class and upper-class females were expected to be able wives and companions for educated husbands. But while we received more years of schooling, the curriculum content with its emphasis on household subjects such as needlework differed little from that provided for black lower-class girls (Ellis, 1986).

Women reformers challenged this conservative view of our education and societal role. Feminist literature of the late nineteenth and early twentieth centuries debated the nature of women's education and shared information about common struggles for change in Third World countries as well as Europe. For example, Iranian women could read *Knowledge* (from about 1906); Chinese women, *The Chinese Women's Journal* (1907); Japanese women, *Seito* or "Bluestocking" (1911); while Egyptian women had fifteen Arabic journals from which to choose by 1914. Nonetheless, readership in this period was limited to learned women (Jayawardena, 1986).

The end of colonialism after World War II was achieved with the active support of women in the independence movements and wars of liberation (see Chapter 14). New nations in Asia, Africa, the Middle East, the Caribbean, and Latin America have made a concerted effort to transform their educational systems as a first step toward development. Since the 1960s, primary school enrollment for girls has doubled, with significant increases for women in secondary, vocational, and higher education. Thus more women have greater access to formal education and are completing more years of schooling. However, as these countries in the postcolonial world represent a wide range of cultures, religions, political ideologies, and economic resources, their individual capacity to extend educational opportunities varies, and in some nations wide discrepancies remain between women and men (Kelly and Elliott, 1982).

Third World feminists have begun to address issues of curriculum content and the tracking of women into specialized fields that become gender-specific in a given society. Since the 1970s, economic development has been the key concern of Third World nations. Many states, particularly nonaligned countries in the Cold War era, initiated policies to involve women in the development process at all levels on the basis of equal opportunities and responsibilities (Hune, 1980). Viewing the context of women's education and role within the framework of development, Third World feminists have criticized specific development strategies, especially the Western capitalist model, as being detrimental to the status, participation, and training of women. They have pointed out that instead of liberating women, development planning that imposes Western values and standards upon traditional ones has perpetuated gender roles that discriminate against women, undermine our historical economic activities, deprive us of access to new economic resources, and relegate us to the domestic sphere as our primary role. This continuation of gender inequality has had its most severe impact on poor, rural, and illiterate women (Rogers, 1980; Mount Holyoke, 1987).

The Present State of Women's Literacy and Education

Increased access to formal education has been one of our greatest gains globally over the past three decades. Yet, inequalities continue to exist. Table 11.1 reveals some of the disparities at the secondary school level where girls from poorer countries and agricultural societies receive less schooling than those of us in wealthy, industrialized nations. Hidden

Table 11.1 Female and Male Enrollment in Secondary School, 1985

Region	% Female	% Male
Africa	16	26
Northern	31	43
Western	—	—
Eastern	8	14
Middle	11	28
Southern	28	23
Asia	29	44
Southwest	33	52
Middle south	18	36
Southeast	35	41
East	38	54
North America	96	94
Latin America	44	42
Caribbean	49	46
Europe	80	76
Northern	89	85
Western	92	82
Eastern	71	64
Southern	77	78
USSR (former)	98	99

Source: The Population Reference Bureau, Inc., *The World's Women: A Profile, 1985.*

within national averages are differences based on locale and family resources. Girls from rural communities and poor families get less education. Moreover, while in absolute numbers more of us are in school, the gap between males and females, especially at the higher educational levels, has not closed.

Literacy rates, school enrollment, and policies of equal access do not tell the entire story. Cultural attitudes, women's marginal status in the economy, and teaching methods in the schools have been identified as three significant obstacles to women's educational participation. In parts of Asia, Africa, and the Arab world where religious practices and cultural values consider the appropriate role for women as within the domestic sphere, many families restrict the schooling of girls (Tinker and Bramsen, 1976). Such attitudes can limit educated wives of the elite from pursuing professions in order to maintain households for the ornament and pleasure of husbands. Government policies have also contributed to marginalizing women who work outside the home to low-level positions. Altogether, it is not surprising that many women come to lack confidence in our own abilities, which in turn can lead women to restrict our educational goals and ambitions (Conway and Bourque, 1993; Mount Holyoke, 1987).

The existing limitations on women's economic roles tend to reinforce the vocational choices of girls. With so many occupational opportunities before us today, girls in Eastern Europe and Sweden are still choosing typing and beauty care over mechanical and electrical work as vocational subjects (Finn et al., 1982). Literate African women are generally white collar workers, nurses' aides, typists, telephone operators, and saleswomen. Uneducated women in the cities work at light industry or turn to petty trading, brewing, or prostitution (Van Allen, 1976).

Gender differentiation in the classroom and through curriculum materials (see below) also serves to discourage girls' intellectual development and educational attainment. Even in the industrialized nations of North America and Western Europe where literacy is high for both women and men, girls still take fewer mathematics and science courses than do boys. In Eastern Europe and the states of the former Soviet Union, where female literacy and employment rates are equally high, women are still overrepresented in fields identified with our gender. Here both medicine and teaching are seen as appropriate for women, but our participation at the higher levels of authority and prestige disappears. There continues to be "the belief that women

do not have the necessary time for demanding positions" (Lapidus, 1976; Springer, 1976:197; Bianchi and Spain, 1986).

Women who have acquired formal education have not easily achieved the positions of power open to men. Here, too, stereotypical assumptions about gender roles intervene. Today, more and more women in the United States, for example, have achieved male-associated educational credentials; yet we find ourselves with disproportionately fewer of the rewards conventionally attached to them. The gains women once made and continue to make in formal education do not automatically create social acceptance. Many occupations are still identified only for or largely with men.

Education and Career Choices in the United States

Women's Education and Women's Realities

In the United States, women have made significant gains in higher education at all levels particularly since the passage of Title IX in 1972, which outlawed sex discrimination within educational programs receiving federal funds. Table 11.2 reveals that women now receive the majority of B.A. and M.A. degrees, which reflects our representation in the population. However, while more of us are obtaining doctorates and professional degrees,

Table 11.2 Degrees Awarded to U.S. Women as a Percentage of the Total Awarded, 1971 and 1989

	1971	1989
B.A.	44%	53%
M.A.	41%	52%
Ph.D.	14%	37%
Professional	7%	36%

Copyright © 1971/92 by the New York Times Company. Reprinted by permission.

we remain underrepresented at the highest levels. We also remain undersupported in our graduate education. Of the 1991 doctorates, more than half of the women listed personal resources as the primary sources of support (Ries and Thurgood, 1993).

The increase in the number of doctorates is only part of the story. As Figure 11.1 points out, women are both entering traditionally male-dominated fields such as engineering in larger numbers and continuing to obtain Ph.D.s in education, the social sciences, and the humanities.

Choices are even more limited for women of color. While minority women earned slightly more bachelor's and master's degrees than minority men, we fall behind at the doctorate level. In 1991, of United States Ph.D.s, the proportion of Asian American, African American, Latina, and Native American women doctorates was 1.2 percent, 2.2 percent, 1.4 percent, and 0.2 percent, respectively (Ries and Thurgood, 1993).

Women are entering the labor force in larger numbers than ever before and we are more educated. Yet at every educational level, women earn less and have fewer opportunities for choice and advancement than men. In 1890, a woman earned 46 cents for every dollar a man earned. A century later, we still earn only 69 cents (*New York Times*, October 18, 1991).

As educators, women are still the majority of elementary and secondary school teachers, but we continue to be strikingly underrepresented at administrative and policy-making levels. In fact, the proportion of women administrators in education has declined since 1930. In 1978, three-quarters of all college and graduate school administrators were men (Howard, 1978; National Research Council, 1980). By 1990, only 12 percent of all college presidents were women, but this was up from 5 percent in 1975. In 1985, women numbered fewer than 10 percent of deans at coeducational institutions. In 1989, we were 28.3 percent of the faculty, an increase from 21.4 percent in 1971. However, the largest proportion

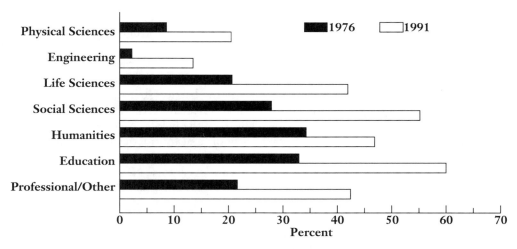

Figure 11.1 Percentage of doctorates awarded to U.S. women in each broad field in 1976 and 1991.
Source: Ries and Thurgood, 1993:31.

of women are in untenured and part-time positions. In 1989, women were 14 percent of the full professors, 26 percent of the associate professors, 38.1 percent of the assistant professors, 53.5 percent of the lecturers, and 49.7 percent of the instructors (Milem and Astin, 1993). Our salary levels at every level remain several thousand dollars below those of men.

Professional Advancement

The traditional professions requiring higher education have been the ministry, law, and medicine. Because the practice of these professions takes place outside the domestic sphere, in the nineteenth century they were viewed as men's activities. That definition, in the late twentieth century, is still slow to change. Not only have men guarded the custom and privilege of the professions as their "right," but women have been socialized to agree with them. Our efforts to break through these barriers have taken such sheer determination that it is more surprising that many achieved our goals than that many more were deterred from trying.

Female ministers were rare in the last century because the largest churches—Roman Catholic, Episcopalian, Lutheran, Presbyterian, Methodist, and Baptist—would neither ordain women nor allow us to occupy their pulpits. Those who did by 1890 were the Congregationalists, Universalists, Protestant Methodists, and German Methodists (Harris, 1978). The continuing struggle of women to achieve theological degrees and become ordained in the modern era is discussed in Chapter 10.

Becoming a lawyer in America proved just as difficult for women. The first woman admitted to the bar was Arabella Babb Mansfield, in Iowa in 1869. A struggle was necessary in nearly all the states where women sought to become lawyers, and it took years for the first woman to be allowed to practice

before the U.S. Supreme Court, in 1879. By 1920, only 3 percent of lawyers were women (Harris, 1978). The real change in women's access to legal training came with the women's liberation movement in the 1970s. By 1989, women were 22.2 percent of the profession and 40.4 percent of the new graduates in 1988 (*New York Times*, October 18, 1992). However, once in practice, women lawyers are finding a two-tier system, especially in the country's leading law firms. Because law as a profession is modeled for men's careers, those of us who choose to become working mothers are viewed as less serious about our work. We tend to be tracked into associate and part-time positions and not to be considered for partnerships and choice assignments (*New York Times*, August 8, 1988). Male-dominated values about women's traditional roles undermine the belief that a woman can be a professional and a good wife and mother. This creates a double standard that penalizes a female lawyer more for becoming a parent than a male lawyer, whose fathering role is not expected to conflict with his professional obligations.

The struggle by women to obtain medical degrees has also been marked by continual setbacks. Mary Roth Walsh (1977) has written a history of this struggle, appropriately titled (from a 1946 newspaper advertisement) "*Doctors Wanted: No Women Need Apply.*" Occasionally wartime and personnel shortages lowered the barriers, but they were always raised again once the crisis was past. Women pioneers in the field were forced to create female schools and infirmaries before all-male medical schools began to admit us early in the twentieth century. New medical schools seeking enrollment would admit women, only to reduce our numbers as soon as qualified male applicants appeared.

Feminism played a crucial role among the women who sought to become physicians in the nineteenth and early twentieth centuries.

At the end of the nineteenth century, 96 percent of women physicians were affiliated with women's institutions. In 1892, 63 percent of women in medical schools attended all-female ones. In time, the nineteenth-century women's medical colleges merged with men's medical schools, to the detriment of the women. Within twelve years of the merger of the New York Infirmary and Cornell University Medical School, for example, there were no women left on the staff (Walsh, 1977).

Although the number of women applicants to American medical schools increased 300 percent between 1930 and 1966, the proportion of women accepted in male-run medical schools decreased while that of male students increased. Quotas restricting women had become common practice, which meant that the small number of women actually admitted were far better qualified than the men (ibid.).

One might wonder why the pioneer medical women so readily gave up all-female institutions for inclusion in schools and hospitals run by men. Lulled into thinking that our struggle for advancement was won, women allowed the very sources of our strength, our independent institutions, to slip away. When the number of medical schools run by men declined from 162 in 1906 to 69 in 1944, women not only had to compete for fewer places but were also subjected to arbitrary and unpublished quotas, as were all black and Jewish students (ibid.). Mistaking a temporary and calculated welcome for a permanent commitment on the part of the male medical establishment, women found we could as easily be closed out again.

Women have now made a comeback in the medical profession. In the first flush of a renewed women's movement in the 1970s, the number of women as medical students increased dramatically. The breakthrough came as a result of a class action suit brought by the Women's Equity Action League (WEAL) against all medical schools on the charge of illegal discrimination in admission practices. By 1988, women were 33 percent of the new graduates and 17.9 percent of the profession in 1989 (*New York Times*, October 18, 1992).

Women have also begun to question the nature of the medical training that we receive at male-dominated medical schools. We have become more conscious of the sexist language and innuendos of standard medical textbooks, and of the male-centered focus of the curriculum. Women medical students have begun to protest the absence of female role models among those who train us. We have even questioned the premises of the health care delivery system into which we are indoctrinated as medical students (ibid.).

The Limitation of Women's Choices

Educational Experiences in the Early Years. Despite extensive education and academic achievement, women are still faced with a pattern of limited career choices. Why should this be so? Some feminists have analyzed the content of children's books to see what sorts of aspirations are held out to young girls. Elizabeth Fisher (1974) pointed out that the fantasy world of the much-admired picture books used widely with small children, such as those of Maurice Sendak, Dr. Seuss, and Richard Scarry, is primarily a male world. In Sendak's and Seuss's books, the characters are almost entirely male, and friendships occur between boys or even boys and girls, but never between girls. In Scarry, male characters are busy digging, building, breaking, pushing, and pulling, while female characters sit and watch.

A report called *Women on Words and Images* (1974), which analyzed 134 elementary school readers with 2,760 stories, found that stories in which boys were the center of focus outnumbered stories about girls five to two. Stories in which male adults took center stage outnumbered stories focusing on female adults by three to one. Male and female characters in animal stories appeared in a ratio of two to one and in folk and fantasy tales in a ratio of four to one. Moreover, in stories about cruelty or meanness, 65 out of 67 were at the expense of girls. There were 147 role possibilities for male characters in contrast to 25 for girls.

School textbooks, especially in science and mathematics, made it clear that girls would grow up to be passive mothers and boys active fathers. In mathematics texts, the wording of the problems themselves revealed gender bias. Girls were off to the store to buy materials for sewing or cooking; men and boys did woodwork, sailed, climbed mountains, and went to the moon. In "new math" texts, which arranged people in *sets*, groups of men appeared as doctors, firefighters, chefs, astronauts, pilots, letter carriers, painters, and police officers, ignoring the existence of women in several of these occupations. Women, on the other hand, were grouped as waitresses, nurses, stewardesses, and funny-hat wearers (Federbush, 1974). The role of the male achiever dominated textbooks in general. Girls were rarely depicted as capable of independent thinking. Such books were often written by women; their messages reflected our own well-internalized socialization (U'Ren, 1971).

Generally, school curricula and texts continue to have "sexism as their subtext" (Sadker and Sadker, 1994; Smithson, 1990:2–3). Only recently, for example, have introductory social studies and history texts begun to use gender-neutral terms such "Political Behavior" and "Industrial Life" in their chapter titles in place of "Political Man" and "Industrial Man."

Later Educational Experiences. The books by which little girls begin to learn about the world and to acquire formal knowledge lay the groundwork for the limiting of choices later in school. Teacher expectations and teaching methods also reinforce gender stereotypes. From elementary school through graduate school, most teachers still expect less of female students and give more time and attention to male students in the classroom and in academic guidance (Sadker and Sadker, 1986, 1994). Hence girls are not encouraged and supported intellectually, especially in mathematics and the sciences. Gender bias in the use of educational technology is also leaving girls behind, as studies document that girls are less likely than boys to use computers and to enroll in computer programming courses in high schools (Smithson, 1990). High school counselors have sometimes urged girls to avoid the more rigorous courses of study and to set our sights on traditional female roles, including teacher, nurse, and secretary.

Two recent studies point to the serious and pervasive unsupportive environment in which girls learn. The American Association of University Women in its report "How Schools Shortchange Girls" (AAUW, 1992) cites the unequal treatment girls receive in a wide range of areas, including curricula, materials used in classrooms, testing, and teacher attention. Its recommendations for action places girls at the center of education planning to alleviate inequities. A joint NOW Legal Defense and Education Fund and Wellesley College Center for Research on Women study (1993) is a shocking revelation on how extensively girls are sexually harassed every day in public by male classmates and by their teachers and how the schools' "evaded curriculum" teaches young women to accept this abuse and young men to remain unchallenged in their intimidating behavior (Stein et al., 1993).

In college, women again receive vocational counseling that sets us on traditional career paths. Male professors often make it clear that they do not expect women to pursue "serious" work (Roby, 1973). Women's academic success has regularly been attributed to diligence, not brilliance (Schwartz and Lever, 1973). In graduate school, more women than men drop out, even though women represent a smaller percentage of graduate students. It has been found that when graduate students marry each other, the woman is likely to undertake all the household tasks; and once we become mothers, we find it very difficult to continue our studies. Women who dropped out often cited as reasons not only new burdens that we assumed but also the emotional strain involved, pressure from our husbands, and a belief that our professors did not take us seriously anyway (Patterson and Sells, 1973). These experiences and others in which the academic pursuits of young women are trivialized and marginalized are discussed in a series of reports on the chilly classroom and campus climate for women in higher education published by the Project on the Status and Education of Women Association of American Colleges (Hall and Sandler, 1982, 1984; Sandler and Hall, 1986).

Exceptions: Women Who Achieved

What kind of educational experiences *do* encourage achievement in women? M. Elizabeth Tidball investigated the college background of women whose achievements were listed in *Who's Who of American Women* and whose college experience occurred between 1910 and 1960. She concluded that women's colleges produced more achieving women in each of the five decades than did coeducational institutions. She decided that a chief reason for this significant difference was the greater number of women faculty and administrators in women's colleges who provided role models (Tidball, 1973, 1980). Advocates of single-sex education who lamented over the excessively high number of women's colleges that either closed or became coeducational during the 1960s and 1970s (sixty-eight alone between June and December 1968), and who welcomed the surge of interest in women's ed-

ucational institutions in the 1980s, have referred to Tidball's conclusions (Rice and Hemmings, 1988).

Oates and Williamson (1978) categorized the achieving women—using Tidball's measurement—into graduates of women's Ivy League colleges (called the "Seven Sisters"), graduates of other women's colleges and graduates of coeducational institutions. They found that during the 1930s, the decade of the highest representation of women achievers, the Seven Sisters produced sixty-one achievers per ten thousand students, while the other women's colleges and small coeducational schools produced eighteen per ten thousand. The larger colleges in every case produced fewer achieving women. On the other hand, women graduates of coeducational colleges achieved greater prominence as government officials and as faculty members and administrators in professional schools, producing teachers, librarians, and home economists.

Rice and Hemmings (1988) in their update of the Tidball study propose other factors to explain Tidball's and Oates and Williamson's findings. They suggest that historically the kind of student recruited by the Seven Sisters is distinct. Women graduates of the Seven Sisters came from families with social and economic advantages and with the highly competitive selection process of these private institutions were more likely to be academically motivated. They conclude that both the college environment including women role models, as Tidball's study suggests, and the selective recruitment process of a college are influential factors. In short, "The student who applies to the women's college is already a self-selected quantity; probably brighter and more advantaged, she may pick a special environment that in turn nurtures and reinforces her later success" (ibid.:558). Rice and Hemmings note that coeducational institutions can also provide a supportive women's environment through the increased presence of

---

Women's Education at Hunter College

A study of undergraduate institutions that ranked highest in the number of female and male graduates who obtained doctorates in the period 1920–1973 placed Hunter College first among all institutions educating women, with a total number of 1,110. Hunter College also ranked within the first four among those institutions whose women graduates obtained doctorates in physical sciences and engineering, life sciences, social sciences, arts and humanities, and education (Tidball and Kistiakowsky, 1976). Established in 1870 as New York City's first public normal college for women, Hunter had developed by 1914 into a full liberal arts college named after its first president, Thomas Hunter. Hunter College became fully coeducational in 1964. As part of the City University of New York, it remains committed to giving women the kind of education that allowed its earlier women graduates to outnumber the women of other institutions in the pursuit of higher education. The women's studies program at Hunter College was initiated in 1971 and by 1976 offered both a collateral major and minor (Helly, 1983). The student body at Hunter taught by the authors of this text is still composed of three-quarters women. Hunter students reflect the many cultural, ethnic, and religious groups who make up New York City and include a large proportion of adult students. Beginning in 1993, all students will complete a course that focuses on gender or sexual orientation as part of their general education requirements.

---

women faculty. However, the factors that aid women to become achievers after college are still under consideration.

Reentry Women

In the 1960s, there began a trend for adult women to "drop back in" to colleges to complete unfinished educational goals and to prepare ourselves for employment or career transitions. Women were enabled to do this where there existed flexible and part-time course schedules, counseling and efforts to help us adjust to educational requirements, and special programs aimed at building our self-confidence. Denmark and Guttentag (1955, 1967) showed that even attending college for only one semester was significant in reducing the discrepancy between the mature woman's ideal and actual self-concepts.

Two models emerged in the 1960s. One was the Radcliffe (now Bunting) Institute for Independent Study, which sought to give individual women support for independent projects pursued part-time or full-time, depending on our needs, surrounded by other women at similar career stages. The other model was the program for returning women in separate centers for the continuing education of women, pioneered by Sarah Lawrence College in the East and farther west in the big city centers of the universities of Minnesota, Wisconsin, and Michigan (Campbell, 1973). These programs gave special assistance to adult students to help build up our self-confidence and to help us with the problems of combining studies and family responsibilities. Since the 1970s, colleges and universities across the country have been finding new and flexible ways of accommodating "nontraditional" students, a large number of whom continue to be adult women.

New Beginnings for Women

As women became more self-conscious and we began to explore our experiences with each other, we also began to question the assumptions about women we learned in traditional disciplines. Ad hoc courses on women and gender roles and gender differences sprang up in the second half of the 1960s because women wanted to learn more about ourselves and our assigned place in society. California State University at San Diego was the first institution to develop a program of women's studies courses by 1970 (Boxer, 1982; Zinsser, 1993). The first graduate seminar in the psychology of women was organized by Florence Denmark and her students at Hunter College. Increasingly, it became clear that education at every level delivered knowledge that reflected the gender of the writer, and that the very theories used to explain the world were theories seen through a male perspective. These insights generated new courses and research and have initiated a serious and sustained reevaluation of all knowledge.

At first, women scholars sought to correct the distortions and omissions that were found to underpin theories of knowledge, our knowledge of the past, and our understanding of contemporary society. Women's studies courses developed just as women were "dropping back in" to colleges and universities and were very eager to find out more about ourselves. Women's studies not only contribute to the new feminist critique of knowledge but also to the raising of women's consciousness of our realities and our choices.

The scholarship in women's studies began to be disseminated through new journals such as *Signs*, *Feminist Studies*, and *Women's Studies*. Women's issues became the subject of new courses and the focus of new centers for research on women at such institutions as Wellesley, Stanford, and the Eagleton Institute at Rutgers University, which has a special program for "policy research on women." A National Council for Research on Women was formed. Articles, monographs, and anthologies brought new reading lists to courses on women. The assumptions underlying past research were looked at anew, and every field from literary criticism to psychology of women to history, anthropology, economics, sociology, biology, and education itself received a scrutiny that questioned the traditional framework of knowledge. The whole world of knowledge suddenly seemed open for reassessment, including the vocabularies that have communicated traditional male perspectives. Mary Field Belenky and her colleagues (1986), Elizabeth Minnich (1990), Patricia Hill Collins (1991), and Sandra Harding (1991) are among those who question the assumption that there is a universal path of development, learning, and construction of knowledge. Christie Farnham (1987), Ellen DuBois (1987), and Susan Aiken (1988) and their collaborators have assessed the influence of feminist scholars and feminist scholarship on teaching, research, publications, and curriculum reform in higher education. They find that while great strides have been and are being made to increase women's presence in higher education, resistance persists. The vocal opposition and national attention given to Stanford University's decision in 1988 to replace its core course in Western Civilization, which emphasized "classic texts" by primarily male contributors, with a new course on "Cultures, Ideas and Values" that requires students to read works by "women, minorities and persons of color" is indicative of this process.

Once courses in women's studies appeared in significant numbers, majors and minors in women's studies programs and even advanced degrees began to take shape. When the first National Women's Studies Association convention took place at San Diego, California, in 1977, it was estimated that some four thousand such courses existed across the country (Tobias, 1978). By 1990 there were over 500 women's studies programs and three departments at institutions public and private, large and small, single-sex and coeducational. Many of these programs were concerned about larger issues in their academic and social communities, including reentry women students; sex discrimination in faculty appointments, promotion, and retention; the free expression of sexual preferences; health care; legal services; child care; and transforming the knowledge base itself to reflect the perspectives not only through gender but other prisms of diversity such as race and class and sexual orientation (Fiol-Matta and Chamberlain, 1994).

The future of women's studies, in part, is contingent upon ensuring our continued presence in higher education. Women students can take the initiative to ensure their institutions respond to their needs. Women faculty remain underrepresented at the full professor level and, as in other professions, continue to find gender discrimination in tenure, promotion, and wages. Aisenberg and Harrington (1988) also find that women's greater familial responsibilities and our historic exclusion in the academic community deny to us an understanding of specific male-defined cultural norms of the profession that serve to limit our capacity to participate. As with other occupations and professions where women remain in subordinate positions, mutual support and advocacy—among students and faculty—are viewed as essential to overcoming organizational barriers in higher education.

A discipline new unto itself is emerging, challenging some of the assumptions of traditional disciplines such as literature, history, or biology, in which until recent decades women have been largely ignored or else "measured in masculine terms" (Westkott, 1979:423). If we find that in the light of our new focus on women's realities and the new theories that emerge we are reordering the universe, if we find that our new theories help us to order and organize the findings of other disciplines to our own use, we have indeed embarked upon an exciting adventure. The future holds the possibility that by means of women's studies we will find a way to restructure knowledge, to make it resonant with women's perceptions of the world in all their diversity, with women's consciousness, as well as men's. If we do so, we will indeed have wrought an intellectual revolution.

Summary

Throughout the world, the pattern today is for women to be less literate than men, either because we have limited access to formal education or because we have been socialized to believe it is not necessary. Even when women make gains in formal education, we still are shut out of many occupations identified with men.

Formal education in the past has been directed primarily to males, although occasionally some women studied and practiced various professions. During the early middle ages, women in Europe were more literate than men in secular society, since boys were taught martial and sports skills while scholarship was left to the clergy and the young women who attended convent schools.

Although the Renaissance period valued cultivated women, most women had to decide between abandoning studies for marriage and continuing studies in the convent or in solitude. More educational opportunities for upper-class women opened up in the sixteenth century, but it took considerable determination to be a serious scholar. Feminists in France in the seventeenth century challenged the social hierarchy by calling into question the authority of tradition, custom, and religion.

From the seventeenth century on, the goals of women's education were given serious consideration. Many schools and tutors decided that the "proper" education was one that would train women to obey and please our future husbands. Some feminists in seventeenth- and eighteenth-century England protested this view and advocated serious education for women.

In the last two hundred years, an educational revolution has taken place globally. Many nations have undertaken the obligation of providing free elementary and secondary education to both girls and boys. But the questions of how much education women should have and for what purposes are still debated. The all-female schools of nineteenth-century America produced many educated women who went into the teaching profession. Many of us were subject to discrimination by local school boards. African American women—as well as other women of color and new immigrants—have had to fight both racism and sexism in our struggle to get educated.

In the last century, most male institutions of higher education refused to admit women because higher education was considered preparation for professions still reserved for males. Those women who did enroll in these colleges were often prohibited from full participation in the curriculum. Separate private women's colleges were established to enable women to enjoy the same kind of education men were receiving, but the price these all-female institutions had to pay for social approval was strict conformity to traditional ideas of feminine decorum.

Although women today are achieving higher levels of education and training than ever before, we are still finding our career choices far more limited than men's. In this century, women have had to struggle to enter the ministry, law, and medicine. Part of the reason women are so limited in our choices is that from childhood we have been exposed to books and teacher expectations that stress the submissive role of girls and the active role of boys. With this exposure, girls are less likely to pursue subjects such as mathematics and science they identify as "male," but choose fields such as education and home economics because we consider them gender-appropriate. The "chilly classroom climate" and sexual harassment are part of the hostile environment for female students. Those women who are achievers have tended to come from women's colleges and smaller coeducational schools. A recent and growing trend is the reentry of women into college to complete unfinished educations and to prepare for new careers.

Women's studies programs have allowed women to learn more about ourselves and about the ways that knowledge has been delivered through male perspectives. Using our new focus on women's realities, we may find we are rethinking everything we have learned.

Discussion Questions

1. How do the world figures for literacy and enrollment in secondary school reflect the position of women in various societies? Why did early feminists believe that education was important for women—and why was this idea resisted?

2. Do you think the expansion of educational opportunities for women in the United States since 1800—at the elementary, secondary, and college levels and in professional training—would have occurred without special efforts by women?

3. Evaluate the education of women at your college. Do you think there are any special advantages or disadvantages to gender-segregated education?

4. Trace the history of education of the women in your family as far back as you can go. What were the educational experiences of specific women (your grandmothers, aunts, mother, and so forth)? How do their experiences compare with your own, and how do you account for the differences and similarities?

5. What are the opportunities and obstacles in education for the career of your choice? Start with early education, even at the preschool level, and continue through all the other levels of educational training. (If you

haven't yet decided on a career, select an interesting one to think about.)

Recommended Readings

Belenky, Mary Field, et al. *Women's Ways of Knowing*. New York: Basic Books, 1986. Challenges the traditional male model of knowing that renders women "voiceless" and considers how women's ways of knowing are legitimate although different because of our experiences and place in society.

Howe, Florence. *Myths of Coeducation*. Bloomington: Indiana University Press, 1984. A collection of selected essays spanning two decades, 1964–1983, by a distinguished feminist, literary scholar, historian, and teacher, covering key issues in the education of women in the United States and refuting the myth that access to education alone will solve sexual inequity.

Conway, Jill Kerr, and Bourque, Susan C., editors. *The Politics of Women's Education: Perspectives from Asia, Africa, and Latin America*. Ann Arbor: University of Michigan Press, 1993. An excellent collection of interdisciplinary articles on the undereducation of women in Asia, Africa, Latin America, and the Middle East focusing on the determinants, nature, and outcomes of women's education in Third World nations.

Lightfoot, Sara Lawrence. *Balm in Gilead: Journey of a Healer*. Radcliffe Biography Series. Reading, Mass.: Addison-Wesley Publishing, 1988. The biography of an African American woman whose educational experiences in the South and the North reveal a moving personal story behind the analysis offered in this chapter. Born in Mississippi in 1914, she eventually attends Cornell University and goes on to become a physician and child psychiatrist.

Woolf, Virginia. *A Room of One's Own*. 1929.

Reprint. New York: Harcourt, Brace, 1957. The now classic exploration of the ways women have been prevented from achieving higher education and what this has meant for our lives, independence, and creativity.

References

The AAUW Report: How Schools Shortchange Girls. Washington, D.C.: American Association of University Women, 1992.

Aiken, Susan Hardy, Anderson, Karen, Dinnerstein, Myra, Lensink, Judy Nolte, and MacCorquodale, Patricia, editors. *Changing Our Minds: Feminist Transformations of Knowledge*. Albany: State University of New York, 1988.

Aisenberg, Nadya, and Harrington, Mona. *Women of Academe: Outsiders in the Sacred Grove*. Amherst: University of Massachusetts, 1988.

Belenky, Mary Field, Clinchey, Blythe McVicker, Goldberger, Nancy Rule, and Tarule, Jill Mattuck. *Women's Ways of Knowing: The Development of Self, Voice, and Mind*. New York: Basic Books, 1986.

Bianchi, Suzanne M., and Spain, Daphne. *American Women in Transition*. New York: Russell Sage Foundation, 1986.

Boos, Florence S. "Catherine Macaulay's *Letters on Education* (1970): An Early Feminist Polemic." *University of Michigan Papers in Women's Studies* 2 (1976):64–78.

Boxer, Marilyn. "For and About Women: The Theory and Practice of Women's Studies in the United States." *Signs* 7 (1982):661–95.

Burstyn, Joan N. "Education and Sex: The Medical Case Against Higher Education for Women in England, 1870–1900." *Proceedings of the American Philosophical Society* 117 (1973):79–89.

Campbell, Jean. "Women Drop Back In: Educational Innovation in the Sixties." In *Academic Women on the Move*, edited by Alice S. Rossi and Ann Calderwood. New York: Russell Sage, 1973.

Cole, Susan Guettel. "Could Greek Women Read

and Write?" In *Reflections of Women in Antiquity*, edited by Helene P. Foley. New York: Gordon and Breach Science Publishers, 1981.

Collins, Patricia Hill. *Black Feminist Thought*. New York: Routledge, 1991.

Conable, Charlotte Williams. *Women at Cornell: The Myth of Equal Education*. Ithaca: Cornell University Press, 1977.

Conway, Jill Kerr, and Bourque, Susan C., editors. *The Politics of Women's Education: Perspectives from Asia, Africa, and Latin America*. Ann Arbor: University of Michigan Press, 1993.

Cott, Nancy F. *The Bonds of Womanhood: "Woman's Sphere" in New England, 1780–1835*. New Haven: Yale University Press, 1977.

Davis, Natalie Z. "Gender and Genre: Women as Historical Writers, 1400–1820." In *Beyond Their Sex: Learned Women of the European Past*, edited by Patricia H. Labalme. New York: New York University Press, 1980.

———. *Society and Culture in Early Modern France*. Stanford: Stanford University Press, 1975.

Delamont, Sara. "The Contradictions in Ladies' Education." In *The Nineteenth-Century Woman: Her Cultural and Physical World*, edited by Sara Delamont and Lorna Duffin. New York: Barnes & Noble, 1978.

———. "The Domestic Ideology and Women's Education." In *The Nineteenth-Century Woman*, edited by Sara Delamont and Lorna Duffin. New York: Barnes & Noble, 1978.

Denmark, Florence L., and Guttentag, Marcia. "Dissonance in the Self-Concepts and Educational Concepts of College and Non-College-Oriented Women." *Journal of Counseling Psychology* 14 (1967):113–15.

———. "The Effect of College Attendance on Mature Women: Changes in Self Concept and Evaluation of Student Role." *Journal of Social Psychology* 69 (1955):155–58.

Department of Education. National Center for Education Statistics. *Digest of Education Statistics*. Washington, D.C.: U.S. Government Printing Office, 1981.

DuBois, Ellen Carol, Kelly, Gail Paradise, Kennedy, Elizabeth Lapovksy, Korsmeyer, Carolyn W., and Robinson, Lillian S. *Feminist Scholarship: Kindling in the Groves of Academe*. Urbana: University of Illinois, 1987.

Ellis, Pat, ed. *Women of the Caribbean*. London: Zed Publishers, 1986.

Farnham, Christie, editor. *The Impact of Feminist Research in the Academy*. Bloomington: Indiana University Press, 1987.

Federbush, Marsha. "The Sex Problems of School Math Books." In *And Jill Came Tumbling After: Sexism in American Education*, edited by Judith Stacey, Susan Bereaud, and Joan Daniels. New York: Dell, 1974.

Ferguson, Moira, editor. *First Feminists: British Women Writers 1578–1799*. Bloomington: Indiana University Press, 1985.

——— and Todd, Janet. *Mary Wollstonecraft*. Boston: Twayne Publishers, 1984.

Ferrante, Joan M. "The Education of Women in the Middle Ages in Theory, Fact, and Fantasy." In *Beyond Their Sex*, edited by Patricia H. Labalme. New York: New York University Press, 1980.

Finn, Jeremy D., Reis, Janet, and Dulberg, Loretta. "Sex Differences in Educational Attainment: The Process." In *Women's Education in the Third World: Comparative Perspectives*, edited by Gail P. Kelly and Carolyn M. Elliott. Albany: State University of New York, 1982.

Finn, Jeremy D., Dulberg, Loretta, and Reis, Janet. "Sex Differences in Educational Attainment: A Cross-National Perspective." *Harvard Educational Review* 49 (1979):477–503.

Fiol-Matta, Lisa and Chamberlain, Mariam K., *Women of Color and the Multicultural Curriculum: Transforming the College Classroom*. New York: The Feminist Press at the City University of New York, 1994.

Fisher, Elizabeth. "Children's Books: The Second Sex, Junior Division." In *And Jill Came Tumbling After*, edited by Stacey et al. New York: Dell, 1974.

Frankfort, Roberta. *Collegiate Women: Domesticity and Career in Turn-of-the-Century America*. New York: New York University Press, 1977.

Garrison, Dee. *Apostles of Culture: The Public Librarian and American Society, 1876–1920*. New York: Free Press, 1979.

Gibson, Margaret, and Ogbu, John, editors. *Minority Status and Schooling: A Comparative Study of Immigrant and Involuntary Minorities*. New York: Garland Publishing, 1991.

Giddings, Paula. *When and Where I Enter: The Impact of Black Women on Race and Sex in America*. New York: Bantam, 1984.

Hall, Roberta M., and Sandler, Bernice R. "The Classroom Climate: A Chilly One for Women?" Washington, D.C.: Project on the Status and Education of Women, Association of American Colleges, 1982.

———. "Out of the Classroom: A Chilly Campus Climate for Women?" Washington, D.C.: Project on the Status and Education of Women, Association of American Colleges, 1984.

Hallett, Judith P. "Sappho and Her Social Context: Sense and Sensuality." *Signs* 4 (1979):447–64.

Hansot, Elisabeth, and Tyack, David. "Gender in American Public Schools: Thinking Institutionally." *Signs* 13 (1988):741–60.

Harding, Sandra. *Whose Science? Whose Knowledge?* Ithaca: Cornell University Press, 1991.

Harris, Barbara. *Beyond Her Sphere: Women and the Professions in American History*. Westport, Conn.: Greenwood, 1978.

Hellerstein, Erna Olafson, Hume, Leslie Parker, and Offren, Karen M., editors. *Victorian Women: A Documentary Account of Women's Lives in Nineteenth-Century England, France, and the United States*. Stanford: Stanford University Press, 1981.

Helly, Dorothy O. "Women's Studies at Hunter College: Strategies in an Institutional Environment." *Women's Studies Quarterly* XI (1983):41–44.

Hill, Bridget, editor. *The First English Feminist: Reflections Upon Marriage and Other Writings by Mary Astell*. Aldershot, England: Gower/Maurice Temple Smith, 1986.

Hobby, Elaine. *Virtue of Necessity: English Women's Writing 1649–88*. Ann Arbor: The University of Michigan Press, 1988.

Hoffman, Nancy, editor. *Woman's "True" Profession: Voices from the History of Teaching*. New York: The Feminist Press, 1981.

Hogeland, Ronald W. "Coeducation of the Sexes at Oberlin: A Study of Social Ideas in Mid-Nineteenth Century America." *Journal of Social History* 6 (1972–1973):160–76.

Horowitz, Helen Lefkowitz. *Alma Mater: Design and Experience in the Women's Colleges from Their Nineteenth-Century Beginnings to the 1930s*. Boston: Beacon Press, 1984.

Howard, Suzanne. *But We Will Persist: A Comparative Research Report on the Status of Women in Academe*. Washington, D.C.: American Association of University Women, 1978.

Hune, Shirley. "The Non-aligned Movement and Women's Equality." *Man & Development* 2 (March 1980):64–75.

Ihle, Elizabeth L. "History of Black Women's Education in the South, 1865–present: Instruction Modules for Educators." Washington, D.C.: U.S. Department of Education, I–IV, 1986.

Ireson, Carol. "Girls' Socialization for Work." In *Women Working: Theories and Facts in Perspective*, edited by Ann H. Stromberg and Shirley Harkness. Palo Alto, Calif.: Mayfield, 1978.

Jayawardena, Kumari. *Feminism and Nationalism in the Third World*. London: Zed Books, 1986.

Kaufman, Gloria. "Juan Luis Vives on the Education of Women." *Signs* 3 (1978):891–96.

Kaufman, Polly Welts. *Women Teachers on the Frontier*. New Haven: Yale University Press, 1984.

Kelly, Gail P., and Elliott, Carolyn M., editors. *Women's Education in the Third World: Comparative Perspectives*. Albany: State University of New York, 1982.

Keohane, Nannerl O. " 'But for Her Sex . . .': The Domestication of Sophie." *University of Ottawa Quarterly* 49 (1980):390–400.

Kerber, Linda. "Daughters of Columbia: Educating Women for the Republic, 1787–1805." In *The Hofstadter Aegis*, edited by Eric L. McKitrick and Stanley M. Elkins. New York: Knopf, 1974.

———. *Women of the Republic: Intellect and Ideology in Revolutionary America*. Chapel Hill: The University of North Carolina Press, 1980.

King, Margaret L. "Book-Lined Cells: Women and Humanism in the Early Italian Renaissance." In *Beyond Their Sex*, edited by Patricia H. Labalme. New York: New York University Press, 1980.

Kinnaird, Joan K. "Mary Astell and the Conservative Contribution to English Feminism." *Journal of British Studies* 19 (1979):53–75.

Lapidus, Gail W. "Changing Women's Roles in the USSR." In *Women in the World: A Comparative Study*, edited by Lynne B. Iglitzin and Ruth Ross. Santa Barbara, Calif.: Clio, 1976.

Lee, Vera. *The Reign of Women in Eighteenth-Century France.* Cambridge, Mass.: Schenckman, 1975.

Lerner, Gerda. *Black Women in White America: A Documentary History.* New York: Pantheon, 1972.

———. *The Female Experience: An American Documentary.* Indianapolis: Bobbs-Merrill, 1977.

Lindsay, Beverly, editor. *Comparative Perspectives of Third World Women.* New York: Praeger Publishers, 1980.

Litoff, Judy Barrett, and McDonell, Judith. *European Immigrant Women in the United States: A Biographical Dictionary.* New York: Garland Publishing, 1994.

Loewenberg, Bert James, and Bogin, Ruth, editors. *Black Women in Nineteenth-Century Life: Their Words, Their Thoughts, Their Feelings.* University Park: Pennsylvania State University Press, 1976.

Lougee, Carolyn C. *Le Paradis des Femmes: Women, Salons, and Social Stratification in Seventeenth-Century France.* Princeton: Princeton University Press, 1976.

———. "Modern European History," *Signs* 2 (1977):628–50.

Lucas, Angela M. *Women in the Middle Ages: Religion, Marriage and Letters.* Brighton, England: The Harvester Press, 1983.

Mahl, Mary R., and Koon, Helene, editors. *The Female Spectator: English Women Writers Before 1800.* Bloomington: Indiana University Press and Old Westbury, N.Y.: Feminist Press, 1977.

Milem, Jeffrey F., and Astin, Helen S. "The Changing Composition of the Faculty." *Change* (March/April 1993).

Minnich, Elizabeth Kamarck. *Transforming Knowledge.* Philadelphia: Temple University Press, 1990.

Mount Holyoke College. Papers prepared for Mount Holyoke College's International Conference on Worldwide Education for Women, 1987.

National Research Council. *Science, Engineering, and Humanities Doctorates in the United States: 1979 Profile.* Washington, D.C.: National Academy of Sciences, Commission on Human Resources, 1980.

New York Times. "Women's Progress Stalled? Just Not So." October 18, 1992.

Newby, Elizabeth Loza. *A Migrant with Hope.* Nashville: Broadman Press, 1977.

Newcomer, Mabel. *A Century of Higher Education for American Women.* New York: Harper, 1959.

Oates, Mary J., and Williamson, Susan. "Women's Colleges and Women Achievers." *Signs* 3 (1978):795–806.

Osen, Lynne M. *Women in Mathematics.* Cambridge, Mass.: MIT Press, 1974.

Patterson, Michelle, and Sells, Lucy. "Women Dropouts from Higher Education." In *Academic Women on the Move*, edited by Alice S. Rossi and Ann Calderwood. New York: Russell Sage Foundation, 1973.

Pizan, Christine de. *The Book of the City of Ladies.* 1405. Translated by Earl Jeffrey Richards. New York: Persea, 1982.

Pomeroy, Sarah. *Goddesses, Whores, Wives, and Slaves: Women in Classical Antiquity.* New York: Schocken, 1975.

———. "Technicai Kai Mousikai: The Education of Women in the Fourth Century and in the Hellenistic Period." *American Journal of Ancient History* 2 (1977):51–68.

Rice, Joy K., and Hemmings, Annette. "Women's Colleges and Women Achievers: An Update." *Signs* 13:3 (Spring 1988).

Ries, P., and Thurgood, D. H. *Summary Report 1991: Doctorate Recipients from University States Universities.* Washington, D.C.: National Academy Press, 1993.

Roby, Pamela. "Institutional Barriers to Women Students in Higher Education." In *Academic Women on the Move*, edited by Alice S. Rossi and Ann Calderwood. New York: Russell Sage, 1973.

Rogers, Barbara. *The Domestication of Women: Discrimination in Developing Countries.* London: Kogan Page, 1980.

Ross, Ruth. "Tradition and the Role of Women in

Great Britain." In *Women in the World*, edited by Iglitzin and Ross. Santa Barbara, Calif.: Clio, 1976.

Rousmaniere, John P. "Cultural Hybrid in the Slums: The College Woman and the Settlement House, 1889–1894." *American Quarterly* 22 (1970):45–66.

Rousseau, Jean-Jacques. *Emile*. Translated by Barbara Foxley. New York: Dutton, 1974.

Sadker, Myra, and Sadker, David. *Failing at Fairness: How America's Schools Cheat Girls*. New York: Charles Scribner's Sons, 1994.

———. "Sexism in the Classroom: From Grade School to Graduate School." *Phi Delta Kappan* 67:7 (March 1986).

Sandler, Bernice R., and Hall, Roberta M. "The Campus Climate Revisited: Chilly for Women Faculty, Administrators, and Graduate Students." Washington, D.C.: Project on the Status and Education for Women, Association of American Colleges, 1986.

Sapiro, Virginia. "Feminist Studies and the Discipline: A Study of Mary Wollstonecraft." *University of Michigan Papers in Women's Studies* I (1974):178–200.

———. *A Vindication of Political Virtue: The Political Theory of Mary Wollstonecraft*. Chicago: University of Chicago Press, 1992.

Schwager, Sally. "Educating Women in America." *Signs* 12 (1987):333–72.

Schwartz, Pepper, and Lever, Janet. "Women in the Male World of Higher Education." In *Academic Women on the Move*, edited by Alice S. Rossi and Ann Calderwood. New York: Russell Sage, 1973.

Scott, Anne Firor. "The Ever-Widening Circle: The Diffusion of Feminist Values from the Troy Female Seminary, 1822–1872." *History of Education Quarterly* 19 (1979):3–26.

Seager, Joni, and Olson, Ann. *Women in the World: An International Atlas*. New York: Simon & Schuster, 1986.

Seller, Maxine Schwartz, editor. *Immigrant Women*. Philadelphia: Temple University Press, 1981.

———. *To Seek America*. Englewood: Jerome S. Ozer, 1977.

Smithson, Isaiah. "Introduction: Investigating Gender, Power, and Pedagogy." In *Gender in the Classroom*, edited by Susan L. Gabriel and Isaiah Smithson. Urbana: University of Illinois Press, 1990.

Snyder, Jane McIntosh. "Public Occasion and Private Passion in the Lyrics of Sappho of Lesbos." In *Women's History, Ancient History*, edited by Sarah Pomeroy. Chapel Hill: University of North Carolina Press, 1991.

———. *The Woman and the Lyre: Women Writers in Classical Greece and Rome*. Carbondale: Southern Illinois University Press, 1989.

Solomon, Barbara Miller. *In the Company of Educated Women: A History of Women and Higher Education in America*. New Haven: Yale University Press, 1985.

Sone, Monica. *Nisei Daughter*. Seattle: University of Washington Press, 1979.

Springer, Beverly. "Yugoslav Women." In *Women in the World*, edited by Iglitzin and Ross. Santa Barbara, Calif.: Clio, 1976.

Stein, Nan, Marshall, Nancy L., and Tropp, Linda R. *Secrets in Public: Sexual Harassment in Our Schools*. Center for Research on Women, Wellesley College and NOW Legal Defense and Education Fund, 1993.

Stock, Phyllis. *Better than Rubies: A History of Women's Education*. New York: Putnam, 1978.

Thiébaux, Marcelle, editor. *The Writings of Medieval Women: An Anthology*. Translations and Introductions by Marcelle Thiébaux. New York and London: Garland Publishing, 1994.

Tidball, M. Elizabeth. "Perspective on Academic Women and Affirmative Action." *Educational Record* 54 (1973):130–35.

———. "Women's Colleges and Women Achievers Revisited." *Signs* 5 (1980):504–17.

Tidball, M. Elizabeth, and Kistiakowsky, Vera. "Baccalaureate Origins of American Scientists and Scholars." *Science* 193 (August 20, 1976):646–52.

Tinker, Irene, and Bramsen, Michele B., editors. *Women and World Development*. New York: Praeger, 1976.

Tobias, Sheila. "Women's Studies: Its Origins, Its Organization and Its Prospects." *Women's Studies International Quarterly* I (1978):85–97.

Trennert, Robert A. "Educating Indian Girls at

Nonreservation Boarding Schools, 1878–1920." In *Unequal Sisters: A Multicultural Reader in U.S. Women's History*, edited by Ellen Carol DuBois and Vicki L. Ruiz, 2d ed. New York and London: Routledge, 1994.

United Nations. *The World's Women 1970–1990: Trends and Statistics*. New York, 1991.

U'Ren, Marjorie B. "The Image of Women in Textbooks." In *Women in Sexist Society: Studies in Power and Powerlessness*, edited by Vivian Gornick and Barbara K. Moran. New York: New American Library, 1971.

Van Allen, Judith. "African Women." In *Women in the World*, edited by Iglitzin and Ross. Santa Barbara, Calif.: Clio, 1976.

Walsh, Mary Roth. *"Doctors Wanted: No Women Need Apply:" Sexual Barriers in the Medical Profession, 1835–1975*. New Haven: Yale University Press, 1977.

———. "The Rediscovery of the Need for a Feminist Medical Education." *Harvard Educational Review* 49 (1979):447–66.

Wein, Roberta. "Women's Colleges and Domesticity, 1875–1918." *History of Education Quarterly* 14 (1974):31–47.

Westkott, Marcia. "Feminist Criticism of the Social Sciences." *Harvard Educational Review* 49 (1979):442–30.

Wider, Kathleen. "Women Philosophers in the Ancient Greek World: Donning the Mantle." *Hypatia* 1 (Spring 1986):21–62.

Women on Words and Images. "Look Jane Look. See Sex Stereotypes." In *And Jill Came Tumbling After*, edited by Stacey et al., New York: Dell, 1974.

Women's Studies Newsletter 8 (1980):19–26.

Woody, Thomas. *A History of Women's Education in the United States*. 1929. 2 volumes. Reprint. New York: Octagon, 1966.

Woolf, Virginia. *A Room of One's Own*. 1929. New York: Harcourt, Brace, 1957.

Yates, Barbara A. "Church, State and Education in Belgian Africa: Implications for Contemporary Third World Women." In *Women's Education in the Third World: Comparative Perspectives*, edited by Gail P. Kelly and Carolyn M. Elliott. Albany: State University of New York, 1982.

Zinsser, Judith P. *History and Feminism: A Glass Half Full*. New York: Twayne Publishers, 1993.

Women, Health, and the Health Care System

Issues surrounding our health have galvanized political consciousness among women as none other. In part, this is because these issues relate to the most fundamental of political questions: Who is to control our own bodies, our physical selves? Additionally, such issues relate to the ways in which the health care system operates to reinforce and sustain power hierarchies within a given class, race, age, and gender structure. Finally, health issues revolve about axiomatic statements of how women "should" be: how we should act, feel, look and relate to others. The health care system serves to promote norms about these matters by correcting deviation from "ideal" womanhood and directing us toward achievement of a particular socially ordained condition.

The publication in 1971 of *Our Bodies, Ourselves*, by the Boston Women's Health Collective, marked the coming of age of the modern women's movement. Not "just" a health movement, the activities represented in this volume involved an analysis of the implications of patriarchal society for our total well-being, and provided three critical routes to change: (1) empowerment through self-knowledge, (2) establishment of our right and obligation to choose what to do with our own bodies, and (3) reliance on mutual support among women.

The women's health movement brings together a variety of different approaches to knowledge, research, reform, and change. On the one hand, it involves a personal reappraisal of our bodies and our health; on the other, it calls for change in the services our society provides. We are required to ask: What is a state of health for women and how do we obtain and sustain such a condition? What are the appropriate means of dealing with illness or disease? The first question is essential, both because women's health has been perceived differently from men's and because women's bodies and biological processes are different in some respects from men's. The second question is essential because we have cause to believe that women have been discriminated against not only as recipients but also as providers of health care services. For example, medication and treatment for medical conditions not specific to women, such as heart disease, have been tested and norms established primarily on men. They are then often prescribed to women although there is an absence of data on appropriate amounts, side effects, and effectiveness of the treatment for women.

What Is a Healthy Woman?

Knowledge and Health

In most societies, at most times, and in most places, women have been the primary caretakers of human bodies from birth to death. It has been women's work to tend to birthing, to infants and children, and to teach basic habits of sanitation and nutrition to young people. Women care for the sick and wounded, the ailing and weak, and the infirm elderly; we also tend to the treatment of the dead. While male authorities from time to time in some societies may have had some part in these activities, the day-to-day concerns have been largely those of women.

The women's health movement has argued that modern Western society has separated women from one another and allocated to men responsibility for, and knowledge about, our bodies. Men have been dominant not only as the physicians, but as obstetricians and gynecologists as well. American society has made "medical" events out of what were once thought to be normal, healthy processes. Women in our society have been told that we do not possess the requisite information to make decisions about our own bodies. When we have asked, that information has been denied to us. Ignorant, we have been discouraged from learning from other women because we have also been taught that normal biological processes are "dirty" and "shameful": not proper subjects of conversation even among women. Thus, there is a connection between our knowledge (or lack of it) of what a healthy state for a woman is or ought to be, and the allocation of responsibility for professional health care to men.

There is yet another connection. The patriarchal society that assigns health care authority to men also perceives of women as "other." As a result, we may be viewed as "abnormal," or even unhealthy. For men, who do not menstruate, menstruation may seem unhealthy, abnormal, and dangerous. For men, who cannot experience pregnancy and childbirth, these conditions may seem mysterious, frightening, and threatening. If men are the authorities to whom women turn for infor-

mation about these events, certainly men's subjective interpretations are conveyed to women, who learn to perceive the world through men's eyes. Moreover, it is in the interest of patriarchal society that women are seen as weak, vulnerable, and aberrant, making it seem necessary for women to turn to men for assistance. Women's dependence upon men is essential to the maintenance of a patriarchal society.

Because Western society has for so long been patriarchal, and because Western health care systems so closely reflect patriarchy, some feminist activists in the women's health movement claim we must reject the medical establishment's view of women. An entirely new perspective must be applied in the consideration of women's health and illness. Others believe that while there may be some value to some products of our health care establishment, we need to tread cautiously, accepting some of what it has to offer with great care, and rejecting a great deal else. Still others think that our health care system might be enormously improved if only women were more active in positions of authority (Fee, 1983; Ruzek, 1978; Dreifus, 1977b; Travis, 1988a,b).

The Female as Deviant

One of the earliest writers on the subject of the health of women was Soranus of Ephesus (28–138 A.D.), in whose work the topics of obstetrics and gynecology are treated as but one aspect of that health. Soranus declared that women and men had the same physical and health problems with the sole exception of the areas of reproduction (Marieskind, 1977). A more misogynist view was taken by Galen (c. 130–200 A.D.), a Greek physician whose writings influenced Western medicine for centuries thereafter. He taught that women were "inside-out men." According to Galen, women have insufficient body heat to

In 1916 Margaret Sanger opened a clinic in Brooklyn, New York, to provide birth control information. In consequence, she was arrested for "maintaining a public nuisance" and accordingly sentenced to thirty days in a workhouse. Five years later, undaunted by such setbacks, she founded the American Birth Control League. (The Sophia Smith Collection [Women's History Archive], Smith College, Northampton, Mass. 01063)

Women and Madness

Women are impaled on the cross of self-sacrifice. Unlike men, they are categorically denied the experience of cultural supremacy, humanity, and renewal based on their sexual identity—and on the blood sacrifice, in some way, of a member of the opposite sex. In different ways, some women are driven mad by this fact. Such madness is essentially an intense experience of female biological, sexual, and cultural castration, and a doomed search for potency. The search often involves "delusions" or displays of physical aggression, grandeur, sexuality, and emotionality—all traits which would probably be more acceptable in female-dominated cultures. Such traits in women are feared and punished in patriarchal mental asylums. . . .

Neither genuinely mad women, nor women who are hospitalized for conditioned female behavior, are powerful revolutionaries. Their insights and behavior are as debilitating (for social reasons) as they are profound. Such women act alone, according to rules that make no "sense" and are contrary to those of our culture. Their behavior is "mad" because it represents a socially powerless individual's attempt to unite body and feeling. . . .

What we consider "madness," whether it appears in women or in men, is either the acting out of the devalued female role or the total or partial rejection of one's sex-role stereotype.

(Chesler, 1972:31,56)

---

force our genitals outward. Thus, using man as his measure, Galen viewed women (as Aristotle had) as "defective" persons. Since women were "inferior," it followed that our diseases were caused, almost entirely, by our inferior genitalia (Veith, 1965).

As the Industrial Revolution began to change the structure of Western society, women were placed in an illogical, dichotomous position. While women's bodies continued to be considered pathologic, women were considered the moral guardians of society (Ehrenreich and English, 1977; Martin, 1987). During the nineteenth century, medicine became an organized profession controlled by men, many of whom built their medical fame on their ability to control women and women's bodies (Barker-Benfield, 1977).

By the end of the nineteenth century, our current health care system had begun to crystallize into the form it would finally take today. By then, men had come to prevail as leaders of the professional health care system, and to propagate ideals about what a normal woman's health was like. These men's ideals reflected not only gender bias but class, race, and heterosexist biases as well. Upper- and middle-class women were perceived as physically weak, of delicate health, and vulnerable to a great variety of ailments arising from the fact that we had wombs. The uterus itself was believed to be the source of a vast array of illnesses both of the body and of the mind. Excessive physical and mental challenges were thought to be damaging to women's most exalted function: procreation. Women of the upper classes were believed to have little or no sex drive (although if we did exhibit some, this was thought to be symptomatic of severe illness, to be treated surgically). Any form of rebelliousness or deviance from expected gender roles was met with severe medical measures (Barker-Benfield, 1977). Refusal to be satisfied with housework, a tendency to practice masturbation, an overeagerness to be educated, or a desire for the vote might be deemed cause for surgical practices ranging from clitoridectomy to hysterectomy (Maries-kind, 1977). These actions or their threat kept women of the more privileged classes more or less in line. Women of the lower classes and women of color were less vulnerable to such strictures, for we were not thought to share the weakness of those of privilege. Only grad-ually were working-class women denied knowledge about and access to our own bod-ies. By the end of the nineteenth century, women health care specialists, healers, and midwives were prohibited from practicing even among the poor (Petchesky, 1990). The assumption of healing roles by the medical es-tablishment had special repercussions for poor women, who did not have the same access as wealthy women to the medicines so central to professionalized medical practices.

The Medicalization of Life Processes

Three life processes that Western society has medicalized, menstruation, childbirth, and menopause, are indeed normal parts of the normal life cycle of most women. Neverthe-less, some women rarely, if ever, menstruate; some women never give birth; some women do not experience menopause. Among those who do experience these processes, there are wide variations in the experience. Menarche can occur when a girl is only ten years old, or may occur later, at eighteen; menstruation may occur every twenty-eight days, or be less regular; it may last a whole week or only a couple of days; it may be accompanied by a blood flow that is heavy or light, with strong abdominal cramps or none at all; it may be preceded by a variety of changes in her body or in her emotions or it may not. The question is, is it necessary for her to *do* something if she does have one variant or another of menstrual experience? If she does, what will be the

consequences? And if she does not? And what are her options?

It was once thought essential for women of the privileged classes to take to bed while menstruating, during the latter phases of pregnancy (confinement), and for several weeks after childbirth. However, no such strictures applied to women of the working classes. Despite class disparities, menstruation was persistently conceptualized as a form of illness; and pregnancy, childbirth, and meno-pause became medicalized events.

As childbirth fell into the hands of profes-sionalizing male medical specialists and was experienced ever more passively by women in hospitals it became a medical event. It now involved medicines and instruments and pro-cedures that served to remove childbirth from the realm of normal experience. Once women were perceived as incapable of giving birth without help from a doctor, we were made so. With the application of anesthetics, the plac-ing of the woman in a prone (lithotomy) po-sition, and a variety of other procedures, the birthing mother became literally incapable of giving birth, and now had to be "delivered." Until recently, this meant the routine use of forceps. Increasingly, in recent decades, deliv-ery has meant the routine performance of ce-sarean sections (surgical delivery of the fetus). While these procedures are convenient and profitable for physicians and hospitals, and ex-tremely useful in medical emergencies, they are disabling for the larger number of women (Martin, 1987).

Pregnancy and childbirth are experienced by women in a wide range of different ways. *Doing* something to control these processes may have serious consequences for both preg-nant women and children. Medications to counteract a tendency to miscarry or for "morning sickness" have been the cause of birth defects in infants, as well as the cause of grave illnesses such as cancer later in their lives. For example, the synthetic hormone diethylstilbestrol (DES), prescribed to those of us at risk of miscarriage (and also used in large doses as a "morning after" contraceptive), turned out to be the cause of a rare type of (vaginal) cancer in our daughters when they reached adolescence; and other abnormalities have been demonstrated in the reproductive organs of both our sons and daughters. This disaster became exposed only through the diligent efforts of the women's health movement, which charged the medical establishment with faulty research, ineffective controls, and delayed dissemination of information to the public (Ruzek, 1978).

Of at least equal concern is the avoidance of pregnancy and childbirth—birth control. This is also a medicalized process in Western society. First, tremendous efforts were made to deny women access to birth control, when the concern was to increase the population among the "better classes" to exercise greater control over women. Then, with growing concern about "overpopulation," especially among the "lower" classes and less-favored races, and about birth control for the families of the upwardly mobile middle classes, there came a dramatic reversal of public policy involving dangerous experimentation with women's bodies (Dowie and Johnston, 1977). Hormone pills and intrauterine devices were distributed freely among millions of women before adequate testing and other precautions were taken. Some of these devices were later found to be damaging to women's health (Seaman, 1977; Ruzek, 1978). No parallel experimentation with men was ever undertaken.

Similarly, abortion, a last resort for women for whom birth control has failed, has been placed in the hands of medical practitioners. It was through the efforts of the nascent American Medical Association that control of abortion was wrested from midwives, and ultimately suppressed as a legal option (Luker, 1984). Once available, abortion was used by medical practitioners to exploit and, through their power over reproductive processes, to

control women (Dreifus, 1977a). There is a consensus in the women's health movement that the decision to have or not to have an abortion should be in the hands of the pregnant woman (Ruzek, 1978). While legalization of abortion in several countries has allowed many women to decide for ourselves and vastly improved the conditions of abortion for many who once might have sought unsafe, illegal measures, abusive treatment of women seeking abortions (and those women and men who aid us) continues. For example, the right of women to this ultimate control over our own bodies has been one of the first issues to be challenged in formerly communist countries of Eastern Europe and the former Soviet Union (Funk and Mueller, 1993). In the United States, harassment of abortion clinic staff has even escalated to the point of killing physicians and support personnel connected with such clinics.

Finally, there is the issue of menopause: the cessation of menstruation. Here again, the medical establishment has sought to medically manage an event perceived through images created to support a patriarchal view of women. If it is claimed women's principal function in life is to reproduce, then cessation of menstruation, and hence of fertility, means the cessation of women's reason for existence. In a society where women's dependency, immaturity, and association with children are our idealized characteristics, the mature woman with adult children is regarded as socially useless, unattractive, and morbid. The biological shifts that come with menopause, seen through this medical perspective, are regarded as pathological (though in fact a wide range of different experiences are quite "normal") and in need of medical management—dosing with hormones, even surgical removal of the uterus, among other measures. While it is true that many women do suffer discomforts that might be relieved medically, there remains the question whether such measures are needed, whether they are worth the cost in terms of risk, and whether alternative measures have been adequately considered.

In order to make choices: We need to know about our own bodies, and how they work, and about the varieties of experience of other women; we need also to know the signs or symptoms of illness or malfunction in our bodies and what might be done about these. We need to know the range of options and the consequences of choosing one or another. What must we do to attain this knowledge? This has been a fundamental issue for the women's health movement.

Health Risks to Women

Women's bodies and men's bodies are more alike than they are different from one another. We are subject, for the most part, to the same hazards to our health—illnesses, accidents, disabilities. However, there are some significant differences. Some hazards are unique to women because they concern our reproductive organs and reproductive experiences. Other hazards are shared by women and men but are experienced differently because of different roles assigned to us (such as different jobs resulting in different workplace hazards) or because society treats us differently (for example, women are more often victims of domestic violence).

In the past (and still today in the poorer countries of the world) men, on the average, have lived longer than women. In the United States today, however, for every age group, women, on the average, outlive men. The leading cause of death for both women and men is coronary heart disease, but more men die of it than women, as is true of the other leading causes of death (Rodin and Ickovics, 1990; see Table 12.1). However, according to indicators such as disability days, hospitalization, and visits to physicians, women display greater rates of illness than men (ibid.; Table 12.2).

How are the differences to be explained?

The facts are that although more males are conceived, there is a higher incidence of death among males in utero and in the first year of life, which suggests some genetic basis for difference. One such possible basis for difference is that males have only one X chromosome (Travis, 1988a). Testosterone might pose higher risks for heart disease, while estrogen might afford protection. But variation in time and between cultures and classes suggests that biological difference alone is inadequate to account for difference in mortality and morbidity. Behavioral differences that affect health risks, such as substance abuse and driving behavior, also clearly are patterned by gender (Travis, 1988a).

Poverty

Two out of three women around the world presently suffer from the most debilitating disease known to humanity. Common symptoms of this fast-spreading ailment include chronic anemia, malnutrition, and severe fatigue. Sufferers exhibit an increased susceptibility to infections of the respiratory and reproductive tracts. And premature death is a frequent outcome. In the absence of direct intervention, the disease is often communicated from mother to child, with markedly higher transmission rates among females than males. Yet, while studies confirm the efficacy of numerous prevention and treatment strategies, to date few have been vigorously pursued. The disease is poverty. (Jacobson, 1993:3)

Probably the most pervasive explanation for general differences in health between different groups of humans is poverty. Poor women are likely to be poorly educated, hence unlikely to have sufficient knowledge to identify and avoid risks or respond adequately to them (even if we had the means to do so). Poor women are unlikely to have the financial resources to pay for medical treatment or the means of obtaining it even when it is offered

Guidelines for the Woman Who Is Going to See Her Health Care Practitioner

These suggestions for what to consider before, during, and after going to a clinician are written for women who share the following assumptions.

—It is healthy to be skeptical of our medical system.

—It is healthy to know about ourselves.

—It is healthy to make our own decisions about what we do with our bodies.

1. Before going:
   A. Figure out what you want specifically. Ask yourself what you'll be content to get out of this visit:
      —a specific medication or lab test?
      —reassurance that it's not serious?
      —to know what it is?
      —validation of your present self-treatment?
      —eradication of a specific symptom?
   B. Make a list of the things you've already done for this problem: first aid, over-the-counter medication, rest, diet.
   C. Give the dates of previous such episodes. What was the diagnosis and treatment given? How did the treatment work? How is this time different?
   D. What important events have just happened or are coming up soon in your life?
   E. List all the medications you are taking.
   F. Figure out the date of your last menstrual period.
   G. Make a list of what you think could possibly be wrong. Which do you consider most likely? Which scares you the most?
   H. Why do you think this happened just now?
2. In the office:
   Take your answers to A. through H. [above], a pad, and a pencil. If you're very nervous, a friend or a tape recorder might help.

   In a well-taken medical history, your concerns should come up. If they don't, you may be able to sneak them in. " Do you think ＿ might have anything to do with this?" "You know, I just got back from Mexico." "My sister told me she has the same thing, and her doctor said ＿ ."
   A. When you're given a diagnosis, ask the following:
      —What are all the names for this condition?
      —Are you absolutely sure that's what I have? If not, what else might it be? What's the worst it could be?
      —How did I get it? Is it contagious or hereditary?
      —Do you see a lot of this? Is it rare or common?
      —Is this something that will come back, or never quite get better?
      —Is there anything I could have done to prevent it, or to save myself the office visit?
      —Where can I read more about this?
      —How long will it take to get better or go away? When should I decide it's not getting better fast enough?
      —How will this interfere with my work and the things I like to do?

B. If given a medication, ask the following:
  —Is this optional? What would happen if I don't take it, or if I stop taking it when I feel better?
  —Are there ways to speed recovery without medication?
  —How can this medication kill me?
  —What will I feel when I take this? Will it interfere with my activities?
  —What will I feel if I'm getting a serious side effect?
  —Is this the cheapest brand?
  —(When the problem is recurrent) If I get this again, can I refill the prescription without seeing you?
C. If given a return appointment, ask the following:
  —What is the followup visit for?
  —What is the reason for its timing? (Why three days, not three months?)
  —Could I just call you instead of coming in?
  —Should I come back even if I'm feeling fine?
3. When you get home:
A. Think about your practitioner.
  —How did you feel in the clinician's company?
  —Was it difficult to say what you were concerned about?
  —Do you believe what you were told? To double-check information, consider getting a second opinion from another practitioner, or a friend in health care, going to the library, asking the pharmacist about any drugs which were prescribed, or looking in the phone book for such groups as the Arthritis Foundation or Alcholics Anonymous.
B. Think about being a woman:
  —How were you treated differently from a man with the same complaint?
  —If you saw a man clinician, do you think a woman would have treated you differently? Why?
  —Could this problem actually be part of every woman's development, and not a disease? If so, what are other women doing about it or for it?
C. Evaluate your health knowledge:
  —How did your diagnosis and self-care compare to what you were told in the office? If they were different, why?
  —What key information did they have that you didn't have or overlooked? If they coincided, was the visit a waste of time, or did you get something else out of it?
D. Other things to think about:
  —How much did it all cost?
  —Is there anything occupational or environmental about this problem?
  —Is the diagnosis a "label" that will make people treat you differently? If so, how will you handle that?
  —If you like that approach to health care, how can you "spread it around"? What about women who can't read this handout, or those who have no choice of which practitioner they will see? (Martin, 1982).

Table 12.1 Age- and Sex-Specific Mortality Rates and Sex Ratios in the United States in 1987

Age	Deaths per 100,000 Males	Deaths per 100,000 Females	Sex ratio (Male/female)
Under 1	1,129	902	1.25
1–4	58	45	1.29
5–14	32	19	1.68
15–24	146	52	2.81
25–34	193	74	2.61
35–44	292	139	2.10
45–54	644	360	1.79
55–64	1,624	900	1.80
65–74	3,618	2,063	1.75
75–84	8,232	5,118	1.61
85 older	18,031	14,261	1.26
All ages	935	813	1.15

Note. From *Statistical Abstract of the United States: 1990,* by the U.S. Bureau of the Census, 1990. Rodin and Ickovics, 1990:1019.

free because of the costs of transportation or time lost from work. Poverty means lack of adequate housing for shelter, and adequate clothing and shoes for protection. It means inadequate sanitation due to insufficient or unclean water, food storage, and waste removal. It means exposure to risky, often illicit means of making a living, including prostitution. And it means exposure to risks of violence as a result of such work, living in unprotected neighborhoods, and dependence on others for survival. Poverty is probably the single greatest hazard to women's health; it is often lethal when combined with other serious hazards.

Women are more likely than men to be poor, and women who head our own households are much more likely to be poor than male heads of household (Wilson, 1988). Poverty poses special health risks to disabled and elderly women, especially if we live alone.

Racial/Ethnic Discrimination

Race or ethnic status comprises another independent variable affecting the health risks of women. According to William Dressler (1993), health statistics show that African Americans are subject to higher rates of morbidity (such as cardiovascular disease, diabetes, and cancer) and mortality (including infant mortality due to low birth weight) than white Americans. These differentials persist even when the data are controlled for socioeconomic status, such that with both African Americans and whites earning the same income, African Americans still have higher rates of illness in many categories. While researchers have often attributed these health

Table 12.2 Morbidity Indicators by Sex and Sex Ratios in the United States in 1987

Indicator	Females	Males	Sex ratio (Female/male)
Restricted activity days			
Total days of disability (millions)	1,984	1,464	1.35
Days/person	16.1	12.7	1.28
Bed disability days			
Total days of disability (millions)	879	595	1.48
Days/person	7.1	5.2	1.36
Work loss days			
Total (millions)	304	299	1.02
Days/person	6.1	4.8	1.27
Hospital utilization rates			
Patients discharged per 1,000 persons	159	116	1.37
Days of care per 1,000 persons	968	860	1.20
Average stay (days)	6.1	6.9	0.88
Physician visits			
Total (millions)	765	523	1.46
Visits/person	6.2	4.5	1.38

Note. From *Statistical Abstract of the United States: 1990,* by the U.S. Bureau of the Census, 1990. Rodin and Ickovics, 1990:1021.

Kathe Kollwitz (1867–1945) lived in Germany. She is known for her stark black-and-white drawings of the victims of hunger and war. This self-portrait (1934), one of over a hundred made throughout her life, catches the beauty and strength in the face of a woman as she ages. (Los Angeles County Museum of Art, Los Angeles County Funds)

differentials to biological factors, Dressler demonstrates that race is a social configuration, having no biological common denominators. In other words, the genetic difference between two people classified as black will be approximately the same as the difference between two people classified as belonging to two different racial groups. Thus, it is unlikely that genetics plays a role in increasing health risks.

Yet models that account for differences in wealth or life-style are equally inadequate to explain the persistence of racial differentials in health. Instead, Dressler proposes a "social structural model," wherein wealth or class as well as status combine to affect life-chances. The stress of race status affects physical (e.g., cardiovascular disease) as well as mental (e.g., depression) health. This stress, combined with preconceptions and misconceptions within the health care industry about the health needs and risks of African Americans, conspires to maintain health inequalities even when controlling for heredity and poverty. This model would help to explain the health risks of other racial or ethnic groups as well, whose perceived "difference" exposes them to the same risks faced by African Americans (Dressler, 1993). While all women face additional health risks because of their gender, poverty and racial or ethnic status combine to pose even greater health risks for some of us.

Occupational Health Risks

Women suffer from different occupational health risks than men. Although men get injured at work more often than women, women suffer illness related to work conditions that are harder to detect and less often reported (Muller, 1990). Often women's occupational health risks are related to the hazards of working while pregnant.

Pregnant and childrearing women experience difficulties in the workplace because many employers do not permit paid leave for pregnancy, do not allow rest breaks or snacking for expectant women at work, and have a negative attitude about breast-feeding at work (Chavkin, 1984). In addition, women who work at video display terminals may be at higher risk for birth defects and miscarriages (Henifin, 1984). There have been cases where women were coerced—by the threat of reduction of our wages or dismissal—into undergoing sterilization in workplaces where substances dangerous to fetuses were used (Scott, 1984). The home as workplace is also a source of occupational hazards where chemical pollutants (such as cleaning solutions) are a key danger (Rosenberg, 1984).

Leith Mullings (1984) points out that higher rates of illness among people of color are often attributed to factors related to biology or culture, rather than being sought in our work roles. African American women work in riskier and lower-paying jobs as compared to white women. As a result, we experience more work-related injuries and illnesses. A large number of African American women work at low-paid, menial health service jobs, and studies show that workers at these jobs experience a high rate of occupational illness. Many Latina and Asian American women work in the garment industry, often in sweatshops where workers face health risks from overcrowding, lack of adequate ventilation, danger of fire due to inadequate escape routes and fire prevention features in the work facility, and other hazards. Work and pregnancy have been more problematic for women of color in the United States than for white women because more of the former have had to work during childbearing years, and more of those jobs have required us to stand at our work during pregnancy (Mullings, 1984).

The Reproductive System

Women's reproductive organs have significant consequences for our health. After heart disease, the next-greatest cause of death in the

United States is cancer. The major types of cancer in North American women are breast, lung, colon, uterine, ovarian, and cervical. Four of these six are associated directly with our reproductive organs. In addition, we run risks associated with childbirth and changes in hormone levels after menopause.

Cancer. The most common type of cancer among women is breast cancer (which only very rarely occurs in men). Incidence of breast cancer varies substantially among different ethnic groups (Table 12.3) (Swanson, 1992). Risk of breast cancer increases with age (Table 12.4) (ibid.).

A variety of different possible factors causing higher risk for cancer has been investigated. Dietary fat and obesity are factors that can be affected by behavioral change, but so far, it is not clear whether, or to what extent, either fat or calories increase the risk of breast cancer. Alcohol consumption has been implicated, but questions remain about how the age of onset of drinking or continuing to drink is related to risk (Swanson, 1992).

Table 12.3 Breast Cancer Incidence, Mortality, and Survival Among Diverse Ethnic Groups in the United States

Ethnic Group	Incidence*	Survival**	Mortality*
Hispanic	52.1	70.6%	19.4
Native American	21.3	46.3%	9.0
Alaskan Native	44.2	...	...
Hawaiian	106.1	68.0%	37.2
Chinese	57.8	80.8%	12.0
Japanese	55.0	85.4%	10.2
Filipino	41.3	73.7%	7.8
White	96.8	78.3%	26.8

*Rates are per 100,000 women and age-adjusted to the 1970 U.S. standard population, average annual incidence or mortality rate in 1977–1983.
**Five-year relative survival rates for cases diagnosed in 1975–1984.
Source: National Cancer Institute SEER Program. Swanson, 1990:141.

The effects of hormones, specifically estrogens, on breast cancer, have been examined in numerous studies. Endogenous hormones (those produced by our bodies) may contribute to risk, but the interaction of different hormones is complex, and their relation to breast cancer not entirely clear. Exogenous hormones (in the form of medication) are commonly prescribed as oral contraceptives and as estrogen replacement therapy for treatment of the effects of menopause. The majority of recent studies show no association between oral contraceptive use and breast cancer. A similar lack of association has been found for estrogen replacement therapy except possibly among women who have used very high doses or have used it for very long periods—fifteen to twenty years—(Swanson, 1992)—or have a family history of breast cancer. Many physicians and researchers argue that the health benefits of estrogen replacement therapy outweigh the risks (see below).

Breast cancer will strike one out of every nine American women; its incidence has gone up dramatically in recent years (Swanson, 1992). However, if detected early, it can be treated effectively. Most breast cancers are detected by self-examination, and women who examine themselves regularly have a better chance of detecting breast cancer early (Travis, 1988a). Physicians also can detect breast cancers through manual examination, which should be performed at regular gynecological examinations. Other technologies for detecting breast cancer exist. Probably the most commonly used today is mammography, which involves taking an image using radiation to identify abnormal tissue masses. Once one of these techniques reveals a possible malignancy, additional methods are used to confirm the diagnosis. These involve taking a sample of cells from the suspicious mass (Travis, 1988a).

Radical mastectomy, which means the removal of the breast, lymph nodes, and surrounding muscle tissue, was the procedure

Table 12.4 Age-Specific Incidence of Female Breast Cancer, 1984–1988

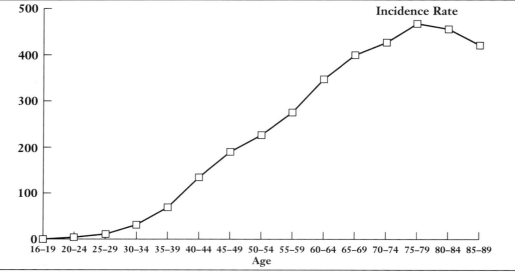

Swanson, 1992:141

first proposed by the physician for whom it was named, Halsted, in 1894. It had a dramatic effect on reducing local recurrence of the disease, but most patients died of cancer at other locations anyway (Layhe and Dimitrov, 1992). It was the most common form of treatment of breast cancer, and more common in the United States than in European countries. Yet there are other options, including modified radical mastectomy (removal of the breast and lymph nodes only) and "lumpectomy," removal of the cancerous lump only. The last and simplest of these options was resisted for a long period in the United States, even though it can be accompanied by other treatments, such as radiation therapy, with great effectiveness. North American women were not only subjected, almost exclusively, to the more radical treatment, but in a particularly traumatic manner. When a lump was discovered, a biopsy would be performed while the patient was under anesthesia; if the lump

was judged to be a malignant tumor, the breast was removed immediately, in the same operation. This meant that the patient would be put under anesthesia for an exploratory investigation not knowing whether she would wake up with a breast or not. Yet there seemed little justification for this treatment other than reducing the woman's own participation in decision making. Today, strong resistance on the part of women, thanks largely to the women's health care movement, has somewhat altered the approach to treatment, and fewer women are being subjected to radical and even modified radical mastectomies (Travis, 1988a). Today, more attention is being paid to the psychological effects of learning one has the disease, and dealing with treatment, to the interaction between physician and patient, and to supports for women in recovery (Travis, 1988a; Layhe and Dimitrov, 1992; Swanson, 1992; Given and Given, 1990; Langer, 1992).

Breast cancer research remains underfunded. Breast cancer develops up to eight years before lumps are detectable. Breast cancer specialists believe that with more research, technologies could be developed to detect these malignancies at an earlier stage (Langer, 1992).

Cancers of the ovaries, uterus, and cervix cannot be detected by self-examination. Early detection is possible, however, by use of a regular PAP smear, which detects abnormalities in sampled cells. This test should be administered at regular gynecological examinations. An abnormal PAP smear is an indication that further examination is warranted, not direct evidence that there is a cancer.

Sexually Transmitted Disease. Sexually transmitted diseases are quite prevalent in the world today, with major repercussions for women's health (Table 12.5). They are a major cause of infertility and can contribute to blindness and brain damage as well as to difficulties in childbearing. Most cause detectable lesions or discharges, which, if a woman has sufficient knowledge and access to medical care, are a signal that it is time to seek medical treatment, and most can be treated simply and effectively with medication. Genital herpes is at present incurable, and this disease, along with some other reproductive tract diseases, when left untreated, has been found to be associated with cervical cancer (McDermott et al., 1993).

More lethal, and still incurable, is human immunodeficiency virus (HIV), the precursor of acquired immune deficiency syndrome (AIDS), which is transmitted through genital secretions or through blood. It is estimated that, globally, one-third of those infected (about 2 million) are women (Smyke, 1991). It is very common among women in sub-Saharan Africa (McDermott et al., 1993), and is growing rapidly in the Caribbean. It particularly strikes the young, especially adolescents, and is transmissible to fetuses.

The epidemiology of AIDS and HIV differs from region to region. In the United States, the poorest populations, including ethnic and racial minorities, as well as gay men are disproportionately affected by AIDS, and pediatric AIDS is most widespread among the poor of the inner cities (Kiefer, 1990). Although African Americans and Latinos comprise only 20 percent of the total population, these groups account for about 50 percent of adult AIDS cases and more than 75 percent of pediatric AIDS (Kiefer, 1990). More than a million women in the United States are infected with the HIV virus, and of these, 52 percent are African Americans and 16 percent are Latinas. More than 30 percent of these adult women acquired the virus through sexual contact (others acquired it primarily through shared use of needles for intravenous drugs or through blood transfusions). Studies indicate that the existence of other sexually transmitted diseases facilitates transmission of the HIV virus. Although African Americans made up only 12 percent of the U.S. population in 1980, African Americans accounted for 76 percent of the syphilis cases and 78 percent of the gonorrhea cases at that time (Hinkle et al., 1992). Consequently, African American women may be particularly at risk. Poverty is the critical factor accounting for these racial group differences; that poverty itself is

Table 12.5 The Annual Total of Sexually Transmitted Infections: 250 Million New Cases

Disease	1990
Inchromoniasis	120 million
Genital Chlamydia	50 million
Genital Papillomavirus	30 million
Gonorrhea	25 million
Genital Herpes	20 million
HIV infection	1 million
Syphilis	3.5 million
Chancroid	2 million

Source: *World Health Organization*, 1990; Smyke, 1991:97.

disproportionately found among African Americans is the product of a history of racial discrimination.

AIDS, like other sexually transmitted diseases, is avoidable for adults who have control over their own bodies. Sexual abstinence and refusal to share needles will protect any adult (infants born to AIDS-infected mothers have no such avoidance options), but most adults prefer not to abstain entirely from sexual intercourse. Protected sex (using a condom) is the most common effective alternative (although "safe sex" alternatives, using fantasy and masturbation have also been recommended). Readily available and most effective are condoms for men, made of latex. The effectiveness of these condoms can be enhanced by application of the spermicide nonoxynol 9. Unfortunately, many women engage in casual sexual relations without using condoms. The reasons we give include inconvenience, shame, and refusal by our male partners (see Eversly et al., 1990; Hinkle et al., 1992). In sub-Saharan Africa, for example, where problems of HIV transmission are acute, women run high risks of abuse by male partners for insisting on condom use. There, poverty forces large numbers of women into sex work, hence into extreme vulnerability to exposure to AIDS and abuse (Smyke, 1991).

Women who engage in heterosexual intercourse with an HIV carrier are at greater risk of contracting HIV than are males who have sexual intercourse with an HIV-positive woman. Condoms for women (which are inserted in the vagina) can help women exert greater control over prevention of HIV transmission. While these are available in some parts of the world, they are difficult to use and not nearly as effective as male condoms.

Childbirth. Until recently, the risks of childbirth were grave for women everywhere; they remain serious for poor women in the modern industrial world as well as in less industrially developed countries. Mortality rates for Latinas in the United States and our infants, for example, are higher than for other groups. The health risks for pregnant and childbearing adolescents and our infants are also great, since teenage mothers are found disproportionately among the poor (Zambrana, 1988).

Women in less economically developed countries face grave health risks in our childbearing years. Of the half million women who die each year in childbirth, 99 percent live in these poor countries. For each maternal death, 100 serious illnesses are contracted by women worldwide. This results in approximately 62 million serious childbirth-related health problems every year. Other illnesses caused by childbirth that only appear later are uncounted in these estimates (Koblinsky et al., 1993).

The immediate causes of maternal death are, in the main, hemorrhage, sepsis (infection), toxemia, obstructed labor, and complications of abortion. Underlying these are causes related to poverty: lack of prenatal care; lack of trained personnel, equipment, blood, or transport at the time of obstetrical emergency; lack of family planning to avoid unwanted pregnancies, too many or too closely spaced births; preexisting conditions like malaria, anemia, fatigue, and malnutrition that predispose to obstetrical complications (Smyke, 1991).

Birth Control and Abortion. The dictation to women of the means of birth control and abortion has long been a social device for the control of women: to allocate to men control over women. Through decisions to deny or to provide these services to women, physicians and politicians are able to assert their own moral positions, to use their power over women to control women's sexual behavior as well as the consequences of that behavior.

Birth control options for women have been limited in part owing to the lack of research into effective new technologies. When this research has been done, it has been tested on impoverished and nonwhite women. For example, Norplant, a new contraceptive implant, has been distributed among Native American women (Native American Women's Health Education Resource Center, 1993). The complications and side effects experienced by these women will undoubtedly lead to modifications in Norplant use.

Sterilization abuse in the United States has been inextricably tied to racist beliefs and practices. It has a history dating back to the eugenics of the early twentieth century when physicians sterilized impoverished women whom they judged to be genetically unfit to reproduce. This practice was modified after World War II, when forced sterilization was judged to be acceptable only in the case of developmentally disabled women (Reilly, 1987; see section on disabled women below).

Although now regarded as medically unethical, forced sterilization, or sterilization without informed consent, has continued to be practiced upon women of low socioeconomic status, particularly those classified as nonwhite. During the 1960s, for example, Puerto Rican women in the United States were sterilized without informed consent in large numbers. Even where sterilization was not technically forced, its use was prescribed in the propaganda used by the government of Puerto Rico to combat overpopulation; and where other birth control alternatives were lacking, sterilization became the only family planning "choice" available. As a result, in Hartford, Connecticut, for example, in the mid-1980s, 51 percent of Puerto Rican women of childbearing age had been sterilized (Lopez, 1987). Native American women have also been sterilized in extremely high numbers relative to our population size, according to a General Accounting Office (U.S. Senate) Report (Rodriguez-Trias, 1978). Significantly, the denial of abortion reimbursement by Medic-

aid also contributes to making sterilization the only viable "option" for impoverished women (Lopez, 1987).

The availability of legal abortion, in light of the realities of the limitations and failures of birth control, is vital to the health of women. When hygienically and correctly induced, abortion is extremely safe. It has been estimated that at least 200,000 women die annually as a result of poorly performed abortions, and hundreds of thousands more suffer serious complications, including sepsis, hemorrhage, uterine perforation, and cervical trauma, often leading to permanent physical damage. These unnecessary consequences are largely the result of women still resorting to clandestine and illegal means of terminating unwanted pregnancies. We still suffer from a shortage of facilities that can provide safe, prompt, and affordable abortions, and that can also safeguard our anonymity if we desire it (Coeytaux et al., 1993).

Menopause. Perhaps no reproductive system process has been so mystified and confused in the public mind during recent times as that known as *menopause*. Generally speaking, the term refers to what happens in a woman's body as she reaches the end of her childbearing years. In Western society and others affected by the values of Western culture, this stage of a woman's life has been regarded as tragic, a kind of "living death," in that menopause ends her whole purpose in life. No parallel exists in popular consciousness for men, who apparently have other purposes. The increased life span for women means that more of us now reach menopause. Our problems related to menopause, and their treatment, have therefore become more central as a health issue.

Most women cease menstruating between the ages of forty-five and fifty-five. During, or just prior to that time, for a period of some months or years, we usually experience some irregularity in the timing and character of our menstrual cycles; a percentage of women also experience other physical changes or sensations. These experiences are thought to relate in large part to the reduced production of estrogen, which also result in eventual cessation of the menstrual cycle. While cessation of the cycle is inevitable, negative experiences in relation to the process are neither universal nor inevitable.

The negative experiences of menopause are not an illusion, but there is documentation of the psychological and cultural shaping of these experiences. A number of sensations and bodily conditions associated with menopause have been linked directly to shifts in the body's production of estrogen. Other conditions, headaches or depression, for example, which may occur at any age and from a number of causes, seem to be attributed to menopause by physicians (and sometimes patients) simply because they occur at this time.

While a great many women report no special physiological experiences during the menopausal years, others report a wide variety of them. The most widely reported negative experiences related to estrogen changes is the *hot flash*, a feeling of body heat that spreads from one point in the body to other areas, often accompanied by flushing, sometimes by intense perspiration, and in some women, a feeling of great embarrassment or discomfort. Very little is known about the hot flash, since few medical scientists have taken this subject seriously enough to study it (Voda, 1982).

Another process associated with estrogen changes has been more closely examined, although its rate of occurrence is difficult to gauge. *Osteoporosis*, associated with decrease in bone density, occurs in all humans after the age of thirty-five, but it is greatly accelerated in some women after menopause, resulting in bone ailments and a highly increased vulnerability to bone fractures. It is estimated that some 20 million Americans currently have osteoporosis, and that we sustain 1.2 million bone fractures annually as a result (AMWA, 1990). It is further estimated that osteoporosis will cause one woman out of three over the age of sixty-five to develop a vertebral fracture and one out of three over the age of seventy-five to develop a hip fracture. Mortality rates resulting from hip fractures are quite high, and morbidity is some 50 percent. Osteoporosis is a major cause of physical disability in older women (twice as common as for older men) (ibid.). There is now evidence that estrogen replacement therapy may alleviate this accelerated bone loss if used in time (Gordon, 1984). The risk of osteoporosis, however, is not uniform among women: African Americans and some African groups rarely show symptoms of this disease (Gilsanz et al., 1991; Gordon, 1984; Mijiyawa et al., 1991).

The use of estrogen replacement therapy to relieve a variety of consequences of the changes in women's endocrine functions with menopause has become increasingly common in the Western world. For this reason, concern has been expressed about its possible negative consequences, including possible increased risk of cancer, particularly in the reproductive organs of the women who use it. Current research (cited above) does not support this suspicion, but women need to educate ourselves about the risks and benefits involved to make informed choices for ourselves. We need to know, for example, that other ways to reduce the risk of osteoporosis include maintenance of a high-calcium diet, regular exercise, and the avoidance of smoking, excessive alcohol, and caffeine (AMWA 1990).

Hysterectomy. The hysterectomy, or removal of the uterus, has been the second most frequently performed form of surgery among the population of the United States for about the past century. Since only half that population has a uterus, this statistic demonstrates how common this operation has been for women.

We are bound to ask why hysterectomies are so common. In the nineteenth century, the uterus was thought to be the principal source of women's ailments; its removal was the obvious cure. Although modern medical science rejects this idea, hysterectomies continue to be performed on women possessed of healthy uteri. Physicians have offered to perform this "service" for women who no longer wish to bear children, citing two primary reasons: It is an effective form of sterilization, and it is a preventive measure, since the uterus *may* be the site of cancer at some future time. Organ removal as a form of surgical prophylaxis against possible cancer, however, has its limits as a rationale. We are still left with the question of why hysterectomy is so prevalent a surgical intervention.

Gena Corea (1985), citing medical references, points to greed as the principal motivation behind the performance of hysterectomy. Doctors make more money performing hysterectomies than using other approaches to deal with either uterine disease or birth control. Moreover, they feel justified in exploiting women in this way because they do not regard the uterus as serving any function other than reproduction, believing that it is a "useless" organ and can be removed without any negative consequences. The removal of ovaries in postmenopausal women is frequently regarded in the same way. Among reasons commonly cited today for hysterectomies, therefore, are uterine fibroids, abnormal uterine bleeding, endometriosis, genital prolapse, and chronic pelvic pain. Alternatives to surgical removal of the uterus are possible for many of these ailments. As a consequence of the medical profession's own self-criticism of the large number of hysterectomies being performed, there began to be an actual drop in their numbers. In 1980, 750,000 such operations were performed in the United States; in 1990, there were 590,000 (Brody, 1993). Women who undergo the procedure risk death at the rate of 16 (at the most) to 11 per 10,000. In addition, women risk postoperative complications (24 to 48 per 10,000) and a worsening of sexual function (20 per 10,000) (ibid.). These statistics suggest that hysterectomies are often avoidable, and moreover pose a considerable risk to women's health.

Violence

A fairly large proportion of women who show up in emergency rooms of hospitals for treatment of injuries are victims of a phenomenon known as *wife-battering*. Estimates vary for the rate of spouse or partner abuse; some estimates have placed it between 3 million and 4 million women in the United States annually (Stark et al., 1983). In the United States, battering is the greatest single cause of injury to women (Stark and Flitcraft, 1991). These women are treated for broken bones and other bodily wounds, and then sent home again without comment. It is likely that in a large number of cases, the cause of injuries—battering—is not reported in the medical record and is not noted by the physician. However, after women repeatedly appear for treatment for such injuries, medical practitioners may respond by blaming the victims. Discovering that many of the battered women who reappear for treatment also use alcohol or other drugs, medical practitioners begin to regard this behavior as the cause of the patients' problems. If such cases are followed up, then, it is the victim who is regarded as "sick," and in need of treatment by various therapies that will change her ways so she will not "cause herself to be beaten."

This common and widespread response to battering contributes actively to the oppression of women by systematic compliance to the patriarchal family structure enforced through physical threat and abuse. The "helping professions" in general inadvertently play this role in capitalist society, by filling the roles that the family no longer provides, such as education of children, and health care, while at the same time actually reinforcing patriarchal gender role expectations (Stark et al., 1983).

Nations and cultures vary in the extent of their domestic violence against women, but the phenomenon appears pervasive worldwide, with few minor, small-society exceptions (Heise, 1993). Rape and sexual assault are also pervasive, and while not usually included in the statistics covering domestic violence, the perpetrators of these violent acts are known to the victims in the majority of cases, often friends, relatives, and household members (Heise, 1993). Both nonsexual and sexual assault results in severe health consequences for women, including not only chronic disabilities, both physical and mental, but also death. It is estimated, for example, that in the United States, "every 15 seconds a woman is beaten, and four battered women die each day" (Smyke, 1991:53). It is also estimated that at least one out of ten women has been sexually abused as a child (Finkelhor, 1984).

Rape, while not a "health" issue per se, has obvious health consequences, both physical and mental, including subjection of the victim to exposure to sexually transmitted diseases, including AIDS. But a further consequence, resulting from the stigma attached to loss of virginity by unmarried women in some cultures, has often been missed. Rape victims may become unwanted, "unmarriageable" members of the household, hence further victimized; we may even be murdered by our own male kin for our loss of "honor" (Heise, 1993). In addition, rape victims are among the highest risk groups for posttraumatic stress disorder, a debilitating psychological syndrome that involves detailed reliving of the traumatic event, panic attacks, depression, nightmares, and sleep disorders. Therapeutic measures designed to help patients overcome posttraumatic stress disorder include systematic desensitization training, cognitive-behavioral treatment, group therapy, and self-help therapy (Foa et al., 1991; Petit, 1991). (At particular risk for such violence are women in war and refugee women [see below].)

Women at Special Risk

While exacerbated by and often contributing to poverty, other factors place some women at higher risk of ill health than others. Being a member of an ethnic or racial group that is subject to discrimination is an obvious risk. Three groups have been singled out for special attention here: disabled women, elderly women, and refugee women.

Disabled Women. Disabled women tend to be stigmatized everywhere. Disabilities include impairments ranging from vision and hearing to mobility at various levels. Poverty and isolation from a supportive family unit generally compound disability. It has only been in recent years that many high-income countries have made accommodations to empower the disabled to participate "in the mainstream," by providing means of access in public places; lower-income countries lag far behind. Even with these accommodations, stigma and prejudice persist, and to a greater extent for disabled women than for disabled men (Boylan, 1991).

It is estimated that over 100 million people are currently disabled as a result of malnutrition (Boylan, 1991). A very high proportion of blindness, mental retardation, and other disabilities could be avoided by proper nutrition. Additional numbers of individuals could avoid disabilities of various sorts by improvements in prenatal care, proper care at birth, and care in early infancy. Safer basic living and working conditions could prevent millions of disabilities in the future. Because female infants and girls are more likely than boys to suffer mal-

The Legal Bias against Rape Victims

Few rapists are punished for their crime simply because the law itself discriminates against their victims. According to a note in 61 *California Law Review* 919 (1973), "A man who rapes a woman who reports the crime to police has roughly seven chances out of eight of walking away without a conviction. Assuming only one woman in five reports the crime, his chances increase to thirty-nine out of forty."

In urging the House of Delegates to approve a resolution calling for a redefinition of rape, Connie K. Borkenhagen of Albuquerque, New Mexico, pointed out one reason why most rape victims prefer not to press charges by imagining how it might sound if a robbery victim were subjected to the kind of cross-examination that the rape victim usually must undergo:

"Mr. Smith, you were held up at gunpoint on the corner of First and Main?"

"Yes."

"Did you struggle with the robber?"

"No."

"Why not?"

"He was armed."

"Then you made a conscious decision to comply with his demands rather than resist?"

"Yes."

"Did you scream? Cry out?"

"No. I was afraid."

"I see. Have you ever been held up before?"

"No."

"Have you ever *given* money away?"

"Yes, of course."

"And you did so willingly?"

"What are you getting at?"

"Well, let's put it like this, Mr. Smith. You've given money away in the past. In fact, you have quite a reputation for philanthropy. How can we be sure that you weren't *contriving* to have your money taken from you by force?"

"Listen, if I wanted . . ."

"Never mind. What time did this holdup take place, Mr. Smith?"

"About 11:00 P.M."

"You were out on the street at 11:00 P.M.? Doing what?"

"Just walking."

"Just walking? You know that it's dangerous being out on the street that late at night. Weren't you aware that you could have been held up?"

"I hadn't thought about it."

"What were you wearing at the time, Mr. Smith?"

"Let's see . . . a suit. Yes, a suit."

"An *expensive* suit?"

"Well—yes. I'm a successful lawyer, you know."

"In other words, Mr. Smith, you were walking around the streets late at night in a suit that practically advertised the fact that you might be a good target for some easy money, isn't that so? I mean, if we didn't know better, Mr. Smith, we might even think that you were *asking* for this to happen, mightn't we?"

(*American Bar Association Journal*, 1975)

nutrition through neglect, they are more prone to avoidable, unnecessary disability as a result; but because the mothers of both girls and boys experience malnutrition as a result of poverty and gender discrimination, both girls and boys are subject to unnecessary, avoidable disability.

Society often concentrates more on what disabled women *can't* do rather than on what we *can* do. Impairment of vision, hearing, mobility, or certain mental functions does not necessarily mean total disability. Given an education and specific training, there are many jobs we can do for a living, and many ways we can help ourselves in daily life, even ways we can help others. Prejudice often places unnecessary barriers in our path. Larger numbers of women with disabilities are today showing the way in professional, skilled, and semiskilled occupations.

Recently, disabled women have protested neglect and prejudice in two important areas of their lives: sexuality and reproduction. It is often assumed, falsely, that disabled women are asexual, neither desiring sex nor being sexually attractive to others. This denies an important human right to disabled women (Boylan, 1991). Disabled women have claimed the right to marry and to bear children, and have shown that we, our spouses, and our children can thrive as families.

Elderly Women. Much of what has been said of disabled women could also be (and has been) said of elderly women, who are often treated as disabled persons, with all the stigma that go with assumptions about disability. The difference is that, with improvement in health care, there are more of us all the time (Smyke, 1991; Heisel, 1989). But we are frequently disabled, too, with chronic diseases such as arthritis, hypertension, diabetes, and osteoporosis, as well as age-related loss of hearing and vision. Isolation often exacerbates our difficulties in cop-

ing with disability, as we live longer than our male partners and, in urban areas, often live apart from our families, despite our potential to contribute importantly to their well-being. Nevertheless, many of us wish to challenge the idea that we are "helpless" in our old age (Boylan, 1991).

Membership in an ethnic or racial minority group may exacerbate problems we experience as aging persons who are female and poor. However, it should be pointed out, we also have coping strategies within our families and communities that counteract larger societal disadvantages (Padgett, 1989; Sánchez-Ayéndez, 1989). Often, our families need our help, and we offer one another support.

In the modern world, we become increasingly dependent on public institutions to provide us with health care and the means of paying for it. Our choices may be reduced, our treatment may become impersonal, and we may have to learn to cope with a barrage of bureaucratic procedures to receive the benefits to which we are entitled. Despite the fact that we constitute an increasing proportion of the general population, little is understood about our situation (Muller, 1990).

Refugee Women. Some 75 percent of the world's 18 million refugees are women (Heise, 1993). Homeless, impoverished, terrified, our tragedy is compounded by special vulnerabilities, particularly to violence, especially rape. "Refugee women are subject to sexual violence and abduction at every step of their escape, from flight to border crossings to life in the camps. . . . Many refugee women who have been raped are shunned by their families and isolated from other members of their community" (ibid.:178). Warfare in our home regions may have already subjected us to rape, torture, kidnapping, and the loss of close family members, as is the case for women in the currently ongoing wars in Bosnia and Herzegovina and Haiti (Sontag, 1993). We often find ourselves settled temporarily in camps with minimal sanitation and health care, little shelter from the elements, little nutritious food or clean water, and rough treatment on the part of camp officials. Finally, when we are resettled, we find ourselves in a strange new land, frightened and lonely, not knowing the language and customs, resorting to health care workers whose understanding of illness and disease might be very different from our own (Smyke, 1991). Thus, refugee women comprise another group that faces exaggerated health risks, but whose needs, like those of the disabled and elderly, are poorly understood and inadequately addressed.

Women and Mental Health

In the realm of mental health, the interconnections between perceptions of health, diagnoses of the causes of illness, and women's place in society seem unavoidable. Critical literature in this field is extremely extensive. In 1972, in a work that is now called a "classic," Phyllis Chesler brought both academic and public attention to the use of ideas about madness and psychiatric institutions in society to oppress and control women. While the interpretation of human behavior as mentally healthy or mentally ill clearly contains a subjective element, it equally clearly reflects social values.

Earlier reflections on the subject of culture, mental health, and deviance by Ruth Benedict (1934a, b) suggested that what any society perceives as normal and abnormal is culturally defined. Benedict's interest in, and sensitivity to, the variable cultural labeling of the "normal" and the "deviant" might have stemmed from her own personal identity struggles as a professional in a society that assigned women to a homemaker role, a childless woman in a society that claimed that motherhood was women's greatest fulfillment, and a lesbian in a society that regarded all homosexuality as criminal and a sign of mental illness.

Human nature is extremely plastic, and most individuals in a society will tend to fit themselves into a pattern of behavior they are taught is "normal." But behavior that is considered "normal" in one society might be interpreted as "insane" or at least "neurotic" in another. Notions and behaviors associated with female modesty in Western society, if found in, say, a woman in a traditional Middle Eastern rural village, would indicate fairly extreme deviance, and vice versa. Just as a Muslim woman parading about in shorts and a halter top in such a village might be thought to be behaving "crazily," a modern Western Christian woman who was ashamed to show her face in public might be suspected of having a "mental problem."

Because different societies express and label mental illness differently, it is not a simple matter to describe universals of mental health and illness, nor is it clear whether there are forms of illness that are distinctive to specific societies that have their own terms for forms of illness they recognize. A number of societies recognize forms of mental illness (for which they have specific terms) that differentially strike women and men. Greenland Eskimos, for example, recognize a mental disorder called *pibloktoq*, to which women seem to be especially prone; the victim becomes oblivious to her surroundings and acts in peculiar ways. It is not clear whether this disorder is one culture's manifestations of a form of mental illness found in other cultures, or whether it has its roots in physiological processes. Some anthropologists have theorized that certain mental illnesses found in a variety of societies are the result of specific vitamin deficiencies (Wallace, 1972). Still others have suggested that certain mental abnormalities such as schizophrenia are found cross-culturally and are described in similar ways regardless of cultural setting (Murphy, 1981), having a biological rather than a cultural basis.

Gender Differences in Mental Health

As in the case of physical health, women and men are more similar than different in most respects in mental health and illness; it is in the area of difference that feminist criticism is most brought to bear. However, some of this criticism has implications for an understanding of mental health, illness, and treatment in areas other than where gender differences are found.

In a very useful review of the literature, Karen Pugliesi (1992) depicts two basic positions regarding gender differences in mental health. One, which she terms the "social causation approach," looks at aspects of women's experience in society that affect women's mental well-being. Thus, the social conditions mentioned earlier, such as greater likelihood of experiencing poverty, sexual abuse, violence, and the double discrimination of gender and race, produce stresses that endanger women's mental as well as physical well-being, with the results that can be expected to appear in the statistical distribution of mental health and illness among women and men. Mental health advantages can also be attributed to social conditions differentially affecting women and men. The fact that women might be encouraged to express emotions while men are encouraged to repress them, might well have specific mental health repercussions.

The second position Pugliesi describes, the "social constructionist approach," finds a major source of difference between women and men in methods of conception and diagnosis of mental health and illness. Phyllis Chesler's *Women and Madness* (1972) falls squarely in this category of critique. Certain behaviors by women are labeled as the product of mental disorders by sexist psychiatrists and psychologists. Gender differences in mental health are, then, largely an artifact of bias on the part of a profession, its practitioners, and the society that produced them.

Thus, while both approaches locate the source of difference in women's and men's mental health in sexism, one approach takes the discovery of gender differences as "real," the product of different experiences in gender-biased society, the other approach treats this discovery as an artifact of biased diagnosis, a misinterpretation of what actually exists. These approaches complement one another in possibilities for dealing with treatment. We shall return to this point later.

Women and men differ with regard to many aspects of behavior that fall into the mental health realm, which clearly reflect social circumstances. Substance abuse is one such. Research indicates that women are less likely than men to be abusers of alcohol and tobacco, for example, but when our life-styles more closely resemble those of men, so do our substance abuse patterns. As women entered the workforce, for example, we more frequently used alcohol and tobacco. On the other hand, women make greater use of prescription drugs, again, most likely as a reflection of social patterns. Women are more likely to request psychotropic drugs from physicians, and physicians are more likely to locate women's complaints in the psychological domain. Hence, with greater access to the drugs, women are more likely to use and abuse them (see Travis, 1988b, for a review of the research).

Depression. One of the most consistent findings in the literature on gender differences in mental health is that women are at about twice the risk for depression as men, and this finding applies not only to the United States but on a global basis (see McGrath et al., 1990, for a major review of the literature in this field). Depression is characterized by the persistence over a prolonged time—two weeks according to current diagnostic procedures—of a number of symptoms from a list. Typical symptoms are given in Table 12.6. Psychiatrists and psychologists recognize a variety of types of depression. The report of the American Psychological Association's National Task Force on Women and Depression (McGrath et al., 1990) urges a "biopsychosocial" perspective on depression, with regard to both diagnosis of causes and prescription for treatment. The biological component of this perspective includes a consideration of the biological and

Table 12.6 Symptoms of Depression

Affective

Depressed mood, feeling sad, despondent, gloomy

Anxiety

Decreased capacity to experience pleasure

Feelings of worthlessness, self-reproach, or shame

Cognitive

Retardation of speech and thought

Loss of interest in work and usual activities

Diminished ability to think or concentrate

Fall in self-esteem

Pessimism and helplessness

Thoughts of death

Behavior

Changes in posture

Indifferent grooming

Agitation, restlessness

Decreased sexual activity

Physical Functioning

Change in appetite, usually leading to weight loss

Sleep disturbance, hyposomnia or hypersomnia

Loss of energy, fatigue, lethargy

Bodily complaints

From *Women and Health Psychology* (p. 40), by Cheryl Brown Travis, 1988, Hillsdale, N.J., Lawrence Erlbaum Associates. Copyright © 1988 by Lawrence Erlbaum Associates. Reprinted by permission.

psychological consequences of reproductive-related events, including menstruation, pregnancy, childbirth, infertility, abortion, and menopause. The psychological component also refers to characteristics of female personality as constructed by society and the ways that women are oriented by this construction toward certain patterns of perception, social interaction, and coping with stress. The social component refers to the stresses produced by the roles to which women are assigned by society, and to the risks to which women are subject as women, such as rape and other violence, and poverty as single parents of low socioeconomic status. The Task Force reviewed research literature on specific factors in each of these general categories, but also took into account the observation that many of the diagnostics are prone to sexist interpretation.

Consequently, a woman might feel she needs to seek help because she feels "depressed," locating the source of the problem in herself, but not recognizing that her social situation might be the major contributor to her feeling. On the other hand, her consultant, psychiatrist, or psychologist, might compound this "blaming of the victim" by characterizing a perfectly normal reaction to a terrible situation as a symptom of mental illness. For example, a woman might exhibit all the symptoms of depression if she were a battered wife; to treat her for mental illness so she could live contentedly with her violent husband would surely be to compound her victimization.

If the risk of depression and diagnosis for depression are higher among women than among men, the risk for members of racial and ethnic minority groups is also high, and higher for women of these groups than men. But the conditions affecting rates of depression for African Americans, Latinas, Asian Americans, and Native Americans vary according to the situation of the groups and subgroups in question; while discrimination produces stress and depression at a greater rate than for the population of women in general, the ways in which they are experienced and expressed are specific to each group. For example, the categories of Latina and Asian American include some groups that are recent immigrants and refugees, who have been subject to situational stresses quite different from those affecting, say, working-class urban African American women, on the one hand, and Native American women living in impoverished rural reservations, on the other.

A second important dimension for variation in risk of depression for women is age. Adolescence and old age are considered high-risk categories, life stages characterized by both biological changes accompanying changes in reproductive status, and social changes resulting in adjustment challenges. Again, while internal adjustments to altered circumstances might be stressful, external circumstances may

be a major source of serious problems, which, if ignored, would result in double victimization of the depressed woman. For example, teenage girls may be subject to sexual harassment and abuse, which leads to depression; older women are likely to be suffering from loss of spouses, leading not only to loneliness but impoverishment and despair.

A final dimension of risk for depression is sexual orientation. The Task Force reports, however, that virtually no research has been done on depression among lesbians. It speculates, however, that this dimension is an important one requiring more attention. The report speculates further that positive factors reducing the likelihood of depression for lesbians include group support from the lesbian community (among those who have come out, and have a community to turn to) and the sharing of housework and child care in lesbian households. We return to the topic of implications for therapy on page 434.

An early focus of the contemporary women's movement was the organization of political agitation to make abortion legal and a matter of a woman's decision over what happened to her own body. The group pictured here rallied in New York City, May 7, 1972. (Photo by Bettye Lane)

Eating Disorders. While depression, as a mental disorder or illness, suggests some social correlates, it is in the realm of eating disorders that the impact of social construction of gender on mental health is most conspicuous. Two related eating disorders, anorexia and bulimia, are marked in the literature on mental health. The ratio of females to males exhibiting anorexia is estimated to be 15:1. Because males are more likely to be hospitalized for the condition when it is recognized, the female-to-male ratio among the hospitalized population is approximately 8:1 (Travis, 1988b). The occurrence of bulimia is harder to detect, because it tends to be concealed. The age at which anorexia and bulimia is found is, most frequently, middle and late adolescence. Eating disorders are found primarily in the middle and upper classes, typically among the offspring of professional and managerial workers.

Simply put, anorexia involves self-starvation to the point of illness, and sometimes, death. Bulimia is a variant; the bulimic person eats ravenously in binges, then purges herself by self-induced vomiting and laxatives. She tends to maintain her body weight but becomes ill through her efforts to remain thin by continuous and repeated purging. There is some overlap in behavior between anorexics and bulimics (see Table 12.7 on signs and symptoms of anorexia and bulimia).

However, eating disorders are not caused simply by social images of women. Eating disorders have their roots in other causes, such as families characterized by a veneer of niceties beneath which anger and conflict are sublimated (MacLeod, 1982). By controlling food and our own bodies, women with eating disorders put order in our own lives.

Dieting and other practices geared to maintaining a slender physique are ordinary, everyday activities urged upon women (and to a lesser extent, men) by the media, by parents and peers, by the medical profession itself. The fact that young women are more likely to

Table 12.7 Diagnostic Symptoms of Anorexia and Bulimia

Anorexia	*Bulimia*
Cognition	
Denial of illness	Awareness of abnormal eating
Preoccupation with dieting and being thin	Self-deprecating thoughts after a binge
Distorted body image	Distorted body image
Affect	
Morbid fear of fatness	Morbid fear of fatness
Anxiety fear & depression	Anxiety fear & depression
Food phobia	Powerful urges to overeat
Pleasure in losing weight & being thin	Fear of being unable to stop eating
Behavior	
Self-imposed starvation	Inconspicuous binge eating
Self-induced vomiting	Self-induced vomiting
Use of laxatives and diuretics	Use of laxatives and diuretics
Hyperactivity and vigorous exercise	Impulsive behavior, drug use
Bulimic episodes	
Physical Signs	
Significant weight loss (20%–25%)	Weight fluctuations (10 or more lbs.)
Amenorrhea	Menstrual irregularity
Lanugo	Strong appetite
Bradycardia	Gastrointestinal complaints
Hypotension	Gastric dilation, rupture
Constipation	Dental enamel erosion
Breast atrophy	Headaches, dizziness, aura preceding binge

From *Women and Health Psychology* (p. 137) by Cheryl Brown Travis, 1988, Hillsdale, N.J., Lawrence Erlbaum Associates. Copyright © 1988 by Lawrence Erlbaum Associates. Reprinted by permission.

have eating disorders than young men results from the obvious emphasis our society places on female appearance and the less obvious tendency to prefer infantilized women (who look more like preadolescent boys).

Anorexics often do not believe they are ill, or deny it. Bulimics, on the other hand, realize that there is a problem and take great pains to cover it up. But binge eating, like dieting, is not at all uncommon; in fact, a large proportion of women have, at some time or another, engaged in this form of behavior. Thus, eating disorders are an extreme expression of a range of behaviors that are merely part of being a woman in modern (probably middle-class) industrial society.

Issues in Therapy

Feminist critiques of psychotherapy generally argue that the fundamental error of traditional therapy is one of attribution. The cause of the client's problem is in the person, and so is the source of the "cure." This ignores social conditions and processes outside the individual and beyond her control. The critical social condition is the fact of male dominance; any woman's identity and behavior, whether regarded as "healthy" or "abnormal," must be understood in light of that fact. So must the concepts and tools of traditional therapy.

One important consequence of male dominance is that what is defined as "male" is the norm of mental health, while what is "female" is deviant. Negative traits, such as masochism, tend to be classified as "female." This places women in the double bind of being psychologically "sick" if they act and feel in accordance with the construction of "female" but at the same time, if they act and feel like males, they are also "sick" because they are then abnormal females. Further, the mental health of women has generally been judged in terms of women's happy and voluntary compliance in the roles assigned to us as wife and mother. As a result, therapy becomes an instrument of social control to keep us in our place, acting as good, subordinate wives and mothers (for a review of these critiques, see Travis, 1988b, and Russo and Green, 1993).

Feminist Therapy. Feminist alternatives to traditional therapy demand recognition of two basic points: first, that women must be viewed in our own terms, not as deviations from a male norm, nor in terms of our fulfilling roles in relation to males, and second, that our experience, like all human experience, must be located in a social context, and that social context has been, until the present, one of inequality. Different feminist philosophies argue for different applications of these basic principles.

Greater awareness of the effects of social bias, and the nature and consequences of gender-related dominance and dependency are essential aspects of feminist analysis of the human psychic condition. Helping women clients through feminist therapy includes assisting us to understand our circumstances at least in part in terms of societal conditions and gender relationships. It also includes helping us to determine means of coping with the stresses that are posed to us by our life conditions that do not deny our worth as human beings, do not require our acceptance of behavior or roles simply because society has assigned them to us, and do not require our perpetual subordination simply because we are women. This may mean actively changing our social interactions and even our social conditions. As Beverly Greene points out, feminist therapists, to be effective, must recognize and validate the biases experienced by women as a result of gender, race, and class discrimination (Greene, 1993).

Addressing Homophobic Bias. Issues related to homophobic bias in the realm of mental health and illness are important in and of themselves, but they also bring into focus more general issues of gender construction and bias relevant to people of any sexual orientation. However, as in the case of racial or ethnic bias, the problems facing a lesbian seeking assistance

Has Feminism Aided Mental Health?

In little more than a decade the feminist movement, some recent research suggests, has already had a beneficial effect on the mental health of women.

That observation has been made repeatedly as scientists take on the difficult job of assessing how an improving job market for women has affected their emotional well-being. The conclusion persists, despite criticism that it is premature and that the elements in the issue are too vague to define rigorously.

Among those who see a clear relationship between feminism and mental health is Dr. Grace Baruch, a Wellesley College psychologist. Following her new study, she declared: "The mental health of women has improved with the women's movement. Feminism leads to equality and equality to mental health."

In 1978, Dr. Baruch and Dr. Rosalind Barnett began to study almost 300 women from the ages of 35 to 55. Interviewers asked the women about their work and family life, their expectations and satisfactions. They found, reports Dr. Baruch, that "woman who work enjoy greater self-esteem and suffer less anxiety and depression than women who do not work."

The prestige of a woman's work, as one might expect, had an added impact: Those in high status occupations showed a greater sense of mastery—a feeling of control over what is important to them—than other women.

"Marriage and children did not affect feelings of mastery," Dr. Baruch says. "Nor did the presumed strain of multiple roles. The women with the highest rates of life satisfaction had both families and high prestige jobs."

The sense that good jobs may serve as a kind of preventive medicine emerged from a National Institute of Mental Health study of 2,300 Chicago adults. Dr. Frederic Ilfeld, a psychiatrist at the University of California at Davis, found that high status occupations tended to protect women from psychiatric symptoms.

The research showed, Dr. Ilfeld explained, that "women suffered twice as many symptoms as men," and that "only among women with high status jobs were symptoms as infrequent as among men."

Dr. Ilfeld speculated that this select group of women perceived themselves as having more control over their lives and enjoyed a greater sense of self-esteem and self-sufficiency. "It makes clinical sense that equality and mental health are related," he said. "When there is not equality, self-image suffers."

The idea that work plays a central role in life satisfaction is not new but is given a novel twist by research showing that it applies to women as well as to men. The customary thinking has been that satisfaction for a woman comes largely from her role in the family and home and not in the outside world, and most of the research on job satisfaction has focused on men.

(Albin, 1981)

through therapy may be compounded as a consequence of negative bias in the larger social environment, struggles with negative self-image resulting from taught prejudice, and therapeutic practices that are inappropriate to the situation because they are based on an assumption of heterosexuality.

The Final Report of the Task Force on Psychotherapy with Lesbians and Gay Men of the American Psychological Association (1991) reviews a variety of ways in which bias affects psychotherapy with lesbians and gay men. Their survey of therapists practicing in the United States identified some twenty-five themes. In the area of assessment, for example, the therapist might believe that homosexuality itself is a form of psychopathology, attribute a client's problems to homosexuality without evidence that this is the case, fail to recognize that the influence of the client's own negative attitudes about homosexuality may influence the client's symptoms or distress, automatically assume that a client is heterosexual, or discount homosexual orientation.

In the realm of intervention, the survey contained the following examples of bias: a therapist focuses on sexual orientation when it is not relevant, discourages a client from having a lesbian or gay orientation, seeks to change the sexual orientation of the client, trivializes or demeans lesbian or gay experience, terminates therapy upon disclosure of homosexuality, makes renouncing homosexuality a condition of treatment, or inappropriately discloses the client's sexual orientation. Other issues of bias involve poor understanding of issues of identity, intimate relationships, family relationships, and problems due to social prejudice and discrimination. A lesbian client might experience even further stress from her interaction with a biased or ignorant therapist than the problems that brought her to seek professional help in the first place!

The Task Force also discovered a variety of different ways that therapists can positively respond to the needs of lesbian and gay male clients. The therapist can begin with an understanding that homosexuality is not necessarily a psychological disorder but is one of many attributes characterizing a client's life, and at the same time may or may not be relevant to the specific problem at hand. The therapist can recognize the problems that social prejudice presents lesbian and gay male clients, recognize the compounding effects of racial/ethnic identities, and that lesbians and gay men can live happy and fulfilling lives. Therapists can be helpful by understanding social homophobia and assisting clients to overcome their own negative attitudes about homosexuality, by recognizing the ways their own sexual orientation and attitudes may be relevant to the therapeutic situation, and by becoming more knowledgeable about lesbian and gay lives and community resources.

Drug Therapy. Research has revealed that psychotropic drugs (tranquilizers, sedatives, hypnotics, and stimulants) are prescribed more frequently, and for longer durations, for women than for men. This pattern becomes marked after the age of forty-five. The most frequent prescribers of these drugs are general practitioners (Travis, 1988b). There are considerable risks in the use of these drugs, including undesirable side effects, negative drug interactions, overdose, and dependence.

Gender differences in this phenomenon can be traced to two sources: the patients and the physicians. Women are more likely to go to a physician for help. This may be because we experience more problems, or because we more readily admit we have problems, or feel less able to cope with these problems without help, or simply, because we have readier access to physicians due to more flexible working hours. It may be a combination of some or all of these factors that explains why women seek physician assistance more frequently than men. Physicians, on the other hand, are more likely to attribute problems reported by women to psychic causes, and deal with these problems with prescriptions for psychotropic drugs (Travis, 1988b).

Feminist analysis of this situation suggests a variety of remedies on several fronts. Women's medical complaints should not be readily "dismissed" as something that is "all in your head." Because with respect to so many physiological features males have been the norm, many physicians are not trained adequately to recognize problems in the physiologies and physiological processes of women. Improved research and training provide only part of the answer. Improvement in physicians' attitudes is also required. However, this is only part of the picture, for physicians reflect and participate in the larger social situation. Ultimately, the differences in drug prescription and use between women and men can only be expected to change with a reduction of sexism and its consequences.

The Structure of Health Care Services

Hierarchy in Health Care

Health care in the Western world and in the Third World that emulates the industrially developed countries has evolved during the past century into an entrenched hierarchy that expresses pervasive sexism, classism, and racism (Weaver and Garrett, 1983). At the top of the hierarchy are mostly men drawn from the privileged classes, who make decisions and who get well paid for doing so. At the bottom of the hierarchy are mostly women, drawn from the less privileged classes, often nonwhite, who are poorly paid for our services, which consist of doing the actual work of taking care of sick and disabled people. This work involves, for example, preparing food and feeding the sick and cleaning up after

meals; it means making beds and changing sheets and clothes and emptying bedpans; it means cleaning up. It means keeping vigil over ill people to watch for signs of improvement or decline. It also means providing conversation, a sympathetic ear or touch, or even just company.

These many tasks have always been "women's work" (Sacks, 1988). What has changed, however, is women's control over decisions about what we, as health care providers, are allowed and obliged to do. The primary health care providers—mothers, housewives, nurses, and various aides—are no longer expected to play a decision-making role in diagnosis or prescription of treatment: We are only to administer the decision of an "expert," a licensed physician.

The hierarchy in Western health care clearly reflects a patriarchal ideological origin. The all-knowing stern but benevolent physician-father gives orders to a dependent, submissive, undemanding nurse-mother, to serve the best interests of the patient-child, who is entirely ignorant and entirely passive. This hierarchy has only rarely been questioned or challenged by any of the participants, yet the system only evolved in recent history.

Women Physicians. Ellen More's brief history of the American Medical Women's Association (AMWA) and the role of women physicians in the United States provides a good background for looking at some of the key issues that face women doctors today. The number of women physicians in the United States had grown from just a handful in the 1830s to 5–6 percent of physicians in 1915, the year women were first accepted into the American Medical Association (AMA). Later that same year, though, women physicians formed our own organization, the AMWA (originally the Medical Women's National Association—MWNA), since we felt we lacked a voice in the AMA, and the community of women physicians was worried about the implications of a recent decline in the number of women graduating from medical schools (More, 1990). Women's recently gained suffrage led to the passage of the Sheppard-Towner Act in 1920, which financed the opening of prenatal and child health centers in rural areas (until 1929), temporarily creating jobs for female physicians who had previously been confined to a special sphere of jobs that were considered appropriate for women such as assistants to surgeons and positions in state institution for the insane (More, 1990). The conservative mood and the woman-as-homemaker ideal of the 1950s were detrimental to women physicians, but an increase in population, the building of hospitals, and the aging of the American population (which meant more labor-intensive, chronic illnesses) after World War II led to an increased demand for doctors, which women, inspired by the 1960s women's movement, rushed to fill: from 1961–1962 to 1971–1972, the percentage of women in medical school nearly doubled (More, 1990).

Following the lead of Carol Lopate's 1968 *Women In Medicine*, the AMWA in the late sixties and early seventies started to attack the social structural constraints on women's role in the medical professions. The AMWA began a campaign, which continues today, against gender discrimination in the workplace, lack of facilities and economic support for child care, and the assignment of household and child-rearing responsibilities to women (More, 1990).

A special sphere of jobs for women physicians that existed around the 1920s exists today in a different form. Judith Lorber has explained that women were encouraged to go into obstetrics and gynecology, pediatrics, psychiatry, and family medicine (Lorber, 1984). These specialties provide lower incomes and carry less prestige than areas in which men specialize, such as surgery and radiology (Lucas et al., 1992).

Women today are branching out in greater numbers in other specialties, such as surgery (Ramos and Feiner, 1989; Geer, 1993), but a "glass ceiling" effect has continued to impede women's progress into the top levels in medical institutions (Lorber, 1984). "The bottleneck begins a little higher up," says Ann Bernstein, who points out that only 5 percent of full professors in academic medicine are women (Bernstein, 1989:84).

Family obligations and child care have always been key issues for women physicians. We have been discriminated against by male doctors and the medical community who fear that maternity leave and family responsibilities might make us neglect our work obligations (Ramos and Feiner, 1989; Lorber, 1984). A survey of women in academic medicine shows that women physicians feel the institutions where we work fail to meet the needs of women with children, citing problems such as lack of child care and maternity leave policies (Bennett and Nickerson, 1992).

Of course, a large part of the problem of child care for women physicians comes from the fact that family responsibilities continue to be assigned primarily to women rather than to men. A survey of the perceived causes of stress among female and male physicians indicates that many women (but very few men) worry about conflicts between career and family concerns. Also, women physicians generally have household and child care responsibilities while 90 percent of male physicians have someone such as a wife to take care of these obligations (Gross, 1992). Among the other gender differences in physician stress, women were more likely to be concerned about the responsibility of being a doctor, while men worry more about their inability to effect cures and the possibility of malpractice suits.

African American women physicians experience the same problems that are faced by women physicians in general coupled with the additional burden of racial discrimination. A study of African American alumni of Howard University Medical School shows that although African American women physicians had as much residency experience and completed more postgraduate fellowships and traineeships than African American male physicians, more African American women than men worked in urban settings (a less desirable place to work, according to physicians) and practiced in the lower-income, less prestigious field of primary care (Titus-Dillon and Johnson, 1989).

Women Healers and Midwives. The transition from health care in the home to the hospital and/or physician's premises accompanied the shift of locus of decision making from women to men. This was the case both for routine health care, as in childbirth, and for illness, and the shift took place in similar ways for both. This is not to say that there were no specialists in health care. Midwifery as a specialization is very widespread. Curers and healers are found as specialists in virtually all societies. These are very often women, who have special experience, training, and recognized talent. There is often a psychological and spiritual component to our healing practices, as well as a pharmacopeia of medicines that we prepare ourselves, and a variety of methods and procedures for particular situations.

Such specialists, particularly when women, were at times seen as threats to other prevailing authorities. This was markedly the case in Western civilization, which viewed us as threats to the authority of the church, and branded us as witches (Marieskind, 1977). Today, new attitudes govern health care policies in some regions of the Third World. While untrained local health practitioners are sharply criticized as the cause of continued ill health among women, there are a number of programs to train local midwives and health

practitioners to collaborate with modern medical specialists (Smyke, 1991).

Women, even leaders in medicine, were not historically in accord over women healers and midwives. Gena Corea (1985) documents the conflict through the personal histories of two such leaders: Clemence Lozier (1813–1888) and Elizabeth Blackwell (1821–1910). Lozier was a pioneer medical practitioner in the United States, having graduated from the Eclectic New York Central Medical College in Syracuse and subsequently set up a very successful homeopathic medical practice. Later, in 1863, she founded a medical school of her own, the New York Medical College and Hospital for Women, the third woman's medical college in the United States. The college survived, despite obstacles placed in its way by the male medical establishment, until 1878. Lozier's approach to medicine was to stress preventive health care and to promote healthful habits of exercise, diet, cleanliness, and rest.

Elizabeth Blackwell, in contrast, identified more closely with the "regular" medical profession establishment. She had to fight hard for admission to medical school and for the right to practice as a medical professional. She also promoted preventive medicine, and trained health care workers who instructed poor mothers in their homes. In 1857 she founded the New York Infirmary for Women and Children. Since she accepted the caste hierarchy of "regular" medicine, the establishment viewed her as less of a threat than Lozier. She, for example, joined her male colleagues in their opposition to midwifery, and supported the takeover by obstetricians (who were, primarily, white, privileged males, accepted to formal medical training).

Yet rigorous formal training for midwives had been available. A novel, *The Midwife*, by Gay Courter (1981), chronicles the professional life of a Russian-trained midwife who immigrated to the United States, to find her credentials useless in her new home. While it remained possible for some years for some women to become licensed midwives, the medical profession eventually succeeded in virtually banishing this specialization for many decades.

Beginning around 1980, midwifery began to reemerge as a specialization. Many of us have decided we prefer midwives for ideological reasons. Disenchanted with the impersonal nature of modern biomedicine, we have sought out midwives who provide a more personal, and often holistic, approach to obstetric care: delivering children at home and allowing couples to have more decision-making power (Sullivan and Weitz, 1988). Midwives are also in demand today for more material and economic reasons. For instance, some authors have stressed the need to find midwives to serve the many rural and poor areas in the United States that currently lack adequate obstetrical care (Taylor and Ricketts, 1993).

Nurses and Nursing. If physicians sit at the top of the medical hierarchy in modern Western health care, nurses occupy positions from the middle on down. Professional nursing took shape in the latter nineteenth century alongside of the development of professional doctoring. The role of Florence Nightingale (1820–1910) in the advancement of professional nursing is well known. It must be pointed out that part of her strategy in establishing the standards of nursing included a hierarchical organization (like the military) that insisted on subordinate, utterly obedient conduct for nurses. Although nurses received their own professional training, part of this training was to perceive themselves as subject to both the authority of their nursing supervisors and the authority of the physician. This subordination did not render them incapable of making decisions, but heavily circumscribed the limits of these decisions and obliged them absolutely to carry out the decisions of physicians (Melash, 1982). While this strategy may have made professional nursing acceptable to physicians because it left it unthreatening to them—and made the presence of professional women health practitioners acceptable in the Victorian patriarchal setting—it also established an ideology of nursing that firmly entrenched a practical gender hierarchy. This ideology, equally accepted by physicians and nurses, resulted in the professional exploitation and oppression of nurses.

Nurses earn a very small fraction of the income that the physicians they serve earn. Nurses are ordered about, instructed to carry out all routine care of patients, and expected to take care of all the "dirty work," unless there are lowlier aides and orderlies to assume these tasks. That nurses are oppressed may be less obvious, but equally true. Nurses are treated as inferiors by physicians, often addressed by first names by people who must be addressed as "Doctor." They are expected to show deference in every respect to physicians, sometimes extended to such conduct as rising when the physician enters the room and opening doors for the physician, all in the name of hospital discipline.

Ideologies that reproduce gender hierarchies in nursing also reinforce racial hierarchies. Yet racism within the nursing profession, toward both nurses and patients, has been largely unexamined because the ideology of nursing itself emphasizes the caring and status-blind role of the caretaker, as well as values of "homogeneity and conflict-avoidance" (Barbee, 1993). Nurses' training excludes conflict-laden dialogue about race. At the same time, dominant social and scientific beliefs about health and illness, which individualize problems, contribute to an inability of health professionals to conceptualize the structural nature (specifically as related to socioeconomic and environmental conditions) of health problems among racial and ethnic groups (Jackson, 1993).

The acquiescence of nurses in such a system has been the subject of some scholarly exploration (Roberts, 1983). The submissiveness expected from nurses is clearly associated with gender hierarchy. But nurses have among ourselves a hierarchy, in which head nurses hold administrative positions and authoritative sway over junior nurses, and which mimics the hierarchy into which nursing is incorporated (Cleland, 1971; Grissum and Spengler, 1976). We acquiesce in the system because it rewards those of us at the top for doing so, in that we can view ourselves as a kind of elite in an elitist organization. For those of us at the bottom, it is fairly common to identify with our oppressors. This phenomenon can be seen as a reflection of the structure of the larger system, in which women in general are taught to be submissive and to identify with our oppressors.

This problem has not gone unnoticed by feminist members of the nursing profession. Various groups and networks have formed to change the system. One group, for example, called Cassandra, is a national network established in 1982 at an American Nursing Association convention in Washington, D.C., for the purpose of advancing communication about a feminist approach to nursing. It puts out a news journal and has periodic gatherings at the local, regional, and national level, as the opportunity arises. Other groups have worked to promote higher pay and better working conditions for nurses.

Women and Health Insurance. Americans, since World War II, have usually obtained health insurance through their employer (or labor union), the employer of a family member, or—especially if they work part-time or are in school—by buying their own health insurance. At a time when married women were mostly homemakers we were insured by our husbands' employers, but now that we constitute a major part of the workforce, both married and unmarried women often have our own insurance and are involved in issues that relate to health insurance and the workplace (Muller, 1990).

Although health care benefits do not vary much by sex, the range of benefits offered by an employer and the portion of the premium that must be paid by the employee vary by job, the lower-paid and more "feminized" positions more often receiving fewer benefits and requiring more employee contribution for the premium. Women more frequently work in low-paying jobs that have health plans "where a larger share of the premium comes from the employee, and the employer contributes little or nothing to the coverage of dependents of the employee" (Muller, 1990:80). In addition, more women than men work in part-time jobs where few employees receive any health benefits.

Health insurance is a particularly difficult issue for poor women. The employed poor often do not have employers who pay for health insurance, and we cannot afford to buy our own insurance. Also, being employed we usually do not qualify for Medicaid since almost any job, no matter how meager the pay, puts us over the extremely low poverty line that determines whether we can receive benefits such as Medicaid and AFDC (Muller, 1990).

Pregnancy and maternity have caused problems for women at the workplace and with our health insurers. Women used to be dismissed from jobs for taking maternity leave, but steps have been taken to require employers to provide job security for us when we go on pregnancy leave. Women on maternity leave were also at risk with insurers. The Pregnancy Discrimination Act of 1978 helped somewhat to guarantee insurance for women on maternity leave, but if a woman takes a leave from work to care for her child in the early months of its life she may have to pay the full premium for her health insurance (Muller, 1990).

However, at present, we are witnessing a social and political recognition of the problems inherent in the private health insurance structure. First Lady Hillary Rodham Clinton has headed an ambitious investigation of the health care system. She advocates for major changes in the way we insure our health. While there is widespread public recognition of the inadequacy of our current system, it remains to be seen what a new system will look like, and how it will affect the deployment of health care services to women.

Caring for Others/Caring for Ourselves

Women in virtually all societies are taught to be caregivers, and this role is cast as a duty of all women, as an extension of their roles as daughters and mothers. It is not surprising that even in complex societies where many responsibilities that formerly fell to households are now dealt with by nondomestic institutions, it is still taken for granted that caregiving will be attended to by women. Professional experts, such as social workers, also do not question the assumption that women will be the primary caretakers of the family (Briar and Ryan, 1986).

In addition, low socioeconomic status and cultural background may give extra reinforcement to the role of women in "household health production" (Clark, 1993). For example, cultural beliefs about women's natural skills and women's proper role contribute to the fact that poor Mexican American women take more responsibility for home health care of their families than do both their own partners and poor white women. Both Mexican and white women conceive of gender in such a way that our own caretaker roles seem "nat-ural." However, Mexican women receive less help from male partners and more help from female relatives than white women (Clark, 1993).

Understandably, because we have been taught it is our duty to take care of family members, women are reluctant to turn over our loved ones to institutions or strangers. Indeed, few could afford to do so if we had the desire. But as a consequence, we find ourselves also the victims of disease or disability, for "unlike wage earners who can negotiate boundaries and limits for their work, caregivers who strive to meet the personal care needs of disabled [family] members have no laws, unions, or governmental regulations to protect them. There is no legislation to regulate the number of hours in a week that they are permitted to work which would give them some respite" (Briar and Ryan, 1986:26).

Fortunately, in some rare instances, some relief can be found in community services. Rochelle Distelheim (1987) tells of the devastation brought to a middle-aged wife when her husband developed Alzheimer's disease, and of the assistance she found in an Alzheimer's Family Center in southern California. Here, for a fee, she can leave her husband for a day or two a week, so she can attend to her own needs—shopping, going to the library, or just being alone.

Finding time to take care of ourselves is a problem. While we have been taught to take care of others, we have not also been taught that we have a duty to look after our own well-being, and very few of us know how. We are taught almost nothing about our bodies or our nutritional or exercise needs, nor do we often have the means to implement such knowledge. It is an important objective of the women's health movement to provide access to knowledge of how to take care of ourselves, and the means to put this knowledge to use.

The Women's Health Movement

It is deceptive to speak of a single women's health movement (see Ruzek, 1978; Fee, 1983; Lenz and Meyerhoff, 1985; Travis, 1988a, b). In fact, there are many women's health movements, associated with different philosophies and different issues, though all agree about certain main points such as the need for women to know, the need for women to choose for themselves, and the damage done to women by patriarchal, phallocentric health care systems.

The literature about women and health care points to three different approaches within the movement in general. On one side is what we can refer to as the "reform" approach, which seeks to improve the ways that health care is provided to women within the framework that already exists. The means it uses involve a variety of changes. One is to increase the proportion of women physicians, in the expectation that a woman physician will be more sensitive to the needs and interests of her clients than men will. A second is to educate women clients, and to demand that physicians be helpful to women clients in our search for knowledge. A third is to promote egalitarian interactions between physicians and clients, so information flow will be improved, with the consequence that better health care will be possible. A fourth is to apply stringent legal controls over medications (drugs, for example), medical devices (such as birth control devices), and procedures that can be used by physicians on women clients. This is so women can no longer be experimented on with inadequately tested drugs, devices, and procedures that can harm us. This approach, then, seeks to retain the benefits of the existing health care system, but to improve it by various reforms.

An alternative approach, often called "radical" in the literature, rejects the existing system and seeks to set up a different mode of health care delivery for women entirely. It rejects the existing medical hierarchy as harmful to women and discriminatory against us. For healthy women, at least, it rejects physicians as specialists, and all their training; it rejects physicians' medicines, medical devices, and medical procedures. It rejects hospitals and doctors' offices as appropriate places to conduct routine health care service delivery. Instead, it seeks to offer appropriate health care for women by women, using a variety of techniques inherited from the past, discovered by women today through our own experience, and learned from one another by "comparing notes." It does not hesitate to borrow from the medical establishment where appropriate. For example, this approach urges women to learn to observe and examine ourselves by touching and looking. In particular, we are advised to examine the workings of our "inside" parts, such as the cervix, using a physician's device, a *speculum*. In this way, we can get to know what it looks like and how it changes from day to day throughout the month, and to recognize our own abnormalities, such as infections, should they occur. Should we get an infection of some sort, the appropriate remedy might be a physician's type of medication, but alternatively, for some types of infection, application of ordinary yoghurt might be recommended.

This approach is tentative and gentle and attempts to approximate natural processes and intervene minimally if at all. Childbirth, for example, should be attended by women, preferably some with experience; it should avoid such interventions as administration of drugs to accelerate labor, or to anesthetize the childbearer unnecessarily, but rather allow the labor process to proceed at its own pace. On the other hand, it does allow for intervention in "natural" processes such as abortion, but using simple, inexpensive devices under clean and controlled conditions. Neither process requires the assistance of a physician unless ex-

A bold statement that appeared in the Pro-Choice March in New York, in 1992. (Photo, Hope H. Wurmfeld, *In the Streets* series)

Members of the Los Angeles Feminist Health Center demonstrate to some women in New York City the techniques of vaginal self-examination. One of the results of new feminist questioning of the unlimited control male medical professionals have asserted over women patients has been a movement by women to take back control over our bodies and health. (Photo by Bettye Lane)

ceptional circumstances arise. In such emergency instances, the physician is regarded as a consultant or specialist whose services are specified and requested by the client or the client's helpers, not the managing authority.

Several writers have described problems that "radically" oriented women's health care centers have experienced as a consequence of attempts to adapt themselves to the context of a wider health care system. In some cases, health care activists have met with fierce, sometimes violent resistance, sometimes legal, sometimes not. In other cases, the initial aims of the health care group may be undermined by a process of co-optation. Members of a health care group may find themselves shifting their programs, their style, and their procedures in ways antithetical to their original philosophy, to take advantage of resources such as establishment-trained physicians (which the law requires for dispensing prescribed medications) and, perhaps more important, funding from public agencies. Sandra Morgen (1986) provides a case study of the process whereby apparent support from public agencies eventually results in approximation of conformity to medical establishment standards.

A third critique of the medical establishment comes from socialist and Marxist feminists (see Travis, 1988a, for a discussion). Marxist analyses argue that significant changes in the health care system cannot be isolated from larger changes in the structure of society, particularly its economic system. Socialist critics emphasize sex-gender systems more than economic class, but agree with Marxists that the health care system's domination and control of women is simply part of a larger social system. Both argue that changing women's health care is not a matter of individual choice, but they locate forces of change in society as a whole, and see social institutions like health care systems as instruments of social control.

The concerns of the women's health movement are not subsumed strictly under the rubrics "reform" and "radical" because these approaches are cross-cut by other concerns. An important perspective takes into account the concerns of poor women worldwide. Health care concerns for them involve not simply the conduct of physician-client interaction, but quality-of-life questions. We are talking now about critical health issues such as the adequacy of food and shelter. If these are inadequate, no improvement in the medical establishment can improve the health of victims of poverty. Among women who have no clean water to drink and insufficient food for their children, why worry about whether doctors are male or female?

Even if food, water, and shelter are minimally available, there may be inadequate health care to provide inoculations against disease, minimal hygiene for infected wounds, and the like; there may be no hospitals, no surgical implements, no medicines. In these circumstances, the issues argued by participants in health care for the middle classes of prosperous countries seem irrelevant. The efforts of health care movements under these conditions are oriented to provision of any care that can alleviate the suffering of the weak and the poor.

A related perspective points out that even health care for the prosperous reflects a social structure and social process that is necessarily damaging to the well-being of women, if the system is one of fee for service in a capitalist, profit-oriented system. That is to say, as long as doctors profit by prescribing medicines and performing operations, they will continue to be motivated to do these things, even to the detriment of their patients. In fact, they will find rationales to continue to prescribe medicines, to perform operations, to guard against competition in the delivery of health care services, and to prevent dissemination of knowledge, since it is their monopoly of knowledge that prevents competition.

The contradictions of providing good health care for women are not limited to the problems of capitalism. They are pervasive in patriarchal social systems of all sorts. Good health, furthermore, depends on the ability of a person to live a "good life," with enough good food to eat, good shelter, clean water for drinking and bathing, healthful work conditions, and positive physical and emotional support as well as the provision of actual health care services. In sum, a society must have the capacity to provide the means to a healthful life and the commitment to implement any policies it may have regarding good health care, in order to benefit women and, indeed, all its members.

Summary

Because of the political importance of the question of who is to control our bodies, the issues surrounding women's health and our health care systems have been central to the modern women's movement. Globally, feminists have sought change in this realm both to improve our material conditions and to empower women through self-knowledge, establishment of our rights to choose, and mutual support. Within this broad framework, there have been a variety of approaches to understanding women's health conditions and to bringing about change.

Feminist theory argues that patriarchal society regards women as "abnormal" (both biologically and mentally); the treatment of women in patriarchal health care systems reflects this assumption. The domination of health care systems by privileged heterosexist males has reflected not only gender bias, but race, class, and heterosexist bias as well. Furthermore, the professionalization of health care has led to discrimination against traditional care of women by other women, and to

the "medicalization" of normal life processes experienced by women. Medical intervention in such processes has often proven problematic, in part because "treatment" reduces women's control over our own bodies by increasing our sense of ignorance and dependence on "experts."

While women and men are subject to similar health hazards in most respects, there are some areas in which women are at greater risk than men; this chapter examines those areas in which women and men differ. It has been argued that women's greater life expectancy in modern industrial societies is due in part to biological differences, but historical and cross-cultural variation point to the importance of social factors as principal causes of gender differences in mortality and morbidity.

Probably the most pervasive and fundamental condition affecting women's health is poverty; most other risks associated with women's vulnerability to illness, disease, and early death can be related directly or indirectly to poor nutrition and sanitation, poor education and health care, hazardous working conditions and violence, all resulting from poverty. Occupational health risks are highest among poor women of color, for example, because we have been forced into hazardous job conditions with employers who are unlikely to hold to occupational safety standards.

Most attention to women's health risks is brought to bear on matters related to our reproductive systems. Breast cancer, for example, is a leading cause of death among women in modern industrial societies. Methods of early detection have improved, increasing rates of survival, and methods of treatment became less radical, hence less traumatic. Sexually transmitted diseases are pervasive and pernicious, particularly among poor women. The rapid spread of HIV and AIDS has been tragic for women and children, because no cure is yet available. The tragedy is compounded by the fact that these, like other sexually transmitted diseases, are avoidable. Childbirth poses great health risks to women in less developed countries, which might be substantially reduced by improved health care delivery, family planning, and alleviation of conditions of poverty.

Lack of access to birth control and legal abortion accounts for a great deal of suffering, but research on improved birth control has reflected gender, class, and racial biases that have been severely criticized by feminists, as has the persistent denial of safe abortions, particularly to poor women. Finally, menopause has been a subject of medical controversy in recent years. As more women reach menopausal age, the medical profession has been challenged to alter its previous neglect of this subject. While hormone replacement therapy has been suspected of increasing risks of cancer, there is increasing evidence that these risks are negligible in most women in comparison to its benefits in reducing risks of osteoporosis and heart disease. Many women run the risk of having apparently unnecessary hysterectomies, particularly at the end of our childbearing years; this also has been the subject of feminist criticism.

Not directly related to our reproductive system risks is the general hazard of violence toward women, a matter of increasing concern. Domestic violence, sexual abuse, and rape pose serious hazards to hundreds of thousands of women, and treatment has tended to be oriented to the victim, but to neglect the cause, hence perpetuating the victimization.

Some women are at special risk for ill health; this chapter examines the problems of women with disabilities, elderly women, and refugee women.

The field of mental health makes particularly clear the interconnections between sexist social conditions, women's health hazards, and gender-biased health care. Social labeling of deviance creates unfavorable conditions for women, who may be regarded as mentally unwell if we rebel against the gender roles we have been assigned, or have difficulty coping with these roles. Some critics of patriarchal society have argued that ideas about mental health have been used to control and punish women. Two approaches to the critique of mental health care are delineated here: One argues that women's experience in sexist society produces differences in mental well-being between women and men; the other locates the source of difference in how behavior is labeled and diagnosed by gender-biased mental health care professionals.

One consistent finding (whether because of social conditions or biased diagnosis) is that women are twice as likely as men to suffer from clinical depression. Ethnic or racial discrimination and ageism are factors contributing to even higher rates for certain groups of women. Reasons for this are explored in this chapter. Eating disorders are found disproportionately among women (particularly of privileged classes in industrialized societies); anorexia and bulimia are discussed here.

Mental health care issues relate to biased psychotherapy. The American Psychological Association's Task Force on Psychotherapy with Lesbians and Gay Men reviewed problems related to homophobic bias in the areas of assessment and intervention, and recommends a variety of appropriate ways to help lesbian and gay clients. Feminist critiques of psychotherapy demand recognition (1) of women's value in our own terms, not by reference to men, and (2) of the social context of inequality that conditions all our lives. Gender differences in the use of psychotropic drugs (prescribed more frequently and longer for women than for men) suggest a variety of socially related causes and several kinds of remedies.

Modern health care institutions reflect the society that created them: They are hierarchical, dominated by males of privileged groups whose ill-paid subordinates tend to be women drawn from less privileged groups. The few women physicians in the nineteenth century struggled to earn acceptance and recognition. During the twentieth century, the percentage of women physicians increased, but we tend to be concentrated in certain fields and rarely do we achieve positions of power in the profession. Both professional discrimination and general social conditions continue to place obstacles in the way of professional advancement for women physicians; this is more so for women of color.

Physicians, even women physicians, have long found themselves in conflict with women healers and midwives who were the traditional health care specialists, and still are in many Third World countries. Today, more cooperative relationships are being encouraged.

The nursing profession, almost entirely female, has been relegated to a subordinate status by the medical establishment. Historical and social reasons for this have been explored, and remedies sought by nurses and other feminist critics.

Health insurance is an integral part of our contemporary health care system. While discrimination against women in insurance is no longer legal, women tend to be underinsured because we tend to be in low-paying, part-time, or temporary jobs that offer little or no health care benefits.

Most health care, of children, the elderly, the disabled, the chronically ill, even the temporarily slightly ill, falls to ordinary women as an extension of our roles as wives, mothers, and daughters. Because it is assumed that this is our duty, the personal costs to us tend to be ignored. Finding time and energy to take care of ourselves can be a serious problem.

Subsumed under the generic label "the women's health movement" are, in fact, many movements, with different concerns and approaches. Generally, critical approaches have been characterized as reformist, radical, and socialist/Marxist. All agree that poverty and sexism are the principal concerns that must be addressed in any solution to problems of health care provision for all members of society.

Discussion Questions

1. What would be the consequences for women's health if women had greater control of reproduction? What factors affect our control; how might our control be increased?

2. Select a group of women at special risk for health problems as a consequence of disability, age, political status, or other factors. Discuss problems, their causes, how they are addressed in the present health care system, and how health care delivery might be improved.

3. Describe health care in a society very different from your own, say, in a Third World country, a traditional indigenous society, a socialist or communist country, or during a time period in the distant past. Who are the health care practitioners? How does treatment differ from that with which you are familiar?

4. Discuss gender segregation in the health care professions. What specialties are female physicians likely to hold; in what specialties are female physicians likely to be rare? Why? What are the patterns of gender segregation in other health care professions; what accounts for this segregation and what are the consequences?

5. Select one health problem (other than one directly involving the reproductive system) whose incidence or expression differs in women and men. What accounts for the difference?

6. It has been suggested that interactions between physicians and patients vary with the gender of each. How do these interactions

vary, and what might be the consequences for treatment?

Recommended Readings

Leavitt, Judith Walzer. *Women and Health in America: Historical Readings.* Madison: University of Wisconsin Press, 1984. A historical overview that brings together some of the more important articles written since the early 1970s demonstrating the impact of feminist scholarship in reshaping the questions being asked about women and health in the American past.

Tronto, Joan C. *Moral Boundaries: A Political Argument for an Ethic of Care.* New York and London: Routledge, 1993. A carefully reasoned response to the issues of women and caring based on the idea that care is a central aspect of human life and that its traditional associations with "women's morality" must be reexamined and reconceived.

Gilman, Charlotte Perkins. *The Yellow Wall-Paper.* The Feminist Press at the City University of New York, 1892/1973. This classic narrative, written in 1892, tells the story of a woman who, discontent with wife- and motherhood, is placed in a country home as a rest cure for a "nervous condition." Yearning for intellectual stimulation and work, she is forbidden to write and prescribed complete passivity. Confined to her bedroom, she creates a reality of her own beyond the patterns of the fading yellow wallpaper. As the afterword, written by Elaine R. Hedges, describes, Gilman was one of the major intellectuals of the first women's movement.

Ehrenreich, Barbara, and English, Deirdre. *Witches, Midwives and Nurses: A History of Women Healers.* The Feminist Press at the City University of New York, 1973. This book explores two important phases in the male takeover of health care: the suppression of witches in medieval Europe and the rise of the male medical profession in the United States in the nineteenth century.

References

American Bar Association Journal 61(1975):464.

American Medical Women's Association. "AMWA Position Statement on Osteoporosis." *Journal of the American Medical Women's Association* 45(3) (1990):75–79.

Barbee, Evelyn L. "Racism in U.S. Nursing." *Medical Anthropology Quarterly* 7(4) (1993):346–62.

Barker-Benfield, G. J. "Sexual Surgery in Late Nineteenth-Century America." *In Seizing Our Bodies: The Politics of Women's Health,* edited by Claudia Dreifus, New York: Vintage Books, 1977.

Benedict, Ruth. "Anthropology and the Abnormal." *Journal of General Psychology* 10(1934a):59–80.

———. *Patterns of Culture.* Boston: Houghton Mifflin, 1934b.

Bennett, Nancy M., and Nickerson, Katherine G. "Women in Academic Medicine: Perceived Obstacles to Advancement." *Journal of the American Medical Women's Association* 47, 4(1992):115–118.

Bernstein, Anne E. "Gender Equity." *Journal of the American Medical Women's Association* 44, 3(1989):84–85.

Boston Women's Health Collective. *Our Bodies, Ourselves.* New York: Simon & Schuster, 1971.

Boylan, Esther. *Women and Disability.* Women and World Development Series. Atlantic Highlands, N.J.: Zed Books, 1991.

Briar, Katharine, and Ryan, Rosemary. "The Anti-Institution Movement and Women Caregivers." *Affilia: Journal of Women and Social Work* 1:1 (1986).

Brody, Jane. "Rate of Hysterectomy Drops, but Not Enough." *New York Times,* C14, June 30, 1993.

Chavkin, Wendy. "Walking a Tightrope: Pregnancy, Parenting, and Work." In *Double Ex-*

posure: Women's Health Hazards on the Job and at Home, edited by Wendy Chavkin. New York: Monthly Review Press, 1984, 196–213.

Chesler, Phyllis. *Women and Madness*. Garden City, NY: Doubleday, 1972.

Clark, Lauren. "Gender and Generation in Poor Women's Household Health Production Experiences." *Medical Anthropology Quarterly* 7(4) (1993):385–401.

Cleland, V. "Sex Discrimination: Nursing's Most Pervasive Problem." *American Journal of Nursing* 71(1971):1542–47.

Coeytaux, Francine, Leonard, Ann, and Bloomer, Carolyn. "Abortion." In *The Health of Women: A Global Perspective*, edited by Marge Koblinsky, Judith Timyan, and Jill Gay. Boulder: Westview Press, 1993, 133–46.

Corea, Gena. *The Hidden Malpractice: How American Medicine Mistreats Women*. New York: Harper and Row, 1985.

Courter, Gay. *The Midwife*. New York: Houghton Mifflin, 1981.

Denmark, Florence L., and Paludi, Michele A. *Psychology of Women: A Handbook of Issues and Theories*. Westport: Greenwood Press, 1993.

Distelheim, Rochelle. "Ambushed by Alzheimer's." *Woman's Day* (November 24, 1987).

Dowie, Mark, and Johnston, Tracy. "A Case of Corporate Malpractice and the Dalkan Shield." In *Seizing Our Bodies: The Politics of Women's Health*, edited by Claudia Dreifus. New York: Vintage Books, 1977.

Dreifus, Claudia. "Abortion: This Piece is for Remembrance." In *Seizing Our Bodies: The Politics of Women's Health*, edited by Claudia Dreifus. New York: Vintage Books, 1977a.

———. *Seizing Our Bodies: The Politics of Women's Health*. New York: Vintage Books, 1977b.

Dressler, William W. "Health in the African American Community: Accounting for Health Inequalities." *Medical Anthropology Quarterly* 7:4 (1993):325–45.

Drinkwater, Barbara. "Physical Exercise and Bone Health." *Journal of American Medical Women's Association* 45 (1990):91–97.

Ehrenreich, Barbara, and English, Deirdre. "Com-

plaints and Disorders: The Sexual Politics of Sickness." In *Seizing Our Bodies: The Politics of Women's Health*, edited by Claudia Dreifus. New York: Vintage Books, 1977.

Eversley, Ravi, Beirnes, D., Newstetter, A., Wingood, G., Hembry, K., Gotch, L., and Avins, A. "Ethnic Predictors of Sexual HIV Risk Among Young Adult Women Attending Family Planning Clinics." *Multicultural Inquiry and Research on AIDS* 4:3 (1990): 4–5.

Fee, Elizabeth. "Women and Health Care: A Comparison of Theories." In *Women and Health: The Politics of Sex in Medicine*, edited by Elizabeth Fee. Farmingdale, NY: Baywood Publishing, 1983.

Finkelhor, David. *Child Sexual Abuse: New Theory and Research*. New York: Free Press, 1984.

Fisher, Sue. *In the Patient's Best Interest: Women and the Politics of Medical Decisions*. New Brunswick: Rutgers University Press, 1986.

Foa, Edna B., Rothbaum, Barbara Olasov, Riggs, David S., and Murdock, Tamera B. "Treatment of Posttraumatic Stress Disorder in Rape Victims: A Comparison Between Cognitive-Behavorial Procedures and Counseling." *Journal of Consulting and Clinical Psychology* 59:5 (1991):715–23.

Funk, Nanette, and Mueller, Magda. *Gender Politics and Post-Communism: Reflections From Eastern Europe and the Former Soviet Union*. New York and London: Routledge, 1993.

Geer, Deborah A. "Women in Surgery." *Journal of the American Medical Women's Association* 48:2 (1993):47–50.

Gilsanz, V., Roe, T., Mora, S., Costin, G., and Goodman, W. "Changes in Vertebral Bone Density in Black Girls and White Girls During Childhood and Puberty." *New England Journal of Medicine* 325:23 (1991):1597–1600.

Given, Barbara, and Given, Charles. "Patient and Family Caregiver Reaction to New and Recurrent Breast Cancer." *Journal of the American Medical Women's Association* 47:5 (1990):201–6.

Goodman, Madeline. "A Critique of Menopausal Research." *Changing Perspectives on Menopause*, edited by Ann M. Voda, Myra Dinnerstein, and Sheryl R. O'Donnell. Austin: University of Texas Press, 1982.

Gordan, G. S. "Prevention of Bone Loss and Fractures in Women." *Maturitas* 6 (1984):225–42.

Greene, Beverly. "Psychotherapy with African-American Women: Integrating Feminist and Psychodynamic Models." *Journal of Training & Practice in Professional Psychology* 7:1 (1993):49–66.

Grissum, M., and Spengler, C. *Women, Power, and Health Care.* Boston: Little, Brown, 1976.

Gross, Edith. "Gender Differences in Physician Stress." *Journal of the American Medical Women's Association* 47:4 (1992):107–14.

Heise, Lori. "Violence Against Women: The Missing Health Agenda." *The Health of Women: A Global Perspective,* edited by Marge Koblinsky, Judith Timyan, and Jill Gay. Boulder: Westview Press, 1993, 171–95.

Heisel, Marsel A. "Older Women in Developing Countries." In *Women in the Later Years: Health, Social and Cultural Perspectives,* edited by Lois Grau and Ida Susser. New York: Harrington Park Press, 1989, 253–72.

Henifin, Mary Sue. "The Particular Problems of Video Display Terminals." In *Double Exposure: Women's Health Hazards on the Job and at Home,* edited by Wendy Chavkin. New York: Monthly Review Press, 1984, 69–80.

Hinkle, Yvonne, Johnson, Ernest, Gilbert, Douglas, Jackson, Linda, and Lollis, Charles. "African-American Women Who Always Use Condoms: Attitudes, Knowledge about AIDS, and Sexual Behavior. *Journal of American Medical Women's Association* 47:6 (1992):230–37.

Jackson, Eileen M. "Whiting-Out Difference: Why U.S. Nursing Research Fails Black Families." *Medical Anthropology Quarterly* 7:4 (1993):363–84.

Jacobson, Jodi. "Women's Health: The Price of Poverty." In *The Health of Women: A Global Perspective,* edited by Marge Koblinsky, Judith Timyan, and Jill Gay. Boulder: Westview Press, 1993, 3–31.

Kiefer, Renata. "Issues in Pediatric AIDS and HIV Infection." *Multicultural Inquiry and Research on AIDS* 4:3 (1990):1–8.

Koblinsky, M. A., Campbell, Oona, and Harlow, Siobán. "Mother and More: A Broader Perspective on Women's Health." In *The Health of Women: A Global Perspective,* edited by Marge Koblinsky, Judith Timyan, and Jill Gay. Boulder: Westview Press, 1993, 33–62.

Langer, Amy. "The Politics of Breast Cancer." *Journal of the American Medical Women's Association* 47:5 (1992):207–9.

Layhe, Beth, and Dimitrov, Nikolay. "Systemic Therapy of Breast Cancer in Early and Advanced Disease." *Journal of the American Medical Women's Association* 47:5 (1992):188–93.

Lenz, Elinor, and Meyerhoff, Barbara. "Feminizing Health Care." In *The Feminization of America,* edited by Elinor Lenz. New York: St. Martin's Press, 1985.

Lopate, Carol. *Women and Medicine.* Baltimore: Johns Hopkins, 1968.

Lopez, Iris. "Sterilization Among Puerto Rican Women in New York City: Public Policy and Social Constraints." In *Cities of the United States,* edited by Leith Mullings. New York: Columbia University Press, 1987.

Lorber, Judith. *Women Physicians: Career, Status and Power.* New York and London: Tavistock Publications, 1984.

Lucas, Linda F., Thomas, Mary H., and Rigor, Benjamin M., Sr. "Women and Specialty Choice: Why Not Anesthesiology?" *Journal of the American Medical Women's Association* 47:2 (1992):54–57.

Luker, Kristin. *Abortion and the Politics of Motherhood.* Berkeley: University of California Press, 1984.

Macklin, Eleanor, ed. *Aids and Families.* New York: Harworth Press, 1989.

MacLeod, Sheila. *The Art of Starvation: A Story of Anorexia and Survival.* New York: Schocken Books, 1982.

Maltseva, Natasha. "The Other Side of the Coin." In *Women and Russia: Feminist Writings from the Soviet Union,* edited by Tatyana Mamonova. Boston: Beacon Press, 1984.

Marieskind, Helen. "The Women's Health Movement: Past Roots." In *Seizing Our Bodies: The Politics of Women's Health*, edited by Claudia Dreifus. New York: Vintage Books, 1977.

Martin, Emily. *The Woman in the Body*. Boston: Beacon Press, 1987.

Martin, Judith. "Guidelines for the Woman Who Is Going to See Her Health Care Practitioner." Unpublished ms. Stanford University Medical Center, 1982.

McDermott, Jeanne, Bangser, Maggie, Ngugi, Elizabeth, and Sandvold, Irene. "Infection: Social and Medical Realities." In *The Health of Women: A Global Perspective*, edited by Marge Koblinsky, Judith Timyan, and Jill Gay. Boulder: Westview Press, 1993.

McGrath, Ellen, Keita, Gwendolyn, Strickland, Bonnie R., and Russo, Nancy F., editors. *Women and Depression: Risk Factors and Treatment Issues*. Final Report of the American Psychological Association's Task Force on Women and Depression. Washington D.C.: American Psychological Association, 1990.

Melash, Barbara. *"The Physician's Hand": Work, Culture and Conflict in American Nursing*. Philadelphia: Temple University Press, 1982.

Mijiyawa, M., Djagnikpo, A. K., Agbanouvi, A. E., Koumouvi, K., and Agbetra, A. "Rheumatic Diseases in Hospital Outpatients in Lome (Togo)" (title translated from French). *Revue du Rhumatisme et des Malades Osteoartic* 58:5 (1991):349–54.

More, Ellen. "The American Medical Women's Association and the Role of the Woman Physician." *Journal of the American Medical Women's Association* 45:5 (1990):165–80.

Morgen, Sandra. "The Dynamics of Co-optation in a Feminist Health Clinic." *Social Science Medicine* 23:2 (1986):201–10.

Muller, Charlotte. *Health Care and Gender*. New York: Russell Sage Foundation, 1990.

Mullings, Leith. "Minority Women, Work, and Health." In *Double Exposure: Women's Health Hazards on the Job and at Home*, edited by Wendy Chavkin. New York: Monthly Review Press, 1984, 121–38.

Murphy, Jane. "Abnormal Behavior in Traditional Societies: Labels, Explanations, and Social Reactions." In *Handbook of Cross-Cultural Human Development*, edited by Ruth Monroe, Robert Monroe, and Beatrice Whiting. New York: Garland Press, 1981.

Native American Women's Health Education Resource Center. "Native American Women Uncover Norplant Abuses." *MS* 4:2 (1993):69.

Padgett, Deborah. "Aging Minority Women: Issues in Research and Health Policy." In *Women in the Later Years: Health, Social and Cultural Perspectives*, edited by Lois Grau and Ida Susser. New York: Harrington Park Press, 1989, 213–69.

Petchesky, Rosalind P. *Abortion and Woman's Choice: The State, Sexuality, and Reproductive Freedom*. rev. ed. Boston: Northeastern University Press, 1990.

Petit, Marilynn. "Recognizing Post-Traumatic Stress." *RN* 54:3 (1991):56–58.

Pugliesi, Karen. "Women and Mental Health: Two Traditions of Feminist Research." *Women and Health* 19:2–3 (1992):43–68.

Ramos, Sylvia M., and Feiner, Cheryl J. "Women Surgeons: A National Survey." *Journal of the American Medical Women's Association* 44:1 (1989):21–25.

Reilly, Philip. "Involuntary Sterilization in the United States." *Quarterly Review of Biology* 62 (1987).

Roberto, Karen. "Stress and Adaptation Patterns of Older Osteoporotic Women." In *Women in the Later Years*, edited by Lois Grau and Ida Susser. New York: Harrington Park Press, 1989, 105–19.

Roberts, Susan Jo. "Oppressed Group Behavior: Implications for Nursing." *Advances in Nursing Science* (July 1983):21–30.

Rodin, Judith, and Ickovics, Jeannette. "Women's Health: Review and Research Agenda as We Approach the 21st Century." *American Psychologist* 45:9 (1990):1018–34.

Rodriguez-Trias, Helen. "Sterilization Abuse." *Women and Health* 10 (1978).

Rosenberg, Harriet G. "The Home Is the Workplace: Hazards, Stress, and Pollutants in the Household." In *Double Exposure: Women's*

Health Hazards on the Job and at Home, edited by Wendy Chavkin. New York: Monthly Review Press, 1984, 219–45.

Russo, Nancy F., and Green, Beth L. "Women and Mental Health." In *Psychology of Women: A Handbook of Issues and Theories*, edited by Florence Denmark and Michele Paludi. Westport, CT: Greenwood Press, 1993, 379–436.

Ruzek, Sheryl Burt. *The Women's Health Movement: Feminist Alternatives to Medical Control*. New York: Praeger, 1978.

Sacks, Karen. *Caring by the Hour: Women, Work, and Organizing at Duke Medical Center*. Urbana: University of Illinois Press, 1988.

Sánchez-Ayéndez, Melba. "Puerto Rican Elderly Women: The Cultural Dimension of Social Support Networks." In *Women in the Later Years*, edited by Lois Grau and Ida Susser. New York: Harrington Park Press, 1989, 239–52.

Scott, Judith A. "Keeping Women in Their Place: Exclusionary Policies and Reproduction." In *Double Exposure: Women's Health Hazards on the Job and at Home*, edited by Wendy Chavkin. New York: Monthly Review Press, 1984, 180–95.

Seaman, Barbara. "The Dangers of Oral Contraception." In *Seizing Our Bodies: The Politics of Women's Health*, edited by Claudia Dreifus. New York: Vintage Books, 1977.

Smyke, Patricia. *Women and Health*. London: Zed Books, 1991.

Sontag, Deborah. "Asking for Asylum in U.S., Women Tread New Territory." *New York Times*, Sept. 27, 1993, late edition. "A National Desk" Section.

Stark, Evan, and Flitcraft, Anne. "Spouse Abuse." In *Violence in America: A Public Health Approach*, edited by Mark Rosenberg and Mary Ann Fenley. New York: Oxford University Press, 1991.

Stark, Evan, Flitcraft, Anne, and Fraizer, William. "Medicine and Patriarchal Violence: The Social Construction of a 'Private' Event." In *Women and Health: The Politics of Sex in Medicine*, edited by Elizabeth Fee. Farmingdale, NY: Baywood Publishing, 1983.

Sullivan, Deborah, and Weitz, Rose. *Labor Pains: Modern Midwives and Home Birth*. New Haven: Yale University Press, 1988.

Swanson, G. Marie. "Breast Cancer in the 1990's." *Journal of the American Medical Women's Association* 47:5 (1992):140–48.

Task Force on Bias in Psychotherapy With Lesbians and Gay Men. *Bias in Psychotherapy With Lesbians and Gay Men*. Washington, D.C.: American Psychological Association, 1991.

Taylor, Donald, and Ricketts, Thomas. "Helping Nurse-Midwives Provide Obstetrical Care in Rural North Carolina." *American Journal of Public Health* 83:6 (1993):904–5.

Titus-Dillon, P. Y., and Johnson, D. G. "Female Graduates of a Predominately Black College of Medicine: Their Characteristics and Challenges." *Journal of the American Medical Women's Association* 44:6 (1989):175–82.

Travis, Cheryl Brown. *Women and Health Psychology: Biomedical Issues*. Hillsdale, NJ: Erlbaum, 1988a.

———. *Women and Health Psychology: Mental Health Issues*. Hillsdale, NJ: Erlbaum, 1988b.

———. "Women and Health." In *Psychology of Women: A Handbook of Issues and Theories*, edited by Florence Denmark and Michele Paludi. Westport, CT: Greenwood Press, 1993.

Ulstad, Valerie K. "How Women Are Changing Medicine." *Journal of the American Medical Women's Association* 48:3 (1993):75–78.

Veith, Izla. *Hysteria: The History of a Disease*. Chicago: University of Chicago Press, 1965.

Voda, Ann. "The Menopausal Hot Flash." In *Changing Perspectives on Menopause*, edited by Ann Voda et al. Austin: University of Texas Press, 1982.

Voda, Ann M., Dinnerstein, Myra, and O'Donnell, Sheryl R., editors. *Changing Perspectives on Menopause*. Austin: University of Texas Press, 1982.

Wallace, Anthony. "Mental Illness, Biology, and Culture." In *Psychological Anthropology*, 2nd ed., edited by F.L.K. Hsu. Cambridge: Schenkman, 1972, 363–402.

Weaver, Jerry, and Garrett, Sharon. "Sexism and Racism in the American Health Care Industry: A Comparable Analysis." In *Women and Health: The Politics of Sex in Medicine*, edited by Elizabeth Fee. Farmingdale, NY: Baywood Publishing, 1983.

Wilson, Julie Boatright. "Women and Poverty: A Demographic Overview." In *Women, Health, and Poverty*, edited by Cesar Perales and Lauren Young. London: Haworth Press, 1988, 21–40.

Zambrana, Ruth. "A Research Agenda on Issues Affecting Poor and Minority Women: A Model for Understanding Their Health Needs." In *Women, Health, and Poverty*, edited by Cesar Perales and Lauren Young. New York: Haworth Press, 1988, 137–60.

Women and Work

Human societies generally organize the work needed for survival by dividing the tasks among their members. Individual work assignments are decided in a variety of ways: Strength and skill are obvious and basic determinants. In addition, considerations of status and value also influence work patterns. Some tasks are thought to merit higher rewards, both concrete and intangible, than others. All known societies have used gender as a criterion for work assignment. That the assignment is largely arbitrary becomes clear when we discover how greatly the content of the role varies from culture to culture and time to time. In nonagricultural societies, for example, hunting of big game might be done by men and gathering of vegetable foods largely by women. In a pastoral society, herding might be assigned to men and farming to women. Yet we can find certain societies in which herding is women's work, and societies in which farming is men's work. In our society, secretarial work and primary school teaching are assigned mainly to women. But less than a century and a half ago, these jobs were assigned almost exclusively to men.

Not only does gender affect who is assigned what tasks, but other variables such as class and race/ethnicity further intervene so that women of color or poor women are usually found in the most undervalued work. In countries like South Africa, Brazil, and the United States, the racial and class system has created a social structure in which women of color work as domestics for white families, freeing masses of white women to find work outside of the home.

Many societies, including our own, judge the value of work in terms of economic rewards to those who buy and sell labor. To ask the question "Do you work?" means, for many people, "Do you earn money?" That is why the idea that a housewife does not "work" is common in our society. Although the labor involved in housekeeping can be bought and sold, when this labor is performed for "free," it is not considered "work." To question this idea, as many feminists have done during the past century, is to challenge basic assumptions most people hold about the nature and definition of "work" itself.

The tendency to undervalue unpaid labor, however, does not correctly express the significance of that labor for the economy, much less for the society. Unpaid labor often contributes enormously to the provision of goods and services that are necessary to keep people and society alive, well, and functioning. Masking the economic value of women's unpaid labor serves the interests of those who have property and power. If women's unpaid household tasks were included in national income accounts, world economic output would increase by 20 to 30 percent (UNDP, 1993). Failing to acknowledge the value of such work in economic terms both distorts an accurate assessment of a country's gross national product and keeps in place a system that undervalues producers of this labor, women.

Many social theories about relationships between people hold that they are fundamentally based on economic power. Social inequalities between women and men, in particular, are often seen to be based largely on economic inequalities. The economic inequality between men and women has contributed to a widely held stereotype of women as dependent. A vicious cycle develops in which a social trait is then cited as the reason for the economic inequality. This chapter examines some aspects of these ideals in order to understand women's roles in society.

We will examine the relationships between production and reproduction, particularly the implications for women's status, of the ways that society integrates the tasks of raising and maintaining a family with other kinds of work. We will be concerned with the impact of economic change on women's roles within and outside the family. Shifting from general theoretical concerns to the more concrete realities of women's work, we will consider in detail the various types of work women have done and the obstacles we have faced as women workers. Finally, we will look at the roles played by support groups of various sorts, by government, and by the women's movement in influencing women's opportunities to work.

The Labor of Women

Division of Labor by Gender

We have seen that every known society has had some sort of division of labor by gender.

Although the work done by women and by men has varied from society to society, the work done by women has almost always been valued less than the work done by men. An activity that is highly regarded in one society, when done by men, may be considered unimportant in another society, when done by women.

The division of labor by gender has often been related, not surprisingly, to the differences in the roles in reproduction assigned women and men. Since women necessarily bear, and until recent times have necessarily nursed, infants, we have always been assigned the additional social role of caring for the young, even though this assignment is not necessitated by either function. Yet the physical burdens we bear while pregnant and nursing are often assumed to place some limitation on our ability to participate fully in the productive economy. An examination of women's roles in a variety of preindustrial as well as developing societies, however, shows that we do engage in fairly strenuous economic activities even while pregnant and nursing.

The labor involved in reproduction itself is essential for any society. With the exception of those employed to care for the young, most of us receive no economic compensation for mothering, even though societies could not exist without the work involved. Using the Department of Labor's figures for the hourly wages paid for certain types of work, Table 13.1 is an estimate of what women in the United States would earn if we were paid for our unpaid labor.

Maintenance of the Domestic Unit

To the extent that women are involved in the care of young children—and this extent varies historically and cross-culturally—the other work we do must be possible to do at the same time. What is defined as "housework," such

"Women's Work"—Work Typically Defined as Women's

Country	"Women's Work"
Uganda	Charcoal selling
Ghana	Market trading
Turkey	Tobacco processing
Iran	Weaving
India	Lace working, cashew cleaning, cigarette production
Nepal	Road building
China	Cotton and rice harvesting
Hungary	Electronics assembly
Portugal	Domestic service
United Kingdom	Secretarial, office cleaning
Guatemala	Crafts
Nicaragua	Coffee picking
United States	Bank tellers, garment industry

Source: *Women in the World Atlas*, 1986

as cooking and cleaning, generally falls into this category. Like reproduction, this work serves an important function: It "services" the male worker so he can return, fed and refreshed, to the workplace the next day. But the housewife is not compensated for this work either.

In most parts of the world for most of human history, virtually all productive labor was domestic, performed without compensation for the benefit of family members. Under these conditions, the labor done by women and men, although often differentiated, was viewed as making equivalent contributions. *Social labor*, labor done for the good of the larger social unit beyond the family, did have social value, earning an esteem for the laborer that went beyond family rewards.

As the social labor sector grew with increasing urbanization and capitalism, it became an increasingly large component of the economy as a whole. With *this* change, women began

to lose ground. That part of our efforts confined to domestic work not only had no social value but also diminished our opportunities to

Table 13.1 What Women Would Earn if We Were Paid for Our Unpaid Labor in the United States

Role	Number of Hours per Week	Hourly Rate	Dollar Amount
Food preparer	18.5	$6	$111
Cleaner	6.0	10	60
Washer	2.0	5	10
Ironer	3.0	5	15
Chauffeur	3.0	12	36
Social secretary	.5	20	10
Psychologist	4.0	100	400
Child care worker	51.0	8	408
Health care worker	.5	30	15
Repairer	1.5	15	22.5
Total Weekly Earnings			$1087.50

Source: Calculations are based on data found in the U. S. Department of Labor, Bureau of Labor Statistics. *Employment and Earnings,* January 1993.

participate in valued social labor outside the home. While the work women have performed has been essential to the economy in providing and servicing workers, it has generally not been recognized as having either economic or social value (Dalla Costa, 1972). Feminists in recent years have called attention to how misleading, and damaging to women, are many traditional conceptions of the "private" and "domestic" spheres of life.

The fact that many sorts of work can be combined with child care is often overlooked. Work that is done in or near the home, such as weaving and making pottery, is a good example. Businesses such as beauty parlors or family grocery stores can be run in or near the home. Alternatively, societies may take responsibility for making child care facilities available so that both parents can work at other jobs.

Women's Work in the Marketplace

Even though women's participation in the market economy has been limited by our assigned responsibilities in the domestic sphere, many of us have managed to sell some of our labor, and larger numbers are continuing to do so. However, because of the devaluation of women, resulting at least in part from the devaluation of our domestic labor, the labor we have sold in the marketplace has also been devalued. That is, when a job was done by a woman, it was valued less than the same work done by a man. In addition, women have often been excluded from a wide variety of jobs open to men.

A more insidious pattern of integrating women into the labor market is illustrated by an early-twentieth-century example. This pattern encouraged women's entry into bookkeeping, which had been formerly occupied by men. Compensation was lowered and the traditional authority associated with the position, office management, was eliminated. A new office position, accountant, was established and became a male-identified occupation (Machung, 1988). The conclusion we are obliged to draw is that when work is divided along gender lines, it is not the work itself that determines its value, but the gender of the person doing it.

The Contribution of Women to Economic Development

Consequently, as long as we are expected to be the primary caretakers of our children, we will be forced into a choice between child care, wage labor, or a compromise, part-time work. In Western societies, part-time work, as a solution to problems associated with the lack of day care, penalizes the female wage earner. Employers of part-time personnel typically pay part-time workers lower hourly wages and provide few, if any, benefits as compared to full-time workers in the same job. For those of us who must work for wages or who choose to do so, the problems of arranging for adequate child care may be severe, especially when fathers continue to maintain that these are the mothers' problems.

In contemporary Third World countries, models of economic growth and change have tended to follow patterns set by Western industrialism. Where women were once heavily involved in small-scale agriculture based on intensive labor and simple technology, there is now a tendency to consolidate land holdings (hence economic growth), to use industrial machinery, and to emphasize production for the market rather than for the home. It has consistently been men who have been taught to use the new machinery (such as tractors) and given the means to acquire it. As a result of being excluded from modernized agricultural production, we have lost our former voice or control over the deployment of resources, even within the home.

Men who have lost their "jobs" through the

shift from labor-intensive to capital-intensive production are viewed as "unemployed," while women in a similar economic position are altogether disenfranchised. We are not considered an economic casualty but are simply invisible. Whereas our work was one of the mainstays of the economy, what we do outside the home now is considered by our societies at best a negligible economic contribution and at worst a hindrance to economic development to be targeted for elimination. Feminist analyses allow us to become aware of many mistakes in standard interpretations of economic "development" (Acosta-Belén and Bose, 1990; Boserup, 1970; Enloe, 1988; Sen and Grown, 1987).

The Domestic Mode of Production: An Integrated System

Anthropologists use the term *domestic mode of production* to describe the organization of economic systems such as hunting-gathering, small-scale, frontier, and peasant economies. In such systems, the household is the basic unit of both production and consumption. The division of labor in the domestic mode of production is by age and gender, with relatively little specialization within these two categories. Women's contributions in economies organized by the domestic mode of production are variable in type and extent. But in all these systems, economic roles are integrated into other domestic roles, both for women and men.

Food Production

While women's roles in food production (subsistence) are quite variable, some general patterns can be found. In hunting-gathering societies, women are primarily responsible for the collection and processing of plant foods; in some cases, we do fishing. Men hunt large game. In horticultural societies that depend on cultivated plants, women tend to be mostly responsible for planting, weeding, and harvesting, while men are often assigned the more sporadic tasks of clearing forest for new gardens and the like. In pastoral societies that depend on herding large animals (sheep, goats, cattle, yak, horse, llamas, alpacas, reindeer), women are often assigned tasks associated with milking, preparation of butter and cheese, and care of the young herd animals, while men are in charge of defense and protection of the herd from raiders and predators. Increased technology curtails to some extent the participation of women in those traditional activities. For example, while women in a number of herding societies participate in caring for herd animals, we are rarely directly involved in ranching operations, which are oriented toward markets rather than household consumption. When agricultural production is intensified by the use of plow and oxen, men take on the tasks of cultivation. While the digging stick is often a woman's tool, the plow rarely is. Women are generally credited with the invention of most of the techniques of agriculture and storage (pottery and baskets). It is even more probable that we were the inventors of spinning (and later of the spinning wheel), weaving, and other techniques of cloth production. But as with so many of the genuinely creative people in world history, our names and records have been forgotten while the records of profitless military adventures, the activity of men, survive.

Maintenance

Simply producing food by gathering, cultivating, fishing, or herding is not enough to provide for the needs of a family. Researchers who attempt to find a relationship between subsistence activities (food production) and women's status often overlook this point. Food processing, for example, may be a critical task in subsistence. While Mexican peasant men are primarily responsible for growing their food staple, corn, Mexican peasant women spend considerable amounts of time and energy turning corn into food—husking and shelling it, grinding it, forming and cooking tortillas. Food preservation and storage may also be critical tasks: Fish and meat may be dried or smoked or preserved in oil. Such tasks often are assigned to women.

Women also tend to take on the tasks of making and maintaining clothing. The Eskimo men who hunt for sea mammals and caribou could not do so unless provided with warm parkas, leggings, and boots made by women. In societies that use plant or animal fibers for clothing, women generally do the spinning, weaving, and sewing. Women also construct tents and houses in many societies. In addition to food and shelter, women also have considerable responsibility for the care and health of our families. In many societies, women play important roles as healers of the sick, as midwives, and as "morticians" (laying out the dead).

Exchange and Marketing

While economies based on the domestic mode of production are geared toward production for use in the household, some commodities are often exchanged to obtain goods and services not produced in the household.

In some societies, most notably in West Africa and in the Caribbean, women play a significant role as traders, merchants, and brokers. Women's participation in the market has tended (though not invariably) to be limited to relatively short-distance trade in necessities such as food and utensils rather than long-distance "luxury" items such as precious metals, gems, and ivory. Where women do engage in mercantile activities, we tend to retain considerable control over our income, enhancing our own autonomy and status.

The Capitalist Mode of Production: An Alienated System

Urbanization and Class Distinctions

Cities depend on migrants for population growth and maintenance. They attract that part of the population that is often desperately poor. Younger daughters and sons of the rural population come to the city with the hope of finding employment and social mobility. The development of social stratification, the division of a society into layers of social classes that commanded vastly different shares of the economic resources of the community, was one of the by-products of the development of civilization.

Women migrating into a city rarely found a dazzling array of choices open to us. We usually entered into the class structure only as the appendages of fathers or husbands. If we were totally on our own, we probably found work most readily as servants, or we entered into the ranks of the "unskilled" laborers. We were ill-paid, transient, and obliged by the discrimination of most societies against working women to supplement our meager incomes with prostitution.

The idea of selling "labor" introduces a distinctive set of notions about work. It distinguishes members of a family (whose labor is not "sold") from those who interact outside the family (where labor *is* sold). Such distinctions are especially applicable in urban contexts, where people interact with others who are mostly nonkin.

Working for Wages: Its Organizational Prerequisites

In order to "free" labor from the household, which requires work to sustain itself, certain basic arrangements must be made. One kind of arrangement involves a division of labor in the social sphere whereby some workers pro-

Elizabeth Gurley Flynn was a labor organizer and leader by the time she was sixteen years old. The child of Irish immigrants, Flynn devoted her life to radical and social causes. Here she addresses strikers from Paterson, New Jersey, silk mills in 1913. (Brown Brothers)

vide, on a regular basis, goods and services once produced only in the home for family consumption.

Labor directed strictly to household use profits only the family. When the same labor is sold in specialized production, the owner of the resources, tools, and products takes part of the profit of labor and allows the worker to take only a small share back to the family in the form of wages. The profit taken by the owner is accumulated and reinvested in the production of more materials, tools, and products to increase future profits.

To the extent that women workers are paid lower wages for our work than men (as has invariably been the case), we can say that women have "subsidized" the development of industry and capitalist economics as a whole. This has especially been the case in the recent development of Third World nations. Women there not only provide cheap labor in industry but also continue to produce food and clothing in the rural countryside for our families, who also work for industry. The African or Latin American male laborer who works for low wages in a mine or a factory depends on his wife to grow food to feed the family. The wife's efforts, however, are rarely appreciated as contributing—as they do—to the Gross National Product of the nation: They are a free subsidy to the nation's development. It is doubtful that any country now considered "developed" could have achieved economic development through industrialization had it not been for a similar subsidy—an absorption by women of costs (Acosta-Belén and Bose, 1990; Beneria and Sen, 1982; Mbinlinyi, 1987).

Women's Work

Slaves and Serfs. In some economic systems, the lowest levels of the working class were slaves, including both women and men who were not paid at all for working.

In the American South, African American slaves were worked to obtain the maximum amount of labor possible, generally by means of coercion. Women were overworked to an even greater degree than men. In addition to the work we performed for our masters, we also cooked and cared for our own families and produced more slaves for our owners. Unlike other women in this era, slave women were defined first as workers (Jones, 1985; White, 1985).

Slavery, however, was often not the mainstay of an economic system. In Europe, the slave-based economic system of the Roman empire was overturned in the fifth century and replaced by small-scale economies made up of free and slave labor. There also developed a system of serfdom binding workers to the soil; it existed for centuries. Serfdom gradually gave way to economic systems based on "free" wage labor. "Free" labor has been the most effective source of work in West European economies since the fourteenth century. The broad base of most contemporary economies is the "working class." With the development of industrial capitalism, the vast majority of workers outside the home sell their labor for wages and cannot exist without doing so. They are "free" to accept what work they can find, but not free *not* to sell their labor for wages.

Prostitution. Prostitution is defined as the sale of sexual services. The role of prostitution in national economies varies from country to country. The United States views prostitution as a crime for both prostitute and client or "john." Some countries, such as Holland, use regulation and yet others, such as Germany, use licensing as a measure of government responsibility, policing brothels and guaranteeing the sanitary conditions of activities and workers. In the United States, historically prostitution has primarily been organized with relationships of economic dependency, very often with third parties as the employers or "bosses," as in the case of procurers, pimps, or madams. Either women or men (husbands, lovers, employers, brothel owners) play these intermediary roles and both gain by the dependent relationship involved (Butler, 1985; Hirata, 1979; Rosen, 1982).

Most women do not intend or aspire to become prostitutes; rather, in circumstances in which a woman feels desperate, prostitution may provide the only means of generating an income. Poor women are the most vulnerable group (Miller, 1988). It is not uncommon for poor women from Bombay to Bangkok to be trapped into international prostitution rings lured by false promises of good wages working as "entertainers." Considered deviant by "good women," prostitutes are vulnerable to crime and diseases such as syphilis and AIDS, are brutalized by pimps, madams, and clients, and do not control economic remuneration for services.

Working-Class Women: Skilled Labor. Until the development of the factory system and of workplaces designed to fit the industrial model, production, as we have seen, was generally a household enterprise.

Although all the family shared the work, members did not do the same things and were not equally recognized for their contributions. In small-scale craft enterprises, it was commonplace for the man to work at the craft, producing goods, while his wife ran the shop, selling goods and keeping the books. This division of labor was even more pronounced in Europe, where the more elite, urban professions and crafts organized themselves into guilds by the thirteenth century. Most of the better, more skilled, and lucrative occupations barred women from membership. The knowledge of the craft was a "mystery" theoretically opened only to licensed apprentices (male).

There were some guilds in which women did participate as independent and fully active working members. Out of several hundred crafts registered in thirteenth-century Paris, six were composed exclusively of women: silk spinners, wool spinners, silk weavers, silk-train makers, milliners of gold-braided caps, and makers of alms purses. In England, fourteenth-century guilds listed women as brewers, bakers, corders, and spinners and as working in wool, linen, and silk. Women never appear to have been eligible for office in these guilds. Indeed it is more likely that the guilds were organized by employers or by civil authorities for the purpose of placing women under surveillance to prevent pilfering the materials provided to take home and work on (Shahar, 1983).

Working-Class Women: Domestic Wage Labor. A vast proportion of wage-earning women have worked as domestic laborers: maids, cooks, and nursemaids. We have contributed to the maintenance of a distinctive standard of living for men and women of the middle and upper classes, enabling them to occupy large, sometimes sumptuous residences and to enjoy elaborate social life-styles.

Domestics had only a little more freedom than slaves. Our personal lives were closely supervised, and our working hours were ill-defined and long, with very little time off. The less skilled were treated with little respect; indeed, we were often "invisible" to our employers. We had little or no job security or bargaining power, nor opportunity to organize to protest our working conditions or low wages.

Today, in the industrially developed nations, at least, the role of female domestics has greatly diminished. Many of the tasks formerly performed by domestics are provided by the service industries such as hospitals, day care centers, and hotels and restaurants. Were it not for the availability of relatively cheap domestic labor, most of which is provided by immigrant women, many middle-

(Opposite top) An illustration depicting women working at the surface of a coal mine in Wigan, England. It appeared in *The Pictorial World*, Saturday, April 18, 1874, reminding Victorian readers that English women worked at hard, outdoor manual labor. (Birmingham Public Libraries)

(Opposite bottom) Workers in a fruit cannery in Australia in the early twentieth century. As countries industrialized, women often found jobs outside the home in areas that were extensions of the work traditionally done in the home. (Culver Pictures, Inc.)

(Above) In debates about the gender segregation of the workforce, a case has often been made that women do not have the physical strength to do "men's work." These women in modern Lesotho, a land-locked African state surrounded by the Republic of South Africa, make up a work crew building a cross-country road. As Sojourner Truth commented about her own life of hard physical labor, "and ain't I a woman too?" (United Nations/Mudden)

There are approximately 3,000 women coal miners in the United States—just over one percent of the workforce. They are often given the heaviest, dirtiest entry-level jobs and kept there long after men would have been promoted to machine operators. Despite this, many prefer going in the mines in order to be paid three times what they would make in a non-union shirt factory. ("Sisterhood." Three Women Coal Miners, Buchanan County, Va. Photo by Earl Dotter/American Labor)

class professional women would be obliged to stay at home to care for our families since few men are yet willing to do so or even to share equally the responsibility of parenting. As women climb the career ladder in politics today, their choices regarding child care expose them to new problems, as the first woman nominee for Attorney General of the United States discovered in 1993. Many women acknowledge not only our dependence on childcare workers but also some sense of guilt. We are conscious that our own ability to pursue careers is built upon a form of exploitation: paying poorer women relatively low wages for this domestic labor. In some areas, domestic workers have begun to form associations to enforce minimum-wage levels.

Working-Class Women: Factory Workers. After 1900, the proportion of workers among women of working age in the United States rose (Table 13.2), due in large part to a major influx of

Table 13.2 Women in the U.S. Labor Force: Selected Years

| | | Women in the Labor Force as a percent of: | |
Year	Women in the Labor Force (thousands)	Total Labor Force	All Women of Working Age
1900	4,999	18.1	20.0
1910	8,076	21.2	23.4
1920	8,229	20.4	22.7
1930	10,396	21.9	23.6
1940	13,007	24.6	25.8
1945	19,304	29.2	35.8
1950	18,412	28.8	33.9
1955	20,584	30.2	35.7
1960	23,272	32.3	37.9
1965	26,232	34.0	39.3
1970	31,560	36.7	43.4
1975	37,087	39.1	47.4
1980	41,283	42.0	52.4
1985	43,506	44.1	56.4
1990	56,554	45.3	60.0

Source: U.S. Department of Labor, Bureau of Labor Statistics. *Employment and Earnings*, Selected Years

European immigrants, most of whom worked in factories. Many immigrants from Italy or Jews from Russia had previous experience in the needle trade and garment factories.

Female factory workers were not new to the American economy in 1900. In the 1820s and 1830s, single women were employed in textile mills throughout New England. The mill owners could recruit us at half or less the pay of men. Mostly young women and the daughters of farmers, we came to work for a short period before marriage to help support our families and ourselves. We generally began in our teens, working twelve to thirteen hours daily, six days a week. At the new model factory at Lowell, Massachusetts, our lives were closely supervised: We were required to live in company housing and to attend church regularly. Many devoted spare time to studying, reading, and writing. Some had high ambitions, going on to become teachers and writers.

But factory conditions gradually deteriorated in the New England towns. Owners began to demand more and give less to their workers. When textile prices fell, the owners lowered wage rates to keep up their profits. From time to time, the workers staged protests, walkouts, and strikes. However, our efforts to improve conditions through protest, organization, and alliance with men's groups met with little success. By midcentury, native-born female factory workers were rapidly outnumbered by poorer immigrant women, initially Irish. These women in turn took over the struggle to organize and protect factory workers. We produced women labor leaders later in the century, like Mary Harris ("Mother") Jones (1830–1930) and Elizabeth Gurley Flynn (1890–1964). Both traveled throughout the country as labor organizers, participating in strikes.

While women immigrants worked in a wide variety of industries, we were clearly predominant in the garment industry—and still are.

It was in this industry that our union activities had the greatest impact. When Rose Schneiderman (1882–1972) arrived as an immigrant, she found work in factories and went on to become a union organizer among garment workers. A strike of women shirtwaist workers in New York City in 1909 brought tens of thousands of members to the International Ladies' Garment Workers Union (ILGWU). Although beaten by hired thugs, the picketing women managed to win an increase in wages. Another goal, recognition for the union, was not achieved until 1913. Despite the fact that 80 percent of the garment workers were women, the ILGWU was dominated by men; not surprisingly, it classified the male-dominated crafts of cutting and pressing as highly paid skilled labor and the female-dominated tasks of joining, draping, and trimming as unskilled, and we were paid accordingly. The union leaders did not press for safety regulations demanded by the women in 1909 and many women perished in the Triangle Shirtwaist Factory fire in 1911 (Kennedy, 1979). The garment sweatshop did not disappear in the United States, but was revitalized beginning in the 1970s in cities like New York, Miami, and Los Angeles, utilizing a new immigrant force—women from East Asia, South America, and the Caribbean. Part of a global workforce in the apparel industry, women have little voice in work conditions or union issues, and exploitation through low wages has remained largely unchanged over the decades (Louie, 1992).

During the Depression in the 1930s, a great deal of propaganda told employed women that we were taking jobs from men. This propaganda ignored the fact that many of the jobs women held were traditionally female jobs. After the Second World War in the 1940s, women were told that for us to work away from home was unfeminine and harmful to our families. The women who had worked in heavy industry during both wars by no means welcomed the opportunity to be relieved of their high-paying jobs. But we had no power to resist layoffs, no means to fight for our interests.

In the 1970s, a few women began to obtain high-paying heavy industrial jobs at twice the wages we could earn as secretaries. Many women have fought for legal reforms to ban gender discrimination in hiring and promotion. Today, only about one-sixth of American working women are factory workers. Women are still only rarely employed or trained in technical or industrial trades and are still routinely excluded from many "skilled" trades. To increase our participation in the skilled trades, the United States Department of Labor in 1978 established regulations that required companies receiving any federal funding to adhere to goals and timetables. For example, of all workers hired as apprentices, that is, those receiving good on-the-job training for the skilled trades, an immediate 20 percent were to be women.

However, our participation rate in trades did not increase, partly due to the failure of the Reagan and Bush administrations to enforce the Department of Labor regulation. Those few women who have entered the nontraditional trades report job isolation and sexual harassment, despite Department of Labor regulations against such activities, with the effect of further reducing our participation in the skilled trades.

The argument made by employers is that women do not have the aptitude or vocational training required for many of the jobs men have traditionally held. Therefore, they choose to hire men and pay them higher wages. But this proposition contradicts a basic rule of capitalism: The employer always seeks to purchase labor at the lowest possible cost and thus increase profits. If women are the cheapest source of labor, why don't employers reduce costs by recruiting and training women for the higher-wage jobs held by men? Employers tend not to hire female workers because they believe the social stereotyping that assures them women would perform those jobs poorly, because they understand the difficulties of introducing women into a world identified as a male sphere, and because they view women as identified with family and home and see nontraditional jobs for us as inappropriate.

The Pink Collar Worker. Women today predominate in clerical work, sales, and services. Gender segregation in the workplace is as emphatic as ever: The range of jobs open to women is narrower than those open to men; the jobs largely filled by women are rarely taken by men; and women's jobs are stereotyped in the workplace just as they are in the home (Table 13.3). The largest proportion of working women are

clerical workers. The secretarial and nursing professions are almost exclusively female. While both women and men work as salespeople, we sell different things. Men, for example, sell cars and insurance; women sell cosmetics and women's clothing. In the United States, most women who work do so in the service sector of the economy. The service sector involves the sale and distribution of goods and services themselves. These exclusively female jobs are called *pink collar* work.

Pink collar workers include female office workers who are often poorly paid. As most such workers are female, often part of our "job" is to look "feminine": to show up for work in attractive clothing, well-coiffed and groomed, or to wear clothes that will appeal to customers. The pink collar worker labors

Table 13.3 U.S. Employment in Selected Occupations, 1950, 1970, and 1990

Occupation	Women and Men (numbers in 000s)			Women as a Percent of All Workers in That Occupation		
	1950	1970	1990	1950	1970	1990
Professional-technical	4,858	11,452	15,818	40.1	40.0	51.2
Engineers	518	1,233	1,862	1.2	1.6	8.0
Lawyers-judges	171	277	756	4.1	4.7	20.8
Physicians-osteopaths	184	280	575	6.5	8.9	19.3
Registered nurses	403	836	1,673	97.8	97.4	94.5
Teachers (prim. and second.)	1,123	2,750	3,993	74.5	70.4	73.7
Teachers (college and univ.)	123	492	765	22.8	28.3	37.7
Writers, artists-entertainers	124	761	1,941	40.3	30.1	47.7
Managerial-admin., except farm	4,894	6,387	30,657	13.8	16.6	45.8
Bank officials-financial managers	111	313	1,189	11.7	17.6	44.6
Buyers-purchasing agents	64	361	219	9.4	20.8	50.7
Food service workers	343	323	5,359	27.1	33.7	59.5
Sales managers-dept. heads; retail trade	142	212	3,812	24.6	24.1	34.8
Clerical	6,865	13,783	18,641	62.2	73.6	79.8
Bank tellers	62	251	468	45.2	86.1	90.4
Bookkeepers	716	1,552	1,912	77.7	82.1	92.2
Cashiers	230	824	2,492	81.3	84.0	81.4
Office machine operators	143	563	72	82.1	73.5	62.4
Secretaries-typists	1,580	3,814	3,956	94.6	96.6	99.0
Shipping-receiving clerks	287	413	546	6.6	14.3	26.8

Source: U.S. Department of Labor, Bureau of Labor Statistics. *Employment and Earnings,* selected years

in an office or beauty parlor or restaurant but gets paid at rates comparable to those of an unskilled blue collar worker. The work is often highly impersonal and routine, as in a typing pool.

Clerical and secretarial work became available to women late in the nineteenth century, especially with the introduction of the typewriter, which both speeded up paperwork and contributed to its volume. With the opening of this new opportunity, thousands of women with a high-school education were drawn to secretarial work as an attractive alternative to becoming salesclerks or telephone operators, the other new service occupations opening up to women with education.

Today, despite the fact that women of color are well represented in pink collar jobs, we are still relegated to lower-level office work (as data entry workers, file clerks, and typists) compared to those office jobs held by European American women.

With the arrival of technology in the workplace, changes in office work have affected different types of jobs. Computers along with office automation have changed the nature and conditions of clerical work. Office automation may provide a woman with the opportunity to gain computer skills, if the employer provides her with training and she is able to use time on the job to enhance her skills. For many clerical word processors, however, little if any on-the-job training is provided. Also, learning a word processing program does not establish a basic level of skills that progresses toward more advanced computer skills, such as operations, programming, or systems (Gutek and Bikson, 1985). The lowest-level clerical jobs, jobs in which women are highly concentrated, are the jobs most likely to slowly disappear from the arena of work (Feldberg and Glenn, 1983). More educated white women tend to benefit the most from "upgrading" to a computer; again, however, many of these positions are simply "jobs," not "opportunities" (Baran and Teegarden, 1983).

What is worse for women in jobs that entail extensive computer use is that office work has been redesigned. We no long perform a variety of duties with diversified body movement, such as opening mail, answering phones, writing correspondence, etc. Instead, challenging and traditional tasks have been reduced (Murphree, 1987). Female office workers today often spend long periods of time in front of the keyboard and computer. These long hours of word processing production have been linked to reproductive disorders, eye fatigue, wrist soreness, nausea, and neck and back aches (Stellman and Henifin, 1983). Just as employers identified women with the office machines of production, the typewriter and word processor, so employers expect these women to produce in a machinelike manner. There is much dehumanization associated with the "back office" word processing production centers where 30–100 or more women may work. In a highly controlled environment, women have to raise their hands to be excused and electronic monitoring devices count each person's keystrokes. It is a grim reminder of the textile mills of the early nineteenth century and a warning that the new technologies have served to reinforce the gender and economic status quo.

Gender attributes are often considered part of job qualifications; preference may be given to women who are young, deferential, and sexually attractive. Pink collar workers are trained in deference and expected to be self-effacing rather than ambitious. What might happen when such social expectations are turned on their head was the plot of the film *Nine to Five*.

In part, the gender segregation of office workers is something of an illusion, a product of labeling the things done by women and men differently. In insurance companies, for example, both women and men process policy applications. The men are higher paid and called "underwriters," while the women are paid less and called "raters." By giving the same job two different titles, one for men and one for women, companies can classify the title used for women at a lower wage rate.

Women who work in pink collar jobs rarely have any significant opportunity for promotion, despite films such as *Working Girl*. Women do not advance to the top. Women working full-time and year-round now earn about 70 percent of what men earn (Table 13.4). The differential has improved only slightly in some twenty years, although women are entering the workforce in greatly increased numbers and are working in jobs formerly held only by men. In other countries, the pay differential between women and men is even greater. In the Republic of Korea and Japan, women earn only 47 and 51 percent (respectively) of what their male colleagues earn (UNDP, 1993). One argument sometimes made is that the pay differential results from the fact that the entering women are less experienced rather than from discrimination. To test this argument, economists hold constant the variables of age, experience, and duration of the job, and find that women still get paid less than men, and are still promoted more slowly (Rotella, 1980).

The Contingent Worker. During the late 1970s and early 1980s, an older form of work became increasingly prevalent in the United States: contingent work. Contingent workers include part-time, temporary, and free-lance workers, as well as leased employees and home-workers. Contingent workers are a "flexible" workforce: that is, employers rely on these workers only when they perceive there is a need and release these workers when there is no further need. Some contingent workers are voluntary, preferring their particular work arrangement, while others are involuntary and are looking for full-time regular employment.

"Leased" employees work for one company (the leasing company), but perform all their job duties for a different company. Because the leased employee is *not* an employee of the

Table 13.4 Earnings of Women and Men*

	1970	1980	1990
All workers	$130	$266	$415
Male	151	322	485
16–24 years old	112	214	283
25 years and over	160	346	514
Husbands	159	349	532
Men who maintain families		314	444
Female	94	204	348
16–24 years old	88	171	254
25 years and over	96	217	370
Wives	95	208	363
Women who maintain families		210	339
White	134	273	427
Male	157	329	497
Female	95	206	355
Black and Other	99	219	329
Male	113	247	360
Female	81	190	355
Latino		214	307
Male		238	322
Female		177	308
Occupation			
Professional-technical	181	341	534
Managers, administrators†	190	380	511
Salesworkers	133	279	292
Clerical workers	109	215	332
Craft and kindred workers	157	328	316
Operatives, except transport	(NA)	225	262
Transport equipment operatives	(NA)	286	314
Nonfarm laborers	110	220	250
Private household workers	38		171
Service workers		180	231
Farm workers	71	169	216

*Median Weekly Earnings of Full-Time Wage and Salary Workers, by Selected Characteristics: 1970–1990 [In current dollars of usual weekly earnings. Due to changes in data collection procedures, data are not strictly comparable with earlier years.]
†Excludes farm.
NA = Not available.
Source: U.S. Bureau of Labor, Department of Labor Statistics. *Employment and Earnings,* January 1993.

firm in which she works, she faces a number of issues: Who am I an employee of? What rights do I have? What will be the effect on my earnings? In many cases, employee leasing, as a cost saving to the employer, is a means of reducing benefits or breaking unions (Axelrod, 1987).

Home-workers and independent contractors are another part of the flexible workforce. Most home-based white collar workers are self-employed (75 percent) and married women (75 percent). Home-workers list four major reasons to work at home: (1) family responsibilities; (2) control over work hours and setting; (3) eliminating the expense of traveling and office politics; and (4) the need to earn extra money (Christensen, 1988). Women performing home-work report stress in trying to balance work at home with other responsibilities at home. Usually there is very little independence for the home-worker, as such workers usually work for only one company. Yet, since home-workers have little contact with the company and work in isolation, they are rarely considered for advancement or training. On average, home-workers receive lower wages than on-site employees.

Contingent work raises many disturbing issues concerning the development of a new workforce of women dependent on the capricious demands of employers. Contingent workers rarely receive the benefits and security associated with full-time employment. Training and occupational advancement is considered a low priority by employers for many contingent workers and some of these workers report feeling "out of it" at their place of work (Barker, 1988); many receive lower wages than full-time workers performing comparable work. Yet, for many of us, a contingent job with a weak attachment to an employer is the only solution to the problems of inadequate child care, partial retirement, or continuing education.

The Professions. The professions include the arts, law, medicine, teaching, and management. Work in them often requires more training and education than other kinds of work, although critics claim that the structure of the

professions is often designed to preserve class privileges (by requiring, for instance, lengthy training that only the rich can afford) more than to enhance the quality of the work performed. Most of the professions set their own standards for qualifications and performance and generally pay more than blue and pink collar workers make.

Work in the professions, like other forms of work, is highly segregated by gender. Women professionals tend to hold lower-paying jobs and positions of less authority, power, and prestige. In the United States, women outnumber men in the professions of nursing, elementary and secondary school teaching, social work, and library work. Women are underrepresented in most other professions, especially in medicine, science, engineering, higher management, and stockbroking. While many women have been trained and are active in the arts, few have held top-ranking positions in architecture or design, or as producers or directors in theater or film. Women have also experienced systematic discrimination against our work as writers and artists, so it is harder for us than for men to gain recognition and make a living in the arts. In recent years, thanks in part to consciousness-raising by the women's movement and in part to anti-discrimination laws, increasing numbers of women have entered and achieved success in professions formerly barred to us.

It is appropriate to consider women in the professions from two points of view: women in those professions that society deems "female," and those in professions that society deems "male." The issues in each are somewhat different.

Within the "women's" professions (nursing, social work, elementary and secondary school teaching, and library work), there is a gender segregation that places men at the highest decision-making levels. More men than women are principals, superintendents, chief officers, and faculty and administrators of professional schools. For the most part, these female professions offer limited career mobility; they are the lowest-paying and least "powerful" of the professions. Yet they are enormously important to society, and they provide large numbers of women with the opportunity to pursue gratifying careers, although society has not elected to reward us with high pay or status. It is likely that we are poorly paid and often belittled *because* we are in women's professions.

For female professionals who pursue both career and family, there are many role conflicts, since both our jobs and our families make demands on our time and energy (Barnett and Baruch, 1985; Frieze et al., 1978). Many professions and employers of professionals, especially male-dominated ones, assume that individuals dedicate most of our time and energies to work. The male model of professional development is especially problematic for women who are raising a family.

Women who enter a "male" profession are likely to encounter a series of social obstacles. Not only will we be in the minority among our peers, but our subordinates, whether female or male, may have difficulty relating to us and we to them as superiors or bosses. The more negative a male subordinate's opinion is of women in general, the less likely he will be to attribute the success of a female manager to her own ability or effort (Garland et al., 1982). While women who are leaders have just as much need as men to enhance their personal power, women tend to express a more helpful style of leadership and inhibit the exhibition of power (Colwill, 1982; Chusmir and Parker, 1984).

There is a tendency for gender segregation within "male" professions as well. Female physicians tend to go into pediatrics; female lawyers into probate (dealing with wills and property dispositions to widows and offspring); and female professors into the humanities and social sciences rather than the physical sciences. The segregation of genders between and within the professions is in part the result of gender discrimination in education.

Women in male-dominated professions gain many benefits beyond the higher salaries associated with professional work. Women have many opportunities to observe a broad range of female and male work models (Lemkau, 1983) and have opportunities to develop self-esteem and competency that have been typically reserved for men. Studies indicate that many of these women have not only been privileged in their early background, but have been encouraged by their parents to achieve in male-dominated fields (Tangri, 1972). Many report having been the firstborn child (Hennig, 1973; Standley and Soule, 1974), and it appears the absence of brothers facilitates a woman's aspiring to a nontraditional career (Helson, 1971; Hennig, 1973).

Race, Ethnicity, and Work in the United States

The experience of gender discrimination in the labor force has been felt by all women. In addition, women of color have been further victimized by racial/ethnic discrimination. *Women of color* refers to African American, Latina, Asian, and Native American women. The term *women of color* lends a sense of diversity about the members belonging to this group and underlines the importance of understanding the different experiences of women within this group.

African American women often have career expectations and pursuits (Ladner, 1972; Collins, 1991). In the United States, we have been a significant part of the labor force since the days of slavery. Our labor was expected in the fields, inside the master's house, and for our own families. African American women slaves were also expected to be compliant sexual objects for white masters. When slavery was abolished many African American women turned to employment as domestics, laundresses, and child care workers to help maintain our families, and continued to work alongside our men in the fields when necessary. Because African American men often found it more difficult to gain employment in cities, African American women quickly recognized our importance in economic survival. We became heads of households when necessary. African American women experienced high labor force participation along with family responsibilities through the periods when fewer white women carried this double burden.

Because of racism, African American women have generally been employed at the lowest rung of the labor market—working long hours for meager wages with few job benefits except at the benevolence of an employer, usually a white family or boss. African American women migrated north in search of employment, but only rarely found jobs in factories or offices open to us except during wartime crises. The legislation establishing a minimum wage in the 1930s explicitly exempted household workers and farmhands, and therefore little affected African American women.

When African American women have received training funded by the government, such as under the Manpower Development and Training Act (MDTA), under the Comprehensive Employment and Training Act (CETA), or under the Job Training Partnership Act (JTPA), our participation in these programs has increased neither our employment rate nor the conditions of our employment. Under the MDTA, African American women were forced into two narrow occupation fields, health and clerical occupations. African American women enrolled in the CETA program received lower incomes after training than either white and black males, or white women (Wallace, 1980).

Despite these handicaps, African American families have always stressed the value of education, especially for daughters (see Chapter 11). Civil rights legislation such as Title IX has increased access for African American children and adults to educational and job opportunities and has allowed many African American women to prepare for careers in teaching and nursing, the female-dominated occupations open to us.

Three major places of origin of women of Latino origin in the United States are Mexico, Puerto Rico, and Cuba. Latino cultural patterns are built around the values of *machismo* for men and *marianismo* for women (Comas-Diaz, 1987). *Machismo*, with its emphasis on the display of male power and authority, means literally maleness or virility. This norm places males in a privileged position in which they are the breadwinner and overseer of the family. *Marianismo* expects us to be spiritually superior to men as well as to adjust selflessly to their *macho* behavior and to our own role in childbearing and motherhood.

This cultural message exhorts boys and men to exercise their freedom and restricts girls and women by the lack of emphasis on education for women, promoting instead large families without fertility control and the development of a passive female disposition, willingly subordinated to male authority. These conditions often discourage women from entering the labor force (Almquist, 1979). Yet paid employment or participation in the informal economy has been a traditional role for most working-class and peasant women in Latin America. Despite the dictates of *machismo*, Puerto Rican women found employment in the cigar, tobacco, and garment industries. By the 1930s, Puerto Rican women outnumbered Puerto Rican men in the cigar and needlework industries (Ammott and Matthaei, 1991). Confinement of Latina women to the home is *machismo* ideology; the reality is that women have a long tradition of contributing to the family economy (Kessler-Harris, 1975; Safa, 1981). In this country, Latina women who are either immigrants or first- or second-generation citizens find that language barriers frequently persist, reinforced by residential patterns, and make difficult their ability to find decent and good-paying jobs.

In the United States today, a large number of Latina women are undocumented workers; in order to avoid apprehension, these women often live in very isolated situations. Many Latina women work as migrant farm laborers, traveling all over the country picking fruits and vegetables, and in factory work (sweatshops) doing piece work. Both of these endeavors are generally conducted in an exploitative fashion, giving the women little power to shape our work environment.

Second- and third-generation Puerto Rican women are less traditional—more assertive—than first-generation Puerto Rican women, and education is considered the major reason (Rosario, 1982; Soto and Shaver, 1983). Nationally, however, only 7.3 percent of all Latina women achieved a college degree in 1985 (Rix, 1987). However, Puerto Rican women have recently increased their labor force participation as they have become more educated and geographically dispersed. Not only is there an indication that there is a shift of Latinas into white collar jobs, there is an emerging split within some Latino communities. For example, in the Puerto Rican community, recent migrants are found in lower-level jobs and mainland-born Puerto Ricans, having attained more education, are relatively upwardly mobile, although not assimilated (Safa, 1981).

Are gains in employment of Latina women more difficult because of unbending sex-role stereotypes associated with ethnicity and expectations associated with the role of mother? One study of professional Latinas—Mexican American, Puerto Rican, Cuban, and women

from other Latino groups—indicates that 82 percent reported discrimination. This discrimination was related to increased stress in balancing roles, lower personal life satisfaction, and increased psychological distress (Amaro et al., 1987). Many of these professional Latinas reported working forty to fifty hours per week.

Compared to Latinas, Asian American women in general have higher labor participation, education, and economic status. Aggregate data on occupational profiles reveals that in 1990 the five largest categories of employment for Asian American women were administrative support, including clerical (24.2%); professional specialty (16.5%); executive, administrative, and managerial (14.3%); service workers, except private household (11.8%); and sales workers (10.4%) (U.S. Bureau of the Census, 1992). These categories are misleading, as Asian American women are often employed in small family-owned businesses as an alternative to limited employment opportunities. Experiences and choices also vary widely, reflective of class, ethnic, and national grouping, English language facility, and immigrant/refugee/native-born status.

Aggregate data hides and distorts disparities. For example, Filipinas and Asian Indians tend to be professionals, particularly in health care, and Chinese and Japanese Americans are found in white-collar, non-professional jobs. Many Chinese, Korean, and Vietnamese American women are unpaid or low-paid workers in small family businesses; a few head their own businesses. Yet there are also Vietnamese, Cambodians, Hmong, and Chinese American women employed as factory operatives or service workers who exist below the poverty line or are among the working poor.

What role does culture play? Historically, Asian cultures have privileged males dissuading women from developing "masculine" traits of competitiveness, independence, and activism. Females are socialized to be obedient, modest, responsible, and self-sacrificing, and to assume traditional roles at home (Fillmore and Cheong, 1980; Mau, 1990). Asian American feminist scholars have argued that structural factors in the United States, as well as cultural factors, contribute to their work roles. Asian American women work as an economic necessity to support families and supplement the low income of spouses (Chu, 1988; Woo, 1985). Sociologist Deborah Woo (1989) finds that highly educated Asian American women are not economically rewarded and that education has served to protect Asian American women from jobs as service or assembly workers or machine operators rather than to provide opportunities for upward mobility. Asian American women who have developed both feminine and masculine aspects of their self-concept experience higher self-esteem, work satisfaction, and occupational attainment (Chow, 1987).

Native American women are the most economically disadvantaged group in the United States. Unemployment rates are high (12 percent) and for those that do work more than two-thirds of Native American women hold part-time jobs. While those lucky enough to have completed higher education have found jobs in the public sector working as professionals and technicians on reservations, cutbacks at all levels of government have made it difficult for Native American women to secure employment opportunities. Native American women must constantly struggle against inadequate education and discrimination in the labor market (Amott and Matthaei, 1991).

The Multinational Corporation

One of the most powerful forces affecting our shrinking world is the multinational corporation. These corporations locate their operations in areas where they can tap cheap, docile labor. Third World women have become the prime targets of the search for cheap labor on the global assembly line. The governments in the Caribbean and South America, and in many countries of Asia, advertise the availability of a large supply of female labor. Often women in these countries do not have equal rights of citizenship, much less rights to control our work environment. To take advantage of this cheap female labor, factories making computer chips or piece goods are springing up all over the world.

Work in multinational corporation factories compromises the health and life expectancy of workers; women perform repetitious and monotonous tasks and are exposed to dangerous chemicals. But the women who enter the labor force in these countries face extreme poverty. We need even the lowest wages for survival, and we have almost no ability to resist exploitation.

Often, the status of women has deteriorated as Third World nations develop within the world capitalist system (Hess and Ferree, 1987). While development of a regional economy indicates an association with an increase in female employment, women's opportunities in that economy decline relative to men (Leon de Leal and Deere, 1982). Women's importance in subsistence-based production has shrunk with the erosion of subsistence agriculture in "developing" nations (Hess and Ferree, 1987). Crafts, traditionally considered women's domain, have been undermined by the mass production of inferior goods and women's incomes have suffered (Tinker, 1976). These changes have been especially felt in rural communities. Lace-making in India is an example of a craft becoming integrated into a wider world market economy. Lace is sold by women to traders or exporters, who are men, and who reap the profits (Mies, 1982). Women who make lace and contribute to the economy of the family are viewed by society and our own husbands as nonworking housewives. Hence, the lace-maker's work is invisible even to those who profit from our work: exporters, traders, and husbands.

The products produced by our Third World sisters earning very low wages enable others to purchase food, clothing, and other goods very cheaply. But many feminists do not wish to achieve economic advancement for ourselves at the expense of our sisters elsewhere. The avoidance of this dilemma will require the development of more enlightened policies on the part of corporations and better foreign economic policies by the United States than are now present.

Self-Employment

The fact that relatively few women are self-employed can be traced in part to the different socialization of girls and boys. Girls tend not to be taught to take the initiative, or to be assertive or independent. When we do show these qualities, which underlie successful self-employment, we receive fewer rewards than boys or even negative sanctions.

In addition, women have less access to sufficient material or monetary resources to establish independent enterprises. Because we earn less, we can save less. Financial institutions have long maintained discriminatory practices, denying loans and credit to women simply on the basis of gender. Discriminatory practices against women in business are found not only in the United States, but also in Africa, Asia, and Latin America. In parts of Africa and Asia, many women are not allowed to own property or to put up collateral for bank loans. Without loans and credit, an individual cannot start or run a business in the United States. As women in the industrialized countries campaign to legislate against such discrimination, it is not easy to end traditional attitudes translated into business practices.

Despite the obstacles, quite a few ambitious women have managed to overcome many of the financial barriers to self-employment. More and more women who must work and who have children are entering the workforce as self-employed workers. Self-employed women, whether working as professionals or nonprofessionals, tend to experience higher autonomy, self-development, and satisfaction from working than women who are employees (Mannheim and Schriffrin, 1984). But as in the case of other sorts of work, there is considerable gender segregation. A self-employed woman is more likely to be found as a woman's boutique owner or a free-lance illustrator of children's books or an interior decorator than as a machine-parts distributor or a tax consultant. Women have tended to go into businesses and services long identified with our traditional roles related to home, family, and personal care. In the United States about 32 percent of small businesses are owned by women.

Women in Corporations

Some feminists hope to reform the corporation from within by gaining positions of power. Our ability to do so remains questionable. Corporations have traditionally employed men in the management of the business enterprise. Women's gains in employment have been mostly dead-end clerical and service jobs (Smith, 1984). In 1985, approximately less than 10 percent of all working women were found in executive and managerial jobs and less than 17 percent were in professional and technical jobs.

Because women are identifiably different from men who usually wield power in the corporation, they experience difficulty in attaining positions of authority and responsibility in the corporate setting. Women have to try to "fit in," and since many women have not had the opportunities to acquire skills associated with upper-management jobs, for example, independent judgment and even nonverbal behaviors, they are seen as incompetent (Kanter, 1977). The pressures toward conformity in the corporate or bureaucratic setting minimize uncertainty but emphasize shaping oneself in the boss's image.

As a result of affirmative action suits and the affirmative action policies of companies, some women are climbing the corporate ladder and attaining more remunerative and prestigious corporate positions. In the past women in corporations found themselves hitting the "glass ceiling." That is, when it came time to be promoted to the highest positions, such as chief executive officer, we found ourselves being skipped over while our male peers or juniors were chosen for these positions. More recent studies indicate that top executive positions are opening up for women. A 1992 survey of 400 top female executives conducted by UCLA's Anderson Graduate School of Management found that 9 percent hold the rank of executive vice president in American companies (compared to 4 percent in 1982); and 23 percent are senior vice presidents (up from 13 percent in 1982). Though our percentages at the highest levels in corporate America are rising, female executives' average total compensation at $187,000 is still quite a bit less than the $289,000 in average total compensation earned by our male colleagues.

As more women work in the corporate world at the executive level, will the corporate environment change? Some feminists hope that the presence of women in corporations and bureaucracies will soften or humanize the corporate culture. However, other feminists believe that if women enter the corporate world primarily in lower-ranking positions, this will perpetuate institutional relationships of dominance and subordination (Ferguson, 1984). A recent study (Denmark, 1993) supports the latter view, indicating that only 25 percent of females have achieved management positions and that these positions are not top management.

Unemployment

The most serious difficulty women who wish to work may face is the inability to find a job. In most countries, whether capitalist, socialist, or communist, governments recognize the responsibility to provide jobs to those who cannot find them. The United States is almost alone in denying this obligation, though even those countries that acknowledge it may also fail to avoid high levels of unemployment. Government attempts to encourage or stimulate so-called private sector employment are often unsuccessful, especially for women, working class, and minorities who are routinely "last hired and first fired." It has been argued that the right of an individual to employment, provided by the government if not available otherwise, should be recognized as a human right (Nickel, 1978).

Unemployment rates are almost always higher for women than for men. If women are to be able to lead decent, productive lives, among our first priorities must be the assurance that when we seek employment, jobs will be available. To be able to compete on equal terms with men for an inadequate number of actual jobs will not be enough.

The Politics of Work: Barriers and Strategies

Conflict and Competition between Women and Men

Women and men have special relationships that are not replicated in any other kind of social relationship. As daughters, sisters, wives, and mothers of men, we are not simply competitors with them for resources, and we cannot entirely separate our own interests from those of the men to whom we are in some way related.

This is a multifaceted issue. First, men may feel that having their wives work for wages will threaten their own authority within the household. Second, women at home usually perform tasks that enhance the status of men and secure their leisure time: We keep house, like servants, freeing men from drudgery. Third, men's social status often relies on their being the primary breadwinner in the family. This situation is beginning to change.

Many households require more than one wage earner. Almost 60 percent of American men who are married with children have wives who work. Then why do not men whose wives *must* work for wages support advancement for women in the workplace? Men's concern for having a status superior to that of their wives operates here too. But the explanation must also incorporate a broader view of the economic system. In industrialized economies, jobs—or at least "good" jobs—are scarce: There are generally more workers available than there are attractive jobs. By reducing the pool from which prospective employers can draw, those who have or could have "good" jobs hope to reduce competition, to better their chances and force up their pay. By supporting both sexist and racist discrimination in employment, white male workers may believe they are improving their own lot, even though such discrimination undermines their own daughters, wives, sisters, and mothers, and their own positions.

Some hope for the future cooperation of men and women is encouraged by studies of children in homes where mothers work outside the home and mothers who work at home. These studies indicate that daughters and sons of working women have less traditional views of marriage (Stephen and Corder, 1985) and that children of working mothers view both women and their employment more positively than children of nonworking mothers (Powell and Steelman, 1982). Finally, there is evidence that men who have high self-esteem and are comfortable with their own masculinity accept the changing role of women at home and at work (Archer, 1984; Corder and Stephen, 1984).

Nuclear Families, Labor, and the State

The argument frequently given to rationalize lower pay for women is that our pay is supplementary; we do not need to support a household because men do. Increasingly, that is not the case: Many households have no men; others have men who are unemployed; many others are "supported" by men who do not earn enough.

The perpetuation of a domestic situation in which women are responsible for all household tasks and childrearing and men are viewed as the primary breadwinners is favorable to the dominant class in a capitalist system: It helps to keep workers in line. If men cooperated with women, supporting social services to relieve parents of some household responsibilities and working for rights to actual employment and equal treatment, both female and male workers would benefit.

The problem of pregnancy and employment provides another area of difficulty that is gender-specific. In many areas of employment in the past, pregnant employees were fired when the condition became apparent. Paid maternity leave is still rare. However, it is unlawful for us to be denied a reasonable period of absence when such leaves are allowed for other disability-related conditions.

One way to eliminate the discrimination that women face after giving birth is parental leave legislation. Such legislation acknowledges the need to have time off to give birth and to recover after having given birth. In 1993, the United States finally overcame executive opposition to parental leave rights and the Family Leave Bill was signed by President Clinton. Under the provisions of this law, companies with at least fifty employees must offer up to twelve weeks of unpaid leave and continue to maintain the health coverage of employees who request time off to care for a newborn or an adopted child. In addition, upon return to their jobs employees must be guaranteed their same job or one comparable to their former one.

Women and the State in Socialist and Communist Societies. Feminist proposals have often included arguments for social reform or revolution that would eradicate the exploitative effects of capitalism and make production more directly responsive to social interests. In addition, these proposals call upon the state to play a more active role in eradicating inequalities between women and men. A number of countries, including countries in Eastern Europe and within the former Soviet Union, Cuba, and Mozambique, have experimented with socialism and communism, and claimed to have reduced the exploitation of women. What have women achieved in such societies?

In various social-democratic, socialist, and communist countries, the state has taken on some of the domestic responsibility formerly borne by women, such as regular provision of child care and support for time off for mothers. Women and men have more nearly equal opportunity and pay on the job, at least in the lower and middle levels of employment.

Until the demise of the Soviet Union, in 1991, women enjoyed a variety of legal advantages not shared by women in the United States. Legislation provided benefits for pregnant and nursing mothers, and the government was committed to providing child care for working mothers.

On the other hand, these social experiments have not removed all of women's exploitation. A study of the former Soviet Union showed how government policy that claimed to be socialist fell short of achieving feminist goals (Lapidus, 1978). Even with the provision of these social services, many mothers were not satisfied; the demand for child care exceeded the supply and parents complained of inadequately trained child care workers.

In the area of gender-role socialization, socialist and communist countries have been less than successful in socializing children to accept gender-neutral roles for females. Women are portrayed in primarily maternal roles while men are seen in a broad range of activities outside the home. In Eastern Europe, girls demonstrate consistently higher levels of academic performance, as in the United States, but by the end of secondary school, girls and boys differ in career orientation. Boys tend to prefer natural and technical sciences and girls, the humanities; boys select technical occupations and girls, teaching.

Given gender segregation in types of work and the scarcity of women in managerial and other attractive positions, it is not surprising that women's pay overall is less than that of men. The fact that women in socialist and communist societies have not achieved equality in the workplace, some analysts attribute to the lack of attention to relieving women from housework (Funk and Mueller, 1993; Posadskaya et al., 1994).

In socialist and communist countries women spend more than twice as much time as men doing housework and have much less free time. Women's household tasks (shopping, cleaning, cooking, repairing, and laundering) leave us with less time than men to pursue other activities; furthermore, these tasks increase radically with marriage and children. In Cuba, women call the burden of working at home and outside of the home the "double day."

Examples from the former Soviet Union, Eastern Europe, China, Cuba, and elsewhere show that discrepancies still exist, but that these discrepancies vary for each country. However, it is generally true that the gender division of labor persists at the household level, and there is disparagement of women's abilities at high levels. More important, policies made by socialist and communist regimes have not been permanent. The profound political changes within former socialist and communist states have swept away whatever gains women secured through socialist and communist state policies and practices. As socialist and communist regimes fell during the late 1980s and early 1990s, unemployment rates for women in Russia, Eastern Europe, and Mozambique rose dramatically compared to those of men, and welfare services such as child care were cut or eliminated. The lesson for feminists is that even with the best intentions of the state, women have no guarantees that progressive social policies will be either sufficiently developed and executed or will endure beyond the end of the regimes that implemented them.

Sexual and Gender Harassment

The issue of sexual and gender harassment has only recently come under legal scrutiny. This pervasive problem for women workers is very much underreported, though the recent testimony given by Attorney Anita Hill against the Supreme Court nominee Clarence Thomas has encouraged more women to come forward about their own experiences with sexual and gender harassment.

Sexual harassment is an abuse of power. In the workplace, sexual harassment occurs when an employer or supervisor demands sexual favors from a female employee under threat of dismissal or other reprisal, often not made explicit, or when a woman is subjected to persistent unwelcome sexual advances or innuendoes. Sexual harassment includes not only the harassment of females by males, but also the harassment by customers of women who must wear sexually provocative clothing, male employees by female supervisors, and homosexual advances as well (Christensen, 1988). Studies have found that many men view certain sexual behaviors (sexual advances or solicitation of sex in exchange for a reward) as flattery. To the contrary, these behaviors are anything but innocent, and may inflict great harm upon a victim. Sexual harassment can interfere with our ability to meet financial obligations; block our career choices; and may damage our self-esteem and personal security (Paludi, 1990).

Women who are victimized by sexual harassment are unlikely to complain, much less take the employer or supervisor to court. In the past, women felt that speaking up or confronting a harasser would make no difference. But as more workplaces establish codes of conduct to regulate such offensive behaviors, women are increasingly seeking redress at their workplace and in the courts.

Social Support for Working Women

Unions. The principal organized support group for working people outside the family is the labor union. In the past, however, unions have not always been particularly supportive of women workers. It is noteworthy that many primary fields of women's employment, whether blue collar, pink collar, or professional, are not unionized. A large proportion of working women have the additional disadvantage of racial and ethnic discrimination; many unions have tended to leave out or discriminate against minority groups, including African Americans, Latinos, and all immigrants.

The conditions militating against women's participation in trade union activity today are much the same as they were over a century ago. Women are seen as dependents, whose primary roles are in the home. The demands of domestic responsibility leave us little time to devote to union activities. We traditionally lack training and experience in public speaking and self-assertion, important aspects of union activity. As the least skilled and lowest-

Levels of Sexual Harassment

- Gender harassment: generalized sexist statements and behavior not designed to elicit sexual cooperation but convey insulting, degrading, and/or sexist attitudes at women or homosexual people.
- Seductive behavior: unwanted, inappropriate, and offensive physical or verbal sexual advances.
- Sexual bribery: solicitation of sexual activity or other sex-linked behavior by promise of reward.
- Sexual coercion: coercion of sexual activity or other sex-linked behavior by promise of reward.
- Sexual assault: assault and/or rape.

(Zalk, 1991:13)

paid workers, we have had little bargaining leverage with employers. We have also faced considerable hostility from working men, who often view us as direct competitors for jobs or union positions and are made uneasy at home by wives who are too "independent" (Kennedy, 1979).

Despite these obstacles, many women have organized ourselves or joined with men to fight for unions and collective-bargaining issues. One of the earliest successful women's trade unions was the Collar Laundry Union of Troy, New York, which had some four hundred members at its peak and lasted nearly six years in the 1860s (Kennedy, 1979). Like many other women trade unionists, these workers were immigrants, in this case Irish. Elsewhere, other largely immigrant women joined to found and support unions. The Knights of Labor, a national union founded in 1869, offered support to women and African American workers but was soon replaced by the more conservative crafts union, the American Federation of Labor, which was interested mainly in skilled white male workers. Despite union organization among women who worked during World War I in machine

shops, foundries, railroad yards and offices, on streetcars, and at telephone exchanges, union support for women subsequently fell. Men feared that the presence of women in these workplaces would change working conditions at their expense. Where they could, men defended traditions that barred women from such employment. Women either were relegated to auxiliary groups in unions or remained unorganized (Greenwald, 1980). The highest levels of leadership of labor unions have remained male preserves.

Although unions have been extremely slow in overcoming discrimination in their own ranks, unionization has proven beneficial to working women, and existing unions are gradually becoming more aware of women's issues. The United Auto Workers, for example, has endorsed equal pay, gender-integrated seniority lists, day care, and the Equal Rights Amendment. Despite unions' growing awareness of the importance of organizing for working women's rights, most women do not join unions. In the United States only 6 million out of a total of 47.5 million working women (13 percent) belong to unions or pro-

Excerpts from EEOC Harassment Rules

Following are excerpts from interim guidelines forbidding sexual harassment of employees by their supervisors, issued by the Equal Employment Opportunity Commission:

Harassment on the basis of sex is a violation of Section 703 of Title VII (of the Civil Rights Acts of 1961, as amended). Unwelcome sexual advances, request for sexual favors, and other verbal or physical conduct of a sexual nature constitutes sexual harassment when (1) submission to such conduct is made either explicitly or implicitly a term or condition of an individual's employment, (2) submission to or rejection of such conduct by an individual is used for the basis for employment decisions affecting such individual, or (3) such conduct has the purpose or effect of unreasonably interfering with an individual's work performance or creating an intimidating, hostile, or offensive working environment.

In determining whether alleged conduct constitutes sexual harassment, the commission will look at the record as a whole and at the totality of the circumstances, such as the nature of the sexual advances and the context in which the alleged incidents occurred. The determination of the legality of a particular action will be made from the facts, on a case by case basis.

Applying general Title VII principles, an employer, employment agency, joint apprenticeship committee or labor organization is responsible for its acts and those of its agents and supervisory employees with respect to sexual harassment regardless of whether the specific acts complained of were authorized or even forbidden by the employer and regardless of whether the employer knew or should have known of their occurrence.

(New York Times, 1980)

fessional associations. One such association, the Coalition of Labor Union Women (CLUW), was formed in 1974 by three thousand women representing fifty-eight trade unions to improve the status of all working women. During the past decade, a number of significant efforts have been made to organize clerical women workers and to negotiate contracts that would address the interests of such workers, including improved opportunities for advancement as well as higher wages. The difficulties faced by a few women who worked in a small-town bank as teller and bookkeepers, organized a union, and went on strike are vividly depicted in the documentary film *The Willmar Eight.*

One model for a trade union association sensitive to the productive and reproductive needs of women is the Self-Employed Women's Association (SEWA) in India. Formed in 1972, SEWA is a trade union of women who work as petty vendors and home-based producers. SEWA establishes savings and credit cooperatives to provide working capital to its members. Its producer cooperatives help women secure a higher price for their goods. Through SEWA, members have been able to learn about plumbing, carpentry, radio repair, and accounting and management, thereby upgrading their skills. SEWA also provides legal services so its members can obtain the benefits of labor legislation enacted by the Indian government. Besides the improvements SEWA has made in the income-earning capacity of its membership, welfare services such as maternal protection schemes, widows' benefits, child care, and the training of midwives are also provided (UNDP, 1993).

Professional Organizations. Since women have not been well represented in the professions in the past, we have not figured conspicuously in the leadership of professional organizations. Beginning in 1969, groups of organized professional women began to take responsibility for raising the consciousness of the members of our professional organizations to the problems and rights of women and to the need to include us in leadership positions. One of the authors of this text, Florence Denmark, helped develop a section on the psychology of women in the American Psychological Association and became president of the APA for 1980–1981. Many other professional organizations, such as the American Historical Association, the American Philosophical Association, the American Anthropological Association, and the American Political Science Association have experienced the development of women's caucuses. As a result, women are playing a greater role than in the past in keeping these groups alert to the problems of women professionals.

Networks. The family, the union, and the professional association are formal organizations that have a legal standing: Networks are informal and have no legal standing. A network is a loose connection among individuals who know one another (or of one another), support one another, and pass along information. They are, for many, the most significant support group in the workplace. They are at once powerful and "invisible," operating to influence career opportunities and the workings of the business and professional worlds but not legally liable or open to attack.

Men in power have always relied on networks. Often they begin at school, especially private schools, or at colleges, where young men get to know others who share their in-

terests. These acquaintances are often kept up through a lifetime. They are sometimes broadened and shaped through other associations: clubs, civic groups, and special membership organizations. Networks provide their members with access to important information and resources. Leaders in virtually all fields—business, the arts, politics, the professions—rely on them for their continued success. For the most part, women have been excluded from these networks. Men have worked to keep outsiders (including women and minorities) out.

Groups of women who share experiences and interests are now attempting to develop ongoing relationships for mutual aid, sometimes on a formal but more often on an informal basis. The women's movement has created a particularly good climate for the formation of women's networks by keeping women aware of our need for one another and by encouraging our mutual support. Women use professional caucuses, newsletters, and regular meetings as more or less formal networking instruments.

Networking of this type is certainly not new to poor women, who have often relied on kin and friends among women to help adapt to a harsh social environment. For these women, household income is not simply low, but unreliable; getting by during hard times requires being able to depend on one's network. When poor women have jobs, we turn to our friends, and especially our kin, for help with child care; when we are out of work, we may receive material help from the network—loans or gifts of food, cash, and the like. Thus the poorest strata of our society, like the wealthiest and most powerful, have long used networks.

Protective Legislation

The rationale behind "protective" legislation applied to women's employment, both in this and other countries, has almost invariably been phrased in terms of women's "maternal functions." Conditions that exploited workers in the United States led many progressive reformers—including women leaders—to attempt to regulate industry. They sponsored state laws that prohibited women from such occupations as mining and bartending; limited total hours or days that we might work; prohibited night work; limited the amount of weight we could lift on the job; and so on. They also attempted, unsuccessfully, to guarantee women a minimum wage. A landmark Supreme Court decision, *Muller* v. *Oregon* (1908), upholding a state law restricting women's work hours, reasoned that overwork was injurious to women's physical capacity as mothers, hence threatening to the public interest. Similar arguments have been used in other industrializing countries.

Despite the good intentions of the reformers, such protective laws have in fact restricted our opportunities in the workplace and encouraged other sorts of discrimination against working women. In effect, they were a means of reducing competition with men, of keeping women in certain types of work—and out of others—and of paying us less. If women were prohibited from night work, men would be hired instead. Protective legislation therefore served to protect men and employers more than women. Some restrictions made little sense at all. For example, while women might by law be restricted from jobs requiring us to lift weights of twenty or thirty pounds, we were assumed quite capable of carrying children weighing more.

While laws are certainly needed to protect all workers against unsafe conditions, feminists have viewed many "protective" laws as mere excuses for discrimination. These laws were targeted for abolition by the authors of the Equal Rights Amendment, first introduced in Congress in 1923, but they were not addressed until 1964, with the equal employ-

ment opportunity provisions of Title VII of the Civil Rights Act (Eastwood, 1978).

Laws against Sexist Job Discrimination

Although no constitutional amendment yet guarantees to women equality under law, two federal statutes enacted in the 1960s provide the legal basis for women's equality in the workplace. One is Title VII of the Civil Rights Acts of 1964, amended by the Equal Opportunity Act of 1972; the other is the Equal Pay Act of 1963, amended by the Education Amendments of 1972 (Higher Education Act). The Equal Pay Act guarantees to women equal pay for work equal to that of male employees. Title VII of the Civil Rights Act of 1964, particularly Section 703(a), prohibits discrimination on the basis of sex in hiring or discharging individuals and in terms of compensation and conditions of work. It also prohibits classifying (on the basis of sex) either applicants or employees, to avoid adversely affecting our opportunities. The 1972 amendments extended coverage of both acts to executive, professional, and other job categories.

Responsibility for enforcing Title VII is in the hands of the Equal Employment Opportunity Commission, which has the power to initiate court action against an employer. Early court actions in 1969 resulted in substantial payments by Southern Bell Telephone Company and Colgate Palmolive to women and minorities who had been discriminated against, as well as in affirmative action programs to recruit and promote qualified women and minority members. An accord signed by the American Telephone and Telegraph Company with the EEOC and the Labor Department in 1973 set goals and timetables for the hiring and promotion of women and minorities in non-gender-segregated job areas and agreed to some 15 million dollars in back pay for almost fifteen thousand employees.

Affirmative action requires that employers who have discriminated against women and minorities set goals for reducing or ending such discrimination. For instance, if it can be shown on the basis of population figures or numbers of qualified applicants that a nondiscriminatory hiring policy would have resulted in about a quarter of the workers in a given category being women, an employer may be required to set a goal of 25 percent women employees in that category. In choosing between qualified women and qualified men, the employer might favor women until such a goal had been reached. Preference has often been given to groups such as veterans, to compensate for their previous personal sacrifices in the national interest (though many individual veterans suffered little). Affirmative action is an effort to compensate for past wrongs done by employers, both public and private, to women and members of minority groups.

White males often charge that affirmative action subjects them to "reverse discrimination." Often, it is younger white men who feel this way because they have not yet established themselves in jobs or careers. Older white males with seniority may be relatively unaffected by affirmative action; yet, they are the ones who have benefited most from past discrimination against women and minorities. Instead of attacking affirmative action as unfair, as many have, fairness would require its burdens to be more equally shared among all white males. It is clear that without evidence of the decrease of discrimination, as can be provided by the meeting of goals for women and minorities in employment, employers can go back to excluding women and minorities, no matter how qualified, from all the better-paying and most desirable kinds of work (Bishop and Weinzweig, 1979).

Many of the gains women achieved during the late 1960s and 1970s were reversed under the Reagan administration. This administration came into office with the support of various groups bitterly opposed to affirmative action. During the Reagan administration, both the Equal Employment Opportunity Commission and the Civil Rights Commission rejected the concept of comparable worth. In addition, the success of conservatives in reducing the number of permanent government employees had an unfortunate effect on women, since those who seek new jobs in the private sector will encounter greater discrimination and salary inequities than in government employment. In Washington, D.C., the federal government is now one of the largest employers of temporary workers who do not enjoy the same benefits or security as permanent federal employees with whom they work side by side.

Equal Pay—Comparable Worth

Those who have enforced laws against discrimination in the past have applied them only to persons doing the same work. It was illegal for an employer to pay a man more than a woman for doing exactly the same job with the same job specifications. This interpretation may be in the process of changing. Only if it does will a real attack on the inequities faced by women in the labor force be possible, for few women do the same work as men. "Women's work" is generally compensated at rates substantially lower than what men get for work of comparable value. Discrimination against women begins with the initial gender segregation of the tasks and persists into the sphere of remuneration.

If only economic forces were at work, there would be a uniform pay scale, since capitalists would seek to raise their profit by utilizing cheap labor. This does not happen. Instead, *institutional* features of the job market have acquired the gender discrimination of society. The gender discrimination of a society is found in the traditional customs, prejudices, and belief systems about the way one group of workers should be paid because of their sex, ethnicity, age, or race.

The labor market is split into the primary segment and the secondary segment. Institutional features of the primary segment are career ladders, on-the-job training and retraining, education requirements, higher rates of pay, good working conditions, and security. These jobs are typically found in industries with large investments, unionization, and advanced technology. Jobs in the secondary segment do not have any of the benefits of the primary segment and typically provide poor rates of compensation, little or no training, lack of security, poor working conditions, and unpredictable work rules. Most important, jobs in the secondary segment do not have career ladders to the primary segment (Ammott and Matthaei, 1991; Treiman and Hartmann, 1981). Women are traditionally found in the secondary segment and men are most often employed in the primary segment.

Juanita Kreps, secretary of labor in the Carter administration, has pointed out "that many of the occupational groups in which women are concentrated pay low wages while requiring higher than average educational achievement. . . . These higher levels of education do not pay off for either men or women in these 'female' occupations" (Kreps, 1971:40). Demands have developed for "equal pay for work of comparable value."

Comparable worth proceeds beyond equal pay for men and women in the same job, as men and women are rarely found in the same job category. Instead, the theory of comparable worth states that wages be reflective of the skills, the training, and the conditions of the work, with men and women receiving equal pay for positions assessed as having equivalent value.

There are four anomalies regarding women's low-wage position in the economy, none of which relate to economic forces (Feldberg, 1983). The first anomaly is typified by the fact that women are not judged on the actual work we perform or the value of our work to the employer, but instead we are often compensated according to widely held beliefs about the female labor force participation. The second anomaly is related to popular views that increasing the demand for workers will increase pay rates. This seems to be true only for men's jobs. The occupation of nursing illustrates both the difficulty women have in receiving compensation for jobs of comparable worth and that shortages of skilled female workers do not sufficiently increase their wages.

The third anomaly is that many of the skills women bring, acquire, and use on their jobs are not recognized as skills. Interpersonal and nurturing skills, skills typically associated with nursing, teaching, and social work, are undervalued and hence devalued. Diplomacy, tact, and masking one's feelings are skills associated with both executive positions and secretarial work. Yet it is only the executive or administrator who is compensated for these skills; these same skills in secretarial positions are "invisible" (Machung, 1988). Because women hold these positions, their compensation is tied to their gender, not to their "skills."

Finally, are women supposed to live a different, less advantaged life than men are supposed to live? A consistent stereotype of the working woman is that she is only "helping out," or working to "make friends." Increasingly, however, women are the sole support of their families and are not economically dependent on a male. In the *Lemons* v. *Denver* case, the judge acknowledged the existence of wage discrimination but ruled that women would have to acquiesce to poor rates of pay because the disruption to the economy, i.e., the cost, would be too great for employers.

To date, the Supreme Court has been unwilling to rule on comparable worth. However, it if can be proved that an employer *intentionally* discriminates in pay rates between men and women performing similar jobs, the courts will rule that violation of Title VII has occurred. In 1983, in *AFSCME* v. *State of Washington*, a favorable comparable worth decision was awarded the public sector union because positions held by female state employees were paid less than comparable jobs held by men. In a posttrial settlement, the State of Washington agreed to pay $482.4 million to correct discrepancies in female-dominated state jobs. However, the Ninth Circuit Court of Appeals held that comparable worth was a theory not protected by law and reversed the decision that employers should compensate workers for discriminatory wage differences (Christensen, 1988). The failure of the federal government and its agencies to adopt comparable worth as a viable theory has led many groups to seek state legislative action. To date, only Washington and Minnesota (Christensen, 1988) have acted on comparable worth and have applied the theory only to jobs in the public sector.

The future of comparable worth is best summed up by Feldberg (1983):

> The whole strength of the comparable worth approach rests on cooperation among women. As long as some areas of women's paid work are devalued, the potential exists for all women's work to be devalued; consider the way in which arguments about married women not needing a living wage have been used against all women (p. 325).

Toni Morrison, recipient of the Nobel Prize in 1993 for literature and Robert F. Goheen Professor at Princeton University, started to work at 13 years of age, at a job that was available to a young African American girl: cleaning house after school. When asked if she "felt a sense of triumph" when she received the Nobel Prize, she answered, "I felt a lot of 'we' excitement. It was as if the whole category of 'female writer' and 'black writer' had been redeemed. I felt I represented a whole world of women who either were silenced or who had never received the imprimatur of the established literary world." (Quoted in *The New York Times Magazine*, September 11, 1994)

New Directions

Impact of the Women's Movement

From the start, the current women's movement has demanded recognition of a woman's right to engage in useful, meaningful, and rewarding work. It has also stood for equal pay and respect for women in the workplace, for equal opportunity in advancement in jobs and careers, and for improvement in opportunity, pay, and recognition for minority women. Many feminists have realized that even deeper and more fundamental changes than these in the structures of economic activity are needed, especially in the United States.

Practical arrangements to relieve the burdens of women who work outside the home have been few and far between. The number of day care centers has increased but not nearly enough to accommodate all working mothers, and they are still too costly. A few work organizations have experimented with "flextime," instituting a system of flexible work hours so that women and men could carry out home and family responsibilities during the day and work as well. But such arrangements are unusual. While consciousness and gender images have changed somewhat, practical accommodations have changed rather little.

One of the most important developments within the women's movement in the United States in recent years is the growing recognition that what women want will require *structural* changes in the American economy. Women cannot achieve feminist objectives without a substantial breakdown of the class differences that pit the interests of advantaged women against those of less advantaged sisters. An equal opportunity to exploit the weak is not the aim of the women's movement. More humane and less hierarchical organizations of work are needed along with a concern on the part of society with what work is for— what investments shall be made, what prod-

ucts produced. Work that serves human needs and interests while respecting the environment is better for both women and men than work for increased profits. Progress toward these objectives will require fundamental changes in the way the work of both women and men is conducted.

Summary

Every known society has assigned work by gender, and the work done by women has traditionally been valued less than that done by men. Women's reproductive functions have been used as an excuse for division of labor by gender. Although the labor involved in reproduction itself is essential for any society, it is seldom recognized or compensated as such.

Maintaining the domestic unit is also essential to the functioning of society and the economy, but it has been given neither economic nor social value. Women who sell our labor in the marketplace also find our jobs devalued; we have been restricted in our choice of jobs and paid less than men.

When a society's economy is based on a simple domestic mode of production, economic and domestic roles tend to be integrated for both women and men. But as a society modernizes and work becomes capital-intensive rather than labor-intensive, women tend to be phased out of the economy and confined to the domestic sphere. Women "subsidize" capitalist enterprises by servicing workers for free and by providing a cheap pool of labor when needed.

As slavery and serfdom gave way to "free" wage labor, a working class evolved. Within this class, women have been barred from most trades of skilled labor by guilds and craft organizations. Most working-class women have been employed as domestic wage labor. In this century, greater numbers of women, particularly immigrants, have found work in factories. Most women today are employed as pink collar workers, involved in clerical work, sales, and services, in jobs considered "female." A growing economic trend is the use of contingent workers, many of whom are women, who do not receive the benefits, security, and earnings of full-time workers.

The professions are also segregated by gender, with women tending to enter nursing, teaching, and social work while men become engineers, architects, and administrators, Within the "female" professions, most top-level jobs are held by men. Women sometimes find it difficult to enter a "male" profession, much less to rise within it, but improvement is occurring.

African American, Latina, Native American, and Asian American women encounter various obstacles in the job market, but nearly all of us have been exploited and have had little power. Multinational corporations exploit the labor of women living in the Third World.

Few women are self-employed, perhaps because we have not been socialized to be assertive and independent. Women have less access than men to the financial resources needed to establish an enterprise. Some women have advanced to high levels within corporations; those who do so are under pressure to conform to corporate standards.

Women find it difficult to compete with men for jobs because our interests are nearly always related to those of men in some way. Men tend not to support our attempt to gain economic equality because they think this would threaten their superior status in the job market. These conditions favor the capitalist system by creating a need for the male worker to depend on his employer in order to support his family.

Women on the job may be subject to forms of sexual or gender harassment, such as pressures for sexual favors, that men are not faced with. Women who work find social support in unions and professional organizations to some extent, but the strongest support systems are found in the informal networks organized by women.

Many laws that were passed to "protect" women in the workplace have instead protected the jobs of men. The Equal Opportunity Act and Equal Pay Act were passed to lessen job discrimination against women. Affirmative action programs attempt to improve the opportunities of those who have been discriminated against. Many women today are calling for laws that will require equal pay for work of comparable value.

The women's movement has raised women's aspirations and brought about some changes in attitudes. However, it appears that feminist objectives will not be achieved without structural changes in the economy and society.

Discussion Questions

1. Choose three households you know that vary in a number of ways: income, educational level, race/ethnicity, age of adults, age of children, or other variables. Interview a woman in each household to find out what she does each week with her time. How can you account for differences and similarities in the work that the three women do?

2. Select a place of work—a hospital, a business firm, a school—to which you have access. Try to list all the types of positions and who holds them, for females and males. Are there particular types of work done mainly or exclusively by women? Also observe ranking: Are women found mainly at some levels and not at others?

3. Many women feel that our family obligations pose special problems for us in our pursuit of careers. In what ways does our society provide "relief" for women who work or study outside the home; to what extent are these services satisfactory or un-

satisfactory? What alternative means for alleviating this problem can you think of?

4. What are the experiences of working women in another country or region of the world? What kinds of work do women do? What child care options do women have? How do women balance family and work responsibilities? What are the similarities and differences between women in this society and the one you chose to study?

5. What is affirmative action? How does it work? Is it necessary?

6. If you have a particular career goal, study the roles of women in that career or profession in the past and at present. What proportion of people in the field are women? If there are obstacles to women's success in this field, might they be overcome?

Recommended Readings

Amott, Teresa L., and Matthaei, Julie A. *Race, Gender, and Work.* Boston: South End Press, 1991. The book explores how race-ethnicity, class, and gender shape the working experiences of women in the United States. It provides a historical look at the types of work performed by Native Americans, Chicana, European American, African American, Asian American, and Puerto Rican women.

Janiewski, Dolores E. *Sisterhood Denied.: Race, Gender and Class in a New South Community.* Philadelphia: Temple University Press, 1985. This study explores the experiences of African American and white working-class women after the abolition of slavery in the South in the tobacco and textile industries. The hardships and social life for women in a small community.

Nash, June, and Fernández-Kelly, María Patricia, editors. *Women, Men, and the International Division of Labor.* Albany: State University of New York Press, 1983. An examination of how the changing international division of labor affects women and men in the labor force. Case studies include countries in Asia and Latin America, and the United States.

Ruddick, Sara, and Daniels, Pamela, editors. *Working It Out: 23 Women Writers, Artists, Scientists and Scholars Talk About Their Lives and Work.* New York: Pantheon 1977. Personal accounts of the problems faced by women who had to carve out their work against the grain of society's expectations. An extraordinary roster of creative women in all fields of work.

Wertheimer, Barbara M. *We Were There: The Story of Working Women in America.* New York: Pantheon, 1977. A history of women working from colonial beginnings to the mid-twentieth century in the United States. The focus is on wage-earning women; the book includes African American women workers during colonial times and as slaves in the nineteenth century.

References

Acosta-Belén, Edna, and Bose Christine. "From Structural Subordination to Empowerment: Women and Development in Third World Contexts." *Gender & Society* 4:3 (September 1990):299–320.

Amaro, Hortensia, Russo, Nancy F., and Johnson, Julie. "Family and Work Predictors of Psychological Well-Being Among Hispanic Women Professionals." *Psychology of Women Quarterly* 11/4 (1987):505–21.

Amott, Teresa L., and Matthaei, Julie A. *Race, Gender, and Work.* Boston: South End Press, 1991.

Applebaum, Eileen. Profile of a New Workforce. Paper presented at *Unions Keep Pace: Strategies on Part-time and Temporary Work.* Cornell University, New York, March 1988.

Archer, C. J. "Children's Attitudes Toward Sex Role Division in Adult Occupational Roles." *Sex Roles* 10 (1984):1–10.

Axelrod, J. G. "Who's the Boss? Employee Leasing and the Joint Employer Relationship." *The Labor Lawyer* 3 (1987):853–72.

Baran, B., and Teegarden, S. *Women's Labor in the Office of the Future: Changes in the Occupational Structure of the Insurance Industry.* New Brunswick, N.J.: Rutgers University Press, 1983.

Barker, K. M. *Peripheral, Marginal, Disposable, Contingent or Flexible? Women in the New Work Force.* Unpublished manuscript. 1988.

Barnett, Rosalind C., and Baruch, Grace K. "Women's Involvement in Multiple Roles and Psychological Distress." *Journal of Personality and Social Psychology* 49 (1985):135–45.

Beneria, Lourdes, and Sen, Gita. "Class and Gender Inequalities and Women's Role in Economic Development—Theoretical and Practical Implications." *Feminist Studies* (Spring 1982):157–75.

Bishop, Sharon, and Weinzweig, Marjorie. Section 7. "Preferential Treatment." *Philosophy and Women.* Belmont, Calif.: Wadsworth, 1979.

Boserup, Esther. *Women's Role in Economic Development.* New York: St. Martin's Press, 1970.

Butler, Anne M. *Daughters of Joy, Sisters of Misery: Prostitutes in the American West, 1865–90.* Urbana: University of Illinois, 1985.

Chow, Esther N. L. "The Influence of Sex-Role Identity and Occupational Attainment on the Psychological Well-Being of Asian-American Women." *Psychology of Women Quarterly* 11 (1987):69–82.

Christensen, A. S. "Sex Discrimination and the Law." In *Women Working: Theories and Facts in Perspective*, edited by Ann H. Stromberg and Shirley Harkess. Mountain View, Calif.: Mayfield, 1988.

Chu, Judy. "Social and Economic Profile of Asian Pacific American Women: Los Angeles County." In *Reflections on Shattered Windows*, edited by Gary Y. Okihiro et al. Pullman: Washington State University Press, 1988.

Chusmir, Leonard H., and Parker, Barbara. "Dimensions of Need for Power: Personalized vs. Socialized Power in Female and Male Managers." *Sex Roles* 11 (1984):759–69.

Collins, Patricia Hill. *Black Feminist Thought: Knowledge Consciousness, and the Politics of Empowerment.* New York and London: Routledge, 1991.

Colwill, Nina L. *The New Partnership: Women and Men in Organizations.* Palo Alto, Calif.: Mayfield, 1982.

Comas-Diaz, Lillian. "Feminist Therapy with Mainland Puerto Rican Women." *Psychology of Women Quarterly* 11 (1987):461–74.

Corder, Judy, and Stephen, Cookie W. "Females' Combination of Work and Family Roles: Adolescents' Aspirations." *Journal of Marriage and the Family* 46 (1984):391–402.

County of Washington v. *Gunther* 101 S. Ct. 2242 (1981).

Dalla Costa, Mariarosa. "Women and the Subversion of the Community." In *The Power of Women.* Bristol, Conn.: Falling Wall Press, 1972.

Denmark, F. "Women, Leadership, and Empowerment." *Psychology of Women Quarterly* 17 (1993), p. 355.

Eastwood, Mary. "Legal Protection Against Sex Discrimination." In *Women Working: Theories and Facts in Perspective*, edited by Ann H. Stromberg and Shirley Harkness. Palo Alto, Calif.: Mayfield, 1978.

EEOC. *Sex Discrimination Guidelines*, 29 CFR 1604.11 (a) (3) 1980.

Enloe, Cynthia. *Beaches, Bananas, and Bases: Making Feminist Sense of International Politics.* Berkeley: University of California Press, 1988.

Feldberg, Roslyn L., and Glenn, Evelyn N. "Technology and Work Degradation: Effects of Office Automation on Women Clerical Workers." In *Machina Ex Dea: Feminist Perspectives on Technology*, edited by Joan Rothschild. New York: Pergamon Press, 1983.

Ferguson, Katherine E. *The Feminist Case Against Bureaucracy.* Philadelphia: Temple University Press, 1984.

Fillmore, Lily Wong, and Cheong, Jacqueline Leong. "The Early Socialization of Asian-American Female Children." In *Conference on the Educational and Occupational Needs of*

Asian-Pacific-American Women. Washington, D.C.: U.S. Department of Education, National Institute of Education, 1980.

Freedman, Estelle B. "Women's Network and Women's Loyalties: Reflections on a Tenure Case." *Frontiers* 8 (1986):50–54.

Frieze, Irene H., Parsons, Jacquelynne E., Johnson, P. B., Ruble, Diane N., and Zellman, G. L. *Women and Sex Roles: A Social Psychological Perspective*. New York: Norton, 1978.

Funk, Nanette, and Mueller, Magda, editors. *Gender Politics and Post-Communism: Reflections from Eastern Europe and the Former Soviet Union*. New York and London: Routledge, 1993.

Garland, Howard, Hale, Karen F., and Burnson, Michael. "Attributes for the Success and Failure of Female Managers: A Replication and Extension." *Psychology of Women Quarterly* 7 (1982):155–62.

Gaylord, M. "Relocation and the Corporate Family." In *Work and Family: Changing Roles of Men and Women*, edited by P. Voyandoff. Palo Alto, Calif.: Mayfield, 1984.

Greenwald, Maurine Weiner. *Women, War, and Work: The Impact of World War I on Women Workers in the United States*. Westport, Conn.: Greenwood, 1980.

Gutek, Barbara A., and Bikson, Tora K. "Differential Experiences of Men and Women in Computerized Offices." *Sex Roles* 13 (1985):123–36.

Hartmann, Heidi. "Capitalism, Patriarchy and Job Segregation by Sex." In *Women and the Workplace*, edited by M. Blaxall and B. Reagan. Chicago: University of Chicago Press, 1976.

Hess, Beth B., and Ferree, Myra M., editors. *Analyzing Gender: A Handbook of Social Science Research*. Beverly Hills, Calif.: Sage Publications, 1987.

Hirata, Lucie Cheng. "Free, Enslaved, and Indentured Workers in Nineteenth-Century Chinese Prostitution." *Signs* 5 (1979):3–29.

Jones, Jacqueline. *Labor of Love, Labor of Sorrow: Black Women, Work, and the Family from Slavery to the Present*. New York: Basic Books, 1985.

Kanter, Rosabath M. *Men and Women of the Corporation*. New York: Basic Books, 1977.

Kennedy, Susan Estabrook. *If All We Did Was to Weep at Home. A History of White Working Class Women in America*. Bloomington: Indiana University Press, 1979.

Kessler-Harris, Alice. "Stratifying By Sex: Understanding the History of Working Women." In *Labor Market Segmentation*, edited by R. C. Edwards, M. Reich, and D. M. Gordon. Lexington, MA: Health, 1975.

Kreps, Juanita M. *Sex in the Marketplace. American Women at Work*. Baltimore: Johns Hopkins University Press, 1971.

Ladner, Joyce. *Tomorrow's Tomorrow. The Black Woman*. Garden City, NY: Doubleday, Anchor, 1972.

Lapidus, Gail Warshofsky. *Women in Soviet Society. Equality, Development and Social Change*. Berkeley: University of California Press, 1978.

Lemkau, Jeanne P. "Women in Male-Dominated Professions: Distinguishing Personality and Background Characteristics." *Psychology of Women Quarterly* 8 (1983):144–65.

Leon de Leal, M., and Deere, C. D. "Peasant Production, Proletarianization, and the Sexual Division of Labor in the Andes." In *Women and Development: The Sexual Division of Labor in Rural Societies*, edited by Lourdes Beneria. New York: Praeger, 1982.

Louie, Miriam Ching. "Immigrant Asian Women in Bay Area Garment Sweatshops: 'After Sewing, Laundry, Cleaning and Cooking, I have no Breath Left to Sing.'" *Amerasia* June 17, 1 (1992):1:1–26.

Machung, A. *The Politics of Office Work*. Philadelphia: Temple University Press, 1988.

Mannheim, B., and Schiffrin, M. "The Temporary Help Industry: Response to the Dual Internal Labor Market." *Industrial and Labor Relations Review* 5 (1984):83–101.

Mau, Rosalind Y. "Barriers to Higher Education for Asian/Pacific American Females." *The Urban Review* 22:3 (1990):183–197.

Mbinlinyi, Marjorie. "'Women in Development' Ideology and Marketplace." In *Competition: A Feminist Taboo?* edited by Valerie Miner and Helen E. Longino. New York: The Feminist Press of the City University of New York, 1987.

Mies, Maria. "The Dynamics of the Sexual Division of Labor and Integration of Rural Women into the World Market." In *Women and Development: The Sexual Division of Labor in Rural Societies*, edited by Lourdes Beneria. New York: Praeger, 1982.

Miller, Eleanor M. " 'Some Peoples Calls It Crime': Hustling, the Illegal Work of Underclass Women." In *The Worth of Women's Work: A Qualitative Analysis*, edited by Anne Statham, Eleanor M. Miller, and Hans O. Mauksch. Albany: State University of New York Press, 1988.

Muller v. *Oregon.* 208 U.S. 412, 422 (1908).

Murphee, Mary C. "New Technology and Office Tradition: The Not-So-Changing World of the Secretary." In *Computer Chips and Paper Clips: Technology and Women's Employment.* vol. II, edited by Heidi I. Hartmann, Robert E. Kraut, and Louise Tilly. Washington, D.C.: National Academy Press, 1987.

Nash, June, and Fernández-Kelly, María Patricia, editors. *Women, Men, and the International Division of Labor.* Albany: State University of New York Press, 1983.

New York Times. "Excerpts from Harassment Rules." April 12, 1:1 (1980).

Nickel, James W. "Is There a Human Right to Employment?" *The Philosophical Forum* 10 (1978–79):149–70.

Paludi, Michele, ed. *Ivory Power.* Albany: State University of New York Press, 1990.

Posadskaya, Anastasia, et al., editors. *Women in Russia: A New Era in Russian Feminism.* Translated by Kate Clark. London and New York: Verso, 1994.

Powell, B., and Steelman, L. C. "Testing an Undertested Comparison: Maternal Effects on Sons' and Daughters' Attitudes Toward Women in the Labor Force." *Journal of Marriage and the Family* 44 (1982):349–55.

Rix, Sara E., editor. *The American Woman, 1987–88: A Report in Depth.* New York: Norton, 1987.

Rosario, L. M. "The Self-Perception of Puerto Rican Women Toward Their Societal Roles." In *Work, Family and Health: Latina Women in Transition*, edited by R. E. Zambrana. New York: Hispanic Research Center, 1982.

Rosen, Ruth. *The Lost Sisterhood: Prostitution in America, 1900–1918.* Baltimore: Johns Hopkins Press, 1982.

Rotella, Elyce J. "Women's Roles in Economic Life." In *Issues and Feminism: A First Course in Women's Studies*, edited by Sheila Ruth. Boston: Houghton Mifflin, 1980.

Safa, Helen I. "The Differential Incorporation of Hispanic Women Migrants into the United States Labor Force." In *Female Immigrants to the United States: Caribbean, Latin American, and African Experiences.* Occasional Papers No. 2, edited by Delores M. Mortimer and Roy S. Bryce-Laporte. Prepared for the Research Institute on Immigration and Ethnic Studies, Smithsonian Institution, Washington, D.C.: 1981.

Sassen-Koob, Saskia. "Exporting Capital and Importing Labor: The Role of Women." In *Female Immigrants to the United States: Caribbean, Latin American, and African Experiences.* Occasional Papers No. 2, edited by Delores M. Mortimer and Roy S. Bryce-Laporte. Prepared for the Research Institute on Immigration and Ethnic Studies, Smithsonian Institution, Washington, D.C.: 1981.

Sen, Gita, and Grown, Caren. *Development, Crises and Alternate Visions: Third World Women's Perceptions for Development Alternatives with Women for a New Era—DAWN.* London: Earthscan Publications, 1987.

Shahar, Shulamith. *The Fourth Estate: A History of Women in the Middle Ages.* trans. Chaya Galai. London and New York: Methuen, 1983.

Smith, Joan. "The Paradox of Women's Poverty: Wage-earning Women and Economic Transformation." *Signs* 10 (1984):291–310.

Soto, E. S., and Shaver, P. "Sex-role Traditionalism and Assertiveness in Puerto Rican Women Living in the United States." *Journal of Community Psychology* 11 (1983):346–54.

Stellman and Henifin. *Office Work Can Be Danger-*

ous to Your Health. New York: Pantheon, 1983.

Stephen, Cookie W., and Corder, Judy. "The Effects of Dual-Career Families on Adolescents: Sex-role Attitudes, Work and Family Plans, and Choices of Important Others." *Journal of Marriage and the Family* 47 (1985):921–29.

Stromberg, Ann H., and Harkness, Shirley. *Women Working: Theories and Facts in Perspective.* 2nd ed. Mountain View, CA: Mayfield, 1988.

Tinker, Irene. "The Adverse Impact of Development on Women." In *Women and World Development*, edited by Irene Tinker and M. B. Bramson. Washington, D.C.: Overseas Development Council, 1976.

Treiman, Donald J., and Hartmann, Heidi I. *Women, Work, and Wages: Equal Pay for Jobs of Equal Value.* Washington, D.C.: National Academy Press, 1981.

UNDP. *Human Development Report 1993.* New York: Oxford University Press, 1993.

U. S. Bureau of Labor, Department of Labor Statistics. *Employment and Earnings*, January 1993 and other selected years.

U.S. Bureau of the Census, Current Population Reports, P20-459. *The Asian and Pacific Islander Population in the United States: March 1991 and 1990.* U.S. Government Printing Office, Washington, D.C., 1992.

Wallace, Phyllis A., editor. *Black Women in the Labor Force.* Cambridge: MIT Press, 1980.

Washington Post, November 13, 1979.

Wertheimer, Barbara M. *We Were There: The Story of Working Women in America.* New York: Pantheon, 1977.

White, Deborah Gray. *Ain't I A Woman: Female Slaves in the Plantation South.* New York: Norton, 1985.

Woo, Deborah. "The Socioeconomic Status of Asian American Women in the Labor Force: An Alternative View." *Sociological Perspectives* 28:3 (July 1985):307–338.

Woo, Deborah. "The Gap between Striving and Achieving: The Case of Asian American Women." In *Making Waves*, edited by Asian Women United of California. Boston: Beacon Press, 1989.

Zalk, Sue Rosenberg. "Harassment on the Job." *Dental Teamwork* (1991):10–15.

Women and Political Power

There has never been a state government, as far as we know, that was explicitly designed or run according to feminist principles, but feminist utopian writers have revealed, in their imagined alternative societies, both critiques of patriarchal society and visions of new, more just and caring social orders. These writers draw from women's experiences of cooperative organizing to achieve our goals in our families and communities (Garland, 1988; Moser and Peake, 1987). In her review of a number of feminist utopias, Carole Pearson (1977) found that they often depict social orders without government, laws, force, or hierarchy. Decisions in feminist utopian societies tend to be made by consensus, and order is kept not by force but by persuasion.

Sultana's Dream, 1905, a feminist utopia written by an Indian Muslim woman, Rokeya Sakhawat Hossain (1880–1932), was perhaps the earliest published in English. In this utopia, "Ladyland," men have been relegated to purdah (seclusion) within the home and violent crime and wars eliminated. The women of "Ladyland" attend two universities and their research has ended the problems of the environment and society, natural disasters, and poverty.

While such imagined societies have no counterpart in actual human history, governments have varied considerably in the extent to which women have been allowed participation in public power. This chapter will examine these variations in political organization and power, and the roles that women have played in them.

Feminism and Politics

Women are underrepresented in *formal* political participation everywhere in the world. Historically, subordinated groups are closed out of formal institutions and structures. Can direct participation of women in "politics" make a real difference? If women occupied more positions of political power, particularly at the top, would public affairs be different (Diamond, 1977)? Those who would answer yes come from both feminist and sexist camps. The former argue that women's equal participation would lead to greater sensitivity to human interests (an end to war, perhaps), while the latter argue that it would lead to inefficiency and ineffectiveness (such as an inability to make war).

Can women achieve political power without following a male model of success? Can we reshape political power to address women's concerns? Do women, as a group, actually have particular priorities and a common set of values relating to political power? Are we a "class"? On one hand, women belong to dif-

Sultana's Dream (1905)

I became very curious to know where the men were. I met more than a hundred women while walking there, but not a single man.

"Where are the men?" I asked her.

"In their proper places, where they ought to be."

"Pray let me know what you mean by 'their proper places.'"

"Oh, I see my mistake, you cannot know our customs, as you were never here before. We shut our men indoors."

"Just as we are kept in the *zenana?*"*

"Exactly so."

"How funny." I burst into a laugh. Sister Sara laughed too.

"But, dear Sultana, how unfair it is to shut in the harmless women and let loose the men."

"Why? It is not safe for us to come out of the *zenana*, as we are naturally weak."

"Yes, it is not safe so long as there are men about the streets, nor is it so when a wild animal enters a marketplace."

"Of course not."

"Suppose some lunatics escape from the asylum and begin to do all sorts of mischief to men, horses, and other creatures: in that case what will your countrymen do?"

"They will try to capture them and put them back into their asylum."

"Thank you! And you do not think it wise to keep sane people inside an asylum and let loose the insane?"

"Of course not!" said I, laughing lightly.

"As a matter of fact, in your country this very thing is done! Men, who do or at least are capable of doing no end of mischief, are let loose and the innocent women shut up in the *zenana!* How can you trust those untrained men out of doors?"

"We have no hand or management of our social affairs. In India man is lord and master. He has taken to himself all powers and privileges and shut up women in the *zenana.*"

"Why do you allow yourselves to be shut up?"

"Because it cannot be helped as they are stronger than women."

"A lion is stronger than a man, but it does not enable him to dominate the human race. You have neglected the duty you owe yourselves, and you have lost your natural rights by shutting your eyes to your own interests."

"But my dear Sister Sara, if we do everything by ourselves, what will the men do then?"

"They should not do anything, excuse me; they are fit for nothing. Only catch them and put them into the *zenana.*"

"But would it be very easy to catch and put them inside the four walls?" said I. "And even if this were done, would all their business—political and commercial—also go with them into the *zenana?*"

Sister Sara made no reply. She only smiled sweetly. Perhaps she thought it was useless to argue with one who was no better than a frog in a well.

*The *zenana* is the women's living quarters in a household.

ferent social classes, traditionally defined by the class membership of our fathers or husbands. On the other hand, all women have a common relationship to the economic system, regardless of social class membership. With a few exceptions, we own—or control—little or no capital, and we contribute free labor for basic social maintenance—household management and reproduction—all of which are seen as our "private" responsibility. All women suffer discrimination by virtue of our gender in jobs and social benefits. Does this make women a "class"? Feminist legal theorist Catharine MacKinnon argues that there is only one "unmodified" feminism: Women are at the bottom, irrespective of race or class or mode of production (MacKinnon, 1987).

Politics and the "Public" Sphere

Feminists trained in political science have begun to examine the history and theoretical assumptions that characterize scholarship in this field. Paula Baker, for example, in her study of late-nineteenth-century rural New York, found two very different political cultures. Men's public activity involved loyalty to a particular political party and voting for its candidates on the basis of their character and willingness to work for their friends rather than on their stands on issues and programs. In contrast, women participated in nonpartisan voluntary associations, organized around specific concerns. What women did in the public arena was not viewed by men as "politics" (Baker, 1987). It is "politics" as defined by men that continues to be privileged.

Most political scientists, being largely middle class and male, have viewed women as of little consequence to their concerns (Freeman, 1976). In their ideology, "politics" is what takes place in the "public" sphere of life, and political activity is identified as inherently "masculine." Traits said to characterize a proper citizen in a liberal democracy, for ex-

ample, include qualities identified in the culture of the United States as "masculine": individualistic, independent, aggressive, competitive (Freeman, 1976; Reverby and Helly, 1992). In contrast, "feminine" traits are identified as egalitarian, caring, pacific, and cooperative. The "citizen" with whom most male political scientists identify is in their own image. They define what women do in public as philanthropic or public service work, not "real politics." On occasion, women's politics in the public arena have even been viewed as "disorderly conduct" (Lebsock, 1992). Hence, feminists have advocated for formal political participation, in part to change its male-centered and male-dominated construction.

American political scientists who have studied women's political behavior have measured our voting performance, our participation in political campaigns and political parties, and our presence in political office. On all counts, women have been found less visible than men. When women express opinions about public issues, we are assumed to have borrowed them from fathers or husbands. Women have been characterized as more conservative and emotional than men and immature in conceptualizing the political realm (Freeman, 1976). When women vote, we are described as "gullible," responding to the candidate's surface personality and easily duped by media images. Women's lack of visibility in politics in the past is explained away as the direct consequence of our domestic roles and our reproductive function (Lovenduski, 1981). In short, our place is in the "private" sphere to which, it has been said, our temperament and "nature" are better suited. Feminist social scientists have a different viewpoint and are exploring the roles women play in formal and grass roots or community-level organizations, women's leadership styles, intraparty roles and power, and how women organize on issues we consider important (Bookman and Morgen, 1988).

Women Do Not Belong in the Public Sphere

Mr. Justice Bradley:

The civil law, as well as nature herself, has always recognized a wide difference in the respective spheres and destinies of man and woman. Man is or should be woman's protector and defender. The natural and proper timidity and delicacy which belongs to the female sex evidently unfits it for many of the occupations of civil life. The constitution of the family organization, which is founded in the divine ordinance, as well as in the nature of things, indicates the domestic sphere as that which properly belongs to the domain and functions of womanhood. The harmony, not to say identity, of interests and views which belong or should belong to the family institution, is repugnant to the idea of a woman adopting a distinct and independent career from that of her husband . . .

. . . It is true many women are unmarried and not affected by any other duties, complications, and incapacities arising out of the married state, but these are exceptions to the general rule. The paramount destiny and mission of women are to fulfill the noble and benign offices of wife and mother. This is the law of the Creator. And the rules of civil society must be adapted to the general constitution of things, and cannot be based upon exceptional cases.

. . . In my opinion, in view of the peculiar characteristics, destiny, and mission of women, it is within the province of the legislature to ordain what offices, positions, and callings shall be filled and discharged by men and shall receive the benefit of those energies and responsibilities, and that decision and firmness which are presumed to predominate in the sterner sex.

(*Bradwell* v. *Illinois*, 1873, in Goldstein, 1979:49–51)

"The Personal Is Political"

Consciousness-raising efforts of the women's movement of the late 1960s and early 1970s made women, and sometimes men, aware of the political components of our personal lives. A power differential pervades the relations between women and men. The artificial distinction between a "public" sphere of politics and a "private" sphere of domestic life obscures the inescapable fact that excluding women from the public sphere deprives us of control over our presumably private existence. The spheres are, in fact, so linked that in order for changes to take place in the private relations between women and men, it may be necessary to make changes in the political structure of society.

Public laws, made and enforced largely by men, have determined women's sexual and reproductive rights by defining marriage, when sexual relations are or are not legal, and whether a woman must continue a pregnancy. Because it was assumed to be a "private" matter, domestic violence was largely ignored by "public" law enforcement, and the seriousness of rape minimized, except of "our" women by a subordinate minority. Public policy, made largely by men, determines women's rights and obligations to our children and women's ability to carry out our wishes with regard to our children's care, education, and safety. Public policy also restricts and shapes women's rights and capacities to select ways to support ourselves, and it determines the conditions under which we work. In other words, nearly everything we have been brought up to regard as personal is a matter of public concern. To the extent that the private sphere has been the domain of women, and the public sphere has been the domain of men, politics has been a means for men to control women's lives.

Feminist legal theorists of color have expanded the critique on the concept of separate public/private spheres. Kimberle Crenshaw (1991) argues for an intersectional approach to domination that incorporates racism and sexism. The dualism of "masculinity" and "femininity" as described above (Crenshaw, 1991; see also A. Harris, 1991; Williams, 1991) does not reflect the complexity of the African American experience. African American women are generally stereotyped as overly assertive, while African American men lack

the power that white men have to control their own lives.

This is not to say that men's private lives are not also politically controlled. Nor do all men have an equal opportunity to participate in the determination of public policy, laws, and enforcement. Many feminists of this and the last century have been particularly sensitive to the exclusion of anyone—male or female—from power on the basis of race, ethnicity, sexual orientation, and class. Yet, while feminists have been conspicuous in the abolitionist, socialist, and civil rights movements, male support from these movements for feminists' goals has not been prominent.

In the civil rights and antiwar movements of the 1960s, women's place was in the kitchen

As a black woman and a Congressional Representative elected from Texas, Barbara Jordan was well prepared to deliver the keynote address at the first plenary session of the National Women's Conference held in Houston, Texas, November 18–21, 1977. In her remarks she said, "American history is peppered with efforts by women to be recognized as human beings and as citizens and to be included in the whole of our national life." (*The Spirit of Houston*, Washington, D.C.: March, 1978: 223. Photo by Bettye Lane)

and the bedroom just as it was outside the movement. Women made coffee and sandwiches, provided men with sexual comfort, and were excluded from central decision making (Evans, 1980; Brown, 1993). It was the realization that all relations between women and men, including sexual relations, were as political as any relations traditionally so labeled, that led to the saying of the women's movement of the 1970s that "the personal is political."

Political Power

What Is Power?

Power is the capacity to get something done, whether directly or indirectly. Women may exercise power in the domestic sphere in terms of our influence within our families. Men's power, in contrast, is "more co-ordinated and structured within an institutionalized framework" (Ridd and Callaway, 1987:3). Political power is usually exercised by means of institutionalized structures, including the military, the government, the economy, and religious, educational, and legal systems. Such structures protect those who wield power and enable them to disperse their power more widely (ibid.; Hartsock, 1983).

The power that individuals or groups possess involves ". . . a social relationship between groups that determines access to, use of, and control over the basic material and ideological resources in society" (Bookman and Morgen, 1988:4). Except in small-scale agricultural societies (Sanday, 1981), men generally have greater access to and control over resources. Power over others fosters relationships of social distance and subordination.

Power is also the capacity not to do something—not to marry, not to bear or be responsible for a child, not to engage in physical labor, and not to have sexual intercourse when another demands it. Only those who have sufficient power to protect themselves from the aggression of others can ensure they will not be coerced to the will of others.

A particular class, group, or gender may also possess "unintentional power" because of its "position within a set of social structures and arrangements." The benefits of a privileged position belong to all those within the group. Thus, any white person in a racist society possesses greater unintentional power than does a person of color. Similarly, men, regardless of race and class position, have greater unintentional power in a sexist society. Both women and men may exercise the power to persuade, manipulate, or coerce the other gender within a personal or familial relationship, "but the male is the sole possessor of unintentional power within a public meaning having political consequences. When he exerts power, it is considered legitimate—perhaps neither wise nor beneficent, but legitimate" (Elshtain, 1979:246).

Feminists have pointed out that power need not imply dominance. Power—to get things done—can be shared and distributed evenly. This is the notion behind the organizations of most feminist utopias. The sharing of power has been attempted on a small scale in communes and simple societies throughout the world. In a complex industrial society, the sharing of power has been difficult even to imagine. Feminists seek, at the very least, to *reduce* the extent to which society is organized hierarchically, with vast disparities of power between those who command and those who must obey.

Some individuals often conclude that because men have such power over women, women are powerless. But this is not quite true; power is a social relationship. Power can be wielded by the "powerless," despite the fact that they possess fewer resources and must often organize in larger numbers to offset their "powerlessness." As long as the analysis of power and politics is confined to the study of institutions in which fewer female faces are present—in the courts, the bureaucracies, the legislatures, and at the executive levels—women will be perceived as more powerless than we are. A more fruitful approach to gain a better understanding of women and politics would be to look to arenas where women can be found—neighborhoods, schools, associations, and organizations (Bookman and Morgen, 1988; Moser and Peake, 1987; Dalley, 1988; and Cott, 1992.)

Power and Authority

There is an important distinction between *power* and *authority*. Those with authority are accepted as being justified in having power. People who seize power need eventually to find a way of legitimizing it in order to command obedience to decisions without resorting to the continued use or threat of force. Economic power and authority are the ability and accepted right to control the production and distribution of resources; political power and authority are the ability and accepted right to control or influence decisions about war and peace, legal protection and punishment, and group decision making in general, including the assignment of leadership roles. In complex societies, political power usually includes a great deal of economic power, but political and economic power can and do operate separately. Sometimes they function in a complementary way; at other times, they are at odds.

Although power and authority often are exercised by the same person, they are distinct, and each may be exercised without the other. Women have from time to time exercised power (the ability to get someone to do something) but often do not hold authority, due to cultural beliefs that we do not possess a legitimate right to power (O'Barr, 1984).

History provides many examples of women who held power by virtue of our relationships with powerful men. Royal mistresses in the courts of European kings in early modern times even had official status. In the United States in the twentieth century, women married to presidents have occasionally exercised notable political power. When Woodrow Wilson collapsed in office in 1919, his wife, Edith Axson Wilson, played a crucial role in helping him maintain the presidency. Eleanor Roosevelt was able to undertake major humanitarian programs because of her influence over her husband, Franklin Delano Roosevelt, and his associates. When some of her ideas were not endorsed by the president, she pursued them through women's networks (Cook, 1992).

Hillary Rodham Clinton's influence is far reaching and directly public. As an attorney with a distinguished career, she was appointed by her husband, President Bill Clinton, to head a task force to draft a national health care policy for the nation. She is the first "First Lady" to have a visible role in political appointments to the administration.

This kind of political power, the exercise of influence, is difficult to establish or assess. Reference to the power of the "women behind the throne" has often been used by those who wish to justify a status quo in which women have little direct power—or authority—in our own right.

Types of Government

As societies have become larger and more complex, forms of government have become more specialized and exclusionary. Full participation occurs only in the smallest, simplest societies, such as hunting and gathering bands, where political decisions are made by public discussion and consensus. There are no government specialists, and leaders arise in particular situations according to need and skills. An older woman with experience and skill might organize and direct others in food gathering. A good public speaker might assume responsibility for expressing the will of the community.

Similar principles apply in slightly larger and more complex societies, but on a more restricted basis. Some individuals hold positions of authority as "chief" or "war leader" or "council member." In these societies, women tend to be more segregated as a group. If women do play a role in political processes, we tend to do so as *women*, not as ordinary and equal group members. Among the Iroquois in North America, certain women, and not men, were entitled to select male group leaders. Men, on the other hand, were entitled to hold the leadership positions; women were not (Sanday, 1981).

The most complex forms of government are nation-states, which exclude most members of society from direct participation in making governmental decisions. This includes capitalist and socialist nations who both refer to their governments as "democratic." At the higher levels of a hierarchical structure, few can participate. But on the local level, the smaller communities conduct much of their business themselves. Here, participatory democracy may be possible even in a large complex state. It is at the local level where women's voices are most likely to be heard, if at all. For example, women are found in China in public councils in rural communities and in the United States in school boards and town councils and in greater numbers at the level of state legislatures than at the federal level.

Women's Political Power in the Past

Women have occasionally exercised authority and political power in the past, both in dynastic states in Europe and in some preindustrial societies. Such power often derived from our kinship positions as daughters, sisters, wives, and mothers. There was, for example, Queen Nzinga of Angola (?–1663) (White, 1990) and Akyaawa Yi Kwan, an influential queen mother, or *asantehemae* (in her fifties in the 1820s) (Wilks, 1980). The latter became an important mediator between the ruler, or *asantehene*, and British forces, bringing about a peace treaty (White, 1990). During Japan's early history, royal women held powerful po-

---

Queen Nzinga of Seventeenth-Century Angola

The instability of the region allowed an extraordinary woman, Nzinga, to step out of the role most women played to gain control over her own state. Her success stands out particularly because she was able to transform herself from a palace slave into a queen of a new state, Matamba. She began life as a slave in the *Ngola a Kiluanje* palace to the south of Kongo. As a palace slave and half-sister of the last *ngola a kiluanje*, or king, Nzinga was closely related to the sources of power in the Ngola kingdom. . . . The court slaves chose Nzinga as an able emissary to the Portuguese in the early 1620s. . . .

Eventually Nzinga moved to the northwest, where she established herself as queen of Matamba. As a woman, former slave, and immigrant to the region, she could not call on the local matrilineage to establish her power. Instead, she . . . developed a system of military rule. . . . Shifting alliances characterized the region until Nzinga made a final pact with the Portuguese in 1655. Their support enabled her to reign in Matamba until she died in 1663.

(White, 1990:58–59)

sitions as imperial rulers; between the sixth and seventh centuries 50 percent of the rulers in the imperial family were women (Sievers, 1990; Sugisaki, 1986).

In the early Middle Ages in Europe, when a ruler's officials were actually royal household servants (and the head of the household governed the domestic affairs of the royal estate, which was the kingdom), it was considered perfectly natural to place the ruler's wife, or queen, at the head of these servants. When Henry II of England went to war (which was a great deal of the time), he left his queen, Eleanor of Aquitaine (1122?–1204), in charge of his kingdom. All his officials were ordered to report to her whenever he was away. As regents for their husbands or sons, queens could wield significant political power. Only when Henry II began to suspect that his queen favored their sons over him did he discontinue making her England's ruler in his absence (Kelly, 1957).

As the governments of European states and elsewhere became more bureaucratically organized, women were less likely to share in political power. The recognized offices that might have been delegated to the queen gradually shifted to ministers, judges, councilors, and other functionaries, who were never women. Even in the reign of Queen Elizabeth I (1533–1603), who governed by virtue of inherited right, not a single woman was ever appointed to a ministerial post (Neale, 1957).

Similarly, European colonial rule precipitated erosion of women's power where it had existed. Among the Iroquois of North America, for example, both women and men participated in village decision making. Women were entitled to demand publicly that a murdered relative be replaced by a captive from a non-Iroquoian tribe and male relatives were morally obligated to join a war party to secure captives. Women also appointed men to official positions in the League of the Iroquois and could veto their decisions, although men controlled League deliberations. Women dominated village life and left interethnic affairs to men, exercising separate but equal political power during the height of the Iroquois confederacy (Sanday, 1981).

In the early nineteenth century, after a steady encroachment on their power by the colonizing British and French over a period of two hundred years, the Iroquois became unable to sustain themselves economically. English Quakers, who actually sought to preserve the Iroquoian culture, suggested solutions that fundamentally restructured Iroquoian gender relationships. Quaker missionaries urged men to cultivate the soil, a sphere hitherto dominated by women. They also insisted on husband-wife nuclear family relationships, which shut out the traditional power of the wife's mother in the family. In imposing their own cultural assumptions, the Quakers helped develop a new pattern of male dominance where it had not existed before (ibid.).

Another example of the erosion of women's political power under colonial rule is that of the Igbo of southern Nigeria in West Africa where precolonial social arrangements included women's councils. By tradition, these councils exercised peacekeeping powers, including the corporal punishment and public humiliation of the offender and the destruction of the offender's property. Local women's councils had no formal links with one another, but Igbo women maintained a network of rapid communication through an overlapping presence in different marketplaces each week (ibid.).

British colonial rule in the late nineteenth century disrupted these cultural patterns, which had afforded women real power. British authorities bypassed women's councils as irrelevant and created new "warrant" chiefs where none had existed, giving the position to local men. After imposing a new tax on all males, the colonial government proposed to take a census of women, children, and animals to assess other taxable wealth. When the local "warrant" chief sought to carry out this task, he tangled with an elderly woman who put up a fight to resist him. Her call for help went out along the women's network, and women from everywhere marched to her aid. The women punished the offending chief, mobbing him, damaging his house, and demanding that he lose his cap of office and be arrested by the British district officer for assaulting the elderly woman. The incident turned into a "war" when some ten thousand women attacked British property—some stores and a bank—released prisoners from the jail, and generally rioted for two days before being dispersed by troops. When an official investigation was conducted, the women were reported as saying, "We are not so happy as we were before. . . . Our grievance is that the land is changed—we are all dying" (ibid.:139–40; Van Allen, 1976; Ifeka-Moller, 1977). What had been "dying" was women's public power.

Patterns of Male Dominance

Anthropologist Ernestine Friedl has defined male dominance as a pattern in which men have better access, if not exclusive rights, to those activities to which society accords the greatest value and by which control and influence are exercised over others (Sanday, 1981). Thus male dominance means excluding women from political and economic decision making and includes aggression against women.

Male dominance occurs in various patterns of social relationships. It may consist of cultural assumptions about natural male aggressiveness, about being "tough" and "brave." It may involve designating specific places where only males may congregate, like men's clubs and bars, street corners, legislative chambers, courts, or boardrooms. It may involve wife-

beating and battering (Gordon, 1988). It may result in murder, as in India where "bride burning" has increased in recent years with husbands seeking to remarry to acquire another dowry. Still other patterns exist in "raiding" enemy groups for wives. The Yanomamo Indians of Brazil and Venezuela practiced warfare for the purpose of abducting women up through the 1960s (Chagnon, 1983). Then there is the regular occurrence of rape (and sometimes its institutionalization as gang rape). The ethnic group rape of Muslim women of Bosnia and Croatia in 1992 and 1993 by Serbian men as part of a general policy of "ethnic cleansing" is an extreme example of the extent to which male dominance is rationalized as a condition of warfare. This pattern of control reminds us that although women may wield some political and economic power and authority, we do so by the implicit or explicit consent of men, not from an independent power base or because of authority invested in women as such.

Women as Political Leaders

Throughout history, women leaders have emerged. In modern times such powerful female political figures have included Margaret Thatcher (England), Indira Gandhi (India), Benazir Bhutto (Pakistan), Eva Perón (Argentina), Gro Harlem Bruntland (Norway), Sirimarvo Bandaranaike (Sri Lanka), Corazon Aquino (Philippines), Golda Meir (Israel), and Eugenia Charles (Dominica). In the early 1990s, Bangladesh, Poland, Nicaragua, Canada, and Turkey elected women as heads of state. While it is rare to see women at the summit of power, increasingly we are taking our places in national, state, and local politics.

Generally, there is an inverse relationship between higher political offices and the presence of women in those offices. Universally, there are many more women in lower-level political offices than in high political offices.

On the average, women comprise 10 percent of national legislatures and 7 percent of executive cabinet ministers worldwide. Table 14.1 reveals that the most promising picture comes from the Scandinavian countries, with their mixed economies, and their concerns for both social welfare and fairness. Socialist and former socialist states also have made great efforts to recruit women into national legislatures. However, these bodies are more cosmetic than functional as the important policies are made by the central committees where few women sit. In the Middle East, South Asia, and Africa, women are the least likely to be found in high-level political positions.

The few women who hold high cabinet positions are most likely to be housed within traditional women's fields, such as health and welfare, education, culture, the family, and consumer affairs (Randall, 1987). Worldwide, women are ignored when it comes to certain ministerial positions: defense, treasury, or foreign affairs, despite the fact that highly capa-

Table 14.1 Women in National Legislature and Executive Offices in 1987

Country	National Legislature %	Executive Offices %	Country	National Legislature %	Executive Offices %
Western Europe			East Asia		
Austria	12	6	China	21	5
Denmark	29	4	Indonesia	9	—
France	6	3	Japan	3	0
R. of Germany	15	5	N. Korea	20	—
Greece	4	0	S. Korea	3	4
Norway	34	19	Philippines	4	7
Portugal	8	5	Africa		
Spain	6	0	Algeria	2	0
Sweden	29	25	Cameroon	14	3
United Kingdom	6	4	Ghana	—	—
Eastern Europe			Kenya	2	0
Bulgaria	22	4	Mauritius	6	5
D.R. of Germany	32	2	Mozambique	16	5
Hungary	31	0	Senegal	12	7
Poland	25	—	Tunisia	6	2
U.S.S.R.	33	0	Zimbabwe	9	7
Middle East			North America		
Iraq	6	—	Canada	10	6
Israel	8	—	United States	5	12
Jordan	0	4	South America		
Saudi Arabia	—	—	Argentina	5	2
United Arab Emirates	0	—	Bolivia	4	0
South Asia			Cuba	34	3
India	7	—	Dominican Republic	5	0
Nepal	5	—	Paraguay	2	0
Sri Lanka	3	7	Trinidad & Tobago	17	13
			Venezuela	4	5

0 = None or negligible— = Not available
Source: U.N. *The World's Women 1970–1990 Trends and Statistics.* New York: United Nations, 1992. Inc. 1985

ble women can be found in these traditionally male-dominated fields.

Recent Political Gains of Women in the United States

In view of the gender socialization women undergo, the effects of the contemporary women's movement on the pattern of female officeholding are striking. Women's increased political participation in 1992 was largely a result of our deciding it was time to change the face of the U. S. Congress and the state legislatures. National attention was given to the dominance of white males in Congress and their male bias during the Senate hearings to confirm Clarence Thomas as nominee to the U.S. Supreme Court in 1991. Angered by the insensitive treatment of both Anita Hill and the issue of sexual harassment by an all-white male Senate Committee, women entered the political arena with a new energy. Many more women decided to run for office. Many more made financial contributions. In addition, we feared the further erosion of specific rights, for example, our reproductive rights.

Women's alienation from the male-centered politics and policies of the 1980s contributed to a "gender gap." It was after the 1980 election that analysts began to note significant differences between women and men in political viewpoints, party identification, and voting decisions. Women have been registering in increasing numbers as Democrats rather than as Republicans, and in the 1980, 1984, 1988, and 1992 presidential elections equaled or exceeded men in voter turnout rates. In public opinion polls, women ex-

Table 14.2 Women Candidates for the U.S. Congress 1970–1992

	Party and Seat Summary for Democratic and Republican Party Nominees*			
	Senate		House of Representatives	
	Candidates	Winners	Candidates	Winners
1970	1 (1R)	0	25(15D,10R)	12 (9D,3R)
1972	2 (2R)	0	32(24D,8R)	14(12D,2R)
1974	3 (2D,1R)	0	44(30D,14R)	18(14D,4R)
1976	1 (1D)	0	54(34D,20R)	18(13D,5R)
1978	2 (1D,1R)	1(1R)	46(27D,19R)	16(11D,5R)
1980	5 (2D,3R)	1(1R)	52(27D,25R)	19(10D,9R)
1982	3 (1D,2R)	0	55(27D,28R)	21(12D,9R)
1984	10 (6D,4R)	1(1R)	65(30D,35R)	22(11D,11R)
1986	6 (3D,3R)	1(1D)	64 (30D,34R)	23(12D,11R)
1988	2 (2R)	0	59 (33D,26R)	25(14D,11R)
1990	8 (2D,6R)	1(1D)	69†(39D,30R)	28†(19D,9R)
1992	11(10D,1R)	5(5D)	106‡(70D,36R)	47‡(35D,12R)

*Includes major party nominees for the general elections, not those running in special elections.
†Does not include a Democratic candidate for nonvoting delegate of Washington, D.C., who won her race.
‡Does not include 2 (1D, 1R) candidates, 1 incumbent who won her race and 1 challenger for nonvoting delegate of Washington, D.C.
Source: National Information Bank on Women in Public Office, Center for the American Woman and Politics (CAWP), Eagleton Institute of Politics, Rutgers University, 1992.

pressed greater dissatisfaction than men with the presidencies of Ronald Reagan and George Bush and favored public policies that support the protection of the environment, less militaristic resolutions to disputes, and programs for quality health care, racial equality, and family support. As women, we concluded that new legislators, particularly women legislators, were needed: 1992 became known as the "Year of the Woman" (Abzug, 1984; Center for the American Woman and Politics, 1992). Table 14.2 demonstrates the increased representation of women Democrats and Republicans, the two major political parties in the United States, as candidates and winners for Congress in the period 1970–1992.

The 1992 election gave us the largest number of women to serve in the Senate simultaneously to date: six, more than the previous four, including the first African American woman, Carol Mosely Braun, of Illinois. We enlarged our numbers in the House of Representatives from the previous election, increasing from twenty-eight to forty-eight with twenty-four returning incumbents and twenty-four newly elected women, including one nonvoting delegate, Eleanor Holmes Norton, from the District of Columbia. Of these representatives, thirteen are women of color: nine African American women, where it had been formerly four; three Latinas, which was an increase of two; and one Asian Pacific American woman. Shirley Chisholm (D-New York), elected in 1968 and serving until 1983, was the first African American Congresswoman (See **Shirley Chisholm: "I'm a Politician."**) Elected first in a special election in August 1989, and reelected in 1990 and 1992, Ileana Ros-Lehtinen (R-Florida) is the first Latina and the first Cuban American, female or male, to be elected. She was joined by Lucille Roybal-Allard (D-California) and Nydia Velazquez (D-New York) in 1992. Patsy Takemoto Mink (D-Hawaii), the first Asian Pacific American woman elected to the House, has a long history of service from 1965 to 1977 and from 1990 through the 1992 election. A second Asian American congresswoman, Patricia Saiki (R-Hawaii), served from 1987 to 1991 (Center for the American Woman and Politics, 1993).

Shirley Chisholm*: "I'm a Politician"

I'm a politician. I detest the word because of the connotations that cling like slime to it. But for want of a better term, I must use it. I have been in politics for 20 years, and in the time I have learned about the role of women in power. And the major thing that I have learned is that women are the backbone of America's political organizations. They are: the letter writers, the envelope stuffers, the telephone answerers; they're the campaign workers and the organizers. . . . When I first announced that I was running for the United States Congress, both males and females advised me, as they had when I ran for the New York State legislature, to go back to teaching—a woman's vocation—and leave the politics to the men.

(In Martin, 1972:148–49)

*The first African American congresswoman, serving from 1968 to 1983, and the first woman to declare her candidacy for the U.S. presidency, in the 1972 election.

Women have been even more successful in state legislatures, where our presence has increased fivefold over the past two decades. From 301 legislators in 1969, or 4 percent of the total, we have grown to 1,516 in 1993, or 20.4 percent of the total state legislators. While the increase of women is significant, in 1993, women were still only 6 percent of the Senate, 10.8 percent of the House of Representatives, and 20.4 percent of state legislatures. It remains to be seen to what extent women's presence, women's voices, and women's priorities make a difference (Kathlene, 1992).

Do Women in Office Make a Difference?

If women make a difference, what kind of difference do we make in office? Irrespective of political party or label, women officeholders generally take more feminist positions on women's issues than our male colleagues. Studies conducted of women parliamentarians in Europe provide corroborative support for this argument (Randall, 1987). Women officeholders are more open and inclusive than our male counterparts. In place of carrying out business behind closed doors, women favor involving the general public in the political process and providing increased access to constituent groups often left out of policy-making (Center for the American Woman and Politics, 1991, 1992; Kathlene, 1992). In a study of Colorado's House of Representatives in 1989, Lyn Kathlene also noted that female legislators sponsored more "innovative" legislation rather than simply modified or updated existing laws as was the tendency of male legislators (Kathlene, 1992). Women legislators also willingly work collectively across party lines to accomplish specific goals. Former New York Congresswoman Bella Abzug found greater support among her female colleagues, both Democrats and Republicans,

than from the male members of her own party on issues of concern to women (Abzug, 1984).

Women are, in short, changing the way government works, how politics is conducted, and reshaping the public agenda. Nonetheless, Congresswoman Patricia Schroeder of Colorado expressed her difficulties as recently as 1992 with getting legislation through a male-dominated legislature. Women in office have faced greater problems than male colleagues in getting access to information, influence, and avenues of advancement (Githens and Prestage, 1977).

Obstacles Facing Women in Politics

Why is there a dearth of women in political office? The reasons have to do both with the supply (women) and the demand (the institutions themselves). Because we have been socialized to think in terms of a public/private dichotomy that locates women in the domestic sphere, we do not expect women to hold political decision-making positions. The question raised about female, but not male, candidates is: "Who is taking care of the family?" As a result, social norms and expectations about women's proper roles still act as a brake to recruitment into politics and political advancement.

It is also more difficult for women to devote the time to running for and holding political office or even to acquire the direct political experience of men of a comparable age given that we bear the brunt of family and child care. Many women and men do not think it is "proper" for us to run for public office at any age. If interested in formal politics, we tend to become involved at the organizational and support level for other candidates (Lee, 1977).

Institutional impediments compound women's situational and socialization barriers to political office. Traditionally, male politicians have sought campaign funds from business and community leaders who are interested in backing candidates as a way of establishing future access to them. Women candidates face difficulties in finding backers, raising funds, and creating large-scale organizations of devoted followers who see possible benefits in our election.

In part to overcome this particular obstacle, EMILY ("early money is like yeast") was founded in 1982 to support prochoice Democratic women candidates through raising money to launch campaigns in the first stages. EMILY's List is a network of donors and was one of the largest contributors in the 1992 election. If traditional financial backers do not take women seriously as political candidates, irrespective of our political philosophies, women are creating our own opportunities to fund ourselves.

If women's issues are to be dealt with effectively, more women must seek political office at every level of government, and do so again and again. This is the lesson taught us by the failure to ratify the Equal Rights Amendment in the United States in 1982. The political circumstances that have brought a lone woman to a place of high political authority, like Margaret Thatcher in England, Golda Meir in Israel, and Indira Gandhi in India, have resulted in producing women leaders of anomalous gender positions. Only significant numbers of women at the highest levels will ensure that women of strong feminist beliefs will be among them. At such time, the standards of leadership—social change, empowerment, and collective action—identified by Helen Astin and Carole Leland (1991) among women leaders who worked for educational and social justice in the United States from the 1960s through the 1980s, are likely to become more commonplace for both men and women.

Women as Citizens

Women have been subject to the decisions of male political leaders and to a male model of citizenship. In this section, we examine women's political subordination in terms of our historical absence from combat warfare, the pattern of women's subjection to man-made laws, and women's participation in voluntary associations.

Women and War

Many of the explanations, both popular and scientific, for the widespread political subordination of women are connected with the observation that we lack physical strength and rarely engage directly in combat warfare. More often, women are the victims of war; we are killed, maimed, raped, and captured. Because women have not entered into combat, we rarely participated in councils of war and relatively few have shared in any "spoils" of war or special (veteran) postwar benefits.

The effects of war on women may extend far beyond the denial of a voice in government. Anthropologist Marvin Harris, for example, has argued that the "male supremacy complex" is a direct product of warfare. He points to the high degree of correlation between institutionalized female subordination and polygyny, female infanticide, and endemic warfare in tribal societies. In simpler societies, population pressure led people to fight one another for limited environmental resources. As these groups came to depend on male aggression for their survival, they came to value aggression and not nurturance, and men rather than women. A wide variety of institutions and beliefs were developed to foster and encourage male aggressiveness, including, for example, polygyny as a reward for male success. At the same time, the devaluation of women and feminine activities fostered such practices as female infanticide and institutions for the subordination and control of women (Harris, 1977).

During World War I (1914–1918) and World War II (1939–1945), women in North

America and Europe were recruited to work in supporting industries and were given much encouragement, relatively high pay, and other social rewards for our patriotic contribution to the war effort. Women in the United States were provided with opportunities to develop new skills by enlisting in the Women's Army Corps, the Women Marines, the Women's Army Air Corps, the WAVEs, and the Coast Guard SPARS during World War II, in part, to free men for combat. Many volunteers were lesbians. For the most part, the armed services sought to manage homophobia—against both lesbians and gays—during the war. However, after producing food, building machines, and working in dangerous occupations such as field nurses, ambulance drivers, and resistance fighters in enemy-occupied territory, when the men came home, women were encouraged to return to the household. "Rosie the Riveter" became "Betty Crocker." And lesbians, like gays who chose not to return to a former life in a small town, began to form communities primarily in large cities (Berube, 1990). Lesbians who remained in the military in peacetime faced increased repression and the likelihood of a dishonorable discharge in spite of years of dedicated service.

Women have served as fighting soldiers, as documented in antiquity and in modern times, but these instances have been exceptional. The biblical figure Deborah was a general, as was Joan of Arc in France in the fifteenth century. The modern armies of Israel and Vietnam train all their women in combat duties, although women soldiers have rarely been deployed in actual combat. Women fighters are more commonly found in the informal armies of rebellions, revolutions, and resistance movements as in the Warsaw Ghetto uprising, the French Resistance of World War II, the Algerian Revolution, the Chinese Revolution, Zimbabwe's war for independence, and revolutions in Nicaragua during the twentieth century. Typically in postrevolutionary societies, women revolutionaries are often told to return to traditional duties of wife and mother. For example, Zimbabwean women who fought violently and valiantly for independence have since received discriminatory treatment in the allocation of plots of land awarded to those who fought in the war (Jacobs, 1984).

Wars today no longer depend on physical strength, which disqualified most women previously. Some modern armies employ women on a regular basis for combat warfare using high technology, such as piloting jet fighters or operating long-range missile installations. American women largely serve in the armed forces in the same positions we do in civilian life: as clerical staff and nurses. More recently,

---

"War Is a Man's Work"

On the question of the admission of women to combat positions in the United States Marines, General Robert H. Barrow has remarked, "War is a man's work. Biological convergence on the battlefield would not only be dissatisfying in terms of what women could do, but it would be an enormous psychological distraction for the male, who wants to think that he's fighting for that woman somewhere behind, not up there in the foxhole with him. It tramples the male ego. When you get right down to it, you have to protect the manliness of war."

(Lloyd, 1986)

women have been admitted to the West Point Military Academy, which produces the highest-ranking army officers, and to the other service academies (Stiehm, 1981). Women were first employed in a war zone during the Persian Gulf War in 1990–91, although none were in direct combat.

Some people feel that if women are to receive equal rights and benefits, women must assume equal responsibilities; if men get drafted, so should women. Others argue that no one should be drafted, nor should anyone go to war—women or men. Many also argue that *until* women are granted equality, we should not have to bear the burden of military service in addition to our other burdens. The U.S. Supreme Court decided (*Rostker* v. *Goldberg*, 1981) that it was constitutional for Congress to call for the registration of men and not women, but the issues raised by the question go to the heart of gender relationships and the issues of autonomy and power.

Does the willingness of women who are career military officers to serve in combat in wartime and the willingness of governments to permit them to do so portend a change in women's participation in warfare in the future? Will our presence and perspectives make a difference in the conduct and strategy of warfare?

Women and the Law

Laws are the governing rules of every human society. The "law" is sometimes conceived to be a force above the vagaries of human will and impulse, an almost divine, implacable, impersonal force. In fact, laws have a history, just as people do. They develop from several sources: ancient custom, legislative bodies, judicial decisions, and administrative agencies.

Feminists are asking new questions about the function of law in society. A feminist jurisprudence is evolving that views the law as a social construction of male dominance.

Catharine MacKinnon argues that "the law sees and treats women the way men see and treat women" (MacKinnon, 1991:186). Critical race theorists also conclude that the law is inherently racist. Hence Mari Matsuda (1989) seeks a jurisprudential method that would incorporate a "multiple consciousness" to give voice to those historically rendered silent and invisible in the law, for example, because of race, sex, class, sexual orientation, or physical abilities.

In its regulation of the family, the law's concern has been to create a space in which the male head of the household can exercise power and authority (O'Donovan, 1981). By viewing women as belonging to a "private" domestic sphere, the men who make and interpret laws, like the men who theorize about political power, act on assumptions that make women less than full legal citizens and political beings. These assumptions about women's rightful place are intimately linked to the patriarchal political philosophies that underpin our societies (Okin, 1979). For example, laws have existed that explicitly commanded husbands and fathers to control their families. Colonial Americans used ducking stools, stocks, and other instruments of humiliation and torture to correct women found guilty of scolding, nagging, or disturbing the peace with our clamor. When women are thus classified as a group, we are subject to gender-based social policies, and our social roles are reinforced by political and legal sanctions.

Traditional moral codes have been based on a double standard for women and men that has affected criminal law and a large amount of civil law, especially family law. Moreover, the laws, a society's moral code, and popular conceptions of social norms reinforce each other. Lawmakers and those who enforce the law start from an idea of what the "normal" family is. They act on the basis of their notions of what women are like and ought to do, and their unexamined assumptions about what women need and want. Anyone who does not conform to their assumptions is either treated as invisible (as battered wives, incest victims, and working female heads of households tend to be) or is sought out and made the object of pressures to conform (as are lesbians and "welfare mothers").

In studying the lives of young working-class and poor African American women, sociologist Joyce Ladner (1972) has pointed out that our lives are in large part governed by laws, customs, and restrictions that are based on a white middle-class male perception of what is normal and what is deviant. For example, until recently, white middle-class norms associated "working mothers" with deviance, yet it was very common for African American mothers to hold jobs.

Based on a double standard of sexual morality, laws have treated prostitutes as "deviant," labeling such women "criminals," but have considered male customers of female prostitutes to be "normal" men indulging a natural appetite. Laws have customarily treated adultery as a serious crime when committed by women, while it is often disregarded when committed by men. The prejudice in favor of the "unwritten law," which excuses husbands who murder adulterous wives, is still not entirely eradicated from society's practice of law.

The law still acts to oppress women and treat us unfairly in many ways. Laws regulate women's reproductive rights. Lawmakers determine the respective priorities of health services, day care centers, education, job creation, and the defense budget. The government shapes welfare regulations that may force women to choose between husbands and money to feed our children.

Women as Interpreters and Enforcers of the Law. We have already pointed out the low levels of representation of women in legislative bodies (which introduce and pass laws) worldwide. In the United States, laws are interpreted by local judges, whose decisions can be overturned by judges at higher federal levels. At each level, women judges are rare, although our numbers are increasing. In the U.S. Supreme Court, there had never been a woman judge until the appointment of Sandra Day O'Connor in 1981. She was joined by Ruth Bader Ginsburg in 1993. Women are also underrepresented in police forces everywhere. Thus, a woman criminal is likely to be a person arrested and taken into custody by male police officers, to be tried by a male judge, and accused and defended by male lawyers for having broken a law made by male legislators (Adler, 1975; Smart, 1978; Chesney-Lind, 1986).

Women's Voluntary Associations

Prior to achieving the vote for women in the United States, women's primary form of political participation was the voluntary association, which we continue to utilize. Women had, in fact, little choice if we wanted to effect change in the political arena. Women's organizations have lobbied the government and other institutions, effectively innovating the strategy of pressure-group politics, now a commonly recognized political practice in the United States (Lebsock, 1990; Cott, 1990; Scott, 1991).

In the 1790s, women organized societies to assist the poor. In the antebellum period, women organized against the evils of alcohol, the most notable organization being the Women's Christian Temperance Union. Women called for the abolition of slavery, educational opportunities for women, better working conditions, and help for "fallen" women. Beginning in the 1860s, women developed the club movement culminating in such national organizations as the National Council of Jewish Women, 1893; the National Association of Colored Women, 1896; the National Association of Collegiate

Women, 1896; and the National Congress of Mothers, 1897, which later became the PTA (ibid).

In the twentieth century, radical women became pacificists and socialists led by Emma Goldman (1869–1940) and Elizabeth Gurley Flynn (1890–1964). Others supported Margaret Sanger (1879–1966) in her campaign for legalizing birth control. When the labor movement resisted women's participation, we formed the National Women's Trade Union League (NWTUL) in 1903. The NWTUL supported the woman suffrage campaign. The campaign became a movement with about 2 million members at the time the National American Woman Suffrage Association (NAWSA) was formed in 1917. Women organized to reform the city and the evils of industrialization, and to prevent the exploitation of children, working women, and immigrants. In this regard, we helped lay the foundation for the modern welfare state (Lebsock, 1990).

Bettina Aptheker (1989) has summarized the "lesbian connection" brought to light by new historical studies on women's organizations. Deeply embedded in the reform efforts of abolitionists, educators, club members, labor organizers, founders of settlement houses, suffragists, and civil rights and peace activists were women who shared emotional and political bonds, and most important, who envisioned a different kind of social structure, one that was woman-centered and caring.

Formal histories have also tended to ignore the importance of grass roots activism. Patricia Hill Collins has written about definitions of power and resistance and of the activist traditions in the African American community. She emphasizes the individual and group actions "that directly challenge the legal and customary rules governing African-American women's subordination . . ." (Collins, 1991:142). Bernice McNair Barnett has explored the leadership qualities displayed by many ordinary African American women in the South during the civil rights movement of the 1950s and 1960s, looking beyond the women (and men) whose names are usually singled out (Barnett, 1993).

Women and Peace Movements. Women have expressed our political disagreement with many men about the excessive use of force, the priority given to militarism versus social agendas, and the effects of nuclear weapons on societies. Peace has been one issue around which women have historically utilized voluntary associations.

In the last two centuries, especially in Europe and the United States, women have organized a number of national and international peace societies. In the late nineteenth century, international socialist leaders Clara Zetkin (1857–1953) and Rosa Luxembourg (1870–1919) were committed to breaking down national borders and ending military competition between nations, positions that were not always taken by their male colleagues. An Austrian woman, Bertha von Suttner (1843–1914), wrote a major book about disarmament, *Down with Arms* (1894), and suggested the creation of the Nobel peace prize. She received it herself in 1905 (Boulding, 1977). Other significant women recipients have been Alva Myrdal in 1982 for her work to further disarmament and peace in international organizations (Bok, 1991) and Rigoberta Menchu in 1992 for her heroism in opposing the cultural genocide of the Indian peoples of Guatemala (Burgos-Debray, 1984).

Harriet Hyman Alonso has noted that U.S. feminist peace organizations from the 1920s to the present have shared four consistent themes. We make connections between militarism and violence against women; utilize our unique perspective of "motherhood," that is, its values of creation, caring, and sharing to secure a world of greater social justice; seek to be responsible citizens, domestically and globally; and strive for independence from male

518

Sandra Day O'Connor (left) and Ruth Bader Ginsburg. The first woman to sit on the United States Supreme Court, Associate Justice O'Connor breaks an all-male tradition that dates to the founding of the country. Ruth Bader Ginsburg was appointed to the Court in 1993 by President Clinton. (The Supreme Court Historical Society)

Sisters in Struggle: African American Women Civil Rights Leaders

Black women in their homes, churches, social clubs, organizations, and communities throughout the South performed valuable leadership roles during the modern civil rights movement in the United States. Although race, gender, and class constraints generally prohibited their being the recognized articulators, spokespersons, and media favorites, these women did perform a multiplicity of significant leadership roles, such as the initiation and organization of action, the formulation of tactics, and the provision of crucial resources (e.g., money, communication channels, personnel) necessary to sustain the movement. Sisters in struggle, they were empowered through their activism.

. . . In countless ways, Black women who lived and worked in the South in the 1950s and 1960s led the way in the fight against oppression, in spite of and because of their race, gender, and class. The blood, sweat, and tears that they shed generated protest and activism by other disadvantaged groups—women, farm workers, gays and lesbians, the handicapped, welfare rights activists—all of whom have been in profound ways the beneficiaries of the civil rights movement. The roles that they performed, whether at the grass-roots level or behind the scenes, represent profiles in courage and suggest that they were *leaders* in their communities, *leaders* in the day-to-day fight against various forms of oppression, and *leaders* in the modern civil rights movement.

(Barnett, 1993:177)

control in the establishment of women-centered and -run organizations (Alonso, 1993). However, not all women have sought peace. Women's peace organizations have often been challenged by women's patriotic organizations, such as the American War Mothers and the Daughters of the American Revolution, who favored military preparedness and joined other organizations in anticommunist and red-baiting activities (Cott, 1992).

World War I (1914–18) galvanized individual women, particularly suffragists, into forming peace organizations. Jane Addams, founder of the first settlement house in the Chicago slums in the 1890s, became a leader in the women's international peace movement during this war. A cofounder of the Women's International League for Peace and Freedom (WILPF), an organization that remains active to this day, Addams called for a women's peace conference in 1915 and helped to form the Woman's Peace Party (WPP) (Steinson,

1980). Mary Church Terrell, a founder of the National Association of Colored Women, became a member of the WPP's executive committee in 1915 (Alonso, 1993).

During the 1960s, Women Strike for Peace and Another Mother for Peace (now defunct) were founded in response to threats to the world's atmosphere from nuclear testing and to protest United States involvement in Vietnam. One founder of Women Strike for Peace, Bella Abzug, became a congresswoman. Many women who became involved in feminist consciousness-raising in the contemporary women's liberation movement were first active in peace efforts. In the 1970s, Women for Racial and Economic Equality (WREE) linked the concerns of women of color and the poor—including racism, welfare reform, reproductive rights, employment, housing, health care, and others—to peace and the conversion of military expenditures to social ones. WILPF, Women Strike for

Peace, and WREE all have global perspectives and were active in the United Nations Decade for Women (Alonso, 1993; Swerdlow, 1982; Boulding, 1977).

The peace movement has been global. In the early twentieth century, peace was a concern of women's suffrage and internationalist socialist movements worldwide, including the Pan Pacific and Southeast Asia Women's Association and, after World War II, the All Africa Women's Conference and the Federation of Asian Women's Associations (Boulding, 1977).

During the 1980s, women organized the first peace encampment at Greenham Common in 1981 to protest the placement of U.S. Cruise missiles in England (Snitow, 1985); Nordic women sponsored a peace march across Europe; and women of the Pacific Islands campaigned against nuclear testing in the Pacific, which contributes to the high incidence of birth defects and miscarriages among women in the region. In the United States, we have marched on Washington, encircled the Pentagon, petitioned Congress, and sought the closure of nuclear power plants. In our peace organizations, as in our formal politics, women have experienced difficulties in finding time for organizing, in fund-raising, and in meeting opposition to our goals (Alonso, 1993).

Equal Rights

The movement in the United States for the abolition of slavery raised women's consciousness, showing white women that oppression took many forms. Sarah M. Grimké (1792–1873), a leader in the abolitionist movement, was an early champion of women's emancipation. She expressed her feminist views as early as 1837:

All history attests that man has subjugated woman to his will, used her as a means to pro-

mote his selfish gratification, to minister to his sensual pleasures, to be instrumental in promoting his comfort; but never has he desired to elevate her to that rank she was created to fill. He has done all he could to debase and enslave her mind; and now he looks triumphantly on the ruin he has wrought, and says, the being he has thus deeply injured is his inferior. . . . But I ask no favors for my sex. . . . All I ask of our brethren is, that they will take their feet off from our necks and permit us to stand upright on that ground which God designed us to occupy. (Hole and Levine, 1971:4–5)

The Declaration of Sentiments drawn up in Seneca Falls, New York, in 1848, at a meeting to further women's rights reflected the sense of unfinished business women felt as part of a young republican nation dedicated to equality and to the pursuit of happiness for all.

We hold these truths to be self-evident: that all men and women are created equal. . . . The history of mankind is a history of repeated injuries and usurpations on the part of man toward woman. . . . Now, in view of this entire disfranchisement of one-half the people of this country, . . . we insist that they have immediate admission to all the rights and privileges which belong to them as citizens of the United States. (Schneir, 1972:77, 78, 80)

Our right to political personhood remains unfinished business for feminists today.

The Struggle for the Vote

The Thirteenth Amendment brought an end to slavery in the United States in 1865. When feminists attempted to eliminate the word *male* in the proposed Fourteenth Amendment, which would ensure the "rights, privileges, and immunities of citizens" to freed slaves, we were advised by male abolitionists that it was not yet our turn. After decades of unceasing work in the cause of black emancipation, women found that we could count on no support from our male colleagues when the matter concerned women's rights, in this case, the right to vote.

In 1869, Susan B. Anthony (1820–1906) and Elizabeth Cady Stanton (1815–1902) organized the National Woman Suffrage Association (NWSA), devoted to achieving national suffrage by a state-by-state effort to change the law. In 1875, the Supreme Court ruled unanimously that the St. Louis registrar of voters could not be compelled to register Virginia Minor as a voter just because she was a citizen. This court ruling made it clear that only a constitutional amendment could achieve the vote for women. By 1878, the Stanton amendment was introduced into Congress: It was this proposal that would be ratified more than forty years later as the Nineteenth Amendment. In 1890, the National American Woman Suffrage Association (NAWSA) was formed.

To dramatize the hypocrisy of Woodrow Wilson's words when he led the United States into World War I "to make the world safe for democracy," Alice Paul's (1885–1977) suffrage group organized a silent picket in front of the White House in 1916. After several months, demonstrators were forcibly removed by the police for obstructing the public way, and 218 women from twenty-six states were arrested in 1917. In prison, they went on a hunger strike. The government ordered them

Elizabeth Cady Stanton (1815–1902), bottom row, center, with suffragist committee. Although she advocated women's suffrage at Seneca Falls in 1843, Stanton became a politically active leader in the cause only after twenty years of being a wife and mother (of seven). Susan B. Anthony, whose unceasing political agitation on behalf of suffrage was sustained by her longtime friendship with Stanton, is second from the left in the front row. (Culver Pictures, Inc.)

forcibly fed. The courts ordered their release several months later, on the grounds that both arrests and convictions were illegal. Despite last-minute efforts by antisuffrage groups after the war, proclaiming that enfranchising women would open up a Pandora's box of evils, the Nineteenth Amendment was passed by Congress in 1918 and ratified by three-fourths of the state governments by August 26, 1920. Finally, American women could vote.

Women's suffrage was achieved in England after an equally long, but far more militant struggle. In 1918, women age thirty and above were allowed to vote. In 1928, women under thirty were given the vote. Women gained political enfranchisement on equal terms with men as early as 1893 in New Zealand and 1902 in Australia, but only as recently as 1946 in France and 1971 in Switzerland. In some countries, women are still not permitted to vote (United Arab Emirates, Kuwait, Saudi Arabia, and Bahrain).

The Modern Women's Liberation Movement

The origins of the modern women's liberation movement in the United States are usually traced to two strands of feminist activism beginning in the 1960s. The first strand is identified with national organizations and follows a liberal tradition with an emphasis on women's rights. It had its impetus in the National Commission on the Status of Women, chaired by Eleanor Roosevelt. This commission was established in December 1961 by President John F. Kennedy on the advice of Esther Peterson of the Women's Bureau of the U.S. Labor Department, the only woman he appointed to a federal office. She urged this action as a way for Kennedy to pay his political debt to the many women who actively supported his campaign. The commission's report focused on the second-class nature of women's status in the United States and led to the formation of a Citizen's Advisory Council on the Status of Women in 1963 and, by 1967, to fifty state commissions (Freeman, 1976; Hole and Levine, 1971)

Women dissatisfied with our inability to use these commissions to achieve any gains founded the National Organization for Women (NOW) in 1966. NOW was initiated by a group of professional women, as were other associations of women that developed, including the Women's Equity Action League

---

Carrie Chapman Catt Remembers

To get the word *"male"* in effect out of the constitution cost the women of the country 52 years of pauseless campaign . . . during that time they were forced to conduct 56 campaigns of referenda to male voters; 480 campaigns to get [state] legislatures to submit suffrage amendments to voters; 47 campaigns to get state constitutional conventions to write woman suffrage into state constitutions; 277 campaigns to get state party conventions to include woman suffrage planks; 30 campaigns to get presidential party conventions to adopt woman suffrage planks in party platforms, and 19 campaigns with 19 successive Congresses.

(Goldstein, 1979:62)

From *Woman Suffrage and Politics* by Carrie Chapman Catt and Bettie Rogers Shuler (New York: Charles Scribner's Sons, 1923). Reprinted with the permission of Charles Scribner's Sons.

When Woodrow Wilson refused to endorse women's suffrage at the Democratic Party convention in 1916, militant suffrage leaders Harriet Stanton Blatch and Alice Paul stationed pickets in front of the White House in Washington, D.C., around the clock. When the suffrage amendment passed the House of Representatives but not the Senate in January 1919, suffrage leaders again posted pickets, and brought an urn with a perpetual fire. They put up a poster mocking Wilson's defense of democracy abroad while denying it to women at home. Whenever Wilson made such a speech, his words were burned in the fire. (National Archives)

(WEAL) and Federally Employed Women (FEW). Conceived originally as a pressure group to force the government to take seriously the sex discrimination guidelines (Title VII of the 1964 Civil Rights Act) administered by the Equal Employment Opportunity Commission (EEOC), NOW filed a gender discrimination complaint against 1,300 corporations receiving federal funds in 1970. It also became a strong political lobby for many other women's rights issues, including the Equal Rights Amendment, child care centers, and abortion rights (Hole and Levine, 1971; Deitch, 1993).

The second source of the modern women's movement in the United States was a rela-tively younger group active in the civil rights and New Left organizations of the 1960s. More radical and grass roots and local in orientation, these organizations focused on women's liberation and structural change. Young white women from the South and the North, young African American women, mainly from the South, and other women of color from across the nation developed a feminist consciousness working in the ranks of the Student Non-Violent Coordinating Committee (SNCC) in 1963–1964. Women helped run the organization, yet SNCC's top leadership was male. In being relegated to clerical and housekeeping chores, women were made aware of our relative powerlessness in the

NOW Statement of Purpose: 1966

... To take action to bring women into full participation in the mainstream of American society now, exercising all the privileges and responsibilities thereof in truly equal partnership with men.

... We do not accept the traditional assumption that a woman has to choose between marriage and motherhood, on the one hand, and serious participation in industry or the professions on the other.

male-controlled decision-making process (Evans, 1980; Brown, 1993).

Similarly, women who participated in the Students for a Democratic Society (SDS), which had developed in northern states in 1960, found even fewer opportunities than in SNCC to take up much responsibility. The style of the primary male leadership was intellectually competitive and aggressive. Women were viewed as attached to particular men, or as "implementers and listeners" (Evans, 1980:108, 113).

When the male leadership at the National Conference for a New Politics in Chicago in

Left to right, Bella Abzug, Gloria Steinem, and Betty Friedan were in the forefront of the early days of the Women's Liberation Movement in the United States in the 1960s and 1970s. The three women contributed to women's growing political self-confidence.

August 1967 ignored a militant resolution demanding 51 percent of convention votes for women because women numbered 51 percent of the population in the country, the women went home and organized. A paper addressed "To the Women of the Left" was circulated calling on women "to organize a movement for women's liberation" (ibid.:200). Gatherings of women became consciousness-raising groups across the nation. *MS.* magazine, founded in 1971 by Gloria Steinem and others, gave women a growing feminist voice that drew national attention. By the 1970s, the two main strands of events had merged to form a movement of great political significance.

Contemporary lesbian feminist organizations are also identified with the radical feminist tradition of the modern women's movement. Local lesbian feminist communities are linked nationally to form a social movement that provides a collective identity to encourage women to participate in a wide range of social and political activities to challenge all forms of domination (Taylor and Whittier, 1992). The political strength of women was particularly significant in the 1992 national presidential election.

The Equal Rights Amendment (ERA). An important symbol for all parts of the new women's liberation movement was the passage in the U.S. Congress in 1972 of a constitutional amendment guaranteeing equal rights under the law to all regardless of gender. The National Woman's Party first proposed an Equal Rights Amendment (ERA) at the seventy-fifth anniversary conference of the Seneca Falls Convention, in 1923. It was introduced into Congress that year, and repeatedly, for the next forty years. The proposed amendment was controversial even among women in public political life. For example, the Women's Bureau of the U.S. Department of Labor, established in 1920, opposed the amendment on the grounds that it would invalidate the protective labor legislation of the early twentieth century. The Women's Party, however, believed

---

Consciousness-Raising and Political Change

Small-group consciousness raising at the beginnings of the contemporary women's movement—with its stress on clarifying the links between the personal and the political—led women to conclude that change in consciousness and in the social relations of the individual is one of the most important components of political change. Women talked to each other to understand and share experiences and to set out a firsthand account of women's oppression.

But a great deal of unexpected energy and method came out of these groups. We learned that it was important to build an analysis of sexual politics from the ground up—from our own experiences. The idea that the personal lives of women should be analyzed in political terms both grew out of the experience of women in these groups and served as a focus for continued small-group activity. We drew connections between personal experience and political generalities about the oppression of women: we took up our experience and transformed it through reflection. This transformation of experience by reflection and the subsequent alterations in women's lives laid the groundwork for the idea that liberation must pervade aspects of life not considered politically important in the past.

(Hartsock, 1981:7)

that such legislation discriminated against women's labor participation more than it protected us on the job (Hole and Levine, 1971). The Citizens' Advisory Council on the Status of Women recommended passage of the ERA in 1970. Hearings were held by the Senate Judiciary Committee after pressure from NOW. Seriously debated by Congress for the first time in 1971, the ERA was finally adopted on March 22, 1972. However, it still required the support of thirty-eight states—three-fourths of the state legislatures—before becoming law.

What were the legal issues raised by the ERA? It would not have outlawed all gender-based legislation. It would have required that any legislation passed by the state and federal governments that discriminated on the basis of gender alone be justified by compelling reasons. The Fifth and Fourteenth amendments to the Constitution, guaranteeing due process and equal protection under the law, as they have been interpreted by the Supreme Court to date, are not adequate to assure this.

The ERA received a great deal of media coverage. While obtaining the ratification of the first thirty states was achieved with some ease, the process began to slow down as opponents mounted their campaign. Ultraconservative groups, in particular, presented the ERA as a threat to personal, social, and religious values (Newland, 1979). Many women also feared changes in family structure, traditional roles, and sexual mores. With the election of a conservative Republican president, Ronald Reagan, in 1980, it proved impossible to marshal support for the ERA from the needed number of states. And time ran out for its ratification by the end of June 1982.

Accompanying opposition to the ERA in the 1970s was an unwillingness on the part of the U.S. Supreme Court to press for women's rights. The judicial system is not immune to the political climate. The passage of the ERA was not just symbolically important, but substantially important to the achievement of equal justice for women under the law. As in the past, every failure to achieve that equality has brought forward renewed efforts. This remains our task today.

Global Feminism

Throughout the 1970s and 1980s, the development of feminist consciousness and women's increased participation in nation-building globally led individuals and groups to place pressure on the United Nations to take up a year of intensive discussion on our position worldwide. While agreement was reached on a United Nations–sponsored examination of the status of women, disagreement arose as to how to focus the discussions. Western women emphasized the issue of equality, especially individual rights; socialist women stressed peace as the defining concern; and Third World

---

The Equal Rights Amendment

Section 1. Equality of rights under the law shall not be denied or abridged by the United States or by any State on account of sex.

Section 2. The Congress shall have the power to enforce, by appropriate legislation, the provisions of this article.

Section 3. This amendment shall take effect two years after the date of ratification.

women underscored economic development and the right of women to be active and full participants at all levels. Out of these three definitions of women's issues came the theme and ten years of attention to our concerns: the United Nations Decade for Women, 1975–1985—equality, peace, and development.

The decade's three world conferences, held in 1975 (Mexico), 1980 (Copenhagen), and 1985 (Nairobi), enabled women from all over the globe to share experiences and views. The official UN conferences brought together government representatives (some of whom were men). At the conclusion of the decade, a comprehensive document, *Report of the World Conference to Review and Appraise the Achievements of the United Nations Decade For Women: Equality, Development and Peace*, was approved overwhelmingly by the United Nations General Assembly. The document is a blueprint for action on the part of the United Nations, governments, and communities to eliminate all forms of discrimination against women and to work to improve the lives of women worldwide (United Nations, 1985).

In addition to the official meetings, the United Nations organized nongovernmental conferences for the participation of grass roots organizations. Women of all backgrounds—students, office workers, peasants, teachers, health care specialists, businesswomen, community activists, and professionals—participated in plenary sessions, workshops, and panels. These conferences enabled women from around the world to learn about one another's similarities and differences, a process that was not always free of either conflict or pain. Organizers of the Nairobi Conference established a Peace Tent to bring together women whose state or ethnic loyalties conflicted with those of others. In this way, Irish Catholic and Northern Irish women, American and Soviet women, Western and Third World women, Arab and Jewish women,

women of color and white women met to attempt to resolve our conflicts, misunderstandings, and disagreements. The Conference on the Decade for Women served as a global consciousness-raising process as women came away with new insights on the varieties of patriarchal oppression, and developed a healthy respect for our differences.

Feminism and Internal Conflicts

This book has often referred to potential conflicts among women who count ourselves feminists. Feminists are divided by national origin, race, ethnicity, class, religion, age, sexual orientation, and experiences of all sorts. Many of the conflicts between and among women stem from what we bring to our discussion of feminism, what we view as the reasons for and the solutions to overcoming our oppression. In the United States, disparities in our lives (differences between white women and African American, Asian American, Latinas, and Native American women, between upper-middle-, and working-class women, between lesbian and heterosexual women, between older and younger women, between native-born, immigrants, and refugees) present problems for feminist unity. There is also more than one kind of feminist: there are cultural feminists, lesbian feminists, radical feminists, socialist feminists, and ecofeminists. The latter gathered support in the 1980s and connect peace activism, radical and socialist feminism, and the ecology movement. Ecofeminists view men's domination of women as a parallel of their attempts to dominate nature (Donovan, 1992; Alonso, 1993). But to begin to understand such differences is to begin to open ways of exploring solutions.

Those who study the history of reform movements and revolutionary societies learn the cost for women of not demanding gains for ourselves until the men of the group to

In Search of African Feminism

The power of social conventions notwithstanding, feminism in Africa is constantly faced with three seemingly divergent challenges. On the international arena, predominant voices of western white feminists insist on a universal brand of feminism whose agenda for action should be concentrated at, and limited to, the elimination of gender hierarchies. Internally, there are those who argue that feminism is a western phenomena with no relevance to Africa. Finally, there are those forces who in principle accept the need for the elimination of inequalities and hence reluctantly accept "feminism" preferably under another label "the women question" but relegate it to a low level of priority. In other words women are told not to be divisive by raising the contradictions within the movement and to wait until the victory of the national liberation movement!

Having been defensive, intimidated and silenced, there are now new and confident voices on the horizon with answers to all three currents and no longer based on instinct and anger . . . but a careful reading of our history and simultaneously sharing of experience with third world feminists and those western feminists who are willing to accept differences and collectively define commonalities.

In the same way that we deny gender hierarchy as a divine or natural ordinance and argue that it is a human and social construct, we oppose any form of cultural hegemony that is based on a dogmatic concept of universality and thus negates variations in the human experience. The realization that gender is a social construct and thus a product of our history and culture has led to a quantum leap in consciousness and has given feminism in Africa its specific character.

. . . To accept the existence of class, race, ethnicity and generational differences among women and to devise multiple fronts of struggle in order to eliminate domination in any of its forms is what gives feminism its vitality.

(AAWORD, 1985:1–3)

which we belong have achieved justice (see Chapter 15). But putting the concerns of women first should still mean considering the needs and goals of *all* women, and not letting racism and class privileges that divide people undermine the growing sisterhood among women.

Feminists from developing countries and those from minority communities in the developed countries have struggled with the problems of multiple oppression—as members of groups who have been victimized because of our race, class, nationality, or religion, as well as because we are women. At a meeting of the National Black Feminist Organization (NBFO) in 1973, African American feminists acknowledged that sexual oppression is a constant factor, but racism is also a daily problem in our lives. Sorting out the nature of the multiple oppression we experience has not been easy or painless. African American feminists see the need for continued solidarity with people of African descent. As one group has expressed it, "We struggle together with black men about sexism" (Combahee River Collective, 1979:366). This struggle is also shared by other women of color in our respective communities.

The Political Climate of the 1990s

More progress toward feminist goals has been made in the past twenty-five years than in any other period of modern history. Such success set off a strong reaction within American society. The rejection of the ERA by the successful Republican Party in the 1980 election, its subsequent failure to be ratified, and the efforts of Presidents Reagan and Bush and their administrations to dismantle legislative, judicial, and economic gains made over the previous decade presented a new challenge to feminists of every kind. When the Reagan administration eliminated the right of abortion for Medicaid recipients and opposed abortion globally, it was a loss for all women's rights. Making abortions difficult for some of us (poor women) to obtain makes it easier down the road for the same conservative forces to eliminate reproductive rights for all of us. The government's opposition to reproductive rights in the 1980s has also contributed to dividing women who are supportive of many feminist concerns, but who, for religious and political beliefs, oppose government funding of abortion.

To preserve the gains women have made against assaults from those who would turn back the clock necessitates our setting aside differences and working together. The phrase made popular during the Black Power liberation movement, "If they come for you in the morning, they will come for me in the afternoon," is a guidepost. Women must continue to struggle together on issues confronting us as women, while we simultaneously struggle to work to transcend our divisions.

We came together in 1992. The election of President Bill Clinton was heavily dependent on women's activism. The "Year of the Woman" was a demonstration of the power of women to mobilize ourselves and others to elect legislators who would pursue a political agenda of social justice and equality for all and particularly to promote policies and practices that would attend to women's issues. Consequently President Clinton's first actions included easing restrictions on access to abortion imposed by previous administrations and efforts to end discrimination against lesbians and gays in the military. In addition, the Clinton administration has made health care and other social concerns primary issues. Among his women Cabinet members is Donna Shalala, the Secretary of Health and Human Services, a post with the largest budget in the government.

Can women build together a significant political force to oppose further incursions on the gains made? Have women developed the networks, the organizations, the ways of offering support to one another to marshal our forces, get our opinions heard, and make our presence felt in the American political process? Can we protect and further our gains in the workplace and in our institutions? Can we make further progress toward the goals we have begun to define for ourselves? The answer depends on women.

Summary

Until recently, most political scientists viewed women as of little consequence in politics. The stereotyped view of women is that we are naturally unsuited to act in the "public" sphere and that we adopt the views of our fathers and husbands.

Women have been far less visible than men in formal political activity. Feminist political scientists call attention to the crucial role women play in community-level organizations and the ways we have been socialized to follow rather than lead. The women's movement has brought out the relation between women's exclusion from the "public" sphere and the lack of control over our "private" lives, arguing that "the personal is political."

Power is distinct from authority. Women

have seldom exercised either power or authority.

As societies become more complex, governmental power tends to be exercised by the few on behalf of the many. Women tend to be segregated as a group, and excluded from political power, along with subordinated racial, ethnic, and religious groups. Women who do participate in government tend to do so on the local level.

In the past, some women have exercised political power in our own right in dynastic states and in precolonial African societies. But as government became more bureaucratic and as colonial powers altered these societies, the power of these women leaders eroded.

Male dominance is associated with increasing complexity of societies and societal response to stress and change. It is manifested in the exclusion of women from economic and political decision making and aggression against women.

The women's movement has encouraged increasing numbers of American women to seek public office. In the 1980s, a "gender gap" emerged with women and men differing in political viewpoints, party affiliation, and voting behavior. Studies show that regardless of party label or level of office, women officeholders take more feminist positions on women's issues than men. Nonetheless, we still face opposition, some of which we are attempting to resolve ourselves, for example, through raising our own funds to support candidates with feminist viewpoints.

One attempt to justify women's political subordination to men asserts that it is men who possess the physical strength to wage wars, and thereby to make critical decisions affecting government. Aggression is valued more than nurturance; and men more than women. Nonetheless, women have been motivated to fight in informal armies of rebellions, revolutions, and resistance movements and to support their government or state in other war-related efforts. For the most part, however, women have been pressed to return to the traditional roles of wives and mothers after we have made our sacrifices and contributions.

Laws tend to have a sexist bias because they are based on male-defined norms. Many laws and moral codes are based on a double standard. Family law often coerces women into traditional roles. Laws designed to "protect" women often have the effect of restricting our choices and activities. Women criminals are subjected to laws made by male legislators, enforced by male police officers, and interpreted by male judges.

Marginalized from "politics" as men define it, women sought to influence government policies through a wide range of voluntary associations. Our involvement in peace movements testifies to our political opposition to men's wars. While women do tend to be more "pacific" than men, this does not mean that we cannot be motivated to fight.

Our chief struggle at the beginning of the twentieth century was to obtain female suffrage—the right to vote.

The modern women's liberation movement derived from two sources: organizations formed to work for women's equality and a younger, more radical group developing out of the civil rights and New Left movements, and concerned with liberation from male domination.

The Equal Rights Amendment took half a century to pass Congress; in June 1982, it failed to win the necessary ratification by three-fourths of the states. Opposition to ERA centers in ultraconservative groups that fear disruption in traditional social norms. The U.S. Supreme Court's willingness to press for women's rights beginning in the early 1970s slowed as the political climate became more conservative throughout the 1980s. Yet more women than ever have joined the political process.

In the 1980s, a global feminism emerged with the aid of the United Nations Decade for Women Conference, which brought together women worldwide to share experiences and to develop strategies to eliminate global patriarchy.

Feminist unity is made more difficult by the fact that women have different ethnic, national, religious, class, and racial backgrounds, and different sexual orientations, and so have different priorities. African American, Asian American, Latina, Native American feminists, and women from developing countries carry a double burden in having to deal with both sexism and racism. The need for all women to engage in the political process and to focus clearly on our necessary goals is paramount if we are to ensure that recent gains will not be lost and that new gains will be won. Women's unity will benefit from understanding all kinds of sexism.

The "Year of the Woman" in 1992 demonstrated our power to mobilize ourselves and others to elect legislators supportive of women's issues. Future progress in all areas of women's rights and liberation depends to a large part on us.

Discussion Questions

1. Document the life of a woman political leader of your choice. How did she manage to succeed, given the obstacles to women's political leadership?
2. Find out which women hold political offices or leadership positions in your town, county, or congressional district. On the basis of what you have read in this chapter, design a questionnaire to find out what positions these women hold on a variety of feminist issues.
3. Do an oral-history interview with women in your own family on their role in and views on key women's movements. Were members of your family suffragettes? Were any participants in the social movements of the 1960s? How many have been involved in voluntary organizations? Which ones? Have any participated in electoral politics? If not, why not?
4. What kinds of organizations exist in your locality to deal with issues concerning women, violence, and the law (such as a rape crisis center, a "battered wife" center, or a group concerned with women in prison)?
5. How do women from different racial or ethnic groups or economic classes differ in our perceptions and attitudes on feminist issues? Select one issue as a "problem" and suggest "solutions." How might women from two groups argue from the perspectives of our different backgrounds?

Recommended Readings

Alonso, Harriet Hyman. *Peace as a Women's Issue: A History of the U.S. Movement for World Peace and Women's Rights.* Syracuse: Syracuse University Press, 1993. As the first comprehensive history of the feminist peace movement in the United States, it provides an analysis of the role, activities, and inner workings of key women's peace organizations. It traces the development of the women's campaign for peace from its roots in nineteenth-century abolitionist and suffrage movements to its expression during the 1990–91 Persian Gulf War.

Dubois, Ellen. *Feminism and Suffrage: The Emergence of an Independent Women's Movement in America, 1848–1869.* Ithaca: Cornell University Press, 1978. An analysis of the political strategies of Elizabeth Cady Stanton and Susan B. Anthony, early suffrage leaders who saw the Fifteenth Amendment, enfranchising only black men, as poor reward for women's abolitionist efforts. Dubois explores the way the stage was set for a broad critique of patriarchal America by these women's rights reformers.

Evans, Sarah. *Personal Politics, The Roots of Women's Liberation in the Civil Rights Movement and the New Left.* New York: Knopf, 1979. A discussion of the emergence of the women's movement in the context of women's activities in the civil rights and antiwar movements in the 1960s. It tells of women's changing roles in these movements as they grew larger and more successful, and of the contradictions that emerged.

I, Rigoberta Menchu: An Indian Woman in Guatemala, edited by Elisabeth Burgos-Debray (trans. Ann Wright). London and New York: Verso, 1984, 1993. The life story of a young peasant woman, now famous as a leader in her country, telling in simple, compelling language about her experiences of injustice, the culture of her people, and her determination to end the brutal oppression of her family and her people.

References

AAWORD. *Feminism in Africa.* vol.II/III, 1985.

Abzug, Bella, with Mim Kelber. *Gender Gap.* Boston: Houghton Mifflin, 1984.

Adler, Frieda. *Sisters in Crime: The Rise of the New Female Criminal.* New York: McGraw-Hill, 1975.

Alonso, Harriet Hyman. *Peace as a Women's Issue.* Syracuse: Syracuse University Press, 1993.

Aptheker, Bettina. *Tapestries of Life.* Amherst: University of Massachusetts Press, 1989.

Astin, Helen, and Leland, Carole. *Women of Influence, Women of Vision.* San Francisco and Oxford: Jossey-Bass, 1991.

Baker, Paula. "The Moral Framework of Public Life: Gender and Politics in Rural New York, 1870–1930." Unpublished doctoral dissertation, Rutgers University, 1987.

Barnett, Bernice McNair. "Invisible Southern Black Women Leaders in the Civil Rights Movement: The Triple Constraints of Gender, Race and Class." *Gender & Society* 7:2 (June 1993):162–82.

Berube, Allan. "Marching to a Different Drummer: Lesbian and Gay GIs in World War II." In *Hidden from History: Reclaiming the Gay and Lesbian Past,* edited by Martin Duberman et al. New York: Meridian, 1990:383–94.

Bok, Sissela. *Alva Myrdal.* Reading, Mass.: Addison-Wesley, 1991.

Bookman, Ann, and Morgen, Sandra, editors. *Woman and the Politics of Empowerment.* Philadelphia: Temple University Press, 1988.

Boulding, Elise. *Women in the Twentieth Century World.* New York: Wiley, 1977.

Brown, Elaine. *A Taste of Power: A Black Woman's Story.* New York: Pantheon, 1992.

Burgos-Debray, Elisabeth, editor. *I, Rigoberta Menchu.* London and New York: Verso, 1984.

Center for the American Woman and Politics. *The Impact of Women in Public Office: An Overview.* Eagleton Institute of Politics, Rutgers University, 1991.

———. *The Gender Gap.* Fact Sheet. Eagleton Institute of Politics, Rutgers University, 1992.

———. *Women Candidates for Congress 1970–1992.* Fact Sheet. Eagleton Institute of Politics, Rutgers University, 1992.

———. *Women in the U.S. Congress 1993; Women in the U.S. Senate 1922–1993; Women in the U.S. House of Representatives 1993; Women in State Legislatures 1993; Statewide Elective Executive Women 1993.* Fact Sheets. Eagleton Institute of Politics, Rutgers University, 1993.

Chagnon, Napoleon. *Yanomamo: The Fierce People.* New York: CBS College Publishing (Holt, Rinehart, Winston), 1983.

Chesney-Lind, Meda. "Women and Crime: The Female Offender." *Signs* 12:1 (Autumn 1986):78–96.

Collins, Patricia Hill. *Black Feminist Thought: Knowledge, Consciousness, and the Politics of Empowerment.* New York: Routledge, 1991.

Combahee River Collective. "A Black Feminist Statement." In *Capitalist Patriarchy and the Case of Socialist Feminism*, edited by Zilah R. Eisenstein. New York: Monthly Review Press, 1979.

Cook, Blanche Wiesen. *Eleanor Roosevelt*. Penguin, 1992.

Cott, Nancy F. "Across the Great Divide: Women in Politics Before and After 1920." In *Women, Politics, and Change*, edited by Louise A. Tilly and Patricia Gurin. New York: Russell Sage Foundation, 1990.

Crenshaw, Kimberle. "Demarginalizing the Intersection of Race and Sex: A Black Feminist Critique of Antidiscrimination Doctrine, Feminist Theory and Antiracist Politics." In *Feminist Legal Theory*, edited by Katharine T. Bartlett and Rosanne Kennedy. Boulder: Westview Press, 1991.

Dalley, Gillian. *Ideologies of Caring: Rethinking Community and Collectivism*. London: Macmillan Education, 1988.

Deitch, Cynthia. "Gender, Race, and Class Politics and the Inclusion of Women in Title VII of the 1964 Civil Rights Act." *Gender & Society* 7:2 (June 1993):183–203.

Diamond, Irene. *Sex Roles in the State House*. New Haven: Yale University Press, 1977.

Donovan, Josephine. *Feminist Theory*. New expanded edition. New York: Continuum, 1992.

Elshtain, Jean Bethke. "Methodological Sophistication and Conceptual Confusion: A Critique of Mainstream Political Science." In *The Prism of Sex: Essays in the Sociology of Knowledge*, edited by Julia A. Sherman and Evelyn Torton Beck. Madison: University of Wisconsin Press, 1979.

Evans, Sarah. *Personal Politics: The Roots of Women's Liberation in the Civil Rights Movement and the New Left*. New York: Vintage, 1980.

Freeman, Bonnie Cook. "Power, Patriarch, and Political Primitives." In *Beyond Intellectual Sexism: A New Woman, a New Reality*, edited by Joan I. Roberts. New York: McKay, 1976.

Garland, Anne Witte. *Women Activists: Challenging the Abuse of Power*. New York: The Feminist Press at the City University of New York, 1988.

Githens, Marianne, and Prestage, Jewel L., editors. *A Portrait of Marginality*. New York: McKay, 1977.

Goldstein, Leslie Friedman. *The Constitutional Rights of Women: Cases in Law and Social Change*. New York: Longman, 1979.

Gordon, Linda. *Heroes of Their Own Lives*. New York: Penguin, 1988.

Harris, Alice P. "Race and Essentialism in Feminist Legal Theory." In *Feminist Legal Theory*, edited by Katharine T. Bartlett and Rosanne Kennedy. Boulder, Co.: Westview Press, 1991.

Harris, Marvin. *Cannibals and Kings: The Origins of Cultures*. New York: Random House, Vintage Books, 1977.

Hartsock, Nancy. "Political Change: Two Perspectives on Power." In *Building Feminist Theory: Essays from Quest; A Feminist Quarterly*. New York: Longman, 1981.

———. *Money, Sex and Power*, New York: Longman, 1983.

Hole, Judith, and Levine, Ellen. *Rebirth of Feminism*. New York: Quadrangle, 1971.

Hossain, Rokeya Sakhawat. *Sultana's Dream and Selections from the Secluded Ones*, edited and translated by Roushan Jahan; afterword by Hanna Papanek. New York: The Feminist Press at The City University of New York, 1988.

Ifeka-Moller, Caroline. "Female Militancy and Colonial Revolt: The Women's War of 1929, Eastern Nigeria." In *Perceiving Women*, edited by Shirley Ardener. New York: Wiley, 1977.

Jacobs, Susie. "Women and Land Resettlement in Zimbabwe." *Review of African Political Economy* 27/28, 1984.

Kathlene, Lyn. "Studying the New Voice of Women in Politics." *Chronicle of Higher Education*, November 18, 1992, B1-2.

Kelly, Amy. *Eleanor of Aquitaine and the Four Kings*. New York: Vintage, 1957.

Ladner, Joyce A. *Tomorrow's Tomorrow. The Black Woman*. Garden City, N.Y.: Doubleday, 1972.

Lebsock, Suzanne. "Women and American Politics, 1880–1920." In *Women, Politics and Change*, edited by Louise A. Tilly and Patricia Gurin. New York: Russell Sage Foundation, 1990.

Lee, Marcia M. "Toward Understanding Why Few Women Hold Public Office: Factors Affecting the Participation of Women in Local Politics." In *A Portrait of Marginality*, edited by Marianne Githens and Jewel Prestage. New York: McKay, 1977.

Lloyd, Genevieve. "Selfhood, War and Masculinity." In *Feminist Challenges: Social and Political Theory*, edited by Carole Pateman and Elizabeth Gross. Sydney: Allen & Unwin, 1986.

Lovenduski, Joni. "Toward the Emasculation of Political Science: The Impact of Feminism." In *Men's Studies Modified: The Impact of Feminism on the Academic Disciplines*, edited by Dale Spender. New York: Pergamon, 1981.

MacKinnon, Catharine A. *Feminism Unmodified: Discourses on Life and Law*. Cambridge, Mass.: Harvard University Press, 1987.

———. "Feminism, Marxism, Method and the State: Toward Feminist Jurisprudence." In *Feminist Legal Theory*, edited by Katharine T. Bartlett and Rosanne Kennedy. Boulder, Co.: Westview, 1991.

Martin, Wendy, editor. *The American Sisterhood*. New York: Harper & Row, 1972.

Matsuda, Mari. "When the First Quail Calls: Multiple Consciousness as Jurisprudential Method." *Women's Rights L. Rep.* 7, 9 (1989).

Moser, Caroline O. N., and Peake, Linda. *Women, Human Settlements, and Housing*. London: Tavistock Publications, 1987.

Neale, John E. *Queen Elizabeth I: A Biography*. 1934. Reprint. Garden City, N.Y.: Doubleday, 1957.

Newland, Kathleen. *The Sisterhood of Man*. New York: Norton, 1979.

O'Barr, Jean. "African Women in Politics." In *African Women South of the Sahara*, edited by Margaret Jean Hay and Sharon Stichter. New York: Longman, 1984.

O'Donovan, Katherine. "Before and After: The Impact of Feminism on the Academic Discipline of Law." In *Men's Studies Modified: The Impact of Feminism on the Academic Disciplines*, edited by Dale Spender. New York: Pergamon, 1981.

Okin, Susan Moller. *Women in Western Political Thought*. Princeton: Princeton University Press, 1979.

Pearson, Carol. "Women's Fantasies and Feminist Utopias." *Frontiers* 2 (1977):50–61.

Randall, Vicky. *Women and Politics*. 2nd ed. Chicago: University of Chicago Press, 1987.

Reverby, Susan, and Helly, Dorothy O. "Converging on History." In *Gendered Domains: Rethinking Public and Private in Women's History*, edited by Dorothy O. Helly and Susan Reverby. Ithaca: Cornell University Press, 1992, 1–24.

Ridd, Rosemary, and Callaway, Helen. *Women and Political Conflict*. New York: New York University Press, 1987.

Rostker v. *Goldberg*, 1981.

Ruddick, Sara. *Maternal Thinking: Toward a Politics of Peace*. Boston: Beacon Press, 1989.

Sanday, Peggy Reeves. *Female Power and Male Dominance: On the Origins of Sexual Inequality*. Cambridge: Cambridge University Press, 1981.

Schneir, Miriam, editor. *Feminism: The Essential Historical Writings*. New York: Random House, 1972.

Scott, Anne Firor. *Natural Allies: Women's Associations in American History*. Urbana: University of Illinois Press, 1991.

Sievers, Sharon L. "Women in China, Japan, and Korea." In *Restoring Women to History* (Teaching Packets for Integrating Women's History into Courses in Africa, Asia, Latin America and the Caribbean and the Middle East). Bloomington: Organization of American Historians, rev. ed., 1990, ASIA:55–101.

Smart, Carol. *Women, Crime and Criminology: A Feminist Critique*. London: Routledge & Kegan Paul, 1978.

Snitow, Ann. "Holding the Line at Greenham: Being Joyously Political in Dangerous

Times." *Mother Jones* (February/March 1985):30–47.

Steinson, Barbara J. " 'The Mother Half of Humanity': American Women in the Peace and Preparedness Movements in World War I." In *Women, War and Revolution*, edited by Carol R. Berkin and Clara M. Lovett. New York: Holmes & Meiers, 1980.

Stiehm, Judith H. *Bring Me Men and Women: Mandated Change at the U.S. Air Force Academy.* Berkeley: University of California Press, 1981.

Sugisaki, Kazuko. "From the Moon to the Sun: Women's Liberation in Japan." In *Women in the World*, 2nd rev. ed., edited by Lynne B. Iglitzin and Ruth Ross. Santa Barbara and Oxford: ABC-CLIO, 1986:109–24.

Swerdlow, Amy. "Ladies' Day at the Capitol: Women Strike for Peace versus HUAC." *Feminist Studies* 8:3 (Fall 1982):493–520.

Taylor, Verta, and Whittier, Nancy E. "Collective Identity in Social Movement Communities: Lesbian Feminist Mobilization." In *Frontiers in Social Movement Theory*, edited by Aldon D. Morris and Carol McClurg Mueller. New Haven: Yale University Press, 1992.

United Nations. *United Nations Report of the World Conference to Review and Appraise the Achievements of the United Nations Decade for Women: Equality, Development and Peace.* New York: United Nations, 1985.

———. *The World's Women 1970–1990 Trends and Statistics.* New York: United Nations, 1992.

Van Allen, Judith. " 'Aba Riots' or Igbo 'Women's War'? Ideology, Stratification, and the Invisibility of Women." In *Women in Africa: Studies in Social and Economic Change*, edited by Nancy J. Hafkin and Edna G. Bay. Stanford, Calif.: Stanford University Press, 1976.

White, E. Frances. "Women of Western and Western Central Africa." In *Restoring Women to History* (Teaching Packets for Integrating Women's History into Courses on Africa, Asia, Latin America and the Caribbean, and the Middle East). Bloomington, Ind.: Organization of American Historians, rev. ed. 1990, AFRICA:49–99.

Wilks, Ivor. "She Who Blazed a Trail: Akyaawa Yi Kwan of Asante." In *Life Histories of African Women*, edited by Patricia Romero. London: Ashfield Press, 1980.

Williams, Patricia J. *The Alchemy of Race and Rights.* Cambridge, Mass.: Harvard University Press, 1991.

chapter **15**

Changing the Present:
A Look to the Future

> The hand that rocks the cradle should also rock the boat.
> WILMA SCOTT HEIDE

What do we see for the future? Do we look ahead with optimism, anticipating a better world for women? Or does a cloud of pessimism shadow our visions?

Feminists hold different views on whether the major causes of the oppression of women are economic, psychological, political, or other, and thus on how best to overcome that oppression (Jaggar, 1983). Our predictions about the future vary. But all feminists seek the liberation of women, and almost all believe that patriarchy is not inevitable and will be overcome eventually.

The preceding chapters have addressed many aspects of women's existence. We have explored our roles in the family and our relationships to the larger society. We have seen changes over time, and we have noted similarities among women as well as differences. Over and over, feminist attempts to change society in ways helpful to women have met with defeat. Yet, the women's movement of recent years and of the present has achieved extraordinary gains. It holds out more hope for women than any previous social movement; it may even offer the only hope for the survival of humanity.

Women and Social Change

The Early Years

The eighteenth century was full of rhetoric and literature about human rights and equality for men. The Declaration of Independence asserted that "all men are created equal"; women, however, were given little consideration in the egalitarian movement. Still, even then, women voiced the belief that principles of equality should be applied to us. In 1776, Abigail Adams wrote to her husband John, soon to be the second president of the United States of America:

> I long to hear that you have declared an independency—and by the way, in the new Code of Laws which I suppose it will be necessary for you to make, I desire you would Remember the Ladies, and be more generous and favourable to them than your ancestors. Do not put such unlimited power into the hands of the Husbands. Remember all Men would be tyrants if they could. If particular care and attention is not paid to the Ladies we are determined to foment a Rebellion, and will not hold ourselves bound by any Laws in which we have no voice, or Representation. (Rossi, 1973:10–11)

In 1792, a similar call was heard in England. In *The Vindication of the Rights of Woman*, Mary Wollstonecraft demanded for women the same rights and freedoms that men were claiming during this period. The eighteenth century in which Abigail Adams and Mary Wollstonecraft lived has been called the Age of Enlightenment, the era of the American and French revolutions, with their themes of liberty, equality, and fraternity. Women who understood we were being excluded in the application of these principles raised our voices in protest. But the exclusion continued.

The French Revolution between 1789 and 1795 overthrew the monarchy and created a republic. During these years, French women's voices loudly called for political liberty and equality that included a legal identity for women in marriage, divorce rights, widows' rights to property and child custody, and more educational opportunities for girls. Working-class women in Paris created political networks while engaging in women's usual activities in the streets, cafes, markets, and breadlines. In this way, women were able to keep abreast of revolutionary events and form crowds for demonstrations (Levy et al., 1979). One short-lived political club was created exclusively by women. But patriarchy yielded not at all though the monarchy was overthrown, and men of the revolution joined in defeating the demands of women.

Women's Organizations

In the nineteenth century, the United States saw an increasing number of women's organizations run by volunteers. Not paid for our efforts, yet outspoken in favor of our ideals, we worked for humanitarian principles. Afri-

---

The Declaration of the Rights of Woman and the Female Citizen (France 1791)

Women have resolved to set forth in a solemn declaration the natural, inalienable, and sacred rights of woman. . . .

Article I
Woman is born free and lives equal to man in her rights. . . .

Article VI
The law must be the expression of the general will; all female and male citizens must contribute either personally or through their representatives to its formation; it must be the same for all: male and female citizens, being equal in the eyes of the law, must be equally admitted to all honors, positions, and public employment according to their capacity and without other distinctions besides those of their virtues and talents. . . .

Postscript
Women, wake up; the tocsin of reason is being heard throughout the whole universe; discover your rights. . . . Regardless of what barriers confront you, it is in your power to free yourselves; you have only to want to.

(Levy et al., 1979:89–90, 92)

can American women made many churches into effective social organizations. Many middle-class white women identified with such causes as the abolition of slavery, prison reform, the expansion of education, and changing the inhumane working conditions of factories and sweatshops. In 1874, the largest national organization of women the country had known, the Women's Christian Temperance Union, formed to protest the abuse of alcohol. Because the WCTU saw the hard-drinking habits of the day as the source of the woes of many women and children, it was actually concerned with many social ills (Berg, 1978; Kolb, 1976).

Far from merely advocating humanitarian principles, women actively tried to implement reforms. The first settlement house in the United States was founded by Jane Addams in 1889 (see Chapter 11). This institution brought together people from all social classes, provided numerous community services, and eventually lobbied for child protection, labor laws, and female suffrage. Many women activists sought to help workers achieve better wages and working conditions, and women joined organizations to apply pressure for reform in government and businesses, thus succeeding in bringing about many improvements for workers.

When the Civil War was over, Congress granted black men the right to vote. Feminists, requesting the same human right for white and black women, were turned down (see Chapter 14).

Though women's efforts for reform have been tireless, the benefits to us have been slow in coming. Many of the volunteer organizations founded by women were taken over by men when these organizations became powerful and politically credible (Heilbrun, 1979). But women did see some improvements. The reform movements brought more women into the public sphere and taught us how to organize and effect change. These skills served us

in finally obtaining the vote in the United States in 1920.

Early Radical Feminists

In the early 1900s, radical feminists were writing and organizing to bring about a new kind of society. One such woman was Charlotte Perkins Gilman, who published *Women and Economics* in 1898 (1966). She analyzed women's roles within the family, the restrictions on our participation in public life, and the social obstructions we faced in realizing personal goals, pointing out how detrimental this situation was to both women and society at large.

The radical feminists were asking for genuine freedom for women, including the freedom to lead gratifying lives in ways previously considered socially unacceptable. We sought a revision in, even elimination of, the marriage arrangement; freedom from the total responsibility for child care; sexual freedom; and control over our own bodies. These demands sound very similar to some we hear from feminists today.

The writings of Emma Goldman reflected many of the beliefs of the radical feminists. She was an anarchist who advocated radical change in the social system, particularly in capitalism, which she viewed as a major source of women's oppression. Margaret Sanger, another radical feminist, worked tirelessly throughout her life for the right of every woman "to control her body," to obtain sexual pleasure without the fear of pregnancy, and to be free to make choices about motherhood (see Chapter 12).

After the Vote

It has been said that feminism died once the vote was won. Indeed, large-scale organized activity diminished, perhaps due to the Depression (starting in 1929), world political turmoil, and the belief that obtaining the vote

Portrait of a Negress by Marie Guillemine Benoist (c. 1800) is one of the rare depictions of a black person in European painting. It is apt for a woman artist to have chosen to immortalize a black woman to symbolize the French revolutionary slogan of liberty and equality. The sitter's dignified, regal beauty dominates the picture despite her semi-nudity, which was the European artistic convention during this period for "exotic" people. (Musée National du Louvre)

Charlotte Perkins Gilman devoted her life to feminist scholarship, analyzing the role economics plays in women's position in society and advocating women's freedom and liberation from family constraints. Her own divorce and relinquishment of the custody of her daughter made her an outcast in the society of her day. (Brown Brothers)

would solve women's problems (Freeman, 1976). One way feminism flourished in the 1920s was that new organizations were created for social reform. For example, the planned parenthood and birth control movement grew. Unfortunately, it is true that women's gains in the educational and work spheres diminished in the struggling economy of the 1930s, and most of the demands of the feminists of the previous decades were rarely heard.

During World War II, when men had to leave their jobs to join the army, women again filled the labor market gap, as we had in World War I. Women successfully took over jobs previously considered appropriate for men only. When the war ended, however, the work gains made by women were snatched away from us. Day care facilities and training programs—to the extent that they had existed—disappeared. Women who continued to work were generally overqualified for the jobs we held and were underpaid. In short, women were sent back to the home, and the late 1940s and the 1950s saw a reemergence of traditional family values and constricting definitions of "femininity" (Freeman, 1976).

Patterns of the Past

A review of the decades preceding the 1960s reveals some historical patterns in women's reform movements. Women have traditionally been connected with "charities." As volunteer workers, we have served as a link between the male power structure and its victims and have acted on behalf of children, the poor, workers, and other groups of people oppressed by the system. Economically advantaged women have assisted women from different social classes, and women in all social classes have to a significant degree banded together to fight for our rights.

Yet other, less comforting patterns also appear. Women have often been divided by class and race, and have allowed such divisions to hinder our understanding and our progress. We have been used to fight the battles of others' causes, and then been denied a fair share of the gains. Finally, periods of progress have usually been followed by lulls or reversals. Carolyn Heilbrun notes that the women's movement seems to defeat itself after each gain. "Each cycle of progress for women seems to end after a decade or two with precious little real advance toward equality. The complacency in women that a few steps forward induces drains the movement of its energy. Progress halts or is even reversed" (1979:24).

Taking Stock of the Present

The status of women today encourages two views—one optimistic and the other more pessimistic. How mixed the picture is can be illustrated by a study reported on in 1989. The study found that between 1980 and 1986, wages for working women increased from 60 percent of men's wages to 65 percent, and estimates that by the year 2000, women will still earn only 74 percent of what men earn. Will this be enormous progress over past inequities, or a disappointing failure to achieve equality? How fast is it reasonable to expect social change to occur? How long should women be expected to wait for equality?

An Optimistic Picture?

Women and Society. As the 1990s proceed, women's issues in the United States and around the world are covered regularly in newspapers; when women suffer some obstacle to our achievement of equality, this event is often noticed rather than ignored, and our efforts to overcome such obstacles are often seen as newsworthy. Many magazines take women seriously and offer their readers stories about successful women in political life or business, and women with serious careers are no longer a novelty in movies and on television. Such problems for women as domestic violence are often discussed, and efforts are often made to address them.

In the creative arts, women's productions are receiving growing attention. More than in the past, our work depicts the female experience. Women's art galleries, craft centers, and bookstores appear with some regularity.

In religious organizations feminists are taking (we are not being "given") positions of authority in the church and are rewriting the Scriptures (see Chapter 10). Women are dissenting in Third World countries as well as in the Western world, and are trying to change traditional religious practices that harm women.

Areas in which women are underrepresented, such as in police forces, corporate hierarchies, and government, show a slight increase of women in high-ranking positions. Women are demanding training programs that will facilitate our advancement, and we are increasingly performing nontraditional jobs. "Displaced homemaker" programs have been established to counsel women who have spent years as homemakers and now seek job training or retraining.

More women are acquiring professional training previously reserved for men. At colleges, women's studies programs have increased and, in the face of a considerable struggle for academic credibility, have gained respect (Denmark, 1994). As the preceding chapters indicate, many trained in the older academic disciplines are critically reviewing old assumptions and raising new questions (Denmark, 1980; Harding and Hintikka, 1983; Zalk and Gordon-Kelter, 1989). Sexism is on the defensive.

Women and the Family. Women's roles in the family are also changing (Rubin, 1984; Shreve, 1987). A growing number of women with preschool children are working at paid jobs, and dual-career families are common (see Chapters 9 and 13). Fathers are playing an increasingly active role in child care. Childrearing practices are still largely sexist, but nonsexist ideas are increasingly being communicated in children's entertainment and education. Many young men want to be more involved in the bringing up of their children than their fathers were with them (Herzog and Mali, 1980).

Mature Women. More attention is being paid to women in midlife, and negative social attitudes are decreasing. A study of women between the ages of thirty-five and fifty-five indicates that many now feel positive about this new stage of life and about the future (Baruch and Barnett, 1980:199). The researchers note that "contrary to the traditional notion that marriage is the most important pillar of a woman's happiness, our study is finding that, for employed women, a high-prestige job, rather than a husband, is the best prediction of well-being."

The Popular View. Surveys find that people are expressing a greater acceptance of such things as mothers' working and women's moving up to higher positions in politics, business, and the professions. More people are now supportive of programs to help women, including more and better day care facilities both at work and in the community.

The Other Side of the Picture

Are We Witnessing a Backlash? Or should we realize that the status quo was *never* better than now so it is not backlash, but an indication of how much further we need to go? Studies show that women still do most of the housework. American women put in two hours of cooking, laundering, and housecleaning for every one hour done by men (*New York Times*, 12/8/88, A28). (According to another study, women

Working Mother Is Now Norm, Study Shows

WASHINGTON, June 15 (AP)—For the first time, more than half of new mothers are remaining in the job market, the Census Bureau reported today.

"Every time a statistic approaches the 50 percent mark of the labor force, it's not an oddity anymore, it's a way of life," said Martin O'Connell, chief of the Bureau's Fertility Statistics Branch.

In 1987, 50.8 percent of new mothers remained in the job market, marking the first time a majority of women reported they were working or actively seeking employment within a year of giving birth.

The figure was 49.9 percent in 1986. In 1976, the first year the Census Bureau calculated the statistic, it was 31 percent.

The percentage has grown steadily in the last decade, Mr. O'Connell said, as a result of women's increasing inclination to delay marriage and childbearing in favor of jobs and education.

Women who accumulate more years of schooling and work experience before having children have "greater financial resources to enable them, once they have a child, to obtain child care services and get back to the labor force much quicker," he said in the telephone interview.

In addition, Mr. O'Connell said such women have "increased career commitment and increased cost of staying out of the labor force, compared to an 18- or 19-year-old who had a child earlier" in life.

Mr. O'Connell cited findings that 68 percent of women who had the first child after turning 30 remained in the job market, as against 54 percent of those 18 to 24 years old.

Education a Factor

Sixty-three percent of new mothers with college degrees remained in the work force, as against 38 percent for those whose education ended in high school.

The study, "Fertility of American Women: June 1987," also said that 53 percent of black new mothers returned to the work force within a year of giving birth, 51 percent of white mothers did and 36 percent of Hispanic mothers.

It also said that widowed, divorced and separated mothers were most likely to be working, at 66 percent. Married women were second at 49.8 percent, followed by single mothers at 49.5 percent.

The report also disclosed a substantial increase in the number of two-income families with children. It concentrated on women 18 to 44 years old, the normal childbearing age.

The increasing number of mothers returning to jobs led to a total of 13.4 million two-worker families with children last year, the report said, up from 8.3 million in 1976.

Two-income couples with children make up more that 40 percent of all married couples in the childbearing ages, Mr. O'Connell said, adding that as a result American businesses would have to pay close attention to the needs of these workers and families.

In a privately published analysis, "Juggling Jobs and Babies: America's Child-Care Challenge," Mr. O'Connell said last year that businesses must begin to cope with the needs of working mothers, including such possibilities as flexible work schedules, employer-sponsored child care, flexible benefit plans and other new approaches.

(*New York Times*, June 16, 1988)

Bishops Denounce Abuse of Spouses: Statement Condemns Sexism and Encourages Priests to Help Battered Women

In their first official statement on spouse abuse, the nation's Roman Catholic bishops have declared that there is nothing in the Bible requiring women to submit to abusive husbands or to remain in abusive relationships.

The statement condemns sexism and encourages parish priests to be ready with "a safe place" for battered women who seek help.

Distorting the Biblical Text

In the document, the bishops say that what particularly concerns them is the way biblical passages encouraging wives to be submissive to their husbands have sometimes been taken out of context to justify spouse abuse. Addressing this point, the statement says:

"Abused women say 'I can't leave this relationship. The Bible says it would be wrong.' Abusive men say 'The Bible says my wife should be submissive to me.' They take the biblical text and distort it to support their right to batter."

The statement seeks to emphasize that violence against women is never justified and that the parish church must be a place where both abused women and the men who batter them can go for help.

To further reduce domestic violence, the bishops encourage parishes to see that women are well represented in parish leadership positions and to insist that religious education is free of sexual stereotyping. "Battering thrives on sexism," the statement said.

(*New York Times*, October 30, 1992:A12)

did a 3-to-1 share of the housework in 1975, and a 6-to-1 share in 1965.) So although we now live in more egalitarian households than in the past, we have a long way to go. In the United States, women's occupational gains are often thwarted by the absence or inadequacy of parental leaves, and by the often severe difficulties in finding affordable child care meeting even minimally adequate standards.

In terms of legislative gains in the area of violence against women, the courts no longer require a witness for rape accusations. However, the incidence of rape is increasing. Although groups have organized to fight wife-battering, wife-battering has not diminished.

In addition, we cannot minimize the impact of the lack of federal funding for agencies that provide abortions or even abortion counseling; nor the withholding of federal funding from inequitable educational programs but not from the school that houses them.

The push for the Equal Rights Amendment itself has had disappointing results, as feminists have failed to obtain sufficient support in state legislatures to achieve ratification. Many legislators and citizens support a constitutional amendment that would make abortion in almost all circumstances illegal. A basic human right that feminists have been demanding for over a century—the right to control whether our bodies are to be used for reproduction—is thus in jeopardy.

Most women, to a far greater extent than men, still work in low-paying jobs with few prospects for advancement, while the upper levels of social structures throughout the world are dominated by men (Denmark, 1993). In the United States, more so than in most other industrialized countries, women are still highly vulnerable to losing our jobs when we become pregnant (Finley, 1986).

In higher education, a concerted effort is being made to restrict such new fields of inquiry as women's studies and African American studies, and to require students to emphasize the traditional "canon" of "Great Works." What such proposals amount to are demands that students continue to be exposed largely to the expression of Western, white, male authors, and that the humanities be kept from fostering new social changes.

Many young women assume that whatever battles were needed in the past have been won, and that we no longer need the militancy often associated with feminism. This complacency contributes to the belittling of women, and to the continuation of sexist attitudes and practices.

The Myth of the Superwoman. What is a superwoman? She is a woman who does just about everything—and does it well! The superwoman presented in magazines and newspapers is an ambitious and successful professional who also keeps house for her children and spouse and has an active social life. Superwomen are gourmet cooks, pursue interests and hobbies, give elaborate dinner parties, and are at their offices by nine making major decisions, apparently never showing the strains of a person drowning in commitments. Do they sleep? Are they human?

Who can really be a superwoman? Most women must make choices, choices that can be frightening, especially when we did not learn as children that such decisions are ours to make. In addition, we require support from a variety of sources to do those things most important to us. To combine a career with childrearing and family life and still have time for special interests appears to require extraordinary talents. Is that what the women's movement has as its goal? We think not. But societal changes are necessary to free women from this *superwoman syndrome.* It is possible that this image, unattainable in reality, is the reason many women with professional promise find the old traditional roles so appealing.

If normal women are to find fulfillment in pursuits outside of the home as well as within the family, revisions in family structure and social support systems will have to occur. Men are going to have to share fully in childrearing responsibilities, and day care facilities we have confidence in will have to be made available.

A Lesson from History. "Two steps forward, one back." In the history of the women's movement, successes have been followed by reversals or lulls. Is history to repeat itself?

The women's movement has always had strong opposition. As it becomes stronger, so does the resistance. The movement threatens to change the status quo, and any kind of significant change is frightening to many people. Change is even upsetting to people who have little, for they fear they will have even less. Change threatens the power structure, and it threatens men, who fear they will lose their privileged status. It also threatens many women: those who fear losing what is thought of as security; those who believe the women's movement denies domestic values and family life; and those who see a whole pattern of life being questioned by uncomfortable, new points of view.

The women's movement needs to address such fears, not ignore them. The greatest danger facing women is that feminists will become complacent. No situation will improve without organized action. This is a lesson to be learned from the history of the women's

Necessity, Ingenuity, and Gourmet Tomato Sauce Yield a Thriving Company

The tale of how Nancy Battista DiStefano became a businesswoman could begin with the memory of her father bringing home bushels of tomatoes for her and her two sisters to can in Mason jars with a bit of olive oil and basil.

Or it might start with lonely midnight runs in her Volkswagen to the tough-edged Hunts Point market in the Bronx to buy tomatoes to supply a tiny new enterprise. Once she saw a man stabbed a few feet away from her.

But this is an entrepreneurial career that had the starkest of origins. It grew out of the disappointment of a failed marriage and the urgent drive of a mother to insure the well-being of her precious son, Daniel, then 2 years old.

'On a Mission'

"I was on a mission," said the president of Pomodora Fresca Foods, which in January moved from a minuscule former ice-cream parlor in Queens to a 10,000 square-foot factory in West Sayville, L.I.

It is selling gourmet tomato sauce in all 50 states, though mainly in the New York metropolitan region. Sales this year are expected to exceed $500,000.

"And I don't see any problem doubling or tripling that every year," Ms. DiStefano, who is 31, said.

She is part of a tidal wave. Census data from 1987, the latest figures available, indicate that 30 percent of all businesses in the nation are now owned by women, a proportion expected by census officials to increase to 50 percent by the year 2000. Two of every three new businesses, most beginning with just one person, are started by women. Many of them, like Ms. DiStefano, never set out to be entrepreneurs, but, when faced with the necessity of making ends meet, they tap an ingenuity and drive they may not have known they possessed.

'The Only Way'

Marsha Firestone, vice president of the American Woman's Economic Development Corporation, says this surge is the result of women having less chance of making it to the top of big companies, where only 3 percent of top managers are women. "The only way they're going to be at the top is to do it themselves," she said. . . .

Fresh tomatoes were the key. Thus it was that Ms. DiStefano ventured to the Hunts Point market, a place she had not known existed. She arrived in her Volkswagen a little after midnight, when she had been told the selection was greatest.

movement and from that of the well-organized groups that would oppress us.

The World of the Future: What Should It Be?

Feminists have differing views on the changes women should bring about. The issues are nu-merous, and we can only present a few of the key ones here.

Women (and Men) of the Future

Women have been defined narrowly in terms that have tied our being to our reproductive and endocrinological systems. Womanhood,

It was a world she was clearly unprepared for. Wandering aimlessly between the huge trucks, stacks of crates and piles of produce of the world's biggest vegetable market, she pushed sleeping Daniel in a carriage. Her mother walked beside her, waving about a big pocketbook.

"Get out of here!" an alarmed merchant screamed. "Take the baby away! Hide that pocketbook!"

He then led the odd entourage around personally. And gradually, but only gradually, she acquired market smarts. People would show her a sample of beautiful tomatoes, then slip her ones much inferior. When she asked for credit, she was told, "Do you know what we do to people who don't pay their bill?"

"You don't know the humiliation I had to face," Ms. DiStefano said.

But things were improving. In January 1990, she finally quit her job at the design studio. She began taking around her sauce, which retails now for $6 a pint jar, to gourmet stores. Many were interested.

She even got an early nibble from a major food distributor, whose representative mentioned quantities she could not then dream of producing. To hide the facts, she lied and said she was in the process of building a 100,000 square-foot plant and hiring her own sales force.

"In the meantime, I'm hysterical, crying," she said. "Every day, I thought it was going to end."

What happened next is the key to her present success. Louis DaGroza, a businessman she met through friends, was impressed with what Ms. DiStefano was doing. And he was interested in a new plant for his own company, Bruno's Specialty Foods, which makes kosher frozen entrees.

A Blur of Motion

Ms. DiStefano's typical business day is a blur of motion. . . . Not that she doesn't have help, mainly from women. Her accountant, lawyer, production manager and all other supervisors are women. Most of her 30 other workers are local housewives who are welcome to adjust their schedules for personal needs.

Lately, Ms. DiStefano has begun to get inquiries from big companies interested in buying into her dream. She isn't ruling them out, but said "I'd like to keep it a privately owned, profitable company."

She feels this incredible pride. "I walk around the plant, and I still get butterflies in my stomach," Nancy DiStefano said.

however, can be what we say it is and what we make it into. We can formulate proposals for the kinds of social arrangements we believe to be worthy of human loyalty, and we can work to bring them about.

Androgyny vs. Differences. Are human characteristics divided into female and male? If so, are we bound by them? Are differences desirable or not? Some differences can be traced to socialization practices; others may be due to cultural factors, biological ones, or to an interaction between the two.

As we learned in Chapter 3, hormonal levels can be affected by factors in the environment. This suggests that increasingly similar living and working environments for women and men may create greater similarities between the sexes. Nonsexist childrearing will allow women and men to develop our biological potential without the shaping influence of stereotypic beliefs.

Some differences between women and men are not subject to this kind of change: Women become pregnant and men do not. Many feminists are arguing that for even the law to treat women equally, equality should not be interpreted to mean sameness in many cases. Lucinda Finley, a professor of law at Yale, argues that the law should require employers to provide adequate maternity leaves even if job-protected leaves are not provided for every condition. This is not preferential treatment for women, but a recognition that for women to participate fully and equally in the workforce, maternity leaves must be assured (Finley, 1986). It is imperative to realize that if we ignore procreative differences, women are denied equal access to work, for in order to have equal opportunity women must either "become men" or find a way for men to also become pregnant.

We may wish to encourage the development of some characteristics and not others in both women and men. Society has in the past polarized the sexes in terms of many characteristics. Women have been socialized into roles defined by men, and our traits of passivity, dependence, and emotionality have traditionally been considered disadvantageous by both men and women. Might it be better for us to emulate a male model, one focused on

---

Doctors Consider a Specialty Focusing on Women's Health

Dr. Adriane Fugh-Berman, a general practitioner in Washington, says that on her first day in medical school a few years ago, a lab instructor told students to cut off the female cadaver's breasts and discard them. How many of her fellow students, she now asks, took away the message that despite the epidemic of breast cancer, women's breasts had no medical significance.

There is no way of telling how common such attitudes are in medical schools. But incidents like these have convinced many female doctors like Dr. Fugh-Berman that medicine has such a profound male bias that women's health needs are being ignored—and that there needs to be a new medical specialty devoted to women's health.

The new specialty, its proponents say, would be concerned with women's total health needs, much as pediatrics is for children. Its practitioners would be trained in everything from managing menopause to spotting abuse, with a focus on the growing body of research on how diseases and drugs act differently in women than in men.

Ending a Division

They would provide the full spectrum of routine women's health care, so that women would no longer have to pay regular visits to two doctors: a gynecologist for the reproductive organs and an internist or family practitioner for everything else.

"Having a medical specialty in women's health could be viewed much like having a room of one's own," Dr. Karen Johnson, a San Francisco psychiatrist, argued recently in the Journal of Women's Health.

(*New York Times*, November 7, 1992:21A)

assertiveness, independence, and rationality? Should women be more like men?

Feminists reject such a suggestion. What have traditionally been viewed as weaknesses in women may in fact be strengths. Most feminists believe that the world would benefit from an infusion of "female" traits: expressiveness, concern for the emotions, humane social priorities, and greater peacefulness. Humane traits are sorely missing from the power structures erected and controlled by men. We should refer to Gilligan (1982), who pointed out the ethical advantages of morality based on *human* relationships. Women can provide these—if we do not trade our "feminine" characteristics for "male" ones. It seems more reasonable to suggest that men should be more like women. The individual who incorporates both "female" and "male" aspects of personality would be a *whole* individual, a balanced individual.

Psychologists are beginning to view the ideal human as one who balances such traits as assertiveness and cooperativeness (Bem, 1975, 1976; Kaplan, 1979). Sociologists (Bernard, 1981) are coming to emphasize the overlapping of "female" and "male" behavior rather than their mutual exclusiveness. They are reworking social theory and definitions of gender roles, and acknowledging the extent to which socialization processes form such behavior and could form different behavior.

Increasingly, however, feminists are exploring not androgyny but a generalization of feminist values in place of masculinist ones. As Nancy Hartsock writes, "generalizing the activity of women to the social system as a whole would raise, for the first time in human history, the possibility of a fully human community" (Hartsock, 1983a:305). Perhaps we should restructure society so it reflects the priorities of mothering, care, concern for the well-being of children, in place of the preoccupation with competition and destruction that have characterized the history of male domination (Hartsock, 1989; Held, 1987, 1989).

Feminist theory in the 1980s has considered the possibilities of developing feminist moral theories that would be different from and better than the moral theories of the past (Gilligan, 1982; Kittay and Meyers, 1987). They would include a central focus on human caring and connectedness. As we develop such notions, we can imagine that from a feminist perspective the whole world of public institutions and private relations should be reshaped. Whether the world we seek should then be a generalization of the feminine or a blending of masculine and feminine remains to be decided.

The World of the Future. Feminist theory is excitingly diverse (Tong, 1989). Some feminists feel that women's equality should be sought through our advancement in existing institutions. Others see the need for radical changes in these institutions. Some see capitalism as the major source of oppression. To others, racism and sexism are the fundamental problems. Almost all feminists, however, recognize that the causes of women's oppression are multiple, and that dealing with them will require changes in many aspects of life and society.

Feminist theorists will need to develop, in dialogue between women of various racial and ethnic groups and with various class backgrounds and experience, theories that adequately transcend the divisions of race and class (Lugones and Spelman, 1983). We must also stress the belief that the feminist future depends on the recognition of diversity and that feminist goals include the elimination of oppression of all people regardless of race, religion, class, age, or sexual orientation.

Sisterhood and Feminism. The women's movement has sometimes been accused of being a white, middle-class movement, insensitive to and irrelevant for poor and minority women.

There is no question that women's concerns throughout history have been articulated by those of us who had the education and social resources to gain a hearing and the material resources to concern ourselves with more than survival. But the women's movement today represents more than just the concerns of middle-class women. The drive for women to be able to control our own reproduction affects all women. Demands for welfare reform and assistance to the poor, most of whom are women and children, are continuing goals.

Women in all social and ethnic groups have many things in common simply by virtue of being women. *Sisterhood*, a term used by the women's liberation movement, refers to the bonding of all women. The strength of this bond is the strength of the movement. Men may choose to join this movement, just as for many years women contributed our energy to efforts to promote "brotherhood."

"A Piece of the Pie" or a New World? Feminists fall along a continuum as to the extent of change we think is required for society and our sisters. Many feminists regard equality in the present capitalist system to be impossible. We believe the system is structured for the benefit of a few and requires the oppression of most of the world's population. Rather than "make it" in the present system, we envision new systems that would emphasize values other than the corporate interests we see as dominant in society in the United States. We want governing institutions that will represent the interests of all people, and a society in which human beings will treat one another with respect and feel concern for the well-being of one another. Jo Freeman refers to such rhetoric as the *liberation ethic*, which holds that men as well as women have deplorable lives and are oppressed by the present structure. Thus the system must be transformed to provide humane lives for all (Freeman, 1976).

Some feminists are more concerned with getting a piece of the pie that now exists. These feminists among us recognize that major changes have to occur but do not advocate a radical transformation of the system. Freeman refers to the goals at this end of the continuum as the *egalitarian ethic*—equality for the sexes and elimination of gender roles. "This means that there will be an integration of social functions and life-styles of women and men as groups until, ideally, one cannot tell anything relevant about a person's social role by knowing that person's sex" (ibid.:253–54).

Freeman cautions that both the egalitarian ethic and the liberation ethic must work in tandem. "To seek for equality alone, given the current bias of the social values, is to assume that women want to be like men or that men are worth emulating. It is to demand that women be allowed to participate in society . . . without questioning whether that society is worth participating in" (ibid.:254).

By definition, the "male" role necessitates a "female" role; it exists by the oppression of women. Equality, Freeman says, requires the destruction of these roles, which will lead to basic changes in the system itself. However, it should not be assumed that a social revolution will result in equality for women. To work for a revolution without paying equal attention to women's roles would be a mistake. Revolutionary systems proposed by nonfeminist theorists have not eliminated sexual inequality or a gender-role structure (ibid.).

Women's Condition and the Human Condition. The women's movement has always been highly sensitive to the human condition. Women are not, however, limitless sources of energy. As individuals and as a movement, we must often choose what to focus on—the larger concern of the human condition or the more narrow area of women's issues as these touch us in our daily lives. These areas are not, of course, mutually

Backlash (excerpt)

To blame feminism for women's "lesser life" is to miss entirely the point of feminism, which is to win women a wider range of experience. Feminism remains a pretty simple concept, despite repeated—and enormously effective—efforts to dress it up in greasepaint and turn its proponents into gargoyles. As Rebecca West wrote sardonically in 1913, "I myself have never been able to find out precisely what feminism is: I only know that people call me a feminist whenever I express sentiments that differentiate me from a doormat."

The meaning of the word "feminist" has not really changed since it first appeared in a book review in the *Athenaeum* of April 27, 1895, describing a woman who "has in her the capacity of fighting her way back to independence." It is the basic proposition that, as Nora put it in Ibsen's *A Doll's House* a century ago, "Before everything else I'm a human being." It is the simply worded sign hoisted by a little girl in the 1970 Women Strike for Equality: I AM NOT A BARBIE DOLL. Feminism asks the world to recognize at long last that women aren't decorative ornaments, worthy vessels, members of a "special-interest group." They are half (in fact, now more than half) of the national population, and just as deserving of rights and opportunities, just as capable of participating in the world's events, as the other half. Feminism's agenda is basic: It asks that women not be forced to "choose" between public justice and private happiness. It asks that women be free to define themselves—instead of having their identity defined for them, time and again, by their culture and their men.

The fact that these are still such incendiary notions should tell us that American women have a way to go before they enter the promised land of equality.

(Faludi, 1991)

---

exclusive, and the two very often affect each other.

For example, unless the world succeeds in avoiding nuclear war, there may be no survival for either women or men, let alone progress. Hence many women participate in peace movements. On the other hand, some point out that there can be no peace right now for women suffering from domestic violence, so some women devote more energy to curbing such violence. Still others point to the possible connections between these, exploring the ways sexism contributes to militarism (Harris and King, 1989; Reardon, 1985).

Increasingly, feminists are insisting that women's issues must become the primary concern of women. In the past, women's goals have repeatedly taken a backseat to other concerns. Labor rights took precedence over women's concerns in England in the nineteenth century. Efforts to enlarge the franchise in England and in the United States gave the vote to ever wider groups of men before any women were given the right. Women were used and scorned in the French Revolution, in the abolitionist movement, in the Russian Revolution, and in the civil rights movement. Many feel that granting priority to "human" concerns, rather than to women's concerns, may continue to support a male culture and male values.

The dominant culture tends to view women's concerns as trivial. Women have been asked to postpone our demands for even the most elementary aspects of equality because of the supposedly "more pressing" concerns of the proletariat or the poor or the racially disadvantaged. Increasingly there is an understanding among many women that a feminist concern for women should not be used to obscure the ways racism and class privilege and homophobia are oppressive to many women and men. But neither should a concern for other forms of oppression be used to obscure gender oppression.

It is difficult for women, particularly when we lack a strong support group, to articulate the things we feel are important when our demands are continually dismissed as insignificant. Thus, men frequently express impatience when women wish to discuss such "unimportant" issues as the division of household chores. Requests by women for even minimal respect are met with ridicule. When women within scholarly fields do pioneering work in feminist theory, or when we investigate whole areas of economic or historical reality ignored by our male colleagues, our work is often dismissed as "not really scholarly" or as "nonserious."

Vehicles for Change

The Bonding of Women. Women, as well as men, can undermine the momentum of women's liberation. As has been noted, the strength of the women's movement lies in the support and encouragement we give one another. The movement suffers when successful women disavow women's struggles, fail to encourage and admire other women, and are not proud of our female heritage. We have all seen women of great accomplishments disavow women's causes, as though they themselves were not women. Florence Nightingale, Helene Deutsch, Golda Meir, and Margaret Thatcher are examples of women who turned from other women.

Of course, many highly successful women have not felt detached from the feminist movement. Eleanor Roosevelt and Margaret Mead, for example, sympathized with women's struggles. Many successful women have actively contributed to women's causes and received strength from doing so, recognizing our responsibilities to help other women achieve what we have often been able to achieve only by unusual luck and the help of other women. Women's bonding has brought about the greatest gains.

Many feminists warn women against the trap of tokenism, a technique long used by those in power to co-opt or buy off opposition. Including a token woman in government, the professions, and the arts allows men to protect themselves better from charges of discrimination. Many an organization displays pictures showing a black and a woman among its smiling, well-dressed employees, even though statistics reveal blatant patterns of discrimination behind the scenes.

Carolyn Heilbrun calls for solidarity among women this way:

> The failure of women's movements, past and present, to retain the momentum of the years of highest accomplishment can be attributed to three causes. The failure of women to bond; the failure of women to imagine women as autonomous; and the failure of even achieving women to resist, sooner or later, the protection to be obtained by entering the male mainstream. Among these causes, the failure of women to find "support systems" among themselves is certainly close to the heart of the problem. . . . Obviously, it is difficult in a hierarchical society to bond with the powerless against those in power, particularly when the aphrodisiac of power is an added allure. (1979:26–27)

Models for Women. Traditionally, most of our models for achievement and autonomy have been male. In the past, women who followed such models frequently adopted a male value system and were called "unfeminine." This is a powerful form of social pressure, for it suggests that women must choose between being successful and being women. The fact is that whatever women do is womanly, by virtue of the fact that we are women doing it. And we can choose to act cooperatively and together, rather than to try to imitate individual "Great Men."

Feminist writers are creating more female protagonists who are imaginative, ambitious, and adventuresome. To provide female models and to keep them alive, even when the wider culture ignores them, is one of the most important functions women's studies can perform. This can be done through a new look at women's history, through a reinterpretation of women's work in the arts and literature, and through a reexamination of the roles women have taken and are taking in society. With this effort will come the voice of more women, speaking of our own experiences and creating new models.

Revolution in the Family. Family structure so far has been almost universally built on a clear division of labor by gender and sex-stereotyping of female and male behavior. This structure serves a number of purposes: It shapes stereotypical identities in children, encourages passivity in women and dominance in men, ties women to the home and to a dependence on men, and interferes with women's achievement of selfhood and with men's ability to love and nurture (Denmark et al., 1993). The constraints of the traditional family bind women tightly. We need to break these ties and to create a revolution in the structure of the family.

This may be the most difficult task of all. Inherent in the family structure is the definition of *mother* as female, with the social and caretaker roles of *mothering* tied to the biological function, and requiring a woman to be at home, passive, and dependent on the male. To overthrow *motherhood* in this sense is to free women from having the primary responsibility of caring for children. It requires *fathering* chil-

dren to mean something similar to instead of something different from *mothering* them. And it demands that *parenthood* be a shared responsibility (Denmark et al., 1993).

The most revolutionary action most women can take is to refuse to accept "personal" domination by men, especially within the family. Women can often do this only at great personal cost. But the rewards, for individual women as well as for all women and even men, can be great, as we experience how satisfying is a life of self-respect in which we demand recognition of our equal worth as human beings.

The legal system must expand its definition of the family and recognize new arrangements for family life as well. Equitable protection for partners and children needs to be guaranteed, and society must protect families living under less traditional modes, such as households of unrelated persons and one-parent households, from unfair disadvantages (Giele, 1978).

Power and Politics. Power usually acts to maintain itself. The powerful will not give up power voluntarily; it must be taken from them. Power is a word that repels many feminists. It conjures up an image of a male power hierarchy in which the existence of the powerful necessitates the existence of the powerless. We do not wish to be powerless, but we also do not wish to use power as men do to dominate and exploit others.

The political system is one of the most powerful bastions of our sexist social structure. Legislation for various forms of equality has been passed, and continues in effect, but the pace at which actual changes that benefit women are made is painfully slow. Much needed legislation still fails to get support and women who are active in politics are still all too often subordinates (Mezey, 1980).

In the United States presidential election of 1980, for the first time women voted in ways that were significantly different from men. *Far* fewer women than men voted for Ronald Reagan (Steinem, 1981). As more women become aware of how governmental policies affect us, we can use the power of our numbers to achieve changes through the ballot. Unlike minorities, who can always be outvoted, women constitute a majority of voters, a reality that has now been grasped by politicians. Through careful voting we could achieve more than we have. As the courts increasingly reflect the conservative views of judges appointed during the Reagan presidency, hope for progress may depend more and more on legislative initiatives. The power of the vote should not be exaggerated, for many of the political and economic structures of the United States are now relatively immune to electoral change. We must support candidates committed to women's issues, and these issues must become a top priority for voters and candidates. Feminists must run for office and exert pressure. To do so, we must have the active support of other women. Women must make ourselves heard through petitions and organizational work as well as voting.

To call attention to feminist issues when the normal political channels are not responsive, more militant actions, such as demonstrations, boycotts, strikes, and actions involving civil disobedience, may be necessary. Where power is used unjustly to dominate those with little power, disobedience of existing, unjust laws on grounds of conscience may be fully justified (Bedau, 1969; Held, 1984).

Women's Studies and the Feminist Movement

Women's studies is both a result of and a vehicle for the women's movement. It grew out of women's awareness of our past and present roles and communicates this awareness to women. It studies women and encourages the study of women. It takes pride in women and conveys that pride to others. It is the academic discipline of feminism. Women's studies is a growing force in the academic community, a force that sends messages and affects beliefs and behavior far beyond the walls of academic institutions.

In reading this book, you have absorbed a tremendous amount of material. With that background, take a minute to think about the future. What would you like to see happen? Do you think it will happen? How can the changes you hope for be brought about?

Your training in women's studies should provide you with a new perspective when you enter into traditional occupations. It will help prepare you for various newly developing fields. As a result of your awareness of what women have done and are now doing, and your understanding of how societies everywhere subordinate the lives of one gender to another, the world may never look the same to you again. We hope that you will never lose the new perspective that feminism provides.

It is not our intention to leave you at the end of this book feeling either optimistic or pessimistic about the future. Both feelings are dangerous. Optimism can lead to complacency—the feeling that all will turn out well and the future will take care of itself. Pessimism can lead to apathy, a sense of defeat, and the feeling that we have no control over our future. Our hope is that you will finish this book with the belief that women must try to take control of the future, and have the courage to persist. We hope that with the insights you have gained in studying women, you will act to bring about the future that women choose.

Summary

When women have fought for social change, we have frequently contributed to the gains of others but have been denied the realization of our own objectives. This happened after the American and French revolutions.

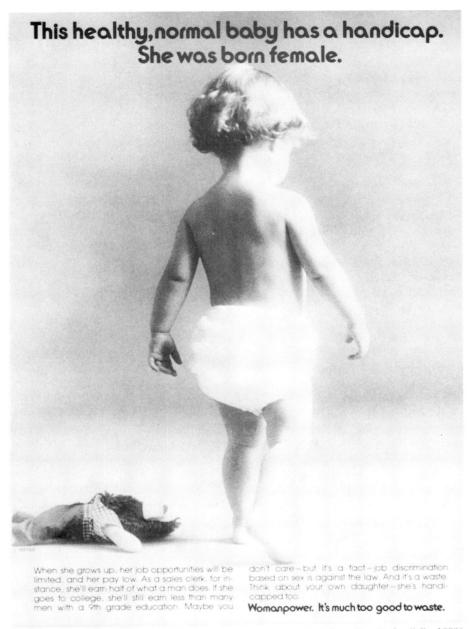

This healthy, normal baby has a handicap. She was born female.

When she grows up, her job opportunities will be limited, and her pay low. As a sales clerk, for instance, she'll earn half of what a man does. If she goes to college, she'll still earn less than many men with a 9th grade education. Maybe you don't care—but it's a fact—job discrimination based on sex is against the law. And it's a waste. Think about your own daughter—she's handicapped too.

Womanpower. It's much too good to waste.

NOW Legal Defense and Education Fund Inc., 132 W. 43rd St., New York, N.Y. 10036

An early NOW poster called "Womanpower. It's much too good to waste." (NOW Legal Defense and Education Fund, Inc.)

After women won the vote in the United States, active feminism continued in the 1920s but diminished with the Depression. Following World War II, women were once again rigidly confined to home and family. In the 1960s, feminism experienced a rebirth. Since then, the women's movement has been increasingly active on behalf of women's rights. Today the movement gets a great deal of publicity, but observers disagree on its effectiveness.

Some women are rejecting the prospective role of the "superwoman," who effortlessly combines family and career, in favor of more traditional and secure roles. In order to free women from having two full-time jobs—one in the home and one in the workplace—major changes in family structure and social support systems will have to take place.

Nonsexist socialization practices will probably result in greater similarities between the sexes, although biological differences will remain and should not be ignored. Some undesirable biological traits may be discouraged and desirable traits enhanced in society. Many feminists believe that the world would benefit from an infusion of such "female" traits as expressiveness, peacefulness, and care for humane social priorities. Society should foster the development of the "good person." Perhaps such a person is one with an androgynous personality incorporating the best traits of both women and men. Or perhaps the concept of "human" should be modeled on that of "woman" rather than on that of "man."

Some feminists urge a radical transformation of the structures of society (the liberation ethic), while others emphasize equality for the sexes and the elimination of discrimination (the egalitarian ethic). It may be that both approaches will lead to similar programs.

Feminists argue that in the future, women must pay more attention to our own needs and give them the importance they deserve.

Change will come about as women create bonds with one another, as we are provided with more role models, and as the family structure is revolutionized so family care is no longer equated with the biological component of motherhood.

Women's studies programs have made an academic discipline of feminism. They enable students to become aware of what women have accomplished and of how we have been oppressed. Once we become conscious of the issues feminists are raising, the world may never appear the same as it did before.

Discussion Questions

1. What factors have led to reversals of the gains made by previous women's movements? Can they be countered in the future?

2. Do you see women as much better off today compared to twenty years ago or as only slightly better off? What components of people's lives are most important for making such judgments?

3. Would you like to have an androgynous personality? Why? Why not?

4. What is meant by "revolution in the family"? Are you for it?

Recommended Readings

Women's studies journals and feminist magazines: *Feminist Studies; Hypatia; Journal of Women's History; Ms.; Quest; Signs; The Women's Review of Books; Women's Studies; Women's Studies International Forum; and Women's Studies Quarterly.*

References

Baruch, Grace, and Barnett, Rosalind. "A New Start for Women at Midlife." *New York Times Magazine,* December 7, 1980.

Bedau, Hugo Adam, editor. *Civil Disobedience: Theory and Practice*. New York: Pegasus, 1969.

Bem, Sandra L. "Probing the Promise of Androgyny." In *Beyond Sex-Role Stereotypes: Readings toward a Psychology of Androgyny*, edited by A. Kaplan and J. Bean. Boston: Little, Brown, 1976.

———. "Sex Role Adaptability: One Consequence of Psychological Androgyny." *Journal of Personality and Social Psychology* 31 (1975):634–43.

Berg, Barbara. *The Remembered Gate: Origins of American Feminism*. Oxford: Oxford University Press, 1978.

Bernard, Jessie. "The Good-Provider Role: Its Rise and Fall." *American Psychologist* 36 (1981):1–12.

Bird, Caroline. *Born Female. The High Cost of Keeping Women Down*. New York: Pocket Books, 1969.

Davidson, Nicholas. *The Failure of Feminism*. Buffalo, N.Y.: Prometheus Books, 1988.

Denmark, Florence. "Psyche. From Rocking the Cradle to Rocking the Boat." *American Psychologist* 35 (1980):1057–65.

———. "Women, Leadership, and Empowerment." *Psychology of Women Quarterly* 17 (1993):343–356.

———. "Engendering Psychology." *American Psychologist* 49 (1994):329–334.

———, Nielson, Karen, and Scholl, Kristin. "United States of America: Gender Roles in the U.S.A." In *International Handbook of Gender Roles*, edited by L. L. Adler, Westport, Conn.: Greenwood Press, 1993.

Eisenstein, Zillah. *The Radical Future of Liberal Feminism*. New York: Longman, 1981.

Elshtain, Jean Bethke. *Public Man, Private Woman*. Princeton, N.J.: Princeton University Press, 1981.

Faludi, Susan. Backlash: *The Undeclared War Against American Women*. New York: Crown, 1991.

Ferguson, Ann. "Androgyny as an Ideal for Human Development." In *Feminism and Philosophy*, edited by Mary Vetterling-Braggin, et al. Totowa, N.J.: Littlefield, Adams, 1977.

Finley, Lucinda M. "Transcending Equality Theory: A Way Out of the Maternity and the Workplace Debate." 86 *Columbia Law Review*. 1118 (1986).

Freeman, Jo. "The Woman's Liberation Movement: Its Origins, Structures, Impact, and Ideas." In *Women's Studies: The Social Realities*, edited by Barbara B. Watson. New York: Harper & Row, 1976.

Friedan, Betty. *The Feminine Mystique*. New York: Dell, 1963.

Giele, Janet Z. *Women and the Future: Changing Sex Roles in Modern America*. New York: Free Press, 1978.

Gilligan, Carol. *In a Different Voice*. Cambridge, Mass.: Harvard University Press, 1982.

Gilman, Charlotte Perkins. *The Living of Charlotte Perkins Gilman: An Autobiography*. 1935. Reprint. New York: Harper & Row, 1975.

———. *Women and Economics*. 1898. Reprint. Edited by Carl N. Degler. New York: Harper & Row, 1966.

Goldman, Emma. "The Tragedy of Women's Emancipation." In *Anarchism and Other Essays*. New York: Dover, 1969.

Gould, Carol. "The Woman Question: Philosophy of Liberation and the Liberation of Philosophy." In *Women and Philosophy*, edited by Carol Gould and Marx Wartofsky. New York: Putnam, 1976.

Harding, Sandra, and Hintikka, Merrill B., editors. *Discovering Reality*. Dordrecht, Holland: Reidel, 1983.

Harris, Adrienne, and King, Ynestra, editors. *Rocking the Ship of State. Toward a Feminist Peace Politics*. Boulder, Co.: Westview, 1989.

Hartsock, Nancy C. M. "The Feminist Standpoint." In *Discovering Reality*, edited by Sandra Harding and Merrill Hintikka. Dordrecht, Holland: Reidel, 1983a.

———. *Money, Sex, and Power: An Essay on Domination and Community*. New York: Longman, 1983b.

———. "Masculinity, Heroism, and the Making of War." In *Rocking the Ship of State*, edited by Adrienne Harris and Ynestra King. Boulder, Co.: Westview, 1989.

Heilbrun, Carolyn. *Reinventing Womanhood*. New York: Norton, 1979.

Held, Virginia. "Birth and Death." *Ethics* 99 (January 1989).

———. "Non-Contractual Society: A Feminist View." In *Science, Morality and Feminist Theory*, edited by Marsha Hanen and Kai Nielsen. Calgary: University of Calgary Press, 1987.

———. *Rights and Goods. Justifying Social Action*. New York: Free Press, 1984.

Herzog, Alison C., and Mali, Jane Lawrence. *Oh, Boy! Babies!* Boston: Little, Brown, 1980.

Jaggar, Alison M. *Feminist Politics and Human Nature*. Totowa, N.J.: Rowman and Allanheld, 1983.

Kaplan, Alexandra. "Changing the Concept of Androgyny: Implications for Therapy." *Psychology of Women Quarterly* 3 (1979):223–30.

Kittay, Eva Feder, and Meyers, Diana T., editors. *Women and Moral Theory*. Totowa, NJ: Rowman and Littlefield, 1987.

Kolb, Frances A. "The Feminist Movement: 1890–1920." In *Women's Studies: The Social Realities*, edited by Barbara B. Watson. New York: Harper & Row, 1976.

Levy, Darline, Applewhite, Harriet, and Johnson, Mary, editors. *Women in Revolutionary Paris, 1789–1795. Selected Documents*. Urbana: University of Illinois Press, 1979.

Littleton, Christine A. "Reconstructing Sexual Equality." 75 *California Law Review* (1987).

Lugones, Maria C., and Spelman, Elizabeth V. "Have We Got a Theory for You! Feminist Imperialism and the Demand for 'The Woman's Voice.'" *Women's Studies International Forum* 6,6 (1983):573–81.

Mansbridge, Jane J. *Beyond Adversary Democracy*. Chicago: University of Chicago Press, 1983.

McKenna, Wendy, and Denmark, Florence. "Women and the University." *International Journal of Group Tensions* 5 (1975):226–34.

Mezey, Susan G. "Women in the Political Process." In *Issues in Feminism*, edited by Sheila Ruth. Boston: Houghton Mifflin, 1980.

Morgan, Robin, editor. *Sisterhood Is Powerful*. New York: Vintage, 1970.

New York Times. "Bishops Denounce Abuse of Spouses." October 30, 1992:A12.

———. "Necessity, Ingenuity and Gourmet Tomato Sauce Yield a Thriving Company." November 9, 1992:19.

———. "Doctors Consider a Specialty Focusing on Women's Health." November 7, 1992:21A.

———. "Milestone for Black Woman in Gaining U.S. Senate Seat." November 4, 1992:40.

———, June 16, 1988.

Nicholson, Linda. *Gender and History*. New York: Columbia University Press, 1986.

Palmer, Judith D. "Stages of Women's Awareness." *Social Change: Ideas and Applications* 9 (1979):1–4, 11.

Postow, Betsy. "Women and Masculine Sports." In *"Femininity," "Masculinity," and "Androgyny": A Modern Philosophical Discussion*, edited by Mary Vetterling-Braggin. Totowa, NJ: Littlefield, Adams, 1981.

Reardon, Betty A. *Sexism and the War System*. New York: Columbia University Teachers College Press, 1985.

Rossi, Alice S. *The Feminist Papers*. New York: Bantam, 1973.

Rubin, Nancy. *The Mother Mirror. How a Generation of Women Is Changing Motherhood in America*. New York: Putnam, 1984.

Ruddick, Sara. "Preservative Love and Military Destruction: Some Reflections on Mothering and Peace." In *Mothering. Essays in Feminist Theory*, edited by Joyce Trebilcot. Totowa, NJ: Rowman and Allanheld, 1983.

———. "Mothers and Men's Wars." In *Rocking the Ship of State*, edited by Adrienne Harris and Ynestra King. Boulder: Westview, 1989.

Shreve, Anita. *Remaking Motherhood. How Working Mothers Are Shaping Our Children's Future*. New York: Viking, 1987.

Steinem, Gloria. "Now That It's Reagan." *Ms.* 9 (1981):28–33.

Stiehm, Judith, editor. *Women and Men's Wars*. Oxford: Pergamon Press, 1983.

Thurow, Lester C. *The Zero-Sum Society*. New York: Penguin, 1981.

Tong, Rosemarie. *Feminist Thought. A Comprehensive Introduction.* Boulder: Westview, 1989.

Treblicot, Joyce. "Two Forms of Androgynism." In *Feminism and Philosophy,* edited by Vetterling et al. Totowa, NJ: Littlefield, Adams, 1977.

Wollstonecraft, Mary. *The Vindication of the Rights of Woman.* 1792. Reprint. Edited by Carol H. Posten. New York: Norton, 1975.

Zalk, Sue Rosenberg, and Gordon-Kelter, Janice, editors. *Revolutions in Knowledge. Feminism in the Social Sciences.* Boulder, Co.: Westview, 1989.

INDEX

"Abandoned Doll, The" (Valadon), *100*

Abolitionist movement: and equal rights for women, 521; women and, 355, 516, 540

Abortion: availability of, 423, 448; and divisions among women, 530; feminist goddess religions and, 339, 341; of fetuses identified as female, 205; and health risks for women, 422–23; lack of federal funding for, 546; laws on, 277; Medicaid denial of reimbursement for, 423; medicalization of, 412; movement to legalize, *432, 444*, 524; spontaneous, sex differences in, 97

Abzug, Bella, 512, 520, *525*

Academic community, role of women's studies in, 4–5. *See also* Higher education of women; Women's studies

Accounting, as male-identified occupation, 460

Acquired immune deficiency syndrome. *See* AIDS

Activities, sex differences in, 141

Adam and Eve story, 27–28, 333

Adam-out-of-Eve myth, 95

Adams, Abigail, 374–75, 538, 539

Addams, Jane, 303, *384*, 520, 540

Adolescence, and risk of depression, 432. *See also* Puberty

Adoption, of girls by daughterless families, 207–208

"Adult" status: marriage and, 231–32; motherhood and, 266

Adultery. *See* Extramarital affairs

Affirmative action, 73, 83, 315, 480, 487–88

Africa: colonial, lack of education in, 386; female circumcision in East and West Africa, 343; feminism in, 529; sub-Saharan, AIDS in, 422; women's role in West African societies, 229. *See also* Igbo of Nigeria

African American children: laws against teaching, 366; of lesbian mothers, 315

African American studies, 547

African American women: cultural perceptions and, 25; daughter-female relatives relationships, *211*; daughter-mother relationship, 213–14; and depression, 432; divorced, 150; education, 377–79, 476; feminists, and struggle against racism, 529; and health issues, 421, 424; and HIV virus infection, 421; and imagery and symbolism, 37; and job training programs, 476; lesbian mothers, 315; and marriage, 238; and organizations for social change in nineteenth century, 540; physicians, 438–39; political leaders, 511, 517, 520; and racist discrimination against African American men, 11; and relationship of gender and race, 64; and "sharing" husbands idea, 315; and slavery, 176–77, 243, 464; socialization of, 140, 143, 145, 146; stereotypes about, 127, 287–88, 503; and teaching profession, 378; and unemployment of African American men, 178–79; and women's networks, 275, 303–304; work and racism, 475–76, 545. *See also* Women of color

African Americans: AIDS incidence, 421; divorce rates, 249; health risks and, 416, 418; and Hill-Thomas hearings, 188; and moral development studies, 126–27; and "popular" religions, 346; and reproductive sexuality, 151; stereotypes about families, 285–88; and unions, 484. *See also* African American children; African American women

AFSCME v. *State of Washington*, 490

Age ranking, and sibling relationships, 218–19, 220, 223–24

Age of Enlightenment: and Wollstonecraft's writings, 68, 70; and women's rights, 68, 539

Aging: and division of labor, 312; of parents, 207, 208; and personality differences, 127; and risk of depression, 432. *See also* Older women